Also by Alan Taylor

The Divided Ground:
Indians, Settlers, and the Northern Borderland of the American Revolution

Writing Early American History

American Colonies

William Cooper's Town:
Power and Persuasion on the Frontier of the Early American Republic

Liberty Men and Great Proprietors:
The Revolutionary Settlement on the Maine Frontier, 1760-1820

THE CIVIL WAR OF 1812

War Party at Fort Douglas, *watercolor by Peter Rindisbacher, 1823. Indian allies of the British discharge their guns to salute the commander, Captain Andrew Bulger, who appears at the far right. This watercolor represents an incident during the War of 1812.* (Courtesy of the Royal Ontario Museum, Canadiana Department, Sigmund Samuel Collections, 951.87.3.)

THE CIVIL WAR OF 1812

AMERICAN CITIZENS, BRITISH SUBJECTS, IRISH REBELS, & INDIAN ALLIES

Alan Taylor

Alfred A. Knopf · New York
2010

This Is a Borzoi Book
Published by Alfred A. Knopf

Knopf, Borzoi Books, and the colophon are
registered trademarks of Random House, Inc.

Library of Congress Cataloging-in-Publication Data
Taylor, Alan, [date]
The civil war of 1812 : American citizens, British subjects, Irish rebels, and Indian
allies / Alan Taylor. — 1st ed.
p.   cm.
Includes bibliographical references and index.
ISBN 978-1-4000-4265-4
1. United States—History—War of 1812—Social aspects.
2. Ontario—History—War of 1812—Social aspects.
3. Northern boundary of the United States—History—19th century. I. Title.
E354.T39 2010
973.5'2—dc22   2010012783

Manufactured in the United States of America
First Edition

For the McIntyre–Von Herffs,

Sheila and Michael,

William, Silas, and Lucy,

and Maggie the Magpie

Contents

THE CIVIL WAR OF 1812

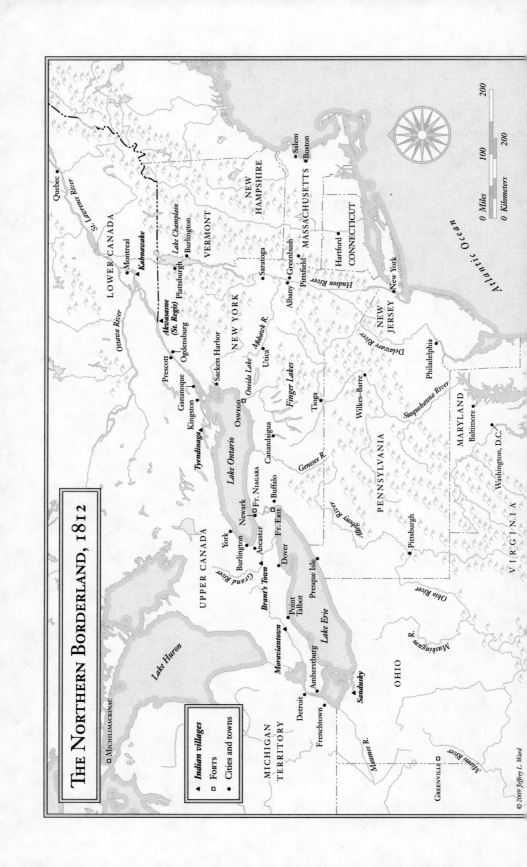

THE NORTHERN BORDERLAND, 1812

Indian villages ▲

Forts □

Cities and towns •

0 Miles   100   200

0 Kilometers   200

© 2009 Jeffrey L. Ward

INTRODUCTION

As much as the people of the two nations resemble each other in face, it is notoriously evident that there are some in America whose souls are perfectly British, and it is believed that there are some in Britain who are Americans at heart. . . . It is not where a man was born, or who he looks like, but what he thinks, which ought at this day to constitute the difference between an American [citizen] and a British subject.

—"An American Farmer," 1813[1]

IN THE FALL OF 1812, Ned Myers, nineteen years old, marched across New York State with a party of fellow sailors bound for Lake Ontario, where the American navy was building warships for an invasion of British Canada. But Myers felt the enemy long before he reached the Canadian border. In northern New York, the sailors came to a village where the inhabitants bitterly opposed the war. On a trumped-up charge, the villagers arrested the officers in command of Myers's party but released them when the sailors threatened to burn the village. Moving on to Oswego Falls, the sailors got caught in a downpour, and sought refuge in a large barn. That night, as Myers recalled, they "caught the owner coming about with a lantern to set fire to the barn, and we carried him down to a boat, and lashed him there until morning, letting the rain wash all the combustible matter out of him." In the War of 1812 Myers had to fight against Americans as well as Britons.[2]

During the following summer on Lake Ontario, a British warship captured the schooner that Myers served on. As a prisoner, Myers dreaded the discovery of his secret: that he had been born a British subject in Quebec in 1793. Abandoned by his father, a German officer serving in the British army, Myers had grown up in Halifax, the capital of Nova Scotia, another British colony. At age eleven he ran away to New York City to become a sailor. Rejecting his birthright as a British subject, Myers *chose* to become an American citizen: "America was, and ever has been, the country of my choice, and while yet a child I may say I decided for myself to sail under the American flag; and if my father had a right to

3

make an Englishman of me by taking service under the English crown, I think I had a right to make myself what I pleased when he left me."[3]

But the British insisted that every "natural-born subject" remained so for life. Before the war, Myers had repeatedly and narrowly dodged the Royal Navy press-gangs, which stopped and boarded American ships in search of any mariner who seemed British. And once the war began, British officers treated former subjects as traitors if they were captured while fighting in the American service. As a British prisoner, Myers feared for his life.[4]

In September at Quebec, a press-gang boarded his prison ship to seize Myers and seven other prisoners. Myers insisted that five of them were Americans by birth, but a British naval officer "pronounced us all Englishmen" obliged to serve in the Royal Navy or face trial and hanging as traitors. All eight refused to serve on a warship, but consented to work on an unarmed transport vessel. They sailed for Bermuda, where naval officers again impressed them to serve on a warship, which threatened "to swallow us all in the enormous maw of the British navy." Refusing again, the captives hazarded a court-martial. Unable to prove that the sailors were subjects, the British transferred them to a prison at Halifax, where Myers worried that the locals would remember and recognize him.[5]

The War of 1812 pivoted on the contentious boundary between the king's subject and the republic's citizen. In the republic, an immigrant chose citizenship—in stark contrast to a British subject, whose status remained defined by birth. That distinction derived from the American Revolution, when the rebelling colonists became republican citizens by rejecting their past as subjects. An immigrant reenacted that revolution by seeking citizenship and forsaking the status of a monarch's subject. But the British denied that the Americans could convert a subject into a citizen by naturalization. By seizing supposed subjects from merchant ships, the Royal Navy threatened to reduce American sailors and commerce to a quasi-colonial status, for every British impressment was an act of counterrevolution. By resisting impressment and declaring war, the Americans defended their revolution.[6]

War raised the stakes in the conflict over subjects and citizens. By converting prisoners or hanging a few as deserters, the British bolstered their contention that any natural-born subject owed allegiance for life, no matter where he went or what nation pretended to naturalize him. Returning the favor, the republic's officers sought to entice captive Britons to enter the American service, thereby reenacting the revolution on an individual scale. Because the line between citizen and subject was so contested, rival commanders promoted the desertion of enemy soldiers, the defection of prisoners, and the subversion of civilians in occupied regions. As much as on any battlefield, the British and the Americans waged the War of 1812 in the hearts and minds of Ned Myers and his fellow soldiers and sailors on both sides.

REVOLUTION

In the American Revolution the victorious Patriots forsook the mixed constitution of Great Britain, where a monarch and aristocrats dominated the common people—then the norm throughout the world. In a radical gamble, the Patriots created a republic premised on the sovereignty of the collective people, rather than of a monarch and his parliament. Meant to protect and promote the liberty, property, and social mobility of ordinary white men, the republic bred a suspicion of government's power as a tool for aristocrats to live as parasites on the labor of the people. But that republic for white men hastened the dispossession of Indians and prolonged the enslavement of African-Americans in the southern states. And the British despised the new republic as a dangerous folly, for they celebrated their mixed constitution as more stable, just, and powerful. Where Americans sought to disperse and reduce the power of government, the British sustained an empire with the coercive "energy" to regulate liberty, particularly that of their colonists and the sailors needed for the Royal Navy.[7]

After the revolution, the British empire and the American republic remained uneasy neighbors in North America. In addition to spawning the republic, the revolution led the British to build a counterrevolutionary regime in Canada, beginning with 38,000 American Loyalists expelled by the Patriot victory. In Upper Canada they developed a Loyalist America meant to set an example of superior stability and prosperity that eventually would entice the rebel Americans to forsake their republican experiment. Loyalists did not believe that their empire had permanently lost the fight against the republican revolution.[8]

Neither Britons nor Americans thought that their rival political systems could coexist for long on a shared continent. Britons predicted that the republic inevitably would collapse into anarchy and civil war. Surely repentant Americans would then beg for readmission into the empire. With equal conviction, Americans insisted that nature destined their republic to dominate the continent. Eventually, they predicted, the

Canadians would join the United States by rejecting the artificial rule of a foreign empire. Created by the revolution, the border between the republic and the empire seemed tenuous and temporary, destined to shift either north or south as one or the other regime collapsed. Paradoxically, until 1812, the parallel convictions of providential inevitability kept relations tense but short of war, for why risk blood and treasure on an invasion when the rival's collapse would come naturally in due time?

Partisan divisions within the republic helped to provoke the war. After 1801, the dominant Republican party challenged the British maritime policies as a threat to American sovereignty. But the minority Federalist party sympathized with Britain's global struggle against the French empire led by the despot Napoleon Bonaparte. The Federalists also despised the Republicans as demagogues who pandered to the common people by weakening the national government. By 1812, the Republicans believed that the Federalists in New England were conspiring with the British to break up the union. And the Republicans accused the Loyalists in Canada of covertly assisting Indian attacks on frontier settlements. By invading Canada and defeating the British, the Republicans hoped to unite and save the republic from a menacing convergence of internal and external enemies. Instead, the war alienated the Federalists, who preferred to smuggle with the British rather than to fight them.[9]

CIVIL WAR

Ned Myers fought in a civil war between kindred peoples, recently and incompletely divided by the revolution. In September 1813, a British lieutenant, John Le Couteur, visited an American army camp, where he marveled upon meeting the enemy officers: "Strange indeed did it appear to me to find so many names, 'familiar household words,' as enemies—the very names of Officers in our own army. How uncomfortably like a civil war." Le Couteur bantered with an American officer, just returned from shooting birds: "Much pleasanter Sport, isn't it, than shooting one's own kindred and language." The American replied, "Indeed, Lieutenant, it is so, I assure you. Believe me when I tell you it so grieves my heart to fire my Guns on your people that I have asked leave to return to Virginia or to serve elsewhere." But a month later, an atrocity by American troops led Le Couteur to denounce them as deserving no mercy in battle: "The rascals, they are worse than Frenchmen." So said the British officer with a French name.[10]

In July 1812 William K. Beall of Kentucky was a prisoner held by the

British at Amherstburg, in the Western District of Upper Canada. Beall "was amused in contrasting the [tavern] signs with those in our Country. Instead of Washington, Green[e] and others might be seen George III, the Lion, the Crown, the King's Bake house, etc. etc." But the allegiance of people was less clear. Beall lodged at "the sign of the harp of Erin," with a landlord named Boyle who had left Ireland for America, where he had served in the republic's army during the early 1790s. Deserting to the British, he had settled at Amherstburg, but in 1812 Boyle fell under official suspicion for expressing sympathy for the Americans. Allegiance was slippery and suspect where so many people had crossed boundaries in geography and identity.[11]

Beall also met William Elliott, a former American officer from Maryland. A Federalist, Elliott had lost his commission in a Republican political purge in 1802. Disgusted with the republic, Elliott moved to Upper Canada, where he swore allegiance to the king, which secured him land and appointment as a captain in the militia. Across the river at Detroit, one of Elliott's brothers served in the American army poised to attack Amherstburg in 1812.[12]

In this North American civil war, brother fought brother in a borderland of mixed peoples. At Kingston, Le Couteur lodged with a Mrs. Elizabeth Robinson: "They are a Yankee family, and have several relatives in the American army and navy." Another British officer, William Dunlop, reported that a Canadian soldier of the Glengarry Light Infantry shot an American rifleman and plundered his corpse, when "he discovered that it was his own brother," and coldly remarked "that it 'served him right for fighting for the rebels, when all the rest of his family fought for King George.'" Like so many on both sides, this Canadian thought of the war as continuing the revolutionary struggle between Loyalists and rebels. Dunlop concluded, "Such is the virulence of political rancour, that it can overcome all the ties of nature."[13]

As Myers found on his march to the front, the war also divided the Americans within the United States. Beall noted that the British "depend more upon party divisions and disturbances among our people than they do on their own strength." Major Daniel McFarland, an Irish-American, insisted that the British were "engaged in the hellish project of creating a civil war" by promoting disaffection within the United States. The British exploited the polarized politics of the republic, where Federalists denounced a war declared by the governing Republicans. A New Yorker concluded, "between the two parties, a hostility existed little short of civil war."[14]

To call the War of 1812 a "civil war" now seems jarring because hindsight has distorted our perspective on the past. Given the later power and prosperity of the United States, we underestimate the fluid uncertainty of the postrevolutionary generation, when the new republic was so precarious and so embattled. We also imagine that the revolution effected a clean break between Americans and Britons as distinct peoples. In fact, the republic and the empire competed for the allegiance of the peoples in North America—native, settler, and immigrant. Americans and Britons spoke the same language and conducted more trade with one another than with other nations, but their overlapping migrations and commerce generated the friction of competition. A British diplomat noted the paradox: "the similarity of habits, language, and manners, between the inhabitants of the two Countries is productive . . . of complaint and regret."[15]

The revolution had divided Americans by creating a new boundary between the victors in the United States and the Loyalists in Canada. And, within the republic, bitter partisan politics led the Republicans to cast the Federalists as crypto-Loyalists. In 1812, a newspaper writer explained that ideology rather than nationality distinguished the North American republican from a Loyalist:

> As much as the people of the two nations resemble each other in face, it is notoriously evident that there are some in America whose souls are perfectly British, and it is believed that there are some in Britain who are Americans at heart. . . . It is not where a man was born, or who he looks like, but what he thinks, which ought at this day to constitute the difference between an American [citizen] and a British subject.

The ideological competition between the republic and the empire blurred the national boundaries and political identities in North America.[16]

After the revolution, the overlap of Britons and Americans became more complicated despite the new border in North America. Thousands of British emigrants poured into American seaports. Primarily from restive Ireland, the newcomers fled from British rule to seek economic opportunity and political liberty in the republic. At the same time (1792–1812), about 30,000 Americans left the republic to seek land in Upper Canada. Euphemistically called "Late Loyalists," these newcomers became the majority in that colony by the eve of war. Invited by the British to help develop Upper Canada, the settlers took an oath of allegiance and received grants of Crown land, the prerogatives of subjects.

In return, they were supposed to defend the colony against any American invasion. But if it was treason for natural-born subjects to fight against the empire, how could the regime expect natural-born citizens to fight against American invaders?

By insisting that the subject was permanent but the citizen fungible, the British asserted the superiority of their empire over the new republic. They implicitly treated Americans as residual or potential subjects, which hedged American independence. But that assertion of power masked the British weakness as a small island running a big empire, 125 times larger than their little homeland. In 1810 a Briton likened the empire to "an oak planted in a flower-pot." To defend that overstretched empire, the British desperately needed every subject who could serve in the British army or Royal Navy. So they insisted on their right to reclaim any subject found on the high seas *and* to make subjects of foreign-born sailors and of American settlers in Canada. This double policy angered Americans hypersensitive to any erosion of their new independence.[17]

The two migration streams—of the Irish to America and of Americans to Canada—collided in the civil war of 1812. Becoming staunch Republicans, the Irish-Americans sought revenge on the empire for dominating Ireland and for treating them as runaway subjects when found on American ships. Irish-Americans served in disproportionate numbers in the armies that invaded Upper Canada, where they sought support from the Late Loyalist majority. But that support withered as the American troops proved more adept at looting than at fighting. Defeats cast scores of Irish-Americans into British prisons, where they had to enlist in the royal forces or face trial as traitors. To save them, the American government threatened to execute a captured Briton for every soldier hanged by the British. In an escalating spiral, most of the prisoners on both sides became hostages for the fate of the Irish-American soldiers threatened with British trial.

The civil war had four overlapping dimensions. In the first, Loyalists and Americans battled for control of Upper Canada. Second, the bitter partisanship within the United States threatened to become a civil war, as many Federalists served the British as spies and smugglers, while their leaders in New England flirted with secession. Third, Irish republicans waged a civil war within the British empire, renewing in Canada their rebellion, which the British had suppressed in Ireland in 1798. Invading Canada, Irish-American soldiers faced British regiments primarily recruited in Ireland, for thousands of Irishmen had fled from poverty by enlisting in the royal forces. Fourth, the war embroiled and divided native peoples. In the Great Lakes country, the Indians allied with the British to roll back American expansion. By intimidating and defeating the invaders, the native warriors obliged the Americans to seek their own Indian allies from reservations within the United States. The fighting especially divided the Shawnee and the Haudenosaunee nations. In the North American civil war of 1812, Americans fought Americans, Irish battled Irish, and Indians attacked one another. They struggled to extend, or to contain, the republicanism spawned by the American Revolution.

HISTORIES

The War of 1812 looms small in American memory, forgotten as insignificant because it apparently ended as a draw that changed no boundary and no policy. At best, Americans barely recall the war for a handful of patriotic episodes: for the resistance of Fort McHenry to British bombardment, which inspired the national anthem; for the victories of the warship dubbed "Old Ironsides"; for the British perfidy in burning the White House and the Capitol; and for the payback taken by Andrew Jackson's Tennessee riflemen at the battle of New Orleans. These images suggest a defensive triumph against British aggression, which obscures the war's origins and primacy as an American invasion of Canada. Of course, Canadians primarily remember what Americans forget, celebrating their victory as a David over the American Goliath, repelled after burning the public buildings of Upper Canada's capital. And Canadians cultivate their own patriotic icons, particularly the martyr Isaac Brock and the plucky Laura Secord, their equivalent of Paul Revere.

But this book attempts a borderlands rather than a national history, for it promotes neither Canadian nor American icons of patriotism. A borderlands history examines the peoples on both sides of a new and artificial border, as they often defied the control of their rival governments. Neither a comprehensive nor a conventional history of the war, this book focuses on the contested region between Montreal on the east and Detroit to the west. In that borderland, two Great Lakes— Ontario and Erie—and three connecting rivers—the St. Lawrence, the Niagara, and the Detroit—served as the porous border between the republic and the empire. That border region featured most of the war's fighting and destruction. Focused there, this book pays only fleeting attention to the war's secondary theaters along the Atlantic and Gulf coasts and on the high seas. To compensate for the limited geographic range, I offer greater depth in time, devoting more attention to the roots of the conflict, during the 1780s and 1790s, and to the postwar consequences during the 1820s and 1830s.

Conventional histories dwell on presidents, diplomats, and generals, and on a few decisive battles which hinged in turn on the characters and intellects of those leading men, cast as either heroes or fools. Although I do narrate battles and do assess the feats and foibles of leaders, I devote more attention to the relationship of soldiers with civilians. For example, the plundering of York by American troops gets more play than does the brief battle that temporarily won that town, for the looting did far more to alienate Canadians than the victory did to impress them.[18]

To prevail in the war, both sides had to win the hearts and minds of civilians, both at home and on the front. Hampered by long supply lines, a short growing season, and sharp seasonal swings in temperature, the rival armies could only sporadically come to grips in battle. Commanders spent most of their time struggling to recruit, train, feed, clothe, motivate, and heal their soldiers or to retake and punish those who ran

Fort George, by Edward Walsh, *1805. A British army surgeon, Walsh had an intimate familiarity with Fort George, which guarded the British side of the Niagara River at its outlet into Lake Ontario. Officers' quarters occupy the center of the background, with drilling soldiers on the right and tamed bears in the left and center foreground.* (Courtesy of the William L. Clements Library, University of Michigan.)

away. To succeed, the commanders needed cooperation from the civilians who raised the food, provided the recruits, wove the cloth, and gave haven to deserters. To woo Upper Canadians, the American generals posed as liberators, but their men behaved too much like the ruthless plunderers described by British propaganda. On the other hand, the British had no better luck restraining their own troops or their Indian allies, who looted the Michigan Territory and the Niagara Valley, alienating the American civilians there.

By telling the story of the borderland war, I seek to illuminate the contrast and the contest between the republic and the empire in the wake of the revolution. Both Republicans and Loyalists suspected that the continent was not big enough for their rival systems: republic and mixed constitution. One or the other would have to prevail in the house divided. Like the revolution, the War of 1812 was a civil war between competing visions of America: one still loyal to the empire and the other defined by its republican revolution against that empire. But neither side would reap what it expected from the war. Frustrated in their fantasies of smashing the other, the Loyalist and the Republican Americans had to learn how to share the continent and to call coexistence victory.[19]

H.M.S. *Pearl* off Quebec, *by William Elliott, 1785. Six years later John Graves Simcoe and Elizabeth Simcoe sailed to Quebec on a similar frigate of the Royal Navy. In the background Quebec's Lower Town appears at the shore, with the Citadel and the Upper Town above.* (Courtesy of the Royal Ontario Museum, 961.2.)

CHAPTER ONE

LOYALISTS

We are in daily expectation of seeing planters on the American side of the [St. Lawrence] river and Great Lakes, and it is much to be wished they should on all occasions perceive how much they are fallen, and the loyalists find, upon every comparison, strong reasons to congratulate themselves upon having persevered in their duty.

—Lord Dorchester, 1788[1]

DESPITE THE 1783 PEACE treaty ending the American Revolutionary War, a cold war persisted between the United States and the British empire. British officials regretted the treaty's new boundary through the Great Lakes as too generous to the United States and detrimental to Canadian security. They longed to shift that flawed boundary southward, and to prevent the Americans from pushing northward to swallow Canada, driving the British from North America. In violation of the peace treaty, the British clung to frontier forts on the American side of the new border, and they supplied weapons and advice to Indian nations resisting the American expansion in the Ohio Valley.[2]

In 1791, at the height of the border tension and near its geographic center, the British established a new colony named Upper Canada. Carved out of the old province of Quebec, Upper Canada occupied the upper reaches of the St. Lawrence River and the northern shores of Lake Ontario and Lake Erie. Downstream belonged to Lower Canada, which retained the old capital at Quebec City, where a governor-general held military command of both provinces. His subordinate, a lieutenant governor, exercised the executive power in Upper Canada.[3]

To serve as Upper Canada's first lieutenant governor, the imperial lords appointed Colonel John Graves Simcoe, who had commanded a regiment of Loyalists during the war. Simcoe had friends in very high places, including Lord Grenville, the secretary of state who made the appointment. Although recently elected to Parliament, Simcoe longed to govern the new colony, which he regarded as ideally positioned to revive the empire by sapping the republic. In 1789 he offered "to consecrate myself to the Service of Great Britain in that Country in preference to any situation of whatever emolument or dignity."[4]

In a gray drizzle on November 11, 1791, the British warship *Triton* ascended the St. Lawrence River to Quebec. The passengers included Simcoe, his wife, Elizabeth, two children, and a handful of servants. Canada's capital and seaport, Quebec rose on a bluff, topped by stone walls with cannon to command the river. At the foot of the bluff lay the lower town, a compact grid of stone houses, shops, and warehouses beside the bustling wharves that hosted the ships. A steep street led up the bluff to the upper town, where a visitor found more houses, Catholic churches and convents, the governor's chateau, a marketplace, and barracks and a parade ground for the soldiers—all surrounded by the most impressive stone walls in Canada. The British clustered their Canadian troops at Quebec to guard the province's maritime gateway and to serve as a citadel should they lose control of the interior.[5]

In 1759 British troops had captured Quebec from the French, who conceded all of Canada to the victors in the peace treaty of 1763. To reconcile the French Canadians to British occupation, in 1774 Parliament adopted the Quebec Act, which endorsed French civil law and protected the Catholic faith. Parliament also dispensed with an elected assembly by mandating government by a military governor with a council of prominent colonists appointed by the Crown. The act also extended Quebec's boundaries south to the Ohio River and west to the Mississippi.[6]

By pleasing the French Canadians, Parliament alienated the empire's English-speaking Protestant colonists settled to the south along the Atlantic Seaboard. In 1763 they had celebrated the conquest of Canada for freeing them from the Indian raids so long promoted by the French. The conquest also promised to open to colonial settlement and speculation the vast, fertile lands to the west in the Ohio Valley and along the shores of the Great Lakes. When the Quebec Act turned those lands over to a military regime based in Quebec, Americans feared confinement east of the Appalachian Mountains, within a boundary patrolled by savage warriors allied to the empire.[7]

That confinement seemed especially menacing because the British had begun to impose new taxes on the colonists, who resented the new levies as unconstitutional. The British sought the money to fund the garrisons needed for the enlarged empire, but the colonists feared a dire spiral of ever higher taxes that would impoverish them. The new taxes combined with the frontier restrictions to alarm the colonists that the empire threatened their status and prosperity as freehold farmers.[8]

In the Quebec Act the Americans saw an arbitrary precedent ominous to their own freedom. As Protestants, they dreaded Catholicism as hostile to liberty and commerce. The provision of French civil law, rather than the English common law, troubled them by discounting trial by jury, freedom of the press, and immunity from arbitrary arrest. And by dispensing with an elected assembly, the Quebec Act aroused suspicions that the British soon would impose authoritarian rule on all of the colonies. In 1776 the American Declaration of Independence denounced the Quebec Act: "For abolishing the free System of English Laws in a neighbouring Province, establishing therein an arbitrary Government, and enlarging its Boundaries, so as to render it at once an Example and fit Instrument for introducing the same absolute Rule into these Colonies."[9]

In 1775 a "Patriot" party seized power in the thirteen colonies and sent troops north to drive the British from Canada. Although cool to the Patriot invasion, the French Canadians also did little to help the British defense. After capturing Montreal, the invasion ground to a halt before the walls of Quebec. In the predawn of December 31, a Patriot attack collapsed with the death of its commander, General Richard Montgomery, an Irish immigrant, while a loyal Irishman, Sir Guy Carleton, led the British defense.[10]

During the spring and summer of 1776, reinforcements arrived from Britain to drive the Patriots out of Canada and back into New York. Although unable to stage another invasion, the Patriots clung to their dream of ousting the British from Canada. Ratified in 1781, the original American federal constitution, the Articles of Confederation, prequalified the Canadian provinces as future states. A sense of weakness and a fear for the republic's security fueled the lingering American longing for Canada. To frustrate that longing, Simcoe came in 1791 to develop Upper Canada into a powerhouse.[11]

Used to the mild and wet climate of England, the Simcoes had to adjust to the sharp and sudden swings in Canada's seasons. They arrived at the start of the long, snowy, and bitterly cold winter that locked up the rivers and lakes in ice, shutting down most business. But winter compensated with a festive social season, as the snow eased travel on skates or in sleighs for both pleasure and visiting. "In winter all is dance and festivity," one newcomer declared. After four months of dinners, plays, concerts, and balls, Elizabeth Simcoe exulted, "How happy I am!" Spring arrived in late April, when the melting snow and ice produced a slippery, muddy mess that paralyzed travel by land. After a brief spring,

Loyalists at Johnstown, *watercolor by James Peachey, 1784. Refugees from the revolution, these men and women encamped in tents on the banks of the St. Lawrence*

a surprisingly hot and humid summer came in a rush. "By the first of June, we were in the midst of summer—a scorching sun, dusty roads, and the woods full of muskitoes, such is the sudden transition from winter to summer in Canada that there's no spring," a traveler marveled.[12]

As the ice melted in the St. Lawrence River, ships returned to Quebec, reviving business as the sudden rush of cargoes, coming and going, made for long and busy days through the brief warm season. That effect rippled upstream to the Great Lakes as boats carried British imports to upper country consumers. Farmers also had to work harder during the brief growing season between the frosts of May and September. In spring and summer, people had no time for socializing. On April 20 Elizabeth Simcoe sulked: "I do not like relinquishing Balls, Concerts, Suppers & Cards."[13]

The flow of information also alternated with the seasons. In summer

while they constructed new log homes. (Courtesy of Library and Archives Canada, C-2001.)

a ship took two months to carry news and goods from England to Quebec, and during the six months of winter the Canadians lived without the news borne by arriving ships. Anxious for information, they welcomed April's burst of letters, newspapers, and travelers from Britain. A visitor remarked, "A Londoner . . . can form no idea what a luxury a packet of papers from England is, at Niagara, when at the beginning of spring, the communication is opened." He recalled Jonathan Swift's satirical account of a "Northern region, where men's words, freezing at the commencement of a frost were thawed at its dissolution, into sounds, tumultuous and indistinct."[14]

In a dependent colony tethered to a powerful empire based in London, the Canadians longed to know the political and market news from Europe. Whether war or peace prevailed would affect their shipments, profits, and fates. A merchant in Canada begged his London supplier for

"Communications" from "your side [of] the Atlantic, where every Day Events happen that are of Importance to all the World, while in this remote Corner we are of importance to No Body but ourselves." Colonial officials particularly longed to know how they stood with their superiors in distant Britain. In June a judge in Canada reminded an official in London: "Remember October corresponds with April, therefore write speedily."[15]

JOURNEY

In June 1792 the Simcoes and their entourage headed up the St. Lawrence River in three bateaux: flat-bottomed boats, each about twenty-four feet long, able to carry two tons of cargo and requiring four men to row and a fifth to steer. As the working men rowed, the gentlemen and ladies examined the riverside landscape of whitewashed stone houses and wooden barns roofed with thatch. Every now and then they could see wooden crosses, a gristmill, a Catholic church, or the manor house of a landlord, known as a *seigneur*. Catholics of French descent, the people settled on long farms with a narrow frontage on the river. Britons regarded the French Canadians as ignorant, superstitious, lazy, and slovenly—but also as cheerful and vivacious.[16]

Five days of rowing brought the travelers to Montreal, "a middle sized country town" by English standards but solidly built of stone beside narrow streets. The crowding made fires frequent, contagious, and devastating, although the people had fortified their houses with slate or tin roofs and with iron shutters for their windows and doors. A visitor reported, "Every house looks like a prison."[17]

After a week at Montreal, the Simcoes resumed their journey by portaging in carts to Lachine, above the rapids, where they returned to their bateaux for the hard ascent up the St. Lawrence for 180 miles to Lake Ontario, the first of the Great Lakes. Rowing hard against the powerful current, the boatmen made a slow headway of about eighteen miles per day. They had to portage around three sets of rocky, foaming, and roaring rapids. Of course their return trip downstream with the current was easy, cutting to two or three days the upriver journey of ten days from Montreal to the lake. The time and labor of the ascent compounded the cost of getting British manufactured goods to consumers in the upper country.[18]

Above Montreal, the party crossed into Upper Canada, where the old French Canadian villages gave way to a thick forest broken by the new clearings of settlers. Passing the "diminutive log-houses, surrounded with a few acres of cleared land," a visitor noted that "a profusion of decayed and half-burnt timber lay around, and the serpentine roots of trees, blown down by tempests, stretched into the air, in the most fantastic forms." With axes to fell the trees, oxen to haul them together, and fire to consume them, the settlers waged war on the surrounding forest: "piles of blazing timber sent forth columns of smoke, which enveloped the forests far and wide. Axes rung in every thicket, and the ear was occasionally startled by the crashing of trees falling to the ground." Elizabeth Simcoe delighted in the fiery spectacle: "Perhaps you have no idea of the pleasure of walking in a burning wood, but I found it so great that I think I shall have some woods set on fire for my Evening walks." Some settlers killed the larger trees by girdling them—stripping away the lower bark, which left fields of leafless, graying, and rotting hulks.[19]

The settlers were Loyalist refugees, fleeing from defeat in the revolution. Most came from New York's Mohawk Valley, where they had been the tenants or clients of the county's wealthiest and most powerful family, the Johnsons. When the rebellion erupted in 1775, the Johnsons stood by the empire that had enriched and empowered them. They rallied their settler clients and the Six Nations' Haudenosaunee (or "Iroquois") in a Loyalist coalition. Disarmed and harassed by Patriots, the Johnsons and their tenants fled north to Canada, where they organized Loyalist regiments. Although averse to British taxation, the Loyalists regarded Patriot domination as far worse, as mob rule destructive to justice and property.[20]

While the Patriots fought for an independent republic, the Loyalists defended the union of the empire. Regarding Catholic and absolutist France as their traditional foe, the Loyalists understood the empire as a bastion of liberty, property, commerce, and Protestantism: values which they understood to be interdependent and fragile. Favoring a social hierarchy and a strong government, the Loyalists cherished the king and the aristocracy as essential elements in a mixed constitution designed to preserve order and property from anarchy. So they feared the Patriots as demagogues driven by greed and ambition to conspire against the freedoms best protected by the union of the empire and by the constitutional balance of king, aristocracy, and commons. The Loyalists felt vindicated when the Patriots brutally suppressed dissent and entered a military alliance with France.[21]

The Indians and the Loyalists fought hard and well, ravaging the

Patriot settlements in the Mohawk Valley in 1780 and 1781. But in July 1782, they received demoralizing orders: to stand down, while British diplomats in Europe negotiated a peace with the United States. The new policy followed a crushing defeat at Yorktown, Virginia, in October 1781, when Lord Cornwallis had surrendered his British army to General George Washington. In 1783 the British concluded a peace treaty that recognized American independence and rewarded the Patriots with a remarkably generous boundary. Although financially bankrupt and defeated on the frontier, the United States secured expansive territory that stretched south to Florida, west to the Mississippi, and north to the Great Lakes. The new boundary sacrificed the empire's primary forts on the Great Lakes: at Oswego, Niagara, Detroit, and Michilimackinac.[22]

The British prime minister, Lord Shelburne, paradoxically believed that indulging the United States with generous bounds would reunite the empire. He reasoned that, if diffused over a vast territory, the Americans would remain farmers, perpetuating their dependence on British manufactured goods. That economic dependence would profit British merchants and soften the American desire for political independence. Soon they would seek some form of renewed union with the empire. Shelburne argued, "If we are to look to regain the affection of America, to reunion in any shape or even to commerce and friendship, is it not of the last degree of consequence to retain every means to gratify America?"[23]

The treaty betrayed the people who had done the most to defend Canada: the Indians and the Loyalists. The Patriot diplomats pledged only to "recommend" that their states welcome back the Loyalists and restore their confiscated property. Everyone but the British negotiators knew that this recommendation was worthless, for the states meant to keep the property and to keep out the Loyalists. And in the weak American confederation, Congress lacked the power to pressure the states. Embittered by wartime raids, the Patriots brutalized any Loyalist refugees who tried to return. In Albany, a public meeting resolved "never to be at peace with those fiends, the Refugees, whose thefts, murders, and treasons have filled the cup of woe." New York's Governor, George Clinton, vowed that he would "rather roast in hell to all eternity than . . . show mercy to a damned Tory"—an insulting name for a Loyalist.[24]

Blocked from returning home, at least 38,000 Loyalists settled in Britain's remaining northern colonies during 1783–84. The great majority (30,000) moved to the maritime provinces of New Brunswick and Nova Scotia. Smaller numbers settled in Quebec (2,000) and the upper country (6,000) west of Montreal as far as Detroit. In the upper country, the Loyalists clustered along the St. Lawrence River and around the Bay of Quinte, at the northeastern corner of Lake Ontario, or along the Niagara Peninsula at that lake's southwestern corner.[25]

To help the Loyalist settlers, the British Crown provided free land, seed grain, tools, and rations for their first two years. The government also built mills to grind their grain into flour and to turn logs into boards for building frame houses. In addition to rewarding loyalty, the British sought to strengthen Canada with people who would transform the forest into farms, which would reduce the costs of feeding the garrisons in the forts. Alienated from the republic, the Loyalists could also provide a militia to help defend Canada should war resume with the Patriots. And the British hoped to score propaganda points by showing to Americans the benefits of clinging to the empire. Canada's governor-general, Lord Dorchester, insisted that they "should on all occasions perceive how much they are fallen, and the loyalists find, upon every comparison, strong reasons to congratulate themselves upon having persevered in their duty."[26]

During the late 1780s, the promise of the Loyalist settlements attracted a second pulse of emigrants from the United States. Many were friends and relatives of the initial emigrants. Others were Germans and Quakers from Pennsylvania and New Jersey. In addition to the pull of free land in Canada, the emigrants responded to the push of political turmoil and economic hard times in the United States. To pay their war debts, the American states levied heavier taxes than the British had ever dared to impose, which dismayed the common people. In welcoming the second wave, British officials adopted a broad definition of Loyalism to include, in Lord Sydney's words, postwar "Sufferers under the ruinous and arbitrary Laws and Constitution of the United States." The British provided the newcomers with two hundred acres of free land but not the tools and provisions given to the original Loyalists. The second wave helped to boost the population in the upper country from 6,000 in 1784 to 14,000 by 1791.[27]

In 1788 a parasite, known as the Hessian fly, devastated the wheat harvest in Canada and the American Northeast, producing rampant hunger during the spring and summer of 1789. On the American side of the border, most settlers muddled through with little or no help from the government, but Canadians benefited from a more paternalistic regime. New York was the lone American state to provide any public relief for the hungry. On the Canadian side, however, the storehouses of the forts provided a reserve, from which commandants advanced barrels of pork, peas, and rice to the needy settlers. Still greater public relief came in the fall, when the Crown purchased in Britain and shipped to Quebec 1,000 tons of flour, 23,000 bushels of wheat, and 24,000 bushels of peas. Although the population of Canada was a third of New York's, the colony received twenty-five times as much public food relief.[28]

By delivering abundant food with a paternalistic flair, the British sought to strengthen loyalty in Canada. Lord Grenville assured Dorchester that the aid would impress "the minds of His Majesty's Subjects under your Lordship's Government with a just sense of His Majesty's paternal regard for the welfare of all his People." In 1791 the Crown canceled that debt with a flourish meant to contrast British benevolence with the crass commercialism of the republic. Upon arriving in Canada, the king's son, Prince Edward, announced: "My father is not a merchant to deal in bread and ask payment for food granted for the relief of his loyal subjects." By contrast, in the republic, the bread merchants ruled and imprinted their names on their towns. In the Mohawk Valley, the people renamed one town as Paris, not after the French metropolis, but to honor Isaac Paris, a merchant and miller who had loaned them food in 1789. The British promoted a Canadian identity framed in contrast with the republic, understood as an amoral land of greedy competition where demagogues flattered the common folk but exploited the poor among them.[29]

NIAGARA

Upon reaching northeastern Lake Ontario, the Simcoes came to Kingston. Founded in 1784, Kingston had a small hilltop fort, barracks, an Anglican church, log wharves, and fifty wood-frame houses. On a rocky point that sheltered the best harbor on the lake, Kingston prospered from the trade of the new farms that, during the 1780s, spread along the shores of the nearby Bay of Quinte. That bay also hosted Tyendinaga, a small reserve occupied by a band of Mohawk Indians. Comprising one of the Haudenosaunee Six Nations, the Mohawks had fled from war-torn New York to join the British in Canada.[30]

To proceed up the country, the Simcoes had to cross Lake Ontario, for no roads penetrated the deep forest, and no bridges crossed the many streams and rivers west of the Bay of Quinte. Rather than risk crossing the big lake in open bateaux, the Simcoes shifted into an eighty-ton schooner, one of several vessels which sailed to Niagara, 160 miles to the southwest. Blessed with a fair wind, the Simcoes made the journey in just three days, but other voyagers battled headwinds for a week or more.[31]

The wooden vessels and the stormy lake made for a dangerous combination. Sudden and powerful storms generated great swells that could drive vessels against the shifting sandbars or the rocky cliffs on the southern shore. In November 1780 a blizzard sank the lake's largest ship, drowning 350 British soldiers and crew and their officers. Hastily built of green wood and poorly maintained, the lake vessels usually rotted to ruin within a decade. Worse still, the mariners were notoriously inept and chronically drunk. A Simcoe servant recognized one sailor as a chicken thief who had fled from justice in England. Another passenger recalled a harrowing passage through a nightlong gale while the drunken captain bellowed, "Let us all go to hell together." Some travelers also swore that they saw "a great Snake, at least thirty feet long, which, from its rearing its head and forepart out of the water . . . meant to attack them!"[32]

On July 25, the Simcoes reached the mouth of the Niagara River, which pours Lake Erie's water into Lake Ontario. On the eastern shore, Fort Niagara occupied a point that controlled the river's mouth and the harbor within. Built by the French during the 1720s but captured by the British in 1759, Fort Niagara featured a stone stronghouse surrounded with extensive earthworks and a stockade to shelter the cannon that commanded the river. Beyond the walls and beside the river, crude taverns, stores, and bordellos sprouted on "the Bottom." A pious Quaker described Niagara as "a strong fortification, but a dark, noisy, confused, dirty place." Across the river on the western bank, the British had built barracks, storehouses, and a wharf, where the schooners and ships disgorged their passengers and cargoes. That bank also had a new Loyalist village, Newark, which in 1792 consisted of about a dozen wooden houses on a grid of muddy streets. Eager to be on the front lines of a probable new conflict with the Americans, Simcoe made Newark his home and the capital for the new colony.[33]

Newark hosted a small elite of regular army officers, retired Loyalist commanders, and local merchants and magistrates (and their wives). Striving to maintain genteel standards in their frontier setting, they hosted dinners, levees, teas, card games, and balls. A traveler marveled at seeing the women wearing the "Feathers, trinkets, and all the paraphernalia" of "the haughty dames of Britain." While the fashions were

British, this little high society included the daughters of Indian women and British officers. Elizabeth Simcoe enjoyed the "pleasant society within a certain circle" defined by a gentility of means and manners. But she complained that the local servants were few, expensive, and uppity: "The worst of people do you a favour if they merely wash dishes for twenty shillings a month."[34]

In the upper country, the mosquitoes of summer carried an endemic malaria known from its symptoms as "ague and fever." Associated with the lowlands, the sickness was more debilitating than deadly. But that sapping debility could last for months and came at the worst of times: during the short warm season when people most needed to work. Given the voracious labor demands of making a new farm in the forest, a family could ill afford the ague and fever. Unaware that mosquitoes carried the pathogens, people blamed their illness on night air around marshes or on drinking too much water in hot weather.[35]

From Newark, the new Loyalist settlements spread west on the fertile plain along the northern shore of the Niagara Peninsula. The new farms also stretched south along the west bank of the Niagara River to the celebrated falls, where the Niagara River pours over an immense escarpment, which extends over two hundred miles, from the Genesee River on the east to the western end of the Niagara Peninsula. A striking feature in an otherwise flat landscape, the escarpment became known as "the mountain."[36]

From Fort Niagara, the river extends thirty-one miles upstream to Lake Erie. Boats could ascend seven miles to the rapids below the falls, where the boatmen had to portage for eight miles to get over the escarpment. On the western side, the portage began at Queenston and terminated, above the falls, at Chippawa, where the boats could reenter the river. While boatmen concentrated on their hard lugging, their genteel passengers exulted in the sublime spectacle of the largest waterfall they had ever seen, as a massive volume of water plunged 144 feet. Miles before reaching the falls, they could hear its thunder and see a thick cloud of mist. Elizabeth Simcoe noted, "The fall itself is the grandest sight imaginable from the immense width of waters & the circular form of the grand fall."[37]

Sixteen miles above the falls, the boatmen reached Lake Erie. On the eastern shore, at the lake's outlet, they found Black Rock, a dark, low outcropping where Indians fished in the river. A few miles up the nearby Buffalo Creek lay a cluster of Indian villages, home to 2,100 natives in 1783. They spoke an Iroquoian language and belonged to the Haudenosaunee (or Six Nations) confederation, which consisted of the Mohawk, Oneida, Tuscarora, Onondaga, Cayuga, and Seneca nations. During the war, most had allied with the British and had fled to Buffalo Creek to escape Patriot raids on their villages. During the mid-1780s the Mohawks founded another set of villages to the west in the nearby Grand River Valley.[38]

Proud of their victories in the war, the Haudenosaunee felt outraged by the shocking peace treaty, which cast their lands within the American boundary. In 1783, at Fort Niagara, a British general reported their insistence "that the Indians were a free People subject to no Power upon Earth, that they were faithful allies of the King of England, but not his Subjects—that he had no right Whatever to grant away to the States of America, their Rights or Properties." The Haudenosaunee wished to live as free people between, rather than be divided by, the republic and the empire.[39]

In 1783 the 2,500,000 Americans greatly outnumbered the 100,000 British subjects in Canada. To even the odds in any renewed war with the republic, the British needed Indian allies. After the loss of the thirteen colonies, Patrick Murray explained, "We are no longer the first landed power in North America. Therefore [we] cannot have too many Indians under our protection and countenance." The British had to treat the Indians with diplomatic respect and to bestow generous presents, including guns and ammunition.[40]

To keep the Americans away from their lands, the Indian nations of the Great Lakes and the Ohio Valley formed a confederation. During the 1780s, by defeating the American army and attacking the settlers in the Ohio Valley, the native confederacy threatened the fragile American union, which needed to expand to survive. Congress relied on the revenue and the patronage derived from selling the Indian lands north and west of the Ohio River. And new settlements provided farms for a rapidly growing American population. Already teetering on bankruptcy and hard pressed to control the states, the republic lost credibility as it lost battles to the Indians. To preserve their union, the Americans needed to defeat and dissolve the Indian confederacy.[41]

While appalling to Americans, the Indian confederacy appealed to Britons embarrassed by the peace treaty's betrayal of their native allies. Under Indian pressure, the British broke the peace treaty with the Americans by keeping the border forts along the Great Lakes. An Indian-controlled borderland also appealed to Canada's powerful merchants, primarily Scots, who traded British manufactures for the furs garnered by Indian hunters around the Great Lakes. Retaining the British posts, defending an Indian borderland, and supporting an Indian confederacy combined to keep away the meddling American traders and game-depleting settlers.[42]

By early 1784, Lord Shelburne's short-lived administration had fallen and the new administration, led by William Pitt the younger, recognized that the flawed peace treaty border compromised the security and economy of Canada. With growing signs that the American confederation was faltering, the British also wanted to be in a strong position for the anticipated collapse. Seeking principled grounds for keeping the posts, the British cited the American violations of the peace treaty, for most of the states had frustrated British merchants from collecting prewar debts and had kept the properties confiscated from the Loyalists.[43]

By retaining the border forts and arming the Indians, the British initiated a cold war. Unwilling to recognize Indian initiative, Americans reflexively blamed their frontier troubles on malicious Britons, who allegedly manipulated ignorant savages in an insidious plot to confine and to subvert the republic. Although outraged, the Americans felt helpless to break the British and Indian hold on the frontier. Nearly bankrupt, the American union could afford an army of only 350 men—too few to fight the Indians, much less renew war on the empire. In 1785 the American foreign secretary, John Jay, sighed, "Our foederal Government is incompetent to its Objects."[44]

Although willing to sustain a cold war, the British hoped to avoid another expensive hot war with the Americans. By holding out the vague prospect that eventually they would surrender the forts, the British strung out diplomatic discussions with the Americans over the tangled issues of the border, the Indians, the merchants' debts, and the Loyalist property. Playing for time, the British waited to see if the United States would collapse, leaving the forts, the Indians, and the fur trade in the British orbit. The American diplomat John Adams explained, "they rely upon it, that we shall not raise an Army to take the Posts . . . and therefore they think they may play with us as long as they please."[45]

DETROIT

Forested on both shores, Lake Erie was a passage between two isolated settlements, Niagara on the east and Detroit to the west, within an Indian world. Wearied by the stormy lake and the wild shores, travelers exulted on reaching the Detroit River, where the French-Canadian *habitants* had crowded the banks with thriving farms. The valley boasted large orchards, which produced Canada's finest apples, pears, plums, peaches, and nectarines. In addition to orchards and farmhouses, the visitors could see thriving fields of wheat and peas, pastures for cattle, and an occasional Catholic chapel and several windmills, which ground grain and cut logs. Beyond the narrow string of riverside farms loomed a dense and immense forest, which seemed disorienting and terrifying because it was so flat, so cloudy, so swampy, so devoid of landmarks for a newcomer, and so full of wolves and Indians.[46]

Delighted by the farms, travelers felt disappointed upon reaching Detroit—a cramped, noisy, and dirty town of 150 low houses crowded within a palisade punctuated by blockhouses. A fort loomed on the hill behind the town, while wharves covered the riverbank. Two carriages could barely pass in the narrow and muddy streets. The French Canadian majority of artisans, boatmen, and laborers shared Detroit with British officers, Scots merchants, and Loyalist settlers. During the day, Indians visited the town to trade and to drink. By 10:00 p.m, the soldiers shooed them out and closed the town gates, shutting in the inhabitants and shutting out the natives. Patrolling the walls and guarding the gates, sentries called out, every fifteen minutes and in succession, "All is well," with the last sentry concluding, "All is very well." Visitors found the nightly performance more unnerving than reassuring. The moral and pious Protestant sorts who kept travel journals also disliked the loose morals and abundant festivity of Detroit, especially in winter. A missionary concluded that the Detroit *habitants* were "a thoughtless and wicked, a cheerful and good-natured people." That good nature certainly appears in their persistent hospitality to such censorious visitors.[47]

Polyglot Detroit represented the transformed British empire of the late eighteenth century. During the Great Imperial War of 1754–63, the British had won a more global and cosmopolitan empire, which included new sugar-producing islands in the Caribbean, slave stations in West Africa, much of India, and all of Canada. Twenty years later, the American Revolution cost the British most of their overseas subjects who spoke English and who professed a British culture. Thereafter, the British retained a disparate set of far-flung colonies, where English-speakers were a small official elite governing diverse natives, enslaved Africans, or conquered French. With a new population of Loyalists, most of the upper country of Canada was both an anomaly and a throwback to an empire where colonists claimed the rights of Britons.[48]

EMPIRE

In the wake of the revolution, the imperial lords struggled to define the best means to preserve the rest of their empire. To avert further revolution, British moderates favored libertarian reforms to appease their colonists. But conservatives believed that indulgence had lost the thirteen colonies, so they favored an authoritarian paternalism that consolidated more power in the royal governors of the colonies. In June 1783 John Adams observed:

> The British Ministry & Nation are in a very unsettled State. They find themselves in a new Situation, and have not digested any Plan. Ireland is in a new Situation. . . . Canada too & Nova Scotia are in a new Situation—the former, they say, must have a new Government. But what Form to give them & indeed what kind of Government they are capable of, or would be agreeable to them, is uncertain.

Ireland was linked to Canada, which in turn affected how the British would treat the newly independent Americans.[49]

Many Irish—both Protestant and Catholic—had identified with the American Patriots during their revolution. Irish reformers shared the Patriot critique of British rule as corrupt, irresponsible, and unresponsive. In 1775 the American Congress adopted an "Address to the People of Ireland" to promote Irish neutrality in the war and to offer emigrants "a safe asylum from poverty and . . . oppression." Irish popular songs celebrated Patriot victories and treated General Richard Montgomery as a martyr for liberty. Irish mobs discouraged recruits for the British army and harbored deserters from regiments ordered to embark for America.[50]

When the war diverted British troops to North America, Ireland became exposed to a French invasion. In 1778, Irish reformers pressured the British by organizing an armed militia, known as the Volunteers, ostensibly to defend the island. Desperate for men, the British reluctantly accepted the Volunteer units, which doubled as political clubs to agitate for reforms. That agitation seemed to triumph in 1782, when the Shelburne administration conceded legislative autonomy to the Irish Parliament. Thereafter, Ireland remained linked to Britain through the Crown, which appointed the Irish executive: a lord lieutenant and his cabinet. Legislation by the Irish Parliament also still required the king's assent. By offering legislative independence but executive dependence, Shelburne hoped that this Irish constitutional reform would entice the Americans back into the empire. To his dismay, the Americans wanted no part of the Irish model, clinging instead to their new independence.[51]

Ireland's supposed legislative autonomy soon proved hollow. The Catholic majority remained barred from voting and from holding office. In partnership with the lord lieutenant, a small elite of Anglican aristocrats continued to dominate the Irish Parliament and to block further reforms. Rather than leading to greater autonomy, the limited concessions of 1782 proved a reactionary firewall that consolidated the recalcitrance of the Anglican elite, which deeply frustrated the Irish reformers.[52]

In 1782 Lord Shelburne had also sought to entice Americans by offering a generous commercial treaty. He proposed opening the empire's colonial ports to American merchant ships, restoring the prewar trade which had been so mutually beneficial to American shippers and to the sugar planters of the British West Indies. But Shelburne's trade proposal appalled conservative Britons, who upheld the protective system mandated by the Navigation Acts. Framed during the seventeenth century, those acts favored British merchant ships at the expense of foreign carriers. That favoritism sought to increase British revenue, stimulate British shipbuilding, and maximize the number of British sailors. Those economic benefits sustained the powerful navy needed to protect the empire's commerce and to enforce the Navigation Acts against foreign interlopers. In a synergy, the Royal Navy secured the swelling commerce that generated the revenue and trained the sailors to sustain the fleet. British prosperity, pride, and power depended on preserving a maritime empire defined by the Navigation Acts.[53]

Conservatives insisted that, if rewarded with free trade, the cunning Americans would supplant the British as the leading carrier of the world's trade. The British would then lose sailors, their navy, and ultimately their empire. Instead of indulging the dangerous Americans, the British should favor Canada's Loyalists who would prosper if freed from American competition by a privileged position to supply fish, livestock, lumber, and grain to the British West Indies. Lord Dorchester insisted: "The only firm hold that Great Britain has upon the remains of the American Dominions is certainly by means of the Loyalists."[54]

In 1783 the British conservatives benefited from the public backlash against Shelburne's peace treaty as appeasement to rebels. British taxpayers felt disgusted by news of American treaty violations, which obliged them to compensate the Loyalists for their losses. The backlash led the Crown to apply the Navigation System to the Americans, which meant that only ships owned, built, and crewed by Britons or their colonists could trade with the West Indies or carry away any colonial produce. American ships could trade at ports in Great Britain, for the British were eager to sell their manufactures to the American market.[55]

By enforcing the Navigation System, the British provoked a commercial depression in the United States during the mid-1780s. Deprived of the West Indian market, American merchants could not pay their mounting debts for British imports. A wave of merchant bankruptcies and farm foreclosures created political turmoil. Unable to coordinate the trade policies of the states, and lacking the revenue for a navy, the Congress could not challenge the British terms of trade. And the American woes and weaknesses compounded British contempt for the republican union, which seemed doomed to collapse.[56]

In 1786 the British sent Lord Dorchester to Quebec as the governor-general. To serve as the colony's new chief justice, Dorchester brought along his American friend, William Smith, Jr., who shared his vision for restoring the union of the empire. In colonial New York, Smith had been a leading lawyer, historian, and politician. A conservative Patriot, he had opposed Parliament's taxes but had cherished Britain's mixed constitution. Balking at independence and republican government, Smith had bolted to join the British in occupied New York City, where he served as a spymaster, political consultant, and jurist. Since the 1760s Smith had promoted a constitutional rearrangement that would unite the colonies under their own parliament, independent of the British Parliament, but yoked to the empire by a Crown-appointed lord lieutenant, as in Ireland.[57]

During the 1780s the American turmoil confirmed Smith's conviction that no republic could survive on a continental scale. He confidently predicted: "We are on the Eve of a Revolution that will lay aside the Congress and the Republican Models. The Change will be either the setting up of the British model with a Reunion, or with a *new King*." To hasten that change, Smith and Dorchester proposed setting up a model constitution in Canada. By displaying the prosperous fruits of stability, the reformed empire would allure their American neighbors to abandon their futile experiment of an independent republic. Sooner rather than later, the Americans would need a king to restore order to their chaos.[58]

Leading Americans felt alarmed by the return of Lord Dorchester to Quebec with an apparent mandate to rebuild the empire in North

America. It seemed more than coincidental that Dorchester and Smith arrived just as rural Massachusetts erupted in Shays's Rebellion, named for a disaffected army officer, Captain Daniel Shays. Hard-pressed to pay their debts and taxes, armed farmers shut down the courts and resisted state troops sent to suppress them. During the winter of 1786–87, Shays and four of his officers visited Dorchester in Quebec, where rumors insisted that they pledged allegiance in return for munitions.[59]

Americans also worried over Dorchester's intrigues with the leading men in the frontier districts of Vermont and Kentucky. Anticipating a collapse of the American union, Lord Grenville secretly advised Dorchester:

> It appears extremely desirable that the turn of Affairs in those Settlements should lead to the establishment of a Government distinct from that of the Atlantic States, and if that should be the case, every means should be taken to improve and cultivate a Connection with the former, as being likely to prove highly advantageous to the Interests of this Country.

But Grenville also warned Dorchester to avoid provoking war with the United States. Preferring to let the republic unravel on its own, the imperial lords wanted to maximize their options without immediately committing themselves to any one of them. By flirting with Dorchester's agents, leading Vermonters and Kentuckians sought favorable trade deals and prepared their own contingency plans for the apparently impending collapse of the American union.[60]

In early 1787 Dorchester sent his aide, Major George Beckwith, to New York City to gather information and to cultivate supporters for a reunion of the empire. During the war, Beckwith had served there as an intelligence officer running spies behind the Patriot lines. In his greatest coup, Beckwith helped to turn Benedict Arnold from a Patriot hero into the war's most infamous traitor. At war's end, Beckwith left behind a network of contacts that he reactivated during his postwar visit.[61]

In March, Beckwith arrived at the low ebb of the American experiment in a republican union. New York's leading merchants and lawyers had lost confidence in the confederation as impotent and in the state governments as prey to reckless demagogues. Alarmed by Shays's Rebellion, these conservatives longed for a stronger national government that could collect taxes, protect creditors, subordinate the states, and revive prosperity in the seaports. But they remained divided over the proper form for a stronger government. Would a reformed republic suffice, or should they emulate Britain's mixed constitution with a king and aristocrats to regulate an elected legislature?[62]

Openly wearing his army uniform, Beckwith ostensibly visited to send Dorchester's dispatches to London via the port of New York. But he lingered, to the dismay of republicans and to the delight of disaffected conservatives. His informants included such prominent men as Alexander Hamilton and his father-in-law, Philip Schuyler, who assured Beckwith that leading Americans longed for a king and for a reunion with the empire. "At this moment, there is not a gentleman in the States from New Hampshire to Georgia, who does not view the present Government with contempt, who is not convinced of its inefficacy, and who is not desirous of changing it for a Monarchy," Beckwith reported. They had found "from experience that a Republican system, however beautiful in theory, is not calculated for an extensive country." He added that some gentlemen planned covertly to visit London to propose that the British provide one of George III's younger sons, of the House of Hanover, to become an American king.[63]

Dorchester eagerly conveyed Beckwith's reports to the imperial lords in London. Although intrigued, they remained cautious, preferring to wait for, rather than hasten, the collapse of the republic. Lord Sydney vaguely replied to Dorchester, "The Report on an Intention on the part of America to apply for a Sovereign of the House of Hanover has been circulated here and should an application of that nature be made it will require a very nice Consideration in what manner so important a subject should be treated." The imperial lords remained loath to make bold decisions lest they backfire as embarrassing mistakes.[64]

Beckwith's informants expected little from the federal convention that met in Philadelphia during the summer of 1787. But, against long odds, the delegates crafted a new federal constitution to replace the Articles of Confederation. While retaining republican institutions, including an elected congress, that constitution had the *potential* to provide a stronger national union that could subordinate the states. The new government could tax the people directly, instead of begging requisitions from the states. And, unlike the Articles, the new constitution had a potentially powerful executive branch headed by a president.[65]

By October 1788, when Beckwith returned to New York for a new visit, eleven states had ratified the federal Constitution, ensuring that the new government would commence in early 1789 with George Washington as the president. Beckwith's informants still preferred a mixed constitution, which Alexander Hamilton had, in vain, proposed to the Philadelphia convention. But they reluctantly accepted the federal Constitution as forming the most powerful government that the American public could abide. Of course Beckwith saw any republican union as eventually doomed for want "of energy sufficient to effect the ends for which it was framed." But he conceded the short-term possibility that the new government could muster just enough energy to raise an army to threaten the British border forts on the Great Lakes.[66]

CANADA ACT

The potential of the new American government obliged the imperial lords to resolve their own constitutional impasse in Quebec. If the Americans got their act together, the British would need greater cohesion and revenue to defend Canada. Under the Quebec Act of 1774, the governor-general and a council of British officials and French *seigneurs* governed without consulting the common *habitants*, who accepted political exclusion so long as they paid no taxes. The officials and *seigneurs* constituted a "French party," which opposed any reforms as the slippery slope to a republican revolution. But the Quebec Act antagonized the colony's small minority of two thousand Protestant Anglophones, primarily tradesmen and merchants who resided in the towns of Quebec and Montreal.[67]

This "British party" championed the British nationalism that upheld the Protestant faith, commercial enterprise, civil liberties, and an elected legislature as interdependent and essential to the wealth, power, and stability of the empire. Reinforced after the revolution by eight thousand Loyalist refugees, the British party pushed for English civil law, freehold land tenures, and an assembly. Their reforms would oblige the French Canadians to learn English, convert to Anglicanism, and become truly loyal subjects. Quebec presented a paradox wherein the British subjects felt restive because their own empire protected French culture and law.[68]

In his previous stint as Quebec's governor (1766–78), Dorchester had championed the Quebec Act, but he subsequently shifted toward the British party position under Smith's influence. In the governing council, Smith acted as Dorchester's prime minister, enraging the French party, which derided the reformers as greedy merchants out to exploit the poor, who were said to prefer a paternalistic and authoritarian government.[69]

The two parties agreed that the proposed reforms would attract more American migrants into Canada. The British party insisted that the newcomers would weaken the United States and strengthen Canada with belated but sincere Loyalists. Optimists of empire, they argued that the British mixed constitution appealed to Americans, as they suffered from the folly of their republican experiment. By escaping from the chaotic states, the migrants could, in the words of Hugh Finlay, "once more [enjoy] a free Government, where the Laws protect the person and property of the Subject." The French party, however, distrusted immigrants from the land of rebellion as subversives who would foment a revolution in Canada. The conservatives preferred the Catholic French Canadians as the best "barrier between our settlements and the United States."[70]

Evenly matched in the governing council, the British and French parties deadlocked in acrimony. Grown arrogant, cold, indecisive, and reclusive in his old age, Lord Dorchester provided little leadership. The squabbling dismayed the imperial lords. Dreading any popular agitation, the lords preferred a top-down solution imposed from London. In 1789 Lord Grenville explained, "I am persuaded that it is a point of true Policy to make these Concessions at a time when they may be received as [a] matter of favour, and when it is in Our own power to regulate and direct the manner of applying them, rather than to wait 'till they shall be extorted from us by a necessity."[71]

Grenville drafted the Canada Constitutional Act, which Parliament passed in 1791. The act divided the immense old colony of Quebec into two new provinces: Upper Canada, along the Great Lakes; and Lower Canada, in the lower St. Lawrence Valley, including the leading towns of Montreal and Quebec. The division was cultural as well as geographic, for Francophones predominated in Lower Canada while English-speaking Loyalists prevailed in Upper Canada. The provinces shared a governor-general based in Quebec, but a lieutenant governor would administer the civil government in Upper Canada, and the two colonies had distinct legislatures.[72]

Canada's constitution reflected the lessons of the American Revolution as understood by its foes, who designed a government meant to avoid internal turmoil and to resist republican subversion. Grenville had examined "the constitution of our former Colonies . . . in order that we may profit by our experience there, & avoid, if possible, in the Government of Canada, those defects which hastened the independence of our antient possession in America." He blamed excessive colonial democracy because "no care was taken to preserve a due mixture of the Monarchical & Aristocratical parts of the British Constitutions."[73]

But Grenville also made concessions to head off popular discontent, for Upper Canada needed to attract and retain American settlers. The Constitutional Act mandated freehold land tenure in Upper Canada and dropped the Crown quitrents that had irritated the prewar colonists. These concessions followed Dorchester's advice, "that all seeds of discord between Great Britain and her Colonies may be prevented." In the Canadian provinces, settlers could obtain two hundred acres by taking the oath of allegiance and paying merely nominal fees.[74]

One of the great ironies of the American Revolution was that it led to virtually free land for settlers in British Canada while rendering land more expensive in the United States. Burdened by public debts incurred to wage the war, the American federal and state governments sold lands to speculators, who could immediately pay the large sums in cash desperately needed to satisfy the public creditors. For example, in 1791 the New York State government sold 5,542,170 acres to land speculators for $1,030,433. Those speculators profited by retailing the land to actual settlers, who had to pay a premium: usually two or three dollars per acre. In sum, postrevolutionary settlers paid higher land prices to enrich the speculators who funded the war that had secured independence. If they disliked that bargain, settlers could immigrate to Canada to procure cheaper land by resuming their allegiance as British subjects.[75]

In a second major concession to American notions, the Constitutional Act reiterated Parliament's 1778 pledge never again to tax the North American colonists for revenue. Indeed, Britain heavily subsidized the government of Upper Canada by bearing the £50,000 annual cost for the military garrisons and the Indian presents. Parliament also funded the salaries drawn by the colony's executive and judicial officers, at a further cost of £7,000 a year. By paying the executive salaries, the Crown ensured control over the colony. This arrangement reflected another British lesson drawn from the revolution: that the elected assemblies of the thirteen colonies had exploited their power over expenditures to intimidate Crown officials by threatening to withhold their salaries. By funding the executive and judicial establishments in Upper Canada, the British made a shrewd investment in colonial dependence and popular passivity.[76]

Because of this British largesse, the Canadian colonists paid minimal taxes, primarily to finance their elected assembly and to construct district courthouses, jails, bridges, and roads. In 1794 Upper Canada's landholders paid only five shillings in tax for every hundred pounds in assessed property, a rate of one-quarter of one percent. This was one-fifth of the tax rate borne by New York's landholders. In 1808 the colony's revenue amounted to a paltry £3,000, about 5 percent of the total paid by British taxpayers to subsidize the colony.[77]

In another great irony of the revolution, the "winners" saddled themselves with higher postwar taxes (as well as higher land prices) to finance their war debts. In 1800 an American emigrating to Upper Canada explained his push factor: "We fought seven years to get rid of taxation, and now we are taxed more than ever!" Although deemed the war's losers, the Loyalists in Upper Canada secured a lighter tax burden than that borne by either the prewar colonists or the postwar citizens of the republic.[78]

Grenville sought a less provocative revenue by reserving one-seventh of the public domain for the Crown. As settlement developed the adjoining lands, the Crown Reserves would appreciate in value, generating enhanced rents to fund the government in lieu of taxes. Grenville believed that such a policy, "if it had been adopted when the Old Colonies were first settled, would have retained them to this hour in obedience and Loyalty." To endow the Anglican church—another bond of loyalty—the British reserved another seventh of the public lands as Clergy Reserves.[79]

In a further concession to American expectations, the British provided each new province with an assembly elected by the owners of land. Grenville concluded that a restricted assembly "would afford a juster & more effectual security against the growth of a republican or independent spirit, than any which could be derived from a Government more arbitrary in its form or principles." The British defined the assembly as a royal favor rather than as a popular right, and as the last, not the first, step toward a republic.[80]

Grenville believed that the revolution had ripened in the thirteen colonies because their assemblies had been too powerful and too democratic. Frequent elections from many paltry districts of small-minded farmers had filled those assemblies with parochial representatives hostile to imperial control. And so many representatives could not be co-opted given the limited patronage available to the colonial governors. Applying those lessons, the British limited the size of the Canadian assemblies by stretching the bounds of electoral districts. In Upper Canada, only sixteen members represented the nineteen counties in the first assembly of 1792–96.[81]

The elected assembly also had to share power with a "legislative council" of colonial notables. Nominated by the lieutenant governor and appointed by the Crown, the legislative councillors held life terms. Grenville hoped, in the future, to bestow titles of provincial nobility on the most worthy councillors: "to establish in the Provinces a Body of Men having that motive of attachment to the existing form of Government, which arises from . . . hereditary distinction." For want of a proper aristocracy, Grenville reasoned, the old colonies had rebelled.[82]

Both houses of the legislature were constrained by a powerful executive branch that served at the Crown's pay and pleasure. The lieutenant governor could summon, prorogue, or dissolve a legislative session. He appointed the speaker of the legislative council and could veto any speaker chosen by the assembly as well as any other bill. And his veto was complete, without provision for the legislature to override. Nor could the legislature review the measures or the expenditures of the executive branch. To become law, an assembly initiative had to survive a formidable gauntlet of increasingly elite and distant power. An assembly bill needed assent by the legislative council, next by the lieutenant governor, and finally by the imperial bureaucracy in London, where the Crown had up to two years to veto a colonial law.[83]

By granting or withholding patronage, the lieutenant governor could manage a small legislature, for the members coveted commissions in the militia or as justices of the peace as well as contracts to supply the military garrisons with provisions. Of course wayward representatives got nothing. In 1793 the province's chief justice advised John Graves Simcoe: "Grain is the sole produce of the Country and a Market the only Benefit required. Give me the Controul of that Market and I will ensure the Result of ev[e]ry Proposition to be made in the House [of Assembly] where ev[e]ry man is a Farmer." Simcoe agreed that the provision contracts were "indispensably necessary to the carrying on [of] the public measures with facility & tranquility." Because the colony's farmers depended on the military market, the lieutenant governor possessed an economic and political power far beyond that of any royal governor in the thirteen colonies.[84]

The mode of election also reduced popular influence in the assembly. The lieutenant governor appointed the sheriffs, who supervised the polling, held at a single location within each district, which kept down the turnout, given the dispersed settlements and miserable roads. Located in a shire town, the lone polling place favored voting by those most dependent upon the government's favor—the nearby lawyers, clerks, and merchants. Upper Canada also retained the traditional

English practice of public, oral voting, which discouraged independent voting by debtors and tenants.[85]

As in Britain, executive and judicial officers could also run for seats in the assembly, and they did not need to reside in their districts. Better educated and more articulate than the farmer-representatives, these officials dominated the legislative proceedings. During the 1790s John White held an assembly seat despite also serving as the attorney general and as a district court judge. Although he lived at Newark, White represented a distant district at the other end of Lake Ontario. In contrast, the American state constitutions required legislators to reside in their districts and banned them from holding executive or judicial office.[86]

The large districts, single polling places, oral voting, and executive eligibility favored pro-government candidates. In 1792 Simcoe recruited his surveyor general, David W. Smith, to stand for an assembly seat in Essex County, which lay on the Detroit River, more than two hundred miles west of Smith's residence at Newark. Simcoe explained, "The persons who shall compose the Assemblies must admittedly be dealt with as our Parliaments are & be purchased to their duty by the participation of the officers of government."[87]

Smith entrusted electioneering to his wealthy "friends," who campaigned in the traditional style by lavishing music, food, and alcohol—rather than policy discussions—upon the voters. A paternalist rather than an egalitarian, Smith advised his campaign manager, "Let the peasants have a fiddle, some beverage and beef." Anticipating victory, he planned a culminating celebration: "I beg an ox be roasted whole on the common and a barrel of rum to be given to the mob, to wash down the beef."[88]

As Simcoe expected, Smith won the seat and became the speaker of the assembly, where he zealously supported the Crown's policies rather than the parochial interests of his distant district. He explained: "We cannot at present exist without the assistance of Great Britain; she has ever shewn herself a foster Mother to her Colonies & any procedure which I conceive tends to divide the Interests of the Parent Kingdom & all her Colonies I will oppose with all my might." His perspective derived from his British birth and upbringing, his military officer's commission, his executive salary, and his loyalty to Simcoe—rather than from the dictates of his constituents.[89]

In 1795 a French traveler, the Duc de La Rochefoucault-Liancourt, passed from the United States into Upper Canada. He marveled when

Simcoe opened the legislative session, although only five of the sixteen assembly members had arrived:

> Where no taxes are to be settled, no accounts to be audited and examined, and no military regulations to be adjusted, public business cannot occupy much time. But, if even all these points were to be discussed, the business would still be trifling, from want of an opposition; which seems to be precluded by the manner in which the two Houses for Upper Canada are framed.

Nothing could have differed more from the avid electioneering and hyperactive legislation that the duke had witnessed in the United States.[90]

CONSTITUTIONS

In sum, the governments of Lower Canada and Upper Canada were more elitist than the thirteen colonies had been. Compared to their prewar predecessors, officials in Canada were more dependent upon the Crown and less beholden to popular pressure. Indeed, the Canadian mixed constitution was a considerable reaction against the republican experiments in the new United States, as a comparison with New York State reveals.[91]

Under the state constitution adopted in 1777, New York's elections became more frequent, more important, and more accessible to a larger electorate. The new constitution permitted polls in every township, rather than in just a single shire town per county, as under the old regime and the Canadian Constitutional Act. In New York, written ballots also replaced the oral voting that had subjected common men to intimidation by their landlords and creditors. Because the colonial governor had been a royal appointee, who, in turn, had named the members of the upper house, New York's colonial voter could only elect representatives to the assembly. After the revolution, however, most men could vote for governor, lieutenant governor, state senators, and federal congressmen as well as for assembly representatives. The colonial system had allocated but two assembly seats for every county no matter how large or small the county. The new state constitution established a more proportional system by allocating from two to ten assembly seats per county depending on population, and by mandating the regular addition and redistribution of county seats as population grew and shifted.

New York's voters chose assemblymen every year, their congressman biennially, their governor and lieutenant governor at triennial intervals, and their state senators every fourth year. Only the state senators were chosen as infrequently as Upper Canada's assemblymen. Republicanism maximized the popular sovereignty that the British mixed constitution sought to contain.[92]

The British designed the Canadian governments to avoid popular discontent *and* to discourage popular participation in politics. On the one hand, the British sought a content and inert public by minimizing taxation and the price of land. On the other hand, they also restricted electoral power to prevent demagogues from fomenting public ferment. Lord Thurlow explained that the British "have given them more civil liberty, without political liberty." He meant that they had granted liberties to Canadians while discouraging their political participation. In sum, the British worked to deny the colonists both the civil motives and the political means for rebellion.[93]

The Canada Constitutional Act culminated a decade of constitutional rearrangement in North America and Ireland. Set in motion by the American Revolution, the reordering included the 1782 reforms in Ireland, the Indian confederacy on the frontier, a new federal constitution for the United States, and the creation of Upper and Lower Canada. All four were related. By blocking American expansion, the Indian confederacy threatened the republican union that prospered by consuming Indian land. During the 1780s Indian victories halted American expansion and land sales, revealing the impotence of the American confederation. That impotence emboldened British leaders, who retained the border forts and revived the Navigation System. The retention embarrassed the United States, while the revival inflicted a trade depression. In turn, the economic troubles increased social conflict, particularly Shays's Rebellion, which further corroded confidence in the confederation.

Dreading a drift to anarchy, many Americans began to fear (and some to welcome) a British design to subvert the republic. Seeing an ominous precedent in the hollow reforms granted to Ireland in 1782, most Americans expected the worst from the similar scheme by Dorchester and Smith to render Canada a model for regenerating the empire. Americans feared the collapse of their weak union into an anarchy that would ultimately recommend a return to imperial rule.

To save their republican union, in 1787–88 the American Federalists crafted and ratified a new constitution. In response, the British endowed the Canadian colonies with a mixed constitution meant to attract American settlers while minimizing their political activity. Anglophone North America became a house divided between American republicanism and the British mixed constitution and between American expansion and the resistance of an Indian confederacy. Would the continent ultimately belong to an expansive republic, an "empire of liberty," or to a renewed British empire allied to a confederation of native peoples? To sway the answer to that question, the British sent John Graves Simcoe to govern Upper Canada.

John Graves Simcoe, *oil painting by Jean Laurent Mosiner, 1791. This portrait captures Simcoe in London shortly before he left for Canada.* (Courtesy of the Toronto Reference Library, Toronto Public Library Board.)

CHAPTER TWO

SIMCOE

His head was filled with vast utopian projects among which the least rational, and ultimately the most ruinous to the Colony, was to restore the old British Colonies to the Empire and a Persuasion that he was to be the Instrument.

—William Dummer Powell, 1815[1]

DEVOTED TO THE EMPIRE and its mixed constitution, John Graves Simcoe bitterly mourned the loss of the thirteen colonies. In 1791 he vowed, "I am one of those who know all the consequence of our late American Dominions. . . . I would die by more than Indian torture to restore my King and his Family to their just Inheritance." Determined to reverse the revolution, Simcoe believed that the new colony of Upper Canada could help to break up the fragile American republic. He assured his superiors:

> It is in the hope of being instrumental to the *Re-union of the Empire*, by sowing the Seeds of a vigorous Colony that I prefer the station I am appointed to & its fair prospects to any Post in his Majesty's Dominions of whatever Emolument. I am persuaded that it is the Interest of Northern America & G[reat] Britain to be united in some mode or other, & that such an Union is neither distant nor impracticable.

Americans would sooner return to their proper allegiance if they could look north to see the fruits of a renewed empire in a prosperous and orderly Upper Canada:

> I mean to prepare for whatever Convulsions may happen in the United States, and the Method I propose is by establishing a free, honourable British Government, and a pure Administration of its Laws, which shall hold out to the solitary Emigrant and to the several

States, advantages that the present form of [American] Government doth not and cannot permit them to enjoy.

Simcoe concluded, "The establishment of the British Constitution in this Province offers the best method gradually to counteract, and ultimately to destroy or to disarm the [American] spirit of democratic subversion." He envisioned Upper Canada as an antidote to the revolution, as an alternative to the republic, and as the model for a revived empire.[2]

Born in 1752, Simcoe revered the memory of his father, a royal naval captain who died in service to the empire during General James Wolfe's conquest of Quebec in 1759. Certain that his father had conceived Wolfe's winning strategy, the son felt driven by a family destiny to lead Canada's development within the empire. Captain Simcoe had drafted nineteen maxims to guide his doting son. Ranking "love of God" first, the captain added: "The love of your Country and King, which necessarily flows from the first maxim, must be your ruling principle." And Simcoe was to enforce the social hierarchy by a firm but fair paternalism: "regard the orderly and deserving; punish inexorably the disobedient and flagitious." Educated at Eton College and Oxford University, Simcoe delighted in classical languages and ancient historians, especially Plutarch. A critic later observed:

The Governor is a man of some reading and a tolerable classical scholar. For a man of the world, he appears to be governed too much by maxims. . . . to me, it appears that His Excellency has proposed to himself, as a model, one of Plutarch's chieftains. It ought, however, to be recollected, that not one of Plutarch's heroes was the governor of a modern British province.

At age eighteen, Simcoe bought an ensign's commission in the British army and joined the war against the American Revolution. An ambitious and dashing young officer, Simcoe served with distinction in the campaigns of 1776 and 1777, in New York, New Jersey, and Pennsylvania.[3]

Promoted to major, he received a daunting new assignment: command of a depleted and disorganized regiment of Loyalists, the Queen's Rangers. Simcoe rebuilt the ranks to four hundred men in an innovative corps that combined light infantry with light cavalry. Belying the stereotype of British redcoats as slow and blundering, the Queen's Rangers wore green uniforms and moved rapidly for hit-and-run raids. Employed in scouting and raiding around New York City, the regiment tangled early and often with Patriot militia and light troops. Aggressive, bold, and opportunistic, Simcoe won dozens of skirmishes, inflicting heavy casualties and taking hundreds of prisoners. Impressed by that record, the British commander, General Sir Henry Clinton, promoted Simcoe to lieutenant colonel.[4]

Simcoe empathized with his Loyalist troops, who had suffered violent persecution by their Patriot neighbors. He explained, "There are few families among them but what can relate some barbarous murder, or atrocious Requisition, which their relatives have undergone from the Rulers of the United States; however those transactions may have been concealed and glossed over in Europe." The Patriots, he charged, "fined, whipt, banished, and hung without mercy all who opposed their resolutions."[5]

Partisan combat by small units was especially ruthless, doubly so when the combatants were fellow Americans. By taking revenge on the Patriots, Simcoe obeyed his father's maxim to punish the "disobedient." Simcoe burned a New Jersey courthouse and jail after finding and liberating a chained and starving Loyalist. He also torched a church for hosting snipers and executed a Patriot militia captain accused of atrocities. Governor William Livingston of New Jersey denounced Simcoe as "a consummate Savage." Wounded and captured in October 1779, he suffered two months of close confinement ordered by Livingston, who wanted to hang him. Instead, a parole and exchange restored Simcoe to the British service.[6]

As a partisan on the front lines with a Loyalist unit, Simcoe depended upon timely insights about local roads, enemy movements, and secret friends. He cultivated closeted Loyalists who provided crucial tips and insights. Impressed by Simcoe's knack and network, General Clinton engaged him in secret service operations supervised by Captain John Andre. In 1780 Simcoe worked on Andre's boldest gambit: a bid to turn General Benedict Arnold from Patriot hero into a Loyalist agent who would betray the fortress at West Point. Andre's capture by Patriot militia foiled that betrayal, but Arnold escaped to British lines. Unable to recover Arnold, Washington settled for hanging Andre as a spy. Infuriated, Simcoe ordered his troops to wear mourning and to seek "the vengeance due to an injured nation and an insulted army."[7]

Instead, the war ended badly for Simcoe and the Loyalists. Sent to Virginia in 1780, Simcoe and most of the Queen's Rangers suffered defeat and surrender as part of Lord Cornwallis's army at Yorktown in 1781. Simcoe escaped captivity when delegated by Cornwallis to take news of the surrender to England. His captured men were less fortunate, with some executed as American deserters. At home, Simcoe fumed at the government's decision to make peace, accept American independence, and abandon the Loyalists. Simcoe also lost his military patron when Clinton resigned, giving up command in America to Sir Guy Carleton. To mend some fences with the Americans, Carleton degraded and disbanded the Queen's Rangers remaining in New York City, which infuriated Simcoe in distant England. After the British evacuated the city in late 1783, the former Queen's Rangers resettled, with their families, in Nova Scotia and New Brunswick.[8]

Meanwhile, Simcoe prospered in England. In 1782 he married a well-educated, artistic, and strong-willed heiress, Elizabeth Posthuma Gwillim. The niece of an admiral and a lord, she provided a five-thousand-acre estate in Devonshire, where the couple built a mansion named Wolford Lodge, and they raised six children born in the decade following their marriage. In 1790 Simcoe won a seat in Parliament, where he consistently supported the Crown. Gregarious and generous, he made many friends.[9]

Despite his domestic happiness, material prosperity, and political success, Simcoe remained haunted by the revolution. A visitor later noted:

> The hatred of the Governor against the United States occasions him, on the slightest occasion, to overleap all the bounds of prudence and decency, which he carefully observes in all other matters. He was a zealous promoter of the American war, in which he took a very active, yet very unfortunate, part. The calamitous issue of the war has still more exasperated his hostility; . . . I listened to his boasting of the numerous houses he had fired during that unfortunate conflict, and of his intention to burn a still greater number in case of a rupture.

Simcoe longed for the chance to fight the war again but on his own terms.[10]

Simcoe became enraged by French (and some British) writers, who championed the Patriot version of the war which cast the Loyalists as corrupt stooges and vicious bandits. In 1787 he published a retort, which denied credit to the victors by blaming defeat on divisions in England. He assured Americans, "The establishment of your independency was not the result of American talents or American courage. It is to be attributed to British credulity and British disunion." He alleged that a misinformed public and petty politicians had hamstrung the British and Loyalist forces by mandating a limited war, when a free hand

and a total war would have crushed the Patriots: "by burning the houses of such peasants as take up arms without being regimented; levying contributions upon towns to save them from plunder; and living upon the country." And yet, in his conclusion, Simcoe urged reconciliation upon the Americans: "let all retrospect be avoided; let all harsh and aggravating expressions cease." But that reconciliation had to be on British terms. Too weak to govern themselves, the Americans needed a European protector. And their natural guardian was Britain, the haven of rational liberty and Protestantism, rather than authoritarian and Catholic France.[11]

Upon taking his new post in Upper Canada, Simcoe employed secret agents to intrigue within the United States. In early 1792 Simcoe sent his close friend Captain Charles Stevenson to New York City to cultivate old Loyalist contacts for a new plot against the republic. Stevenson reported:

> If they were inclined to join us, there would be no difficulty in seizing West Point (where all the cannon and Stores of Gen. Burgoyne's and Lord Cornwallis's Armies are deposited). Fort Montgomery and Stoney Point might be occupied in one night, which would effectually secure the river and protect the Yorkers from the vengeance of Congress. I should like a little mischief amazingly [and] it would give you the opportunity of laying aside the State Robe and of resuming the sword.

Stevenson dreamed of completing Andre's mission by taking West Point, and he longed to reverse the revolution's three greatest setbacks for British arms: Burgoyne's surrender at Saratoga; Cornwallis's capitulation at Yorktown; and the loss of Stony Point to a surprise attack. Sharing that fantasy, Simcoe praised Stevenson's New York mission as performed "in the same manner as if I could have personally attended to the business." Simcoe longed to resume the war against the revolution and to crush the rebel republic in his own way.[12]

LATE LOYALISTS

Simcoe boasted that Upper Canada's constitution was "the very image and transcript of that of Great Britain, by which she has long established and secured for her subjects as much freedom and happiness as is possible to be enjoyed under the subordination necessary to civilized society." Simcoe saw the British empire as "the sacred deposit of power which has preserved the liberties & common happiness of Mankind."

He expressed the Loyalist ideology that true liberty required regulation by an official elite, in contrast to the excessive and hollow liberty of republicanism, which suffered from the power of an ill-educated, penurious, greedy, and volatile majority. In the violent turmoil and property confiscations of the revolution, the Loyalists found ample confirmation that civilized order required a constitutional mix and balance of monarchy, aristocracy, and republicanism.[13]

While Simcoe's plans for Upper Canada confronted the American republic, they also challenged the status quo in the British empire, which sought to keep colonies economically dependent and politically subservient. Simcoe blamed greedy merchants and dull officials for perpetuating Canada's limited economy devoted to the fur trade. Unless developed with a large population of farmers, Upper Canada could never fulfill its potential as an engine of imperial renewal. Reviving the Queen's Rangers for service in Upper Canada, Simcoe employed the new recruits in colony building—constructing roads, bridges, mills, and inns. He vowed to force "the rapid Establishment & Progress of this Colony, beyond the slow, unsystematic & unconnected gradations by which the British colonies in America have usually been formed." Congenitally impatient, Simcoe meant almost overnight to create a powerful and populous colony.[14]

A visionary of empire, Simcoe saw Upper Canada for what it could become rather than for what it was. A smattering of small settlements and ramshackle forts strung along the Great Lakes, Upper Canada lay dangerously near the American republic. In examining a map of Upper Canada, a peninsula thrusting southward amid the Great Lakes, most people saw a dangerously exposed limb of empire ripe for amputation by the aggressive Americans. But Simcoe perceived the powerful arm of a revived empire that could thrust its economic and military power deep into the continent to throttle the republic. He deemed "that Great Peninsula between the Lakes Huron, Erie, and Ontario a Spot destined by Nature, sooner or later, to govern the interior World." Simcoe's chief civil administrator, Peter Russell, predicted that by rendering Upper Canada "the grand Mart and Emporium of that Western World," the British could "extend their Arms round the United States, and hanging as a two edged Sword over their Necks Secure at last to this Country (by the force of Terror) all those advantages" of dominion.[15]

No mere dependency, no exotic appendage, Simcoe's Upper Canada was to be a New Britain—no small task given that the frontier colony stretched for over a thousand miles but had only 14,000 British subjects in 1791. Simcoe assured Secretary of State Henry Dundas "that the utmost Attention should be paid that British Customs, Manners, & Principles in the most trivial, as well as serious matters, should be promoted & inculcated to obtain their due Ascendancy to assimilate the Colony with the parent state." This assimilation ought "*instantaneously* to take place & not to be procrastinated to a future Season."[16]

To promote the resemblance, Simcoe renamed the features and civil jurisdictions of Upper Canada, replacing Indian and French toponyms with English names meant to establish functional equivalents. Working from a map in England a year before he laid eyes on Upper Canada, Simcoe picked an uninhabited site for his future capital and metropolis, which he named London. Of course, its adjoining river, La Tranche, had to be renamed the Thames. For his second city, Simcoe designated York at a place formerly (and now) known as Toronto; the local rivers became the Ouse and the Humber. Some new place-names honored a patron among the British aristocracy, including Dundas County, after Henry Dundas. The Mohawk chief Joseph Brant slyly observed, "Gen. S[imcoe] has done a great deal for this province, he has changed the name of every place in it."[17]

Simcoe also moved to abolish slavery as part of his drive to equate Upper Canada with England, where slavery was illegal. The colony had about three hundred slaves, primarily taken during the war from Patriot settlements by Indian and Loyalist raiders and then sold to merchants and magistrates, who balked at losing valuable property. At least six of the sixteen assembly representatives owned slaves. Obliged to compromise, Simcoe accepted a gradual emancipation law that freed no current slaves but barred further imports. Children subsequently born to slave mothers would become free at age twenty-five. By making Upper Canada the first British colony to abolish slavery, Simcoe reiterated his devotion to a "rational liberty" granted by a paternalistic state to common folk. In contrast, most Americans celebrated an almost unlimited freedom for white men, including their right to hold blacks in slavery.[18]

To create his new Britain, Simcoe needed more people. Despite the modest Loyalist influx of the 1780s, Upper Canada remained dwarfed by the swelling numbers of Americans to the south and east. In 1790 the adjoining state of New York had 340,120 people: more than twenty-four times the residents of Upper Canada. Anticipating another war with the republic, Simcoe sought thousands of immigrants quickly to populate the colony, develop its economy, and provide a militia to augment the regular troops for defense. But where could he get them?[19]

Emigration from distant Great Britain meant crossing the Atlantic and ascending the often ice-choked or fogbound St. Lawrence River, a long, difficult, and expensive voyage. In 1793 renewed war with France added hostile warships to the hazards of transporting Britons across the Atlantic. Moreover, they lacked the experience and skills needed to clear forests and to make frontier farms. At Niagara, a Scot conceded, "The Trade of Farming in this new Country Requires to Europeans as much an Apprenticeship as any handicraft profession."[20]

As an alternative, Simcoe could recruit settlers from the nearby republic. On the plus side, Americans were nearby and experienced at farm-building. They could emigrate cheaply at their own expense and quickly support themselves as frontier farmers. Simcoe also reasoned that every settler drawn into Upper Canada subtracted from the republic's resources as it added to the empire's strength.[21]

But recruiting Americans was a gamble, for they came from a revolutionary republic ideologically hostile to the British empire. In 1793, Captain Stevenson warned, "I could wish we had not so many emigrants from the States as I much fear the turbulent seeds of fanaticism and rebellion are not sufficiently eradicated from their breasts." Instead of strengthening the empire, their growing numbers might subvert Upper Canada from within.[22]

Seeing no evil, Simcoe devoutly believed that the states remained filled with closet Loyalists who longed to escape republicanism by returning to the empire: "There are thousands of the Inhabitants of the United States whose affections are centered in the British Government & the British Name; who are positively enemies of Congress & the late division of the Empire; many of their Connections have already taken refuge in Canada & it will be true Wisdom to invite & facilitate the emigration of this description of people into that Country." To attract settlers, Simcoe promised to exempt them from both taxation and democracy, while providing cheap land. Persuaded that sensible Americans disliked republican electioneering, legislative partisanship, and libelous newspapers, Simcoe assumed that thousands would find Upper Canada's mixed constitution as alluring as its paltry taxes and generous land grants.[23]

On February 7, 1792, Simcoe issued a proclamation, offering at least two hundred acres to every family of newcomers. To obtain a land grant, a settler needed only to take an oath of allegiance to "the King in his Parliament," and to pay some official fees. During the mid-1790s those fees amounted to only six pence per acre, which rendered land in Upper Canada dirt-cheap relative to the two to three dollars per acre charged by land speculators in New York and Pennsylvania. In March 1792 John

Munro reported, "I have the pleasure to inform Your Excellency that Emigrants are flocking in from the States with all their property." During the four years 1792–96, Simcoe's administration fielded four thousand applications for land, about three-quarters from newcomers, euphemistically known as "the Late Loyalists."[24]

Historians doubt the loyalty of the Late Loyalists and consider Simcoe deluded about them. Such scholars narrowly define Loyalists as those who, during the war, fled to join the British and actively assisted their troops. Those overt Loyalists had to depart America with the British withdrawal of 1783.[25]

But Simcoe more broadly defined a Loyalist as anyone who sympathized with and assisted British forces in any way. As a partisan commander, he knew of hundreds who spent the war behind rebel lines while covertly helping the British with information, supplies, and havens for spies, couriers, and escaped prisoners. Many were Quakers or German pietists with scruples against bearing arms but with grievances against bullying Patriot militias and committees. Although reluctant to uproot their families and sacrifice their property by fleeing to the British lines, these soft Loyalists would provide covert assistance.[26]

Most of the emigrants came from New Jersey and Pennsylvania, where soft Loyalists had been especially numerous and familiar to Simcoe. Many derived from Pennsylvania's York and Northumberland Counties, the base for a Loyalist plot led by Colonel William Rankin, a wealthy judge and militia commander. Uneasy with independence and disgusted by the French alliance, Rankin recruited several hundred disaffected men, who entered a secret association, bound by oath, to rebel against the Patriots if assisted by a British foray into their counties. After Andre's death, Simcoe became Rankin's chief correspondent and champion. In March 1781 Patriot authorities tried to arrest Rankin, but he escaped to the British in New York City, where he could do little to rally his supporters stuck behind rebel lines.[27]

In upper Canada Simcoe's drive to attract American settlers clashed with his longing to renew the conflict against the republic, for few would move into a war zone. Consequently, his words often effected a surreal marriage between longing for peace and lusting for war. In June 1792 Simcoe assured the British secretary at war:

> I have no personal views, no personal fears, but those of Peace, Peace, Peace, and as I know the Military Contempt in which I hold Washington and such like cattle may induce people to suppose I should not

dislike war, I beg my friends to understand [that] I think worse of his heart than [of] his head and fear he will urge us into war to support his power.

One of Simcoe's guests noted the same tension in his host's mind: "no hillock catches his eye without exciting in his mind . . . the plan of operations for a campaign, especially of that which is to lead him to Philadelphia. On hearing his professions of an earnest desire of peace, you cannot but suppose, either that his reason must hold an absolute sway over his passion, or that he deceives himself."[28]

CRISIS

In 1794 a diplomatic crisis put Simcoe at the front lines of a looming war. During the previous year, the British began to seize American merchant ships trading with the French West Indies. The seizures compounded American resentments over the withheld border forts and the Indian war. Sympathy for the French Revolution also promoted boisterous public celebrations of French victories over the British. Taking his cue from the hostile American press, Lord Dorchester anticipated that the United States would honor its treaty of alliance with France by attacking the border posts and by invading Canada. In a provocative speech, Lord Dorchester urged the Indians of Lower Canada to prepare for war. Dorchester also directed Simcoe to rally the Indians in his province and to build and garrison a new fort on the Maumee River to guard the southern approaches to Detroit.[29]

While Dorchester sensibly planned for only the defensive war appropriate to the scanty British forces in Canada, Simcoe wanted to conquer the United States. In letters to his superiors in London, he promised within three months to rout the American army in the Ohio country, destroy forts in western Pennsylvania, burn the settlements of western New York, and neutralize Kentucky. During the following year he offered to sweep across Pennsylvania to rout President Washington at Philadelphia. This blitzkrieg would, he explained to an American guest, "destroy the mob; give honest people good government; and thereby produce peace, harmony, and good neighbourhood." At last he would crush the republic and reunite the empire.[30]

Simcoe's longing was double: to escape from his British superiors as well as to settle scores with George Washington. After all, Simcoe blamed defeat in the revolution more on the restraints of dullards in the British high command than on the prowess of the Patriots. Free at last of weak-willed superiors, Simcoe would demonstrate how easily and quickly total war could destroy the republic. In particular, Simcoe longed for freedom from Lord Dorchester, who in 1782–83 had been known as Sir Guy Carleton, the commander who had disgraced the Queen's Rangers before surrendering New York City to the Americans. By plunging deep into republican America, Simcoe would run far and free from Dorchester's control.[31]

Simcoe's rampaging fantasy derived from his wartime experience, when thrice he had sought permission to lead the Loyalist regiments in a breakout from the Atlantic Seaboard. By fighting their way through rebel America, they would find a safe haven on the Great Lakes—the mirror image of his 1794 proposal. He had broached this plan in 1778, when the British evacuated Philadelphia; again in 1779 when Washington's army seemed poised to capture Staten Island; and yet again in 1781 when Cornwallis prepared to surrender Yorktown. Of course, on all three occasions, Simcoe's conventional commanders had nixed his reckless proposals. But those rejections and the subsequent humiliating peace treaty had deepened Simcoe's conviction that his strategy would have led to imperial victory.[32]

In 1794 the three- to four-month lag in transatlantic communication played a cruel trick on Simcoe. During the summer, while the crisis heated up on the North American frontier and in Simcoe's letters, it cooled down in London diplomacy. Not until the fall would Simcoe learn that his bellicose letters had reached a government determined to improve relations with the United States. Faring badly in the war with France, the British could ill afford conflict on another front or to curtail the transatlantic commerce cherished by the British exporters of manufactured goods. Consequently, the British responded favorably when the Washington administration sent a conciliatory special envoy, John Jay, to London to negotiate a solution to the crisis. In July, while Simcoe wrote fiery proposals in Canada, Henry Dundas in London ordered him to back down; their letters crossed on ships in the night.[33]

In early September Dundas's orders reached a chagrined Simcoe. During the following spring, Simcoe further learned that the imperial lords had concluded the Jay Treaty with the United States, resolving the crisis amicably. The British agreed to evacuate the border forts within two years. That prospect completed the collapse of the Indian confederation, as the native nations scrambled to make a separate peace with the victorious Americans. At Greenville in August 1795, General Wayne dictated American terms to the Indians, who had to concede most of Ohio and part of Indiana and to allow the Americans to build forts throughout the native country. By securing American hegemony, the Treaty of Greenville foiled the buffer zone sought by the British and their native allies.[34]

Simcoe grew weary and sour as his grandiose plans for Upper Canada crumbled. Instead of reversing the revolution, Simcoe now faced the triumphant republic on his Canadian doorstep. Deprived of his grand vision, Simcoe could not abide governing a distant and marginal colony. He also suffered from multiple bouts of "ague and fever," the malaria endemic to Upper Canada. The illness sallowed his complexion and deepened his foul mood. Wary subordinates found him "peevish beyond description." The attorney general, John White, bitterly complained, "The Officers of Government seem to have been considered by Gen[era]l Simcoe only as footballs to be kickt' about at his pleasure."[35]

During the summer of 1796, the British surrendered Detroit, Niagara, Oswego, and Michilimackinac to American garrisons. On the eve of those transfers, Simcoe sailed away across Lake Ontario, bound via boat to Quebec and then by ship for England. He left in a hurry, wanting no part of surrendering anything to the Americans lest he too become a Cornwallis or a Dorchester. Soured on Simcoe's ambitious schemes and volatile temper, most officials felt relieved by his departure. The Reverend John Stuart was more tactful: "His Foresight is so great, and his Plans so extensive, that, it is the Opinion of some here, that a man of plain, common Understanding, would suit the Circumstances of this Country as well."[36]

LEGACY

Simcoe left behind the Late Loyalists, who continued to settle in Upper Canada. Through 1811, the American influx persisted at the rate of about five hundred families (or about 2,500 persons) annually. In 1800 Thomas Merritt marveled to his brother, "You would be astonished to see the people from all parts of the States, by land and by water, 250 wagons at a time, with their families, on the road, something like an Army on the move." Thanks to the newcomers, Upper Canada's population swelled from 14,000 in 1791 to 75,000 in 1812. By then, the Late Loyalists comprised three-fifths of the inhabitants, outnumbering both the original, true Loyalists, who had arrived during the 1780s, and the still-small number of immigrants from Great Britain.[37]

Most of the Late Loyalists came from the mid-Atlantic states of New York, New Jersey, and Pennsylvania. Families traveled in horse-drawn wagons laden with beds, bedding, clothing, cooking utensils, and farm tools. The more prosperous also brought along a cow or two. A smaller, secondary flow came from New England and eastern New York. Primarily Yankees, they traveled in bateaux via the Mohawk River before crossing Lake Ontario to Kingston. Some settled among the original Loyalists along the St. Lawrence River, the Bay of Quinte, and the Niagara River. But most of the Late Loyalists opened new settlements along the north shore of Lake Ontario, or to the west in the Grand River and Thames valleys.[38]

Simcoe regarded land grants and low taxes less as incentives to immigration than as due rewards for loyalty. In 1795 La Rochefoucault-Liancourt saw Simcoe greet an arriving family:

"We come," said they, "to the Governor, . . . to see whether he will give us land." "Aye, aye," the Governor replied, "you are tired of the federal government; you like not any longer to have so many kings; you wish again for your old father. . . . You are perfectly right; come along, we love such good royalists as you are, we will give you land."

The colony's surveyor general, David W. Smith, similarly described the American emigrant: "The loyal peasant, sighing after the government he lost by the late revolution, travels from Pennsylvania in search of his former laws and protection; and having his expectations fulfilled by new marks of favor from the Crown, in a grant of lands, he turns his plough at once into these fertile plains, and an abundant crop reminds him of his gratitude to his God and to his King."[39]

Other British officials and travelers had their doubts. Alexander Macdonell warned Simcoe to beware of "the silver-tongued & arsenick-hearted Americans." William Dummer Powell denounced the newcomers as "a base and disloyal Population, the dregs and outcast of other Countries." Colonel Thomas Talbot harshly categorized the newcomers as

1st. Those who were early enticed by a gratuitous offer of land, without any predilection on their part, to the British Constitution. 2nd. Those who have fled from the United States for crimes, or to escape their Creditors. 3rd. Republicans, whose principal motive for settling in that Country, is an anticipation of its shaking off its allegiance to Great Britain.

The British traveler John Maude predicted that they would "form a nest of vipers in the bosom that now so incautiously fosters them."[40]

In fact most of the newcomers lacked ideological commitment to either the empire or the republic. Neither good royalists nor republican vipers, most were bargain hunters. In 1798 Benjamin Mortimer observed, "What has invited people into Canada, is the free gift of 200 acres, which is made by government to every actual settler." In 1800 a British traveler on the St. Lawrence observed, "Five hundred came over this Winter. Their attachment to our Government is the reason they give out for the change; but the cheapness of Land and their not having any Taxes to pay, are the real reasons." In 1805, Julian Niemcewicz, a traveler from Poland, saw American emigrants preparing to cross the border. A committed republican, he lamented:

> Thus having struggled for nine years to shake off the English yoke, and having shaken it off, they go of their own free will to submit themselves again. I believe that, were they to learn that even in Hell there were lands producing excellent wheat and corn and at six cents an acre, despite all the flames and all the torments, they would give up their *liberty and equality* to go and settle there.

In 1808 Michael Smith explained that he had emigrated from Pennsylvania to Upper Canada "in order to obtain land upon easy terms (as did most of the inhabitants now there) and for no other reason." Attracted by the cheap land and low taxes, the Late Loyalists cared little about the regime, so long as it demanded little from them.[41]

HUMBLE VIEWS

Seeking common settlers, the British distrusted genteel migrants from the United States, lest as local leaders they might foment popular disaffection. To discourage their immigration, the government denied large land grants and prestigious offices to genteel Americans. John Cosens Ogden explained:

> The object of the British nation is to people and cultivate this country, and to make it as perfect a part of the Empire as possible. Dreading revolutions, they are cautious in receiving republicans from the States, and wish to encourage husbandmen and labourers only. Clergymen, lawyers, physicians, and schoolmasters from the States are not the first characters who would be fostered.

An Anglican minister from New Hampshire, Ogden spoke from experience. Despite flaunting his loyalty and despite the shortage of Anglican

Old Fort Erie, with the Migrations of the Wild Pidgeon in Spring, *by Edward Walsh, 1804. Walsh depicts the impact of settlement on the forests and wildlife of Upper Canada.* (Courtesy of the Royal Ontario Museum, 952.218.)

clergy in the colony, he failed to secure a parish because Crown officials distrusted his American background.[42]

Impatient to settle the colony, in 1792–93 Simcoe had granted thirty-two townships of land to some American gentlemen, in the naive belief that they represented groups that wanted to settle together to sustain a common church. In fact, the gentlemen were land speculators trolling for cheap lands in large quantities. And they sold shares in their lands to new investors, who included Aaron Burr, a notorious Republican politician from New York. The British minister to the United States, Robert Liston, warned that the new investors possessed "high-flying democratic sentiments" and "would rejoice to see an independent Republick, established in Canada." Infuriated at having conned himself, Simcoe revoked the township grants in 1795–97.[43]

Thereafter, the colonial government offered common Americans two hundred acres of land—perfect for a small farm—while granting larger tracts only to British officials and their friends. A settler explained that the colony attracted "many thousands of my fellow-citizens of the United States, who were without land, and [without any] prospect of obtaining any in the United States upon such easy terms as they might in Upper Canada." Two hundred acres were as much as a common farmer could manage in Canada *and* more than he could afford to buy in the United States.[44]

Most of the newcomers were relatively poor people with modest economic aspirations and little education. As befit a frontier region, which demanded hard labor under great hardships, most of the men were young and hardy, in their late teens or twenties, with a smaller number in their thirties and still fewer older men. And they had humble status. In 1796 the colony's surveyor general assessed 250 male immigrants and concluded that 74 percent were farmers, 18 percent artisans, and 6 percent laborers or sailors. Only one could claim the genteel status of "Esquire," and the only two professionals were barely that: two teachers, then as now an underpaid and undervalued occupation. In 1804 General Peter Hunter described the colony as "principally settled by people who came into it with a very small property." After touring Upper Canada, Lord Selkirk reported that the colonists were "of the lowest order with scarcely any men of the rank of gentlemen."[45]

The predominance of common men gave a plebeian cast to the colony's economic culture. In passing from the United States into Upper Canada in 1798, Benjamin Mortimer, a Moravian missionary, noted a stark difference:

> Most of the inhabitants of Canada are emigrants from the United States; but no sooner did we enter the country, than we perceived that some difference exists between their national characters. In the States, the principal subject of conversation in most public companies which we entered, was the quality of lands. From Tioga to Buffaloe every traveler is supposed to be in quest of them; and little else is cared about, if bargains of that kind can only be made or disposed of to advantage. In Canada, the settlers are more humble in their views. They are mostly poor people, who are chiefly concerned to manage, in the best manner, the farms which have been given them by government.

In Upper Canada, settlers could more easily and cheaply obtain farms, but they faced poorer prospects for speculating their way to greater prosperity, given the two-hundred-acre restriction on Crown land grants.[46]

Upper Canada also offered few incentives for commercial agriculture. To reach the Atlantic export market, Upper Canadian farmers had to boat their produce down the long St. Lawrence River to Quebec.

Rapids above Montreal made that route difficult and expensive for bulky exports and still more so for consumer imports coming upriver. And for half the year, ice shut down the port of Quebec, freezing commerce. Meanwhile, the American frontier farmer benefited from rivers flowing to ports that usually (New York and Philadelphia) or always (Baltimore and New Orleans) remained open through the winter. Consequently, Upper Canadian farmers could rarely compete with their American counterparts in the wheat export trade. The historian Douglas McCalla estimates that in 1803 Upper Canada's wheat exports amounted to only about seventeen bushels per household per year, providing only £3.0.0 ($12.00) in annual income.[47]

Because of the high transportation costs, Canadian farmers felt squeezed between the low price paid for their produce and the high prices they had to pay for imported consumer goods. By American standards, stores were few and far between. Mortimer reported:

> There are no stores or shops in the whole province of Upper Canada, except in the towns of Newark and York, and in the neighbourhood of Detroit. The most common articles to be had in every village in the eastern parts of the United States can hardly be procured here for any money. Br[other] Heckewelder, for instance, was in want of tobacco and could get none. He began at length today to smoke dried leaves of trees.

Upper Canada offered cheap land and paltry taxes, but the settler had to accept a lower standard of living than in the United States. That prospect screened out ambitious men. Simcoe's successor, Peter Russell, warned an Irish gentleman, "This is the best Country in the World for an industrious poor Man, but a bad one for a Man of Fortune, as he cannot possibly obtain either Comforts or Luxuries adequate to his Expences."[48]

The scarcity and high wages of laborers also discouraged prosperous farmers from settling in Upper Canada. Few men remained laborers for wages because they could so easily obtain farms in the land-rich colony. The colony's chief justice, John Elmsley, complained that he could find neither tenants nor laborers to develop his estate: "Who will work long for another, when he can, as he undoubtedly may at present in this Province, earn the fee simple of four Acres by one day's labour?"[49]

Because few men of means immigrated to Upper Canada, the colony had relatively few millers, innkeepers, or commercial farmers, the sort of entrepreneurs who led rural society in the United States. In sum, the colony had a weak "civil society": a network of private associations and institutions beyond government's control. Distrusting such a civil society, the government officials felt strengthened by its weakness in Upper Canada.[50]

The entrepreneurial Benajah Mallory was an exception who proved the rule. From Vermont, he immigrated to Upper Canada in 1795, settling at Burford in the Grand River Valley. A versatile Yankee, he posed as a prominent Loyalist to obtain a Crown grant to 1,400 acres, where he developed a distillery, tannery, and tavern. He became a militia captain, Methodist preacher, and local politician popular among his fellow newcomers. Challenging the older Loyalist elite in the London District, Mallory won election to the assembly in 1804. His opposition politics confirmed the government's distrust of entrepreneurs as potential malcontents. British officials gave thanks that ambitious leaders were so few among the Late Loyalists.[51]

Upper Canada did attract some prosperous families that belonged to pietist denominations with pacifist convictions. In addition to English-speaking Quakers, these pious pacifists included German-speaking Mennonites and Dunkers (or Tunkers). Most came from New Jersey or Pennsylvania. During the revolution, all three groups had suffered persecution for their pacifism, incurring arrests and heavy fines from Patriots who treated them as Loyalists. After the war they continued to suffer fines for avoiding mandatory militia musters. Those with large families and small farms sought new lands on the frontier, but they feared the Indian war that raged in the Ohio Valley until 1795. They preferred Upper Canada, where the British kept the peace by treating the Indians more generously.[52]

The British welcomed the pietists as especially hardworking and orderly farmers endowed with some property. The colonial government exempted them from militia service upon the payment of a modest fee (in peacetime). Upper Canada rewarded them for the supposed Loyalism that had been their curse in the United States. After visiting one newly arrived family of German-speakers, Captain Miles Macdonnell observed, "They were from Pennsylvania & were called *Tories* by the Americans."[53]

The pious pacifists felt threatened by republicanism, which promoted majority rule at the expense of cultural minorities. They suffered from the American paradox, later noted by Alexis de Tocqueville, that the emphasis on individualism led to a majoritarian conformism intolerant of dissent. Having found the American republic "pleasing in theory, but troublesome & frequently factious in execution & practice," the Quaker Peter Lossing immigrated to Upper Canada.[54]

These newcomers felt nostalgic for the colonial social order that had seemed more tolerant of cultural minorities. In 1805 Christopher Beswick explained the appeal to Dunkers of their own township, Uxbridge, in Upper Canada: "[They] have not forgot the happiness they enjoyed under the British Government, and I have taught them to believe that in Uxbridge they will find a second edition of Pennsylvania as it was before the American War." They preferred the rule of a distant king to domination by a local majority intolerant of cultural difference.[55]

Unlike the American republicans, British officials imagined political society in traditional and prenational terms: as a mix of quasi-distinct and quasi-corporate communities, each with varying customs, duties, and privileges. In Canada, imperial officials saw security for their rule in the division of their subjects into distinct ethnocultural communities unlikely to join together in republican revolution.[56]

Upper Canada appealed to the Dunkers, Mennonites, and Quakers because the British promised to leave them alone and leave them distinct. Obtaining entire townships, the pietists could live in ethnocultural clusters—as did the colony's New England Yankees, New York Dutch, and Scots Highlanders. Scattered through an immense forest, Upper Canada's distinctive communities had little cause or desire to cooperate, much less to meld. Upper Canada was an ethnic and religious mosaic rather than a melting pot.[57]

FAITH

British officials believed that true Loyalism required the Anglican faith, for the king headed the Church of England. Canada's Anglican bishop, Jacob Mountain, promised that religious conformity "would prove the best security to Government for the submission, fidelity, and loyalty of its subjects." William Dummer Powell agreed: "That religious Establishments are highly conducive to order, and form an essential link in the chain of every Government, that is designed to be permanent, seems admitted everywhere but in France and the American States." And anything denied in those republics needed to be true in the British empire.[58]

Anglicanism reinforced a social order premised on inequality and deference. The church's hierarchy of laity, priests, bishops, and archbishops reflected an elitist society led by aristocrats and a monarch. Proud of their genteel education, the Anglican clergy preached an organic vision of an unequal society, where God ranked people in distinct classes and then required their cooperation. Poor and ignorant, the lower orders owed respect and obedience to their superiors, who bestowed protection and charity in return. John Strachan preached that the "will of God" rendered most people "obscure in the world [and] of no account or consideration."[59]

Alas, the colony had too few Anglican clergy to minister to the growing population. From three priests in 1793, the Anglican clergy increased to only five in 1812, during a period when the colony's population quintupled. In 1812 the Anglicans had but one resident clergyman per 14,000 inhabitants in the colony, compared to one per 4,667 colonists in 1792. Lacking their own bishop (despite Simcoe's best efforts to secure one), the Anglicans of Upper Canada reported to Bishop Mountain in Montreal.[60]

The Anglican clergy were so few because it was so hard to entice them across the Atlantic to cope with the harsher conditions and lower pay of a frontier parish. In theory, the Anglicans should have derived an abundant support from the one-seventh of the colony's lands reserved for their clergy by the Constitutional Act of 1791. But the Clergy Reserves attracted few tenants because the settlers could so easily obtain their own freehold farms. And the government refused to accept priests ordained in the United States, deeming them security risks—as John Cosens Ogden had discovered.[61]

The Anglican clergy and government officials tolerated those churches which ministered only to their traditional ethnic communities. The Quakers, Mennonites, and Dunkers largely kept to themselves and preached submission to the civil hierarchy. The Presbyterians also got a pass as the national church of Scotland, one of the constituent kingdoms of the empire. And German Lutherans were tolerated as theologically similar to the Anglicans. Catholics were numerous at the two wings of the colony, among the Gaelic-speaking Scots Highlanders of Glengarry County at the eastern margin, and among the Francophones of the Detroit Valley to the far west. Alexander Macdonell, a Catholic priest, urged cooperation with the Anglicans because "both those great churches . . . strenuously uphold subordination of civil ranks, monarchy, and ecclesiastic monarchy." Such a partnership would "ensure subordination in a country receiving daily swarms of republicans into its bosom."[62]

Macdonell and the Anglicans shared a contempt for the Baptists and Methodists, whose plain style, egalitarian brotherhood, evangelical worship, and itinerant preaching seemed to threaten moral and social order. Hannah Peters Jarvis dismissed evangelical religion "as a Veil to cover a Multitude of Sin. They can pray and Pick your Pocket at the same time with as much grace and dexterity." Anglicans equated evangelicalism with republicanism, for both favored individual choice over traditional allegiances defined by inherited status and residence. Because evangelical preachers weakened the deference of common people, Bishop Mountain warned that they would "dissolve the bonds of society," inviting anarchy.[63]

Leading humble lives of poverty, the preachers relied on a trade or a farm to supplement the small contributions from their adherents. Poorly educated, the evangelicals practiced an "experimental religion" that sought direct, transforming encounters with the divine spirit. Seeking an intense and collective feeling of unity with one another and in Christ, their worship was loud, wrenching, twitching, and it alternated joy with despair.[64]

The evangelical message of suffering and redemption resonated with common settlers struggling with frontier hardships. In praise of the preachers, a settler's daughter asked, "were they not the class of men who suited their hearers? They shared their poverty and entered into all their feelings . . . and their lives bore testimony to their sincerity." From just 332 members in 1793, Methodists grew to 2,719 by 1810 to become the colony's largest denomination. Many more settlers attended Methodist preaching but had not yet experienced the emotional "new birth" required of members. And their twelve ordained preachers more than doubled the Anglican clergy in Upper Canada.[65]

The Anglicans felt besieged by the evangelical success. In 1812 Richard Cartwright lamented, "The Country is overrun with itinerant Methodist Preachers & Fanatics of all Descriptions & the Difficulty of reclaiming the Inhabitants to the rational Doctrine and Practices of the Church of England will increase every Day." Anglicans especially disliked the American origins of the itinerants, who belonged to conferences or associations based in New York or Vermont. Anglicans and officials feared that the American evangelical expansion would prepare Canadians for a republican invasion.[66]

During the late 1780s and early 1790s some magistrates and army officers tried to drive evangelical itinerants from the colony. Born in Ireland but raised in the United States, Charles Justin McCarty came to Upper Canada to preach Methodism in 1790. Irish, American, and Methodist meant three strikes against McCarty, and he was out. Prosecuted as a vagrant in Kingston, McCarty was convicted, jailed, and ousted from the province. With only one witness against him and seven for the defense, the verdict hinged upon the animus of the presiding judge, Richard Cartwright, a staunch Anglican. But this overt persecution made McCarty a martyr, which strengthened the Methodist appeal to common people. Thereafter, the authorities avoided evicting evangelical preachers.[67]

Instead, the colonial regime relied on patronage to define respectability as Anglican and to stigmatize Methodism as vulgar. In awarding the coveted commissions as magistrates and militia officers, the government favored Anglicans, and to a lesser degree Presbyterians, rather than evangelicals. Because so many evangelicals were also newcomers from America, they faced a double bias.[68]

To further boost the prestige of Anglicans, the government barred evangelicals from performing marriage ceremonies. Simcoe reasoned that marriage was a civil institution that required government sanction through its favored church. Unthinkable in the American republic, this Anglican marriage monopoly attested to the gap wrought on the two sides of the border by the revolution. In 1798 the government loosened the law to allow marriages conducted by ordained Lutheran, Presbyterian, and other "Calvinist" clergy. But they had to secure a license from their district court, where Anglican magistrates could enforce a strict definition of ordination and Calvinism. Chief Justice John Elmsley excluded Methodist preachers as "the weakest, the most ignorant & in some instances the most depraved of Mankind."[69]

British officials and Anglican clergymen exaggerated the political danger posed by evangelical preachers. Although they challenged the elite style in religion, the evangelicals avoided political controversy as divisive and crass. They came to preach Jesus Christ, not Thomas Jefferson; and they sought the way to heaven rather than the road to a republic. The real danger to Canadian security lay in an overreaction by the elite that might alienate the evangelicals from British rule.

POWER

In leaving the United States for Upper Canada, an emigrant exchanged the assertive liberty of republican citizens for the passive benefits of British subjects: cheap land and low taxes. The activity of a republican citizen contrasted with the passivity of a monarch's subject. Where the citizen had to enact his identity in elections and in office, birth and residence defined the subject.[70]

In Upper Canada, the district was the primary unit of local justice and administration. In 1802 the colony had eight districts, ranging from east to west: Eastern, Johnstown, Midland, Newcastle, Home, Niagara, London, and Western. By design, the districts eclipsed county and town

Gideon Tiffany (*1774–1854*), *photo-graph, unknown date.* (Courtesy of the Archives of Ontario, S-13892.)

governments, which British officials disliked as too small, parochial, and democratic.[71]

With advice from the Upper Canada Executive Council, the lieutenant governor appointed the local magistrates who conducted each district's Court of Quarter Sessions. In addition to hearing minor civil cases and petty criminal complaints, this court handled the district's finances, records, schools, courthouse, jail, poor relief, and orphans. The district court also regulated taverns, markets, roads, bridges, and ferries. Major trials involving large sums or felony crimes fell to a circuit Court of King's Bench, conducted at least once a year by at least one of the three elite judges sojourning from York: the chief justice and two associate judges.[72]

Conferred from above, local status and authority promoted a synergy between district oligarchies and the governing officials at the provincial capital (Newark until 1796; York thereafter). Ambitious men longed to become magistrates or militia officers, for those posts offered some income, an enhanced status, and preferential treatment from the Crown, including larger grants of the best lands. As a consequence, aspiring men curried favor with the lieutenant governor and his executive council. Opposition simply did not pay as well. In naming the district officials, the council favored fellow Britons, where available. Some

Loyalists also passed muster, but very few Late Loyalists won district posts. David McGregor Rogers grumbled:

> An American can have but little chance, let his abilities be what they may, to succeed in his application for preferment. Can it be any wonder, therefore, that they should not feel such a warm attachment to the Constitution or Government of the Country as if they had an equal chance with others[?]

Although Late Loyalists comprised three-fifths of the colony's population, they received less than a third of the local magistracies, and none became a district sheriff or a judge. Upper Canada was a discouraging country for Americans with ambitions beyond running a farm.[73]

Britons and Loyalists got ahead by bad-mouthing American-born rivals as malcontents and closet republicans. Warm and welcoming to the apparently loyal, Simcoe bristled when a newcomer said anything remotely critical. He denied land to one man simply because of a hearsay report "that he had said he supposed the Colony would join the United States." Simcoe's successor, Peter Russell, similarly refused land to Nathaniel H. Tredwell, an American newcomer, for allegedly praising the republic and "preferring the works of Tom Pane to the Holy Bible."[74]

Spooked by the recent revolution, British officials treated criticism as sedition, for they dreaded any public disaffection as potentially deadly, especially in a colony that bordered the republic and that had attracted an American-born majority.[75] To suppress sedition, the government sought to control the flow of public information. In a stark contrast with the republic, the British restricted postal service in Upper Canada to official dispatches and to the letters of favored merchants. An American settler described Upper Canada as the land of "No mails, no post-offices, [and] no post-riders." The officials also jealously guarded their records from public scrutiny. In 1804 Russell's successor, Peter Hunter, canceled printing the assembly's journals, declaring that it "did not produce any essential Benefit to the Province." In 1807 the government sacked the Home District sheriff for publicly reading aloud a letter from the solicitor general. In 1808 London District's clerk refused to answer queries from an agricultural writer without prior approval by the lieutenant governor.[76]

Officials frowned on public gatherings beyond their control. By law, no town in Upper Canada could hold a legal meeting without a warrant from the district court. In 1794 some Niagara District Loyalists sought "to associate for the purpose . . . of discountenancing all seditious or incendiary opinions," but they felt obliged to seek Simcoe's approval first. To reinforce the official hierarchy, lieutenant governors often refused to receive delegations or petitions from public meetings by common people, even when they merely conveyed professions of loyalty. The colony's rulers preferred requests conveyed through local elites: magistrates, militia officers, Anglican priests, or Presbyterian ministers.[77]

The executive council also bristled at, and rejected, any petition pitched in a demanding, rather than a deferential, key. They preferred the obsequious appeal of Robert Short, who sought land by vowing "to render myself as useful as possible & by gratitude, Love, & duty, to convince them how much & how greatly I am their devoted & much obliged servant." In contrast to American Republicans, British officials considered themselves the paternal rulers, rather than the friends, of the people.[78]

Local schools worried officials, who feared that a little knowledge was dangerous in common minds, particularly when their teachers came from the United States. In 1802 William Graham, a Loyalist militia officer, denounced the itinerant teachers:

> They use all their efforts to poison the minds of the youth by teaching them in republican books, and in particular the third part of Webster's History. . . . As I had the misfortune to live in Maryland before the Rebellion in America, I was an eye witness to the steps they took [which] makes me dread any thing that may tend to any enervation of Government.

In narrating the revolution, Noah Webster's school text demonized the British and extolled the Patriots. In 1799 the government required that teachers secure a license from a board of commissioners, but this proved unenforceable in the province's scattered settlements.[79]

Distrusting local, common schools, officials preferred to fund only a few elite schools, one per district, to educate the sons of gentlemen. David W. Smith declared:

> May Loyalty be professed and taught as a necessary combination with good manners and the progress of the Arts and Sciences. May the influence of Religion spread itself among the rising Generation to the credit of the Pastors and to the Honor of the Lord—and may the Youth with hilarity, and their Parents with gratitude, never cease to pray, "God Save the King."

Unlike the common schools, the district schools would be "in all respects under the direction of the Executive Government." In 1807 the government funded eight district schools conducted by trustees appointed by the lieutenant governor, who vowed to veto any American teacher. In 1811 an American visitor noted, "There is a considerable desire to monopolize knowledge as well as riches and power, and the aristocracy, being backed by the military, have more power here probably than in England."[80]

The colony's rulers also blamed unregulated newspapers for promoting the American Revolution. Simcoe derided the republic as "a Government founded upon the Basis of popular Opinion and floating with its very Breath" because newspapers had "alienated their Minds, and severed them from the parent Country." Distrusting common readers as ignorant and volatile, British officials regarded public words as potentially dangerous, exciting emotions that could provoke deadly revolts. Therefore, the publication of political speech needed careful regulation by an elite of superior education and authority.[81]

Until 1799 the colony had but one newspaper, the *Upper Canada Gazette*. Published in the provincial capital, the paper depended upon an official subsidy for its paltry profit. Leaving nothing to chance, the administration subjected that press to both prior censorship and subsequent prosecution for seditious libel, should an erring piece slip through. In 1794 a traveler reported that the press was "carefully guarded against every thing that may excite discontents among the inhabitants or encourage assaults upon religion and government."[82]

Censorship hardly seemed necessary, given that so few colonists—dispersed and isolated by bad roads or boisterous waters—ever read the lone newspaper. Elmsley described the settled part of the colony as

> a parallelogram of near 500 miles by not more than 10 [miles]. Exclusive of the inconvenience of its form, it is hardly possible to conceive [of] anything more scanty, more irregular, or more uncertain, than the means of communication which the extremities of this slender strip have with each other, & with the seat of Government.

Newspapers rarely circulated beyond the three commercial villages of Kingston, Newark, and York to reach the frontier settlements where most people lived. In 1795 a traveler remarked, "As to the interior of the country, no news penetrates into that quarter, a circumstance that excites there very little regret." In 1795, by contrast, New York State had thirty-one newspapers, which collectively reached readers in every county.[83]

The brothers Gideon and Silvester Tiffany struggled to conduct a newspaper in security-obsessed Upper Canada. As Yankee immigrants from New Hampshire, they drew extra suspicion from the official elite. Sensitive to that suspicion, they tried to run the *Upper Canada Gazette* in an innocuous fashion. A traveler aptly described their product as "a short abstract of the newspapers of New York and Albany, accommodated to the principles of the Governor."[84]

And yet the Tiffany brothers repeatedly ran afoul of the official censors. In 1795 Simcoe's chief aide lectured Gideon: "Good sense and discretion . . . would induce you to prefer that [news], if it appears to be true, which is most favorable to the British Government." Instead, the aide complained, the Tiffanys had indiscreetly reprinted "a libel for which the printer was prosecuted in Ireland." In 1797 the government prosecuted Gideon for public blasphemy. Convicted, he paid a twenty-pound fine, spent a month in jail, and had to resign as printer, leaving the press to his brother's sole management. A year later, Chief Justice Elmsley fumed that a speech by King George III, "the finest thing in Modern History, & which ought to be circulated in all his Dominions, & got by heart by all his Subjects, has never made its appearance, while every trifle related to the damned States is printed in large characters." In April 1798 the attorney general, John White, announced, "I think *Silvester Tiffany* (indeed all the Tiffanys) cannot be too soon got rid of." The government promptly sacked him as the official printer.[85]

In 1799 the brothers founded the province's first independent newspaper, the *Canada Constellation* (soon renamed the *Niagara Herald*), which attracted close scrutiny from the official elite. Apparently while drinking in a tavern, Gideon publicly sang "God Save the King" but with his own new verse: "God Save America and keep us from dispotic Powers or Sways till Time shall Cease." Prosecuted for sedition, in 1800 he retired from the press, again leaving Silvester as the sole editor and publisher. But, given the province's few and scattered readers, no newspaper could thrive without a government subsidy. During the summer of 1802, the *Niagara Herald* failed, leaving the official *Upper Canada Gazette* as the colony's lone newspaper—to the government's relief.[86]

ABSENCES

Britons defined Upper Canada as a set of absences: as free from the social and political pathologies attributed to the United States. They celebrated the colony for lacking the land jobbing, Indian warfare, African slavery, republican electioneering, libelous newspapers, majoritarian intolerance, and mob violence that blighted the republic. In 1792 Patrick Campbell boasted that the settler in Upper Canada could "get lands for nothing, be among his countrymen, and run no risk of being ever molested by the Indians, tarred or feathered." The British promoted Upper Canada more for what it was *not*, than for what it was.[87]

Because of that negative appeal, Simcoe was only half successful in recruiting Upper Canada's settlers. He enticed families who did not identify with the republic, but he did not attract many who cared deeply for the empire. Most Upper Canadians lacked both the motives and the means to challenge their rulers—or to support them. Disengaged from politics, most of the newcomers saw little reason to regret (and some cause to celebrate) their settlement in a colony where a British elite would govern them at the king's expense. The newcomers cared much for their families, farms, and communities but far less for the empire, which they regarded as an absence of any demands upon their imagination, emotions, or pockets. In 1812 a British officer noted:

> The settlers thus enclosed by thick woods, are occupied chiefly in the laborious concerns of husbandry. . . . Those events which are related to their own state of life, seem alone worthy of their notice. The tumults of contending nations, or the factions of a distant state . . . are listened to with few emotions of interest.

Designed to remain politically inert, Upper Canada had attracted people averse to mobilizing for war. During the War of 1812 they would disappoint their British rulers. After that war, William Dummer Powell blamed Simcoe's vision: "His head was filled with vast utopian projects among which the least rational, and ultimately the most ruinous to the Colony, was to restore the old British Colonies to the Empire and a Persuasion that he was to be the Instrument."[88]

But Simcoe had died with no such doubts. Appointed in 1806 to command in India, the most prestigious military posting in the overseas empire, he sickened on the outbound voyage, compelling his return to England, where he died on October 26. Simcoe ascended to an Anglican heaven, thanks to a consoling conversation with his sovereign seven years before. Praising Simcoe's service in "the American War," King George III added, in Simcoe's rapturous words, "that had every one acted as I had done, that War would have had a different termination [which] has poured a Balm into my mind that nothing can obliterate & that grateful Remembrance of which will remain as the proudest Inheritance of my Children."[89]

Hannah Peters Jarvis with her daughters, Maria Lavinia and Augusta Honoria, *oil painting attributed to Matthew William Peters, 1791. Hannah (1763–1845) was the daughter of the Reverend Samuel Peters, an Anglican and a Loyalist from Connecticut. In 1785 she married William Jarvis, depicted below.* (Courtesy of the Royal Ontario Museum, 981.79.2.)

William Jarvis with his son, *oil painting attributed to Matthew William Peters, 1791. Proud of his service as an officer in the Queen's Rangers, Jarvis (1756–1817) appears in that uniform—and had a children's version made for his son. The father became the provincial secretary of Upper Canada, under Simcoe, and the boy later fought in the War of 1812.* (Courtesy of the Royal Ontario Museum, 981.79.1.)

William Duane, *engraving by Charles B. J. F. de Saint-Mémin, 1802. Duane edited and owned the* Aurora *of Philadelphia, the nation's most influential Republican newspaper.* (Courtesy of the National Portrait Gallery, Smithsonian Institution; gift of Mr. and Mrs. Paul Mellon.)

CHAPTER THREE

UNITED IRISHMEN

Truly so many unaccountable things happen in this age, that nothing should be considered impossible, however incredible.

—John Richardson, Montreal, Lower Canada, 1802[1]

America with us bears the character of the land of freedom and of liberty and is accounted like the land of promise flowing with milk and honey. Thus how desirable would such a place be to those labouring under Egyptian bondage encreasing and seemingly to encrease every day without the smallest gleam of hope. Such is the state of this Countrey and such are our sentiments with respect to America.

—Margaret Wright, County Tyrone, Ireland, 1808[2]

ALREADY REELING from the American Revolution, the British faced a still greater challenge from the French. In 1792 the French revolutionaries abolished the monarchy and declared a republic. To suppress opposition, they executed the former king and queen as well as hundreds of aristocrats and priests. In early 1793 the British joined the coalition of European monarchies waging war to destroy the French republic. Britain's ruling gentry rejected any reform at home as reckless in a time of revolution and war. "Who would repair their house during a hurricane?" asked William Windham, the secretary at war. "The British constitution is the best that ever was since the creation of the world, and it is not possible to make it better," a Scots judge instructed a jury trying a radical for treason. Abandoning his support for moderate reforms, the prime minister, William Pitt, devoted his administration to waging war abroad and to suppressing dissent at home.[3]

The British rulers worried because the French Revolution appealed to so many artisans, shopkeepers, schoolmasters, writers, and dissenting ministers. Impatient with domination by king and aristocracy, these middle-class and laboring radicals sought equal rights, universal manhood suffrage, annual parliamentary elections, a simplified legal system, a diminished military, and lower taxes. They denounced aristocrats and monarchs as corrupt and lazy parasites preying upon the common people whose labor created property. Radicals defied the government by forming the London Corresponding Society, which coordinated a national network of branch societies to agitate for reforms.[4]

In October 1795, 100,000 angry and hungry people staged an antiwar rally in London. A mob stopped the carriage of King George III as he rode to the opening session of Parliament. Crying "Down With Pitt," "No War," and "Give us Bread," the rioters hurled stones, smashing a window in the carriage. One man wrenched open the door and tried to pull out the king, but troops intervened to save him. Never intended by the radical leaders, the riot led to a popular backlash exploited by the government, which banned public gatherings by its critics. Conservative "Church and King" mobs attacked the homes and churches of radicals, and government prosecution shattered the London Corresponding Society. Rendered furtive in England and Scotland, republican agitation persisted in Ireland, the most restive part of the empire.[5]

In theory, Ireland was an independent kingdom, but the monarch was the king of Great Britain, and his ministers controlled the civil, military, and judicial appointments. The Irish had their own parliament, but it exercised more pomp than power, for real sovereignty lay in London. Thousands of British regulars occupied the country and served as a reserve for deployment overseas.[6]

Catholics comprised three-quarters of the Irish population, while Anglicans and Presbyterians split the Protestant quarter. The ruling Anglicans denied political and property rights to the Catholics, deemed too dangerous for self-government. The Presbyterian dissenters of Ulster, in northern Ireland, also resented domination by the Anglican elite, which owned about 90 percent of the land in Ireland and held virtually all of the government offices, military commissions, and seats in the Irish Parliament.[7]

During the early 1790s, radicals organized the United Irishmen to mobilize popular pressure for an independent republic. Finding inspiration in the American and French revolutions, Irish republicans offered the toast: "A fourth and fourteenth July to Ireland: we will die to achieve them." A mix of Protestants and Catholics, the United Irishmen tried to heal the religious divisions that favored British rule. In the words of one of their newspapers, the United Irishmen sought a republic where "every Irishman shall be a citizen [and] every citizen an Irishman." Primarily middle-class merchants, doctors, master artisans, schoolmasters, and shopkeepers, the United Irishman were bourgeois radicals, who sought an equality of rights rather than a leveling of property. Preparing for revolution, they stockpiled weapons in secret caches and solicited military intervention by the French. Dreading government informers and prosecution, they held clandestine meetings and employed secret oaths and a cell structure for their organization.[8]

In response, Irish Loyalists defended aristocracy, monarchy, and British rule as essential to law, order, and property. The Anglican elite rallied some popular support among the more conservative Presbyterians, who blanched at any alliance with Irish Catholics and French Jacobins. The reactionaries formed Orange Lodges, which mobilized mobs to attack the radicals and to destroy their newspapers. Unity was a dream rather than a reality for Irishmen, who prepared for civil war.[9]

UNITED COLUMBIA

As a Catholic country occupied by British troops, Lower Canada resembled Ireland with a French twist. The governing officials dreaded a French Canadian rebellion with the assistance of a French fleet and army of invasion. In fact, although the *habitants* disliked British rule, they were loath to risk their necks on a rebellion until a massive invasion force really did arrive. And the priests and landlords (*seigneurs*) rallied to the government from a disgust with the French Revolution's attacks on aristocracy and the Catholic Church.[10]

In 1796 British officials expected the worst when *habitants* rioted to resist a new law that drafted their labor to repair streets and roads. That rioting seemed especially ominous in October, when a French fleet did appear in the Gulf of St. Lawrence, producing, in the words of the governor, "a Sensation throughout this Province." Far from promoting the riots, which were local and spontaneous, French agents regretted them as premature, for the naval appearance in the gulf was a mere probe to gather information for a real invasion planned for 1797.[11]

But the invasion plan suffered a crippling blow in November 1796, when a British warship intercepted an American merchant ship two hundred miles south of Ireland. Bound west from Holland, the misnamed *Olive Branch* carried two dozen cannon and 20,000 muskets with bayonets. The weapons belonged to Ira Allen, a clever Vermont politician and land speculator who had previously intrigued with British officials in Canada. Allen claimed that he had bought the cargo for the militia of Vermont, but the British suspected that the weapons were French and intended for the United Irishmen.[12]

In fact, the arms were destined for Vermont, but Allen planned to smuggle them into Canada to promote a rebellion in support of a French invasion by sea. Then Vermont would secede from the United States to join Canada in forming a new republic called United Columbia. Embracing Allen's scheme, the French sent the weapons to Holland, where Allen chartered the *Olive Branch*.[13]

The wildest geopolitical schemes seemed plausible during a generation of revolutions. During the preceding twenty years, American rebels had defeated the mighty British empire; French revolutionaries had destroyed their monarchy; a former slave had led a massive revolt in St. Domingue that would produce the world's first black-ruled republic, Haiti; and an obscure Corsican had risen through the ranks to lead a French republic that defeated the combined might of Europe's monarchies. So why not believe in a United Columbia or a United Ireland?[14]

In the United Columbia scheme, Allen's chief partner was John Andrew Graham. Born in Connecticut in 1764, Graham was the son of a Yankee doctor and the grandson of a Presbyterian minister from Ulster. After studying divinity, Graham shifted to the study of law, which better suited his tastes for women, drink, and money. In 1785 he moved to Vermont, where he became a militia colonel and the chief aide to the governor. Tall, handsome, and charming, Graham had a slick persona. A critic described him as "a very needy, petty Attorney, with a very handsome appearance & an address which would be no disgrace to a European Courtier & an unbounded assurance." He married the daughter of one of Vermont's wealthiest men but, after running through her inheritance, abandoned her for a still wealthier Englishwoman. Writing in the margin of a book by Graham, his first wife retorted: "You have no honour, you liar—to divorce one woman by intrigue and marry another for *her money*." She concluded, "So Good Bye, You Jackall."[15]

Visiting London, Graham published his book to seek British support for a canal to improve Vermont's commercial link to Montreal. Professing Anglophilia, Graham claimed: "I have ever been inclined to regard myself as a citizen of Great Britain as well as of America, and I am persuaded the great majority of my countrymen think in the same manner." Disillusioned with republicanism, he praised Britain's mixed constitution, and urged "the kindred inhabitants of America, Great Britain, and Ireland" to "stretch forth their arms, and spring across the Atlantic to embrace. Not the *fraternizing hug* of France! No! But the tender, the sentimental embrace of children of one family."[16]

Yet, when the imperial lords balked at funding his canal, Graham joined Allen in turning to the French to pitch the United Columbia scheme. They faced disaster when the British intercepted the *Olive Branch*. To save himself, Graham betrayed Allen by revealing that the weapons were meant for rebels in Canada. In December 1797 a court of admiralty condemned the *Olive Branch* and her cargo, which ruined Allen, who fled to France, where the authorities jailed him for fleecing them. Released in 1800, he sailed for the United States, a bankrupt man.[17]

At least Ira Allen was alive, which could not be said for David McLane, who died for his misplaced faith in United Columbia. A militia major and merchant from Rhode Island, McLane was a dimmer version of Graham: tall, handsome, restless, and naive. In the spring of 1796 McLane fled from his creditors and offered his services to the French. Put on their payroll, McLane headed to Vermont, where he crossed into Canada, posing as a horse trader and timber speculator. Few believed his guise, and he lost more credibility by proposing a harebrained scheme to drug the British garrison at Quebec with opium. He also could speak little French, no small liability in an agent sent to rally a French Canadian rebellion. And his mission was pointless, for the French had canceled their invasion after the loss of the *Olive Branch*.[18]

Regarding McLane as hopeless, his Canadian contacts betrayed him to the British authorities at Quebec in May 1797. The British tried McLane for treason, on the grounds that, although an American citizen, he owed a subject's allegiance when in a British province. In July a jury convicted McLane after two witnesses had committed perjury by denying that they received any reward for their testimony. In fact, for each had been promised a township of land by British officials. On July 21, outside of Quebec's walls, McLane died on a well-guarded hill surrounded by a massive crowd. Some American newspapers denounced the trial as rigged and the execution as cruel, but the Federalist administration of John Adams disavowed McLane in favor of good relations with the British.[19]

REBELS

In 1797 McLane's hanging was a rare bit of good news for imperial lords facing defeat in Europe, unrest in Ireland, and mutinies in the Royal Navy. To restore order in Ireland, the British declared martial law in the most disaffected counties. Orange Order volunteers and regular troops disarmed, abused, arrested, and tortured suspected radicals. Some were murdered and had their homes burned. Under duress, the United Irishmen accelerated their plans for an armed uprising in conjunction with a

French invasion. But on March 12, 1798, before their preparations were complete, British troops arrested most of the United Irish leaders.[20]

The arrests sparked a scattered and uncoordinated rebellion, primarily by Catholic peasants south and west of Dublin. Despite poor leadership, the rebels won early victories as large numbers armed with crude pikes overwhelmed better-armed but smaller forces of British troops and Loyalist volunteers. But the Catholic rebels massacred some Protestant prisoners, which the government shrewdly publicized to deflate support for the rebellion in Protestant Ulster. Counterattacking, the royal forces crushed the rebels in June. Two months too late, the French landed a mere thousand men on Ireland's northwest coast. The small French force marched toward Dublin, rallying about five thousand untrained Irish, who were no match for the British regulars commanded by Lord Cornwallis. Avenging his American defeat at Yorktown, Cornwallis routed the invaders and the rebels in September. Thereafter, the rebellion dissipated into social banditry by small groups in isolated forests.[21]

The victors flogged and murdered hundreds, burning their houses and Catholic chapels, making a grim landscape of scorched villages. Executed and rotting bodies hung in chains from the roofs of county courthouses, while city walls bristled with heads stuck on spikes. The rebellion claimed at least 20,000 lives, most of them defeated rebels. Another 3,000 Irish suffered dispossession and transportation to the penal colony at Botany Bay. Others were sent to serve and die in the British army in the West Indies or in the Prussian army in Germany. Primarily driven by Irish Loyalists, the brutal vengeance disgusted Cornwallis as excessive. In 1799 he regretted the whole "wretched business of Courts-martial, hanging, transporting, etc., attended with all the dismal scenes of wives, sisters, fathers, kneeling and crying."[22]

While the common rebels suffered, most of the leading United Irishmen got off lightly. After trying and executing four as traitors, the government negotiated a pact with the remaining ninety state prisoners. In return for confessions to the details of their organization, methods, and goals, the government spared their lives but exiled them from Ireland. Twenty remained in a Scottish prison after Rufus King, the American minister to Great Britain, blocked their bid to immigrate to the United States. King explained: "I certainly do not think they will be a desirable acquisition to any Nation, but in none would they be likely to prove more mischievous than in mine, where from the sameness of language and similarity of Laws and Institutions they have greater opportunities of propagating their principles than in any other Country." Lord

Castlereagh sardonically responded that "the majority of our prisoners are not more dangerous than the general class of American settlers." But to gratify the Federalist administration in the United States, the British kept the twenty state prisoners behind bars until 1802, when a peace treaty halted the war with France. Freed to immigrate to America, they nursed a deep bitterness for the Federalists, especially Rufus King.[23]

The Irish comprised most of the immigrants to the United States from 1783 to 1820: 199,000 of the 366,000 total. Primarily sailing from ports in Ulster, three-quarters were Protestant and only one-quarter were Catholic. Most landed in Philadelphia, New York, or Baltimore. By 1800 the Irish comprised at least 12 percent of Philadelphia's population. Despite their religious tensions in Ireland, the immigrants of both faiths cooperated in politics and benevolent associations in America. During the 1790s, the distinction between Catholic and Protestant Irish was far less significant in America than it has become to historians writing in hindsight. The Protestant immigrants from Ulster never called themselves "Scotch-Irish." Instead, they were as Irish as any Catholic from Wexford.[24]

Economic and political motives merged for immigrants who blamed Ireland's troubles on British misrule and who credited republican equality for American prosperity. One migrant assured a friend in Ulster that "the lowest here (unlike those of poor Ireland) are well fed, well dressed, and happy. . . . They stand erect and crouch not before any man. This my friend is due to the enjoyment of liberty in her proper extent." The immigrants equated republican government with opportunity for hardworking common people. Conversely, they blamed monarchy and aristocracy for the empire's debilitating taxation, chronic warfare, low wages, and high land rents.[25]

FEDERALISTS AND REPUBLICANS

During the 1790s the Irish immigrants landed in the midst of a political struggle between Federalists and Republicans to define the legacy of the American Revolution. During the 1790s the Federalists held national power, controlling the Congress and the presidency under George Washington and John Adams. But they faced growing opposition from the Republicans led by Thomas Jefferson, James Madison, and Aaron Burr. The political partisans were so shrill because the stakes seemed so high: the survival of the republic and its tenuous union of fractious states. Although endowed with an immense potential for economic and demographic growth, the United States was a new and weak country in a dangerous world of powerful empires. And its leaders had gambled their immense union on a republic, a radical form of government notoriously short-lived in the past.[26]

Both Federalists and Republicans denounced political parties as selfish factions bent on perverting the common good. Paradoxically, that dread of parties drove each group to practice an especially bitter partisanship. Claiming exclusively to speak for the people, each party cast rivals as insidious conspirators bent on destroying freedom and the union. Referring to "the parties of honest men and rogues, into which every country is divided," Jefferson insisted, "the republicans are the *nation*."[27]

Seeking social stability, the Federalists hoped to build a stronger national government that could control the states. During the 1790s the Federalists established a national bank, consolidated the national debt, built an army and a navy, and they funded their expensive initiatives with increased taxes. The Federalists agreed with Britons that a true nation needed a central sovereignty invested with the power to act with energy.[28]

Seeking greater equality, the Republican opposition favored a minimal federal government and a decentralized, consensual union, where most power remained with the states. They insisted that dispersing power would frustrate America's would-be aristocrats who expected to dominate a national government. Equality and consent, not central command, should unite the people. Of course, Federalists rejected the Republican vision as dangerously naive and doomed to collapse into anarchy.[29]

The Republicans and Federalists also differed over the proper degree of democracy in a republic. While the Federalists cast themselves as "the Fathers of the People," the Republicans posed as "the Friends of the People." The Federalists insisted that common people should elect, and then defer to, a paternalistic elite defined by their superior education, wealth, and status. Once elected, gentlemen should govern free from "licentious" criticism that eroded public esteem for them. In sharp contrast, the Republicans promised to heed public opinion and to deny special privileges to any elite. They insisted that equal rights and opportunity would elevate the industrious poor rather than perpetuate the idle rich.[30]

But, while pushing for equal rights for white men, most Republicans disdained Indians and African-Americans. In their racial hierarchy, all white men were equal in their rights and superior to blacks and natives. Because the Federalists imagined social hierarchy in class (rather than racial) terms, they regarded Indians and blacks as worthy objects of elite paternalism. Appealing for white votes, the Republicans derided the Federalists as pro-black and pro-Indian.[31]

The Federalist and Republican political struggle became entangled in the global and ideological war between France and Great Britain. Each great power pressured the neutral United States for assistance against the other belligerent. The British played upon the American economic dependence on British imports and on the vulnerability of American merchant ships to the might of the Royal Navy. While Federalists accepted that commercial dependence as mutually profitable, the Republicans dreaded British commerce as corrupting. The French Revolution also reignited the debate among Americans over the proper meaning of their own recent and still unsettled revolution. The Republicans identified with France as a sister republic assailed by the monarchies of Europe, but the Federalists denounced the French Revolution as dangerously radical and violent. With the Federalists tilting toward Britain, the Republicans equated their rivals with Loyalists bent on subverting republicanism in America as well as France.[32]

In 1797 the French provoked a crisis by seizing American merchant ships trading with the British. Adding insult to injury, the French demanded bribes and tribute from American diplomats in Paris. In the United States, news of the seizures and indignities produced a popular backlash against France, which the Federalists exploited to mobilize for war and to tar the Republicans as traitors. In 1798 the crisis enhanced cooperation between the Federalist administration and the British empire. The British supplied munitions to the United States, protected American merchant ships from French privateers, and shared secret information. Preferring Canada in British rather than French hands, the Federalists offered to send troops to help defend Canada in the event of a French invasion.[33]

ALIENS

Leading Irish-Americans identified with the United Irish cause, including a secular vision of politics that downplayed religious differences. In 1797 in Philadelphia, they organized an American Society of United Irishmen, with branch societies ranging from Albany in New York to Charleston in South Carolina. Members swore to seek "the attainment of liberty and equality to mankind in whatever nation I may reside." Thanks to the indulgent voting requirements, the newcomers helped swing elections in favor of the Republicans. And Irish-American leaders and editors built the urban organizations of Jefferson's party. A Federalist congressman declared that "with a very few exceptions," the immigrants were "United Irishmen, Free Masons, and the most God-provoking Democrats on this side of Hell." Indeed, the Federalists charged that the United Irishmen were preparing to assist a French invasion of America.[34]

Recoiling to a nativist position, the Federalists denounced the Irish as too ignorant, poor, and brutish to become citizens. The most vociferous Federalist was an immigrant from England, William Cobbett, a former British army sergeant who had immigrated to Philadelphia, where he became the nation's most popular and polemical journalist. Cobbett declared that "every United Irishman ought to be hunted from the country, as much as a wolf or a tyger." He concluded, "As well might we attempt to tame the Hyena, as to Americanize an Irishman." Espousing a conservative nationalism, Federalists imagined the American people as properly homogeneous and native born. On the one hand, the Federalists distrusted the immigrants as too strongly defined by their distinctive origins and ethnic identity. On the other hand, the Federalists also dreaded the Irish-Americans for championing an international vision of continuing revolution which transcended the nationalism of their adopted country.[35]

In 1798 the Federalists in Congress moved to restrict the naturalization of immigrants. Robert Goodloe Harper insisted, "The time is now come when it will be proper to declare that nothing but birth shall entitle a man to citizenship in this country." Balking at so extreme a measure, Congress instead increased the probationary period for naturalization to fourteen years from the previous five. Congress also authorized the president summarily to expel any alien deemed "dangerous to the peace and safety of the United States."[36]

The Federalists also bristled at criticism in Republican newspapers, especially those edited by Irish immigrants. Passing a Sedition Act, which applied to citizens as well as aliens, Congress criminalized the publication of "any false, scandalous, and malicious writing or writings against the government of the United States or the President of the United States, with intent to defame . . . or to bring them into contempt or disrepute." Those convicted faced up to two years in prison and $2,000 in fines. By allowing jurors to consider the truth of the provocative words as a defense, however, the Federalists insisted that they had liberalized the common law of sedition.[37]

In enforcing the Sedition Law, the secretary of state, Timothy Pickering, targeted "Irish villains," including William Duane, the clever and truculent editor of Philadelphia's *Aurora*, the nation's leading Republican newspaper. Duane's roaming past revealed the global range of the struggle between revolutionary republicanism and the reactionary empire. Born in colonial New York in 1760, he had returned as a child to Ireland with his widowed mother. As a young man, he moved to London, where he worked as a parliamentary reporter for a radical newspaper. When that press failed in 1786, Duane sent his wife and three children back to Ireland. By enlisting in the military service of the East India Company, he secured a free passage to India. Reaching Calcutta in 1787, Duane wriggled out of the military and secured better-paying work as a merchant's clerk. Charming and enterprising, he took up with an English actress, who bore him three more children.[38]

Borrowing money, Duane bought a newspaper in 1790. A staunch republican, he offended the colonial government by denouncing corruption in India and by praising the revolution in France. In 1794 colonial officials deported Duane for "attempting to disseminate the democratic principles of Tom Paine." Unable to sell his paper on short notice, Duane was financially ruined. He sailed back to London as a prisoner in a ship aptly named the *William Pitt* to honor the prime minister who suppressed dissent. Reunited with his original wife and children, Duane briefly edited a radical newspaper. To dodge another arrest by the British government, Duane immigrated with his family to the United States in 1796.[39]

Settling in Philadelphia, Duane wrote essays for the *Aurora*, becoming the editor in 1798 and the owner two years later. Aggressive and resourceful, Duane relentlessly denounced Federalist misdeeds, real and invented. A master of invective, he became a national celebrity at the center of his own narrative of a global struggle for liberty, with Britons and Federalists as the arch-villains. His flair rendered the *Aurora* the most influential paper in the nation, eclipsing Cobbett's Federalist newspaper, *Porcupine's Gazette*. Despised by the Federalists, the *Aurora* became essential reading for Republicans throughout the country. A Federalist writer complained that "on every important subject, the sentiments to be inculcated among the democrats, had been first put into the *Aurora*. This was the heart, the seat of life."[40]

In May 1799 soldiers broke into Duane's office to beat him with their fists, feet, and a cowskin whip. A Federalist insisted that Duane got what he deserved, for he "was not an American but a foreigner, and not merely a foreigner, but a United Irishman, and not merely an United Irishman, but a public convict and fugitive from justice." Where Duane saw himself as a victim of British tyranny, the Federalists upheld British justice by deeming him a renegade outlaw. A Federalist concluded, "Jails and dungeons and pillories are forsooth pretty seminaries of Republicanism!" Defining the revolution as conservative and complete, the Federalists criminalized those who crossed boundaries to renew the struggle. But Duane defined the revolution as radical, democratic, international, and ongoing. So he could claim to be a better American than the Federalists, whom he cast as Loyalists hostile to the republic.[41]

In 1799 Duane foiled the Federalists by obtaining secret dispatches from Robert Liston, the British ambassador, to the colonial government in Upper Canada. In rural Pennsylvania, a Republican magistrate found the documents in the saddlebags of Isaac Swayze, a Loyalist wanted for horse thefts committed during the revolution. Having settled in Upper Canada, Swayze had become an emissary for the colonial government. In the dispatches, Liston boasted of his close cooperation with the Federalist administration. When the purloined documents appeared in the *Aurora*, Pickering ordered Duane prosecuted for seditious libel, but the district attorney had to suspend the case when Duane threatened to reveal another embarrassing letter, by President Adams, in open court.[42]

In the election of 1800 the Republicans exploited the popular backlash against the Sedition Act prosecutions and against the taxes that funded the military escalation by the Federalists. The Republicans won a majority in Congress and appeared to have elected Thomas Jefferson as president and Aaron Burr as vice-president. In early 1801 the lame-duck Federalist Congress toyed with overturning Jefferson's election in favor of Burr, which provoked widespread talk of, and some preparations for, civil war. In mid-February, a moderate Federalist, James Bayard of Delaware, broke the tense stalemate by forsaking Burr to permit Jefferson's election. Burr had to settle for the vice-presidency and for Jefferson's resourceful hatred.[43]

The victorious Republicans reversed the Federalist drive to build a powerful national government. The victors instead favored a decentralized union which entrusted all but foreign affairs to the states. By reducing the army and navy, the Republicans could abolish the unpopular excise and land taxes. Congress also killed the Sedition Act, while Jefferson pardoned those convicted under that law. And his fiscal policy sought to pay down, and eventually to eliminate, the national debt. To reward immigrant voters, the Republicans loosened naturalization, which the Federalists had tightened. The Naturalization Act of 1802 lowered the residence requirement to five years, down from the fourteen years mandated by the Federalists in 1798. The new citizens included Duane, naturalized in July 1802.[44]

The electoral revolution in America inspired a surge in immigration from Ireland: over 28,000 during 1801–2. In New York, the British consul Thomas Barclay blamed "the immense emigrations" on United Irishmen in America, who

> by every conveyance, send over to England, Scotland, and Ireland, seditious, inflammatory publications for the express purpose of rendering His Majesty's Subjects dissatisfied with their present situation and the measures of Government [and] describing their now envied situation in America in the enjoyment of Liberty and equality, free from taxation; and painting these States as a field where wealth is reaped with care and moderate industry.

Barclay dreaded that every Irish emigrant reinforced American republicanism and deprived the British empire of valuable labor and a potential soldier or sailor. In 1803 Parliament limited the number of persons that any vessel could carry away from Great Britain, reducing the Irish migration to America.[45]

The decline came too late to save the Federalists from immigrant voters in the seaports. In 1807 in New York City, Thomas Addison Emmet rallied the immigrant voters to take revenge on Rufus King, who had delayed the release of the Irish state prisoners (including Emmet) in 1799. After King's legislative slate suffered electoral defeat, the victorious Republicans stood outside his house, chanting "Emmet and Liberty!" Indebted to Irish votes, the state's new Republican governor, Daniel D. Tompkins, had Emmet appointed as New York's attorney general.[46]

Meanwhile in Ireland, a "United Kingdom" rose on the ruins of the United Irish dream. With the British abolition of the Irish Parliament, effective on January 1, 1801, the imperial Parliament became the sole sovereign legislature for Ireland, Scotland, Wales, and England. The British union was the inverse consequence of a rebellion that had tried, but failed, to win Irish independence. The British union survived for more than a century because the rebellion's bloody failure had bitterly divided Ireland's Protestants and Catholics. Thereafter, Irish nationalism became increasingly Gaelic and Catholic, while the Protestant minority, including the Presbyterians of Ulster, embraced the union as their safeguard against Catholic domination. The renewed sectarian tension betrayed the United Irish vision of a secular republic with equal rights for all men.[47]

In May 1801 Canada's governor-general, Peter Hunter, celebrated the new United Kingdom in an address to the legislature of Upper Canada. In 1798 General Hunter had suppressed the rebellion in County Wexford, where he had hanged United Irishmen from a bridge and then impaled their heads on iron spikes for display at the county courthouse. Three years later, Hunter extolled the new centralization of power at the heart of the empire:

> The British Nations are now entirely *consolidated*. . . . Every thing that was partial; every thing that was local; every thing that could recall the Recollection that those whom Nature intended to be One, were distinct, is done away, and the most intimate Union is Established on the justest and most liberal Principles. Our strength is increased by being brought to a Centre.

This consolidation of imperial power starkly contrasted with the decentralized union favored by the Republicans in the United States. That difference made the United States a haven for the discontented of Ireland.[48]

WHITE CAPS

If the Irish were the empire's prodigals, the Scots were the favorites. Escaping the constraints of their cramped, cold, rainy, and rocky land, ambitious Scots exploited the global opportunities of the empire. Their regiments became the backbone of the British army; their gentlemen served as colonial governors; and their merchants exploited the colonial trade. During the American Revolution, the Patriots dreaded the Scots as more formidable troops than the English. The United Irishmen learned the same hard lesson in 1798, when most of the British regulars in Ireland came from Scotland.[49]

Born and raised in Scotland, General Hunter had fought against the American Revolution, serving primarily in the West Indies. During the 1790s he rose to brigadier general for his military exploits in the Caribbean, on the European continent, and in Ireland. In 1799 Hunter secured command of the military in both Canadian provinces, and he took charge of the civil government in Upper Canada. Impatient, demanding, and harsh, he terrorized the civil officials at York, the new capital of Upper Canada. His chief whipping boy was the sloppy provincial secretary, William Jarvis, whose wife, Hannah, complained, "For my part, I think the Ministry must have scraped all the fishing Towns of Scotland to have found so great a Devil."[50]

Hunter favored fellow Scots at the expense of American, Irish, and even English rivals for government patronage. Upper Canada's attorney general, the aptly named Thomas Scott, joined Aeneas Shaw and John McGill to form Hunter's inner circle of fellow Scots. An English judge in Canada disliked "the Combinations formed, wherever they gain a footing, to promote themselves . . . and impede all others." This judge concluded that "no man coming from the South or West of the Tweed will flourish in that Territory."[51]

Scots merchants had long dominated Canada's commerce, including the fur trade with the Indians around the Great Lakes. Based in Montreal, Scots firms placed correspondents at the key transit points in the upper country: Kingston, York, Niagara, Detroit, and Michilimackinac. Those firms also sold imported manufactured goods to the settlers in exchange for their pork, wheat, potash, and lumber. For want of banks, the Scots merchants were the prime source of credit and of lawsuits to collect on overdue debts. Upper Canada's most powerful merchants, Richard Cartwright of Kingston and Robert Hamilton of Queenston, were Scots allied to Montreal firms. Recruiting kinsmen from Scotland, Hamilton and Cartwright patronized their ascent in Upper Canada's interlocking economic and political elite.[52]

The key figure in the Scots nexus was John Richardson of Montreal. Shrewd, ambitious, and well connected, Richardson grew up in a mercantile family. After a university education in Aberdeen, Richardson joined a leading firm in the colonial fur trade. Sent to New York, Richardson ran afoul of Patriot committees and mobs enforcing boycotts on British imports. Confirmed in his loyalty, Richardson spent the war supplying the British troops occupying New York, Philadelphia, and Charleston. After the war, Richardson moved to Montreal, where he became a partner in the preeminent fur-trading firm, Forsyth, Richardson, and Company.[53]

Canada's governors entrusted counterintelligence operations to Richardson, a perfect role for his penetrating intelligence, keen attention to detail, ideological zeal, and business connections, which reached across the American border. Possessing a dark sense of human nature as anarchic, Richardson dreaded that French and American agents were busily promoting rebellions and inviting invasions. He believed that only his exertions could keep Canada from the volcanic brink of a republican revolution. Richardson intercepted correspondence, investigated strangers, interrogated suspects, and recruited informants. He built the Crown's case, such as it was, that hanged David McLane for treason in 1797.[54]

In July 1801 Colonel John A. Graham of Vermont appeared in Montreal to reveal a new plot against British Canada. As in the *Olive Branch* case of 1796, Graham fingered French agents in cahoots with Ira Allen's republican circle in Vermont. Graham charged that a newly built ironworks in Upper Canada was preparing for rebellion by making pikes, like those used by the United Irish. Graham also insisted that Allen had sent a schoolteacher, known only as "Rogers," to Montreal to organize a secret society of radicals.[55]

Dodging arrest, Rogers escaped to Vermont, but the magistrates caught some of his associates, who made sensational revelations about the "White Cap Club" or "Civil Society of Montreal." Bound by a blood oath to keep secrets, that society had sixty-one members, primarily transient American artisans and traders. Professing magical powers, Rogers had promised that he could help his initiates find buried treasures by performing elaborate, nocturnal, and occult ceremonies while wearing white caps. But the informants confessed that the "Ceremonies and Mummery" drew the initiates into a deeper plot to plunder and burn Montreal, with the help of one thousand armed men who would rush across the border from nearby Vermont. One imaginative informant suggested that the uprising would begin by "introducing a wire into" the garrison's powder magazine "and thereby conveying the electric fluid" to ignite an explosion.[56]

To abate local alarm, the Montreal magistrates organized a night patrol by armed volunteers, and Richardson sent an agent into Vermont to gather information. Finding no evidence of a plot, that agent dismissed Graham as "a needy Swindler" who never told the truth. Far from leading a rebellion, Ira Allen was in jail in Burlington for his unpaid debts. During the winter the British released the suspects from custody in Montreal for want of credible evidence to prosecute them.[57]

The supposed plot was merely a scam run by Rogers to shake down his initiates. A Connecticut-born schoolteacher, Ransford Rogers claimed an expertise that "descended into the bowels of the earth, and could reveal the secret things of darkness." Peripatetic, Rogers had repeatedly conned people who subscribed to the widespread folk belief that nocturnal magic could wrest buried treasures from guardian spirits. During 1788–89 in Morris County, New Jersey, he collected £500 in contributions from farmers persuaded that he could enrich them by leading prolonged seances and complicated ceremonies involving the wearing of white caps. In Montreal in 1801, Graham probably hired Rogers to organize a similar White Cap Club to lend plausibility to Graham's story of a radical plot. Then Graham covered his tracks by tipping off Rogers so he could escape arrest.[58]

British officials overreacted to the Rogers plot because they expected the worst from a set of signs that evoked the United Irishmen: secret oaths, initiations, and nocturnal ceremonies. Richardson explained, "Truly so many unaccountable things happen in this age, that nothing should be considered impossible, however incredible." Such was the garrison mentality of officials on the margins of an empire imperiled by French war, Irish unrest, and American subversion.[59]

In the end, the Rogers alarm benefited British officials by strengthening their support from French Canadians, who despised the American transients accused of plotting against lives and property in Montreal. The canny Richardson confided:

> It is generally speaking, the scum of the people from the States, with whom the [French] Canadians have had any intercourse in their dealings, and being very frequently cheated by them, they now entertain a hatred of the Americans in general, which is daily increasing and it is good policy at present to encourage them in such sentiments.

During the summer of 1803, when several fires ravaged Montreal, the inhabitants again suspected arson by Vermonters seeking plunder. In 1805 an American visitor to Montreal noted that the inhabitants had "an antipathy to the English, but a still greater one to the people of the United States." Managing ethnic divisions was the essence of empire.[60]

DANFORTH'S ROAD

In January 1802 an informant warned the Upper Canada Executive Council of another plot to overthrow that government and to create a republican state that could join the American union. "The American Government," the informant insisted, "is at the bottom of the plan but will not be seen." Vice-president Burr and Governor George Clinton of New York were the alleged ringleaders. Conveying the shocking news to General Hunter at Quebec, Chief Justice John Elmsley insisted that the plotters had recruited armed volunteers in New York "& that the Invaders will be immediately joined by between One & two thousand of the Inhabitants of this Country." According to Elmsley, the conspirators sought "1 & 2 Millions of Acres, which are to be divided among them & for which Col. Burr had pledged himself to use all his influence to obtain a confirmation from Congress whenever the Conquest is complete."[61]

Upper Canada seemed ripe for republican subversion once Jefferson became the American president, for the British believed that he wanted to export revolution. And many Upper Canadians sensed great unease in their colony. A newcomer, Joseph Willcocks, observed, "the people of Ireland are not more discontented than the Lower Class of People here." An American emigrant, Asa Danforth, Jr., reported that Peter Russell, an executive councillor, had "observed to me . . . that if Mr. Jefferson & Mr. Burr should come in at the Head of affairs in the states, the [Canadian] Provinces must give up to the States." Danforth estimated that in Upper Canada "three fourths of the common people would be happy of a Change."[62]

Originally from Massachusetts, Danforth had invested in the Upper Canada townships granted by John Graves Simcoe. That investment soured in 1795–97, when the government revoked the grants upon discovering that the owners were American speculators rather than true Loyalists. Simcoe's secretary lectured one speculator, "You must perceive that the King's Government is infinitely more desirous of settling a few well-affected Subjects, moral, sober, and religious men, than of a Multitude of Inhabitants & above all that . . . it is careful to prevent this Colony from becoming the Prey of Land Jobbers."[63]

Chief Justice Elmsley had led the push to repossess the townships. An eloquent elitist, Elmsley denounced the speculators as agents of an insidious commerce that corroded stability and hierarchy. He castigated them for rendering Upper Canadian land "as much an Article of Commerce as Corn, and may be bought with equal ease at the store of the merchant." By reclaiming the townships, Elmsley boasted that the government had "Prove[d] that the strong arm of Monarchy is not to be pushed aside by those unprincipled & unattached republicans."[64]

The executive councillors promptly regranted the land to themselves or to their friends and relatives. Claiming ten thousand acres as his share, Elmsley asked,

Can lands be in any hands better than in those of the officers of Government, in a country in which the influence of extensive property is so much wanted to give effect to the Laws, & keep the turbulent in good order? & in whose hands can they be more safely placed than in ours, who depend so entirely upon the King & the Mother Country?

But the dispossessed speculators saw Elmsley as a ruthless competitor who exploited his advantages as an insider. They bristled at officials who, in the name of security, obstructed the enterprise of newcomers.[65]

Despite losing most of his land, Danforth stayed in Upper Canada, where he landed a government contract to build a road along the north shore of Lake Ontario. The new road would link York with the settlements along the Bay of Quinte to the east. By December 1800 his workers had completed all 106 miles, but the official inspector found fault with the quality. Taking a hard line, the executive council withheld Danforth's payment and refused to grant the eight thousand acres due to the workers, who had sold their land rights to Danforth. Certain that Americans were tricksters, the councillors protected themselves by cheating Danforth.[66]

Financially ruined, Danforth sought revenge by heading to New York City to pitch a Canadian rebellion to his chief creditor, Timothy Green, and his political friend, Aaron Burr. Delighted by Burr's apparent interest, Danforth declared, "I am fully of oppinion that the Great Change of Politics in the United States will afford something very handsome to those who were drag[g]ed from home by fair promises of Genl. Simco[e] & the like." Opportunistic and secretive, Burr liked to fish in troubled waters, often flirting with grandiose filibustering expeditions meant to reshape the political geography of North America. And he had a flair for inspiring ambitious young men to take reckless risks on implausible adventures. Danforth gushed, "It has been a pain to him to see genius trampled." As the patron of promising young men of modest means, Burr stood in contrast to Upper Canada's rulers, who defended the entrenched privileges of birth and office.[67]

Danforth recruited other entrepreneurs drawn into Upper Canada during the early 1790s but frustrated in their dreams by government suspicion. They included the millwright Aaron Greeley, the newspaper editors Gideon and Silvester Tiffany, and their brother-in-law, Davenport Phelps, a former Patriot army officer who became a merchant, lawyer, and land speculator. The conspirators saw themselves as able and enterprising men unjustly frustrated by a corrupt and oppressive elite of British officials. The suspects shared a bond as Freemasons: members of a secret society with a meritocratic philosophy that appealed to ambitious freethinkers.[68]

Danforth nicely expressed their eagerness for applause in seeking a republic in Upper Canada: "A Scene will open and many become Actors in the Play. The United States is like a Stage Play. Every Man's Mind is taken up with his part." By contrast, British Canada limited the leading and lucrative roles to imperial officials, who distrusted the American entrepreneurs as grasping for a wealth properly beyond their lowly station and shifty morals. That distrust became a self-fulfilled prophecy when the suspected turned in frustration to a republican plot.[69]

Their scheme fizzled in early 1802, when one of the plotters, the

English-born surveyor and teacher Richard Cockrell, tipped off the executive councillors, and provided his letters from Danforth. The September date for the American invasion and Canadian uprising passed uneventfully, exposing the plot as, in the words of Peter Russell, "a tissue of Absurdity & Improbability."[70]

Most of the conspirators fled to the United States. Back in New York, Danforth landed in a debtors' prison for failing to pay his creditors in either money or a rebellion. Eventually released, Danforth was last documented in 1821 on the lam from another arrest for debt. In the end, Danforth found the commercial republic as hard a taskmaster as the security-obsessed empire. But he remains unwittingly honored in the province that he tried to subvert, for the British kept his name on "the Danforth Road," now a major street in Toronto.[71]

The Danforth plot sought to combine an internal uprising with an external invasion—but both failed. Despite the reports of Canadian discontent, few colonists would risk their lives and properties on overt rebellion. Dispersed over bad roads through an immense forest, the common people took little interest in politics, and few ever learned of the proposed rebellion. Such dispersed and passive settlers could not rebel on their own, without the support of a major American invasion likely to win without them, and no such intervention was forthcoming.[72]

Danforth's wild optimism inflated a bubble of rebellion that burst when an American invasion proved an illusion. Among the Republican leaders, only Burr showed any interest in the plot, and he had no money and little power after his foiled bid to steal the presidency from Jefferson in 1801. At the peak of the plot, Jefferson was undermining Burr's political base in New York rather than seeking to expand it into Canada. And Jefferson was far from the reckless radical of his British reputation. Determined to reduce federal taxes and the national debt, Jefferson did not want to provoke an expensive war with the empire in 1802.[73]

IRISH PARTY

On August 21, 1805, General Hunter suddenly died. In the short term, his successor was an elderly Scot named Alexander Grant, a member of the executive council. With the fearsome Hunter replaced by a nonentity, at last the legislators could protest their long impotence. An assemblyman complained that, during Hunter's reign, "the house had but one thing to do, that is to vote a set of silk caps for themselves, which were to be pulled over their eyes." That passivity dissolved in early 1806, when Grant reported that the assembly was busy "vomiting grievance and

Complaints Against the Administration of General Hunter and plaguing me, and his favoureds."[74]

The opposition rallied around Robert Thorpe, an Irish judge newly arrived in Upper Canada. Ambitious, arrogant, and reckless, Thorpe meant to dominate the government, but he found his path blocked by the Scots officials. In letters to superiors in London, Thorpe posed as the one man who could calm the popular fervor that he did so much to foment: "In a quiet way, I have the reins so as to prevent mischief, tho' like Phaeton, I seized them precipitately. I shall not burn myself & hope to save others."[75]

The colony's official elite denounced Thorpe for playing with republican fire. Alexander Macdonell called Thorpe the "Demon of Anarchy" and "a Revolutionary genius" bent on disaffecting "the lower class of People." He concluded that Thorpe, "like a mole, works in the dark, but communicates with the lowest class through a medium of his . . . friends"—his fellow Irishmen, William Weekes and Joseph Willcocks.[76]

Weekes was an ambitious and passionate lawyer who drank heavily and quarreled frequently. Born in Ireland, he had immigrated to New York City, where he had apprenticed in Burr's law office. In 1798 Weekes moved to Upper Canada, where his Irish origins and his Burr connection aroused suspicions that he had been a United Irishman. In fact, Weekes initially cultivated patronage from the elite, especially Judge Henry Allcock. But Weekes lost his patron in 1805, when Allcock departed for Lower Canada. Feeling blocked by Hunter's Scottish clique, Weekes turned to political opposition and won election to the assembly.[77]

Joseph Willcocks possessed dashing good looks, charm, deep ambition, and flexible morals. Born near Dublin in 1773, the son of a country gentleman, Willcocks had obtained a genteel English education. During the United Irish uprising, he remained loyal, boasting of his "attachment to the King and Constitution and my zealous Exertions to suppress the late Melancholly Rebellion which pervaded my native Country." In 1803 his older brother tipped off the authorities to a revived uprising planned by Robert Emmet, the younger brother of Thomas Addis Emmet.[78]

Facing poor career prospects in Ireland, Willcocks immigrated to Upper Canada, where he secured patronage from his cousin, Peter Russell, as confidential secretary and lodger. Russell helped Willcocks to procure Crown grants to a town lot in York and 1,200 country acres. Writing home to his kin in Ireland, Willcocks boasted of his good life at "Russell Abbey," dwelling with his patron: "the most pleasant and most sensible man I ever met . . . He is all consideration and I believe all goodness—he seems partial to me—we live [like] Father and son." In his diary Willcocks recorded a pleasant round of carriage and sleigh rides, tea parties, card games, ballroom dancing, horse races, fowling, fox chasing, deer hunting, and sailing in the harbor. In November 1801 he drank wine and ate cake at York's fort to celebrate news of the Irish submergence in the British union.[79]

Willcocks flirted with the local belles, but he preferred money in a woman. "Beauty will not make the Pot boil," he explained. Peter Russell's unmarried half-sister, Elizabeth Russell, was no beauty and, at forty-seven in 1801, she was nineteen years older than Willcocks, but she stood to inherit her bachelor brother's considerable estate. Willcocks's diary hinted at a secret courtship with mutual understandings, small presents, and brief spats. In August 1802 he proposed marriage, but Elizabeth snapped. Refusing to see him, she revealed the flirtation to her shocked brother, who angrily discharged Willcocks. He sadly observed, "Mr. Russell, finding that Miss Russell and myself were pulling a cord together, immediately dismissed me and for once left me naked to the world." They no longer lived like father and son, for the Russells meant to keep living as surrogate husband and wife.[80]

A lucky man, Willcocks landed on his feet, taken in by Allcock as lodger and clerk, for the judge wanted to spite his political enemy, Russell. At Allcock's request, General Hunter appointed Willcocks as sheriff of the Home District, with an annual income of £200. Willcocks boasted that, although "the officers of Government disagree very much, I have the good fortune to be always at the strongest side." When Allcock moved to Lower Canada, Willcocks found a new patron in Robert Thorpe, who became his "most particular friend."[81]

In the Whig tradition of Britain, the Irish party extolled the king as a perfect font of benevolence and rational liberty who had accepted constitutional limits on his power. True loyalty obliged resistance to the abuses of colonial officials who betrayed the king by exploiting his subjects in distant Canada. By defending the Whig tradition, the Irish party resisted the more centralized and authoritarian empire that had emerged in reaction against the American and French revolutions.[82]

The Irish party charged the executive with neglecting the colony's economic development. "Nothing has been done for the Colony, no roads, bad water communication, no Post, no Religion, no Morals, no Education, no Trade, no Agriculture, no Industry attended to," Thorpe charged. The Irish party also denounced the executive for corruptly deploying its patronage—appointments, contracts, and land grants—to buy a passive assembly. Ultimately, the opposition blamed a Scots cabal that combined the power of mercantile creditors and executive officials. Thorpe insisted: "This Shopkeeper Aristocracy has stunted the prosperity of the Province & goaded the people until they have turned from the greatest loyalty to the utmost disaffection."[83]

Thorpe argued that the assembly should control land grants and manage their revenue, a radical proposition in a British colony. Seeking what would later be called "responsible government," the dissidents promoted legislative control over the colony's finances and administrators. But the powerful district oligarchies of magistrates and militia officers relied on the government for their offices, contracts, land grants, and social respectability. And the colony's thin population, scattered settlements, and miserable roads encouraged political passivity. A leading Quaker, Peter Lossing, denounced the Irish party for "raising [an] insidious distinction, what they term'd the friends of the People & the friends of Government." Avoiding politics, most of the inhabitants preferred to attend to their families, farms, and religious communities (or to their drinking and swearing).[84]

Alarmed by the rancor in Upper Canada, the imperial lords appointed a new lieutenant governor to supplant the overmatched Grant. An English aristocrat, Francis Gore had served as a major in the British army, capping his career as aide-de-camp to Ireland's lord lieutenant, the Earl of Camden, during the rebellion of 1798. Camden secured Gore's appointment to govern Bermuda in 1804. Transferred to Upper Canada, Gore arrived in August 1806. "I have and ever will contend against Democratic principles," he declared.[85]

Mistaking his man, Thorpe hoped to become Gore's chief adviser. Rejecting Thorpe's officious overtures, Gore noted, "The plain English of all this is, let me dictate to you, and everything will go well. *I, the People* . . . is, in reality, a characteristic motto of Mr. Thorpe and every other factious Demagogue." Dismissing the discontent as limited to "the lower classes of the community," Gore took his stand: "The most respectable People in this Province are looking up to me for protection." Enraged by the brush-off, Thorpe blasted Gore as "imperious, self-sufficient & ignorant."[86]

In October 1806 at Newark, Thorpe presided over a circuit court, where Weekes denounced General Hunter as a "Gothic Barbarian whom the providence of God . . . removed from this world for his tyranny and Iniquity." Alas, a similar providence would soon smite Weekes. Offended by the words, a Scots lawyer, William Dickson, rebuked Weekes, who challenged him to a duel—a fatal mistake.[87]

In the special election to fill Weekes's seat in the assembly, Thorpe mustered his voters beneath a flag with the motto: "The King, the People, the Law, Thorpe & the Constitution." He triumphed over Gore's candidate, Thomas B. Gough, who insisted that the flag also display a harp without a crown, a symbol of the United Irishmen. A sore loser, Gough denounced this "standard of Discord, Anarchy and Rebellion, which in another part of the Empire has led thousands to a premature Death, and many who escaped the horrid carnage of the field expiated their Treasons in a vain attempt to sever the Crown from the Harp, by an ignominious exit at the Gallows, and their heads were affixed as public spectacles to warn the deluded."[88]

By agitating the common people, Thorpe outraged a government haunted by the American and French revolutions. Gore insisted that Thorpe had rendered "the Courts of Justice [into] the theaters for Political harangues" and encouraged "strictures on the Government from every description of persons, however incompetent they might be to form any correct opinion upon the subject." Such conduct contradicted his "peculiar duty" as an official "to inculcate subordination, and to recommend and enforce respect and submission to the Government."[89]

Gore dismissed Thorpe's supporters from their offices, including Willcocks, sacked as the Home District sheriff. An informant insisted that Willcocks had predicted that Napoleon "would carry Republicanism through the world, and till then, the world could never be happy nor at rest, and that he often suppressed his admiration of a Republican Government before any other, and that the poor Rebels in Ireland were not supported as they ought to have been, but were sacrificed." Scant chance that Willcocks said any such thing, but the statement revealed how Gore's partisans perceived their critics: as United Irish republicans who cheered for Napoleon to shatter the British empire.[90]

In July 1807 Gore suspended Thorpe as a judge. Writing to London for support, Gore claimed the highest of stakes: "it now rests with the Ministers, either to support the established Government or permit Mr. T. to erect an independent Republic." Of course the imperial lords supported Gore. Thorpe returned to England, where he lobbied for, and remarkably got, a new post as chief justice in the African colony of Sierra Leone, where he again quarreled with a governor, which led to his dismissal in 1815.[91]

After Thorpe's departure from York, leadership of the opposition passed to Willcocks. In June 1807 a government informant warned that Willcocks had visited New York City to seek moral support and financial backing from Irish-American radicals "to *revolutionize* the

Province." His new friends included Thomas Addis Emmet, the United Irishman who had become a leading lawyer and politician in New York. Ideology trumped blood, for Willcocks's Loyalist brother Richard had doomed Emmet's rebel brother Robert to the Dublin gallows in 1803.[92]

In July 1807 Willcocks returned to Newark in the Niagara District, where he began to publish the *Upper Canada Guardian, or Freeman's Journal.* Declaring himself the "only man in Canada that dare speak the truth," Willcocks championed "the middle and lesser orders of society in this infant and much injured colony." His press attacked the local oligarchies that supported Gore: "Some have sucked the breasts of government 'till they have sucked large tracts of land; some have sucked commissions and great honor." Willcocks claimed to serve the king by revealing his betrayal by corrupt and deceiving officials.[93]

To Gore's dismay, the new press helped Willcocks to win an assembly seat in late 1807. After years of battling phantoms conjured up by Ira Allen, David McLane, Ransford Rogers, and Asa Danforth, the colonial officials now faced a more substantial challenge from the most dangerous of sources: an Irish gentleman with American ties. In Willcocks the British saw the United Irish menace erupting within a weak colony precariously perched beside republican America. Worse still, his ascent coincided in 1807 with a sudden crisis that threatened Upper Canada with an American invasion.[94]

Russell Abbey, *engraving by Henry Scadding.* (Courtesy of the J. Ross Robertson Collection, Toronto Reference Library, Toronto Public Library Board, T-11480.)

H.M.S. *Leopard* attacks U.S.S. *Chesapeake* in June 1807, *sketch by F. S. Cozzens.* (Courtesy of the Naval Historical Foundation, U.S. Naval Historical Center, NH-74526.)

CHAPTER FOUR

DESERTERS

*The true American System will be Peace, eternal Peace: but this very
System will provoke England. In future Times, America at Peace, and
England at War, what will become of her? How many will fly, Sailors
especially, to the standard of the Olive Branch? Will not this excite her
Envy, her Jealousy, her Rage?*

—John Adams, 1780[1]

ON JUNE 22, 1807, while Joseph Willcocks was visiting New York, a
British warship, the frigate *Leopard*, intercepted the American frigate
Chesapeake about eight miles off the coast of Virginia. Bound for the
Mediterranean and expecting no trouble, Commodore James Barron of
the *Chesapeake* had left his cannon stowed and his deck cluttered with
cargo. But Captain Salusbury P. Humphreys of the *Leopard* had orders
from his admiral to stop the *Chesapeake* and to search for deserters from
the Royal Navy. When Barron refused, the *Leopard* unleashed a devastating broadside by twenty-six cannon at close range. The ill-prepared
Chesapeake erupted in flying, deadly splinters. A second British broadside ripped into the American ship before Barron could salvage some
pride by firing a single American cannon, without effect. After a third
British broadside, Barron hauled down the ship's flag to surrender, while
three dead and eighteen wounded Americans wallowed in their blood.[2]

Captain Humphreys took no pleasure in the killing, but he had a
duty to perform. His commander, Admiral Sir George Cranfield Berkeley, had declared that "the conduct of the Americans on the subject of
Deserters must come to a crisis between the two Countries soon." With
the American frigate dead in the water, Humphreys sent across a search
party, which returned with four sailors, deemed deserters. The British
then allowed the ravaged *Chesapeake* to return to port in Virginia for
repairs. Having obtained his crisis, Admiral Berkeley praised Captain
Humphreys for the attack.[3]

The four sailors—David Martin, Jenkin Ratford, John Strachan, and
William Ware—had all served in the Royal Navy, but only Ratford was

a "natural born" British subject. Martin, Strachan, and Ware were Americans. In the spring of 1807, all four men had enlisted to serve on the *Chesapeake* in the belief that an American warship offered greater security from a British press-gang than did an unarmed merchant ship.[4]

Ratford had been especially brazen in his confidence. A former tailor, specializing in breeches, he had been born in London. Thirty-four years old in 1807, Ratford was a short, slender man with a "dark, swarthy complexion." In early March, with four other sailors, he had stolen a boat to escape from a British warship, patrolling off the Virginia coast. Norfolk's magistrates and the *Chesapeake*'s officers had stonewalled British requests that they return the deserters. Parading about the streets of Norfolk under an American flag as part of an enlistment party, Ratford had boasted of his escape to "the land of liberty." By openly defying his superiors, Ratford had set a corrosive example that the British could ill afford to abide. A marked man, he helped to bring on the attack by the *Leopard* on the *Chesapeake*, igniting a crisis between the republic and the empire.[5]

Capture converted Ratford from a dangerous example of contagious defiance into evidence of an inexorable British power to reclaim deserters to their duty. The *Leopard* carried the four prisoners to Halifax, Nova Scotia's premier port and Berkeley's headquarters. A court-martial sentenced Martin, Ware, and Strachan to five hundred lashes each: an agonizing, near-death experience. Suspending that punishment, the British instead kept all three in prison. Ratford got worse: hanged in August from the yardarm of his former vessel, the *Halifax*, before the assembled fleet. The hanging sent a pointed message to the watching sailors: no "land of liberty" offered a safe haven for deserters from the Royal Navy.[6]

IMPRESSMENT

Britain's rulers insisted that no one born a subject could renounce that identity and its duties. Allegiance began at birth and ended only in death. No emigration, not even a legal process of naturalization, could alienate a subject. Throughout life, the "natural-born subject" remained obligated to serve the king in time of war. And the subject became a traitor if he fought against the sovereign of the kingdom of his birth.[7]

American naturalization defied the British concept of the perpetual subject. In the republic, free men chose citizenship, as the Patriots had done by rejecting British rule during the revolution. Immigrants reenacted that revolution by choosing to become American citizens, renouncing their birth allegiance as Britons. Republicans favored quick and easy naturalization, which troubled Federalists and Britons determined to limit that revolution.[8]

British naval officers insisted upon their right and duty to detain and inspect merchant ships, of any nation, to retrieve runaway subjects for impressment. The British desperately needed sailors for the hundreds of warships in the Royal Navy. A relatively small homeland surrounded by the sea, the United Kingdom developed a powerful fleet to keep enemies away and to protect the trade routes of a vast overseas empire, which funneled a lion's share of the world's colonial commerce into British ports. The profits enriched the mother country while generating customs duties to pay for the protecting fleet. Without a well-manned navy of the world's best warships, the maritime empire would collapse. Thomas Barclay, a British consul in America, explained that Britain would never relinquish her subjects because she "owes everything to her Navy & Commerce."[9]

In wartime the navy added new warships, which required more sailors. The Royal Navy grew to a mammoth and unprecedented scale during the long, hard war against the French Revolution and, later, Napoleon's empire. In 1793, when the war began, the Royal Navy had 16,600 sailors. That number soared to 119,000 by 1797, a strength sustained into the next decade. Desertion, illness, injuries, and combat deaths combined to produce a 10 percent annual attrition, which meant that the swollen navy annually needed 12,000 new sailors to replace the losses. Combined with the needs of the British merchant marine, that voracious demand exceeded the British supply by about two to one. As the war intensified and the navy grew, press-gangs expanded their reach beyond mariners to grab common landsmen, including the breeches maker Jenkin Ratford.[10]

Armed with clubs and fists, naval press-gangs scoured ships and wharves, streets and taverns, inns and even homes to grab mariners and haul them away for forcible enlistment. Their catch entered a harsh, dangerous, badly fed, and underpaid servitude that usually lasted until the sailor died or the war ended. Naturally such conscripts were surly and recalcitrant, so the officers resorted to a hard discipline enforced with the whip. As the war dragged on, naval captains increasingly denied shore leave lest the men desert.[11]

The navy's shortage of sailors increased as thousands fled to seek berths in the booming American merchant marine. British merchants faced an intense and growing competition from the shippers of neutral nations, picking up trade routes too dangerous for the belligerents.

While British warships devastated the French merchant marine, French privateers took a toll on British merchant ships and their insurers. Aggressive Americans were happy to fill the gap, becoming the largest of the carriers. To profit from the booming trade, the Americans built more ships, swelling their merchant marine from 558,000 tons in 1802 to 981,000 tons by 1811.[12]

That growth demanded more sailors than America could provide. Awash in profits, the American merchants paid premium wages to attract the sailors of other nations, and the British offered the best sea-men keen to serve under another flag. American shippers paid fifteen to eighteen dollars per month for able sailors, compared to just seven dol-lars in the British navy. In sum, the war generated a growing discrepancy between working conditions and pay in the American merchant marine, on the one hand, and in the Royal Navy, on the other. That discrepancy pushed sailors away from Britain and pulled them to America.[13]

The British claimed that at least 20,000 subjects had fled to crew American merchant ships. In 1807 Albert Gallatin, the U.S. secretary of the treasury, put the number of British sailors in American merchant ships at 9,000, at least a fifth of the total employed. He concluded that, as the merchant marine grew, over half of the new sailors were British by birth. Their loss, he conceded, would cripple the expanded American shipping.[14]

The concentration of British-born sailors was especially great in the American navy, where they expected greater security from British press-gangs. In 1811 the American naval captain John Rodgers noted:

> We never hear of English sailors deserting into the service of any other country than our own. Indeed, from our speaking the same lan-guage & possessing nearly the same habits, they are led to believe there is no actual crime attach'd to their exchange of slavery for free-dom; & every opportunity afforded them of effecting such a change proves this fact.

In early 1808, Captain Isaac Chauncey investigated the naval seamen based in New York City and reported that only 42 percent were Ameri-cans by birth. The rest were naturalized citizens (9 percent) or recent emigrants (49 percent). The great majority of the foreign sailors came from Britain (134 of 150) and especially from Ireland (80 of the 150). Despite the Irish majority, historians persist in the misnomer of calling the contested sailors "English."[15]

Crisis loomed as the empire and the republic competed for a limited pool of sailors in a world at war. The British insisted that they impressed only their own subjects from American merchant ships. But British captains defined American citizens narrowly and British subjects broadly. Often a naval captain simply took the best sailors who spoke English. One captain frankly explained, "It is my duty to keep my ship manned, & I will do so wherever I find men that speak the same language with me." Such captains claimed hundreds born in the republic as well as thousands born within the empire.[16]

While clinging to every "natural-born subject," the British agreed to relinquish any American-born sailors, but placed the burden of proof on the sailors and American authorities. Impressed men languished aboard British warships for years as American consuls and British officials wrangled over standards of proof. In no case would the British surrender anyone born within the empire but naturalized by the Americans, who formed the lion's share of the impressed sailors taken from American ships.[17]

Some of the British-born sailors claimed American citizenship by virtue of a formal naturalization. But most emigrant sailors did not bother with the legal formalities and their cost. Instead, they simply got tattoos of American patriotic symbols, especially the flag or the eagle.[18]

American magistrates, at home, and consuls, abroad, provided sailors with "protection certificates," which attested to birth within the United States. But British captains and judges dismissed the certificates as frauds bought and sold by conniving sailors. In 1807 Thomas Barclay insisted, "for every real American Citizen impressed on board His Majesty's Ships of War, there are at least fifty of His Majesty's Subjects in the Service, civil and naval, of their states, furnished with certificates of American Citizenship." The British felt contempt for the loose authority of the decentralized republic, derided as the glorified anarchy of cheats.[19]

An irritant before 1803, the impressment of Americans soared thereafter, as the British resumed their desperate war with Napoleon. During the next eight years, the British probably impressed ten thousand men who claimed American citizenship, some by birth but most by naturalization either formal or informal. Some won their release by 1807, but about six thousand remained in British service, according to American figures. Five years later, Lord Castlereagh officially reported to Parliament that the Royal Navy held 3,300 seamen who claimed American citizenship. The American navy's Captain Stephen Decatur informed a superior, "It is a well known fact, Sir, that a vast majority of our Seamen have, at some period of their lives, been impressed into the British service."[20]

One of those harried sailors was Ned Myers, born a British subject in Nova Scotia, but a runaway to America as a boy. In early 1806 in New York City, he joined the crew of the merchant ship *Sterling*, where he befriended a young American sailor, the future novelist James Fenimore Cooper, who later helped Myers write his story. On the *Sterling*, Myers found "the mixed character of the crews of American vessels during the height of her neutral trade." Only the captain, the first mate, and four sailors (including Cooper) were Americans by birth. The remaining seven seamen included a Dane, a Portuguese, a Prussian, a Spaniard, a Scot, an Englishman, and a Canadian (Myers).[21]

In return for high wages, these sailors ran the gauntlet through British warships on a voyage to the very heart of the empire: England. Their luck ran out upon approaching the port of Cowes on the Isle of Wight, where a Royal Navy lieutenant led a boarding party forcibly to muster the crew of the *Sterling*. The lieutenant seized the best sailor, although he was American by birth. Deriding his protection certificate, the lieutenant declared, "You are an Englishman, and the King has need of your services." Myers watched his friend depart "with tears in his eyes, and to the regret of all on board." Myers concluded, "Such was often the fate of sailors, in that day, who were with you one day and lost forever the next."[22]

In April 1807, on a return voyage, another press-gang swarmed aboard and compelled the crew to muster. The British officer recognized as English a fifty-year-old sailor, who had immigrated to America twenty years before. Myers recalled, "The poor fellow took an affectionate leave of his shipmates. He told those around him that his fate was sealed. He was too old to outlive a war that appeared to have no end, and [the British officers] would never trust *him* on shore." Taking Cooper by the hand, the old salt lamented, "My foot will never touch the land again and I am to live and die, with a ship for my prison." In 1809 at Limerick, an Irish port, a press-gang nabbed Myers, but "a party of Irishman" appeared, "showed fight and frightened the fellows so much that I got clear." He benefited from the animus of common Irishmen to British press-gangs.[23]

FINE LADS

The empire also lost men along its Canadian border with the alluring republic. A Canadian military historian concludes, "Nowhere else in the empire did so many men flee the colours so easily." Desertion depleted a small force already spread thin: three thousand men scattered over two thousand miles, from Quebec to the western end of Lake Huron. In 1804 John Richardson sighed, "We have so few Troops that we can ill spare any by Desertion."[24]

Both British push and American pull promoted desertion. The deserters fled *from* the tedium, low pay, bad food, and harsh discipline of the British army, while they ran *to* the abundant meat, cheap liquor, and better wages of the United States, where a common laborer earned four times the pay of a British private. Even the best of soldiers could succumb to the temptation of the American border. In October 1803, when "three fine lads" deserted, Colonel Isaac Brock complained, "It's really difficult to determine upon whom to place confidence." Eight months later, five more men fled, and Brock erupted, "I am the more vexed as I did not think I had five better characters in the Regiment." All five were Irish recruits.[25]

Early and often, British officers lamented that a young Irishman was the most likely soldier to desert. Less committed than the Scots and the English to the empire, the Irish most felt the pull of the nearby republic. In 1804 General Peter Hunter complained that desertion in Canada soared after the home government sent over three regiments "composed generally of Irishmen": the Fifth, Forty-first, and Forty-ninth Infantry Regiments. Three years later at Quebec, Colonel Brock expected trouble from the newly arrived Hundredth Regiment because the men, "being nearly all Irish, are, of all others, the most volatile and easily led astray." He kept them within fortress Quebec, away from the temptation of the American border.[26]

Impoverished Ireland had become a prime recruiting ground for the British army. Officers suspected that many Irish recruits joined regiments bound for Canada, intending to desert once they got close to America. By engaging in "emigration enlistment," poor men got the army to pay for their passage across the Atlantic. General Hunter's military secretary begged one recruiter to cease enlisting "Irishmen, as from long experience it has been found that they not only desert themselves frequently, but take others with them." But the shorthanded army could not do without Irish recruits.[27]

Upper Canada offered the easiest access across the American border. In 1800 Hunter predicted "that when the 6th and 41st Regiments are sent to the Frontier Posts, they will lose considerably by Desertion, from being composed of so great a proportion of Irish." Discipline lagged at distant posts with small garrisons and few officers. And at frontier forts, the officers employed the soldiers in small work parties moving equipment and provisions in boats and carts. The men were poorly supervised, and their chores familiarized them with the roads, rivers, boats, and locals—knowledge that facilitated escapes. Nearby, American civilians enticed and assisted the deserters both to spite the British and to recruit wage laborers, who were preciously scarce on the frontier.[28]

The British took tough measures against desertion. In Upper Canada, Hunter secured a law providing six months in prison and either a public whipping or a forty-pound fine for any civilian convicted of enticing or concealing a deserter. British officers also brutally punished recaptured runaways by sentencing them to five hundred or six hundred lashes: an excruciating torment that reduced backs to a bloody mess. The officers assembled the men in ranks and at attention to watch the grim business. If caught, repeat offenders faced exile for life to the harsh penal colony at Botany Bay (in Australia) or death by firing squad. In 1803 the British discovered a massive plot to mutiny and desert by the Irish soldiers of the Forty-ninth Regiment at Fort George on the Niagara River. A court-martial sent eleven to the penal colony and ordered seven shot before the garrison at Quebec.[29]

To discourage desertion, and to capture those who tried, the British employed Indians as trackers, with a license to kill runaways who resisted. One soldier explained that his peers dreaded "being taken up by the savages, who were as thick in the woods as musquitoes." In 1803 Hunter's military secretary directed an officer to reward warriors for catching deserters "in such a manner as to impress upon the mind of the Indians that they are always well rewarded for any service rendered by them to the King—and upon the Soldiers, that the Indians are ever faithful to the Officers." The empire relied on Indians to intimidate the Irish soldiers who defended British Canada.[30]

In October 1800 Francis Pacquette, a French Canadian, escaped from his service in the Royal Canadian Volunteers by crossing the Detroit River. Sergeant Levi P. Cole led a British patrol across the border to catch Pacquette at his new home with an obliging widow. When the soldiers broke down the door, Pacquette struck Cole with an ax, inflicting a glancing blow to his head. Subdued and hauled to the riverbank, Pacquette tried to escape but suffered bayonet thrusts to his stomach. Hauled across to the British shore in a canoe, he died a few hours later. In early 1801 the American government demanded Cole's extradition for murder. Although deserters could not be extradited by the two countries, murderers could per the Jay Treaty of 1794. Tipped off to impending arrest, Cole ran away. The deserter hunter turned deserter. Dodging three British search parties, he vanished.[31]

An advertisement offering a reward for his apprehension revealed that Cole had been born and raised in Rhode Island. A British soldier by trade, Cole was an American by birth, and he had killed a French Canadian deemed a British deserter. Such shifting migrations and allegiances clouded the line between the empire and the republic.[32]

Some discontented American soldiers deserted across the border to seek haven and employment in Upper Canada, where leading locals welcomed them as a precious source of wage labor. Along the border, the dual flow of deserters led British and American officers to make covert, local agreements to help each other recover runaways.[33]

In December 1805 two British officers crossed the Detroit River in pursuit of David Morrison, an Irish deserter. With help from two American army officers, the Britons broke into a Detroit house to nab Morrison. His protecting hosts alarmed the town by firing two pistols in the air and bellowing, "Murder! Fire! Indians!" Dozens of men "rushed from their houses, armed with swords, guns, and shovels." They crowded around Morrison and the officers in the street. The jostling became a brawl as both sides threw fists and discharged pistols, wounding one British officer in the leg. The mob triumphed, spiriting Morrison away to the tavern of Richard Smyth, a radical republican born in Ireland. One impetuous American army officer threatened to fire cannon on the mob "and blow them all to Hell." But the people called his bluff, and the town's magistrates arrested the British and American officers to stand trial for provoking a riot. In September 1806 a jury convicted, and a judge fined, two British and two American officers.[34]

In May 1809 on the St. Lawrence River, the American captain William P. Bennett sent a sergeant and two privates, bearing arms, across the border to seek Isaac Underhill, a deserter who had become a schoolteacher at Elizabeth Town (now Brockville). Breaking into his school, the soldiers hauled out the struggling teacher while the children screamed. Underhill broke free and began to run, but the soldiers shot him and left him to die beside the road, while they rejoined Bennett on a schooner in the river and sailed away.[35]

In 1801 the American government had pressed for the extradition of the British soldier Cole to face a murder trial at Detroit. Eight years later that government rebuffed the British demand for Bennett to stand trial for murder in Upper Canada. Instead, the Americans offered an apology and a cash payment. Dodging a criminal trial in Canada for murder, Bennett instead faced a court-martial by his own peers for the lesser charge of "conduct unbecoming an officer and a gentleman." Bennett got merely a private reprimand: a slap on the wrist that rankled

Britons, who charged the Americans with hypocrisy for screaming bloody murder over seamen seized by British naval officers. Thereafter, military cooperation dissolved along the border, to the dismay of officers and the delight of deserters, both British and American.[36]

WAR IN DISGUISE

Britons also blasted Americans for exploiting their neutral flag to steal commerce from the empire, which so desperately needed the revenue to fund the Royal Navy. In 1805 a British lawyer, James Stephen, published *War in Disguise; or, the Frauds of the Neutral Flags*, which denounced American shipping for aiding Napoleon by weakening the British empire. Another writer, Joseph Marryat, published the aptly titled *Concessions to America, the Bane of Britain*. A popular sensation, these pamphlets led the British to take a harder line on American ships and sailors.[37]

Embroiled in a massive war for the survival of their empire, the British demanded greater understanding and restraint from the Americans. The British diplomat Augustus J. Foster noted, "The two greatest Commercial Nations in the Globe cannot move in the same Spheres without jostling one another a little; where we were aiming blows at the French Marine, we want Elbow room, and these good Neutrals won't give it to us & therefore they get a few side Pushes, which makes them grumble."[38]

Where Americans saw Britain as an imperial bully, the British saw themselves as defending the world's freedom against Napoleon's brutal despotism. In 1806 a Montreal merchant worried that Napoleon was "the Devil Come to Torment the inhabitants of the Earth, and when his reign will end no one knows. I am afraid not until he gets into England, and we are going to have a war with America." Britons charged Americans with vile ingratitude, for the Royal Navy kept the French despot far from North America. Referring to the United States, Thomas Barclay claimed, "we are contending for her Independence and our own." The British argued that at the very least the Americans should repatriate British sailors and tolerate the occasional mistaken impressment of the American-born.[39]

But American diplomats insisted that every merchant ship was an extension of their nation's sovereign territory. The Jefferson administration would concede only the wartime right of a belligerent to stop and search ships for munitions bound to an enemy's port. James Madison, the secretary of state, protested when the British extended those searches to reclaim supposed British subjects. In 1804 the British foreign secretary scoffed, "The Pretension advanced by Mr. Madison that the American Flag should protect every Individual sailing under it on board of a Merchant Ship is too extravagant to require any serious Refutation." The British insisted that, as the world's dominant naval power, they set and enforced international law on the high seas.[40]

Given the weakness of the American navy, Britons marveled at the high and moralistic pretensions of Jeffersonian diplomacy. Deemed a waste of money, the U.S. Navy had been reduced to only two substantial warships—frigates—and about sixty-eight smaller vessels, primarily gunboats, of little or no use against the massive Royal Navy. Given that naval weakness, the Americans could only seethe as British warships hovered off the major seaports to board and inspect every passing ship for suspected subjects. This virtual blockade was tightest around New York City, the nation's leading port and home to thousands of immigrants. A British diplomat conceded that it was "highly grating to the Feelings of an independent Nation to perceive that their whole Coast is watched as closely as if it was blockaded, and every Ship coming in or going out of their Harbours examined rigorously in Sight of the Shore by British Squadrons stationed within their Waters."[41]

To sustain their coastal patrols, the British warships needed provisions and water bought from the American seaports. But when British warships sent boats into those ports to make the purchases, many sailors ran away. If the British naval officers tried to retrieve their seamen, mobs of American sailors and laborers intervened. And local magistrates did little or nothing, for they either applauded the desertions or feared the mobs. Such incidents confirmed the British prejudice against the republic as anarchic. In December 1806 the new prime minister, Lord Grenville, dismissed the United States as "a *Mob Government* and one too weak to carry its own measures into effect."[42]

When British officers and diplomats protested, Madison pointedly replied that, for want of a maritime treaty, the American government could not intervene. He invited the British to forsake impressment at sea in return for an American promise to return recent deserters from the Royal Navy. In effect, American officials winked at the mobs and the desertions as means to pressure the British. That tacit collusion enraged the British as the consummate mix of republican weakness and perfidy.

Rather than accept their losses to desertion, British naval officers recouped them by impressing more sailors from the ships leaving or entering the offending ports, especially New York and Norfolk. In a vicious cycle, Americans enticed deserters while Britons impressed more Americans, fueling a mutual and deepening animus. In June 1807 that cycle culminated in the attack by the *Leopard* on the *Chesapeake*.[43]

The attack initially outraged Federalists as well as Republicans, who convened protest meetings to adopt angry resolutions demanding preparations for war. Meanwhile mobs raged in the seaport streets. At New York, rioters crippled a small British supply boat, smashed the windows at Barclay's house, and threatened to hurl the carriage of another British diplomat, Augustus Foster, into the Hudson River. "The ringleader on this occasion was, as might be expected, an Irish emigrant," Foster noted.[44]

Mob violence, public resolutions, and newspaper fulminations struck the British as the unholy trinity of American republicanism. From the security of his warship, Admiral Berkeley responded with perfect contempt: "The wretched Outcasts & Vagabonds who have been collected by the Glittering Tinsel of American Freedom may wish for a War in which they have nothing to lose but every thing to gain." Berkeley proposed throwing more fuel on the fire by offering "to run up to New York with the squadron before the harbour is secured and wait there for the issue of negotiations, as having the city under the terror of destruction would insure a favourable issue."[45]

The republic was ill prepared for war because Jefferson's administration and the Republican Congress had cut the military to reduce taxes and the national debt. In addition to curtailing the navy, the Republicans had reduced the army to a mere 3,287 men, a paltry force for patrolling a frontier of ten thousand miles and a coastline at least twice that long. And given poor recruiting and the inroads of disease and desertion, the real force was only about two-thirds of the authorized strength.[46]

But the crisis obliged Jefferson to do *something*, so he ordered the gunboats repaired to defend the seaports, and he directed the state governors to prepare 100,000 militia for federal service. A reserve of militia amateurs cost far less than a real army of professional soldiers. By threatening Canada with militia, Jefferson hoped to pressure the British, but his secretary of the treasury, Albert Gallatin, explained that the invasion force would come only from the northern states because "none can be spared from the negro country." The southern states needed their militiamen to guard against a slave revolt. In Jeffersonian plans, the war would liberate Canada while defending slavery in the American South.[47]

During the summer of 1807 some runaway slaves rowed out to the

British warships off Norfolk. The fugitives volunteered to serve in the Royal Navy in return for their freedom. While Irish sailors escaped from the British warships, regarded as floating prisons, American slaves fled to those vessels as portals to freedom. A "land of liberty" for white men, the American republic sustained slavery for African-Americans.[48]

DISTRUST

Anticipating an American invasion of Canada, British officials felt exposed for want of troops. With most of their army pinned down in Europe, only 400 regulars garrisoned Upper Canada and another 2,500 defended Lower Canada, primarily at Quebec. And the quality was poor—"old and worn-out men," in the words of Francis Gore. Desertion contributed to both the small numbers and the poor quality, for the British had decided to post older, less mobile men in Upper Canada because they were less likely to escape into America.[49]

In theory, the provincial militia would supplement the regulars, but Upper Canada's militiamen were few, untrained, badly led, and barely armed. Thinly populated, the colony had only about 12,000 military-age men dispersed over a frontier of one thousand miles. And most of the militiamen were American newcomers of dubious reliability in a war with the United States. In 1807 the Loyalist Thomas Welch estimated that nine-tenths of the people in the London District were "internal Enemies under the cloak of Subjects." Welch warned, "those people do keep the 4th of July annually in the same manner (firing excepted) as we subjects do the 4th of June" (the king's birthday). Far from defending the province, such men might help the invaders.[50]

Given the small regular force and the unreliable militia, British commanders doubted that they could defend Upper Canada against an American invasion. In that event, the governor-general, James Henry Craig, planned to withdraw his regulars into the fortress at Quebec. A great stronghold of stone walls bristling with cannon, Quebec could resist an American siege long enough for the mother country to send ships with reinforcements to repel the invaders. In Upper Canada, Gore privately endorsed Craig's plan but warned that "it must be carefully concealed from persons of almost every description in this colony, for there are few People here that would act with Energy, were it not for the purpose of defending the Lands which they actually possess."[51]

Gore also dreaded internal subversion by Joseph Willcocks, who had formed a "connexion . . . with United Irishmen at New York." Willcocks did welcome the *Chesapeake* crisis as an opportunity to pressure

Upper Canada's officials. On July 24, 1807, he wrote, "We are all thunderstruck here, particularly the great folks. They are between a S[hit] and a Sweat, and the Devil relieve them (I say)." Willcocks hoped that the republic would take a strong stand against the empire: "The honest part of us say that if the States pocket the Indignity now offered them that they can no longer stile themselves a Nation." With the help of New York's corrupt postmaster, Gore intercepted the letter and sent a copy to the imperial lords to document the province's internal danger.[52]

With populist rhetoric and a defiant flair, Willcocks gained popularity by weathering government harassment. In February 1808 Gore's supporters in the assembly tried Willcocks for insulting the dignity of the house by accusing them of taking bribes in land from the government. Convicted, he spent five weeks in the York jail, but he won reelection to the assembly, and his newspaper gained new readers. In 1809, on a circuit through the Niagara and London Districts, Judge William Dummer Powell found the *Upper Canada Guardian* "in almost every house," and Gore lamented that the paper was "relished too much by the good people of Upper Canada."[53]

By helping opposition candidates in other districts, Willcocks reduced the government's majority in the assembly. After the 1808 election, the new parliament lacked Crown officers and had more religious dissenters than known Anglicans, both firsts. Common millers and farmers with no more than a grammar school education outnumbered gentlemen. Most of the representatives still came from old Loyalist families, but an unprecedented number—four of twenty-nine—were Late Loyalists. The trend shocked the government's supporters, including John Strachan, who rued the election of so many "ignorant clowns, for the spirit of leveling seemed to pervade the province."[54]

British officials also dreaded the suspicious presence in America of Jean Victor Moreau, one of Napoleon's victorious generals. The British dismissed, as a cover story, his political exile to America by a vindictive Napoleon. Surely, General Moreau really came to lead an American army of invasion with the help of French troops to be sent by Napoleon. Halifax's garrison commander, General John Skerrett, reported that Moreau was working with "Thomas Addis Emmett and William James McNeven, two dangerous United Irishmen (who gave me much trouble during the Rebellion)." Of late, they had "been very active and industrious in provoking the people in the United States to wage war with England and said that they would arm a force of sixty thousand United Irishmen to aid them in this undertaking." In British minds, the *Chesa-*

peake crisis perfected the three-headed revolutionary monster of American Republicans, French Jacobins, and United Irishmen.[55]

Refining Skerrett's fantasy, Admiral Berkeley warned Gore, "from every information I have received, it is a secret article agreed by the American Government, if the events of War should put them in possession of the English Colonies in America, to transfer them to France or erect them, in a separate Kingdom to be Governed by a Frenchman." Berkeley deployed this fantasy as propaganda to stimulate Anglophones in Canada to resist the American invasion. His report took on a life of its own, echoing through letters and newspapers until it seemed plausible even to many Americans. In March 1808 Senator John Quincy Adams reported widespread gossip, originating in Nova Scotia, of a French plot "to conquer the British Provinces on this continent and form a monarchy of them under General Moreau and at the same time to introduce a more monarchical government in these States, all [of] which was to be effected by means of a war between this country and Great Britain." In an age of revolutions and counterrevolutions, many subscribed to the wild scenarios of powerful conspiracies and geopolitical rearrangement.[56]

EMBARGO

While the British alarm grew in Canada, Jefferson was deflating the crisis within America. He dreaded that a war with the empire would oblige the republic to create a large and expensive army and navy, which would undercut his primary goals: to reduce taxes and the national debt. Averse to war, the president hoped that his nation's blustering meetings and newspapers would scare the British imperial lords into giving him an easy diplomatic victory. As a start, Jefferson and Madison sought cash reparations to the families of the dead and wounded sailors, the return of the men impressed from the *Chesapeake*, and the removal of Admiral Berkeley. But they also wanted much more: a sweeping British commitment to stop impressing sailors from any American vessel, merchant as well as naval.[57]

But British consuls and spies reported how little leverage the president really had. Lacking soldiers, fortifications, and cannon, the seaports were vulnerable to attack by British warships. Tied up for repairs, none of the American frigates were fit for sea. Unable to defend themselves, the Americans were hardly prepared to invade Canada. Phineas Bond concluded, "The Consequences of a Rupture would be serious to us, but ruinous to the United States. . . . Their Commerce, now so extensive and lucrative, would be annihilated, and with these her Revenue would fail, for they are the Sources from which her Coffers are filled."[58]

Britain's rulers wanted to avoid a war in America as a dangerous distraction from the pressing struggle against Napoleon. They sought to limit the controversy with the republic by agreeing to pay reparations, to return the surviving sailors taken from the *Chesapeake*, and to renounce searching neutral *warships*. In late August, the government also recalled Admiral Berkeley and Captain Humphreys to England.[59]

But the British would never relinquish their power to stop and search neutral merchant ships to regulate trade and seize runaway subjects. In October 1807 a royal proclamation reiterated a perpetual claim to all natural-born subjects found in merchant ships on the high seas. A month later, the British adopted "Orders in Council" which tightened their naval blockade on Napoleon's Europe by requiring all neutral ships bound there to visit Britain, pay duties, and take a license before proceeding to the continent. In response, Napoleon decreed that his regime would seize any ship that visited Britain. American ships had to pick their poison: to risk British seizure by sailing directly to French-dominated Europe or follow British regulations at the risk of French confiscation.[60]

Despite the British hard line on core policy, the war fever cooled in the United States. In late 1807 Congress adopted only modest military preparations: $1 million to upgrade seaport fortifications and a boost in the army to ten thousand men, still too little to defend a nation of seven million people. Rather than build more frigates, which were big and costly, Congress authorized more small, cheap, and virtually useless gunboats. Most Republicans balked at building a stronger fleet, for fear that it could never compete with the British and would only invite a preemptive strike, like that recently inflicted by the Royal Navy on neutral Denmark.[61]

But the Republicans had to do something to protect American shipping from predation. Diplomacy had failed to budge either the British or the French, who shared only a contempt for the American republic as weak and whiney. War seemed too expensive, given the Republican phobia for taxes, but Madison and Jefferson believed that they had an economic leverage to pressure the British. Factory workers in Britain and slaves in the West Indies would starve, Jefferson reasoned, if the Americans stopped exporting their wheat, flour, fish, pork, and cattle. In December 1807 he proposed an embargo on all maritime commerce by American ships. While protecting idled American merchant ships from French and British seizure, the embargo would also pressure the belligerents to accept the American position on neutral shipping and sailors.[62]

Relieved to avoid declaring war, the Republicans in Congress passed the Embargo Act on December 22. John Quincy Adams reluctantly supported the embargo as better than nothing, but he doubted that it would sway the belligerents: "Nations which sacrifice men by the hundred thousands and treasure by the hundred millions in War, for *nothing*, or worse than nothing, pay little attention to their real interests." In vain, the Federalists protested a measure that they saw as self-destructive and for a bad cause: to retain British subjects on American ships.[63]

In fact Jefferson had overestimated the British dependence on American commerce. In Latin America, the British found alternative sources of food and a new market for their exports. Meanwhile, British merchants could hardly believe their good fortune: the foolish Americans had withdrawn from the world's oceans, leaving maritime commerce to British ships. In the consummate irony, the American navy discharged its British-born sailors to provide work for unemployed Americans. Many of the discharged had to return to the empire for paying work, to the further delight of British imperialists.[64]

Jefferson also underestimated the American reliance on overseas trade. As the embargo dragged on through 1808, the seaport economy withered, idling thousands of sailors, laborers, and artisans. Seaport employers cut wages in half, while the price of imported consumer goods soared. Unable to export their produce, farmers glutted the domestic market with grain. In New York, the price of wheat fell from two dollars per bushel before the embargo to seventy-five cents a year later.[65]

Along the border, the embargo encouraged smugglers to push American produce into Canada in exchange for British manufactures. They drove over herds of cattle or rowed across rafts and boats laden with potash, wheat, and flour. To suppress the smuggling, Jefferson summoned governors to mobilize militia to patrol the border, but the smugglers took up arms to defy the militia. In one skirmish on Lake Champlain, smugglers killed three militiamen. At Oswego, on Lake Ontario, the smugglers beat and nearly strangled an American army officer. "I had rather encounter war itself than to display our impotence to enforce our laws," Albert Gallatin confessed. Respect for federal authority had ebbed along the border.[66]

The unpopular embargo also revived the Federalist party in the

Northeast, which relied on maritime commerce. Federalists insisted that Jefferson's supposed cure was far worse than the British disease of meddling with ships and sailors. Because the transatlantic trade had been so profitable, the Federalist merchants had become resigned to writing off the loss of some vessels and men to British seizure. But the merchants reaped only losses when Jefferson locked up their vessels. Federalists charged that Jefferson's southern-dominated party had designed the embargo to impoverish New England. Suspicious that Jefferson covertly favored Napoleon, the Federalists celebrated Britain as the world's champion of true liberty against French despotism and Republican hypocrisy. Impressed by the Federalist gains in the New England state elections of 1808, the British balked at making diplomatic concessions to Jefferson's faltering administration.[67]

In New York and Pennsylvania, the Republicans preserved an electoral edge by inflaming bloody memories of the revolution. As the Federalists more openly defended British policy, the Republicans more easily cast them as Loyalists bent on subverting the republic and substituting the mixed constitution of Britain. In New York, a Republican campaign broadside exhorted: "Every Shot's a Vote, and every Vote Kills a Tory! Do your Duty, Republicans, Let your exertions this day Put down the Kings and Tyrants of Britain." This rhetoric played especially well among the Irish immigrants, who despised Federalists associated with the hated Britons.[68]

The Federalist revival fell short in the presidential election of 1808, when Madison won the right to succeed Jefferson as president. The Federalists carried New England (save Vermont), but the southern and western states remained solidly Republican. Once again, the presidential election swung on the populous mid-Atlantic states of New York and Pennsylvania. Both went for Madison, thanks, in large part, to immigrant editors and voters in Philadelphia and New York City. Strategically clustered in the leading cities of the two pivotal states, the immigrant voters possessed an influence disproportionate to their national numbers. Runaway subjects had become especially influential citizens.[69]

By early 1809, however, most northern Republicans had soured on a policy that had weakened them by reviving the Federalists. To hold the party together, the Republicans in Congress terminated the embargo on March 4, 1809, Jefferson's last day in office.[70]

The ill-conceived embargo had weakened the United States. Because duties on foreign trade primarily funded the federal government, the embargo depleted the treasury. And the embargo trained people along the border to defy their own government, which augured poorly for their support in case of war. Once considered easy, an American invasion of Canada became a far trickier proposition in the wake of the embargo. But invasion became the prime American policy option after the embargo had inevitably failed.[71]

While weakening the United States, the embargo boosted the Canadian economy. Diverted from American seaports, farm produce poured into Canada, for export to England and the West Indies. By eliminating most American competition, the embargo also gave Canadians a larger share of the West Indian market for grain, fish, livestock, and lumber. And Canadian lumber and potash exports soared to supply the mother country. At a dinner in Upper Canada, British officers and magistrates offered a toast to "Thomas Jefferson & his Embargo." They explained to a British traveler that the embargo had "done more for Canada than fifty ordinary years would have effected." The traveler concluded, "It has taught Great Britain the value of these provinces, which I sincerely hope will prove a brighter gem in her crown than ever the States were." Meant to coerce the British, the embargo instead increased their resolve to defend Canada as precious to the empire.[72]

PRINCIPLES

Rejecting the Federalist vision of a strong national government, Republicans gloried in the novelty of their diffuse example to the world. In 1812 in Pennsylvania, a Republican meeting celebrated the United States as a loose union of sovereign states "without foreign or domestic wars, without taxation, without any more of the pressure of government than was absolutely necessary to keep the bands of society together." Congressman John A. Harper of New Hampshire concluded, "We are a Republic; ours is a Government of opinion, not of force." He contrasted his republic with Britain, "where more power is concentrated in less compass than ever happened to any other nation on earth, with all her system of vigor and terror, with all her fleets, her custom-house and excise officers." In 1811 the United States government spent only one dollar per capita, a mere twenty-fifth of the public expenditures in Great Britain.[73]

Republicans insisted that less was more, that a minimal and cheap government inspired a commercial prosperity and a passionate popularity that no monarchy could match. Jefferson paradoxically claimed that the United States had the "strongest Government on earth," because its institutional weakness secured popular support. As a militia, the common people would rush to defend a government that demanded so little of them.[74]

By British standards, the United States was a flimsy union of discordant states, a virtual nullity. A British spy, John Henry, dismissed the republic as "that crazy coalition of heterogenous interests, opinions and prejudices." Referring to the number of states and their weak union, Henry concluded, "Seventeen staves and *no hoop* will not make a barrell that can last long." The restive and diverse Americans lived in a fantasy republic that pandered to their illusions that they need not pay for their government. As a result, the United States lacked the military means and coercive "energy" to compel obedience within or to inspire respect abroad.[75]

Britons charged that Americans compounded the weakness of their government by the immorality of their souls. In the pervasive commercialism of American life, Britons saw a cunning greed that sacrificed integrity for rampant speculation in land and banks. Augustus Foster concluded that "from the Province of Maine to the borders of Florida, you would not find 30 men of Truth, Honour, or Integrity. Corruption, Immorality, Irreligion, and above all, self-interest, have corroded the very pillars on which their Liberty rests." Britons charged that the republic promoted legal chicanery and corrupt juries, which rewarded cunning cheats, undermining the legitimate property of respectable men.[76]

Britons also saw that corruption in sordid elections that pivoted on slander, bellowing, bullying, and dirty tricks. Robert Nichol reported, "The Heats & divisions in the United States have got to an alarming height & will, it is thought, plunge that ill-fated Country into all the Horrors of Revolutionary Anarchy." John Howe, a British spy, insisted that bad elections drove good men—by which he meant the Federalists—from politics because they balked at "the servile means necessary to obtain power." Instead, voters elected vulgar demagogues, who prevailed even in Congress, where the British diplomat George H. Rose found

one Sailor [and] one Weaver (Mr. Smilie, and Mr. Finley, both Irishmen and leading orators in the Government Party), six or seven Tavern Keepers, four notorious Swindlers, one Butcher, . . . one Glazier, one Curer of Hams, several School Masters, and several Baptist Preachers. It is impossible to calculate how Short-lived such a system must be. But the excess of the democratic ferment in the people is conspicuously evidenced by the dregs having got up to the top.

A legislature of former tradesmen struck a British gentleman as the consummate republican folly.[77]

British officials also dreaded the influence of Irish immigrants on the republic: "a perpetual source of disease to the body politic," according to John Howe. "The enmity of these Foreigners to Great Britain is kept alive at Philadelphia by Duane, an Irishman, Printer of the *Aurora*, who possesses abilities, and is supposed to be in French pay." Augustus Foster counted ten Irishmen among the Republicans in Congress: "a motley set of imported grumblers from Dublin." Foster concluded, "Irishmen, who live by agitation . . . have an immense influence over all the wild, unruly young adventurers of the western woods especially the Democrats of the slave districts, who are of rather a rakish turn."[78]

The British regarded the southern Republicans as doubly damned for owning black men while preaching the equality of white men. To Britons it seemed odd that race mattered so much, and class so little, in the distribution of political rights in America. In sum, British officials disliked the republic as weak, chaotic, corrupt, rancorous, vulgar, and demagogic. In addition to the republican form of government, they blamed three American social conditions: a violent frontier, the Irish influx, and the exploitation of slaves. John Strachan concluded, "Liberty in such a country becomes worse than an empty name, a mask for oppression."[79]

The American Revolution had generated an ideological rift between the republic and the empire. Republicans defended liberty for white men by restraining national power, while Britons nurtured imperial power by constraining liberty particularly for sailors. To preserve power, the British violently retrieved runaway subjects who claimed to have become American citizens. Jefferson and Madison tried to protect those putative citizens without building a military power deemed hostile to liberty. But the resulting embargo threatened to unravel the union, vindicating British contempt.

At the same time, the *Chesapeake* crisis also revealed the limits of the revolution's legacy. While generating an ideological division, the revolution failed to erase the commercial, cultural, and demographic overlap of the American and British peoples, which derived from their long heritage within a shared empire. They spoke the same language and traded more with one another than with other nations. Far from diminishing, the human overlap grew during the first decade of the nineteenth century. While Britain's Irish subjects poured into American seaports, American farmers immigrated into British Canada. The exchange of people and goods generated both mutual dependence and the frictions of competition. Foster concluded "the similarity of habits, language, and manners, between the inhabitants of the two Countries is productive . . . of complaint and regret." Conflict emerged from that overlap of people.[80]

Citizenship reflected the egalitarian logic of a revolutionary republic, while the concept of the subject reflected an empire predicated on inherited inequality. Republican citizenship was volitional, a matter of choice, unlike the birth status of the subject. At the personal level, an immigrant to America reenacted the revolution by choosing citizenship and rejecting his subject status. Consequently, when impressed by the British he suffered from an act of counterrevolution. By enforcing their maritime power, Britons threatened to reduce American commerce to a quasi-colonial status. The Republicans defended the revolution by asserting the right to create citizens by naturalization and by upholding American sovereignty on the high seas.[81]

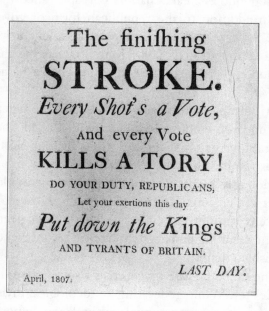

The Finishing Stroke, *New York Republican broadside, 1807. Republicans equated elections with a continuing revolution against the king and his Loyalists.* (Courtesy of the New-York Historical Society.)

The threat of war obliged the British to try to defend Upper Canada with a militia composed primarily of newcomers from America. By giving Late Loyalists the oath of allegiance, granting them land, and enlisting them in the militia, the British adopted a fluid concept of national status that contradicted their rigid insistence on the perpetuity of the "natural-born subject." That insistence had generated the *Chesapeake* crisis, which then obliged the British to contradict it by defending Canada with Americans-by-birth. If it was treason for natural-born subjects to fight against the empire, how could the regime expect natural-born citizens to fight against American invaders?

According to the British, their empire could make subjects of American immigrants, but Americans could not make citizens of emigrants from Britain. That inequality of power implied that Americans remained colonists whenever they passed beyond the republic's terrestrial boundaries. That implication enraged Republicans as undermining the value of their revolution, reducing the republic to an adjunct of the empire. To defy that implication, they would declare war.

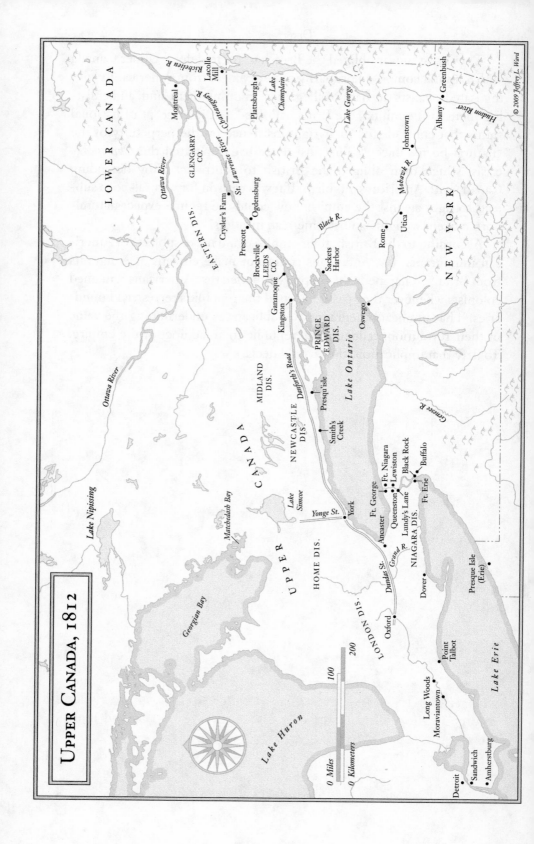

Upper Canada, 1812

© 2009 Jeffrey L. Ward

CHAPTER FIVE

BLOOD

People speaking the same language, having the same laws, manners, and religion, and in all the connections of social intercourse, can never be depended upon as Enemies.

—Baron Frederick de Gaugreben, British officer, 1815[1]

IN THE COUNTRY around the Great Lakes, on both sides of the border, the British and the Indians needed one another. About 50,000 natives, a fifth of them warriors, dominated a heavily forested domain that surrounded the occasional fort or settlement. Dependent on imported firearms and gunpowder, the natives relied on British suppliers to resist the Americans, who were pushing their settlements into the native country, while the British counted on Indian allies to help them defend Canada in the event of war. Michigan's governor William Hull concluded, "The British cannot hold Upper Canada without the assistance of the Indians," but the "Indians cannot conduct a war without the assistance of a civilized nation."[2]

At their Canadian forts, British officers wooed visiting Indians with gifts of food, firearms, and ammunition. At these gatherings the Indian chiefs and British officers also took the measure of one another by exchanging formal speeches and private consultations. They particularly weighed the prospects that the war in Europe would spill over into North America, renewing an overt British alliance with the Indians against the Americans.[3]

Usually the British counseled restraint, lest the Indians provoke a frontier war which the British hoped to avoid as an expensive distraction from their pressing priority: to fight Napoleon in Europe. But in mid-1807, when an American war seemed imminent, the British scrambled to prepare the Indians to fight by offering more presents and more forceful speeches. The British walked a fine line, wooing the Indians while restraining them. At Amherstburg, the lead British agent, Matthew Elliott, told warriors, "keep your eyes fixed on me; my tomahawk is now up; be you ready but do not strike until I give the signal."[4]

Loath to recognize Indian initiative (or British caution), American officials regarded natives as pawns in an insidious British plot to ravage the frontier. Republican journalists recycled the canard that British agents paid bounties to Indians for scalps taken from American heads. In addition to blaming the British officers of the Indian Department, Americans dreaded the influence of British fur traders, who routinely visited Indian villages within the American border, as was their right under the Jay Treaty.[5]

Americans insisted that the natives should be their dependents living within a fixed boundary separating British from American sovereignty. But the British treated the Indians as autonomous peoples dwelling in their own country *between* the empire and the republic—and thereby free to make their own alliances. The frontier inverted the American and British positions on freedom of movement, for at sea the Americans insisted upon a free movement of trade and of sailors, while Britons saw their security as imperiled by indeterminacy at sea, but they needed that fluidity for Indians to defend Canada by land. Americans felt as imperiled by free Indians as the British felt threatened by free sailors. Freedom depended on race and context for both Americans and Britons.[6]

By breaking down Indian sovereignty and cultures, Jefferson sought to absorb them into American society as farm families without tribal identities or allegiances. By giving farm tools as their presents to natives, Republican officials sought to convert Indian men from warriors to farmers and thereby to wean them from seeking British arms and ammunition. Jefferson's vision alarmed natives proud of their autonomy and traditions and of the weaponry that they could extract from the British. The prospect of becoming American-style farmers horrified warriors as emasculating, for women cultivated the crops in Indian villages. And Indian women balked at sharing their fields with clumsy men.[7]

By transforming Indians, Jefferson sought to obtain more land for American settlers. He reasoned that, as American-style farmers bound to small farms, Indians would need less land than as roaming hunters. On Jefferson's orders, the territorial governors of Indiana and Michigan pressured natives to cede millions of acres for a mere penny or two per acre. William Henry Harrison of Indiana was especially relentless, resourceful, and ruthless. He negotiated land cession treaties with older chiefs representing smaller tribes or minorities, outraging most of the Indians, especially the younger warriors. They rallied to the leadership of two Shawnee brothers, Tenskwatawa, a religious prophet, and

Tecumseh, a charismatic war chief. Rejecting Harrison's treaties, the brothers vowed armed resistance and gathered their supporters at Prophetstown, in the Wabash Valley of northern Indiana.[8]

In 1811 Harrison invaded the Indian country to menace Prophetstown with 1,200 soldiers. On the night of November 6, Indian warriors surprised Harrison's slumbering soldiers encamped at Tippecanoe Creek. After suffering heavy casualties, Harrison repulsed the attack, while the fleeing Indians burned and evacuated their village. Rather than pursue the Indians, Harrison retreated to his base at Vincennes. Critics faulted Harrison for provoking the Indian attack and for neglecting to secure his camp against an Indian surprise. But President Madison and the Republican press endorsed Harrison's claims that Tippecanoe was a great and glorious victory over bloodthirsty brutes armed by the British. Madison sought a popular military victory to help prepare the republic for war against the empire.[9]

As the great savage villains of American nightmares, Indian warriors evoked a hatred that could best rally Americans for a war. A Kentucky newspaper declared, "The blood of our fellow-citizens murdered on the Wabash by British intrigue calls aloud for vengeance." Called Malden by Americans, the British post at Amherstburg was cast as the darkest den of British conniving with murderous savages. William Duane's *Aurora* insisted that a war to conquer Canada should begin by seizing "a certain hell upon earth called fort Malden." The invaders should, Duane preached, "demolish that infernal place and put all the garrison to the sword—every man of them."[10]

CONGRESS

On November 5, 1811, Madison had urged Congress to prepare the nation for war against the British empire, which he accused of "trampling on rights which no Independent Nation can relinquish." He insisted that only war could defend the nation's sovereignty, imperiled by the British on the frontier and on the high seas. In support of Madison, Duane asked his readers, "Will you abandon your rights? Will you abandon your independence? Are you willing to become colonies of Great Britain?" Embarrassed by the failure of the embargo, most Republicans concluded that they must threaten the empire with war.[11]

In Congress, the Republicans held 75 percent of the seats in the House and 82 percent in the Senate, but they were divided into feuding factions that reflected regional tensions. John Randolph of Virginia led a few southern traditionalists who adamantly opposed any measures that strengthened the federal government at the expense of the states. At the other extreme of the party, many northeastern Republicans distrusted Madison as weak and indifferent to their commercial interests. A New York Republican, DeWitt Clinton, was preparing to challenge Madison's reelection bid in the fall of 1812. Madison hoped that a push for war would unite the fractious Republicans.[12]

The new speaker of the House, Henry Clay, vigorously supported Madison's call to prepare for war. Although only thirty-four years old and newly elected to the House, Clay possessed charm, eloquence, determination, and political savvy. From Kentucky, a frontier state, Clay urged an American conquest of Canada to "extinguish the torch that lights up savage warfare." To respond to the president's war speech, Clay appointed a Foreign Relations Committee dominated by especially bellicose Republicans known as War Hawks. Like Clay, most were relatively young and new to Congress. They included John C. Calhoun of South Carolina, Joseph Desha of Kentucky, Felix Grundy of Tennessee, John A. Harper of New Hampshire, and Peter B. Porter of New York, who chaired the committee. This new generation longed to prove that they were worthy heirs of the revolutionary fathers, who had fought the British. The War Hawks hoped that war would purify the American character, which they feared had been softened by a long and peaceful indulgence in selfish commerce. On November 29, Porter's committee insisted: "We must now tamely & quietly submit, or, we must resist."[13]

In January 1812, Congress voted to expand the regular army to 35,000 men, but Congress narrowly refused to build new warships for the navy. Most northeastern representatives, both Federalist and Republican, voted for naval expansion, but southern and western Republicans opposed the measure as a waste of money. They deemed it hopeless to challenge the mighty Royal Navy, which had already swallowed up the fleets of France, Spain, and Denmark. In early 1812 the United States had only five substantial warships—frigates—while the North American fleet of the Royal Navy could muster twenty-three frigates plus three still larger "ships-of-the-line" mounting at least seventy-four cannon each. And that fleet was but the tip of the iceberg, for globally the Royal Navy had nearly 1,000 warships, including 102 ships-of-the-line.[14]

By favoring an army over a navy, the Republicans chose a land war to invade Canada, which struck the Federalists as an incoherent folly. "How," they asked, "will war upon the land protect commerce upon the ocean?" The Republican choice deepened the Federalist antipathy for a war that would expose northeastern ships and seaports to attack by the British fleet. Many Federalists also suspected that the Republicans were plotting to ally the United States with the despotic Napoleon. Such an alliance would, they warned, subject Americans to French domination, destroying the republic.[15]

Given the comparable French depredations on commerce, some Republicans suggested that principle demanded a war on France as well as Britain. But the French lulled most Republicans, including Madison, with deceptive hints that they had shifted their policy in favor of American commerce. Taking the French bait proved irresistible, because the weak republic could ill afford to wage a double war. Obliged to choose one enemy, Republicans preferred to smite Britain as the greater sinner. Like the French, the British had seized American ships and cargoes, but the British also impressed American sailors and allegedly fomented Indian raids on the frontier. Plus British Canada offered the closest target. "The one we can strike, the other we cannot reach," Clay explained in favoring war on Britain instead of France.[16]

In mid-January, the secretary of the treasury, Albert Gallatin, stalled the push for war by reporting to Congress the unpopular truth that wars are expensive and require heavy taxes. Gallatin proposed doubling customs duties and adding new internal taxes. The price tag sobered many Republicans, who had hoped to wage war on the cheap. During the winter, the skittish Republicans in Congress would adopt only one internal tax—on salt—and delayed doubling the customs duties until they could muster the nerve to declare war. Of course the Federalists ridiculed the gap between the Republicans' bellicose rhetoric and their reluctance to levy the taxes needed to fund a proper army. James Bayard wondered if "the war [would] float the taxes, or the taxes sink the war."[17]

In January and February, as Congress sputtered over the war, violent earthquakes shook the Mississippi and Ohio valleys, with tremors reaching the national capital. In Ohio a missionary reported that the repeated shocks "produced headache, and a disordered state of the stomach resembling sea-sickness." He added that many people "suppose that the end of the world was near at hand." After the "shock of an Earthquake" hit the capital, a Federalist congressman wrote, "I hope these things are not ominous of national calamity." On February 16 Calhoun noted, "How unusual our earthquakes—we had several shocks last night." The sudden "appearance of a strange comet of the first magnitude" in the night sky added to an ominous sense of dread.[18]

SPY

On March 9, President Madison renewed the push for war by releasing to Congress the revelations of John Henry. Born and educated in Dublin, Henry was a tall, handsome, and charming gentleman in his thirties. During the mid-1790s he had immigrated to Philadelphia, where, unlike most other Irish immigrants, he cultivated Federalist patrons by selling them wine and editing one of their newspapers. The Adams administration rewarded Henry with a captain's commission in the army. Abruptly resigning in 1800, he moved to Montreal, where he wooed British officials with ardent declarations of renewed loyalty to the empire and contempt for the republic.[19]

In late 1807, during the *Chesapeake* crisis, Henry offered, as a British secret agent, to cultivate Federalist disaffection in New England. He predicted, "By good management, a war will make half of America ours. . . . That wretched republic already totters under its own weight." Intrigued by Henry's proposal, the governor-general, Sir James H. Craig, covertly revived Simcoe's dream of dissolving the American union to reattach the northern states to the British empire. Visiting New England in early 1808, Henry reported that the Federalists were prepared to secede and to ally with the empire. But when the *Chesapeake* crisis passed, his British employers decided to let sleeping dogs lie.[20]

Henry sailed to London to seek rewards for his services as a spy. Put off with vague promises from the imperial government, Henry felt sour as he sailed back to America in late 1811. During the voyage he fell in with a French con man who called himself the Comte de Crillon. He persuaded Henry that they could become rich by selling his papers to the American government. Approaching the president and the secretary of state (James Monroe), Henry predicted that his damning letters would discredit the Federalists "and produce a *popular war*." Intoxicated by that promise, Madison and Monroe spent the nation's entire secret service budget for the year—$50,000—to buy Henry's papers.[21]

Initially, the documents sent shock waves through the Federalists. John A. Harper chortled, "The federalists here are in the greatest agony and distress. I never before have seen so restless a set of men." He saw "great drops of sweat" on their faces—despite the cold of March. But a closer reading of Henry's papers both reassured and enraged the Federalists. Long on exaggerated suggestions, his reports were short on real information. Relying on dinner party chitchat and coffeehouse gossip, Henry never brought any prominent Federalists to commit to secession and a British alliance. And he had deleted the names of his contacts.

Peter B. Porter *(1773–1844), oil painting
by Lars Sellstedt, 1870, after a miniature by
Anson Dickinson, 1817.* (Courtesy of the
Buffalo and Erie County Historical Society.)

When congressmen sought to question Henry, Monroe reported that
the spy had already left the country with the administration's blessing
and money. The Federalists promptly denounced the purchase of
Henry's papers as further proof of Republican credulity, incompetence,
and desperation. As a result, historians have dismissed the Henry revelations as inconsequential or counterproductive.[22]

In fact, leading Republicans clung to the Henry documents as sufficient proof that the British and the Federalists were up to no good.
These Republicans concluded that national security demanded the conquest of Canada to uproot a den of covert operations. Calhoun
remarked, "Such is the conduct we have ever to expect from England,
while she retains possession of Canada—such the cause that necessarily
forces us into a state of war." Desha added, "Can any American, after
this discovery, doubt the propriety of ousting the British from the continent[?]" Far from ineffectual, the Henry revelations further polarized
the nation's politics. While the Federalists became more embittered, the
Republicans agitated for war with renewed zeal. Henry's documents
revived the stalled push for war, but ensured that the war would bitterly
divide the nation.[23]

DECLARATION

Peter B. Porter represented New York's westernmost district, along the Niagara River, which would become the vulnerable front line in any war with British Canada. Born in Connecticut and graduated from Yale, he moved to the Niagara frontier in 1795. With his brother Augustus, Peter B. Porter developed the leading mercantile and shipping business on the eastern Great Lakes. He built a mansion and erected wharves and stores at Black Rock, on Lake Erie's outlet into the Niagara River. Initially a Federalist, he shrewdly converted in 1801, just as the Republicans came to power in New York and the nation. He gained office as a county clerk and state legislator before winning election to Congress in 1808 and reelection in 1810. Hard-drinking, Porter was also amiable, gregarious, and popular.[24]

During the winter of 1811–12, Porter had urged the conquest of Canada, but he suddenly reversed himself in the spring. On April 19, 1812, he declared it "an act of madness fatal to the administration to declare war at this time, when, so far from being in a situation to conduct offensive operations, we are completely exposed to attacks in every quarter." Rather than stay in Congress to vote for the declaration of war, he headed home, to become the quartermaster general for the New York militia. Porter also helped his brother to win a federal contract to provision the soldiers at Niagara and Detroit. The British diplomat, Augustus Foster, mocked that "Porter, after being for war, then against it, then for it and anew against it, set out at last for the frontiers of Canada with a commission for supplying the troops."[25]

In fact, his shifting positions pursued a constant goal: to protect his mansion, wharves, and stores, which lay within cannon shot of the British batteries on their side of the Niagara River. Ideally, Porter wanted to secure his property by promoting a rapid and overwhelming American invasion. In the spring, however, recruiting for the army lagged far behind the force needed to conquer Canada. Porter then worried that a weak invasion would only invite a destructive British counterattack on western New York.[26]

Porter's constituents also felt vulnerable to attack. In the Niagara Valley, the only American military base was the ruinous Fort Niagara at the river's outlet, about thirty-five miles north of Black Rock. The fort's paltry garrison of eighty troops could not match the four hundred British regulars across the river at the newer and stronger Fort George. While the Americans had done almost nothing to fortify their side of the border, the British had built new batteries, arms depots, guard-houses, and a set of signal stations to convey alarms. On the American shore, James Harrison worried, "Comparatively speaking, we are few in number, undisciplined, and in fact unarmed." Worst of all, the British could rally hundreds of Indian warriors to ravage the American settlements. In the event of war, Harrison expected the American settlements to fall "Sacrifice to marauders and Indians."[27]

Despite the nation's military weakness and frontier dread, most Republicans felt that they had to declare war or lose their credibility. In Philadelphia, an Irish-American journalist, John Binns, insisted, "The honor of the nation and that of the party are bound up together and both will be sacrificed if war be not declared." Identifying their party with the nation, the Republicans feared that inaction would discredit both as impotent. In turn, that failure would doom liberty by inviting the Federalists to resume power. A Republican worried that if Congress backed away from declaring war, "I think our Doom will be Fix[ed] and we shall become the tame Submisive Vasals of Briton & a Laughing Stock to the world . . . & the Henry Plotters will get the Ascendancy & then we may bid a Long farewell to Libberty & Equall Laws."[28]

Republican leaders desperately hoped that war would galvanize and unify a divided country. Madison later explained that he "knew the unprepared state of the country, but . . . esteemed it necessary to throw forward the flag of the country, sure that the people would press forward and defend it." Robert Wright similarly urged his fellow congressmen to emulate a young couple willing "to get married, & buy the furniture afterwards." Calhoun also defied caution: "So far from being unprepared, sir, I believe that in four weeks from the time that a declaration of war is heard on our frontier, the whole of Upper and a part of Lower Canada will be in our possession."[29]

On June 5, the House voted for war by 79 to 49. After more prolonged debate, the Senate concurred two weeks later by a narrower vote: 19 to 13. On June 18 Madison signed the declaration of war. In both houses of Congress, the vote was primarily partisan, as every Federalist opposed, while 81 percent of the Republicans (98 of 121) voted for the war. The greatest opposition came from New England, New Jersey, and New York, where the Federalists were strongest and where the Republicans felt dismayed by the inadequate preparations for war. Support for the war primarily came from the Republican strongholds in Pennsylvania, the South, and the western states of Ohio, Kentucky, and Tennessee.[30]

Historians have long debated the primary cause for the declaration of war. Early in the twentieth century, they stressed the longing of western politicians to conquer Canada. These historians quoted the provocative antiwar speech by John Randolph: "Agrarian cupidity, not maritime right, urges the war. . . . we have heard but one word—like the whip-poor-will, but one eternal monotonous tone—Canada! Canada! Canada!" But subsequent historians discounted the strength of western interests and of the drive to seize Canada. "The conquest of Canada was primarily a means of waging war, not a reason for starting it," Reginald Horsman claims. Stressing that the three western states had only 10 of the House's 142 members, these scholars insist that southern and Pennsylvania Republicans pushed the war and that they had no particular lust for Canada. According to this interpretation, these congressmen primarily reacted against the British meddling with American ships on the high seas. Stressing the British Orders in Council, these scholars downplay all other issues, even impressment.[31]

In fact, the British commercial restrictions could have been negotiated and compromised, as James Monroe and William Pinkney had done in a London treaty of late 1806. That deal had failed because Jefferson and Madison refused to accept the treaty's silence on the more fundamental and less tractable issue of impressment. Moreover, if the orders had been the sole and pressing cause for declaring war, the conflict would have been brief. On June 16, 1812, just before the Americans declared war, the British suspended the Orders in Council. They acted to improve a depressed economy in Britain and to avoid a costly war with America. Hastening the news by ship across the Atlantic to America, the British expected the Madison administration promptly to restore peace, as it would have done had the orders truly been the sole major cause of the war. But Madison and the Republican Congress fought on, citing impressed sailors and attacking Indians as enduring grievances.[32]

No single cause can explain the declaration of war. Nor was there a single day of decision on June 18, 1812. During the following thirty-one months the Republican administration and the congressional majority repeatedly renewed their commitment to fight against impressment and for frontier security. Taking the longer view, impressed sailors and Indian warriors mattered more than the British orders in sustaining the republic's war with the empire.

The quest for the one true cause—to the detriment of all others—distorts the complex push for war. Instead, we should examine the *interaction* of maritime and frontier issues in producing the profound alarm for the republic which drove the Republicans to declare war. They wove their grievances into a thick fabric, which unravels if we pull out a single thread. Lumpers rather than splitters, the Republicans composed a package of laments, typified in the resolves of a Republican town meeting in upstate New York. That meeting denounced "British spoiliations, British impressments, British intrigues with the Indians, and British murders." That sequence was common, as the Republican bill of indictment moved from the most commercial and abstract grievance to the most visceral and bloody. In building to an emotional climax, the sum was greater than the parts. To understand the declaration of war, we should explore the *synergy* of multiple grievances in producing an explosive combination of fear and loathing by Republicans of Britons and Indians.[33]

At first, in November 1811, the president and Congress did emphasize the British Orders in Council as a justification for war. But the complicated issues of maritime restrictions did not suffice to stir the common Americans needed to win elections, man privateers, and serve in the army. As the push for war intensified, Republicans turned up the rhetorical heat by emphasizing impressment as a primary grievance. Beginning in February, the nation's most influential newspaper, the *Aurora*, devoted far more space to impressment than to the Orders in Council. Duane repeatedly hammered at the theme in emotional language and beneath a bold and provocative number—6,257, the supposed minimum number of citizens held on British warships. Impressment also loomed large in Madison's address of June 1, 1812, and larger still in the response by Calhoun and the House Foreign Relations Committee:

> Our Citizens are wantonly snatched from their Country, and their families; deprived of their liberty and doomed to an ignominious and slavish bondage; compelled to fight the battles of a foreign Country and often to perish in them. . . . While this practice is continued, it is impossible for the United States to consider themselves an independent Nation.

By enforcing a broad definition of British subjects, the Royal Navy devalued American citizenship and sovereignty, reversing the revolution. Impressment roused Republicans for war and precluded compromise with the British, who insisted that their security required the recovery of runaway subjects.[34]

In their most provocative rhetoric, Republicans likened impressed sailors to white slaves. The House Foreign Relations Committee report of November 29, 1811, charged that Britain "enslaves our seamen." An

American mariner complained that British naval officers would "muster the crew, and examine the persons of the sailors as a planter examines a lot of negroes exposed for sale." In western New York, a Republican meeting demanded "the restoration of enslaved freeborn Americans . . . by the dealers in the flesh and blood of white men." Associating the degradation of slavery with blacks, Republicans denounced the British for blurring the racial line between servitude and freedom.[35]

Republicans especially resented the whipping of white Americans by British naval officers. A mariner complained that impressed sailors "were stripped, tied up, and most cruelly and disgracefully whipped like a negro slave. Can any thing be . . . more humiliating to the feelings of men born and brought up as we all are?" Congressman Richard M. Johnson demanded: "Who could number the stripes inflicted upon their naked skin at the yard-arm by a second lieutenant or midshipman? Who could enumerate the ignominious scars left by the cat-o-nine-tails?" A Kentucky slaveholder, Johnson regarded whipping as a mark of slavery. Black slavery generated a hypersensitivity to corporal punishment among whites. That racial polarity accounts for the prominence of slave-state congressmen in pushing for a military crusade to liberate white men from a bondage deemed fit only for blacks.[36]

The denunciation of British whipping raised an embarrassing contradiction: the American army and navy also used the whip to punish white men. In May 1812, Congress sought to ease that embarrassment and increase enlistments by banning flogging in the army. The *Buffalo Gazette* exulted: "*The body of the soldier is now holy:* he suffers no irretrievable disgrace for venial offences." But Congress declined to abolish flogging in the navy.[37]

Republicans linked the cuts of British flogging with the mutilations of Indian warfare. Throughout America, not just in the West, they obsessed on bodily violation by savage knives and tomahawks. In a Fourth of July oration in a New England coastal town in 1808, Nathaniel Cogswell denounced the "hordes of barbarous savages" for "rioting in the murder of defenceless innocence, their tomahawks and scalping knives glutted with the blood of every age, sex and condition." In January 1812 a Republican meeting in New York warned, "we see the infernal engines set in motion by the agents of Great Britain and the bloody tomahawk & Scalping knife suspended over our heads reeking with the blood of our Citizens."[38]

The lurid rhetoric expressed a pervasive anxiety that American men were failing to defend their women and children from bloody violation by another race. In the heat of elections, anywhere in America, Republicans waved the bloody petticoat as their most potent weapon for rally-ing common voters to smite the Federalists, who were cast as defenders of scalping Indians and conniving Britons. "Of what avail will it be for you to oppose them in the field of blood, if you support them at the polls of the election!" demanded a Republican electoral appeal in New York. Conquering Canada would enable American men to fulfill their patriar-chal duty to protect. Congressman Felix Grundy predicted, "We shall drive the British from our Continent—they will no longer have an opportunity of intriguing with our Indian neighbors, and setting on the ruthless savage to tomahawk our women and children."[39]

In the final push for war, Republican rhetoric yoked scalping and impressment as twin faces of British brutality. Both violated white bodies and humiliated white men. A Revolutionary War veteran urged Peter B. Porter to declare war on "those oppressors on the land and tyrants on the seas . . . I think with you the time is come to humble the overgrown monsters and to cause our republic to be respected at home and abroad." To render the war popular, Jefferson advised Madison that he needed, above all, "to stop Indian barbarities. The conquest of Canada will do this." Defending their race and gender, white Republican men sought to save the republic from the empire and her Indian allies.[40]

LIBERATION

Many Republican congressmen longed to oust the British from the con-tinent and to annex Canada. Anticipating the rhetoric of manifest des-tiny, John A. Harper told Congress: "The Author of Nature has marked our limits in the South, by the Gulf of Mexico; and on the north, by the regions of eternal frost." Expansionists argued that annexing Canada would compensate Americans with land for their commercial losses at sea and for the military costs of invasion. Annexation would also deprive the British fleet of a valuable source of timber. Above all, the conquest would sever the British connection to the Indians who blocked Ameri-can expansion westward. Richard M. Johnson explained, "I should not wish to extend the boundary of the United States by war if Great Britain would leave us to the quiet enjoyment of independence; but, consider-ing her deadly and implacable enmity and her continued hostility, I shall never die contented until I see her expulsion from North America, and her territories incorporated with the United States."[41]

But other Republicans worried that a northern expansion would ren-der the union too large to survive. Many southern Republicans feared that annexing Canada would strengthen the North with new states, thereby weakening the South in the Union's precarious balance of regional power. In May 1812, James Bayard of Delaware reported, "No proposition could have been more frightful to the southern men, and it seems they had never thought of what they were to do with Canada before, in case they conquered the country." Some northern Republicans also wondered if an enlarged union could survive a regional imbalance. Gideon Granger of Connecticut, reflected:

> We shall doubtless acquire the Canadas and other northern British possessions, which are of great importance to Ohio, Michigan, Indiana, Illinois, Pennsylvania and all the States to the east. But will not the addition of these Territories accelerate a dissolution of the Union? Or can it spread securely over the continent? I fear, I doubt.

A loose confederation of regions, the union seemed too fragile to stand expansion in only one direction. Many Republicans also balked at taking in Lower Canada's French-speaking Catholics, deemed unfit by faith, language, and illiteracy for republican citizenship.[42]

Lest Republican dithering undermine the American appeal to the Canadians, Porter had urged the Madison administration to pledge "that the Government of the United States should be extended to [Canada] as soon as it should be in a situation to adopt a new form." Harper similarly pressed Congress to issue "an address to the people of Canada that they shall be protected . . . and that they shall be incorporated with and become a part of this Union." He explained, "I have no idea of having a war for years to conquer the British Province[s] then surrender them by negociation, unless we can have a pledge that [if] conquered, they shall be retained." But the House would only authorize a presidential proclamation that promised to secure the "lives, liberty, property, and religion" of Canadians "in as full and ample manner as the same are secured to the people of the United States by their constitutions." This vague resolution said nothing about annexing Canada or establishing a republic there, but even this limited pledge proved too strong for the Senate, which voted 18 to 13 against on June 25.[43]

On July 2, Senator William H. Crawford of Georgia revived the issue by proposing to link Canadian liberation with the military seizure of Spanish Florida to give the South something to balance northern territorial gains. Crawford sought to authorize the president to establish in Canada "a temporary government . . . for the protection and maintenance of the inhabitants . . . in the full enjoyment of their property, liberty, and religion." But Crawford weakened that promise with the caveat that "the principles upon which such temporary government shall be established, shall form no obstacle to the restoration of peace between the two nations." In effect, the president could organize a provisional republic in Canada, but the United States could still ultimately return the Canadians to British rule in a peace treaty. That contradiction soured enough senators to defeat the final bill, 16 opposed to 14 in favor.[44]

In the end, Congress punted on deciding Canada's future. Indecision papered over Republican divisions and kept their options open pending the fortunes of war. Should the conquest prove easy and popular, many Republicans (including Monroe and Clay) expected to keep at least Upper Canada. In June 1812 Monroe warned the British that a republic, driven by popular opinion, would find it "difficult to relinquish Territory which had been conquered." But other Republicans hoped to cash in their conquest as a bargaining chip in a peace treaty, restoring Canada to Britain in exchange for maritime concessions.[45]

The congressional ambivalence and confusion left a vacuum that some border commanders tried to fill by issuing proclamations addressed to the Canadians. On July 13, 1812, General William Hull led the first American army into Canada by crossing the Detroit River. Hull's proclamation promised republican liberation: "Raise not your hands against your brethren. Many of your fathers fought for the freedom & *Independence* we now enjoy. . . . You will be emancipated from Tyranny and oppression and restored to the dignified station of freemen." Hull offered more than Congress and the Madison administration had authorized, but the official nonpolicy remained publicly murky, for while the secretary of war corrected Hull in a private letter, the government did not publicly disavow his proclamation. That ambiguity invited another commander to make an equally bold promise. In November in western New York, General Alexander Smyth assured his soldiers:

> The time is at hand when you will cross the stream of Niagara, to conquer Canada, and to secure the peace of the American frontier. You will enter a country that is to be one of the United States. You will arrive among a people who are to become your fellow-citizens. It is not against *them* that we come to make war. It is against that government which holds them as vassals.

Hull and Smyth recklessly invited Canadians to risk their lives and property for a pledge of liberation that the American government would not honor.[46]

By declaring war, the Republicans tried to overcome their own divisions and contradictions. They hoped to unite the country and discredit the Federalists. But their aversion to taxes locked them into a land war, which they assumed would be cheaper than building a competitive navy. But a land war meant invading Canada, which renewed the Republicans' contradictions with a vengeance. On the one hand, many longed to evict the British from the continent to guarantee the nation's northern security and westward expansion. On the other hand, annexing Canada worried many Republicans, especially in the South, as a menace to republican values and a threat to the union's regional balance of power.

Although uncertain what to do with Canada, the Americans invaded anyway, while failing to offer any clear reason for Canadians to welcome them. A Federalist congressman rebuked the ambiguity of the Republican war aims:

> If the object of this war was the conquest of Canada, the Administration ought to have come out openly and honestly, and avowed it . . . and have pledged themselves to the Canadians that they would not lay down their arms until it was effected, and that they should not be delivered up on a future peace. The Canadians would then have had something to depend upon.

Why should they risk their lives and property to help a conquest that would ultimately return them to British rule? Any collaborating Canadians would be marked as traitors if restored to British rule in a peace settlement. For want of clarity, the Republicans undercut their appeal to the Canadians.[47]

CONQUEST

Republicans expected a quick, easy, and cheap conquest. They reasoned that the 7.7 million Americans would rapidly overwhelm the 300,000 British subjects in Canada. New York State alone had nearly 1,000,000 inhabitants, compared to just 75,000 in neighboring Upper Canada. Clay insisted that "the militia of Kentucky are alone competent to place Montreal and Upper Canada at our feet." Jefferson declared that "the acquisition of Canada, this year, as far as the neighborhood of Quebec, will be a mere matter of marching," and would lead, a year later, to "the final expulsion of England from the American continent."[48]

Glorying in old memories of their triumphant revolution, the

Republicans could not recognize the revived power of the empire. During the preceding twenty years of global war against the French, the British had built a massive military that, in 1812, employed nearly 400,000 soldiers and sailors, triple the peak number deployed during the American Revolution. After that defeat, and those inflicted by the French during the mid-1790s, the British had made major reforms to improve their forces on land and sea. Under Horatio, Lord Nelson, the Royal Navy destroyed the French and Spanish fleets in 1805. Four years later, led by the Duke of Wellington, the British army began to roll back Napoleon's forces in Spain. The long, hard fighting tended to weed out incompetents and to advance battle-tested officers of merit. Honed by prolonged war, the British were far from the bunglers remembered by the Americans from their revolution.[49]

In predicting an easy victory, the Republicans also counted on the Upper Canadians to welcome American troops as liberators, rather than to fight them as invaders. Congressman Harper declared:

> They must revere the principles of our Revolution and Government, they must sigh for an affiliation with the great American family—they must at least in their hearts hail that day, which separates them from a foreign monarch, and unites them by holy and unchangeable bonds, with a nation destined to rule a continent by equal laws, flowing from the free will of a generous and independent people.

After visiting the Niagara District, DeWitt Clinton reported, "A great majority of the people prefer the American government, and on the firing of the first gun would unite their destinies with ours." He offered an ethnic analysis: "The Irish and emigrants from the United States are opposed to the Scotch, who have monopolized the government." A Buffalo resident, Erastus Granger, similarly claimed that "a very large majority of the Inhabitants, say seven-tenths, would greatly rejoice at a union with us."[50]

An American conquest did appeal to some frustrated entrepreneurs in Upper Canada. Many millers, innkeepers, doctors, merchants, surveyors, and petty land speculators felt blocked by an entrenched and suspicious elite. In a vicious cycle, British officials distrusted ambitious Americans as republican malcontents; that suspicion denied them patronage in honorable offices and large land grants, which the government reserved for Loyalists and Britons; so the distrusted became disaffected. Ambitious newcomers also resented the British policy that locked up two-sevenths of the province's land as Crown and Clergy Reserves. Dispersed within almost every township, the reserves slowed settlement, harbored wild predators, and increased the road-building burdens borne by the early settlers.[51]

Some ambitious Canadians did hope that American annexation would shatter British restrictions, accelerate economic development, and open opportunities to all. They sought the sort of liberal revolution won by the United States during the preceding generation. General Hull's proclamation boasted that, thanks to the revolution, the Americans enjoyed greater "wealth and prosperity than ever fell to the Lot of any people." In Upper Canada, the disaffected expected a republican regime to confiscate the Crown and Clergy Reserves for sale at bargain prices. Aspiring men also sought better access to the American market, which would enhance the value of Canadian produce and lands. One such entrepreneur was Simon Zelotes Watson, who ran afoul of Colonel Thomas Talbot.[52]

An Irish-born aristocrat and retired British army officer, Talbot supervised the new settlements along the "Talbot Road," which bisected the London District. A paternalist, he sought to create a Loyalist society by rewarding deferential settlers and by ousting meddling malcontents. He promised to halt "the growing tendency to insubordination and revolt, already manifested by persons brought up in the wilds of America, unaccustomed to any manner of control and ignorant of almost every religious duty." Talbot vowed to encourage only "industrious Settlers . . . excluding all Land Jobbers, the pest of the Province, obliging the Settlers to reside and cultivate." He linked land speculation with social mobility and republican politics—an unholy trinity corrosive to social order and property rights.[53]

Of course, Talbot especially disdained land speculation by a middle-class striver like Watson. A land surveyor, Watson had secured 1,200 acres from the executive council, but with the caveat that his settlers meet Talbot's approval. In 1811 Watson recruited 185 settlers, but Talbot rejected them because most came from the United States, although Talbot had often settled such families on his own lands. Adding insult to injury, Talbot preached to Watson: "His Majesty will in every instance prevent all manner of speculation upon the Crown Lands." Delighted by Talbot's hard line, Lieutenant Governor Francis Gore advised:

> Do not let that Rascal Watson slip through those delicate hands of yours. You acted most prudently and judiciously by warning him of

his danger in my name. Would to God every one in the Province would use it to so good a purpose.

The executive council abruptly withdrew the land grant to Watson and ordered him to post bond to keep the peace.[54]

Deeply indebted for money spent recruiting the settlers, Watson faced ruin. Confronting Talbot, Watson argued "that neither the Governor, Government [n]or any individual had a right to interfere with his private contracts . . . and he would shew the world that he would make such bargains as he thought fit." Common in the commercialized United States, such sentiments were sedition in security-conscious Upper Canada. In a fury, Watson warned Talbot that should Gore "decide against me, that will fix an *indelible seal upon your fate and mine*." Indeed, during the coming war Talbot would lead the British defense of the London District, while Watson would assist the American invasion. By getting rid of Talbot, Watson hoped to establish a republic that would nurture commercial enterprise and social mobility.[55]

But Watson could not count on support from the common settlers of Upper Canada. About a third were true Loyalists, the settlers of the 1780s and their children. They would defend a colony that gave them preferential access to land grants and to commissions as magistrates or militia offices. The Loyalists also nursed bitter memories from the revolution. William Dunlop, a British military surgeon, lodged with a farm family of "good, kind, simple people," who told of unarmed friends and relatives "shot before their own doors, or hanged on the apple trees of their own orchards," while their wives and children "were turned from their homes without remorse or pity." Dunlop concluded, "I found their hatred to the Americans was deep rooted and hearty and their kindness to us and to our wounded (for I never trusted them near the American wounded), in proportion strong and unceasing."[56]

Aside from the disaffected entrepreneurs, the invaders also could not rely on the Late Loyalists, who accounted for three-fifths of the colony's people. Drawn across the border by low taxes and cheap land, most were common farmers and tradesmen with scant interest in politics. A visitor noted:

> Politics, indeed, are scarcely named or known among them. They have very little agency in the affairs of government, except that the freeholders once in four years elect their representatives. The people are not agitated by parties, as they are in the United States, where all

branches of government depend, directly or indirectly, upon frequent popular elections.

Preoccupied with their families, farms, and local churches, the settlers just wished to be left alone by their government. Religion reinforced the aversion to politics among the Mennonites, Dunkers, and Quakers. As pietists and pacifists, they had fled from the United States and had little desire for the republic to reclaim them, but they also would not bear arms to defend the province.[57]

Erastus Granger recognized that most Upper Canadians wanted to fight neither for nor against an American invasion:

> we ought not to calculate with any degree of certainty on a part of his Majesty's Subjects taking up arms in our favor to reduce the rest. The people at present feel no oppression. They have hitherto rather been fostered by their Government. We therefore can only calculate on their neutrality & good wishes for our success.

Granger concluded: "[It is] of no consequence to them who governs if they have good land, light taxes & can raise a plenty of wheat." Preferring to stay home to tend their crops, they might wish the American forces well if they came in overpowering numbers quickly to oust the British. But all bets were off if the Americans invaded with a weak and undisciplined force more adept at looting than at fighting. In July 1812, a Loyalist militia officer, William Hamilton Merritt, confronted two inhabitants in the London District. Merritt asked "Whither they were Americans or British," but they "would not give a direct answer." Caught in the middle, they did not yet know which they were. But the war would turn on their eventual decision.[58]

SCUM

In appeals to Upper Canadians to defend their colony, Loyalist writers insisted that the cheap land and low taxes of a paternalistic empire would not survive an American conquest. They also argued that the Canadian economy benefited from membership within the protected market of the vast and prospering empire. A judge asked: "Is there a freeholder in this district or in the Province so extremely ignorant of commercial affairs as not to know that his farm cannot be of half the value to him or his posterity under any other government than that of Great Britain?"[59]

The Loyalists also depicted the invaders as vicious thieves masquerading as republican liberators. A Kingston writer denounced the American army as "composed of the refuse and scum of the earth, Renegadoes and Vagabonds of all Nations, who having fled from justice in their native land have found an asylum in the United States." He concluded, "Our wives, our children, our property, our all is at stake, and shall we then tamely submit and see ourselves plundered of our well earned property, of property for which we have fought and bled?" To protect their families and farms, Upper Canadians had to repel the invaders.[60]

The Loyalists argued that the invaders ultimately would confiscate the homes and lands of the Upper Canadians. Thomas G. Ridout claimed, "As an inducement for men to enlist, they each receive a grant of two hundred acres of land in Upper Canada, and the whole country is to be given up for plunder or booty, as they term it." Loyalists insisted that the invaders carried maps detailing local properties assigned to particular soldiers once victorious. Some captured Americans assured a Loyalist woman that "we were only coming to set them free, so that those lands might be their own, and not King George's." But she retorted that some invaders "killed at Queenstown had deeds in their pockets for all their best plantations."[61]

According to Loyalist propaganda, the Americans ultimately planned to sell the entire stolen province to the worst of buyers: Napoleon Bonaparte. Far from offering a republican liberation, a conquest would subject Canadians to the French dictator. In a published appeal, General Isaac Brock asked, "Are you prepared, inhabitants of Upper Canada, to become willing subjects, or rather slaves, to the Despot who rules the nations of Europe with a rod of iron?"[62]

Both the Republicans and the Loyalists appealed to the property interests of Canadians. But the American appeal was more speculative and prospective, promising future commercial benefits in a republic vaguely promised, while the British vowed to protect what Upper Canadians had already achieved within the empire. The invasion pleased some frustrated entrepreneurs like Watson, but Loyalism appealed to the caution of most Upper Canadians.

Major General Isaac Brock *(1769–1812)*, *1812*. (Courtesy of Library and Archives Canada, C-36181.)

Brigadier General William Hull *(1753–1825)*, *oil painting by John Trumbull, 1791.* (Courtesy of the Yale University Art Gallery.)

CHAPTER SIX

INVASIONS

The crown will lose another jewil and [the] savage yell [will] disperse, and harmony fill the land. The eagle here shall build her nest, and every subject shall be at peace.

—James Reynolds at Amherstburg, Upper Canada, July 17, 1812[1]

From the Manner the War is conducted, there is much more Probability of this Part of the United States being conquered by and added to Canada than Canada be conquered by the United States.

—Joseph Ellicott, at Batavia, New York, February 26, 1813[2]

ON JUNE 25, 1812, a mounted American courier, James Vosburgh, hurried westward to the Niagara River, bearing urgent news of the American declaration of war. Rather than head to the American Fort Niagara, Vosburgh crossed the river to Queenston, in Upper Canada. He delivered his dispatches to Thomas Clark, a merchant and magistrate, who alerted the British commander, General Isaac Brock. An inverse Paul Revere, Vosburgh had ridden to warn the British that the Americans were coming.[3]

By declaring war, the Americans should have had the advantage of striking first. Instead, the British on the Niagara front learned of the declaration of war a dozen hours before their American counterparts did. Exploiting that advantage, the British seized American visitors and goods on the Canadian side of the border. The detainees included an American army lieutenant socializing at Newark.[4]

Returning to the American side that evening, Vosburgh was arrested and cast into jail by his angry countrymen. Republicans suspected that his dispatches came from Augustus Foster, the British minister at Washington. In fact, his employer was John Jacob Astor, America's leading fur merchant and financier, who had cultivated close ties with the Republicans, particularly Albert Gallatin, the secretary of the treasury.[5]

Tipped off by Gallatin, Astor had hired Vosburgh to rush news of the

Lieutenant General Sir George Prevost (1767–1816), *artist unknown*. (Courtesy of Library and Archives Canada, C-6152.)

war to Clark, a business partner, with directions to protect Astor's furs stored in Canada from British seizure as a prize of war. Loyal to profits rather than Britain, Astor meant no treason, but Clark passed the news on to Brock, who turned the commercial information to military advantage. Vosburgh escaped trial because no law criminalized the passage of commercial news. This folly confirmed the British conviction that

Americans would do anything for money—and that the diffuse republic could do nothing to control them.[6]

BROCK AND PREVOST

Tall, handsome, and powerfully built, General Brock commanded attention, which he confirmed with his magnetic personality and keen mind. A colonist recalled him as "exceedingly affable and gentlemanly, of a cheerful and social habit, partial to dancing, and although never married, extremely devoted to female society." A shrewd judge of men and their motives, Brock understood the political nature of military command. With masterful timing and deft showmanship, he bolstered the morale of civilians and soldiers. At Newark, Charles Askin gushed, "General Brock is much liked here and will be so wherever he is known."[7]

Born in 1769 on the Channel Island of Guernsey, Brock had entered the army at age sixteen as an ensign. He saw combat in 1799 in the Netherlands and again in 1801 with Lord Nelson at Copenhagen. Promoted to lieutenant colonel, he shifted to Lower Canada in 1802. Eight years later he earned promotion to major general in command of the troops in Upper Canada. In 1811, when Francis Gore departed for England, Brock became the colony's acting lieutenant governor. Long frustrated by his isolation from the European battles against Napoleon, where other commanders won fame, Brock felt delighted in June 1812 when war came to him in Upper Canada. He expected to win glory by foiling the American invasion.[8]

To defend the province, Brock needed to heal the divisions provoked by Gore's irascible administration. Upper Canada's leading men were bitterly polarized between the dominant officials, who had reaped Gore's patronage, and a feisty opposition, led by Joseph Willcocks, who resented being marginalized. Brock vowed to "act with the utmost liberality and as if no mistrust existed, for unless the Inhabitants are given an active and efficient aid, it will be utterly impossible . . . to preserve the Province." William Hamilton Merritt applauded Brock's "peculiar faculty of attaching all parties and people to his person."[9]

Brock had to combat a pervasive defeatism, a conviction that superior American numbers would inevitably conquer the colony. He called most of the inhabitants "cool calculators" who held back from the war, waiting to see who would probably win. Brock reported, "Most of the people have lost all confidence. I, however, speak loud and look big."

Making a great show of every new measure, Brock sought "to animate the loyal and control the disaffected."[10]

Brock recognized the interdependence of Upper Canada's three sources of defense: regular soldiers, militiamen, and Indians. Strengthening one promised to bolster the resolve of the other two. In a frontier colony, the Indians were pivotal. If alienated, they could ravage exposed settlements, paralyzing the militia and negating the regulars. But if rallied to defend Upper Canada, the natives could daunt American invaders, who especially dreaded Indians. And native allies would pressure the militia to do their duty. If aligned, the three elements could mount a formidable defense: far more powerful than the Americans bargained on. But assembling and maintaining that coalition would test Brock's abilities.

Despite Brock's pleas for more men, the governor-general, Sir George Prevost, kept most of Canada's regulars to defend his headquarters at the fortress city of Quebec. Prevost explained, "To the final defence of this position, every other Military operation ought to become subservient and the retreat of the Troops upon Quebec must be the primary consideration." By retaining 5,600 regulars at Quebec, Prevost allowed Brock only 1,200 to garrison seven forts, scattered from the St. Lawrence River to Lake Huron.[11]

To supplement his regulars, Brock had to rely on the militia drawn from the civilian population. Upper Canadian law required every able-bodied man (except religious pacifists and government officials), aged sixteen to sixty, to bear arms in the militia. But the province's militiamen lacked weapons, discipline, and professional officers. Local farmers and tradesmen, their training consisted of an annual muster, held on the king's birthday (June 4), which featured more drinking than drilling. In early 1812 Robert Nichol described the militia in the London District as "little better than a legalized mob; the officers without respectability, without intelligence and without authority, and the men without any idea of subordination."[12]

To improve the militia, Brock sought a core of young, active men of reliable loyalty. At his request, the legislature established two elite "flank companies" of up to one hundred men each from every battalion of militia. These men received six days of training per month under the supervision of regular officers. In an emergency, Brock could call the flank companies into service for up to eight months and under the command of regular officers. To Brock's pleasant surprise, two thousand volunteers filled the flank companies, precluding the need for a draft.[13]

While granting militia reform, the assemblymen balked at Brock's proposals to tighten internal security. They narrowly refused to suspend the writ of habeas corpus for eighteen months, a suspension that would have empowered the executive to arrest and detain indefinitely anyone suspected of sedition or treason. Michael Smith, a Late Loyalist, noted, "Had this act passed, there is no doubt but that a rebellion would have taken place." The assembly also rebuffed Brock's bid to require all militiamen to take a new oath to renounce allegiance to the United States in addition to swearing loyalty to the king. Brock sought to prevent newcomers from claiming neutrality in a conflict between their country of birth and their colony of migration.[14]

Short on regulars and reliable militia, Brock especially needed Indians to defend the province. In addition to wooing those within Upper Canada, he appealed to the natives dwelling on the American side of the Great Lakes. Brock's agents offered lavish gifts of food and weapons as well as bellicose speeches. To impress the Indians and to secure his western flank, Brock favored a preemptive strike to seize the American forts at Michilimackinac and Detroit. In early 1812 Brock urged his cautious superior, Sir George Prevost, to abandon "our present inert and neutral" policy toward the Indians.[15]

Brock's aggressive plans troubled Prevost. Born in New Jersey in 1767, he was the eldest son of a Swiss immigrant, who had remained loyal to the empire during the revolution. Sent to England for his education, George returned to North America in 1779 as a British army ensign, to serve his king against the Patriots. During the 1790s he suffered wounds but won renown in the West Indies, where he combated the French revolutionaries. Careful, diligent, and politic, he shone as a military administrator, becoming a major general in 1805. Three years later, during the *Chesapeake* crisis, the imperial government appointed Prevost to command and to govern in Nova Scotia. Tactful and patient, he worked well with the province's elected assembly.[16]

In 1811 the imperial lords promoted Prevost to the command at Quebec as governor-general of the Canadian provinces. He inherited a political mess created by his stubborn and cranky predecessor, Sir James Henry Craig, who had alienated the French Canadian majority in Lower Canada. Treating the assembly with contempt, Craig had arrested leading politicians and shut down the opposition newspaper. Distancing himself from Craig's hard-line advisers, Prevost deftly conciliated the French Canadian leaders with patronage and respect. By appealing to their distrust of the Americans as pushy cheats and Protestant bigots, Prevost won French Canadian support for defending the colony against invasion.[17]

The good feelings nearly dissolved in June 1812, when Prevost called some militia into service at Lachine, near Montreal. The men balked at the draft and gathered in protest because a wild rumor insisted that the British would force the conscripts into the regular army and send them to the West Indies. One militiaman "declared that they were determined upon and prepared for a Civil War." After an exchange of gunshots the crowd dispersed, losing one dead and another wounded. Regular troops arrested twenty-four ringleaders for trial in September, when fourteen were convicted of riot and sentenced to a year or two in jail. By showing resolve in suppressing the riot and restraint in prosecuting the leaders, Prevost calmed the agitation.[18]

News of such riots misled Americans, who concluded that the French Canadians would welcome an American liberation. In fact most of the *habitants* regarded British rule as far better than an American conquest. In October 1812 a British officer reported that the Lower Canadian militia had turned out "with the greatest alacrity, and altho' they abominate the War, they hate the very name of an American." In his subtle way Prevost did as much as the more aggressive Brock to rally Canada against the American invasion.[19]

Prevost heeded his superiors in London, who dictated a defensive policy meant to minimize the troops that the British had to send to North America. The imperial orders fit Prevost's own cautious instincts. He also felt that Canada's defense hinged upon prolonging and deepening the political divisions of the Americans. Fearing that a British offensive would discredit the Federalist opposition, he directed Brock "to avoid every measure which can have the least tendency to unite the people of America, [because] whilst disunion prevails among them, their attempts on the British American Provinces will be feeble." Where Brock sought to unite Upper Canadians, Prevost believed that dividing the Americans was the true key to British victory. In fact the British needed to do both.[20]

MICHILIMACKINAC

In command on the Niagara front, Brock felt bound by Prevost's orders to remain on the defensive. The restraint pained him, for the American Fort Niagara was an undermanned ruin—easy pickings for an aggressive attack. But Brock believed that different rules applied to distant Lake Huron, where Captain Charles Roberts commanded the small British garrison at Fort St. Joseph. In a sly letter, Brock hinted that Roberts had a golden opportunity to surprise the American fort at Michilimackinac, a strategic island that guarded the outlet of Lake Michigan into Lake Huron.[21]

Taking the hint, Roberts mustered 45 regulars, 200 Canadian boatmen, and 400 warriors to overwhelm the 61 American soldiers at Michilimackinac. Shortly before dawn on July 17, Roberts and his men reached the island, forty miles west of Fort St. Joseph. Landing, they quietly occupied the high ground overlooking the American fort. Roberts then shrewdly displayed his Indians to scare the Americans. One spooked man recalled, "[The Indians] discharged their pieces in the air & kept up a most hideous yelling." Roberts warned the American commander, Lieutenant Porter Hanks, "that if a single Indian should be killed before the Fort, it would be impossible to protect them from their fury & thirst for blood." Unaware that his nation had declared war, Hanks was unprepared to defend his post. While Brock had exploited Vosburgh's revelations to rush news of the war to Roberts, the American government had forgotten to inform Hanks. Dreading an Indian massacre, he quickly surrendered.[22]

Without suffering a single casualty, the British had won a victory with immense strategic consequences. From an American perspective, Michilimackinac seemed distant and marginal, but that post lay at the strategic heart of a nexus of native peoples and the fur trade that bound them to the British. By seizing that fort, the British secured the fur trade and impressed the Indians, for British initiative and resolve stood in marked contrast to American weakness and bungling. That impression helped the British to rally the Indians throughout the Great Lakes country. An American Indian agent warned, "There is no calculating on the friendship of the Indians after the loss of Michilimackinac." By swinging most of them decisively into the British alliance, the defeat staggered the American bid to conquer Canada. And that setback exposed the American troops and settlers in the Michigan Territory to attack.[23]

HULL

In 1812 the Michigan Territory was an American oasis on a distant frontier hemmed in by potential enemies. At Detroit a mere one hundred men garrisoned the fort, and the territory's 10,000 Indians outnumbered the 4,700 American citizens, who lived in a narrow band along the Detroit River. At least as many British subjects dwelled across the river in the Western District of Upper Canada. Michigan's chief justice, Augustus B. Woodward, noted: "The whole territory is a double frontier. The British are on one side, the savages on the other. . . . Every individual house is a frontier. No one farm is covered by another farm in the rear of it." Only a long, narrow, and stumpy road connected Detroit through the muddy mire of the "Black Swamp" for nearly two hundred miles to the American settlements in Ohio. One traveler referred to passing through "my great terror, the Black swamp." Avoiding the road, most goods and people moved by boat along Lake Erie and the Detroit River, but the water route was interrupted by ice in winter and by British armed vessels during war.[24]

In addition to external enemies, the territorial officials feared disloyalty within. Four-fifths of the inhabitants were French Canadians. Conquered by the British in 1760, the *habitants* on the western side of the river became reluctant Americans when the British evacuated Detroit in 1796. Catholic and mostly illiterate, few spoke any English, and they had little in common with the American officials sent to govern them. Thanks to visits, trade, and intermarriage, the Detroit French felt much closer to their kin dwelling across the river on the western margin of Upper Canada. On both sides of the river, the *habitants* tried to protect their property by seeking good relations with the surrounding and visiting Indians. An American officer questioned the racial loyalty of the "ignorant French Canadians, attached to no particular Political principal, apparently more of the Disposition of Indians than white people."[25]

The American territorial governor was William Hull, a Yale-educated lawyer who had won distinction as a Patriot officer during the revolution. After the war, he became a Republican politician in Massachusetts and a failed land speculator. Some of his losses came from dabbling in Ira Allen's tangled mix of land speculation in Vermont and rebellion plots in Canada. In 1805 Hull sought to rebuild his fortune by becoming Michigan's governor with an annual salary of $2,000.[26]

Tall, strong, and courtly, he looked the part of a war hero, but he lacked substance, alternating an imperious manner with chronic indecision. Hypersensitive to criticism and quick to lash back, Hull made more enemies than friends. Pompous in print and person, he delighted in long proclamations and in grandiose uniforms rich in gold and silver braid and decked with black plumes and a red sash. But his heroism had long faded, replaced by a haunting terror of Indians, quite a liability in a frontier governor. Distrusting the local *habitants*, he disliked living "surrounded by a Savage foe, in the midst of a people, strangers to our language, our customs and manners."[27]

Early and often, Hull bickered with the other territorial officials, particularly the egocentric chief justice, Augustus B. Woodward. Adept backstabbers, Hull and Woodward derided each other in vitriolic letters written to Jefferson and Madison or to any congressman who could read. Each accused the other of being a closet Federalist working to betray the territory to the British. The *habitants* lost respect for the American officials as their bitter factions exchanged insults and blows in the Detroit streets. "Assassination would be no surprizing occurrence in this Territory and particularly at Detroit," complained the territorial secretary, Stanley Griswold, who battled both Hull and Woodward. At a tavern on St. Patrick's Day in 1808, a witness marveled when Hull and Griswold "attended, dined, and got gay." But three weeks later, the witness added, "This unhappy place is more than ever torn by factions, assaults, [and] batteries. The Magistrates have been these several days buried in binding people to keep the peace."[28]

During the winter of 1812, Hull visited Washington to lobby the president and his cabinet for a military command with authority to invade Canada. Hull rejected the conventional wisdom that an American invasion should concentrate forces on Lake Champlain to strike north against Montreal. Along that relatively short and easy route, an invasion would smite the vital heart of Canada, for capturing Montreal would open the way down the St. Lawrence to besiege the great fortified city of Quebec—as had been the Patriot strategy during the revolution. By comparison, it made far less sense to strike upriver at peripheral Upper Canada, whose loss would do little harm to the British. Indeed, that colony would inevitably fall if the Americans captured Montreal, for Upper Canada relied on the narrow St. Lawrence corridor for trade and reinforcements.[29]

But Hull warned that focusing exclusively on Montreal would leave Detroit vulnerable to attack by the British and their Indian allies. And the loss of Detroit would expose the Indiana and Ohio frontiers to savage raids. So Hull proposed an unorthodox strategy: to invade Upper Canada from Detroit. By neutralizing the Indians, this invasion would, he predicted, "probably induce the Enemy to abandon the province of Upper Canada without Opposition."[30]

Hull also rejected the conventional belief that invading Upper Canada would require naval command of the Great Lakes. To challenge the British edge in armed vessels on the lakes, the Americans would have to build fleets on Lake Erie and Lake Ontario, a costly proposition that daunted the tax-phobic Republicans. Pandering to his audience, Hull insisted that a small army could simply cross into Upper Canada to seize the British vessels in their ports. By that neat and cheap stroke, he boasted, "we should obtain the command of the waters without the

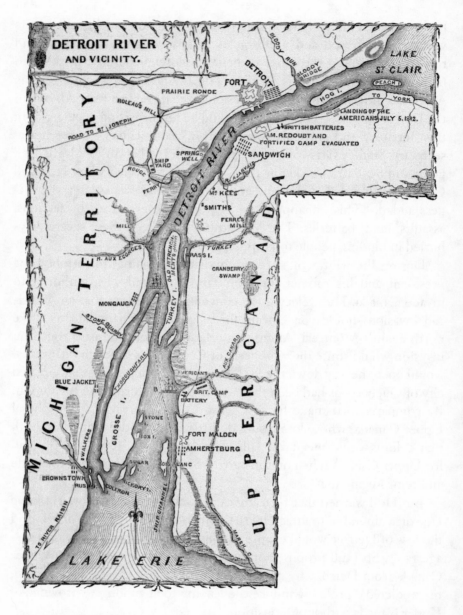

Detroit River and Vicinity, *1812. From Benson J. Lossing,* The Pictorial Field-Book of the War of *1812 (New York, 1869), 266.* (Courtesy of the New York State Library.)

expence of building" a lake fleet. Delighted by that fantasy, Madison appointed Hull a brigadier general and approved his plan.[31]

But Madison also authorized invasions on the Niagara and Lake Champlain fronts. Lacking enough men and supplies for one decent army, he divided the nation's paltry force in three. Indecisive, Madison disliked choosing between conflicting advice and advisers, so he embraced three distinct invasions. That division also reflected the diffuse structure of the nation as governed by the Republicans. A loose alliance of disparate regions, the union lacked the central power (or the logistical means) to concentrate forces on one front. To maintain a fractious coalition of supporters, the Madison administration had to mollify key regional blocs. A Detroit army would please the Ohio and Kentucky Republicans, especially Henry Clay. A Niagara force would soothe the western New Yorkers, particularly Peter B. Porter. And an advance down Lake Champlain to Montreal would appeal to northeastern Republicans, including Governor Daniel D. Tompkins of New York. Although a military folly, the multiple invasions were a political imperative in early 1812. The decentralized republic had to wage a dispersed war, for this was a very political war.[32]

Put into motion even before Congress had declared war, Hull's advance took priority in the strategic plan. Madison wanted Amherstburg taken before the British could rally the Indians to attack the American settlements. As the first invasion force, Hull's little army assumed a critical political importance in a nation divided, especially in the northern states. By winning an early victory, Hull could thrill the people, galvanizing support among the wavering. But a defeat would demoralize the public, disgrace the Madison administration and discredit the war. The Republicans gambled on Hull's leadership.[33]

FEAR

On May 25, in central Ohio, Hull mustered 1,600 militia volunteers and 400 regulars for what he described as a march into the heart of savage darkness. Meant to inspire his assembled troops, his speech must have had a sobering effect, for Hull warned that they would advance "through a wilderness, memorable for savage barbarity," where they would view "the ground stained with the blood of your fellow-citizens." As motivational tool, Indian-hating was double-edged. It initially aroused white men to fight, but it ultimately invited them to fear.[34]

In early June, Hull's army slogged through the ominous "Black Swamp" swollen by almost daily rains and infested by swarms of flies and mosquitoes. Fearing Indians, Hull slowed the march by fortifying his camp every night and by building small forts every twenty miles to guard his supply line. Untrained, undisciplined, and badly clothed, the troops inspired little confidence. And their officers squabbled over rank, while Hull seemed distracted and erratic, preoccupied with his showy uniform while giving pompous and ominous speeches to the men. His slurred speech and frequent drooling showed the effects of a stroke suffered the year before. And he drank too much. One disgusted soldier concluded, "If an army was made up of fiddlers and dancers, and nothing else was to be done but . . . drink wine and brandy, he would make a good general to command it."[35]

On July 1, Hull reached the Maumee River, which flows into Lake Erie. Weary of hauling his heavy baggage overland, he sent it ahead on board a schooner which descended that river, crossed Lake Erie, and ascended the Detroit River bound to Detroit. But he took a great risk, for the schooner had to pass by the British guns of Amherstburg at the mouth of the Detroit River. The British post's commander had learned about the war before Hull had, thanks to Vosburgh's ride to Niagara. Capturing the schooner, the British procured letters in Hull's baggage that revealed the weakness of, and bickering in, his army. Once again, the British proved better prepared for the war than the Americans who had declared it.[36]

On July 5, Hull reached Detroit, where he began to doubt that he had enough men for the invasion that he had so aggressively pitched to his superiors in Washington. Rather than directly attack fortified Amherstburg, he landed at Sandwich, an undefended hamlet closer to Detroit. In terror, the *habitants* fled from Sandwich, abandoning "their homes and property in the greatest confusion." Another soldier added, "Had an army of Cannibals invaded their country, they could not have manifested stronger symptoms of consternation. In fact, many of the ignorant old women, afterwards, acknowledged that they were taught to believe [that] we would *eat* them."[37]

But Hull had come to woo the Canadians, not to eat them. Wary of fighting, the general hoped to win by persuading the Western District militia to desert and go home, leaving Amherstburg thinly defended by a small garrison of regulars. On July 13, he issued a printed proclamation, in both French and English, which announced, "I come to *find* enemies not to *make* them. I come to *protect* not to *injure* you." He primarily sought the inhabitants' neutrality, but he also welcomed volunteers and promised to liberate Canada from British rule, contrary to his government's nonpolicy on that issue.[38]

Although he welcomed help and encouraged neutrality, Hull threatened those who resisted his invasion, particularly if they fought beside Indians:

> If the barbarous and savage policy of Great Britain be pursued, and the savages are let loose to murder our citizens and butcher our women and children, this war will be a war of extermination. The first stroke with the Tomahawk, the first attempt with the scalping knife will be the signal for one indiscriminate scene of desolation. *No white man found fighting by the side of an Indian will be taken prisoner.* Instant destruction will be his Lot.

Hull warned white Canadians to avoid the race treason of allying with Indians against their true "brethren," the Americans. Hull represented a white man's republic premised on subduing Indians as savages—in contrast to the British policy of allying with them as warriors. Because British-led forces in Canada almost always included Indians, any militiaman who did his duty risked execution if captured by Hull.[39]

PROCLAMATION

Waging war by proclamation, Hull aggressively disseminated copies carried by riders along the Detroit and Thames Rivers. To the dismay of British officers, the proclamation impressed the Western District militiamen, who deserted from Amherstburg in droves. From 850 men on July 8, the militia there dwindled to 471 by July 15, and more deserted during the following week. Never keen to fight, they wanted to go home to harvest their ripening wheat. If they lost that crop, their families would suffer for a year. After visiting Sandwich to receive Hull's paroles of "protection," they hastened to their neglected farms. An American reported, "Genl. Hull began to think that his Proclamation would reduce Canada without fighting."[40]

Hull won more active support from the leading Americans settled at Delaware Township up the Thames River. Ebenezer Allan, Simon Zelotes Watson, and Andrew Westbrook were enterprising men and sharp dealers in land, surveys, mills, and whiskey stills—the sort of pushy speculators so distrusted by the British. By toppling British officials, who had checked their ambitions, the three malcontents hoped to get ahead in an Upper Canadian republic. They also meant to dispossess the local Indians protected by British rule. At the Moravian mission to the Indians on the Thames, a missionary reported that Allan and Westbrook were plotting "to destroy this village and our congregation." After visiting Hull in Sandwich, Allan, Watson, and Westbrook returned home to circulate his proclamation and to promote militia desertion.[41]

News of Hull's invasion and proclamation spread eastward, promoting defeatism in the London and Niagara Districts, where most of the militia refused orders to march to Amherstburg. At Long Point, their wives appeared in force and defied Colonel Talbot's efforts to draft their husbands. Brock reported, "The disaffected became more audacious and the wavering more intimidated." According to Michael Smith, a Late Loyalist, most of the people hoped for a quick American conquest to put "an end to the unhappy war."[42]

In the Niagara District, many settlers tried to flee across the Niagara River to New York. In July a traveler, Tilly Buttrick, Jr., reported, "Waggons were daily coming in from the back woods loaded with men, women, and children, many of whom were in a very distressed situation; they begged for permission to cross to the United States." But regular troops barred their departure, for Brock needed every militiaman to defend the colony, and he feared that the refugees would reveal his military weakness to the Americans. So the regulars pressed the refugees and their horses for militia service. "Bad as this may seem," Buttrick remarked, "yet it was far preferable to remaining in the woods among the savages, who assumed the right of plundering whatever came in their way."[43]

In boats and at night, some refugees evaded the guards to cross Lake Erie or Lake Ontario to reach the American shore. To deter flight, the British locked up boats, patrolled the lakes with armed vessels, and employed Indian scouts to watch the shores. "Had not this been done, one half of the people would have left the province, the fear of war was so great," noted Michael Smith. Defending Canada meant keeping subjects in as well as invaders out. To do both, the British relied on the natives, particularly the Haudenosaunee who lived on the Grand River Reserve.[44]

But those Indians began to waver when Hull sent them a message promising to protect their lands if they stayed neutral. The chiefs kept at home all but fifty warriors, a fraction of the four hundred that Brock had expected to join him. The Indians' suspicious restraint alarmed the settlers, who evaded militia service so that they could stay at home to protect their families from a native uprising. Without the Indians, Brock could not raise the militia, and without the militia he could not defend the colony.[45]

Fearing "the impending ruin of the country," Brock again pressed the assembly to suspend the writ of habeas corpus, so that the military could arrest suspected spies and dissidents. Rebuffed again, on July 29 he concluded:

> My situation is most critical, not from anything the enemy can do, but from the disposition of the people—the population, believe me, is essentially bad—a full belief possesses them all that this Province must inevitably succumb—this prepossession is fatal to every exertion. Legislators, magistrates, militia officers, all have imbibed the idea, and are so sluggish and indifferent in their respective offices that the artful and active scoundrel is allowed to parade the country without interruption and commit all imaginable mischief.

In frustration, Brock demanded, "What in the name of heaven can be done with such a vile population[?]" In a desperate bid to turn the tide, he rallied Loyalist volunteers from York and Newark. In early August he led them west in boats along the north shore of Lake Erie to Amherstburg. To save British rule in Upper Canada, Brock would attack Hull, defying Prevost's orders to remain on the defensive.[46]

SURRENDER

Brock exploited a mistake made by Hull, who broke a promise in his proclamation by allowing his troops to plunder Canadians. Angry at the British for seizing his baggage from the captured schooner, Hull took revenge on the property of leading men in Sandwich. The looted homes included that of Colonel François Baby, who had been Hull's prewar friend. The invaders also tore down fences and cut down fruit trees to obtain firewood and to build barricades. And mounted patrols returned with plundered sheep, blankets, boats, and flour. That looting confirmed British propaganda, which cast the invading Americans as larcenous brutes.[47]

Aside from waging war on sheep and orchards, Hull clung to his fortified camp. In mid-July his army outnumbered the British force at Amherstburg by two to one, but Hull feared that an attack was doomed to end in the massacre of his men:

> The army would have been destroyed; if not by the tomahawk of the Indians, they must after a defeat, have perished for want of supplies. . . . A defeat would have been the signal for all the hord[e]s of savages in the surrounding wilderness to fall upon the unsuccessful

troops. Every path would have been filled with these remorseless warriors.

Gripped by dread, Hull refused to attack Amherstburg until he received heavy cannon being prepared at Detroit, work that proceeded at a glacial pace.[48]

Hull did send an advance guard forward to the River aux Canards, about thirteen miles south of Sandwich and five north of Amherstburg. On July 16 those volunteers seized the bridge, but Hull ordered them to fall back. "There appears to be a mystery in these proceedings," grumbled one captain. Another recalled, "Such skirmishing, marching and countermarching by detachments from the army . . . had become irksome to the troops and loud murmuring took place." The loudest complainer was the ambitious Colonel Lewis Cass, who declared, "Instead of having an energetic commander, we have a weak old man."[49]

In return, Hull derided the Ohio volunteers as boastful cowards and their officers as mutinous demagogues. In a subsequent skirmish near the bridge, warriors spooked the volunteers. One officer reported that his men "were Panic Struck at the yells of the savages." When the officers threatened to shoot the fleeing volunteers, "They replied that they would rather be killed by them than by the damned Indians." Hull blamed Cass and his fellow colonels: "My officers, who had seen no service, were impatient at delay, & were destroying my influence with the army, & its discipline, by their complaints & censures."[50]

Prepared to evacuate Amherstburg in mid-July, the British resolved to stand and fight once they saw the incompetence of the invaders. On July 26 an American prisoner at Amherstburg (which the Americans called Malden) sadly recorded, "The British officers and soldiers begin to laugh at Hull, seeing that he sends his men out skirmishing to the bridge and does not take possession of it and keep it, or come to Malden." On the Detroit River, British morale waxed as American confidence waned.[51]

Learning, on July 26, of Michilimackinac's fall, Hull imagined that a horde "of Savages from the North" would soon sweep down upon his army. The real Indian danger lay closer to home, for the Michilimackinac news and British enticement persuaded the Wyandot, who lived just south of Detroit, to cast off their neutrality. On the night of August 2–3 they withdrew their families and cattle to safety on the British side of the river. Their defection exposed Hull's tenuous supply line to distant Ohio. On August 5, Tecumseh led an Indian ambush that routed an

American guard south of Detroit, killing seventeen. The warriors mutilated the corpses, staking them to the ground beside long poles that waved their scalps in the breeze.[52]

Spooked, Hull withdrew his troops from Sandwich, crossing the river to Detroit on the night of August 7–8. Cass protested, "We have wholly left the Canadian shore and have abandoned the miserable inhabitants who depended on our will and power to protect them, to their fate." One captain blasted Hull as "an imbesile or Treacherous Commander." Hull wanted to arrest Colonel Duncan McArthur for his bitter and open complaints, but desisted for fear that his volunteers "would have turned their arms against me . . . I might, and I believe I should, have had a Civil War in my Camp." The civil war in Upper Canada threatened to become, instead, a civil war within the American army. Cass and McArthur began to plot a mutiny to take the command away from Hull.[53]

On August 13 Brock and four hundred men reached Amherstburg. Where Hull was gloomy, passive, irresolute, and dull, Brock was optimistic, active, decisive, and charismatic. Hull made the worst of his difficulties, while Brock found ways to overcome his. Hull depressed or infuriated his subordinates; Brock inspired his men to new exertions. On August 10, a Brock aide noted, "It has rained almost constantly since we encamped last night, and although the men have been completely drenched, they continue in excellent spirits and behave in the most orderly and obedient manner." The same rains fell on Hull's men, who became sicker and more despondent. An American officer reported, "Such Confusion I never Saw in men pretending to be under any Subordination."[54]

Where Hull had dithered at Sandwich for nearly a month without attacking Amherstburg, Brock immediately prepared to assault Detroit. He was emboldened by the mailbags from Detroit captured by Tecumseh's warriors during their ambush. Reading the letters of despairing American officers, Brock felt confident of victory. He also benefited from the return of the local militiamen, for their harvest was over; they resented Hull's plundering; and they welcomed Brock's leadership.[55]

On August 14 Brock had 1,925 men: 385 regulars, 133 lake sailors, 807 militia, and 600 Indians. Although Hull had more men—2,500— Brock put greater stock in morale than in numbers. One of his militia officers, William McKay, reported, "We are told we are to attack the Americans tomorrow, and we all appear well agreed and in high spirits." Meanwhile at Detroit, an American captain wrote, "We are now reduced to a perilous situation, the British are reinforcing, our Communication[s] with the States are cut of[f], our Provisions growing short, and likely to be Surrounded by hosts of Savages. All appears Dark."[56]

On the evening of August 15, Brock's cannon at Sandwich opened fire across the river on Detroit. Fleeing civilians crowded into the fort, adding to the loud, wailing confusion. Within embattled Fort Detroit, Lydia Bacon (an officer's wife) reported that "bombs, shells, & balls . . . were flying in all directions." One cannonball plunged into the officer's mess, dismembering three officers, including Lieutenant Porter Hanks, who had survived Michilimackinac's surrender. "Scattering their brains and blood against the walls," this fatal shot shocked Hull, whose nerves gave way. "His lips [were] quivering, the tobacco juice running from the sides of his mouth upon the frills of his shirt," recalled one officer. Instead of inspiring his men exposed at the walls, Hull cowered in a bomb shelter, drinking heavily.[57]

A shrewd judge of men, Brock knew just how to make Hull crack: with Indians. On August 15 Brock sent Hull a summons to surrender: "It is far from my intention to join in a war of extermination, but you must be aware, that the numerous body of Indians who have attached themselves to my troops, will be beyond controul the moment the contest commences." Although Hull rebuffed this summons, the seed had been planted in his agitated mind. Preoccupied with thoughts of his daughter and grandchildren huddled in the fort, Hull imagined seeing them "bleeding under the Tomahawk of a Savage!"[58]

On the morning of August 16, Brock landed 1,330 men (half of them Indians) on the American shore south of Detroit. Rather than contest the landing, Hull kept his men within the fort. To intimidate the Americans, Brock paraded his warriors within sight of the fort, marching them in a circuit that tripled their apparent numbers. Stripped and painted for battle, they presented a horrifying spectacle to the Americans: "some covered with vermillion, others with blue clay, and still others tattooed in black and white from head to foot." One observer thought "he was standing at the entrance to Hell, with the gates thrown open to let the damned out for an hour's recreation on earth! It was frightful, horrifying beyond expression." He added, "The terrific din was increased by the howls of the savages, impatient to take part in the combat."[59]

The French Canadians of the Detroit militia began to desert, fleeing to Brock rather than face an Indian attack. "From this moment," Hull recalled, "I determined to surrender on the best terms I could obtain." As Brock's troops approached the fort's gates, Hull ordered his men to hold fire and suddenly hoisted a white flag atop the fort. Without consulting his other officers, he hastily accepted terms dictated by Brock. Sent out by Hull on a scouting mission prior to the attack, McArthur and Cass could not stop him from including their five hundred men in the capitulation. Hull explained that he surrendered to avert a bloody massacre of the women and children: "A Savage will have blood for blood, though he draws it from the veins of the defenceless." The American fear of Indians, played upon by Brock, had paralyzed Hull.[60]

Chaos reigned in Detroit. Because Hull had more men and cannon and a stronger position, the sudden surrender stunned his troops, who erupted in curses. "*Treachery—we are sold*—was the cry throughout," reported one disgusted officer. Most of the attackers were also surprised, in the words of William McKay, "to obtain such a strong fortification defended by double our numbers without the loss of a man." A British private, Shadrach Byfield, explored the fort but slipped and nearly fell, for he had stepped onto the brains of Porter Hanks. The victors included Captain Richard Hatt's militia company, in which most of the men were American settlers, who recognized some of Hull's men and asked after their mutual "friends, acquaintances, and relations." Meanwhile, celebrating Indians rode through the town in captured carriages and on stolen horses "hollowing and shouting the whole day." Breaking into houses, they plundered freely despite Brock's pledge to protect private property. "We saw the best of goods and furniture destroyed or carried off by these frightful wretches," reported McKay. But those "wretches" had won the day for the British by the terror of their sound and appearance.[61]

By bluff and bravado, Brock had won an overwhelming victory, capturing men and munitions that the Americans could ill afford to lose. The take included thirty-three cannon, three thousand muskets and rifles, and tons of lead and gunpowder. Brock put the value of the captured public property at about £35,000, but the cannon had a priceless symbolic importance because most had been taken by the Americans from the British during the revolution. An American prisoner watched as "some of the British officers, who in the extacy of joy, saluted [the cannon] with kisses." While the British gloried in their recovery, the Americans felt humiliated by the turnabout, which seemed to mark their decay from the heroic standard of their fathers.[62]

Hull surrendered 2,500 men. The British paroled the 500 Michigan militia and the 1,600 Ohio volunteers. A parole barred men from serving in the war until exchanged for prisoners held by the Americans. The local militia would remain in occupied Detroit, while the British sent the volunteers back to Ohio. Paroling them made sense because Brock lacked the provisions to feed so many prisoners. He also hoped that such dispirited men would demoralize their home communities, further depressing the American war effort. The British sent the four hundred captured regulars, including Hull, via Niagara to prison at Quebec. One victor pitied "the dirty & ragged" prisoners, calling them "the poorest looking sett of men I have seen for a long time."[63]

The victors felt contempt for Hull as a coward and a liar. At the surrender Brock refused to allow the Americans any of the customary "honors of war" granted to men who had mounted a courageous defense. A gabby prisoner, Hull scandalized his fellow officers and his captors by loudly casting all blame on his government for failing to reinforce or to supply him adequately. To make his surrender look better, Hull understated the size of his force and their supply of ammunition. One disgusted Briton concluded, "I believe him to be both rogue and fool." Hull's conduct confirmed British officers in their disdain for Americans as cowardly blowhards who lacked the honor of true officers and gentlemen. In late September, Prevost shrewdly released Hull to return to the states, which embarrassed the Madison administration and deepened the political fissures within the troubled republic.[64]

OCCUPATION

In 1812 Hull's campaign began as an American bid to conquer Upper Canada, severing the British alliance with Indians around the Great Lakes. But the campaign ended with a British conquest of Michigan that deepened the British dependence on their Indian allies. Instead of shifting north, the border was pushed south. But would it stay there? While the Americans prepared to counterattack, the British debated what to do with their conquest.

Prevost wanted to abandon Michigan, after burning the fort at Detroit. He worried that keeping the territory would enrage the Americans, precluding the quick peace that he sought as Canada's best security. And Prevost dreaded becoming entangled in an Indian alliance that would implicate the British in bloody attacks on American frontier settlements. Exploited by American propaganda, atrocities might unite the fractious enemy, rendering them more formidable. Prevost pressed Brock to show "extreme moderation in the use of the Indians, and to keep them in control as much as possible."[65]

Brock better understood that the British needed the Indians to defend Upper Canada. And only patience and concessions could woo fiercely independent warriors who bristled at any attempt to command them. Knowing their importance, the Indians meant to dominate their alliance with the British in occupied Michigan. At Michilimackinac, the chiefs told a British officer "that without them he could never have got up there, pointing to the Fort and . . . that the Future possession of the Fort depended upon them." The Indians expected the British to keep Michilimackinac and Detroit and to help them ravage the American settlements to the south in Indiana and Ohio. They wanted no peace until the British–Indian alliance had pushed the Americans all the way back to the Ohio River, restoring the Indian country of 1783. Despite Prevost's restraining orders, Brock entrusted conquered Michigan to General Henry Procter with instructions to support Indian raids: "The enemy must be kept in a state of constant ferment."[66]

But Brock could spare only 370 regulars for Procter's garrison. A dutiful officer of Irish birth, modest ability, and a hot temper, Procter had to rely on eight hundred Indian warriors. He lamented, "Our Influence over the Indian is just in Proportion to his Opinion of our Strength, which unfortunately has been ever small."[67]

The warriors expected British officers to accept the native mode of war, which sometimes killed women and children and often sacrificed prisoners. An officer reported his impotence when an Indian tomahawked an American captive near Detroit:

Spectators of this disgusting scene, we all stood around overcome by an acute sense of shame! . . . And yet, under the circumstances, what could we do? The government had desperate need of these Indian allies. Our garrison was weak, and these warriors were numerous enough to impose their will upon us.

In vain, Procter begged Brock for more regulars to command greater respect and restraint from the Indians.[68]

The British occupation also suffered from a shortage of food. In the best of times, the farms in the Detroit Valley barely raised enough to subsist the local people. And 1812 was the worst of years, as the war added hundreds of hungry soldiers and Indians to the valley, while subtracting many farmers from their fields for militia service. The belligerents also devastated many farms by looting homes, fences, barns, orchards, and fields. In addition, the unusually cold and rainy spring and summer depressed the grain harvest. In late August a British supply officer, Lieutenant Edward Dewar, reported that the valley farmers had harvested only half of their usual wheat crop and a quarter of their maize and potatoes. Produce prices soared to four times their level of the year before.[69]

Plundering on both sides of the Detroit River, Indians stole horses to sell and they killed cattle and hogs to eat or simply as a wasteful sport. The outnumbered British troops could do little to stop the pillaging for fear of provoking the Indians. Dewar reported that the British impressed a horse and cart belonging to a *habitant* to help them haul military stores, but the Indians stole the beast. When soldiers reclaimed the horse, the Indians "ran their swords thro' the Animals body. Of course, Government will have to pay the value of this horse, as well as perhaps forty or fifty others, that were pressed and have been stolen."[70]

To reduce the pressure on the local farms, Procter sent the warriors south to gather provisions and livestock from the American settlements between Detroit and Ohio. In addition to augmenting his food supply and employing the Indians, Procter meant to discourage the advance of an American army, which would find nothing to subsist on within a hundred miles of Detroit. Command nominally belonged to Major Peter Chambers, but he had too few regulars to gain the warriors' respect. On August 21 Chambers reached Frenchtown, a small settlement of *habitants* on the Raisin River, which flows into Lake Erie. He offered the farmers protection from the Indians in return for their submission. But Chambers could not stop the Indians from pillaging homes, killing cattle, and stealing horses. "Indeed, it was one Universal scene of desolation," he complained.[71]

Chambers headed south to the abandoned settlement at the Maumee Rapids, where the Indians plundered and burned most of the houses. Slaughtering dozens of cattle, the Indians left most to rot, creating "an intolerable stench." Once again Chambers protested in vain. Returning to Amherstburg on August 23, Chambers found that the Indians had stolen his prize horse, which was the last straw. To appease him, Procter sent Chambers east to the Niagara front.[72]

An exasperated Procter threatened to arrest, jail, and try some Indians for larceny under the civil law of Upper Canada. Because Indians detested incarceration, such arrests threatened to blow up the alliance. Appalled by that prospect, Brock warned Procter that arrests would increase "a hundred fold the evil . . . and give a mortal blow to our interest with the Indian Nations in that quarter." Brock instructed Procter to accept Indian depredations as the price of their alliance in a district where warriors outnumbered British regulars. But that Indian domination threatened to alienate Michigan's civilians, who might welcome an American counterattack as liberation.[73]

SHOCK

On the day that Brock attacked Detroit, a nine-year-old boy in distant Virginia expected nothing but American victory, as he wrote to a cousin:

> I have no news to tell you but that General Hull has entered Upper Canada with an army of brave Americans, and it is reported that the inhabitants are generally disposed to join him, chusing to be free Citizens of the United States rather than subjects of the mad King of Great Britain. . . . All appearances seem to promise success to the Righteous cause of our Country.

Given the lavish hopes invested in Hull's expedition, the news of his surrender shocked the nation. Having cast the expedition as a test of their honor and courage, Republicans felt humiliated by the failure. On New York's northern border, Jacob Brown, a militia general, asked, "Do you not think that we are a set of polltroons and Cowards—a set of Speech makers and Proclamation manufacturers destined to become contemptible through the World[?]" If his nation failed to recover Detroit and conquer Canada, Brown vowed, "I will never shew my face again beyond her boundaries, to be pointed at and hear it said there goes an American."[74]

Most Republicans quickly shifted to blaming Hull as the scapegoat in a treasonous melodrama. In Kentucky a congressman's father reported, "The Idea with us is that Hull is a traitor or nearly an Ediot or part of both." Thousands concluded that Hull had sold his soul and his countrymen for British gold.[75]

Hull's humiliated subordinates recalled suspicious conduct leading up to the surrender. At the start of the campaign, he had tipped off the British by shipping his papers on a vessel that invited capture. And three days before the British attack on Detroit, and without telling any of his officers, Hull had sent a boat across the river with a mysterious message for Brock—allegedly to arrange a quick surrender. Thereafter, Hull distinctively decorated his tent "with red and blue stripes painted on the top and sides, bearing a strong resemblance to the British flag." Why would he render his tent more conspicuous just as the British cannonade began? Surely he had prearranged with Brock which tent the British fire should avoid. And despite plenty of provisions on hand, Hull had denied sufficient rations to the troops on the eve of battle.[76]

Rumor also insisted that Hull's children had married British officers or their daughters. Allegedly one of his brothers was a Late Loyalist, who had settled on the Thames River, where he supported British rule. Once hailed as a war hero from the revolution, Hull reappeared as a Judas of the borderland, compromised by family ties to Upper Canada. The rumors also recoded the Canadians. No longer seen as potential Americans, they became nefarious Tories who had corrupted Hull. By losing so spectacularly, Hull unwittingly defined a starker distinction between Americans and Canadians, which the British reinforced by their own response to the surrender of Detroit.[77]

BOLD CANADIANS

About forty disaffected Upper Canadians had retreated to Detroit when Hull evacuated Sandwich. His sudden and shocking surrender threatened to cast them into a British prison for trial as traitors. One despairing man blew his brains out in a Detroit street. Some, including Simon Zelotes Watson and Andrew Westbrook, slipped out of town in the confusion, fleeing south to the American settlements in Ohio. Others became prisoners. The British sent most of them home but made examples of four by trial for treason in September. Ebenezer Allan escaped trial on a technicality, but six months in prison ruined his health. Released in the spring, he went home to die in April 1813.[78]

In early September the trial at Sandwich of the four traitors enabled the presiding judge, Sir William Campbell, to drive home the British interpretation of the victory at Detroit. Campbell congratulated the inhabitants for their "recent rescue from the grasp of an enemy whose principal motive in attacking you seems to have been the base one of acquiring plunder and destroying private property." He insisted that, not only would the British never give up Upper Canada, but they would keep Michigan.[79]

In a similar vein, but in a more popular key, a new ballad, "The Bold Canadian," swung common men toward loyalty:

> *Those Yankees did invade us*
> *To kill and to destroy,*
> *And to distress our country,*
> *Our peace for to annoy.*
> . . . . . .
> *May the news of this great conquest*
> *Go all the province round.*
> *Come all ye bold Canadians,*

Enlisted in the cause,
To defend your country,
And to maintain your laws;
Being all united,
This is the song we'll sing:
Success unto Great Britain,
And God save the King.

Cast as an alien enemy, the Yankees provoked a new "Canadian" nationality, where once there had been diverse settlers from America of dubious loyalty.[80]

Because they had expected Hull to win, most Upper Canadians were stunned by his surrender. Watching the dejected prisoners of Hull's army trudge by, Michael Smith declared, "I could scarcely believe my eyes." Brock's victory depressed the disaffected, thrilled the Loyalists, and pressured the wavering majority to join the winning side. Taking a harder line against the disaffected, Brock's officers arrested any who refused militia service and the oath of allegiance. Cast into the dismal cells of a British fort or Canadian jail, many began to sing a different tune—probably "The Bold Canadian." On September 8, 1812, Fort George held seventeen "Civil Prisoners," but nine of them confessed a new readiness to take the oath and to do militia duty.[81]

Impressed by Brock's victory, the Grand River Haudenosaunee forsook their neutrality and renewed their alliance with the British. Now determined to fight the Americans, the warriors harassed any settlers who seemed disloyal. On the Niagara front, Upper Canadian refugees complained to an American officer:

> Some Indians from Grand River recently observed to Col. Claus at Ft. George, "We raised no corn last Season and our great Father the King must feed us." The answer was, "you know such a rich Farmer?" "Yes." "Well pitch your Camp on his farm & eat what you choose. Do as you please, he is not a Subject, no friend to the King," &c., &c. They are actually now quartered in this manner on our wretched Countrymen whose cattle, provisions, &c. are taken & devoured & who think themselves fortunate to escape with life.

One of the harried farmers was Smith, a pacifist who refused to serve in the militia. During the summer and fall of 1812, passing Indians broke into his house to pull off my hat, then drag me out of the house, then take the hatchet, knock me on the head, say that they would split out my brains, run their scalping knife around my head, then stick a spear through my clothes and sometimes skin. This they would do in order to terrify me, while some would cry out "kill him, kill him, quick."

By playing possum, Smith survived, but some of his pricklier neighbors were less lucky when similarly harassed. The Indians delighted in turning the tables on settlers, who had lorded it over them in peacetime. Smith concluded, "the Indians felt as if they were masters of the country."[82]

British officers encouraged the warriors to harass the disaffected. John Askin, Jr., declared, "Those scoundrels and cut-throats should be pointed out to the Indians, and they will soon make an example of them." Lieutenant Colonel James B. Dennis regarded the Indians as invaluable "to effect intimidation, of which I shall avail myself to its fullest extent." Another officer boasted that he spooked the dissidents in one settlement "by threatening to send my Indians to teach them better manners." In this war, the Indians did double duty by terrifying American invaders and by intimidating dissidents within Upper Canada.[83]

Under Indian and British pressure, most Upper Canadians took the new oath and turned out for militia duty. John Strachan exulted that Brock's victory had "been of infinite service in confirming the wavering & adding spirit to the loyal. Many of our settlers are recently from the States and by no means acquainted with the obligations which they contract when they come to live under this government—a signal advantage gained over the enemy was therefore necessary to keep them to their duty." Smith also noted a great change: "The people now saw that it was as much as their property and lives were worth to disobey orders, and now what they had been compelled to do, after a little while they did from choice." Disgusted by Hull's folly, most concluded that their best hope for peace lay in fighting against any renewed American invasion. They would help the side that seemed most likely to end the war quickly by winning it.[84]

Meanwhile, across the Atlantic, Brock's victory gave the imperial lords greater confidence that Canada could hold out against the invaders. An undersecretary for war, Henry Goulburn, noted, "It was impossible to overrate the importance of this success. By retarding for a whole year the American invasion, it gave time to supply such reinforcements as could be collected from other quarters & for organizing the Militia & Volunteer force of the Provinces." The American consul in

London, Reuben G. Beasley, warned the Madison administration, "This disaster will raise the tone here and lead to much greater exertions than were ever intended to be made for what was considered an hopeless object." An American conquest of Canada would, he sadly concluded, "require a proportionably greater sacrifice of blood and treasure."[85]

Hull and Brock had multiplied the challenge facing the invaders. When the war began, the Republicans had counted on a quick and easy victory to unite the American people by discrediting the Federalist opposition. But Hull's botched campaign produced the inverse effect, increasing loyalty in Upper Canada while worsening divisions within the United States. Having gambled on Hull's expedition, the Republicans lost big, imperiling their war and the republic that it was supposed to save.[86]

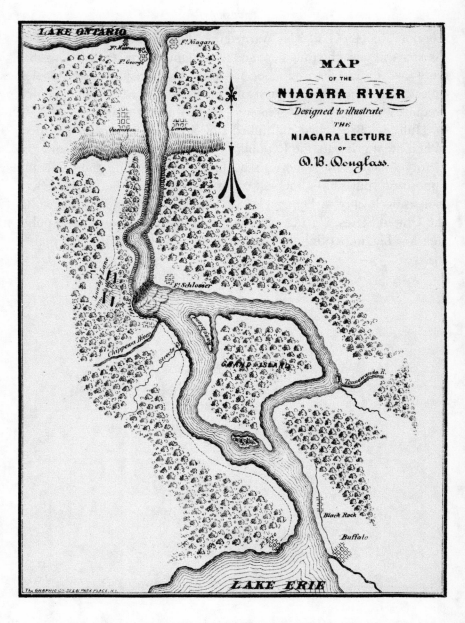

Map of the Niagara River. *Thirty-five miles long, the Niagara River flowed out of Lake Erie, to the south, passing by the British Fort Erie, on the west, and the American villages of Buffalo and Black Rock on the east. About halfway down, the Great Falls compelled travelers to portage around the escarpment to either Queenston, on the Canadian side, or Lewiston, on the American. Flowing northward, the river emptied into Lake Ontario between the American Fort Niagara and the British Fort George and village of Newark. This borderland valley became the chief theater of combat in the war.* (From the *Historical Magazine*, 1873, courtesy of the American Antiquarian Society.)

CHAPTER SEVEN

CROSSINGS

[I]t is not likely that a people enjoying peace and comfort on their farms would, if unmolested, march to attack another people, equally peaceable and with whom they have been accustomed to hold a friendly intercourse, without some objects. If that be plunder, that would raise a mass of inhabitants to resist them.

—Sir Andrew Francis Barnard, 1808[1]

BEGINNING ON AUGUST 23, 1812, General Brock staged a four-day parade along the west bank of the Niagara River. His troops slowly marched north from Fort Erie to Newark, driving four hundred prisoners recently captured at Detroit. Brock displayed the prisoners to American troops watching from Lewiston, on the river's east bank, where Major John Lovett reported:

> I saw my Countrymen, Free born Americans, robbed of the inheritance which their dying Fathers bequeathed [to] them, stripped of the arms which achieved our Independence and marching into a strange land by hundreds as black cattle for the market!! Before and behind on the right and on the left their proud victors gleaming in arms, and their heads erect with the pride of victory.

Lovett reacted exactly as Brock had hoped: disgraced as an American and awed by British prowess.[2]

A Federalist from Albany, Lovett regarded the parade as further proof that the Republicans were reckless fools for declaring the war and for waging it so badly. Writing to a fellow Federalist, Lovett urged: "Now use all these things as battering rams, and the walls of Democrat Jericho must fall." Lovett even hoped that the Republican strongholds would suffer frontier raids and slave uprisings as their just deserts for declaring war: "Between *Negroes* and *Indians*, extirpation may be the price of their folly & rashness." Although an officer in the army, Lovett felt greater animus toward American Republicans than toward the British enemy.[3]

Watching the same parade from Black Rock, Peter B. Porter focused his rage on the British, who prodded the prisoners "with all the parade and pomp of British insolence." Porter and his fellow Republican, Colonel Philetus Swift, longed to attack the British on the other side of the river. But their commander, General Stephen Van Rensselaer, had mandated an armistice along the Niagara front. Defying that order, Swift and Porter looked the other way as their volunteers fired a cannon at the British guards landing the prisoners at Fort Erie. When Van Rensselaer demanded an accounting for the shot, Swift replied that, try as he might, he could not identify the culprits, although "most of the Regiment" had watched the firing. Lovett blamed "our war-hawks, boiling over with wrath, mortification, and despair."[4]

On the night of August 24–25, the Republican volunteers at Black Rock again violated the armistice by surprising and capturing a British guard post on an island in the river. The victors returned with six prisoners: a small but cherished offset for Hull's loss. Embarrassed a second time, General Van Rensselaer sent his fiery cousin, Colonel Solomon Van Rensselaer, to rebuke Swift and Porter and to demand the immediate return of the prisoners to the British. Upon reaching Black Rock, Colonel Van Rensselaer found them "in high spirits," dining at a tavern with their new friends, their supposed guards. Denying any raid, Swift and Porter insisted that the six Britons were not prisoners but deserters, who should be permitted to join the American army. But back they went to the British at Colonel Van Rensselaer's insistence, while Swift and Porter seethed. In parting, the colonel denounced "Peter *Belligerent* Porter" as "a *Damned Scoundrel*."[5]

The confrontation between the Van Rensselaers and Porter highlighted the war within the war between Republicans and Federalists. Despising any armistice, Porter favored aggressive action by partisan volunteers, who offered more fervor than discipline. He regarded the war as an ideological struggle between American republicanism and British monarchy. In that war, common Britons could become Americans by deserting to join the republic. In Porter's war, the most insidious enemy lay within as Federalists clogged the efforts and dampened the zeal of the Republicans.[6]

But Lovett and the Van Rensselaers saw the Republicans as reckless, undisciplined, and dishonorable for defying the hierarchical chain of command, which had mandated an armistice. The Federalists sought a war of civility rather than a civil war. Indeed, they felt more respect for the British officers on the other side of the river than for the Republican volunteers at Black Rock. The Van Rensselaers longed primarily to win Brock's esteem and only secondarily to defeat him.

MOB LAW

By declaring and winning the war, the Republicans hoped to suppress the Federalists. The Baltimore *American* explained that in time of war "there are but two parties, *Citizen Soldiers* and *Enemies—Americans* and *Tories.*" In Philadelphia, John Binns's *Democratic Press* threatened to publish the names and addresses of antiwar men for, in the words of one alarmed Federalist, "correcting the refractory by mob law." Recalling the revolution's brutal treatment of the Loyalists, Thomas Jefferson boasted that mobs armed with tar and feathers would intimidate Federalists in the South. In the North, where they were more numerous, he darkly insisted that their leaders should be hanged and their property confiscated.[7]

The partisan fury peaked in Baltimore, a booming seaport of 41,000 people and a bastion of the Republicans because of the many Irish immigrants. Federalists called Baltimore the "head-quarters of mobocracy," where laboring folk rioted against anyone who criticized the Republicans, while the elected magistrates looked the other way.[8]

Only a fool or a brave man would publish a Federalist newspaper in Republican Baltimore, and Alexander Contee Hanson, Jr., was both. A wealthy and well-educated planter and attorney, Hanson owned and edited the *Federal Republican*, which defended the British as liberty's true defenders and castigated the Republicans as stooges for the French dictator. Hanson also blasted the folly of democracy and the ignorance of immigrants, whom he longed to disenfranchise and deport.[9]

On June 22, news of the declaration of war inspired a mob to tear down Hanson's printing office and to destroy his press. The mob's leader declared, "that house is the Temple of Infamy, it is supported with English gold, and it must and shall come down to the ground!" During the following two weeks, mobs dismantled several ships suspected of trading with the British as well as the homes of free blacks considered pro-British.[10]

A defiant Hanson fortified a new office, a three-story brick building guarded by armed Federalists, including two Revolutionary War heroes, Generals Henry Lee and James Lingan. On the evening of July 27, hundreds of boys and men gathered to stone the building, smashing the windows and shutters. When the mob rushed the house and broke down the front door, the Federalists opened fire, killing one attacker and wounding several others. The rioters retreated, but returned shortly before dawn with a cannon. Their leader bellowed, "The civil authority shall not protect these tory murderers. We will not be satisfied till we put them to death."[11]

The embattled Federalists surrendered to city officials, who promised to protect them and their property, but neither promise could they keep. The mob wrecked and plundered the building, while the officials pushed the Federalists into the city jail. The next day, a mob surrounded the jail, shoved aside the magistrates, broke open the cells, and battered the Federalists while women cried, "Kill the tories!" and the rioters sang:

> We'll feather and tar ev'ry d[amne]d British tory,
> And that is the way for American glory.

The rioters stripped the wounded of their clothing and tortured some with hot wax dripping from lighted candles. Militia officers refused to intervene, fearing for their popularity in the Republican city.[12]

Stabbed in the chest, Lingan died. Eleven others suffered crippling injuries, including Lee, his face cut and blackened by heavy blows. Unwilling to linger in America, he sailed to Barbados, in the British West Indies, where he remained until his premature death in 1818. Hanson suffered a broken nose and finger as well as cuts to his head, hands, and back. Although he never fully recovered his health, Hanson resumed publishing his newspaper within a week, but at safely distant Georgetown, mailing copies to his Baltimore subscribers. A few token prosecutions produced only one conviction, and the lone convict only paid a small fine. A juror explained, "that the affray originated with them tories, and that they all ought to have been killed, and that he would rather starve than find a verdict of guilty against any of the rioters."[13]

Republicans insisted that the Federalists exaggerated the Baltimore violence or had brought it upon themselves. Those who offended the people "must abide by the consequences," preached the *Maryland Republican*. Duane's *Aurora* asked, "Can any reasonable man suppose that in the present crisis the people will suffer presses evidently under British pay to abuse the government with impunity?"[14]

Federalists, however, denounced the riots as the poisonous consequences of democracy and immigration. A Boston town meeting called

Henry Dearborn (*1751–1829*), *engraving by Charles B. J. F. de Saint-Mémin, 1805.* (Courtesy of the National Portrait Gallery, Smithsonian Institution; gift of Mr. and Mrs. Paul Mellon.)

the rioting "a prelude to the dissolution of all free government, and the establishment of a reign of terror." In September a convention of New York Federalists insisted that, by suppressing a free press, the mobs would render the government merely "republican in its forms; in spirit and practise, arbitrary and despotic." The delegates predicted that the Republicans would, "by exasperating party violence to its utmost height, prepare the way for the horrors of a civil war."[15]

Seeing the war as a Republican plot against them, the Federalists discouraged enlistments and loans to the government. They hoped that a weak military effort would reap defeat, exposing the Republicans as reckless and inept. The Federalists reasoned that once the public soured on defeats and taxes, they would cast the Republicans from office. "Things could not get better until they had grown worse," Rufus King explained.[16]

DISTRUST

In a vicious cycle, the Federalists became obstructionists because the Republicans cast any opposition as treasonous. Rejecting the concept of a two-party system, the Republicans insisted that they alone expressed the will of the people. Thomas Jefferson explained to William Duane, "I will not say our *party*, the term is false and degrading, but our *nation* will be undone. For the Republicans are the nation." If the Republicans were the nation, then the Federalists were traitors.[17]

While urging united support for the war, the Republicans gave the Federalists scant reason to cooperate. Indeed, the dominant party monopolized the coveted commissions as officers in the expanding army. Elbridge Gerry argued that commissioning Federalists "would retard the recruiting service, give a triumph to the opposers of the national Government, depress its friends, & weaken their confidence in the national Army." President Madison made a halfhearted effort to commission a few token Federalists in minor roles, but most rejected the overtures as too little and too late. A Republican noted that Madison's tepid attempt had made "enemies of democrats without turning federalists into friends."[18]

The senior command went to Major General Henry Dearborn, a sixty-one-year-old veteran of Jefferson's cabinet and of the political battles in New England. Dearborn's chief career accomplishments had been to execute Jefferson's policy of reducing the army and to secure government patronage for his extensive family. Insecure, fat, slow, and accident-prone, Dearborn inspired little confidence. In March 1812 President Madison's wife, Dolly, reported, "Genl. Dearborn has had a fall which, tho not serious, confines him [t]o his house." Despite the urgency of the impending campaign, Dearborn took his sweet time recovering pleasantly at home.[19]

When the war began, he squandered more precious time by lingering in Boston, frozen there by his dread of a Federalist plot. Dearborn shared Gerry's suspicion that the Federalists were plotting to seek the "secession of the Northern states and the erection over them of a Hanoverian monarchy." Gerry grimly concluded, "If we do not kill them, they will kill us." He welcomed the war as a golden opportunity to destroy the Federalists: "By a war, we should be purified, as by fire." In vain the secretary of war urged Dearborn to hasten to Albany to expedite an invasion of Canada: "The blow must be struck. Congress must not meet without a victory to announce to them." Dearborn replied that first he had to secure New England lest the Federalists "effect a serious and open revolt."[20]

Major General Stephen Van Rensselaer (*1764–1839*), *engraving by T. Gimbrede.*
(Courtesy of the Institute Archives and Special Collections, Rensselaer Polytechnic
Institute, Troy, N.Y.)

The Federalist governors of Connecticut, Massachusetts, and Rhode Island settled for refusing to provide any militia for national service. By defending the New England coast with militia, Dearborn sought to free up the region's regular troops to join his offensive against Montreal. After exchanging rebukes with the governors, Dearborn belatedly headed west to Albany in late July. Taking away the regulars, Dearborn left New England undefended against British coastal raids. Fortunately for the Federalists, the British rewarded them by exempting New England from attack during the first year of the war.[21]

Setting up camp at Greenbush, near Albany, Dearborn struggled to amass enough men for an offensive. His second-in-command, Morgan Lewis, conceded, "We have as yet but the shadow of a regular force— inferior, even in numbers, to half of what the Enemy has already in the field." Enlistments lagged far behind expectations; the new soldiers lacked equipment, ammunition, decent clothing, and pay, and Dearborn did little to bring order to the chaos.[22]

In early August, Sir George Prevost sent Colonel Edward Baynes to negotiate with Dearborn at Greenbush. A military professional, Baynes disdained the American camp, where he found "the greatest contempt and repugnance to the restraint & discipline of a military life." Baynes came to propose an armistice that would freeze military operations while diplomats sought a quick peace. On August 9 Dearborn eagerly embraced the armistice, for he had neither the means nor the will to take the offensive. After hearing Dearborn express an indiscreet longing to retire from his command, Baynes concluded that the American commander lacked both "the energy of mind or activity of body requisite for the important station he fills."[23]

Dearborn rushed news of his armistice to President Madison for his approval. In the interim, Dearborn instructed General Van Rensselaer to avoid any clash with the British along the Niagara River. Van Rensselaer welcomed the truce as a precious chance to strengthen his little army with supplies and reinforcements. But the truce proved short-lived, for Madison abruptly repudiated Dearborn's agreement on August 15. In early September, Van Rensselaer received Dearborn's new orders to renew the war along the Niagara front.[24]

LEWISTON

As a Federalist, Stephen Van Rensselaer was the prime exception to the partisan rule in awarding military commands. Owning thousands of acres worked by hundreds of tenant farmers, Van Rensselaer was the wealthiest landlord in New York. Educated at Yale, he possessed gracious manners and a popularity derived from his "condescension" to common men, including a reluctance to press his tenants to pay their rent. In 1812 he was preparing to run for governor against the Republican incumbent, Daniel D. Tompkins.[25]

In a political game of chicken, Tompkins got the Madison administration to appoint Van Rensselaer to the command on the Niagara front. Tompkins calculated that Van Rensselaer would, by declining, sacrifice his reputation for patriotism or, by accepting, have to mute his opposition to the war. Although a major general in the state militia, Van Rensselaer had never seen combat. Probably to Tompkins's surprise, Van Rensselaer accepted. But he also insisted on naming his own staff, which included his hyperpartisan cousin, Solomon Van Rensselaer, and his boon companion, the poet and lawyer John Lovett. Despite their new positions, the Federalists continued to mock the war as a Republican folly. Solomon Van Rensselaer declared, "If nothing is done, it will not be our fault but that of the Government." And Lovett despised the war as "the deformed, rickety offspring of Mars begotten, in a drunken frolic in the stews, with the hag strumpet democracy."[26]

The Van Rensselaer "military family" meant to run their camp at Lewiston as a model Federalist society where common men deferred to the paternal protection of their superiors. Confusing wish with reality, Lovett praised "the order, the decency, the patience, sobriety & indeed discipline of the troops here." Despite lacking pay and blankets, the troops were "as quiet & dutiful as children," and "fond of pressing about [the general] to tender their homage. All seem to think that where he is, they are safe." The Federalist officers cast their camp as what New York should be, and would be, once their general replaced Tompkins as governor.[27]

Other documents reveal that, in fact, the camp suffered from drunken soldiers who insulted their officers, neglected guard duty, randomly fired their guns, and ran away. Lieutenant Colonel John R. Fenwick confessed, "Our Guard-room is full of prisoners—some for mutiny—others for desertion." Despite repeated orders, bored soldiers shot at men on the opposite bank of the Niagara River, who then returned the fire. In July a rogue sniper claimed the first casualty on the Niagara frontier: John Hendershot, an Upper Canadian militiaman and Late Loyalist who fell victim to a bullet fired by a fellow American.[28]

The sniping irked Van Rensselaer, for it contradicted his illusion of paternal control over deferential soldiers. And the firing led to formal complaints from Brock, which embarrassed the Federalist officers, who longed for his respect. Regarding the campaign as a genteel competition, Van Rensselaer lost whenever a rogue sniper enabled Brock to protest.[29]

Van Rensselaer and his aides welcomed opportunities to shower civilities on Brock's emissaries. Crossing the river on a boat under a white flag of truce, the emissaries officially came to fine-tune the armistice or to propose civilian exchanges. But they also kept their eyes and ears open to assess the strengths and weakness of the enemy camp. A wary commander kept such visits to a minimum, blindfolded visitors except when within a tent, and kept subordinates mum. But the Van Rensselaers treated the emissaries as honored guests due every civility and free access.[30]

One of Brock's officers, Major Thomas Evans, reported meeting privately with Solomon Van Rensselaer: "after some familiar conversation, he threw off his reserve" to declare "that he himself, and the General were Federals, that at the approaching Elections he had no doubt of the Government being in their hands, [then] looking round to see [that] no one was present he enjoined me to secresy, and then declared the Govt to be in the hands of a faction, that the War was obnoxious to a Majority of the people." Although an officer in the U.S. Army, Solomon Van Rensselaer hoped that the British would foil the invasion.[31]

The coziness with British officers alarmed Republican soldiers, who feared a repeat of Hull's betrayal. A Republican activist, John C. Spencer, complained to the governor, "General Van Rensselaer is openly declaring against the war, represents it as undertaken from base, selfish motives, [and] states that General Porter voted for it to make money." Worse still, the commander entrusted management of his army to a "precious couple, Col. Van Rensselaer and John Lovett; the one a political madman and the other a buffoon." Spencer concluded, "The soldiers are disgusted and disheartened, they have no confidence whatever in their officers. They believe that they are in more danger of being surrendered, than of being destroyed in battle." In return, Solomon Van Rensselaer accused Spencer and Porter of spreading malicious rumors "that Gen. Van Rensselaer is a traitor to his Country and the Surrender of the Army when it crosses the River is the price of his Infamy."[32]

The bickering eroded the army's already shaky morale. "Distrust began to whisper; suspicion walked the camp by night," Lovett recalled. In early September an anonymous note warned the Van Rensselaers that the men would mutiny and go home unless they were paid within eight days. The commanders ceased to see the men as dutiful children who loved their general. Lovett later consoled the general: "I know that . . . your very soul was sickened with the motley group of Indians, upstarts, vagabonds, ragamuffins, rap scallions, and slubberdegullians who poured in like flood wood from every stream." No longer a Federalist utopia, the Lewiston camp seemed democracy incarnate.[33]

Morale further deteriorated in late September and early October, when fierce storms ripped through the flimsy tents. On September 22, Lovett reported "the most tremendous storm of cold rain & wind that I ever saw at this season of the year. . . . The wind was terrible—hail—lightning—thunder and the whole army of terrors seemed pressed into requisition. Many Tents blew up and over." Two weeks later he added, "We are, every few days, deluged in water. Such storms of rain and wind I think I never experienced." Lovett concluded, "We eat, drink, and sleep in water."[34]

Debilitating sickness spread among the shivering and dripping soldiers in their ragged tents, while the British were snug in their wooden barracks. On September 28 Brock reported, "Those under my command are in perfect health and spirits." But the Americans had to wage an offensive war on the cheap. Lovett observed, "no one dares speak the word *Barracks* (on this shore) for fear of being hanged for a Tory." Barracks cost money and meant staying on the defensive instead of crossing the river to smite the British. Too weak to move forward and too proud to retreat, the American troops suffered and seethed.[35]

The Niagara border drew together two hostile armies within sight and sound of one another, separated only by a river. In general, the United States was far more populous and prosperous than the frontier colony of Upper Canada. But the Niagara River presented an inversion, for the settlements on the Canadian bank were older, thicker, and more prosperous. On the west bank, broad and open fields, apple and peach orchards, frame houses, and good roads stood in stark contrast to the east side's tangled forest broken by some stumpy pastures and log cabins. An American officer lamented: "This is a very poor country—miserable roads and nothing to be had for love or money. The land opposite is very inviting, it looks well, and I understand they live well." So near and yet so far, the prosperous Canadian side tantalized American troops drenched in rain, mired in mud, pained by hunger, and sickened by exposure.[36]

The Federalist officers blamed their supply problems on Peter B. Porter and his brother Augustus, charging them with negligence and profiteering as the state's quartermaster general (Peter) and primary

Lieutenant Colonel Solomon Van Rensselaer (*1774–1852*), *oil painting by Ezra Ames, c. 1818.* (Courtesy of Historic Cherry Hill, Albany, N.Y.)

military contractor (Augustus). In fact, the Porters struggled against daunting conditions, for the frontier farms were too new and too few to feed hundreds of troops suddenly pushed into the valley. That year's unusually cold and rainy weather further reduced the grain harvest, pushing up the price of wheat, flour, and bread. The miserable weather also clogged the already bad roads with mud, slowing the progress and increasing the cost of hauling provisions from the east. It cost far less to move bulky cargoes in vessels on Lake Ontario: seventy-five cents to transport a barrel of flour one hundred miles by water, compared to five dollars over the same distance by land. But British warships dominated the lake, making it unsafe for the Americans to risk valuable cargoes on unprotected ships.[37]

QUEENSTON

Hull's disaster doubled the stakes in the dangerous political game played at Niagara. The Republicans desperately needed a military victory somewhere, and the Niagara front looked like their only chance, for Dearborn remained stalled at Greenbush, far short of attacking Montreal. Instead of hastening to Niagara to take command, Dearborn diverted men from his army to reinforce Van Rensselaer and exhorted him to cross the river and attack the British as soon as possible: "*At all events, we must calculate on possessing Upper Canada before winter sets in.*" The desperate Republicans invested their resources in a general who despised them and their war. And that Federalist general commanded a restive army of Republican soldiers who feared betrayal. The commanders disliked their soldiers, who distrusted them—a formula for disaster.[38]

On September 29, General Alexander Smyth arrived to compound the divisions in the Niagara army. Irish-born, Virginian, and Republican, Smyth was a stark contrast to Van Rensselaer, the Federalist grandee from New York. High-strung and bombastic, Smyth had shone as a lawyer and state legislator before taking command of an army regiment in 1808. Regarded as a military genius by the president, Smyth won promotion to brigadier general at the start of the war. Although subordinate in rank to Van Rensselaer, Smyth disdained the Federalist general as a military amateur. Rather than submit to his command at Lewiston, Smyth set up his own headquarters upriver at Buffalo, where he led about two thousand men compared to the three thousand downstream under Van Rensselaer. Instead of combining and cooperating, the divided army worked at cross-purposes.[39]

On the night of October 8–9, troops and sailors from Smyth's command pulled off a daring raid, capturing two British vessels near Fort Erie at the outlet into the Niagara River. The rare victory thrilled the Republicans along the Niagara front, increasing the clamor for Van Rensselaer to do something. At the Lewiston camp, the militia officers warned Van Rensselaer that their impatient men would bolt for home unless led into battle within a week.[40]

Van Rensselaer and his staff prepared for a crossing, but they expected to expose Republican folly rather than to defeat Brock's army. Solomon Van Rensselaer vowed to test the "blustering Democrats who pretend to be full of fighting & to cross the river." By dishonoring themselves and losing the battle, the Republicans would vindicate the Federalists for opposing the war.[41]

In the predawn darkness of October 13, an advance force of three hundred militia and three hundred regulars crowded into thirteen boats for the hard rowing against the rapid, twisting current of the powerful river. To the dismay of Republican officers, Van Rensselaer gave command of the advance to his cousin Solomon. But he did not command for long. Upon landing at Queenston, Solomon suffered gunshot wounds to his hip, thigh, and leg, and had to be hauled back across the river to safety in a field hospital. His command nominally fell to a militia brigadier general, William Wadsworth, but he deferred to Lieutenant Colonel Winfield Scott of the regulars.[42]

Despite the difficult crossing, the initial attack proved surprisingly successful. Only a small guard defended Queenston, for Brock had concentrated his forces seven miles to the north at Fort George, where he had expected the Americans to strike. Before Brock could rush south to Queenston, Scott had stormed the nearby heights, capturing a British battery. When Brock arrived with reinforcements, he ordered a hasty charge to retake the high ground. Sword drawn, he rushed into a withering American fire. Shot in the chest, Brock crumpled, dying within a minute. His dismayed troops carried off his corpse as they fled down the hill. An easy victory at Detroit had cost Brock his life at Queenston, for his earlier triumph had reinforced his aggressive overconfidence. He died from his conviction that Americans were undisciplined cowards who would run or surrender whenever boldly attacked.[43]

Succeeding Brock as commander, General Roger Hale Sheaffe rallied the British and brought up more men—a mix of regulars, militia, and warriors—increasing his force to 1,200. While the British gathered their strength, the Americans failed to send enough reinforcements across the river. About 1,200 Americans did cross, but at least 1,800 militia refused to enter the boats. Novices to combat, they felt shocked by "the sight of a considerable number of dead and mangled bodies" brought back to the American shore in the boats. And they flinched at the growing din of battle, especially the screams of Indian warriors. As an excuse, the militiamen insisted that their constitutional duty confined them to defending the state, which barred crossing a border.[44]

Above all, the militiamen balked from distrust of Stephen Van Rensselaer, who had done so little to organize the attack and who made only a cameo appearance on the western shore during the midday lull in the fighting. Unlike Brock, who exposed his body to inspire his troops, Van Rensselaer vainly exhorted men to cross into a danger that he avoided. The Republican militiamen suspected him of mounting a suicide mission meant to kill them instead of Britons. Solomon Van Rensselaer had added to their dread and distrust with an intemperate order on the eve of battle. He threatened that if any men retreated once on the other shore, they would "expiate their crime by the fire of the Artillery and Musketry of the Columns which shall be directed at them to their total Extirpation." Already fearful of the British and the Indians, the militiamen now also dreaded fire from behind directed by their Federalist commanders.[45]

In the late afternoon, Sheaffe led a British counterattack that overwhelmed the Americans on Queenston Heights. By their piercing screams and painted appearance, about 250 Indians turned the American retreat into a bloody rout. An American volunteer confessed, "I thought hell had broken loose and let her dogs of war upon us." A British officer described the scene:

> The Indians hanging upon their rear completed their dismay and those remaining in the batteries, becoming also terror struck, fled in all directions. A terrible slaughter ensued. The Indians were furious. Their war whoops so intimidated the Americans, who expected no quarter, that in despair some leapt the precipice and were seen for some time after suspended halfway down in the branches of the trees, where the Savages had shot them from the brow [of the heights].

Some leapers died from the fall and others drowned in the rampaging river. Most of the routed Americans huddled at the landing, where they found no boats for their evacuation. In a panic, the boatmen had fled, leaving their boats on the far shore or to drift away down the river. To avoid a massacre, Scott surrendered to Sheaffe. The American losses were heavy: 90 killed, 100 wounded, and another 925 captured. By comparison, the British-led force suffered only 19 killed, 77 wounded, and 21 captured.[46]

Adhering to Prevost's defensive policy, Sheaffe declined to exploit his Queenston victory. Instead of countercrossing to smash the demoralized Americans, he negotiated a truce and a prisoner exchange. Sheaffe released the captured militiamen to return home on parole. One parolee marveled that "even the Irishmen were well treated, and to our surprise a parole was given to a major, who had belonged to the United Irish patriots." Sheaffe also exchanged some of the captured regulars for Britons lost with the two vessels captured near Fort Erie on October 9. Sheaffe then sent the rest (including Scott) to Quebec.[47]

Three days after his defeat in battle, Van Rensselaer won the victory he had sought: the respect of the British commander. On the morning of October 16, the British held an elaborate funeral for Brock at Fort George. Van Rensselaer ordered a cannon salute fired in honor of the fallen commander. In a grateful note to the American general, Sheaffe concluded: "Allow me, Sir, to express a hope that the time is not far distant when the restoration of peace and amity between our respective countries may afford me an opportunity of assuring you, personally, of the respect and esteem with which I have the honor [to bear you]." Another British officer observed, "General Van Ranselair, I think, was a good Officer, but he was too liberal and too much of a Gentleman to please his Country." This was the praise that Van Rensselaer coveted: to be deemed too genteel for his vulgar country governed by Republicans.[48]

In this political war, a battle continued to reverberate in the partisan press. The Federalist editors lionized the Van Rensselaers and demonized Republican militia officers as hypocrites who shrank from combat after urging invasion. But the Federalists were two-faced in blasting the militia for refusing to cross. In September a state convention of New York Federalists had denounced "the employment of the militia, for the purpose of offensive war, as a palpable violation of the constitution . . . which it behooves the true friends of our excellent institutions, by all lawful means, firmly to resist." That denunciation had appeared in the *Buffalo Gazette* a week before the battle of Queenston. Yet three weeks later that same Federalist paper blamed the Republicans for the refusal of so many militia to cross.[49]

Counterattacking, the Republicans depicted Van Rensselaer as an empty uniform who had allowed his partisan staff to demoralize the troops. Joseph Ellicott belittled Van Rensselaer as "a good, easy sort of a Man, pretty much under the Guidance of others, without giving himself the Trouble to do the acting or thinking Part . . . of a commanding General." Some Republicans even insinuated that he had tipped off the British to the attack. Far from uniting Republicans and Federalists, the battle had deepened their distrust and animosity.[50]

BUFFALO

Upon Van Rensselaer's abrupt resignation, Smyth assumed command on the Niagara front. He relished the opportunity to execute his strategy of an upriver crossing to attack Fort Erie. This strategy had the advantage of striking where the British were weakest, at the southern

Brigadier General Alexander Smyth *(1767–1830), engraving by Charles B. J. F. de Saint-Mémin, 1805.* (Courtesy of the National Portrait Gallery, Smithsonian Institution; gift of Mr. and Mrs. Paul Mellon.)

end of their defensive line, far from their headquarters at Fort George. But Smyth's strategy had the matching liability of hitting only an appendage instead of a vital organ. Capturing the small British garrison at Fort Erie would do little to weaken the enemy and to win the war. But Dearborn went along with Smyth's plan, for the Republicans desperately needed some military victory on Canadian soil to close the campaign. In June they had expected to conquer most of Canada within six months. By October, however, Dearborn would settle for much less: for Smyth merely to "pass into Canada and secure good winter quarters."[51]

Gathering up the military wreckage at Lewiston, Smyth shifted most of the regulars south to Black Rock and Buffalo. But almost all were raw recruits who had been rushed to the Niagara front without any training.

An army inspector declared, "They are mere militia, and, if possible, even worse; and if taken into action in their present state, will prove more dangerous to themselves than to their enemy." The inspector doubted that they knew "on which shoulder to carry the musket." And their equally raw officers knew more about running a store or arguing a court case than about drilling soldiers or leading an attack.[52]

To bolster his army, Smyth relied on "volunteers": soldiers intermediate between drafted militia and enlisted regulars. Like militia, they were amateurs, but they volunteered for a brief term of service, usually a few weeks or months. Unlike militia, who came reluctantly and from both political parties, volunteers were Republicans, who boasted that their ardor more than compensated for their lack of training.[53]

In mid-November at Buffalo, Smyth welcomed 1,800 volunteers from western Pennsylvania and appealed for more from western New York:

> In a few days the troops under my command will plant the American standard in Canada. . . . They will conquer or they will die. Will you stand by with your arms folded and look on this interesting struggle? Are you not related to the men who fought at Bennington and Saratoga? Has the race degenerated? Or have you, under the baneful influence of contending factions, forgot your country?

Lest shame and patriotism prove insufficient, Smyth offered the promise of booty and a $200 bounty for every horse taken from the British army and $40 "for the arms and spoils of each savage warrior who shall be killed." By this euphemism, Smyth could deny that his government paid for scalps, while persisting in charging the British with doing so. And he assured the volunteers that they had nothing to fear:

> You have seen Indians, such as those hired by the British to murder women and children, and kill and scalp the wounded. You have seen their dances and grimaces and heard their yells. Can you fear *them*? No. You hold them in the utmost contempt.

Smyth expressed the Republicanism of 1812: boastful of superiority but haunted by defeat; mixing patriotism with commercialism; asserting masculine prowess yet fearing failure; and obsessed by fear and loathing for Indians.[54]

With Porter's help, Smyth rallied nine hundred New York volunteers, who came to Buffalo despite the cold rains that mired the roads in mud. Impressed by their zeal, a Republican newspaper boasted, "The friends of England, who have hitherto exulted in our discomfiture will shortly hang their heads in confusion. They may bark and snarl at the gallant Smyth for the present; their tune will soon be changed." Republicans thought of victory in Canada as the means to silence the Federalists at home.[55]

But conditions deteriorated in the military camps at Buffalo and Black Rock. Drenched by rain and frozen by biting winds, the men shivered in thin clothing and flimsy tents. A junior officer lamented:

> It rains almost every day, cold as Greenland. . . . Our troops [are] dieing rapidly, 1500 sick, no boards for tent floors, very little straw, sometimes something to eat, and sometimes nothing, no money . . . and no prospect of getting any.

The Porters could not feed the growing numbers of volunteers, who often went hungry or had to eat rancid beef. "In fine, everything that is sure to rid man of life is here practiced," a soldier complained.[56]

Malnutrition, exposure, and wretched sanitation produced rampant sickness. Afflicted by colds, dysentery, measles, pleurisy, and pneumonia, many soldiers were finished off by a typhoid fever. They died so fast that coffin makers and grave diggers could not keep up, so dogs feasted at shallow, sandy graves. The disease reduced the effective strength of Smyth's army by a third, while demoralizing the rest. In late November an officer was "forcibly struck with the melancholy and desponding state of the troops."[57]

Relations with the local civilians also deteriorated as hungry troops tore down rail fences to build fires to cook stolen cattle, sheep, hogs, and chickens. Joseph Ellicott complained, "The fact is our own Troops have destroyed all the farms within the vicinity of their Encampments, plundered the people of their corn and their potatoes, and many farms are laid in open common by having all their rails consumed." In Buffalo, infuriated civilians established a night watch, which shot and wounded four pilfering soldiers, further inflaming tensions between citizens and their supposed defenders.[58]

Buffalo's Federalist majority especially despised the Irish-American volunteer companies from New York, Albany, and Baltimore. The Buffalo Federalists accused the "Baltimore Greens" of fomenting the bloody riots of their city. In a combustible mix, the officers of the Baltimore Greens lodged in the Buffalo hotel kept by Ralph Pomeroy, an ardent Federalist. A quarrel erupted on November 25, when the officers

Colonel Moses Porter, *1815*. (Courtesy of the Danvers [Mass.] Historical Society.)

demanded free food and drink as their due for defending the village. Enraged, Pomeroy baited his lodgers with the wish "that every volunteer who came to fight the British might be put to death in Canada." Word of his insult spread through the streets into the nearby military camp. Threatening to "kill all the federalists and damned tories," hundreds of angry volunteers rushed into the village to smash the hotel's windows and furniture. Pomeroy escaped death by hiding in the hay of his barn.[59]

To suppress the riot, Smyth sent regulars commanded by Colonel Moses Porter. No relation to Peter, the colonel was known as "Old Blow-Hard" for his loud and eloquent profanity. Ignoring his bellowing demands to stop, the rioters set fire to the wrecked hotel. On Colonel Porter's order, the regulars fired a cannon, wounding at least six rioters, three of them fatally. Swinging swords, the regulars drove the remaining rioters from the blood-spattered ruins of Pomeroy's hotel. Fleeing to their camp, the enraged volunteers "threatened to take vengeance" upon the regulars and the villagers. "The Excitement was Fearfull," recalled one resident. Smyth kept three hundred regulars in Buffalo to guard against a renewed attack by the volunteers in a civil war that had erupted within the army. A visitor remarked, "They will have fighting enough amongst themselves without crossing into Canada."[60]

DUELS

The hotel riot compelled Smyth to do something desperate to unite his distracted army. That evening, he suddenly ordered his troops to prepare for crossing and combat. To inspire them, Smyth fired another broadside of words: "Friends of your country! . . . Think on your country's honors torn; her rights trampled on; her sons enslaved; her infants perishing by the hatchet. Be strong! Be brave! And let the ruffian power of the British King cease on this continent." But these words rang hollow in an army at war within itself.[61]

On the evening of November 27, an advance raid led by Captain William King captured the British battery in front of Fort Erie, but Smyth suddenly lost his nerve and failed to send more men across. Counterattacking, the British retook the battery, capturing Captain King and most of his men. While the initial success had thrilled the volunteers, the subsequent failure infuriated them, as they sat shivering in a snowstorm that engulfed their boats at Black Rock. Belatedly ordered back to their camp, many frustrated men smashed their muskets against stumps.[62]

Trapped by his own vow to conquer or die, Smyth could neither admit failure nor consummate a crossing. For three more days he prolonged the miserable suspense while his band kept playing "Yankee Doodle." One evening he announced to the troops, "Hearts of War! Tomorrow will be memorable in the annals of the United States." But confusion reigned, for Smyth failed to attend to the essentials of an amphibious assault: matching men and supplies with boats. "Nothing was ready—nothing arranged," Colonel Isaac A. Coles complained.

Aloof, Smyth wrapped his plans in a secrecy that maddened his subordinates, who felt disrespected. Major David Campbell lamented, "The General kept himself almost entirely secluded from the Camp and seemed to know but little of our situation." Smyth apparently withdrew to hide his prolonged bouts of depression, which alternated with brief bursts of manic enthusiasm.[63]

Of the 4,500 men in Smyth's force, a third were too sick to move and another third refused to cross the river, leaving only one-third to endure the cold in open boats, waiting for hours for the order to cross and attack. On December 1 Smyth belatedly canceled his final attempt to cross, citing insufficient numbers.[64]

Fed up, the volunteers erupted in outrage, for they felt deceived and ashamed. Frustrated officers broke their swords, and their men "pretended to rave like madmen," while firing at random. "The Balls were whistling in every direction," Coles recalled. Porter saw "4,000 men without order or restraint discharging their muskets in every direction." Confronted by a menacing crowd, Porter shrewdly deflected blame onto Smyth. After treating the thirsty volunteers to "a few barrels of whiskey," he denounced Smyth as "a coward, a traitor, and a villain!" Angry volunteers offered a $200 reward to anyone who would kill the general. Some shot at him as he rode by, but they missed. Others settled for hooting at Smyth as a "damned Tory" and "worse than Hull," while burning his straw-stuffed effigy and copies of his proclamations. His Black Rock landlord threw Smyth out for fear that a mob would tear down the inn. Unable to find another host in town, Smyth had to sleep in a tent guarded by regulars. "I have never seen a man so completely depressed . . . for he has no friends," remarked Major Campbell.[65]

At last, on December 12, Smyth and Porter did cross the river, but they took only one boat with twenty men under flying colors, and they stopped midway across at Grand Island. Instead of attacking the British, they went to shoot at each other. To heal his wounded honor, Smyth challenged Porter to a duel, which proved as ineffectual as their assault on Fort Erie. After each fired and missed, their seconds intervened to persuade Porter to retract his charges against Smyth. In return, Smyth conceded that he respected Porter "as a gentleman and officer. The hand of reconciliation was then offered and received."[66]

To complete the business, their seconds published an account in the *Buffalo Gazette*, for American duels involved a broader republic of readers. Reprinted through the land, the account invited mockery by Federalists, who concluded that Porter and Smyth had too little honor and courage to stand a second fire. Stung by the ridicule, Smyth and Porter resumed their battle in the newspapers by publishing rival accounts of the aborted attacks on Fort Erie. Porter insinuated cowardice and incompetence in Smyth, who countered that Porter had ruined morale by failing to supply the men: "He was too Indolent and too fond of whiskey to attend to his duty."[67]

Defending Porter as one of their own, New York's Republican politicians denounced Smyth as an insulting imbecile. One volunteer officer derided Smyth as "a *demi-brute* or whimsical savage—who ought to be placed in a museum, or sent into the forest with the orang outang." Instead, Smyth returned to Virginia, where he remained in forced military retirement. To conduct a war on the northern frontier, the administration needed the support of New York's Republicans. So the secretary of war and Congress rejected Smyth's appeals for reinstatement or for a court of inquiry to clear his name. A Virginia legislator wrote to his brother, an officer in the army: "Your general still keeps writing. This alone has ruin'd him. Every man in this nation who can think and feel as a rational being is sick to lo[a]thing of *words, words, words*."[68]

While fending off Smyth in Republican politics, Porter also faced attack from the Federalist front. During the winter, Solomon Van Rensselaer sought a duel by posting Porter in a Federalist newspaper as a "*Rascal, Poltroon, and Coward*." Augustus Porter wrote to his brother: "I beg of you not to attempt to fight a duel with him, but abuse him back in the papers, and if you come across him personally kick and cuff him." On a visit to Albany in April, Peter B. Porter settled for accosting Van Rensselaer's friend, John Lovett. The two men whacked at each other in the street with heavy canes until bloodied, when bystanders intervened to separate them. Politics, war, and honor made a bloody mix for Americans, who found it easier to attack one another than the British.[69]

GRAVY

In mid-December Smyth left the Niagara command to Colonel Moses Porter. At last the long-suffering regulars received orders to erect log huts as winter shelters. Meanwhile, the volunteers had already run away home without waiting for official discharges. A few were so disgusted that they fled across the river to join the British. These deserters included David Harvey, who had a brother in Upper Canada. Fed up with the "rascality and tyranny" of the American army, Harvey declared a "preference to be shot by the British rather than return to the United

States." In a civil war that divided families, men could readily change sides.[70]

In upstate New York, the dispersing and contagious volunteers infected hundreds along their route home. Joseph Ellicott deemed that winter "the most sickly, and the sickness the most mortal, we have experienced since I have been in this country," a span of a dozen years. Known as "The *Buffalo Fever*," the deadly disease reached Albany, where it afflicted thirty-three members of the state assembly, killing three by early February. Lovett also blamed the legislators' way of life: "[They] eat like wolves at irregular hours, live in close rooms, broil their foreheads brown by close stoves, until the gravy runs out at their eyes, and exercise none." In the newspapers, doctors fiercely debated whether the best treatment was copious bleeding or large doses of opium, alcohol, and laxatives—probably equally deadly options.[71]

To discourage enlistments, the Federalist press played up the deadly sickness in the army, which led Republican editors to downplay the misery. Federalists cast the epidemic as a divine judgment by a just God enraged at Americans for waging an offensive war against unoffending Canadians. A pious Federalist assured Baptist Irvine, of the Baltimore Greens, that "all our misfortunes were *judgments from Heaven* for going to war." Irvine replied "that the disasters in war were occasioned, I thought, *not by God Almighty*, but by cowardly or treacherous officers." That was the best face a Republican could put on the military disasters of 1812.[72]

Irvine and his fellow Baltimore volunteers stirred up more controversy in February 1813 when they moved east to seek new quarters at Utica, another Federalist village. The landlords united to deny any lodging to the volunteers, which Irvine blasted as emulating "the plan of the *Orange Lodges* in Ireland to wage war against civil and religious liberty." Defying the Federalists, the volunteers seized a hotel "without the consent of its owner, who was then in Albany." Captain Stephen Moore reported that the seizure enraged "the disloyal and disaffected inhabitants, who . . . repeatedly threatened to dispossess me by force." Although the volunteers moved on in the spring, the Federalists made an election issue of "the late violent seizure of the Hotel in the village of Utica, by the Baltimore volunteers and Irish Greens" as evidence of military despotism.[73]

Despite riots, defeats, and epidemics, most voters clung to the Republicans. In late 1812 the citizens reelected Madison, who bested a dissident Republican from New York, DeWitt Clinton, who took an ambiguous position on the war and sought support from the Federalists. Madison prevailed in the southern and western states and in pivotal Pennsylvania, while Clinton carried New England and New York. Although the Republicans lost some northeastern seats in Congress, they retained control of both houses: 63 percent in the House and 78 percent in the Senate.[74]

In April 1813 Stephen Van Rensselaer challenged Daniel D. Tompkins for the governorship of New York. Tompkins narrowly prevailed, securing most of his margin of victory in the state's western counties. Despite bearing the brunt of the war, Niagara County voted for Tompkins by nearly two to one. An outraged Solomon Van Rensselaer assured his defeated cousin: "The die is cast, vice has again triumphed over virtue by the election of D. D. Tompkins! . . . But Jacobinism is the order of the day, and soon, very soon I fear, will this once happy Republic meet the fate of those which have gone before it." Disgusted with America, he vowed to "withdraw from politics" and to flee westward: "Canada would be my place of destination if the times would admit of it. To my native Country you know I owe nothing." Solomon Van Rensselaer felt so betrayed by Americans that he longed to live in British Canada.[75]

GAMBLE

The botched invasion compounded the British contempt for the Americans as bombastic, inept, chaotic, fractious, greedy, and cowardly. Baptist Irvine complained, "The taunts and sarcasms of the tories on both sides of the river are not to be endured." Both sides understood the war as a test of their contrasting political systems, so the British felt thrilled, and the Republicans felt humiliated, by the battles of 1812.[76]

The British also exulted that the Upper Canadian militia had performed so well at Queenston in October and at Fort Erie in November. Few had expected these men to show greater fight and resolve than the invaders. But war morale worked inversely on the belligerents: as Americans blundered and plundered, more Canadians decided to fight them.[77]

Desperate Republicans longed to reverse the spiral of defeat. In early 1813, a Kentuckian warned, "A few more disasters, a few more defeats, and I very much fear . . . disaffection, distraction, [and] disunion will follow. The cause of Republicanism will be lost." Only by conquering Canada could the Republicans cleanse the national honor from the stains inflicted by Hull, Van Rensselaer, and Smyth. And only that con-

Governor Daniel D. Tompkins *(1774–1825), oil painting by Ezra Ames, 1813. New York's Republican governor was a masterful politician who foiled and infuriated the Van Rensselaers.* (Courtesy of the Albany Institute of History and Art.)

quest could save the republic from unraveling. During the next campaign, an officer vowed "to drive before us both British & savages and sing triumphant at the standard of liberty & plant the seed of Washington in that harbour of rogues & tories, viz., Upper & Lower Canada."[78]

Playing a desperate game of double-or-nothing, the Republicans gambled everything on a new campaign planned for the spring and summer of 1813. To improve military administration, Madison eased out the inept and unpopular secretary of war, William Eustis, in favor of

John Armstrong, a veteran of the revolution and of political infighting in New York. In March 1813 Armstrong warned Dearborn that the nation could not stand another defeat: "If our first step in the campaign . . . should fail, the disgrace of our arms will be complete. The public will lose all confidence in us, and we will even cease to have any in ourselves." He exhorted Dearborn to replicate George Washington's victory at Trenton, which had rescued the Patriots at the lowest ebb of the revolution: "We are now in that state of prostration he was in after he crossed the Delaware." According to Armstrong, the fate of the republic hinged on the next campaign.[79]

Grand River Six Nations Warrior, *watercolor by Sempronius Stretton,*
1804. Painted for combat and adorned with gorget, medal, and crucifix,
such warriors terrified Americans. (Courtesy of Library and Archives
Canada, C-14827.)

CHAPTER EIGHT

SCALPS

You may rely on it that without the Indians we never could keep this country and that with them [on the British side] the Americans never will take the upper posts, . . . for in the woods, where the Americans must pass, one Indian is equal to three white men.

—John Askin, January 1813[1]

ON MAY 29, 1813, a British naval officer, James Richardson, saw an astonishing sight. From his warship on Lake Ontario, Richardson watched a boat full of American troops rowing out from the shore under a white flag. They came, he noted, "to surrender and claim our protection as prisoners of war against the savages on the shore." A terrified American officer told Richardson "that the woods were full of Indians, that he had had a fight with them that morning; and rather than fall into their hands and be massacred, he surrendered to us." The officer's alarm seemed incongruous, for he appeared "armed to the teeth, with a hanger by his side and a pair of pistols on his belt." A second boatload of his men soon followed to complete the surrender of 115 well-armed Americans, who had suffered only light casualties skirmishing with a mere thirty-six warriors.[2]

To explain the surrender, Richardson cited an American culture that wallowed in horror stories featuring Indians: "The dread of encounter with Indian foes was a striking feature among many of the Americans. . . . To the effect of nursery tales and fireside legends, aided by 'thrilling narratives' issuing from a mercenary press, the Americans are most indebted for this weakness." A New Yorker confirmed that no child was "allowed to grow up in that region, without imbibing . . . hatred and horror of the Indians. Tales of Indian cruelties were in the mouths of all mothers and nurses."[3]

Britons valued Indian warriors because they scared Americans. A British agent noted, "The Americans . . . are constantly in Alarm either by an Indian War or at least the shadow of Bands of Indians. They imagine their heads in danger of being scalped." At Detroit, an American official agreed, "A war with England has no terrors compared with those arising from their savage allies." Such alarmism gripped the settlers of Canton, Ohio, on the night of August 3–4, 1812, when a stray gunshot at dusk suggested rampaging Indians to the settlers. Benjamin Mortimer, a Moravian missionary, reported that the terrified Cantonians huddled under arms for several days, although "not an Indian was to be seen or heard of." Mortimer blamed the panic on the women, who told "each other the most frightful stories which they had ever heard concerning the cruelties of the Indians in war, and thence to form strong representations of what great evils might befall themselves."[4]

The American dread derived, in part, from the very real prowess of native warriors in guerrilla combat. Masters of sudden raids and deadly ambushes, warriors intimidated far beyond their numbers. Trained from youth in handling firearms, and adept as hunters, the warriors were better shots than almost all Americans or Britons. Warriors terrified both by their silent approach and by their sudden sound and fury in attack, for their piercing screams chilled all but the most hardened foes. In hand-to-hand combat their knives and tomahawks made quick work of their enemies.[5]

In addition to that real prowess, the Indian customs of war terrified the Americans. By scalping the dead, warriors took trophies of victory and dishonored the enemy. Sometimes the victors mutilated corpses to make a terrifying impression on those who would discover them. In the spring of 1812 in Indiana, an American soldier found a settler family of five "shockingly cut up with the tomahawk and scalping knife. The man had his breast opened, his entrails torn out and strewed about the ground." Such displays often spooked entire settlements into flight, for panics were more common than the heroic defense of hearth and home so celebrated in patriotic histories of the settler frontier.[6]

Bodily mutilations horrified Americans as desecrations of the divine image, for they held the Christian belief that an intact and decently buried corpse had a better chance at eventual resurrection in heaven. Americans developed a lurid fascination with mutilation, particularly of women and children. In December 1811 Detroit's inhabitants declared: "The tenderest infant, yet imbibing nutrition from the mamilia of maternal love, and the agonized mother herself, alike wait the stroke of the relentless tomahawk. . . . Nothing which breathes the breath of life is spared. . . . It is in the dead of the night, in the darkness of the moon, in the howling of the [wolf] that the demoniac deed is done." In lurid rhetoric, Americans lumped all native peoples together as brutal savages—although both sides scalped the dead, killed prisoners, and plundered civilians. Americans, however, had a greater and morbid fascination with bodily mutilation. They also had access to printing presses to spread and perpetuate their words to our own time.[7]

The fear of warriors generated loathing, a categorical hatred of all Indians as murderous savages who deserved extermination. Dread and hatred were alternating emotional currents affecting the same people depending on circumstances. When endowed with superior numbers over vulnerable natives, Americans could butcher natives of all ages and both genders, which the vindictive called a just revenge. But fear trumped hatred when Americans ventured into a densely forested country possessed by Indians who had British help. In forest combat, American troops confronted their own nightmares, something far more terrible than real Indians. An American soldier's greatest foe lurked in his own vivid imagination.[8]

DREAD

Conditioned by childhood stories, soldiers expected the worst whenever they heard, saw, or imagined Indians. In July 1812 Captain Charles McNeill ventured into the woods along New York's northern border with Lower Canada:

> It was said to be very dangerous. We heard frightfull storys every day on the road. The last night we lay out in the woods . . . we was allarmed at the Dawn of Day with Dreadfull news of savage depredations—fires, murders, &c., &c., in three miles of us said to be hundreds of Indians.

In September 1812 a Kentucky volunteer recalled marching into the Indian country north of the Ohio River; that advance "seemed to shake the boasted valor of some of our bravest heroes." In July 1813 General James Wilkinson declared that traveling through an Indian country had inflicted "more anxiety, than half a dozen, well fought Battles would produce." While hatred for Indians mobilized Americans to fight the war, that hatred became a paralyzing dread when they went into combat in the northern forest.[9]

During the summer of 1813 an American midshipman landed on the enemy shore of Lake Ontario. Although he saw no Indians before hastily returning to his ship, the midshipman believed that his shore party had nearly "been surrounded and massacred by the Savages and English." His fear derived from news that another American party had been found nearby "most shockingly butchered, their heads skinned, their hearts taken out and put in their mouths, their privates cut off and put in the places of their hearts. We . . . narrowly escaped a similar fate." His privates intact but his nerves shaken, the midshipman blasted his superiors for risking his life in an Indian country.[10]

Playing on the shaky nerves of their foes, clever Indians performed a theater of intimidation. In July 1813 a Canadian captain, William Hamilton Merritt, found Indians holding captive some pitiful Americans: "The poor devils were crying and imploring me to save their lives, as I was the only white they saw." The Indians covertly assured Merritt that they would spare the prisoners but would first *frighten them a great deal to prevent them coming again.*"[11]

Americans bitterly complained that the British failed to protect the prisoners taken by the Indians, but the British dared not alienate their allies, known as "Nitchies" after the Ojibwa greeting, *Shaygo, Niigii* (Hello, Friend). On the Niagara front in 1813 Lieutenant John Le Couteur saw "a poor unfortunate American Soldier" held prisoner by the Mohawk: "The poor fellow implored us to ransom or rescue Him from his sad fate and shed many tears." But the captors refused ransom, and Le Couteur concluded, "Rescue Him we dared not, [for] it would have lost us an alliance of seven hundred Indians, most invaluable allies they were—no surprises with Nitchie on the lookout."[12]

British commanders coveted Indians to harry the flanks of American armies and to harass their retreats into bloody routs or sudden surrenders. After watching a few Indians spook an American army into flight, Major Robert McDouall exulted: "Our Indians prove themselves right worthy & right useful auxiliaries. Macbeth says ' 'tis the eye of childhood that fears a painted devil,' but it is so far lucky that our opponents are mere infants in the sublime science of war."[13]

As American defeats mounted, the frustrated Republicans longed to wipe the Indians out. The *Aurora* concluded, "The hand of vengeance must be raised against them, and a war of extermination waged until they shall disappear from the borders of our extensive country." The *Baltimore Whig* proposed, "Hang *four or five* Indians for every American massacred, and if it does not bring them to their *senses* it will at least go some way towards their *extermination*." Unable to defeat Indians in battle, Republicans indulged in genocidal fantasies.[14]

They also sought consolation in a propaganda that denounced the

British for manipulating bloodthirsty savages. In Congress, Henry Clay refuted Federalists who described Canadians as the unoffending victims of an American invasion:

> Canada innocent? Canada unoffending? Is it not in Canada that the tomahawk of the savage had been moulded into its death-like form? Has it not been from Canadian magazines, Malden and others, that those supplies have been issued? Supplies which have enabled the savage hordes to butcher the garrison of Chicago and to commit other horrid murders?

Even Madison lost his usual measured restraint to vent lurid denunciations of the British alliance with Indians. In March 1813 he assured Congress that the British were "eager to glut their savage thirst with the blood of the vanquished, and to finish the work of torture and death on maimed and defenceless captives."[15]

Republicans praised their own refusal to employ Indians as a pointed contrast to the British, whom they accused of buying scalps at six dollars each. General William Henry Harrison boasted, "Let an account of the

A Bloody Scalp. *From Benson J. Lossing,* The Pictorial Field-Book of the War of 1812 *(New York, 1869), 493.* (Courtesy of the New York State Library.)

murdered innocence be opened in the records of Heaven against our enemies alone; the American soldiers will follow the example of his government, and neither the sword of the one will be raised against the helpless or the fallen, nor the gold of the other paid for the scalp of a massacred enemy." The *Aurora* promoted a new map of Upper Canada to reveal the "country where the scalps of infants, whose flaxen locks scarce afford a hold for the ruffian hand of the ferocious savage, less cruel than the blood-buying monsters, *who pay the premiums* for such butcheries, were taken." Although defeated in battle, the Republicans hoped, to win a propaganda war.[16]

FIRST SCALP

The American propaganda embarrassed British officers, who considered themselves paragons of civilization. The Britons retorted that the Indians had every right to defend their own lands in their own way against American aggression. The British also insisted that they did everything possible to moderate the Indian mode of war. Far from buying scalps, the Crown paid only for captives, which encouraged the warriors to spare lives.[17]

Britons added that the Americans employed their own savages: the frontiersmen from Kentucky. The British regarded Kentuckians as bloodthirsty brutes, who had devolved from civilization by adopting the Indian mode of war. Sergeant James Commins reported:

These Kentucky men are wretches suborned by the Government and capable of the greatest villanies. They are served out with blanket clothing like the Indians, with a long scalloping knife and other barbarous articles and with Red Paint with which they daub themselves all over and in summer nearly went naked. In this manner, they would surprise our piquets and, after engagements, they scallop the killed and wounded that could not get out of their way.... The Americans not being able to flatter their own Indians over to Canada induced them to make a fool of the Kentucky men, being the most barbarous, illiterate beings in America.

When General Hull rebuked a British officer for employing Indians as allies, he retorted "as a justification of such conduct, that our government *would send the Kentuckians into Canada.*"[18]

Kentuckians did take Indian scalps as cherished tokens of masculine prowess. Enlisting as a ranger in June 1812, John Ketcham recalled, "In

General Winchester at Frenchtown, *1813. From the* Morning Chronicle *of London, this caricature mocks the humiliation of an American general, stripped and painted by his Indian captors. The British troops and officers laugh beside an implausible palm tree.* (Courtesy of Library and Archives Canada, C-123432.)

Frenchtown Massacre, *1813. This engraving conveys the far darker American image of the battle as culminating in a massacre, with the burning and scalping of wounded prisoners by drunken savages while Procter's army camps nearby, complicit in the brutality. In fact Procter had withdrawn almost all of his troops to Amherstburg.* (Courtesy of the William L. Clements Library, University of Michigan.)

my first month's service, I killed and scalped an Indian—was very proud of it—got leave to go to Kentucky to show it to my Daddy and Mamma. I guess they thought I had done about right." A Pennsylvania officer reported that Captain Ballard of Kentucky returned from captivity with a hidden treasure:

> He had two Indian scalps that he had taken at Frenchtown, and had concealed them in the waist band of his pantaloons while a prisoner. While in the fort with us, he ripped open his waist band, took out the scalps, fleshed them with his knife, salted them, and set them in hoops in true Indian style. He said he had twenty scalps at home, and . . . that he would raise fifty scalps before he would die.

Ballard had risked his life to keep his precious trophies, for his Indian captors had killed every Kentuckian found with a scalp.[19]

Indians called Kentuckians "Big Knives" because of their especially large scalping knives. An Ottawa chief, Black Bird, assured the British: "If the Big Knives, when they kill people of our color, leave them without hacking them to pieces, we will follow their example. They have themselves to blame." Indians scoffed at the American propaganda that cast frontiersmen as the innocent victims of unprovoked savagery.[20]

Indeed, an American took the first scalp in the war. On July 25, 1812, during Hull's brief invasion of Upper Canada, Captain William McCulloch killed and scalped a Menominee warrior. That mutilation enraged the Menominee, who had honored a British request not to scalp any of Hull's men. Carrying the corpse back to Amherstburg, the angry warriors confronted the British officers and vowed to resume scalping their enemies. Ten days later McCulloch fell into an Indian ambush and lost his own scalp—to the delight of the Menominee.[21]

REMEMBER

A village of twenty houses, Frenchtown lay beside the Raisin River and within the dangerous zone between the British garrisons at Detroit and Amherstburg and the American troops encamped to the south, in the Maumee Valley of Ohio. Fearing an American advance, the British commander, Sir Henry Procter, and his Indian allies pressured the *habitants* of Frenchtown to take up arms as British subjects. Procter began to arrest holdouts while the Indians threatened to kill their livestock and burn their farms. Instead of submitting, the desperate *habitants* sent two emissaries to beg the American forward commander, General James Winchester, to rescue them: "Five hundred true and brave Americans can . . . secure us from being forced to prison and the whole place from being burned by savage fury."[22]

The appeal agitated the volatile Kentuckians who composed Winchester's little army. An officer demanded, "Can we turn a deaf ear to the cries of men, women and children, about to perish under the scalping knife and tomahawk of the savage?" A weak commander, Winchester dared not resist the popular tide among his men. Lurching across the Maumee River, Winchester's volunteers crossed thirty-five miles of snowy ground to Frenchtown. On January 18, their attack routed the small garrison of British regulars and Indian allies. But the reckless volunteers had advanced far beyond the support of their reserves in Ohio, and dangerously close (just twenty-six miles) to the enemy at Detroit and Amherstburg. A feckless commander, Winchester carelessly dispersed his troops around the village and took his own lodging a half-mile away.[23]

At dawn on January 22, the Kentuckians awoke, in the words of one man, to "the thundering of cannon and roar of small arms, and the more terrific yelling of savages." Procter had arrived with 1,200 men, half of them Indians, a quarter regulars, and a quarter militia. At the village, the Americans fought hard, inflicting heavy casualties with rifle fire on the British regulars. But the Indians overwhelmed the camp's exposed right flank, where the volunteers panicked and fled—a fatal mistake, for they foundered in the deep snow, easy marks for mounted warriors. Capturing the terrified Winchester, the Indians stripped off his uniform and painted his skin before surrendering him to Procter. Playing upon the American dread, Procter persuaded Winchester to order his men in the village to surrender as the only way to avert their slaughter. In disgust, the troops threw down their arms. Six hundred became prisoners while another three hundred lay dead or dying.[24]

Procter feared (needlessly) that another larger American army was closing fast, so he hastily retreated to Amherstburg, taking the able-bodied prisoners and almost all of his troops. Stripped of their coats, pants, and shoes by the Indians, the prisoners suffered severely from the bitter cold of the Canadian winter. At Amherstburg they were assaulted by angry women who, Procter reported, hated the Kentuckians "as a band of banditti, who without cause or provocation had invaded their territory." Unable to feed so many prisoners, Procter sent them to the Niagara front for repatriation.[25]

At Frenchtown Procter left behind a handful of militiamen to guard eighty American prisoners too badly wounded to move. The guards proved too few to restrain about two hundred Indians who lingered to plunder the *habitants*. When the prisoners begged for protection against the warriors, the guards replied, "We are afraid of them ourselves." On the morning of January 23, the guards fled, while the warriors set on fire the two houses that held the prisoners. Some died in the flames, and the Indians tomahawked and scalped those who crawled or limped out of the blazing buildings. A shocked British officer recalled the "fierce glare of the flames, the crashing of the roofs, the sacrificing of the dying wretches enveloped in fire, and the savage triumphant yelling" of the Indians. At least thirty, and perhaps sixty, Americans died. A survivor reported that scavenging pigs ran about "with sculls, arms, legs, and other parts of the human system in their mouths." A *habitant* testified, "The hogs appeared to be rendered mad by so profuse a diet of Christian flesh."[26]

The Raisin River massacre again exposed the conflict as a civil war. The overmatched guard had been commanded by a Late Loyalist, Captain William Elliott. Before the war, Elliott had visited Kentucky, where Captain Nathaniel Hart had been his generous host, nursing him through a nearly fatal illness. But at Frenchtown, Elliott could not save the wounded Hart from the warriors.[27]

The Indians did spare the life of the *habitant* Captain Jean Baptiste Beaugrand, but on the condition that he tomahawk a captive Kentuckian. By offering that deadly choice, the Indians sought to compromise the Frenchtown *habitants* as their allies, thereby alienating them from the Americans. When the Americans later recovered Michigan, they tried Beaugrand for murder, but a local jury acquitted him, for they too well knew the duress that he had suffered.[28]

The victory won Procter a promotion to major general, but the sordid aftermath disturbed many British officers, who knew how adept Americans were at turning military defeats into propaganda victories. A military surgeon, Dr. Robert Richardson, sighed, "Be assured we have not heard the last of this shameful transaction." In July Congress published a lurid report that cast the "Raisin River Massacre" as the ultimate war crime and castigated Procter as the evil mastermind of savage depravity. Highlighting the massacre diverted attention from Winchester's humiliating defeat the day before. By waving the bloody scalp, Republicans shifted the focus away from their mistakes onto the misdeeds of the British and their Indian allies.[29]

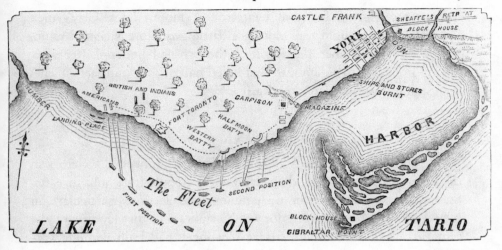

The American Attack on York, *1813. From Benson J. Lossing,* The Pictorial Field-Book of the War of 1812 *(New York, 1869), 590.* (Courtesy of the New York State Library.)

In the propaganda war, the "Raisin River Massacre" became the Republican trump card. When a British official complained that American privateersmen mistreated their prisoners, General John Mason retorted that nothing could match the atrocities committed

> on the Raisin River . . . and elsewhere, when the Indians, in British pay, fighting by the side of British troops, and afterwards thanked in general orders by British officers, were permitted to murder by piecemeal, to hack, to mangle, and to torture unto slow death, and to burn alive, American citizens, their prisoners; and, as if to fill the measure of savage enormity, to expose the bodies of these wretched sufferers to be devoured on the surface by every passing vermin.

In vain Britons tried to dismiss the charges as the exaggerations of hypocrites who also employed tomahawks and scalping knives in the ruthless warfare of the frontier.[30]

"Remember the Raisin!" became a rallying cry to raise recruits. In April 1813 General Green Clay addressed his Kentucky volunteer brigade: "Should we encounter the enemy—REMEMBER THE DREADFUL FATE OF OUR BUTCHERED BROTHERS AT THE RAISIN RIVER—*that British treachery produced their slaughter.*" But such gruesome rhetoric had limits as motivation, for the anger could lead to recklessness followed by terror. A month later, Clay's men ignored orders to hold back during a battle near Fort Meigs in Ohio. Bellowing "Remember the Raisin!," they rushed helter-skelter after fleeing Indians into an ambush that killed half of the volunteers. Clay's men should have forgotten the Raisin.[31]

YORK

By the spring of 1813 the Madison administration needed a victory in the worst way. Otherwise, the war's waning popularity would threaten the Republican candidates in the pending state elections, particularly in New York. The best prospect for a quick military victory lay along Lake Ontario, where Commodore Isaac Chauncey had built enough warships to secure an American edge. Naval command of the lake would permit American troops to take the offensive against Upper Canada once the spring thaw freed the warships from the winter's ice. In preparation for the campaign, General Henry Dearborn had spent the winter concentrating four thousand men at Sackets Harbor, a naval base about thirty-five miles southeast of Kingston, the principal British post on the lake.[32]

Fearing that Kingston had too strong a British garrison, Dearborn sought a surer victory by attacking a secondary target: York. Poorly fortified and lightly defended (by seven hundred men), York also promised a symbolic payoff as the capital of Upper Canada. And there was the allure of a warship, the *Sir Isaac Brock*, under construction at York. By capturing and completing that ship, the Americans could increase and prolong their command of Lake Ontario. Departing from Sackets Harbor on April 25, fourteen American warships carried 1,700 soldiers across the stormy lake to York. During the early morning of April 27, the troops boarded small boats and rowed ashore west of the town. The green-clad riflemen of Major Benjamin Forsyth led the way, dispersing some Mississauga Indians in the woods. Covered by cannon fire from the ships, General Zebulon Pike commanded the main strike along the shore, driving back the British regulars and capturing their batteries. For the first time in the war, American troops fought well in a major battle, albeit against smaller numbers.[33]

Making the best of a bad situation, the British commander, General Roger H. Sheaffe, ordered a retreat by his regulars toward Kingston to the east. He had fires set to destroy the *Sir Isaac Brock* and to blow up a stock of gunpowder in a stone storehouse. The massive explosion sent skyward a deafening fireball and tons of stone, which fell in a deadly rain on the advancing American troops, killing 38 and wounding 222. The dead included General Pike, but some of the wounded fared worse. For forty-eight hours, without food or sleep, an army surgeon operated on "his fellow creatures . . . mashed & mangled in every part, with a leg— an arm—a head, or a body ground to pieces." The wounded screamed, "Oh, Dear! Oh Dear! Oh my God! My God! Do Doctor, Doctor! Do cut of[f] my leg! My arm! My head! To relieve me from misery! I can't live! I can't live!"[34]

The explosion stunned and halted the American troops. Deprived of Pike's leadership, they dreaded more explosions. Aged and ailing, Dearborn failed to leave his ship to take charge of his stalled force. The confusion and delay enabled Sheaffe to make good his escape with the regulars and allowed flames to consume the precious *Sir Isaac Brock*, denying the Americans the fruits of victory.[35]

York's magistrates and militia officers negotiated terms of surrender with the American officers, who agreed to protect private property and to parole the local militiamen, who pledged not to serve until formally exchanged. In return, the town fathers promised to surrender all government and military property. But both sides soon felt betrayed. Dearborn refused to ratify the agreement for a day because he resented the burning of the warship as a violation of the terms. During his delay, American soldiers and sailors looted the town. The town's Anglican priest, John Strachan, blasted Dearborn's hesitation as "a deception calculated to give the riflemen time to plunder, and after the town had been robbed, they would then perhaps sign the capitulation and tell us they respected private property."[36]

Dearborn's belated ratification did little to slow the looting, for the officers could not control their men. The magistrates concluded that "the great degree of insubordination that prevailed among his troops rendered such orders of no effect." York's leading militia officer, William Allan, reported, "Few houses in the town escaped a minute search by two or three parties, under the pretext of looking for public property. Many have been pillaged and some have had everything taken." The sheriff John Beikie noted, "Those who abandoned their Houses found nothing but the bare walls at their return." The looters also hit Strachan's Anglican church and the town's subscription library, and they hauled off the town's fire engines and destroyed the local printing press, casting the type into the harbor.[37]

The most talented looters belonged to Major Forsyth's riflemen, who had been assigned to guard the town against thieves. An American naval officer marveled:

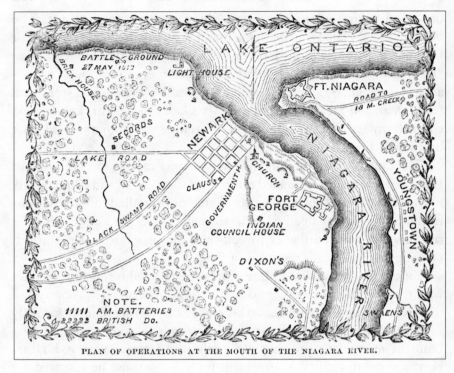

PLAN OF OPERATIONS AT THE MOUTH OF THE NIAGARA RIVER.

Plan of Operations at the Mouth of the Niagara River, 1813. Dearborn's army landed on the lakeshore west of the lighthouse and swept into Newark, while the British evacuated Fort George, retreating south and then west to safety. From Benson J. Lossing, The Pictorial Field-Book of the War of 1812 *(New York, 1869), 599. (Courtesy of the New York State Library.)*

Some of them have had handkerchiefs full, and have made several hundred dollars in one battle. They have mashed up, between two stones, some of the most elegant Silver embost urns, turines and plate of every discription to get them in their napsacks. The officers generally attempt to prevent it; but Forsyth is a perfect savage himself. He, it is said, encourages it.

The riflemen took special pains to ransack the home of Major James Givins, an officer in the Indian Department. Strachan noted: "[Dearborn] confesses that he is not able to protect any family connected with the Indians." While British commanders conceded that they could not control their Indian allies, American commanders failed to restrain their own troops bent on vengeance against natives and their British agents.[38]

Dearborn and Chauncey ordered the burning of the fortifications, barracks, and military storehouses, but freelancing sailors exceeded those orders by also torching the twin Parliament buildings. To justify their arson, they claimed to have found a scalp "suspended near the Speaker's chair, in company with the Mace & other Emblems of Royalty." That brazen placement seemed to confirm the close ties between Indian violence and British rule in Canada. But would British officials truly have given a public place of honor to a scalp? One Upper Canadian plausibly argued that the sailors found the scalp elsewhere and then planted it beside the mace as a joke on their officers. If so, the joke became deadly serious, for Chauncey and Dearborn officially reported the discovery of the damning scalp to their superiors in Washington. In Congress and the press, Republicans pounced on that scalp to excuse the ravaging of York.[39]

FORT GEORGE

On May 1 the invaders embarked in Chauncey's vessels, and York reverted to British control. Rather than leave some men to garrison the town, Dearborn concentrated his forces on the Niagara River for an attack on Fort George. Drawing reinforcements across the lake from Sackets Harbor, Dearborn assembled 4,500 troops at Fort Niagara. To defend Fort George and the adjoining village of Newark, General John Vincent had only 1,000 regulars, 300 militia, and 100 Indians. As at York, the relative paucity of Indians relieved the American attackers from their greatest fear.[40]

Watching from a ship, Dearborn entrusted the attack to Colonel Winfield Scott, the able and ambitious young officer recently returned from his British captivity. At dawn on May 27, under cover of fog on the lake and fire from Chauncey's warships, the American troops rowed ashore in large, open boats. Landing on the beach northwest of Newark, their superior numbers overwhelmed the British, who fell back after suffering heavy casualties. Evacuating Fort George, Vincent retreated to Burlington Heights, sixty miles to the west. He also withdrew the small British garrisons from Queenston, Chippawa, and Fort Erie, abandoning the entire Niagara front to the victorious Americans.[41]

Hungry for a complete victory, Scott began a vigorous pursuit (despite a broken collarbone), but he was called back by his superiors, Generals Morgan Lewis and John Boyd. Fearful men, they preferred not to risk their army on an advance into the heavily forested hinterland, where they dreaded an Indian ambush. Scott groused that before Boyd

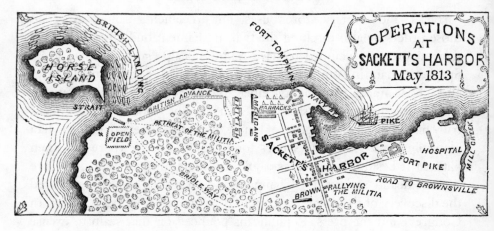

Operations at Sackett's Harbor, May 1813. *Prevost's British force landed on Horse Island and crossed to the shore, routing the militia and heading east to attack the regulars entrenched at the village. From Benson J. Lossing,* The Pictorial Field-Book of the War of 1812 *(New York, 1869), 612. (Courtesy of the New York State Library.)*

and Lewis had landed, there was "no General present to spoil my sport." The delay saved and thrilled the British. Colonel John Harvey recalled, "This display of the total want of Enterprize in the Enemy's Generals gave me a most encouraging impression of their talents." Once again, a showy victory had proved a hollow shell, as the British saved most of their men to fight another day.[42]

Instead of chasing the British, the American troops lingered at Newark to plunder the dead and wounded as well as the houses and stores of civilians. Essential for any further pursuit of the British, Forsyth's riflemen were too busy looting the village. American civilians also rushed across the Niagara River to seek booty. In "many log cabins" on the New York side of the river, an officer later saw expensive tables, chairs, and mirrors taken from the finer homes of Newark. When the villagers returned home, "They found empty rooms and bare walls." Charged with failing to protect the village, Lewis defensively claimed that "every house . . . was plundered by the British Forces previous to our taking possession of it"—an impossibility given the thoroughness of the looting and the hasty British retreat.[43]

SACKETS HARBOR

To counter Dearborn's assault on the Niagara front, Sir George Prevost and Sir James Yeo, the new British naval commander on Lake Ontario, attacked the American naval base at Sackets Harbor. In addition to destroying the fortified dockyard, Prevost and Yeo hoped to capture a powerful new warship, the *General Pike*, then nearing completion. Away supporting Dearborn's attack on Fort George, Chauncey had left his base uncovered by the navy and thinly garrisoned by regular troops.[44]

On May 29, 750 British troops landed at a point west of the harbor. After quickly routing the 700 militia guarding that beachhead, the British pushed eastward until halted by a heavy fire from 750 American regulars entrenched near the harbor. Daunted by the loss of a quarter of his force, Prevost suddenly ordered a retreat. Because the Americans failed to pursue, the British safely reembarked and sailed back to Kingston. Used to victory, the British officers blamed Prevost for their surprising setback, accusing him of losing his nerve at the critical moment.[45]

Although they claimed victory, the Americans paid dearly for it. During the heat of battle, a confused naval lieutenant expected defeat, so he set fires to destroy the dockyard. When the British withdrew, the dock workers saved the new warship from the flames, but they could not rescue the naval supplies in the blazing warehouses. The losses included the plunder taken at York, which reduced the American gain from that costly victory to one old scalp which Dearborn had already sent to the secretary of war.[46]

But the greatest loss was of Chauncey's confidence in the army. Upon learning of the attack, the commodore hastily sailed back to Sackets Harbor, arriving on June 1 to find his supplies in ashes. He bitterly blamed the American generals who had exposed his cherished base to assault by drawing his fleet away to support their attack on Fort George. Thereafter, Chauncey put a higher priority on defending Sackets Harbor than on assisting army offensives. Although Dearborn's troops soon faced a British counterattack, Chauncey refused to come to their rescue. On June 11, he assured the secretary of the navy that "upon more mature reflection I have determined to remain at this place and preserve the new ship at all hazards." Chauncey's priority gave Yeo a free hand to harass Dearborn's army at the western end of the lake. By souring relations between the American army and navy, Chauncey's reaction turned the battle into a British victory.[47]

In the short term, the battle's one clear winner was the militia commander, Jacob Brown. Although most of his men had fled, Brown rallied a few to help the regulars defend the fortifications. Near the end of the battle, the regular commander, Colonel Electus Backus, took a fatal bul-

Commodore Isaac Chauncey (1772–1840). (Courtesy of the Toronto Reference Library, Toronto Public Library Board, T-15206.)

let. Taking command, Brown subsequently wrote the official report, in which he shrewdly amplified his role in the victory. The Republican press and the War Department endorsed that report, for they needed a war hero from New York to popularize the war in that key state. As his reward, Brown won a general's commission in the regular army.[48]

STONEY CREEK

On June 1 Dearborn sent Generals William Winder and John Chandler with 2,500 men westward in belated pursuit of General John Vincent's 1,600 troops. Hemmed in by the Niagara Escarpment, a three-hundred-foot cliff, to the south, the advancing Americans stuck to the road along the north shore of the Niagara Peninsula. The American commanders were military amateurs: a former Baltimore lawyer (Winder) and a Maine blacksmith (Chandler), who had won their com-

U.S.S. General Pike, 1813, *plan by C. Ware.* (Courtesy of the U.S. Naval Historical Center, NH-57006.)

missions as political patronage for their Republican exertions. Late on June 5, their brigades reached Stoney Creek, about fifty miles west of Fort George. After a brief skirmish with British guards, the Americans encamped for the night. Carelessly arranging their camp, Winder and Chandler posted few sentries, which invited a British night attack in the early hours of June 6.[49]

Lacking Indians, the British regulars and Canadian militia simulated warriors by adopting their war scream. A slumbering American awoke to a panicked "sentinel running in among us, screaming 'Indians! Indians!' " Another soldier recalled feeling "surrounded . . . by all the Indians in Canada." An Upper Canadian remembered, "we yelled like Indians. I tell you those simple fellows did run." In the darkness, smoke, and noise, both sides became confused and entangled, firing on their own men as well as the enemy. An American soldier recalled, "The British shouting, Indians yelling, arms clashing, men screaming, begging, groaning, dying, swearing, and fighting." Struggling to find their men, Chandler and Winder instead stumbled upon the British and became prisoners. Leaderless, the Americans retreated, abandoning their cannon.[50]

On June 7 Dearborn sent two more bunglers, Generals Boyd and Lewis, to take command of the advance force. That evening, Yeo's flotilla suddenly appeared at the western end of the lake, while Chauncey remained holed up at Sackets Harbor. Worse still, the British victory at Stoney Creek inspired their Indian allies to return to the fray. While a British fleet menaced the Americans to the north, the Indians appeared ominously along the high escarpment that hemmed in the Americans to the south. Caught between a lake and a hard place, the invaders panicked and fled eastward, seeking the safety of Fort George. In their haste, they abandoned boats, provisions, ammunition, and tents: another expensive loss to a republic that pinched pennies. Amused by the panic, a British officer insisted that a few hundred Indians would suffice "to carry terror & dismay thro' the American army. It is inconceivable the horror & dread which they have of the Indians."[51]

A week before, Dearborn's men assumed that they had virtually conquered Upper Canada. But now they lay cooped up within Fort George and Newark, abandoning the rest of the Niagara District to the resurgent British. After two hollow victories, all Dearborn had to show for his bloody campaign was a single Canadian fort and an adjoining village. An American officer lamented, "Had a map of the United States been published on or about the first of June, it would have exhibited quite a respectable addendum to our territory. But the expansion proved to be only a bubble on the frontiers of New York, which burst after a few weeks' inflation."[52]

A British officer, Colonel John Harvey, understood that Stoney Creek's "most important result was that produced on the Morale of the enemy's Troops." At Fort George an American officer sadly recalled, "Misery was in large company." Crowding, cold rains, and wretched sanitation promoted dysentery, a depleting and sometimes fatal disorder of the bowels. On June 23, a weary Dearborn wrote, "Incessant rains still continue; it is rare to have two dry days in succession." The rainy season bred biting mosquitoes, which conveyed the region's debilitating malaria, which deepened the malaise among the troops, who began to desert in large numbers. An officer reported that the demoralized troops were "more durty and filthy than any set of Men I have ever seen in Service." The sickness and desertion decreased the garrison's able-bodied "effectives" from 4,500 in late May to 3,500 a month later. The incapac-

Lieutenant James FitzGibbon (*1780–1863*), *by an unknown artist*. (Courtesy of the Toronto Reference Library, Toronto Public Library Board.)

itated included Dearborn, who was worn down by fever, age, self-doubt, and the stress of command.[53]

By default, command slipped to Morgan Lewis, who inspired even less confidence than had Dearborn. Fifty-nine years old, Lewis was a wealthy landlord and hack politician who had served as New York's governor until defeated by Daniel D. Tompkins in 1807. On the eve of the war, Lewis was a state senator whose "political stupidity" aggravated the state's Republican kingpin, Judge Ambrose Spencer. To get Lewis out of the state senate, Spencer had him appointed as a general, revealing the priority that the Republicans gave to politics. Lewis also benefited from his ties to John Armstrong, for the two men had married sisters from the prestigious Livingston family. Dull, lazy, and luxurious, Lewis cherished his creature comforts. Peter B. Porter complained that General Lewis lumbered along with "two stately waggons . . . carrying the various furniture of a Secretary of State's office, a lady's dressing chamber, an alderman's dining room, & the contents of a grocer's shop."[54]

On June 20, Lewis departed for Sackets Harbor, which left the active command at Fort George to John Boyd. During the 1790s Boyd had served in India as a mercenary officer employed by native princes.

Returning to America a rich man, he secured a colonel's commission in the U.S. Army in 1808. Showing courage at Tippecanoe in 1811, he won promotion to brigadier general a year later. Able at executing the orders of superiors, Boyd lacked the intelligence, resolve, and imagination to command an army. Scott considered him "respectable, as a subordinate, but vacillating and imbecile, beyond all endurance, as a chief under high responsibilities." More vividly, Lewis derided Boyd as "better adapted to [be] the Bully of a Brothel" than to command an army.[55]

BEAVER DAMS

On the Niagara front, the American troops still outnumbered the British by two to one, but the hunters had become the hunted. Dreading the forest full of Indians and the roads clogged with mud, the Americans waited in vain for Chauncey to recover command of the lake, which would free them to move in boats. Meanwhile, Yeo's British flotilla freely ranged the lake to raid New York villages and pick off American boats carrying supplies to Niagara. Desperate for provisions and fodder, Boyd sent out scouting parties to plunder the farms and mills within a dozen miles of Fort George. But these forays increasingly fell into ambushes set by the British and their Indian allies. An American officer recalled that each probe found "the limits of safe marching more and more contracted."[56]

The lone American to thrive in this petty war was Major Cyrenius Chapin, a forty-four-year-old commander of mounted volunteers recruited at Buffalo. Chapin was a rare Federalist who broke with his party to assist the war. An entrepreneurial Yankee, he had practiced medicine in frontier Buffalo for nearly a decade. Fond of profanity and alcohol, he sought thrills and profits by leading cross-border raids. Chapin insisted that he took only public property kept by notorious Tories, by which he meant magistrates and militia officers who defended British rule. But his volunteers became known as "the Forty Thieves," who made more enemies than friends by their rampant looting.[57]

To counter the Forty Thieves, General Vincent relied on thirty-two-year-old Lieutenant James FitzGibbon. Born poor in Ireland, he was bright, ambitious, and daring. Enlisting in 1796 as a teenage private in the British army, he impressed his regiment's lieutenant colonel, the future general Isaac Brock, who helped FitzGibbon to win an officer's commission. Tall and powerfully built, FitzGibbon commanded attention. His men performed superbly because they trusted in his keen attention, bold decision, and good luck.[58]

In 1813 FitzGibbon organized an independent company of fifty rangers. Because most were fellow Irishmen, they called themselves "the Irish Greens." Their ethnicity and green uniforms confused Americans, who associated the Irish with the republican cause and that color with their own riflemen. But in this civil war, the Irish fought on both sides. To add to their aura of menace, FitzGibbon's rangers also named themselves "the Bloody Boys." To suppress the American foragers, FitzGibbon posted his men at a country crossroads known as De Cou's, about eighteen miles southwest of Fort George.[59]

Because the Bloody Boys were bad for Chapin's looting, he urged General Boyd to attack their post. Boyd cleared the mission with Dearborn, who gave the command to Lieutenant Colonel Charles G. Boerstler. Dashing but dim, Boerstler longed to prove his ability to lead an attack, but he had to rely on Chapin as a guide, and the two men despised each other. Boerstler had 575 men: more than enough to deal with the 60 Indians and 50 Britons that Chapin claimed to have seen at De Cou's. In fact, he had never been there, and about 465 Mohawk Indians awaited along with FitzGibbon's Bloody Boys.[60]

The expedition repeated Winchester's folly by recklessly advancing into the heart of the enemy's country, too close to other British forces and too far from American reinforcement. To compound the folly, Boyd assigned a miscast set of troops to Boerstler's command: several companies of regular infantry, a company of light artillery, a small troop of dragoons, and Chapin's volunteers. Save for the volunteers, these units lacked experience fighting in the woods—unlike Forsyth's riflemen, who remained behind on guard duty at Fort George.[61]

Despite the need for speed and surprise Boerstler's men moved ponderously, hauling along two heavy supply wagons and two cannon through the thick mud of a bad road that ascended the escarpment. It took them nearly two days to cover seventeen miles. Along the way, loose-lipped officers, including Chapin, boasted of their destination to a Canadian woman, Laura Secord, who slipped ahead to alert FitzGibbon.[62]

At a place called Beaver Dams, two miles short of their destination, the American troops plunged into their greatest nightmare: an Indian ambush. Covered by trees, the Indians inflicted heavy casualties, while the Americans wasted their ammunition on erratic volleys into the woods. When Boerstler's regulars charged with bayonets, the nimble Indians dodged out of the way to find new trees as firing posts.[63]

After three hours of fierce combat in blistering heat, thirty Americans lay dead or dying compared to only five Indians. Taking a cue from

Brigadier General John P. Boyd (*1764–1830*),
engraving by Charles B. J. F. de Saint-Mémin,
1802. (Courtesy of the National Portrait Gallery,
Smithsonian Institution; gift of Mr. and Mrs. Paul
Mellon.)

Brock, FitzGibbon sent a white flag with an ominous message to Boerstler: the Americans must surrender to him to avert "a general massacre" by the Indians. A British officer at the parley, Lieutenant John Le Couteur, described Boerstler as "badly wounded and . . . horror struck, the tears roll[ing] down his handsome countenance." Boerstler wanted to surrender but worried that the Britons were too few to protect their prisoners from the Indians. A master bluffer, FitzGibbon claimed that another seven hundred British troops were closing fast, so Boerstler capitulated. "For God's sake, keep the Indians from us," he begged. Although the British generals credited FitzGibbon for the victory, he conceded: "Not a shot was fired on our side by any but the Indians. They beat the American detachment into a state of terror, and the only share I claim is taking advantage of a favorable moment to offer them protection from the tomahawk and scalping knife." The British took 492 prisoners, for only a handful of mounted volunteers escaped to Fort George. The American dead lost their scalps, while the survivors lost their boots, swords, uniforms, and watches to plundering Indians, for the British dared not stop them.[64]

Coming so soon after Stoney Creek, the grim news from Beaver Dams seemed the "climax of continual mismanagement and misfortune," in the words of one dismayed politician. Republican leaders agreed that Dearborn had to go. Despite his mistakes and illness, many officers regretted Dearborn's humiliation. "I really felt for the old buck," Colonel Burn remarked. The officers especially rued Boyd's elevation to full command at Fort George, for he bore greater responsibility for Boerstler's defeat than did Dearborn.[65]

Boerstler blamed the fiasco on Chapin's misinformation and cowardice, but the good doctor won the postbattle debate in the press by making a wily escape on the lake. On July 12, the British loaded Chapin and twenty-eight of his men into two boats bound east to Kingston, but they rose up and overpowered their sixteen guards when they paused to drink grog. Redirecting the boats and eluding Yeo's schooners, the volunteers and their new prisoners rowed to Fort George. A crowd of American troops watched the two boats arrive with Chapin in the lead boat, bearing a "sort of triumph in his look and the cock of his hat." An officer reported, "This gallant little achievement put the whole camp in good humor." The Republican press lionized Chapin as an icon of American daring and cleverness—which left the blame for Beaver Dams to Boerstler.[66]

ELDRIDGE'S BODY

Spooked by Boerstler's disaster, the Americans stayed close within their trenches at Fort George and Newark. Linking town and fort, their earthworks stretched from the Niagara River, on the southeast, to the lakeshore on the northwest, enclosing about one square mile. Under orders from the secretary of war, Boyd had to sit still until a new commander, Major General James Wilkinson, could arrive from the south and until Chauncey could clear the lake of British warships. The idled troops would have been more secure, less crowded, and better supplied if they had blown up Fort George and withdrawn across the river to Fort Niagara. But pride dictated that the Americans cling to their one vestige of victory in Canada. Rather than sacrifice that point of honor, an officer declared, "I had rather be immolated—sacrificed by the fiends of hell, the savages." At Fort George the invaders were too proud to retreat but too scared to advance, so they wallowed in misery.[67]

As an early warning system, Boyd set up six small outposts, half a mile apart and each half a mile beyond the entrenchments. Known as a "picquet" or "picket," each post had about fifty guards. Both night and day, the British and Indians probed the pickets with sudden, fatal strikes that kept the Americans on edge. The new British commander, General Francis de Rottenburg, boasted that his Indians were "daily engaged with the enemy's outposts, harassing and teasing them the whole day long." Rottenburg marveled that his more numerous enemy did "not attempt to drive me from my position, but keeps perfectly quiet and passive within his lines." After visiting Fort George, Peter B. Porter reported, "This army lies panic-struck, shut up and whipped in by a few hundred miserable savages." John Norton, a Mohawk chief, boasted that his warriors "so far intimidated them that they became like prisoners at their own expense."[68]

On July 8, Indians attacked a picket guard commanded by Lieutenant Joseph Eldridge. After repulsing the attack, Eldridge and thirty men foolishly pursued their tormentors deep into the woods. When none of the pursuers returned, a larger American force went out to find fifteen mutilated corpses, including Eldridge's. An officer described the bodies as "utterly stripped and scalped, and mangled in a . . . sort of sportive butchery." The rest of the men had become British prisoners. By conventional standards, the Eldridge butchery was a petty affair eclipsed by grander battles involving more men and more famous commanders. And yet that particular skirmish fixated those who served at Fort George. They long remembered the nightmare scene as an episode of intense emotional importance. A young and handsome officer of great promise, Eldridge aroused the empathetic anger of his peers, who vowed "a war of extermination" against the Indians and any Britons who fought beside them.[69]

After the Eldridge butchery, the American officers decided that they needed their own warriors as allies. They sought to reverse the American policy that had rejected the employment of Indian warriors, derided as savages unwanted in a white man's war. By mid-1813, army officers recognized that the propaganda benefits did not compensate for the defeats suffered for want of warriors to counter the Indians allied to the British. Major Willoughby Morgan concluded, "We have forborne long enough. It is not unjustifiable to fight the enemy upon his own terms."[70]

In particular, the officers wanted help from the 3,800 Haudenosaunee Indians who lived on reservations in western and central New York. The most numerous and influential of their six nations, the Seneca dominated the villages clustered along Buffalo Creek, beside the settler town of Buffalo. During the 1790s the Haudenosaunee within New York had lost most of their lands in exchange for annuities paid by the state or federal governments. The leading Seneca chiefs also received annual pension payments in return for their cooperation. Thanks to the annuities, pensions, and surrounding settlements, the Haudenosaunee within New York could not risk a confrontation with the United States.[71]

Enforced neutrality pained the Buffalo Creek Indians, who feared becoming irrelevant. In addition to the plunder and scalps of war, their warriors coveted the gifts bestowed by the British on their allies. The Buffalo Creek chiefs also worried that their Grand River rivals would exploit the British victories to seize Grand Island in the Niagara River, a valuable hunting ground claimed by both sets of chiefs. The Buffalo Creek spokesman, Red Jacket, shrewdly told American officials, "If we sit still . . . the British (according to the customs of you white people) will hold it by conquest, and should you conquer the Canadas you will claim it upon the same principle, as conquered from the British." Red Jacket also suspected that, unless taken into the American service, many of his warriors would slip across the river to join the Grand River warriors as British allies.[72]

By raiding Black Rock, the British unwittingly pulled the Buffalo Creek Indians into the war. Before dawn on July 11, Lieutenant Colonel Cecil Bisshopp crossed the Niagara River with 250 men, including FitzGibbon and the Bloody Boys. Bisshopp brought along no Indians because the British feared that employing warriors in New York would, in Michael Smith's words, "unite all the people against them." Landing at Black Rock, Bisshopp's men surprised and routed the local militia commanded by Porter, who fled to Buffalo in his underwear. After looting the public stores and Porter's mansion, the British set fire to the blockhouses, barracks, navy yard, and a schooner. Overconfident, the British took their sweet time, "drinking & carousing" while loading the plunder into their boats. A watching American, James Aigen, recalled, "They was having a good time."[73]

But the good times did not last. In borrowed clothes, Porter rallied 250 soldiers and 37 Seneca warriors for a counterattack. For the first time in the war, the British experienced the terror so often felt by the Americans. Spooked by the "appalling war whoop, they were thrown into confusion & fled to their boats with the fleetness of deer." As they rowed away, the British took heavy casualties from rifle fire. "The River was red with Blood," Aigen reported. The thirteen British dead included Bisshopp, who had been a rising star in the British army. Porter implausibly claimed that he prevented the Indians from scalping the dead, which thrilled the Republican press as a new proof that Americans were more humane than the British.[74]

To draw the Buffalo Creek warriors deeper into the war, Porter organized a raid across the Niagara River to arrest Loyalists and to seize supposed "public property." But the warriors also plundered private houses and rustled horses and cattle. To entice the Buffalo Creek Indians into an offensive war, Porter sacrificed the property of Upper Canadian farmers, thereby alienating people whose support had previously been coveted. The Indian agent at Buffalo, Erastus Granger, assured General Boyd at Fort George: "as [the Indians] have now committed themselves, [and] have in fact crossed the river, they may be persuaded to join you."[75]

In return for generous presents, 140 Buffalo Creek warriors proceeded to Fort George, arriving on August 13. Four days later Boyd sent them out, supported by 200 regulars, to attack a British picket guard. Taken by surprise, the enemy mistook the advancing warriors for their own allies. In the melee, the attackers killed a dozen and captured eighteen, most of them Ojibwa. After burning a farm, the attackers retreated to Fort George, where Winfield Scott exulted at the sight of American-allied warriors returning with prisoners "closely pinioned and led by a string. The novel spectacle produced such roars of delight as to be heard from camp to camp." Boyd insisted that his new allies kept their promise to take no scalps, but another American officer reported, "Sundry scalps were exhibited fresh from the heads of the victims."[76]

The prisoners included a battered man, who had been shot in the left thigh, speared in his right shoulder, and tomahawked to the face, losing his right eye. Although dressed as an Indian, the shattered prisoner was an American named Robert Livingston. Born in New Hampshire, Livingston had immigrated to Canada and enlisted in the British army during the 1790s. Posted on the Great Lakes, he had mastered the Ojibwa language and had become a petty trader and an interpreter for the British Indian Department. In 1812 Livingston had helped to rally the native warriors who compelled the Americans to surrender Michilimackinac. A year later he had recruited Ojibwa warriors to join the British army on the Niagara front.[77]

Despite taking Indians into their service, the Americans treated as race traitors any white men captured among the native allies of the British. An American officer explained "that a man is generally known by the company he keeps; that all the captives appearing in breech-cloths and leggings, the color of the skin had not been particularly regarded; that they seemed to be birds of a feather, and had been locked up together." Cast into the dungeon at Fort Niagara, Livingston complained of being treated "with the greatest inhumanity, being refused the least Medical Aid, until his wounds were swarming with worms." Somehow he gathered enough strength to escape and to cross the Niagara River in October. After subsisting for seven days on acorns, he reached the British lines and resumed his service in the Indian Department.[78]

While Livingston attested that Americans fought on both sides of the war, he was captured in a skirmish that pitted Indians against one another. This new dimension to the civil war shocked the British and their native allies. Just as the Americans expected the support of all Irishmen, the British considered themselves the natural ally of all Indians. The skirmish threatened to divide the British allies, for the Ojibwa angrily accused the Grand River Haudenosaunee of colluding with their

A Scene on the Frontiers, *etching by William Charles. A piece of Republican propaganda, this etching depicts British officers paying Indians for American scalps.* (Courtesy of the Library of Congress, Prints and Photographs Division.)

Buffalo Creek kin to spring the nasty surprise. Healing that breach required soothing presents from the British.[79]

But the Indian boost to the Americans proved short-lived, for the warriors suspected their hosts of hanging back for safety while sending them forward to bear the brunt of forest combat. To their further disgust, Boyd reverted to form and clung to his entrenchments instead of leading the breakout promised to allure them to join his army. An American officer reported, "Indians [are] very much dissatisfied—say that Yankees [are] cowards, dare not fight." Bored with inaction, most of the warriors returned to Buffalo Creek by the end of August. Their withdrawal restored the British edge in native allies on the Niagara front.[80]

COMBINATION

A cherished American legend mocks the folly of British regulars fighting as massed men in open fields: easy marks for resourceful American riflemen firing from cover. At Beaver Dams, however, it was the Americans who clumped together and fired pointless volleys, while Indians shot at them from behind trees. After that defeat, Boyd fulminated, "Should the Enemy dare to meet us [as] men, his dastardly practice of assailing us from behind Trees will soon meet its check and the intrepid Yankee again [will] be Triumphant." Inverting the legend, the natives helped the British to defeat the American invaders of Upper Canada.[81]

In the northern borderland, a powerful *combination* of British regulars and Indian warriors repeatedly defeated American troops. Together they made a formidable team. Consummate guerrilla fighters, Indian warriors guarded the British flanks, while the disciplined regulars controlled the center with bayonet charges that also terrified raw American recruits. Colonel Harvey explained the British tactics to a general: with "your flanks secured by light troops, militia, and Indians . . . you must depend upon the superior discipline of the troops under your command for success over an undisciplined though confident and numerous enemy." Whenever the Americans broke and fled, the Indians pounced, making short work of the wounded and the slow. The rare American victories at York and Fort George came beside the lake, where superior American numbers and a devastating fire from warships led the Indians to hold back, leaving the British vulnerable.[82]

Madison later blamed the American defeats on "the forests to be penetrated, the savages to be encountered, and the Lakes and other waters to be passed in order to reach a distant theatre, where the adversary was at home in the midst of all his resources for defence." Wary of

Indian ambushes on land, American commanders preferred the greater ease and security of moving by boat and ship along the Great Lakes. But the American naval command of Lake Ontario proved fleeting, given Chauncey's caution and Yeo's competition. Because both commodores avoided fighting at a disadvantage, the Americans and British became locked into an expensive competition to build more ships at Kingston and Sackets Harbor. Whenever one side surged ahead, the other flotilla withdrew into the fortified safety of its base to build still more warships. This stalemate favored the British, who fought to defend Canada, rather than the Americans, who needed to conquer. Thanks to Indians on land, the British forced the Americans to rely on shipbuilders and warships to fight the war for Canada. And because the Americans' war effort stalled on the water and in the woods, their appeal to Upper Canadians withered.[83]

The Reverend, The Honourable John Strachan *(1778–1867)*, *oil painting by an unknown artist*, *1827*. (Courtesy of the University of Trinity College, Toronto; the gift of Henry W. Davies, D.D.)

CHAPTER NINE

FLAMES

Every thing that is done appears to me to be all hodge podge. All is a chaotic Mass of Disorder, Anarchy, and Confusion.

—Joseph Ellicott, December 30, 1813[1]

BORN IN SCOTLAND IN 1778, John Strachan developed a powerful self-confidence and burning ambition. He recalled, "The day of my birth was accompanied with too many singularities not to portend something great," for he came into this world on a Sunday at the twelfth hour in the twelfth day of April when both the sun and the moon were full and the tide was high. Although the youngest of six children sired by a quarry overseer, Strachan escaped from obscurity and poverty by meriting the liberal education essential to gentility. Graduating from Aberdeen University in 1797, he began to study divinity as a Presbyterian.[2]

Seeking his fortune, the young man sailed across the Atlantic to New York City in 1799, but he quickly soured on the republic. Attending a court session, he noted, "most of the causes respected swindling. The science of cheating seems to be very well understood in the States." Hastening overland to Upper Canada, Strachan settled in Kingston, where he taught school and lodged with the town's leading magistrate, Richard Cartwright, who persuaded Strachan to forsake his Presbyterianism for the Anglicanism favored by the governing elite in Canada. Ordained in 1803, Strachan obtained the Anglican parish at Cornwall in the St. Lawrence Valley. Four years later he married the wealthy widow of a Scots merchant from Montreal. A friend reported, "Mr. Strachan has now been married nearly two months, he lives in great style, and keeps three servants."[3]

At Cornwall, Strachan also developed a private academy to educate the sons of elite families. He hoped "to prevent in future our young men from going to the United States . . . where they learn nothing but anarchy in Politics and infidelity in religion." Although a demanding teacher, Strachan won a remarkable loyalty from his students, who cher-

Major General Sir Roger Hale Sheaffe *(1763–1851)*. (Courtesy of Library and Archives Canada, C-111307.)

ished his gregarious and passionate interest in their well-being. His graduates subsequently helped one another to become the colony's leaders. In 1808 Strachan boasted, "By an[d] by, my pupils will be getting forward, some of them perhaps into the House [of Assembly] & then I shall have more in my power."[4]

At Cornwall, Strachan distrusted most of his common neighbors as crafty Yankees, who had intruded into the land of loyalty: "Plenty of them have now acquired property, but in point of information they are brutes." He complained that they had "little or no religion, and their minds are so prone to low cunning, that it will be difficult to make any thing of them." Despising the United States, Strachan concluded, "This new nation are *vain & rapacious* and without *honour*—they are hurried on to any action provided they gain money by it."[5]

In early 1812, on the eve of war, Strachan won promotion to the parish at York, the colonial capital, where he made himself indispensable to any political, cultural, or social initiative. An adept self-promoter, Strachan wrote fawning letters to powerful men in Montreal, Quebec, and London. In addition to his odes to the king and to British naval victories, Strachan conveyed his prolific advice on public policy. To rally support for defending the colony, he also published addresses and sermons, which exhorted the American-born majority: "You have been recognized as British subjects, you have been adopted into our family and received as children. Let then obedience and submission to the laws mark your conduct, and as you receive protection, our king has a just claim to your service."[6]

Although Strachan urged submission on others, he busily undermined any of his own superiors who seemed soft on the American menace. Blasting Prevost's defensive strategy, Strachan concluded: "The people of Upper Canada . . . have wept to find that he who was sent to protect them has proved their greatest foe, & that their victories have been received with a chilling coldness, & apologies made to the enemy." Making himself Upper Canada's spokesman, Strachan vowed to defeat the enemy despite Prevost and his protégé, Sir Roger Hale Sheaffe, who had succeeded Brock as Upper Canada's acting lieutenant governor.[7]

COUP

Although the son of Loyalists, Sheaffe's American origins aroused the suspicion of Strachan and other hard-liners. During the revolution Sheaffe had left the rebellious colonies to study at an English military academy, where he had been befriended by Prevost, then a fellow student and later his patron. Entering the British army in 1781, Sheaffe served six years in Ireland before coming to Canada. By 1811 he had risen in rank to major general. A year later Prevost sent the cautious Sheaffe to Upper Canada as the second-in-command to help restrain the aggressive Brock.[8]

When the war began, Sheaffe sought a transfer to England, so he could avoid fighting the Americans. Instead, he had to succeed the heroic Brock as Upper Canada's military commander and civil governor. Although Sheaffe won the battle at Queenston, Brock reaped the popular credit and joined Britain's other great battle martyrs: General James Wolfe, who died on the Plains of Abraham at Quebec, and Admiral Horatio Nelson, who fell while destroying an enemy fleet near Trafalgar. By comparison to Brock, the colorless and methodical Sheaffe could only lose.[9]

As commander and governor, Sheaffe followed Prevost's lead by practicing a moderation meant to unify Upper Canada and to divide the enemy. After the battle of Queenston, Sheaffe declined to cross the Niagara River to smash the demoralized Americans. Instead, he made a temporary truce and exchanged or paroled most of his prisoners. In politics, Sheaffe cultivated good relations with Upper Canada's elected assembly, soothing the opposition led by Joseph Willcocks. But Sheaffe's restraint angered Strachan and other hard-liners, who wanted a more aggressive war and a crackdown on dissidents. During the winter of 1812–13, the hard-liners held covert meetings and spread dark rumors to impugn Sheaffe's loyalty. Instead of confronting his critics, Sheaffe turned inward and despondent. A worried friend noticed "an irresistible melancholy on his mind, which is very distressing."[10]

In April 1813, after Sheaffe's defeat at York, the hard-liners pounced. Given the superior American numbers and naval firepower, Sheaffe did well to extricate his regulars for a retreat to Kingston. But Strachan and the other York magistrates blamed Sheaffe for failing to inspire his men as Brock had done: "the disgrace of their defeat . . . was owing entirely to their commander." In private letters they hinted that Sheaffe was a traitor in cahoots with his fellow Americans. Strachan worked his connections with the influential Scots merchants of Montreal, including John Richardson, the spymaster. The merchants passed on the critique to their London correspondents, for conveyance to the Earl of Bathurst, who as secretary of state was Prevost's superior. In a sly bit of political pressure, Strachan advised Richardson privately to show the scathing York report to Prevost with the threat to publish it if he failed to sack Sheaffe.[11]

Rather than take the fall, Prevost sacrificed his protégé on June 19, replacing him with Major General Francis de Rottenburg. A German born in Poland, Rottenburg was a veteran mercenary with broad experience in the British army. In 1798 he had helped to suppress the United Irish rebellion—the framing experience shared by so many British officers who later served in Canada.[12]

Sheaffe's downfall undermined Willcocks, the Irish-born politician who had moderated his opposition since 1811. In June 1812 Willcocks had sold his provocative newspaper, the *Upper Canada Guardian*, to a Scots Loyalist who renamed and reoriented the press. When the war broke out, Willcocks sought to defend the colony without sacrificing traditional liberties. Although he blocked Brock's bid to suspend the writ of habeas corpus, Willcocks also rallied colonists against the invaders. In August, at Brock's request, Willcocks visited the Grand River villages to persuade the warriors to join the British defense of the Niagara frontier. In October at Queenston Heights, Willcocks fought bravely beside them in crushing the American attack. After Brock's death, Willcocks continued to cooperate with Sheaffe. In February 1813 William Hamilton Merritt marveled to his fiancée, "You will be surprised to hear of Joseph Willcocks changing about and becoming a zealous loyalist. He has behaved very well on all occasions and so have all his party."[13]

In June 1813, however, Willcocks faced arrest on a charge of treason pressed by his political foes—Strachan and the other hard-liners. After toppling Sheaffe, they meant to treat all opposition as treason. The hard-liners spread the malicious rumor that Willcocks had guided the American army that advanced to Stoney Creek in early June. They also arrested his friend, Abraham Markle. A versatile and entrepreneurial American, Markle had prospered at Ancaster by running an inn, a stage line, mills, a farm, and a distillery. After winning an assembly seat in 1812, he became Willcocks's closest ally. Charged with treason in June 1813, Markle was hauled onto a British warship and taken to Kingston. Protesting innocence, Markle complained that he had to leave his large family "without my Protection, exposed to the Indians who are daily Distroying the property of our Neighbours." In late June, Prevost ordered Markle released, but by then an alarmed Willcocks had defected to the Americans at Fort George.[14]

His defection delighted the hard-liners as vindicating their insistence that Willcocks had always been a traitor. Driven out, he could no longer lead the assembly opposition, and the hard-liners could claim a mandate for repressing all dissent as treasonous. In fact, his defection showed more desperation than opportunism, more shove by his foes than pull by his new friends. Indeed, if drawn to Fort George by opportunity, his timing was poor, for the Americans were reeling from their recent defeat at Stoney Creek.[15]

In April Willcocks had raised provincial troops to defend the colony, but in July he offered his military services to the Americans to enlist a "Corps of Volunteers to assist in changing the Government of this Province." By accepting that offer and commissioning Willcocks as a major, Dearborn exceeded his government's policy, which remained ambivalent about regime change in Canada as a war goal. While the Madison administration waffled, the frustrated generals at the front sought a conquest that hinged upon rewarding dissidents and punishing Loyalists.[16]

Willcocks recruited his volunteers from refugees who fled to the American lines at Fort George. Primarily settlers from New England known as "Yankees," these refugees related tales of woe to Lieutenant Baptist Irvine:

There is a number of Yankees here from the Grand River. They come to obtain paroles and say that if our army leaves them, they dare not return to their homes for fear of the Indians. Norton and other Scotch chiefs have lists of suspected Yankees whom they will plunder and murder without remorse. What distresses our friends have suffered for refusing to take the oath [of allegiance] and perform militia duty is incredible. Some died in jail and others have been robbed of their property by being fined eighty dollars at every draft.

By late September Willcocks had enlisted 130 volunteers, who honored their Irish commander by wearing green ribbons around the crown of their hats.[17]

The Canadian Volunteers guided the forays by American troops from Fort George into the countryside to seek forage and to arrest and plunder Loyalists. Fearing capture as probable death, the Canadian Volunteers were desperate fighters who impressed their American commanders. In mid-August General Boyd reported, "The Canadian Volunteers, under Major Wilcox, were active and brave as usual." But another American officer suspected that they made more enemies than friends by seeking vengeance in their "private and local feuds" with the Loyalists of the Niagara District.[18]

RETREAT

During the summer of 1813, two thousand British troops and seven hundred Indian allies penned up twice as many American troops at Fort George. Prevost marveled that his Niagara division held "a situation very critical and one novel in the system of war, that of investing a force vastly superior in numbers within a strongly intrenched position." The American commander, General Boyd, had orders to immobilize his army until Chauncey won control of the lake by sweeping away Yeo's British warships.[19]

Day after day, British and American soldiers watched in anxious suspense as Chauncey's and Yeo's rival flotillas maneuvered around the lake. Jockeying for position, both cautiously evaded a decisive battle. One frustrated American likened the two forces as "lying alongside of each other, like two dogs, always growling and snapping, but never biting." An equally frustrated Briton blasted Chauncey as either "a coward or a Jackass" for not seeking battle, but the same could be said of Yeo.[20]

During the stalemate, the British relied on their Indian allies to keep the Americans trapped within Fort George and to keep British soldiers and Upper Canadian settlers from deserting to the invaders. But that reliance proved double-edged, for the warriors demanded that the British keep a substantial army on the Niagara Peninsula, a dangerously exposed position should the Americans regain naval command of the lake. Prevost's chief aide, Edward Baynes, explained that a withdrawal "would have lost us all our wavering friends and would have proved destructive to our Indian alliance."[21]

Encamped beside a mosquito-infested swamp, the Britons sickened with ague and fever as the summer turned hot and nasty. Rottenburg assured another British general, "You must not imagine that we sleep here upon a bed of roses. Sickness and desertion diminish our number daily to the most alarming degree and nothing decisive can be attempted until the Enemy's Fleet is disposed of." He added, "The procrastination of the conflict on the lakes is the cause of all our disasters." In late September, Rottenburg described his little army as "crippled by Disease and dispirited by wants and Misery." Routing both armies, the disease-bearing mosquitoes were winning the war.[22]

Meanwhile, to the west, the Americans were building warships to wrest control of Lake Erie away from the British. So long as the British dominated that lake, they could cling to occupied Michigan as well as the Western District of Upper Canada. But if the Americans built more and better warships, they could break the British supply line and could more quickly, cheaply, and safely ferry troops across the lake to attack Amherstburg and Detroit. Securing Lake Erie became the top American priority because, as the secretary of navy explained, "it at once erects a Naval barrier between our civilised and savage Enemies from Niagara to Michigan." General William Henry Harrison kept his army in Ohio on the defensive until Oliver Hazard Perry completed the American flotilla under construction at Presque Isle in northwestern Pennsylvania.[23]

At Amherstburg, the British commander, General Sir Henry Procter, became anxious and irritable from dread of an American offensive. Lacking regulars, he had to rely on Indian warriors, who meant to call the shots in their alliance with the British. An officer lamented:

As we are now completely in the savages' power, we are obliged in a great measure to act as they think proper. . . . Many dread the war whoop may sound in our ears, if we act contrary to their ideas, which are as wild as themselves. We have spread a net which may catch us.

Procter also distrusted the inhabitants of "that Depot of Treachery, Detroit." When he had marched south to attack General Winchester at Frenchtown, Procter had withdrawn most of the Detroit garrison. Some drunks in the town had then talked of seizing the undermanned fort. Although nothing came of their talk, Procter blamed and ousted the town's leading civilians, sending them across the American lines.[24]

The Indians also increased their harassment of the settlers in occupied Michigan. Lewis Bond of Detroit reported that, after crushing Winchester, the Indians

> returned with encreased fury, elated with their success and exhibiting the Scalps, Prisoners, clothing &c. Amidst the most infernal yells & shouts, [they] danced round from door to door, and we were obliged to be silent Spectators and even to affect pleasure at the sight and give them refreshments of Victuals and drink lest we should share the same fate.

During the next summer, the warriors plundered orchards, gardens, and livestock. One settler reported that the Indians killed "all my pigs to the number of thirty, four Oxen, ten sheep, all our Fowls and burned our hen house." Procter apparently hoped that Indian harassment would drive the citizens from Michigan, tightening the British hold on that conquered territory. By declaring the territory to be "an Indian country," Procter implied that the British would never restore Michigan to American rule.[25]

In late July, Procter led a mixed force of Indians, Britons, and Canadians against Harrison's advanced base at Fort Meigs on the Maumee River in northwestern Ohio. Procter mounted the risky offensive to mollify warriors impatient with inaction. A British officer noted,

> Tis a degrading truth that British soldiers should be so solicitous for the good opinion of Savages, but the ascendance in number of 10 to 1 which they possessed over the Right Division, whose very existence depended upon them, compelled the British General to accede to some wrong measures to preserve their friendship.

Failing to dislodge the Americans from Fort Meigs, Procter next attacked nearby Fort Stephenson. Suffering a bloody defeat, Procter lost many regulars whom he could not replace. The two defeats strained the alliance, as the warriors blamed Procter's bungling, while he complained that they held back from attacks on forts that they had demanded.[26]

Clinging to a defensive policy that saved lives and resources, General Prevost rebuked Procter for allowing "the clamour of the Indian Warriors to induce you to commit a part of your valuable force in an unequal & hopeless conflict." This rebuke exposed the fatal contradiction in Procter's thankless position. His commander denied him enough regulars and supplies to sway the natives. Rendered dependent on the Indians, Procter then had to heed their demands for an offensive that risked his scarce regulars and reaped Prevost's wrath.[27]

Lying near the western end of the chain of command and the line of supplies, Procter's army suffered as Rottenburg and Prevost clung to their men, money, munitions, clothing, and provisions. During the spring, the American attacks on York and Fort George had also disrupted the flow of supplies to Procter. And he could not control the natives, who killed local livestock and demanded army rations beyond the limited capacity of British logistics. To feed the Indians, Procter had to reduce his regulars and sailors to half rations, which sapped their energy and soured their morale.[28]

The situation further deteriorated in August, when the Americans completed their new flotilla and seized command of Lake Erie. By blockading Amherstburg and Detroit, the American naval commander, Captain Oliver Hazard Perry, disrupted Procter's feeble line of supply. Desperate to reopen his supply line, Procter demanded an attack on Perry by the lake's British flotilla. Although dangerously shorthanded and two ships short of Perry's force, the British naval commander, Lieutenant Robert H. Barclay, reluctantly agreed: "That the Risk is very great, I feel very much, but that in the present state of this place, without provisions, without stores, & without Indian Goods (which last is a matter of the highest importance), it is necessary, I fully agree with the Gen[era]l."[29]

Unlike on Lake Ontario, the British and Americans did fight a decisive naval battle on Lake Erie that summer, for Perry was more aggressive than Chauncey, and Barclay was more desperate than Yeo. On September 9, Barclay and his hungry men sailed out onto the lake to seek Perry's flotilla. During the battle, the sound of cannon fire reached Detroit, where Lewis Bond recalled the agonizing suspense over "whether we were to remain in Servility to our Savage masters or to be again free People." Although outgunned and outmanned, Barclay put up a fierce fight before surrendering his battered vessels and surviving men on September 10. News of the American victory thrilled the Detroiters but dismayed their British guards.[30]

After Perry's victory, Harrison could embark his five thousand men to cross Lake Erie and attack the British. To defend Amherstburg and Detroit, Procter had only 850 regulars and 3,000 Indians, and he expected little or no help from the French Canadian militia of the district. Regarding resistance as futile, Procter retreated overland via the Thames Valley toward Burlington Heights, at the head of Lake Ontario. Resenting the withdrawal as a British betrayal, two-thirds of the Indians dispersed to their homes around the Great Lakes. Only a third, led by Tecumseh, reluctantly agreed to join Procter's retreat. On September 24–27, Procter burned the forts, barracks, and storehouses at Amherstburg and Detroit and began his painful march east.[31]

On September 27, Harrison's troops landed near Amherstburg and occupied the village, where his Kentuckians looted and burned the houses of the Indian Department officers, who had wisely retreated with Procter. As at York in April, the American troops treated as race traitors any white men who rallied Indians for war. On September 29, Harrison's troops ascended the Detroit River to liberate Detroit "amidst the joyful acclamations of the People." An American officer noted that the British had allowed the Indians "to pillage the poor miserable inhabitants at pleasure. This Country is totally exhausted of all its resources, and except as a frontier is scarcely worth possessing."[32]

After leaving garrisons at Amherstburg and Detroit, Harrison pushed up the Thames with 3,500 men in pursuit of Procter and Tecumseh. Most of the advancing force consisted of mounted Kentuckians, under their governor, Isaac Shelby, an elderly but fiery veteran of the revolution. Harrison also enjoyed the assistance of two hundred Indians, primarily Shawnee from Ohio, and some Canadian guides led by Simon Zelotes Watson, returning from exile in the United States.[33]

Both the retreating and the advancing forces looted the frontier farms and mills of the Thames Valley. A Moravian missionary reported:

> We heard nothing but wailing and weeping from the inhabitants on this river. Retreating Indians had taken all their horses, slaughtered cattle and pigs to their hearts' content and stole whatever else they could from their homes. . . . After the Indians came [and went], the armies took whatever was left.

The Kentuckians seemed as intent on plundering the farmers as on catching the British. A local boy recalled, "They robbed us of everything they could carry away, even my mother's young baby clothes. They chopped up everything else, including a feather bed." When the boy's father complained to Harrison, the Kentuckians laughed and said, "Who cares for General Harrison? None of his business what we do."[34]

Heavy baggage, muddy roads, and restive Indians slowed Procter's retreat, enabling Harrison's troops to catch up at Moraviantown, an Indian mission village with a church, school, and sixty log houses. Obliged to stand and fight, Procter posted six hundred regulars beside the river, on the east, while Tecumseh and one thousand warriors defended the marshy and forested flank to the west. Outnumbered by about two to one, the British and their allies were hungry, tired, disheartened, and running low on ammunition. Almost everyone had lost confidence in Procter, who had become despondent, erratic, and negligent.[35]

On October 5, a powerful charge by mounted Kentucky riflemen overwhelmed the British regulars, who broke, fled, and surrendered. Desperate to avoid capture by the dreaded Kentuckians, Procter raced away as fast as he could spur his horse. Left behind, the Indians fought desperately until Tecumseh took a fatal bullet. Disheartened, the surviving warriors dispersed deeper into the forest, before heading east to Burlington Heights.[36]

To the victors went the spoils. Harrison exulted in the capture of six cherished cannon, three of them lost by Hull to the British (and previously taken by the Americans during the revolution). Their recovery helped Harrison to cast his victory as erasing Hull's stain to the nation's honor. The victors also paraded about in Procter's captured carriage and rummaged through his abandoned baggage. In addition to scalping the enemy dead, the Kentuckians flayed an Indian corpse—believed to be Tecumseh's—to make razor strops of his skin.[37]

The Kentuckians also ransacked Moraviantown. John Schnall, a missionary, watched as the soldiers even "poured the honey out of the hives without killing the bees first, and swarms of them surrounded the feasting soldiers." The missionaries begged Harrison to intervene "to protect us from the wild mob." But the general could not restrain the Kentuckians, who hated all Indians and despised any white men who consorted with them. "All day long, we had to listen to jeering insults. We had to listen to the atrocities Indian warriors had inflicted upon the American soldiers," Schnall lamented. In vain, the missionaries protested that their Indians were Christian pacifists. Driven away, the missionaries looked back at the rising smoke of Moraviantown: the first village entirely and intentionally destroyed in the war, but it would not be the last.[38]

Instead of pursuing Procter to Burlington Heights, Harrison cautiously withdrew to Detroit, where he made peace with those Indians who had deserted from Procter and Tecumseh. On October 14, the Miami, Potawatomi, Wyandot, Wea, Ottawa, and Ojibwa promised to surrender their American prisoners, to stop raiding the settlements, and to join the fight against the British. In return, the victors agreed to feed the Indians around Detroit, as a cheaper alternative to fighting them. Brigadier General Duncan McArthur explained, "It is certain that I have as little respect for those wretched beings as any other person can have, yet I was of opinion that we might save the lives of many women and Children on our frontier, and the expense of hunting down those savages over a vast wilderness."[39]

At last, on the western front, the tide of war had turned in the Americans' favor. Thanks to Perry's victory on the lake and Harrison's beside the river, the Americans had recovered Michigan and occupied the Western District of Upper Canada. Tecumseh's death devastated his dream of uniting the Indian nations in a confederacy that, in alliance with the British, could roll back the American settlements all the way to the Ohio River. Thereafter, the Americans could more easily divide and conquer the Indians.[40]

McCLURE

In late September on the Lake Ontario front, the new American army commander, General James Wilkinson, shifted most of his troops from Fort George east to Sackets Harbor, where they menaced Kingston. To protect that base, Rottenburg withdrew most of his troops to Kingston, leaving behind General John Vincent with a smaller force to watch the remaining Americans at Fort George. On October 8, Vincent learned that Harrison had crushed Procter's army. A false report added that the victors were marching east to attack Burlington Heights, which threatened to trap Vincent's army on the Niagara Peninsula.[41]

Vincent ordered a withdrawal, to the relief of his men, suffering from hunger and fever. The hasty retreat became chaotic as the sickly men struggled to push their wagons through muddy wallows and up steep ridges. The wagons broke down, so the troops abandoned valuable supplies in their rush to reach Burlington Heights. The waste was especially great because most of the local civilians hid their wagons to prevent impressment by the retreating troops. At Burlington Heights, Vincent's men found 3,500 Indian refugees: about half from the western nations, who had fought beside Tecumseh, and the other half from the Grand River villages. Both burden and asset, the refugees strengthened the

British force but consumed scarce rations and plundered the local farmers.[42]

For a second time, an American surge had pushed the British westward, out of the Niagara District. Once again, most of the local militia despaired of the British cause. Rather than rallying to defend Burlington Heights, the militiamen stayed home to fend off plundering Americans and Indians. And two leading Late Loyalists, Benajah Mallory and Abraham Markle, defected to join Willcocks's volunteers as officers. A British officer confided to Strachan: "Our prospects are very gloomy at present." William Hamilton Merritt added, "our great men had given up the idea of regaining the country."[43]

Rottenburg ordered Vincent to continue his retreat to Kingston, but the Indians refused to follow, and if left behind, they might seek a separate peace with the Americans. Their loss would cripple the British defense of Canada, which hinged upon combining regulars and warriors. Vincent warned Rottenburg: "The Grand River Indians, if they once quit us, they are lost for ever, and from that instant are changed to Enemies." In effect the Indians held the British hostage at Burlington Heights, preventing a further retreat. Rottenburg canceled his withdrawal order and promised to recover the Niagara District.[44]

Meanwhile, the Americans withdrew almost all of their regulars from Fort George to cross Lake Ontario to Sackets Harbor. The Niagara command fell to George McClure, a brigadier general of the New York militia. Born in Ireland and trained as a carpenter, McClure had immigrated as a young man to America, settling at Bath in western New York. Thriving as a miller, farmer, and trader, he also became the local postmaster, county judge, state legislator, and a brigadier general in command of the county militia. A jovial man, he haunted the local taverns to sing romantic ballads and tell heroic stories. McClure personified the Irish emigrant who rose to prosperity and influence by settling in the republican land of opportunity.[45]

Grateful to the republic, McClure longed to smite the British empire in Canada. By leading Republican volunteers to victory, he hoped to vindicate the much-maligned citizen-soldiers. In late 1812 he had commanded some of the volunteers who joined Alexander Smyth at Black Rock. At first, Smyth had seemed a kindred spirit: an ambitious Irishman and rabid Republican with a zeal for bombastic rhetoric and military pomp. But by abruptly canceling his invasion after exposing the volunteers in open boats for hours, Smyth disgusted McClure as a cowardly and "blustering paper warrior."[46]

Desperate for a second chance, McClure was thrilled in August 1813 by an invitation to command at Niagara. That invitation came from the new commander on the northern front, the grandiose (and Irish-descended) General Wilkinson. At last McClure could prove his worth and vindicate his fellow militiamen—so disgraced by the debacles at Queenston and Black Rock: "Let us wipe off the stigma upon the character of militia; let us prove to the world that those who enjoy and appreciate the blessings of liberty are the most competent to defend it." Deeming a republican army no contradiction, McClure sought to prove that militiamen, when properly led, could adopt the discipline of regulars. While inviting men to defend "the rights and liberties of the only free government on earth," McClure added: "Without discipline, an army is no better than a mob without order or restraint, useless to their country and a plague to themselves."[47]

Emulating Smyth, McClure published bombastic appeals for more volunteers to join his crusade against the British and their Indian allies. He promised them revenge for the massacre at Raisin River in January:

> On the west, behold your brethren under faith of a surrender shut up in a combustible dwelling and there burned to death by inches! Or, if they escape the fire, see them tomahawked by savages and their dead bodies kicked about the highway until they are devoured by hogs and dogs! Can the vengeance of God sleep? Can the indignation of man be stifled?

Championing a republican patriarchy, he denounced any men who held back from crossing into Canada with him:

> Let them return amidst the mockery and contempt of their friends and neighbours and wear out their life in sloth and infamy. They shall be standing objects of scorn and their children's children shall blush to acknowledge them! The General desires no faint-hearted, effeminate poltroons.

Instead, he sought "those who love their families and their homes and are resolved to protect them." He concluded, "Advance then, Americans, defenders of your country's rights, avengers of her wrongs, protectors of your wives, your children, and your friends." The best masculine defense of family values, he insisted, was a good offense that would thrust deep into Upper Canada, cast as the heart of savage darkness.[48]

McClure promised both plunder for his men and protection for the

Upper Canadians. To bridge that dangerous contradiction, he distinguished between private property, which he would defend, and public property, which was fair game. In practice, that distinction proved less neat, for he considered as public any cache of provisions. In another slippery distinction, McClure vowed to protect the common people, deemed potential republicans, but to plunder Tories, by which he meant the magistrates and militia officers who upheld British rule. But that distinction also broke down, for a peaceable civilian could seem a rabid Tory in the covetous eyes of a plundering volunteer.[49]

Discipline dissolved as his volunteers looted far and wide in the Niagara District. McClure's aide, William B. Rochester, deemed the men "completely raw, untrained & lawless." Only a fifth remained at Fort George, because the rest scattered through the countryside to seek "flour, pork, salt, arms, &c., of which immense quantities have been already found." Another aide, John C. Spencer, reported that the inhabitants were "wholly defenceless to the rapine and pillage of marauders from our side." The primary threat to the inhabitants came from their supposed liberators. But McClure implausibly believed that annexation to the United States could stem the marauding: "That such protection will be necessary, the pillage by our citizens every day abundantly proves." Despite his boasts of leading disciplined troops, McClure confessed that the inhabitants faced "universal pillage and desolation."[50]

Unable to control his volunteers, McClure made scapegoats of his Haudenosaunee allies, who were rustling livestock, particularly horses. Rebuking the warriors, McClure took away the stolen horses for return to their owners. Feeling insulted, the warriors left in a huff, exposing the volunteers to a counterattack by the Indian allies of the British.[51]

McClure longed to capture the British camp at Burlington Heights, but he needed more men. In apparent answer to his prayers, the great hero of the west, William Henry Harrison, and nine hundred regulars arrived in late October. Leaving Detroit, Harrison had crossed Lake Erie to Buffalo and then marched north along the Niagara River to Fort George. In an appeal for more volunteers, McClure vowed that they would jointly complete "the conquest of this province."[52]

But the secretary of war dashed McClure's dream by ordering Harrison and his regulars away to Sacket's Harbor. Harrison's abrupt departure embarrassed McClure, who had promised a quick and decisive attack. As with Smyth's debacle at Buffalo in late 1812, so with McClure at Fort George a year later: the disgusted volunteers felt misled and "commenced a scene of confusion and disorder beyond description."[53]

To mollify the rioting volunteers, McClure led a smaller foray without Harrison and the regulars. In addition to saving face, McClure sought to give "confidence to the inhabitants, that we have the possession of the country, and the power to protect the well-disposed and overawe those who are inimical." In fact the foolhardy advance by a mere 1,200 men compounded the damage already done by McClure's misbegotten force. Advancing only about twenty miles, McClure turned around when his scouts confirmed that the British at Burlington Heights were too strong to attack. Consoling themselves with more stolen flour and horses, the volunteers retreated to Fort George, where they deserted in droves.[54]

Almost all refused McClure's entreaties to stay on. Waging war on the cheap, the American commanders had never built proper barracks at Fort George. That neglect sentenced the volunteers to icy nights in drafty tents as the Canadian winter came on. Delays in their pay further soured the morale and loosened the tongues of the angry men. McClure lamented that the "best and most subordinate militia that have yet been on this frontier" became "a disaffected and ungovernable multitude."[55]

During the first week of December, his army shrank to merely eighty men, and most of them were Willcocks's Upper Canadians rather than McClure's New Yorkers. A disillusioned McClure blamed the defiant egalitarianism of American citizens:

> But, says a militia man, I will not be commanded and ordered about by such and such officers. I am as good a man as he is. The contagion spreads through the camp, and anarchy and confusion is the consequence.

Bitterly frustrated, McClure confessed to Armstrong: "In spite of all my exertions to ensure subordination, my late detachment ultimately proved to be very little better than an infuriated mob." Instead of vindicating the militia, McClure had confirmed its follies.[56]

REVENGE

On the night of December 9, McClure panicked upon learning that five hundred British troops, led by Lieutenant Colonel John Murray, were nearing Fort George. Unable to defend the fort with a mere eighty men, McClure ordered an evacuation during a snowy December 10. He destroyed most of his equipment and set fire to the fort. In his most controversial decision, McClure also burned the adjoining village of

Fort George, *engraving by Edward Walsh, c. 1805. Seen from the American Fort Niagara, in the foreground, this view of the British fort across the Niagara River reveals the dangerous proximity of the opposing forces in 1813.* (Courtesy of Library and Archives Canada, C-26.)

Newark, affording the people only twelve hours to leave, before the flames consumed ninety-eight houses, two churches, the jail, the court-house, and the library. Ousting the people into a driving snowstorm, he cited instructions from the secretary of war to destroy the town if neces-sary to protect Fort George from attack. But McClure had already abandoned Fort George when he set fire to the town, which he more thoroughly burned than the fort.[57]

Why did McClure order Newark burned? The answer lies in his close relationship with Joseph Willcocks. The two men admired and relied on each other. McClure felt "much indebted to Lt. Col. Wilcox, who with his mounted-men, scoured the country." And Willcocks extolled McClure as "an excellent officer and a true Patriot" who "stands high in the estimation of all those in the Province who are friendly to the American form of Government." McClure shared Will-cocks's radical insistence that the war should be fought to "declare this Province Independent of British influence."[58]

During the fall, McClure gave Willcocks a free hand to range the countryside and appointed him the "Police Officer" for Newark. In that post, Willcocks supervised the arrest and interrogation of prisoners and regulated the movement of civilians. An Upper Canadian officer, William Hamilton Merritt, concluded that Willcocks "had the whole management of civil and, I may say, military affairs" at Fort George. McClure amply followed Harrison's advice to "make use of the zeal, activity, and local knowledge which Col. Wilcox certainly possesses to counteract the machinations of our enemy and assure the confidence of our friends amongst the inhabitants."[59]

On the night of December 9, Willcocks had led a scouting party west, tangling with the advancing British. Before retreating, the Canadian Volunteers suffered one dead and four captured. Willcocks believed a report that the British had allowed the Indians to burn one of their captives to death. Infuriated, he demanded that McClure take revenge on Newark. The next day, Willcocks and his volunteers spread through the town with torches to set the consuming fires. When Cyrenius Chapin protested, Willcocks drove him away by pointing a pistol. Willcocks took special pains to destroy the brick mansion house of his old foe, William Dickson.[60]

After McClure withdrew across the Niagara River, British and Indian patrols scoured the Niagara District to arrest and plunder anyone who had helped the invaders. Merritt confessed that his men shot one suspect who allegedly tried to escape. Convinced that the British had killed at least six of the disaffected, McClure sent Willcocks with a letter to Armstrong, begging for reinforcements to rescue "our friends in Canada . . . They are arrested by the British soldiery and Indians and no sooner arrested than inhumanly butchered." He exaggerated the butchery, but not his own dread.[61]

On December 12, Colonel Murray's troops occupied the smoking ruins of Newark. He declared the inhabitants "delivered from the oppression of a lawless banditti, composed of the disaffected of the country organized under the direct influence of the American Government, who carried terror and dismay into every family." Both sides posed as liberators of the civilians caught in the middle, but both sides competed by intimidating civilians to secure their support. In the wake of Newark's burning, however, the British had the better claim.[62]

Murray led the advance force but reported to an aggressive new commander, Lieutenant General Gordon Drummond, who had supplanted Rottenburg as the colony's presiding general and civil administrator. The son of a Scots merchant, Drummond had been born in

Quebec in 1772. Educated in Britain, Drummond had entered the British army, serving with distinction in the Netherlands, Egypt, Jamaica, and Ireland. A stickler for discipline, he delighted in veteran troops who could wield bayonets with deadly effect. Compared to the deep military experience of Drummond, McClure was an amateur and a poseur.[63]

To avenge the burning of Newark, Drummond prepared to attack the American Fort Niagara and to torch the nearby village of Lewiston. The British meant to deprive their enemy of winter shelter and provisions along the Niagara front. Drummond struck before dawn in the bitter cold of December 19, sending Murray across the river with 550 regulars. Under "the strictest discipline," these veterans maintained "the profoundest silence" as they landed and advanced in the darkness. Obeying orders, these troops were not McClure's wild volunteers.[64]

The Britons quickly overwhelmed two lax picket guards posted outside the fort's gates. The American sentries had retired into a house to warm themselves by a fire, while their officers played cards in another house. One American officer asked another, "What are trumps?" A Briton suddenly answered, "bayonets are trump," as the attackers broke into both houses and quickly killed everyone "in grim silence," preserving the secret.[65]

Advancing to the fort's gate, the attackers found it open and the sentry dozing. Bayoneted, he gave no alarm as the British poured into the fort, at last yelling to break the prolonged tension. A British private recalled that the garrison's women, "supposing we had Indians with us, were greatly frightened and ran around shrieking most piteously." A British officer recalled that his "exasperated men . . . rushed wildly about into every building, bayoneting every American they met." Some died while begging for mercy, before the British officers could intervene. The sixty-five American dead, compared to only twelve wounded, delighted Drummond as proving "how irresistible a weapon the Bayonet is in the hands of British Soldiers." Another three hundred Americans survived as British prisoners, while the victory liberated from the dungeon eight Upper Canadians arrested by Willcocks and a few Indians taken by the Americans.[66]

The booty included twenty-seven cannon, three thousand stands of arms, and massive quantities of ammunition and provisions—virtually all of the American military stores on the Niagara frontier. That booty saved the British force from a hungry winter, for the Niagara District had been stripped of surplus food by American marauders. New York's

Governor Tompkins concluded that the "immense" supplies would "be of the greatest importance to the British, & is an irreparable loss to us." For want of stored food, the Americans would struggle to support a new army on the Niagara frontier to oust the well-stocked victors. The Americans were losing a war that pivoted on which side could better feed its armed men.[67]

Badly maintained, the fort disgusted Drummond, the consummate military professional: "Nothing can be in a more wretched state both as to the defences & the cover than Fort Niagara at the time of its Capture." Because McClure was away at Buffalo, the fort was commanded by Captain Nathaniel Leonard, a veteran officer who had aroused suspicions for fraternizing with British officers before the war. Lazy and often drunk, he lodged with his family in a comfortable farmhouse three miles from his garrison, an unusual arrangement when a powerful enemy lurked nearby. Dozing through the evening's noise, he rode to his fort the next morning to find the British in charge and his men dead or captured. Accepting that twist of fate, Leonard meekly surrendered. McClure concluded, "His uniform attachment to British men and measures . . . strengthens me in a suspicion that there was a secret understanding with regard to this disgraceful transaction."[68]

Although probably not a traitor, Captain Leonard was certainly a fool. Why then was he entrusted with command of Fort Niagara? Almost a year before, Armstrong had ordered Leonard arrested to answer charges of ineptitude and disloyalty. But the area commanders— Dearborn, Boyd, and Wilkinson—had neglected to execute that order, leaving Leonard in command where his folly could inflict the greatest damage in December 1813.[69]

As soon as Murray secured Fort Niagara, Drummond unleashed a second attack that targeted nearby Lewiston. General Phineas Riall led five hundred soldiers and five hundred Indians—a new departure for the British, who had previously barred their allies from crossing into New York for fear of atrocities that would fuel American propaganda. A British officer reported that the sixty American defenders broke and fled "as soon as they heard the yells of the Indians." The shocked villagers joined the rush. One refugee saw scores, "some not more than half dressed, without shoes or stockings together with men on horseback, waggons, carts, sleighs and sleds overturning and crushing each other stimulated by the horrid yells of 900 savages on the pursuit, which lasted eight miles [and] formed a scene awful and terrific in the extreme."[70]

The Indians killed about a dozen of the slower civilians, including at least one child. Breaking into stores and homes, the warriors got drunk on plundered liquor and then wounded two British soldiers and killed two of their own people. So impressive in surprising Fort Niagara, the discipline of the British regulars also broke down at Lewiston. An officer reported, "Indians, Regulars & Militia were plundering every thing they could get hold of. . . . I have never witnessed such a scene before & hope I shall not again." The victors burned every house in Lewiston and the nearby village of the Tuscarora, a Haudenosaunee people who had helped the Americans.[71]

The Lewiston raid was a transaction that typified the war: the British got a military victory while the Republicans reaped a propaganda tale of Indian savagery. When the British withdrew back to their side of the river, an American returned to find the mutilated bodies of his neighbors: "with their heads cut off, their bodies torn open, and their hearts taken out—some scalped, some not, but all hacked and cut in the most brutal manner—with their tongues cut out; some partially eaten by the hogs." While the Republican press played up the atrocity, the Federalists minimized the gore, and the British insisted that they had done everything possible to restrain warriors who could not be restrained.[72]

BUFFALO

To defend Black Rock and Buffalo from the next British attack, McClure again appealed for volunteers by waving the bloody scalp: "The enemy are preparing to invade your frontier and let their savages loose upon your families and property." This call backfired, for most of the militiamen had lost faith in McClure, so they preferred to pack up their families to flee eastward away from the savage menace.[73]

Some militia did gather at Buffalo, but they rejected McClure's orders, preferring Chapin's command. During the fall, the two men had fallen out at Fort George. Chapin blasted McClure as a fool for letting Willcocks loot the countryside and burn Newark. And McClure denounced Chapin as an insidious Federalist who fomented disorder and desertion by the volunteers. At Buffalo on December 20, McClure arrested Chapin on charges of treason and mutiny. "There is not a greater rascal [who] exists than Chapin, and he is supported by a pack of *tories* and enemies to our Government," McClure explained. But the local volunteers rescued Chapin and bellowed at McClure: "Shoot him down, shoot him." The rescuers fired a few guns, while McClure fled. In December 1812 he had applauded as his volunteers drove a frightened

Alexander Smyth from Buffalo. A year later it was McClure's turn to suffer a mob's rage.[74]

To avoid a bloody battle between his supporters (primarily the Canadian Volunteers) and Chapin's volunteers, McClure headed for home, deserting his command. "Each had his friends and a civil war, if I may call it such, was like to be the consequence" of staying, he explained. Denouncing Buffalo as a den of Federalist treason, McClure assured one resident, "they may all be destroyed, and I don't care how soon." His aide, John C. Spencer, had heard and seen enough to declare McClure "wholly incompetent" and almost universally despised.[75]

Another militia general, Amos Hall, hastened to Buffalo to try to save the town. Arriving on December 26, he found "irregular troops of various descriptions, disorganized and confused. Everything wore the appearance of consternation and dismay." Hall tried to bolster his militia by publicly flattering "their civil deportment and soldier-like conduct," but he belied that praise by begging the men to desist from the "idle sport" of randomly firing off their muskets, which squandered scarce ammunition.[76]

On the morning of December 30, General Riall led a British attack by 50 militiamen, 400 Indians, and 965 regulars. Despite the brutality at Lewiston, Drummond repeated the experiment of sending Indians across the river because of their shock value. At Black Rock, Hall had 2,011 men until they heard the war screams of the hostile warriors. Spooked by the "savage yells coming on all sides," the militia broke and ran in a "general stampede," throwing away their muskets without even a parting shot. A witness recalled, "They could no more be stopped than a flock of sheep." Instead of rallying the men, the militia officers joined the race away from the "bursting shells and the rockets . . . the whistling of the bullets and the horrid yells of the savages." A regular officer, Lieutenant Riddle, rallied a few militia, but General Hall, a fatalist and a Federalist, told the men that "all was lost, all was gone" and "if they went with Riddle, they would be cut to pieces. What few had been collected then fled in almost every direction."[77]

The civilians also ran for their lives. At Buffalo, Chapin found "all was confusion and alarm, women and children running in every direction, to avoid the fury of British savages, which were rapidly infesting the village." Compounding to that confusion, Chapin bellowed, "Every Man for himself & the Devil for us all." A boy recalled fleeing with his mother: "As we went out the Side Door, the Indians come into the front Door." The warriors tomahawked Sarah Lovejoy, who foolishly lingered to wrench her dresses away from plundering Indians. Laid on a bed in a black silk dress, her corpse impressed a boy, who reported: "Her long Black hair reached to the Floor clotted with Blood."[78]

The Indians pillaged and burned every building in Black Rock and Buffalo save one, spared because they had killed a child who had lived there. In the two villages, the fires destroyed 104 homes, 43 barns, and 18 stores. The British also burned four schooners trapped in the ice at Black Rock. To spite Peter B. Porter, the victors blew up his stone mansion and stone storehouse. The British took away 130 prisoners including Chapin, who was sent to prison in Quebec. Making a political distinction, the British released any captured Federalists who helped them locate caches of valuable property. The freed men included Ralph Pomeroy, who assured his captors that he was "a friend to the British Government." A year before, Pomeroy had suffered for that friendship when Republican volunteers demolished his inn. Although freed by his British friends, Pomeroy had lost his rebuilt inn to their torches.[79]

On January 1, the British and their allies withdrew to the Canadian side of the Niagara River—save for Fort Niagara, which Drummond kept with a strong garrison. His raids had dispossessed 12,000 inhabitants, whose flight depopulated a tract of 160 square miles. Families became scrambled in the terrified confusion of flight, as "mothers [found] themselves wandering with strange children."[80]

The refugees included John Haddock, a furniture maker and grocer. Initially, he had prospered from the war by supplying troops with coffins, an especially lucrative business given the diseases of the camp. By late 1813 he had "gained a very Handsome Property, a Decent House" and "Plenty of Every thing to Live on." But on "that Fatal Day" of December 30, the war turned on Haddock. His gains dissolved as "merciless British troops & Indians" pillaged and burned his house and store. Fleeing from "Death and Destruction," Haddock was reduced to the charity of strangers.[81]

With the villages and farms along the Niagara River abandoned and burned, the American front receded about eleven miles to the east to Williamsville, where four hundred militiamen kept an uneasy watch. A western New York Republican lamented, "Every thing that is done appears to me to be all hodge podge. All is a chaotic Mass of Disorder, Anarchy, and Confusion."[82]

The best American troops on that front were, in fact, the Canadian Volunteers, who had fought bravely at Lewiston and Black Rock. Instead of liberating Canadians, the Americans depended on some of them to protect their own ravaged frontier. But General Hall blamed Willcocks and his volunteers for the war's nasty turn. By waging their civil war in Upper Canada, and especially by burning Newark, the Canadian Volunteers had drawn British retribution across the river, devastating New York farms and villages. Despising them as renegades, Hall dissolved their regiment and demanded their weapons. Benajah Mallory concluded, "Genl. McClure was our friend but Genl. Hall being distinctly opposed to the War is in direct opposition not only to us but to the Cause in which we are engaged."[83]

In Washington, D.C., Willcocks lobbied to save the Canadian Volunteers. He had Porter's ringing endorsement conveyed to the secretary of war: "This corps, although small at present, has distinguished itself by its bravery & good conduct and much reliance might be placed on this description of troops as they have literally no alternative but victory or death." Impressed by that case, Congress spared the Canadian Volunteers, and Armstrong issued commissions in the regular army to the officers, including Willcocks as the lieutenant colonel in command. But he was restricted to recruiting only Canadians, which would be difficult with the American forces ousted from the Niagara District. Thanks to desertion, Hall's meddling, and the restriction on recruiting, the unit shrank to a mere thirty-six men by June 1814.[84]

RETALIATION

The destruction of the Niagara Valley villages shocked Americans. "Such is the horrid character which this war has assumed—a war of plunder and of burning," concluded a newspaper in western New York. Lusting for revenge, Armstrong proposed to recruit Indians to ravage Upper Canada:

> These settlements must be broken up and converted into a desert. . . . We should not by the 1st day of June have a British settler west of Kingston. . . . All the horrors brought to our firesides ought to be carried to theirs.

General Harrison and Governor Tompkins endorsed Armstrong's plan, but President Madison balked, for he remained wedded to the American propaganda which cast Britons as uniquely vicious for employing savages.[85]

Armstrong's bloody proposal revealed the polarization wrought by the war as Americans and Upper Canadians soured on one another. At the start of the war, Republicans had empathized with Upper Canadians as brethren who warranted liberation. But after the disasters on the Niagara front, Armstrong longed to obliterate their homes in a fantasy of revenge. While plundering and burning had hardened most Upper Canadians against the invaders, Drummond's destructive counterattack led Republicans to see their northern neighbors as bitter foes rather than as natural friends. The escalating and interacting horrors of war created a new boundary in minds on both sides.

In this highly political war, waged in newspapers as well as on the battlefield, both sides jockeyed for a propaganda edge. Britons and Americans each blamed the other for violating the "laws of war" which in European theory (but rarely in European practice) exempted civilians and their property from military violence. The British regarded the American republic as a rogue state too weak to govern its own people and restrain them within the bounds of international law. In a proclamation issued on January 12, 1814, Prevost denounced them as the aggressors and cast the British as their punishing teachers. He described Drummond's attacks as just retaliation for the previous looting and burning by American troops at Sandwich in 1812 and at York, Moraviantown, and the Niagara District in 1813: "this departure from the established usages of war has originated with America herself, and . . . to her alone are justly chargeable all the awful and unhappy consequences." He concluded that "a full measure of retaliation has taken place, such as, it is hoped, will teach the enemy to respect in future the laws of war."[86]

Outraged by Prevost's presumption, Republicans insisted on their own moral superiority as the original victims. They claimed that the British began the destructive spiral by promoting Indian atrocities on the frontier and by ravaging Havre de Grace and Hampton, coastal towns on Chesapeake Bay. Some mercenaries in British employ had raped women at Hampton, which made that town another American symbol of British barbarity. And the Republicans regarded the British destruction of four villages in the Niagara Valley as a disproportionate revenge for Newark's burning.[87]

The Madison administration also denied responsibility for the plundering at Sandwich and York, dismissed as the unauthorized misdeeds of undisciplined troops. The government blamed Newark's destruction on McClure, cast as a rogue commander who misunderstood his orders. And the U.S. secretary of state, James Monroe, dismissed Moraviantown as a worthless Indian village that should not be avenged by burning a civilized American town. Besides, he insisted, the Moraviantown Indians got what they deserved for ravaging the American frontier. In fact,

Moraviantown's people were Christian pacifists who had built homes, barns, and fences more valuable than those of their white neighbors in the Thames Valley.[88]

The Madison administration offered flimsy excuses, for the republic had sent undisciplined troops and reckless generals across the border to plunder and burn with impunity. In September General Wilkinson had applauded "the patriotism and enterprise of Major Chapin" and declared that "all [the] enemy's property should be good prize for any of our citizens who may take it." And the government never punished their wayward troops and officers for the looting and burning. Not even McClure faced a court-martial. Desperate for political support, the Republicans dared not punish one of their own. No one bore public responsibility for the destruction inflicted on Upper Canadians.[89]

The disasters on the Niagara front became the key issue in New York's spring legislative election. Federalists blamed the Republicans for ineptly waging an unjust war. In an appeal to the voters, the Federalists demanded: "Where was the protection of the government, when your villages were in flames, and your wives and children driven from home in the severity of winter, to seek refuge at the door of charity?" The Federalists insisted that true security lay in electing Federalists to seek a prompt peace. In response, the Republicans shifted the focus from their defeats to the atrocities of Indian warfare, dwelling on the bodily mutilations that so disturbed Americans. Again casting the issue in familial terms, Governor Tompkins insisted:

> Many of our fellow citizens, who were at peace with their families, were murdered and scalped. The bodies of many of those who were wounded or taken prisoners in the engagement at Black Rock, have been found mangled in the most shocking manner by the tomahawk and scalping knife.

He urged voters to unite behind the Republicans, who vowed to push the British away from the Niagara frontier.[90]

In a landslide, the voters endorsed the Republican promise of revenge rather than the Federalist insistence on peace. Even the county that had suffered the most, Niagara, strongly supported the Republicans, as did adjoining Genesee County, which had taken in most of the refugees. Statewide, the Federalists lost their majority in the assembly, and the Republicans won every seat but one in the state senate. For the first time since the war began, Tompkins enjoyed Republican majorities

Major Andrew H. Holmes, *died 1814.* (Courtesy of Mackinac State Historic Parks, Michigan.)

in both houses of the legislature, which promised the state's full support for a new military campaign in 1814.[91]

DETROIT

After Drummond's victorious campaign, the Americans retained one foothold in Upper Canada: the Western District in the Detroit Valley, which Harrison had captured in October. But the American hold on the valley was tenuous, for their occupying troops were demoralized by hard work, cold rains, scarce rations, delays in their pay, and disease in their bodies. Crowded into filthy forts, the men suffered from cholera and dysentery, which incapacitated two-thirds of the garrison in December. By April at least six hundred soldiers had died of disease, more than combat had killed during the preceding year. Worn out by the burials, the weary survivors stopped making coffins, casting the dead directly into pits. The force dwindled further as enlistments expired for many of the men, "none of whom reenlist," their commander lamented.[92]

The Americans also inherited a logistical dilemma that had bedeviled the British: how to feed an occupying army without alienating the local farmers. In October the new territorial governor, Lewis Cass, reported: "The whole resources of the country are exhausted. . . . The principal part of the resources was consumed by the British; and the savages gleaned the residue." To provision the civilians, Indians, and troops for six months, the Americans had to ship 500,000 rations to Detroit from Ohio and western Pennsylvania. Transporting the bulky provisions was manageable from May through October, when ships could navigate Lake Erie. But when winter's ice locked the waters, shipments had to crawl in wagons along the miserable road through the Black Swamp between Ohio and Detroit. Feeding the draft animals cost more than the value of the provisions that they could pull through the slush and mud. When contractors could not make a profit, they halted their shipments and declared bankruptcy, which left the troops to starve. An exasperated general declared, "I would hang half of the quartermasters and all the contractors if I was to remain in service much longer."[93]

To supplement their erratic shipments from the south, Detroit's commanders extorted food from the Canadian farmers. Armed patrols ascended the Detroit and Thames Rivers to collect and carry away wheat and flour. The farmers and millers had to accept the prices offered and the quantities demanded by the American troops. The troops also crippled farming operations by requisitioning—and rarely returning—horses, sleighs, and wagons to haul away the provisions.[94]

Dropping the pretense of liberation, the occupiers sought to intimidate the Canadians. Governor Cass explained, "we must trust to secret agents, of whom I have several employed, and to the terror of military punishment." The local military commander, Colonel Anthony Butler, agreed that the Canadians should be managed "with sufficient severity to inspire terror."[95]

Captain Andrew H. Holmes treated the civilians with particular rigor. To shame those who violated his regulations, Holmes marched them through the village of Amherstburg at the point of a bayonet while drummers beat "the Rogue's march." Regarding the inhabitants as the accomplices of Indians rather than as the brethren of Americans, he demanded: "Did you not join hands with the Savage in his career of Murder and desolation upon the opposite Frontier[?] Did you not participate in the dark Tragedy at the River Raisin, where demons might have blushed in witnessing unresisting innocence[?]" Unless they submitted to his orders, he threatened to inflict "one scene of devastations from Hartley's to Point-au-Plait. Savages have been put under my command for this special purpose, and it rests with you to give the signal." Holmes saw no contradiction in employing Indians to brutalize people whom he blamed for fighting beside warriors allied to the British.[96]

In January 1814 the American officers learned that General Drummond was preparing a winter expedition by 1,760 men in sleighs to retake the Detroit Valley. Victory would restore the Indian alliance on his western flank and enable the native refugees at Burlington Heights to return home. By repatriating them, Drummond meant to alleviate their plundering pressure on the farmers of the Niagara District. A scarcity of food drove strategy on both sides in early 1814.[97]

Dreading Drummond's approach, Colonel Butler ordered Amherstburg and Sandwich burned to deprive the British of winter shelter—the same rationale cited by McClure for destroying Newark. According to a witness, Butler's announcement panicked the inhabitants: "the confusion was great, People running in every direction carrying their effects out of the Town." At the last minute, Butler rescinded his order to burn the towns, upon learning that the British had canceled their expedition. Unusually mild weather had melted the snow cover that Drummond needed to glide his sleighs westward to Detroit.[98]

To keep the British from trying again, the American commanders sent armed patrols up the Thames River and along the north shore of Lake Erie to seize surplus food. The patrols sought to create a buffer zone, where an advancing enemy would starve. The patrols also arrested and removed militia officers who might rally the local people to support a British comeback. Increasingly destructive, the raids slaughtered livestock and burned farms, barns, mills, and distilleries. The destructive turn delighted Andrew Westbrook, a tall, muscular, red-haired, brooding man who guided the patrols. A disaffected Late Loyalist, Westbrook sought vengeance against the London District's leading magistrates and officers. In Delaware Township, Westbrook burned his own house and barn, "rather than that they should be enjoyed by his implacable persecutors."[99]

To counter the Americans' "incendiary system," Drummond sent three hundred regulars and militia volunteers, with a few Indians, to the Thames Valley. On March 4, at the Long Woods, 110 miles northeast of Detroit, the British attacked about 150 American troops led by Captain Holmes, the bully of Amherstburg. Strongly posted behind a log barricade on a hill, the Americans leveled a withering fire. "Shot to pieces," the British retreated eastward, abandoning the valley. A rare American

Brigadier General Duncan McArthur
(*1772–1839*), *engraving by an unknoan
artist. From Benson J. Lossing,* The Pictorial Field-Book of the War of 1812
(*New York, 1869*), *267.* (Courtesy of the
New York State Library.)

victory, the bloody skirmish at the Long Woods made a war hero of
Holmes, who was promoted to major.[100]

McARTHUR

The American hold on the Detroit Valley remained weak so long as the
British retained Michilimackinac, which they had captured at the start
of the war. An island at the confluence of Lake Michigan and Lake
Huron, Michilimackinac lay at the strategic nexus of the fur trade and
Indian alliances extending west from British Montreal across the upper
Great Lakes to the Mississippi Valley. The British General Prevost
insisted: "I consider it as of vital importance as respects our Indian
alliance, it being the rallying point, the last link by which their Warriors
still faithfully cling to our interest." The American general Duncan
McArthur agreed that "nothing can break off the intercourse and connection between the British and Indians short of having possession of
that post." If distant and marginal from a coastal view, Michilimackinac
was central and pivotal from a continental perspective.[101]

In July 1814 the American expedition sailed north from the Detroit River into Lake Huron. Commodore Arthur Sinclair led the five naval vessels, while Colonel George Croghan commanded the 770 troops. On August 4, Croghan's troops landed on the west end of Michili-mackinac Island and marched eastward to attack the British fort. In the woods at mid-island, the Americans tangled with fewer than half of their own numbers: one hundred British regulars and two hundred Indians. Early in the fight, Major Holmes died, which disheartened Croghan, who ordered a retreat to the ships after his men had suffered sixty-one casualties.[102]

Sailing back to Detroit, Croghan and Sinclair left behind two war-ships to blockade the fort, in hopes of starving the garrison into a sur-render. Instead, in early September, British troops and their Indian allies surprised the negligent American crews, capturing both ships, which secured Michilimackinac from further attack. In the reflexive American response to an embarrassing defeat, Sinclair accused the Indians of atrocities against captured Americans, who allegedly "had their *hearts* and *livers* taken out, which were actually cooked and feasted on (and that too in the quarters of the British officers sanctioned by Colo. [Robert] McDouall) by the Savages." Even atrocity stories pivoted on scarce food in the Great Lakes country of 1814.[103]

After Croghan's failure, the Americans at Detroit felt vulnerable to a British attack and an Indian uprising that would repeat "the catastrophe of 1812." Their alarm grew as some roaming warriors killed cattle and a few farmers on the outskirts of town. To bolster Detroit, the Madison administration sent reinforcements commanded by General McArthur, a gruff, tough, and barely educated Ohioan of Ulster Irish descent. One Briton disdained McArthur as "dirty and butcher-like, . . . seeming half-savage and dressed like a backwoodsman," but he had prospered as a land speculator and politician in a classic American rise from homespun to riches.[104]

By raiding deep into Upper Canada, McArthur meant to destroy the flour mills that supplied British troops—and thereby to discourage an attack on Detroit for want of food. Starting from Detroit on October 22, McArthur led 70 Indians and 650 mounted volunteers, half from Ohio and half from Kentucky. His warriors were Shawnee, Delaware, and Wyandot from enclaves in Ohio. Moving quickly, the mounted men pushed up the Thames River 150 miles to Oxford County. When two local men bolted to warn the British of the American advance, McArthur burned their homes and barns. Refreshing his force with stolen horses, McArthur pushed east another fifty miles to the Grand River.[105]

Finding that river too swollen by heavy rains to cross, McArthur turned south to the Lake Erie shore, and then west to return to Detroit. On the way, his men stole more horses and arms and burned five mills and took and paroled 111 militiamen. The only resistance came on November 6, at Malcolm's Mills, where the raiders routed a few militiamen. Eleven days later, McArthur reached Detroit after losing only one dead man while wreaking havoc through the London District. The chagrined Britons resorted to the American practice of turning a defeat into a propaganda of atrocity. Casting the Americans as hypocrites, British officers dwelled on two men scalped and mutilated by McArthur's warriors at Malcolm's Mills.[106]

To augment McArthur's raid, Colonel John Miller sent probes from Detroit up the Thames River as far as Oxford to intimidate Loyalists, destroy munitions, and grab provisions. Miller needed to control the valley's promising wheat harvest, estimated at 150,000 bushels, for that crop could be either Detroit's great liability or best asset. If left to the settlers, the crop would invite a British advance to attack Detroit during the winter. But that attack could be discouraged, and the Detroit garrison fed, by taking the harvest. Returning home to Ohio in late November, General McArthur reported, "When I left Detroit, the troops subsisted entirely on the resources of the Country." But by January the rations again fell short at Detroit. Not even hunger, however, could stop the traditional festivities of the winter season, as an American official reported: "The country exhibits a strange mixture of starving & jolity."[107]

The American extortions alienated the Canadian farmers, who hid their crops and sent information to the British at Burlington Heights. Feeling betrayed, Governor Cass vowed to destroy all of the farms in the Western and London Districts to create "a desert between us and them." He concluded, "It appears to be a harsh and rigorous step, but it is certainly no time for weak, timid, and irresolute measures." Colonel Butler agreed: "A little blood letting may do them good and make the Country tranquil," for "the safest course is to depopulate the Territory."[108]

McArthur wanted to go even farther by including Michigan in the proposed devastation. He advised removing the citizens and burning their homes, "leaving nothing but the Garrison posts. From my observation, the Territory appears to me not worth defending and merely a den for Indians and traitors." Disgusted that the Michigan militia had refused to assist his Canadian raid, McArthur insisted, "Some of those people from choice and others perhaps to save their scalps, feed, harbour, and communicate every information to [the Indians] and through them to the British." Indeed, he denounced the territory's people as "the most dangerous of our enemies." Fortunately, the war ended before McArthur could depopulate and ravage Michigan as well as western Upper Canada.[109]

At the start of the war, Cass and McArthur had helped Hull's invasion, which they described as a liberation of their oppressed brethren in Upper Canada. Two years later, however, Cass recast the Upper Canadians as foes who should be uprooted, and McArthur wanted to treat even the people of Michigan as traitors. Meanwhile, British officials applauded the grim new determination by Canadians to fight the invaders, who had turned potential friends into bitter enemies.[110]

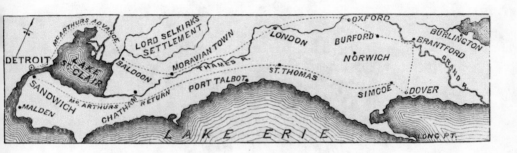

McArthur's Raid, *1814, engraving by an unknown artist. From Benson J. Lossing,* The Pictorial Field-Book of the War of 1812 *(New York, 1869), 852.* (Courtesy of the New York State Library.)

Judge Nathan Ford *(1763–1829), engraving by J. C. Buttre. From Franklin B. Hough*, A History of St. Lawrence and Franklin Counties New York from the Earliest Period to the Present Time *(Albany: Little, 1853), 591.* (Courtesy of the New York State Library.)

CHAPTER TEN

NORTHERN LIGHTS

*Poor little half-starved Upper Canada alone could carry on a war
against the whole gang of cowardly, stupid Democrats to all eternity.*

—Nathan Ford, July 5, 1813[1]

BRITISH MILITARY OFFICERS marveled at the American failure to contest the St. Lawrence River, which served as the critical supply line of
British Canada. Along the northern boundary of New York, American
troops might have commanded the river by erecting batteries of cannon
along their shore and by filling the river with gunboats. Better still,
they could have crossed the river to seize and fortify the key Upper
Canadian river town of Prescott, giving the invaders secure control of
both banks. "If they had done so with any kind of spirit, we must have
abandoned Upper Canada, Kingston, and the fleet on [Lake] Ontario
included," a British officer explained. With that supply line severed, the
British forces upstream would have run out of ammunition, provisions,
naval supplies, and pay. Desertion by the regulars would have surged,
and militia and Indian support would have faltered. But only once, in
late 1813, did the main American army enter the St. Lawrence Valley—
and then only briefly and disastrously. For most of the war, the Americans instead frittered away their resources by attacking Niagara and
Detroit at the western fringes of Upper Canada. Why did they resist
the obvious?[2]

A savvy British officer, who had served at Prescott, hinted that the
Madison administration kept troops away from the valley to appease
"the private interests of a very influential individual in the States."
Unnamed in the officer's account, that "very influential individual" was
David Parish, a German capitalist who had immigrated to the United
States in 1806, settling in Philadelphia. Two years later, he procured
200,000 acres of land in the St. Lawrence Valley, where he sought prof-
its by retailing farms to settlers. His agents, Joseph Rosseel and John
Ross, resided in the valley's leading town, Ogdensburg, New York, on

the river across from Prescott. By loaning millions of dollars to the Madison administration, Parish procured a tacit understanding that the government would keep its troops away from Ogdensburg. Neutrality in the St. Lawrence Valley best protected his property, but it compromised the war effort that his loan money kept barely afloat.[3]

While Parish worked behind the scenes, his outspoken friend Nathan Ford led the Federalists in the St. Lawrence Valley. Born in New Jersey, Ford had served as a quartermaster during the revolution. After the war he had joined a cartel of land speculators led by the Ogden family. During the early 1790s he had moved north to the valley to supervise the settlement of their holdings and especially the town of Ogdensburg. Recognizing his clout, the state government made Ford the county's presiding judge, a role in which he became "a terror to evil doers." An especially partisan Federalist, Ford clashed with Alexander Richards, the leading Republican in the county. As the national government's customs collector for the valley, Richards struggled to suppress the illicit commerce pouring across the long border.[4]

The smugglers included Judge Ford and Parish's agents, Ross and Rosseel. The landlords regarded the trade as a profitable resistance to unjust laws enacted by foolish Republicans. Without the Montreal market for their flour, lumber, and potash the valley's settlers could not pay their landlords for their farms. Reliant on that profitable cross-border trade, the great landowners balked at the conquest of Canada. David A. Ogden explained to a friend that he "would regret much (between ourselves) that Quebec should not remain in the possession of the English."[5]

Ogdensburg served as the market center and courthouse town for the surrounding county. By 1810 the town had 1,245 inhabitants and a neat grid of streets. The brick or wood-frame houses and stores, many two or three stories tall, attested to the prosperity of the land agents, merchants, and lawyers. In the surrounding country towns, the settlers struggled to raise grain and livestock in small fields still bristling with stumps. They depended on Ogdensburg's land agents and merchants for the credit to buy store goods and their farms. In politics, most followed the Federalist lead of the Ogdensburg gentry who served as their patrons. Smuggling strengthened that bond by buoying the local economy, which averted litigation between the town creditors and their country debtors.[6]

War threatened to disrupt that town–country alliance for if the common folk crossed the river to attack and plunder the Canadians, the British would counterattack to destroy the valuable homes and stores of

Ogdensburg. And if the British employed Indians to raid the American shore, that would trigger a massive, panicky flight by the settlers to the ruin of their gentry creditors.[7]

To keep the local peace, the Ogdensburg gentry sought an understanding with the British officers at Prescott. A Briton reported that Ford and the Ogdens proposed "a neutrality between the Inhabitants on the St. Lawrence Frontier in the event of War. It seems this idea has originated with themselves, and arose in a great measure from their dread of the Indians." In that spirit, some Canadians erected on the border a large sign depicting an American eagle and the British lion with the slogan: "If you don't scratch, I won't bite."[8]

In July 1812 that neutrality threatened to collapse with the arrival of Captain Benjamin Forsyth and his company of riflemen. A staunch Republican from North Carolina, Forsyth meant to wage an aggressive partisan war across the border into Canada. Recruited in North Carolina and Virginia, Forsyth's riflemen wore green coats faced with brown and yellow, and leather caps topped with black plumes. Although crack shots, they had little discipline, which suited Forsyth just fine. An inspecting officer concluded that Forsyth "was a brave, intrepid, ardent, eccentric officer . . . Order, discipline and subordination were totally neglected by him, consequently his men appear more like outlaws than soldiers." Another officer scoffed, "They are little better than savages in battle." Fighting more for plunder than for country, his riflemen picked off enemy officers and then dashed up to strip them of their money, watches, and epaulets.[9]

For his first raid, Forsyth targeted the compound of Joel Stone, the leading man of Gananoque. A Loyalist refugee from Connecticut, Stone owned a set of mills, presided over the local court, and commanded the Leeds County militia. When the war broke out, Stone aggressively drafted militiamen to defend his mills and the flow of British supplies along the river. His drafts irritated the American newcomers, who formed half of the county's population. Some fled across the border, to convey their tales of woe to Forsyth. Empathizing with them, Forsyth vowed to punish Stone, "a tory in [the] time of the revolutionary war" who had "remained since [a] notorious enemy and opposer to the Government of the United States." Both Stone and Forsyth regarded the new war as a renewal of the revolution.[10]

On the night of September 20–21, Forsyth and 104 men rowed across the river to surprise Stone's compound. Twelve militia guards surrendered, while the rest ran away. Stone was absent, so the victorious riflemen saluted him by firing a volley into his home, smashing his windows and wounding his wife. After burning Stone's storehouse and a large stock of provisions, Forsyth withdrew with 12 prisoners, 30 barrels of flour, 41 muskets, and the plundered contents of Stone's trunks.[11]

In his second cross-border attack, Forsyth surprised the riverfront village of Brockville in the wee hours of February 7, 1813. The raiders broke open the district jail to liberate sixteen Late Loyalists jailed for resisting the hated militia draft. Although petty victories, Forsyth's raids thrilled Republicans, who desperately needed a war hero in the wake of Hull's, Van Rensselaer's, and Smyth's follies. Forsyth won rapid promotion to major after the first raid and to lieutenant colonel after the second. But the British and the Federalists vilified him as a reckless outlaw and "a man-killing idiot" whose raids provoked British retaliation on the innocent.[12]

To stem Forsyth's raids, the Reverend John Strachan pointed out the best pressure point to a British official:

These marauding parties are very dangerous, but if they continue, you must burn Ogdensburgh. I believe that, if Mr. Parish were informed that his House & Stores shall pay the forfeit of the next marauding expedition, and Judge Ford's new house, there should be no more. These people have the power to prevent them, and they ought to be informed that it is [in] their interest to do so. . . . They must feel their danger, and then they will exert themselves.

At Prescott, the fiery British commander, Colonel Thomas Pearson, seethed at Forsyth's exploits and resented the safe haven that he offered to militiamen fleeing from service in Upper Canada. During the last week of January, fifty-eight refugees, primarily "poor farmers' sons," reached Ogdensburg. "Deserters from Canada cross almost every evening," the *Ogdensburgh Palladium* reported on February 3.[13]

Emulating Forsyth, some private marauders crossed the river to steal horses from Canadian farms. Under a flag of truce, Pearson sent a blunt warning to Forsyth at Ogdensburg. Demanding the return of the horses, Pearson threatened, if refused, to "send his Indians over to Scalp as many American Officers as they took horses." According to Rosseel, "Nothing but the protection of a flag saved the british officer from being mobbed, so much the Threat of sending Indians is provoking." Forsyth replied "that the british commander might send his Indians and be d[amne]d"—an answer calculated to hasten a confrontation.[14]

Pearson entrusted the attack to Lieutenant Colonel George Mac-

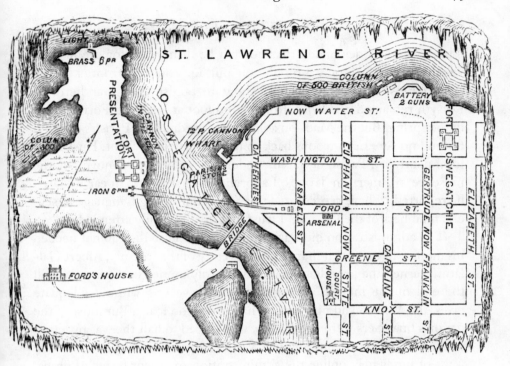

Map of Operations at Ogdensburg. *This map locates the American batteries, the British columns of attack, the streets of the town, and Parish's store and Judge Ford's house. From Benson J. Lossing,* The Pictorial Field-Book of the War of 1812 *(New York, 1869), 580.* (Courtesy of the New York State Library.)

donell, one of the many Macdonells among the Highland Scots settled in Upper Canada's Glengarry County. As brave as Forsyth but more clever, Macdonell commanded the Glengarry Light Infantry. On the morning of February 22, he pretended to drill five hundred men on the frozen St. Lawrence River. Suddenly they charged across the ice under the cover of an artillery fire that pounded Ogdensburg. After a brief firefight, Forsyth and his riflemen retreated to Sackets Harbor, leaving Ogdensburg in British hands.[15]

Most of the inhabitants had fled, abandoning their homes and shops to a thorough ransacking "by swarms of the abandoned of both sexes from Canada, and by numbers of the dissolute class who belonged to the American side." Judge Ford noted, "Many families have been stripped to the last shirt." The British officers protected only the houses of Ford and Parish from the looting. After burning the barracks and four vessels stuck in the ice, the British returned to Prescott, hauling away provisions, munitions, eleven cannon, and fifty-two prisoners.[16]

NEUTRALITY

The Federalists demanded that Forsyth be dismissed "for the distress which he has wantonly brought on our unprotected frontier." The Republicans, however, were not about to punish their war hero, so Forsyth remained in service, to fight and loot at York and Fort George in the spring. But the Madison administration did heed Parish's demand to send no American troops back to the St. Lawrence front. Favoring a local neutrality, Parish declared, "as long as we are not annoyed by the presence of American Troops, I apprehend no danger." In early March he reported, "I have represented this Subject in strong Language to several members of the Cabinet. I trust that it will be duly attended to."[17]

The administration did Parish's bidding because the cabinet needed his money. In early March the U.S. secretary of the treasury, Albert Gallatin, warned the president: "We have hardly money enough to last till the end of the month." Waging an expensive war without adequate taxes, the Madison administration had to rely on loans. But most of the nation's financiers were Federalists, who hoped to halt the war by bankrupting the government. Stephen Van Rensselaer assured Parish, "The want of funds may oblige the administration to accept terms of peace. Nothing but the failure of means will coerce them to terminate the unfortunate war." In March Parish agreed, but he flip-flopped in early April, suddenly agreeing (with partners) to advance $7.5 million—most of the loan.[18]

What had changed for Parish? In part, he was a good capitalist who saw the loan as a secure investment with an alluring interest rate of 7.5 percent. But Parish also expected to buy political leverage, for he insisted on neutrality in the valley and peace negotiations in Europe. In both cases the Madison administration dutifully complied. In early April the administration sent Parish's friend, Gallatin, to New York City to close the deal, which included a commitment to send Gallatin to Europe as the lead American negotiator.[19]

Parish's deal appalled other Federalists as dangerously naive, for they did not trust the administration to negotiate in good faith. Judge Ford declared that "as you furnish the fiddles," the administration would "be sure not to give up the dance." But the dance did move away from Ogdensburg. During the following spring and summer, the American army kept clear of the St. Lawrence Valley, instead attacking strategically marginal places to the west around Lake Ontario and Lake Erie.[20]

David Parish wove a tangled web. Although he privately denounced "this foolish & iniquitous War," Parish also sought a government contract to supply the navy at Sackets Harbor with cannonballs made by his ironworks near Ogdensburg. But Rosseel warned Parish that the British would attack that foundry once they got wind of any contract. Reconsidering, Parish wrote to Prevost, vowing to produce no munitions if the British would promise to protect the ironworks. Prevost agreed. While sustaining the war with money, Parish also worked to keep the fighting away from his property in the valley.[21]

After their Ogdensburg raid, the British played nice, allowing the villagers to return home and inviting them to resume trading with the Canadian side. Ross reported that they "promised protection and security to the country, provided there is no more troops sent to Ogdensburgh." With relief he concluded, "We are entirely at the mercy of the British," for he had despised Forsyth's occupation as "a System not unlike anarchy." Judge Ford agreed, "I feel safer than when Forsyth was here."[22]

Bearing white flags of truce, the Ogdensburg gentry exchanged polite visits and genteel dinners with the British officers at Prescott. On March 2, Rosseel reported, "The british officers rode thro' this village yesterday in sleighs for pleasure as if Ogdensburgh was [under] british dominion." On March 13, Ross added, "we are all as quiet as lambs and are dayly visited by some enemy officers." At the end of the month he concluded, "The frequent communications, if continued, will do good to our Villagers. The [British] officers, for instance, are getting new Boots made & old ones mended here."[23]

Ford worked hard to enforce the neutrality on the valley people. In late March he published an appeal to the inhabitants: "if forbearance is extended [by the enemy], it is not unmanly to receive it with becoming thankfulness. . . . If each remain upon their own side of the river, and each zealously discountenance marauding parties, we shall very much ameliorate our condition." Ford also covertly fed information to the British to help them catch cross-border counterfeiters and horse thieves. Writing to his superiors, Colonel Pearson noted that Ford's "name must of course be buried in our breasts, and too much caution cannot be observed in the treatment of this Fellow to prevent a suspicion of where my Information comes [from]."[24]

But the judge's antiwar politics and his cozy ties with British officers were no secrets. The Republican press denounced Ford as the ultimate "Tory" and Ogdensburg as "a Damd. Tory hole" and the domain of "treason, treachery, and toryism." Ford published an angry rejoinder: "I care not who knows that I was opposed to the war, and I hope I ever shall be opposed to shedding one drop of native American blood, to

protect (upon the high seas) the renegadoes of any nation." As a Federalist, he promoted a substitute enemy: the Irish "renegadoes" blamed
for causing the war.[25]

Most of the local people supported Ford, but a Republican minority
wanted revenge instead of neutrality. Plundered by the British raid, they
sought to even scores by crossing the river to steal horses and boats.
Such revenge raids terrified Rosseel because Colonel Macdonell had
warned "that nothing less than the total distruction, by fire & arms, of
this Place should atone for any hostile operation" across the river into
Canada. Ford concluded, "I have every passion & every prejudice to
grapple with, and public feeling runs pretty high."[26]

Passions ran higher in mid-March, when six Indians crossed the river
in pursuit of British deserters. To dissuade the terrified settlers from
fleeing, Ford and Ross protested to Colonel Macdonell, who agreed to
keep his warriors on his side of the river. Ford also pressed Macdonell to
compensate the villagers for their losses. But the British canceled the
negotiations in late April, when American troops, including Forsyth,
captured and plundered York. Once again, Ford cursed Forsyth.[27]

By reopening the border, the British attracted a steady flow of American cattle and produce to supply their troops at Prescott. The smugglers included Judge Ford and the Parish agents. Ross explained that
they paused only during the local court sessions, when it was "prudent
for the Judge & myself to be cautious." Ford also promoted British propaganda within America by forwarding British general orders to the
Federalist press. And he helped the British acquire a new printing press,
to replace that destroyed at York by the invaders. In a war that pivoted
on printed words as well as pointed bayonets, the new press helped the
British to attack the Americans.[28]

The Ogdensburg gentry also fed military information to their
British friends. During the summer of 1813 Parish visited Ogdensburg
and met with British officers, informing them of the American troop
strength at Sackets Harbor and Fort George. Ross provided the officers
with Federalist newspapers, which routinely detailed the location, quantity, destinations, disputes, and supply and disease problems of American armies. Ross assured Parish that it was "of great importance by me
to be copiously supplied with papers" to convey to Prescott's officers,
who could then "curry favour with their superiors to whom they are
quickly dispatched." Ross noted that the British were "most minutely
informed of all preparations & movements throughout the States." A
local Republican grumbled, "One thing is certain, nothing transpires on
this Side of the River, but it is immediately known on theirs."[29]

Although a net asset to the British, the open border also facilitated desertion, the great bane of their army when posted near the United States, which beckoned as the land of good wages and cheap whiskey. The crisscrossing boats, canoes, and rafts of smugglers enhanced the chances of escaping to Ogdensburg, and the restraint on Indian pursuit removed the chief deterrent. In late May, an irritated Macdonell sent an abrupt message to Ford, demanding the arrest and return of the two latest cross-border deserters. Otherwise, Macdonell threatened to burn Ogdensburg. When the judge refused to comply, the colonel backed down. Losing some deserters became the price that the British had to pay for preserving Ogdensburg as a neutral conduit into the republic.[30]

PIKE'S PIQUE

Along the border, customs officers were too few and too weak to suppress smugglers, who enjoyed popular support. Prosecutions failed because of intimidated witnesses and alienated jurors. In northern New York, General Zebulon Pike complained:

> The commanding officers on the lines are placed in a very delicate situation from the imbecility of the Laws, more especially in this Country where the thirst of gain is such that from the Judges on the bench to the drayman in the street you find persons either directly or indirectly engaged in trading with the enemy.

Indeed, the New York State courts preferred to punish the customs officers rather than the smugglers. In January 1813 Judge Ford's court convicted and fined Alexander Richards and his assistants of assault for their interference. Obliged to pull back, the customs officers watched the smuggling surge. Richards worried, "If a speedy stop is not put to this nefarious traffic, I fear the whole County will become disaffected to the Government and engage in it."[31]

To help Richards, General Pike sent forty soldiers into St. Lawrence County. They arrested nine suspected smugglers and cast them into a military brig at Sackets Harbor. But Pike had underestimated Judge Ford, who retaliated by arresting two army officers on charges of "trespass, assault, and false imprisonment." By setting a prohibitive bail of $10,000 on each, Ford kept both in his jail. Lieutenant Loring Austin sputtered that he was the victim of Ford's "legal patronage of *absolute treason*." Amused, Ford declared, "It is a little funny." But the judge was

Major General James Wilkinson *(1757–1826)*, *oil painting by an unknown artist, ca. 1820.* (Courtesy of the National Portrait Gallery, Smithsonian Institution, NPG 75-5.)

playing for serious stakes: "We are determined to . . . know if a military despotism is really to be the order of the day. They will find we shall die hard." The civil law triumphed when the Jefferson County court (which had jurisdiction at Sackets Harbor) dismissed the charges for want of evidence against the suspects, who returned home in triumph. And, after Parish complained to Gallatin, the Madison administration disavowed the use of troops to enforce the customs laws.[32]

By favoring smuggling, the Federalists promoted an economic interest hostile to the Republicans and their war. Otherwise, the Federalists feared, the common people might seek profits by raiding the Canadian shore or by attacking the British boats passing along the river. Denouncing the war as illegitimate, the Federalists insisted that peacetime law should prevail, which defined raiding as a crime and cross-border trade as proper. Reversing that stance, the Republicans denounced smuggling as treason, while they defended raiding as patriotism in a just war.[33]

In July two ambitious Republicans, Captains Dixon and Dimock, armed two small vessels as privateers to attack and capture sixteen British supply boats passing up the river. The local Federalists denounced the captains as selfish criminals who inspired copycats. To Ford's disgust, some American marauders seized and sold a lumber raft in which he had invested. To avert British retaliation, the judge vigorously prosecuted cross-border raiders, and the Parish agents threatened to evict any of their settler-debtors who so transgressed. In the St. Lawrence Valley, one man's patriotism was another's predation.[34]

THE PLAYER

In late August, General James Wilkinson took command of the American troops around Lake Ontario. Affable, effusive, energetic, and self-assured, Wilkinson dazzled officers sick of their enforced inertia since Boerstler's defeat in June. Lieutenant Mathew Hughes reported that Wilkinson "produced a general joy amongst us." Impressed by Wilkinson's "marked attention and politeness," General Jacob Brown concluded, "He is no common Man. He views things as they really are, and I do not doubt but that, with the smiles of Heaven, something will yet be done worthy of the American Name." At Sackets Harbor a captain marveled, "Gen. Wilkerson has infused new spirit into the troops at this post. He inspired a degree of confidence in every officer & soldier that I never saw equaled."[35]

Historians of the American stage often identify Edwin Booth (older brother of the infamous John Wilkes Booth) as the first great American actor. But those theater historians underestimate the earlier genius of James Wilkinson, who persuaded thousands, including presidents, congressmen, and most of the army's officers, that he was a military genius and a paragon of patriotism. Loving pomp and pageantry, he looked great in a uniform—even as his appetite for liquor and food stretched the fabric. And he issued vivid orders and bombastic proclamations that put Alexander Smyth and George McClure to shame. Wilkinson's many indiscretions charmed friends as the precious candor of an open heart. Only gradually, through painful experience, did they discover that Wilkinson cared only for his own enrichment and power. And, aside from a gift for conning others, Wilkinson had no talent.[36]

Of Irish descent, Wilkinson grew up on a farm in Maryland. He trained to become a physician, but medicine bored him. In 1775 the revolution rescued Wilkinson by offering the excitement and flashier clothes of an army officer's life. Cultivating patrons, he rose by serving as an aide to leading generals: Nathanael Greene, Benedict Arnold, and Horatio Gates. Their influence and his self-promotion won Wilkinson elevation to brigadier general. Put in charge of clothing the army, he lost the post in 1781, when Congress discovered funds missing. But Wilkinson prospered by marrying the daughter of a wealthy merchant from Philadelphia.[37]

After the war he moved west to Kentucky, where his wife's money bought plantations near Lexington. Dabbling in merchandising and politics, Wilkinson visited New Orleans, then under Spanish rule, where he charmed the governor and promised to promote Spanish possession of Kentucky. In return he reaped lucrative trading concessions and an annual pension of $2,000. But he delivered little to the Spanish beyond fawning letters and vague promises. In 1791 he returned to the American army as second-in-command, but he intrigued against his commander, Anthony Wayne, who despised Wilkinson as "that worst of all bad men." Wayne's death in 1796 put Wilkinson in charge of the army, while still on the take from the Spanish.[38]

A political gymnast, Wilkinson became a loud Republican just in time to survive Jefferson's 1801–2 purge of most of the army's Federalist officers. Dazzled by his banter, Gideon Granger praised Wilkinson as "one of the most agreeable, best informed, most genteel, moderate, and sensible Republicans in the nation." By wooing and promoting junior officers, Wilkinson cultivated a devoted following in the army, but he made nearly as many foes by punishing any critics. In 1809 a major noted, "There is a great division among the officers of the army concerning him. Some are his warm advocates, whilst others are his deadly enemies."[39]

In 1805, after the United States acquired the Louisiana Territory, Jefferson made Wilkinson the governor, although he also remained in command of the army. Playing the role of "a petty tyrant," he ran Louisiana as his personal fiefdom, embezzling government funds and lands while illicitly trading with the Spanish in Texas and Cuba. Playing a double game, he also promoted Zebulon Pike's western explorations, which served as a cover for probing Spanish defenses in New Mexico. By having others make trouble for the Spanish, Wilkinson drove up his own value as their informant.[40]

Wilkinson cooperated with the vice-president, Aaron Burr, who proposed to rally adventurers to seize Texas and perhaps Mexico from the

Spanish. When the press blew their cover, Wilkinson saved himself by betraying Burr's plans to Jefferson. To further damn Burr, Wilkinson also charged that the vice-president meant to detach the Mississippi Valley from the union. Smitten with Wilkinson, Jefferson discounted evidence of his double-dealing, even when Burr won acquittal in his treason trial of 1807.[41]

Returning to his command in Louisiana, Wilkinson posted most of his men at Terre-aux-Boeufs, a swamp where bad food, heavy rains, clouds of mosquitoes, and miserable sanitation inflicted malnutrition, malaria, yellow fever, dysentery, and scurvy. Neglecting his troops, Wilkinson lived grandly in New Orleans. He also profited by withholding pay due to the soldiers and by favoring a corrupt contractor who supplied worm-infested meat to them. In two years Wilkinson lost nearly a thousand men, about half his force, to disease and desertion.[42]

This debacle infuriated his second-in-command, the imperious Wade Hampton, and the army's rising young star, Winfield Scott, then a captain. Reckless in his contempt, Scott announced that serving under Wilkinson "was as disgraceful as being married to a prostitute." If they went into battle together, Scott vowed to bring two pistols, one to shoot the enemy and the other to shoot his general. Determined to be thorough, Scott also denounced Wilkinson as a liar, scoundrel, and traitor. In 1810 a court-martial convicted Scott of insubordination and suspended him for one year without pay.[43]

A year later the general faced his own court-martial on charges of illicit dealings with the Spanish, but the court consisted of friendly officers, who despised the secretary of war, William Eustis, who had mustered the government's case. The court cleared Wilkinson, citing a want of evidence, although even a defender conceded that "many very queer transactions of a political and mercantile character were exposed."[44]

Leading Republicans regarded Wilkinson as the best of generals afflicted by the worst of enemies. In 1812 and early 1813, as the northern armies suffered one disastrous defeat after another, a clamor grew in the press and Congress for Wilkinson to take command on the Canadian front. William Duane extolled Wilkinson as "the man of all others best adapted to save the country from such disasters as ignorance and imbecility have brought upon us."[45]

Wilkinson's military star was rising in the spring of 1813, when he won an easy and bloodless victory by seizing West Florida from his old friends, the Spanish, who got precious little return on their investment in him. Wilkinson also had become a political liability in Louisiana, which became a state in 1812. Weary of his corruption, the new state's congressional delegation demanded Wilkinson's removal. The secretary of war, John Armstrong, fancied himself a genius, so he thought it brilliant to solve the Louisiana political problem by transferring Wilkinson to military command in the North. And Madison, to his discredit, went along with that plan, in part from the want of any other veteran generals not yet tainted by defeat.[46]

In mid-March, Armstrong summoned Wilkinson to Washington, D.C., but the general dawdled along the way in every town that offered a grand reception and fancy meals. At last, on July 31, Wilkinson and his entourage pulled into the capital, where he lingered for another eleven days. While waiting for Wilkinson, the northern troops spent two months in enforced inactivity in filthy, rancorous, and disease-ridden camps. But still they longed to believe in their new commander when he belatedly appeared at Sackets Harbor on August 20.[47]

DEMONS OF DISCORD

To unite his officers, Wilkinson issued a general order in the third person: "He will cherish harmony, Union & a Manly fraternal Spirit, as the precursor of triumph & fame, but should Intrigue & faction, those demons of discord, ever shew their Heads within the limits of command it will be his duty to strangle them in the Birth." Alas, some officers knew Wilkinson too well from past service in Louisiana. They included his archenemy, Wade Hampton, who led the American force on Lake Champlain, which fell within Wilkinson's military district. Determined to remain independent, Hampton would take no direct orders from his foe, so Armstrong had to act as a go-between, slowing communication and decisions.[48]

Armstrong wanted Wilkinson to attack Kingston, the main British base on Lake Ontario. But Wilkinson believed that he—and not Armstrong—was the republic's great military genius. He proposed a more daring plan, to load his men into boats to bypass Kingston and Prescott, floating down the St. Lawrence to attack Montreal. A successful attack would cut the supply line that sustained the British forces left behind in Upper Canada. And this advance would bring Wilkinson into Hampton's vicinity, compelling his submission. Best of all, if the scheme worked, Wilkinson—and not Armstrong—would reap the credit.[49]

But October was awfully late in the year, with the Canadian winter closing in, to risk such an offensive. What would become of the army if trapped deep within Canada, far beyond reinforcement and supply? In inviting Wilkinson to come north, Armstrong had enticed, "If our cards are well played, we may renew the scenes of Saratoga." Indeed they might, but with Wilkinson playing the surrendering role of the trapped Burgoyne. The scheme to strike deep behind enemy lines was Napoleonic, but Wilkinson was no Napoleon, and even the emperor had just played that trick once too often, destroying his Grand Army in the Russian winter of 1812–13.[50]

In mid-October Wilkinson shifted his men from Sackets Harbor to Grenadier Island, near the mouth of the St. Lawrence, where gales of driving rain wrecked a third of the boats, drenched the men, and ruined half of their provisions. Wilkinson became bedridden with fever and dysentery, which he treated with whiskey and opium, worsening his erratic orders and delusions of grandeur.[51]

At last, on November 2, Wilkinson began to descend the St. Lawrence in three hundred boats carrying seven thousand men and their food, equipment, and cannon. But the spectacle inspired more pity than awe. A civilian described the boats as resembling a "moving Hospital much more than they did an invading army." To reach Montreal, the expedition would have to descend 150 miles through five sets of dangerous rapids. If they made it, the troops would find Prevost waiting with three thousand regulars and five thousand militia in strong fortifications. And by then the invaders would have exhausted their provisions. If they failed to take the city quickly, they would starve or freeze to death in their flimsy tents. Wilkinson assured his troops that, at Montreal, "our artillery, bayonets and swords must secure our triumph or provide us honorable graves." A wit in his army declared that Wilkinson "delighted in swelling sentences . . . most of them ending with victory or death."[52]

The Republican press assured the nation that at last the American army would win a great victory. On November 3, the *National Intelligencer* predicted "that in ten days hence the enemy will be entirely dispossessed of Upper Canada." Jefferson declared, "we are rejoicing in the expectation that all Canada above the Sorel is ours, and that the earlier disgraces of the war are now wiped away." But Judge Ford knew better, for Wilkinson's army appeared "weak beyond measure . . . Those who live upon the lines know & see the shameful deception which is played off upon the credulity of those who are remote from the scene." Ford awarded to Wilkinson "a pattent right for superior stupidity."[53]

At last, on the night of November 6–7, Wilkinson's boats bypassed Prescott and Ogdensburg in the night. The erratic British cannon fire hit only one boat, killing a soldier and wounding two others, while

Ogdensburg suffered scant damage. A greater threat came from Wilkinson's mouth during the night he spent in the village. Rebuking the general, Ford recalled "your wish that Ogdensburgh might be burnt, and as for Judge Ford, you would hang him, and if the enemy did not burn his property, you would be God damned if you did not." Drunk and drug-addled, Wilkinson entertained (or shocked) his hosts by showing off his gold watches and a picture of his young wife, while singing,

> *I am now a going to Canada.*
> *And there I will get money.*
> *And there I'll kiss the pretty squaws.*
> *They are as sweet as honey.*

Even a defender conceded that the performance "was not of the dignified deportment to be expected from the commander." The next morning his aides sobered Wilkinson enough to stow him aboard his schooner, now safely downstream from the big guns at Prescott.[54]

Upon crossing into Canada with his expedition, Wilkinson issued a forceful general order to his troops:

> It will be the pride and the glory of this Army to conquer not to destroy. Its character, its honor, and that of the American people are intrusted, deeply intrusted, in its magnanimity, its forbearance, and its sacred regard of private property. . . . And as marauding is punishable by death, the General is solemnly determined to hang the first person who shall be detected in plundering an inhabitant of Canada of the smallest Article of property.

But orders are only as good as their enforcement, and Wilkinson punished no one although his troops, led by Forsyth's riflemen, widely looted farms and stores. The plundered included Reverend Strachan's wife, who had gone to Cornwall, mistaking it as a refuge from the war. In a protest sent to Wilkinson, the British Lieutenant Colonel John Harvey denounced "that system of rapine and plunder of the property of the peaceful and unoffending Inhabitants which has marked the progress of the American army."[55]

Lieutenant Colonel Joseph Morrison commanded 1,200 British troops who chased and harassed Wilkinson's descent. On November 11, Wilkinson turned to attack his pursuers at Crysler's Farm on the Canadian side of the river. While Wilkinson remained safely on board his schooner, command of the land attack fell to General John P. Boyd, the senior but least respected brigadier in the army. To the confusion of the troops, Boyd added his own contradictory orders to those already issued by Wilkinson. An officer complained, "We were marched now here, now there, without any system, or apparent design, but to learn whether the army liked cannon shot as little as certain generals."[56]

Although the 2,100 Americans sent into battle outnumbered their foes by almost two to one, the attackers lacked discipline and coordination. Their ragged and erratic fire proved less lethal than the coordinated volleys unleashed by the well-trained British regulars. Exhausting their ammunition too quickly, the Americans broke and fled to the riverbank. Boyd evacuated his demoralized troops to safety on the American side of the river. Their losses—102 killed and 237 wounded—exceeded the 22 dead and 148 wounded suffered by the British.[57]

In his report, Wilkinson spun the battle as a glorious American victory over superior numbers. Judge Ford mocked:

Never was there a more vapid, ill-told lie than he has put his name to. The most funny part of it is, he sais he was worn down with disease to be a mear skeleton. If he had said he was bloated like a toad, he would have discribed himself more accurately.

The report fooled few, for letters from American officers vividly conveyed how badly they had been led. A disgusted General Brown declared, "I would prefer the Glory which Col. Morrison and his gallant *Little Band* so fairly earned on Christler's Fields to . . . the bungling and expensive manner in which we proceed."[58]

On November 12, the day after the defeat, Wilkinson received a second blow in a letter from General Hampton, who was supposed to bring reinforcements from Lake Champlain to a rendezvous on the St. Lawrence. Instead, Hampton reported that he was returning to his base after suffering a defeat on the Châteauguay River, southwest of Montreal. On October 26, a mere 460 French Canadians and 22 Abenaki warriors, led by Lieutenant Colonel Charles de Salaberry, had rebuffed Hampton's 4,500 men.[59]

Salaberry had posted his men behind a log barricade between the river, on the east, and a swamp, to the west. To roust the defenders, Hampton sent one brigade, under Colonel Robert Purdy, across the river with orders to march north to seize the ford behind Salaberry's line. While Purdy's brigade attacked the enemy from the rear, another brigade, led by General George Izard, prepared to assault the barricade from the front. It was one of those nice plans on a neat map that fell apart in the dark and wooded swamp that clogged Purdy's advance. Hampered by inept guides who could not find the ford, Purdy's meandering troops traveled twenty-five miles but made only five miles of forward progress.[60]

Detected at dawn by the French Canadians, Purdy's men suffered from snipers. In returning fire, the confused Americans fired on one another. Hearing the musketry, Hampton falsely concluded that Purdy had seized the ford and had the enemy trapped, so the general ordered Izard to attack the barricade but without supporting artillery fire. More exposed, the Americans suffered heavier casualties. Meanwhile, 1,100 Canadians and Indians arrived to reinforce Salaberry. Disheartened, Hampton ordered his troops to disengage and retreat.[61]

Afflicted by Indians, the swamp, a cold heavy rain, and vivid imaginations, Purdy's men panicked as they fled to the river. Captain Thayer reported, "Officers deserted their posts & their commands fled from the scene of action, threw away their arms & swam the river." Thayer concluded:

> The margin of the river, for 3/4 of a mile was covered with stragglers endeavoring to cross it; some by the help of poles; some on logs; others to their hips in water, exclaiming "we shall all be tommahawk[e]d," begging & offering rewards to be helped over the river. . . . The neighboring woods rang with an incessant roar of musketry, the sound of bugles, & the yell of Indians.

When Purdy's men straggled into Hampton's camp, they were "in a most pitifull plight, numbers without hats, knapsacks, or arms & their clothing torn to tatters." Once again, the sound and fury of Indians terrified troops who too readily imagined the loss of their scalps.[62]

The battle claimed only 84 American casualties out of 4,500 men, and the attackers still enjoyed an edge of nearly three to one over the defenders, but psychologically Hampton and his men were whipped, for officers and men had lost all confidence in one another. Rather than mount a second attack, Hampton abruptly retreated back across the border to Plattsburgh on Lake Champlain. By leaving Wilkinson in the lurch, Hampton gave his old foe an excuse to halt his own advance and to make a scapegoat of Hampton. Retreating from the St. Lawrence River, Wilkinson moved his army six miles up a winding tributary, the Salmon River, to French Mills, just within the New York border.[63]

French Mills consisted of two sawmills, a tavern, a dozen ramshackle houses, and a blockhouse, all surrounded by a dense forest of hemlock and pine. Wilkinson chose that miserable location for his camp to maintain the pretense that he would soon renew his offensive against Canada. Wilkinson's army then had to protect their boats, locked up as winter froze the Salmon River. The tail wagged the dog, when an army stood guard over ice-locked boats in northernmost New York. Wilkinson had found the perfect cul-de-sac to render impotent the main American army at a critical period in the war, freeing up the enemy to shift troops west to ravage the Niagara frontier.[64]

At that dreary camp, the weary men had to build log barracks for their winter shelter. Food was scarce and expensive because of the 230 miles of bad roads between French Mills and the nearest supply depot at Plattsburgh. Hunger, cold, exhaustion, worn-out clothes, and bad sanitation sickened 2,000 men and killed 216 during December. Funeral dirges became so frequent and demoralizing that Wilkinson banned playing them at burials. Wilkinson's favorite officers got furloughs to go home or to go to Washington, to lobby for promotions and to champion their commander. Their departure soured the mood of those who had to stay behind.[65]

In grandiose letters to Armstrong, Wilkinson proposed mounting a winter offensive that would in a single blow capture Kingston, destroy Yeo's squadron, capture four thousand enemy troops, "recover what we have lost, save much blood and treasure to the nation, and conquer a province." In fact, his broken army was in no condition to attack anything. Seeing through the farce and staggered by the transportation costs to feed the army at isolated French Mills, Armstrong ordered Wilkinson to withdraw his men: half to Sackets Harbor and half to Plattsburgh. On February 12, the evacuation began, with the burning of the boats, which had cost the nation so much to build. The next day proved chaotic, as an officer lamented:

> This morning the men appeared to anticipate what was to be done (soldiers always delight in destroying). Fire was communicated to the barracks before the baggage was loaded, parties were sent to put out the fire and guards sent to prevent firing the buildings until the proper time, but no sooner than the fire was got under [control] in one place than it broke out in two or three other places, so that in a little time the whole cantonments were enveloped in flames and smoke, so that some of the troops had some difficulty in getting out without being burnt up.

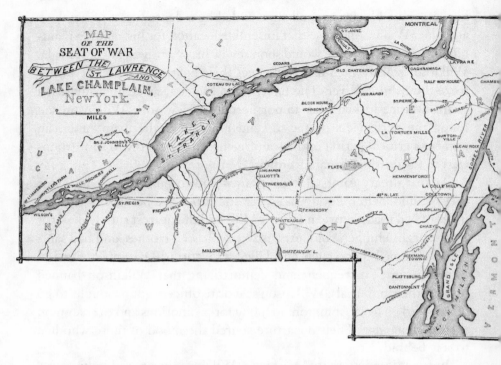

Map of the Seat of War Between the St. Lawrence and Lake Champlain, New York. *From Benson J. Lossing,* The Pictorial Field-Book of the War of 1812 *(New York, 1869), 881.* (Courtesy of the New York State Library.)

At last the soldiers could vent their disgust and defy their officers by destroying whatever would burn. Their chaotic fires provided an apocalyptic spectacle to conclude the misbegotten campaign.[66]

IMPOSTER

To embarrass the Madison administration and discourage army recruiting, Ogdensburg's gentry vividly reported Wilkinson's follies. In the Federalist press, the gentry dwelled on the cudgels used to beat weary soldiers and on the criminal neglect of wounded men. Judge Ford insisted, "Our wounded soldiers are dying like sheep, and the disentary rages in the army and the little attention which is paid to the sick beggers discription." He saw hundreds of ragged, unpaid, discharged soldiers "stringing along the road begging as they go."[67]

Firing back in the Republican newspapers, Wilkinson and his supporters dismissed the grim reports as concocted by the malicious Judge Ford. The counterattacks accused Ford of conducting a "traitorous correspondence" and of engaging in "habits of intimacy with the British officers on the Canada shore." He had helped runaway British prisoners return to Canada, and he had betrayed caches of military property in Ogdensburg to British patrols. Worst of all, during Wilkinson's dangerous passage by Prescott and Ogdensburg, Ford allegedly had signaled his British friends by setting a blue lantern in his window, exposing the American troops to British fire. This accusation linked Ford to the notorious "Blue Lights" employed by Federalists to signal to British warships off the Connecticut coast. His notoriety spilled into Congress, where the Republican George M. Troup of Georgia charged Ford with treason, citing the newspaper report that he had "hoisted a light in his upper story, which gave the British information, and that Wilkinson's army was soon fired on."[68]

A federal district judge issued an arrest warrant for treason, served on Ford in late January by two officers with drawn swords. They hauled him in a sleigh four hundred miles south to New York City for arraignment, but the district judge released Ford on bail and, in early April, dismissed the charges because the government had failed to produce any witnesses.[69]

While Ford triumphed, Wilkinson fell. Because so many resources and such high (if false) hopes had been invested in his campaign, its humiliating failure seemed all the more damning. Although a core of supporters clung to him, including William Duane, the tide had turned in the army. One disillusioned officer branded Wilkinson "an Imposter." Once a great admirer, Jacob Brown became a fierce critic, bitter at having been duped: "James Wilkinson is, in my opinion, totally and utterly unfit for command."[70]

After a second year of military failure, someone had to take the political fall. Determined to survive, Armstrong shunted blame onto Hampton and Wilkinson. Desperate to save his command, Wilkinson threw the dice one more time, in hopes of restoring his popularity with an easy victory. In March 1814 he advanced north from Plattsburgh to attack a small British post at La Colle. Defended by a mere five hundred men, the post should have been easy pickings for Wilkinson's army of four thousand, but the British defended a mill with thick stone walls, which defied the attackers because Wilkinson had failed to bring sufficient cannon. After wasting much ammunition, the Americans withdrew. Of course, Wilkinson issued a battle report that spun his latest setback as another glorious triumph. A disgusted officer commented, "His talent is in *writing* his own exploits as they *did not* happen."[71]

Save for Duane's *Aurora*, Republican newspapers erupted in outrage, so Armstrong relieved Wilkinson from command. General George Izard replaced him on the Lake Champlain front, while Brown took charge of the troops at Sackets Harbor. Once again Wilkinson faced a court-martial, this time charged with conduct unbecoming an officer and a gentleman. But the court did not meet until January 1815. By then Armstrong had suffered his own fall from political grace. Preferring to blame the secretary of war for the fiascoes of 1813, the military court acquitted Wilkinson. In a political war, Wilkinson was the great survivor.[72]

SMUGGLERS

After the removal of American troops from the valley, smuggling again surged in 1814. New Yorkers and Vermonters drove thousands of head of cattle across the border, or they loaded rafts with potash, grains, flour, and salt pork. The British commissariat enticed the smugglers by offering high prices for American produce. They returned with British manufactured goods, which sold for a pretty penny in the United States. In July General Izard complained:

> From the St. Lawrence to the ocean, an open disregard prevails for the laws prohibiting intercourse with the enemy. The road to St. Regis is covered with droves of cattle and the river with rafts destined for the enemy. The revenue officers see these things but acknowledge their inability to put a stop to such outrageous proceedings. On the eastern side of Lake Champlain the high roads are found insufficient for the supplies of cattle which are pouring into Canada. Like herds of buffaloes, they press through the forest making paths for themselves.

A visitor to northern New York concluded, "It is as much impossible to stop the smugling here as it would be to prevent the water from running down stream."[73]

The smuggled produce and livestock sustained the British army in Canada. Reinforced from Europe, the British troop strength had nearly tripled from 5,720 soldiers in June 1812 to 14,157 in March 1814. That increase exceeded the agricultural capacity in Upper Canada, where the farms had suffered from American invasion, Indian predation, and militia drafts. American smugglers filled the gap. In January 1814 at Cornwall, the commissariat officer Thomas G. Ridout reported, "The country is so excessively poor that our supplies are all drawn from the American side of the river." In August 1814 Prevost informed Lord

Bathurst: "In fact, my Lord, two-thirds of the army in Canada are at this moment eating beef provided by American contractors drawn principally from the States of Vermont and New York."[74]

The smuggling doubly damned the American war effort, for while supplying the enemy, the diverted supplies increased the costs of feeding American troops, a grave concern given the financial distress of the national government. By late 1814 a government contractor reported a severe "scarcity of Beef & Pork occasioned by exports to the Provinces of Canada." Another lamented that the smuggling would "drain our country of those resources which will be wanted for the subsistence of the army [during the] next campaign."[75]

The smuggling also sapped popular support for the war on the home front, as thousands preferred to smuggle rather than enlist in the army or assist the customs officers. Smuggling also corrupted the virtues that Republicans deemed essential to free government. In declaring war they had hoped to purify the nation of commercial greed by inviting Americans to sacrifice for the common good. But on the northern frontier, the war produced the opposite effect, creating new incentives for Americans to profit in defiance of their government and to the detriment of their troops. General John Chandler lamented, "Our citizens are, by their ready communication with the Enemy, becoming familiar with treason, corruption & perjury, which with their characteristic avarice, will soon annihilate every estimable quality they may have possessed as citizens & prepare them for submission."[76]

British officers saw this corrupting process at Cornwall, a major destination for American cattle drovers. In June 1814 Ridout "contracted with a Yankee magistrate to furnish this post with fresh beef. A major came with him to make the agreement, but, as he was foreman to the grand jury at the court" in his home county, "he turned his back and would not see the paper signed." At the same post, a military surgeon watched Lieutenant Colonel Macdonell receive "a tall, good-looking, middle-aged man," a militia major from Vermont, who had just brought across one hundred head of cattle to sell to the British. After sealing their bargain with a glass of wine, the smuggling major declared:

Well, Colonel, I must say you are a leetle the genteelest man to deal with ever I met with, and I'll tell my friends how handsome you behaved to me. . . . They do say that it is wrong to supply an innimy, and I think so too; but I don't call that man my innimy who buys what I have to sell, and gives a genteel price for it. We have worse innimies than you Britishers.

Among rural people on both sides of the border, personal relationships mattered more than abstract allegiance to nationalism.[77]

Posted along the border at the northern end of Lake Champlain in 1814, Lieutenant Colonel Forsyth tried to reduce the smuggling. Playing cat-and-mouse games with American smugglers and British border guards, he set an ambush near Odelltown on June 28. Ever impetuous, Forsyth sprang the trap prematurely, exposing himself to an Indian's fatal bullet.[78]

Polarizing in life, Forsyth remained so in death. Attending the funeral, a local citizen recorded: "He was a fine man. His soldiers all loved him." But his superiors did not. Recalling "the gallant but excentrical & irregular Forsyth," General Izard noted "the many Instances in which the Indiscretion of the late Forsyth prepared Embarrassment for his commanding officers." Britons and Loyalists celebrated his death. William Hamilton Merritt reported, "When I heard of that fellow's death, I was really pleased, a greater brute never existed." When Forsyth's successor imposed greater discipline on the riflemen, some deserted across the British lines to Canada. Like the smugglers, the deserting riflemen cared more about personal relationships (and chances to plunder) than about allegiance to their nation.[79]

The porous northern border became a debilitating open sore for the United States. Instead of serving as the primary invasion route into Canada, that sector became the smugglers' thoroughfare, feeding the enemy, distorting the American economy, and sapping support at home for the war. That open border had many makers, but none more important than David Parish, who lobbied to keep American soldiers away from the St. Lawrence Valley.

Parish was so effective because the republican union was so weak and diffuse. Averse to levying adequate taxes, the Madison administration struggled to raise the money to recruit and supply a sufficient army. And waging war on the cheap turned out to be surprisingly expensive, as inept commanders and indifferent soldiers wasted supplies and equipment such as those three hundred boats and the barracks burned by Wilkinson's men at French Mills. In a dire spiral, those losses increased the administration's dependence on a handful of financiers, especially Parish, who gained leverage over policy.

In the decentralized republic, the administration was reactive, investing money and men where the Republican leaders were most powerful and demanding. Madison favored the Detroit front because of his own dread of Indian warfare and because of the clout of western politicians, particularly William Henry Harrison and Henry Clay. And,

Lieutenant Colonel Thomas Pearson
*(1780–1847), watercolor on ivory by Robert
Field, 1811. Despite his benign appearance
here, Pearson won a prickly reputation as
Prescott's commander in 1813.* (Courtesy of
Royal Ontario Museum, #980.277.)

except for the Wilkinson interlude of late 1813, the Niagara front
eclipsed the St. Lawrence at the insistence of New York's powerful
politicians, Peter B. Porter, Ambrose Spencer, and Daniel D. Tompkins.
In contrast to western New Yorkers, who usually voted Republican,
northern New Yorkers favored the Federalists. Consequently, St.
Lawrence County lacked any influential constituency in favor of waging
war. While Porter pushed for more troops on the Niagara, Parish
wanted none along the St. Lawrence. Consequently, in the 1814 campaign, the Madison administration would once again concentrate its
limited forces on the Niagara front—where the war could never be won.

Lieutenant General Sir Gordon Drummond (*1772–1854*), *oil painting by George Berhan.* (Courtesy of the Government of Ontario Art Collection, Toronto.)

CHAPTER ELEVEN

TRAITORS

The United States have Many Friends in that Country. There is more Friends to the present [Madison] administration in Canada, according to the Number of inhabitants, than in this Country. [They] are Anxiously waiting for the change of Government. Many have Suffered in Consequence of their Friendship towards this Country, but they still hold out in Confidence that the American standard will be hoisted in that unhappy Country.

—William Graves, March 24, 1814[1]

A LOYALIST DURING THE revolution, Joel Stone lost his property in Connecticut to confiscation by the Patriots. After that war he became a refugee in Canada, settling at Gananoque on the St. Lawrence River, where, in reward for his loyalty, the Crown granted him 1,110 acres. During the late 1780s and early 1790s he rebuilt his fortune by developing a farm, distillery, sawmill, gristmill, inn, blacksmith's shop, and retail store. Appointed by the government as a militia colonel, customs collector, postmaster, coroner, and the presiding justice of the local court, Stone became the leading man in Leeds County. Grateful to the empire, Stone despised the republic.[2]

When the new war began, Stone struggled to maintain order in a county where half of the settlers were newcomers from America. Lieutenant Colonel Thomas Pearson described Leeds County as "a strongly disaffected part of the province." And the county lay beside the St. Lawrence River, an especially porous border with the United States. Despite militia patrols along the river, Stone could do little to halt the outflow of refugees and the influx of counterfeiters, horse thieves, and spies.[3]

On both sides of the border, the common people balked at the new attempts to limit their movement to and fro across the river. When accused of "treasonable practices," Asahel Geralds protested that he had crossed the border "to speculate or make property, but if every person was called in question and punished for commiting treasonable practices

that has been across since the declaration of war for the purpose of speculation, and in fact for the good of their Country & themselves, I believe
there would be but very few enterprising men but what would be
guilty." Geralds equated his self-interest with the good of his country,
by which he meant the valley, rather than something larger, either
republic or empire. As circumstances shifted, the valley people readily
switched sides of the river and of the war, only to switch again later. In
early 1814 three Leeds County militiamen returned home after deserting to the enemy. At their trial, an officer testified that the people were
"in the habit of Crossing and recrossing on friendly visits to the people
of the other Shore." They saw no reason to stop during the war.[4]

In addition to providing a border, the St. Lawrence River served as
the logistical lifeline for Upper Canada, which depended on the flow of
boats from Montreal with supplies and reinforcements. As a result, the
Leeds County militia bore a heavy burden in drafts to operate and guard
the boats and to repair the roads used by sleighs in winter, when ice
locked down the river. The county's proximity to Kingston also meant
heavy militia drafts to supplement the garrison so critical to Upper
Canada's defense.

Zealous in his duty, Stone vigorously enforced the drafts and threatened to punish anyone "vain enough . . . to wish to be excused from
bearing an Eaqual share of the burthens Incidental to this wicked war."
He defined the war as wicked because it was imposed by Americans,
allegedly to benefit the despot Napoleon. Stone also regarded the war as
a second round against the hated Patriots who had dispossessed and
exiled him. Self-righteous and self-pitying, he felt both martyred and
vindicated in September 1812, when Forsyth's riflemen raided his
Gananoque property. Stone also felt "surrounded at that time with seditious neighbours, by whom, as well as by the enemy, his own person had
been marked out with singular Malice."[5]

Stone's zeal impressed British governors and generals, but it irritated
his neighbors, who wanted to be left alone. In a frontier county, labor
was preciously scarce, and every boy or man taken into the militia subtracted from the hands needed to sustain a farm. The widow Metty
Douglas begged another officer to overrule Stone's enforcement of the
draft:

I am a poor, helpless and sickly old Woman and no one to help me
but one boy. I have three sons in the army and Now I am like to have
the last taken away and if he is gone, I shall inevitably suffer. And now

if it is in your pow[e]r to help me, I beg of you to show some pity—
that is, to let my son stay at home and take care of his poor and helpless Mother.

Seventy-four men signed another petition, declaring that "from the
oppressive and Tyranical conduct of Col. Joel Stone, more than one half
of the effective men have fled either to the enemy or [to] other parts of
the Province in order to avoid his Tyranny." They insisted that Stone
had compelled even the deaf, lame, and elderly to serve, but that Colonel
Pearson had sent them home, "judging that Col. Stone was a lunatic."[6]

Stone's second-in-command, Benoni Wiltse, had also suffered for his
loyalty during the revolution, but he remained a poorly educated farmer
more closely attuned to his neighbors than to external power. Wiltse
warned Stone

of the Ceartain Calamity that must befall us if the Militia are thus
continued to be Cawled from their familes. If they are Cawled one
month or six weeks from their farms, they can put no spring grain in
the ground and . . . their families must inevitably suffer. The famine
even threatens before the ensuing harvest. . . . for if they sow not,
neither can they reap and what must be the felings of a poor man that
is forced from his plough when he sees nothing but distruction and
death awaits his wife [and] tender Children.

Feeding and defending the country worked at odds during the harvest
season. Wiltse warned Stone "that his impolitick and illegal proceedings would drive many to the enemy; and might possabily make some
hypocrits."[7]

In June 1814 Stone's captains reported that ninety-four men, or 27
percent of the regiment, were "deserters to the enemy." Most were
American-born, single, and landless laborers or artisans. If a deserter
owned any land, it was usually only a new and stumpy farm of a hundred
acres. Such men had little to lose by bolting across the river to escape
from militia service. Many later returned "to see their friends." If caught
and court-martialed, they explained that they had "considered the draft
as unfair."[8]

Holding a contractual view of their service, these militiamen claimed
the right to abscond if mistreated, just as they would quit working for an
abusive employer. In February 1813 Stone ordered John Landries to
escort to Kingston some government sleighs laden with stores. But the

weather was brutally cold, and Landries lacked a greatcoat, so he fled across the border. Two months later Uriah Kelsey deserted because the officers had broken their promise to promote him to sergeant. Landries, Kelsey, and two other deserters returned to Leeds County to steal horses to sell on the American side of the river. Caught by a militia patrol in September 1814, they faced a court-martial, which convicted and sentenced them to transportation for seven years, which usually meant exile to the penal colony at Botany Bay.[9]

Stone disdained the complaints of his men and officers as insubordination and defeatism. Dismissing the petition against him as "a very Mutinous writing," he blamed local resistance on "the Elderly persons in the Country—such as Fathers, Mothers, and other heads of Familys, [who] had (By their Examples and bad Counsel) Poisoned the minds of the Youth." He arrested and jailed an elderly critic as the author and organizer of the offending petition.[10]

In late October 1813, when General Wilkinson's American army descended the St. Lawrence, Colonel Pearson ordered Stone to call out his entire regiment, about 368 men. Despite the crisis, only seventy turned out, and most of them quickly deserted, citing a rumor that the Americans would confiscate the farm of any man who bore arms against them, but that "such as Remaind at home should be secured in their property and caresed as friends." Dreading exposure to the cold rains of fall, most preferred to stay at home by the fire and to store their corn and potato harvest for the winter.[11]

Embarrassed by the poor turnout, Stone blamed and arrested Wiltse, the regiment's second-in-command. Stone denounced Wiltse for telling the men that "I had got a flea in my ear, and that I was calling them out at a time when there was no necessity for it." Stone also accused Wiltse of encouraging the militiamen to sue their commander for abuse of power. In April 1814 a court-martial in Kingston vindicated Stone by convicting Wiltse, who lost his commission and faced a fifty-pound fine. Unable to pay, he suffered six months in jail. His wife, Rachel, complained that their six children were deprived of "their aged and almost toothless father, thus unjustly thrust into a Crimonel cell, gnashing his gums" for want of decent food.[12]

Stone had a far harder time tracking down "that obstinate man Isaac Simpson, who has never yet performed a Tour of duty in my Regt.—has uniformly Deserted—in doing which he has proved himself very capable." Although an illiterate young farmer, Simpson shrewdly and repeatedly dodged arrest. According to Stone, Simpson would "Tantalize and abuse his Neighbours who had performed their Duty, pointing at— laughing at—and calling them Dam[ne]d fools for doing their Duty and exultingly saying that the whole Reg[i]ment could not make him do his Duty." Once, Stone's men thought that they had trapped Simpson at his cabin in the bush, but as they closed in, "he so escaped by means of a secret passage he had provided through the floor and Earth under his own house." Sputtering with fury, Stone vowed to capture Simpson "or to have his life."[13]

At last, in October 1814, Stone captured and sent his nemesis to Kingston in irons. After two months in jail awaiting trial, Simpson sweet-talked an officer into releasing him to work as a boatman for the military. Once sprung, he ran away home. Arrested again, Simpson at last came to trial in January 1815, when he cleverly argued that "the length of time" between the charges against him and his trial was "a presumption of my having been forgiven . . . particularly as I have been since permitted to do my duty" on those boats. Flummoxed by his argument, the court acquitted him, which outraged General Drummond, who denounced the verdict as "directly at variance with the evidence." But, rather than hazard another trial, Drummond let Simpson go home, where he relished recounting his ultimate triumph over Stone.[14]

While battling horse thieves, mutineers, deserters, spies, and subversives, Stone also suffered from the vandalism of British troops, sailors, and boatmen who camped on his property during their passage up and down the river. They pilfered from his gardens, wrecked his outbuildings, chopped down his orchard, and toppled his fences for firewood. In November 1814 a drunken soldier roughed Stone up. Left with a ruined farm, he felt "Age and Infirm[ities] increasing daily and cast my Eyes to the Right or left, Destruction and Loss of almost all Comforts of life and property stare me in the face."[15]

Happiest when miserable, Stone exulted in suffering for his loyalty. Although he had devoted "every exertion of Body & Mind—in my Civil and Military Capacity—for the Defence and Preservation of this Country—totally neglecting every Branch of business for my own Benefit," he also knew "there is a certain part of Human Society who say— he is a Vain fool who Volunteers his Service for any Government whatever." Stone blamed "the too prevelant insubordination and inordinate Covitous Desires of Many of those of considerable note, woolves in Sheap's Cloathing I *must* call them, resident within this County." He referred to other magistrates who reaped greater popularity by letting their neighbors evade militia service.[16]

AMBIVALENCE

In Upper Canada most of the common people felt ambivalent about taking sides in the war. Drawn to the colony by low taxes and cheap land, the American-born majority had scant interest in politics and a great dread of war. Localist, pragmatic, and self-interested, they balked at making sacrifices for any larger political cause, whether for an empire or a republic. The common folk were loyal enough to Britain so long as the colonial government left them alone, but they felt shocked by the sudden wartime demand for their service in the militia. British officials mistook their reticence for disloyalty, and the Americans misunderstood it as longing for a republic. In fact, most of the people just wanted to be left alone to tend their farms, so they hoped that one side or the other would win the war quickly.[17]

During the summer and fall of 1812, Brock's victory at Detroit and Sheaffe's at Queenston had persuaded most of the people to defend the colony. But they grew restive during the following winter as the colony's economy staggered under the burdens of war. Food became scarce after a shortfall in the grain harvest, and the typhoid fever epidemic sickened many families. With men called away to the militia, wives struggled to thresh wheat, chop wood, and tend the cattle, in addition to their usual "charge of nursing helpless infancy & guarding heedless childhood." And many men feared leaving their families and farms unprotected from plundering soldiers and warriors. The militiamen also suffered from erratic pay, bad food, and poor clothing, and most disliked the prospect of fighting against their former countrymen.[18]

In early 1813 British officers noted the growing resistance to militia service. In January, Colonel Pearson complained of "the constant and numerous desertions of the Militia." In March, Sir George Prevost noted the

> growing discontent and undissembled dissatisfaction of the mass of the people of Upper Canada in consequence of the effects of the militia laws upon a population thinly scattered over an extensive range of country, whose zeal was exhausted and whose exertions had brought want and ruin to the doors of many, and had in various instances produced a considerable emigration of settlers to the United States, from whence most of them originally came.

Some desperate men dodged militia service by hiding in the Canadian bush. During the winter of 1812–13 about twenty armed men holed up in a cave at the head of Yonge Street near Lake Simcoe. Found by pursuing Indians and Loyalists, the refugees lost a firefight and landed in jail at York.[19]

The British had to suppress draft dodging, lest it become contagious. Captain Simeon Washburn noted, "The Truth is that if one is favoured or given leave to stay in his Turn of duty, there is no such thing as getting another [to go], and they are all alike." Colonel Richard Beasley complained that Philip Shaver had refused to serve and had, "by his actions, Conversation, and threats, been the means of Deterring many of his Majesty's Subjects from doing their duty." To avoid arrest, Shaver had been "skulking in the woods . . . thretening to shoot any person that would attempt to take him." To Beasley's dismay, Shaver escaped to New York in March 1813, risking the storms of Lake Ontario in an open boat with fourteen other refugees.[20]

But a harsh enforcement of the draft threatened to complete the alienation of the people. A refugee from arrest for draft dodging, William Biggar, boasted "that he was determined in Peace or War to be revenged on Richard Hatt & Robert Nichol, Esquires" by burning their homes. Biggar's war was intensely local and personal, rather than driven by any larger allegiance to a national cause. Another Upper Canadian dissident promised to "take away the officers, that the militia may be at peace and that the [people] might go to work." Rather than seeking American rule or a Canadian republic, he simply wanted to be left alone to work on his farm.[21]

During the spring the invaders sought popular support by offering paroles to militiamen. The paroles barred them from fighting until exchanged, which the recipients hoped would not come until the end of the war. Paroled militiamen achieved their fondest hope: to stay at home, immune from drafts. In addition to the 241 militiamen captured at York on the day of battle, hundreds more flocked in from the countryside to receive paroles before the Americans departed on May 1.[22]

Some common people also joined the Americans in plundering the officers and officials of York. William Dummer Powell blasted the "wretches of our own population, whose thirst for plunder was more alarming to the [genteel] inhabitants than the presence of the enemy." The York magistrates noted, "a great number of traitorous people had come from the country and pillaged nearly as much from the King's stores and from private individuals as the enemy." After helping the Americans cart stores to their ships, the farmers returned home with their loot.[23]

In the Niagara District, the American victory at York persuaded most of the inhabitants that British rule was nearly finished in Upper Canada. General John Vincent lamented:

> With respect to the Militia, it is with regret that I can neither report favorably of their numbers nor of their willing cooperation. Every exertion has been used and every expedient resorted to, to bring them forward and unite their efforts to those of His Majesty's Forces with but little effect, and desertion beyond all conception continues to mark their indifference.

Driven from Fort George and Newark on May 27, Vincent retreated to Burlington Heights, abandoning the district to the invaders. Rather than join the retreat, most of the militiamen kept to their homes. A retreating British officer complained, "The disaffection of the settlers is shocking and deserves an exemplary chastisement."[24]

Giddy with victory, the American officers insisted that the local people welcomed them as liberators. On May 30 at Newark, Lieutenant Irvine claimed, "Our friends hereabouts are greatly relieved by our visit—they had been terribly persecuted by the Scotch myrmidons of England. Their present joy is equal to their past misery." General Dearborn similarly reported, "A large majority are friendly to the United States and fixed in their hatred to the Government of Great Britain."[25]

In fact, relatively few felt committed to the republic; a larger minority of Loyalists longed to oust the invaders; and the great majority simply hated militia service and wanted the war to end. In late May the American momentum appeared irresistible, so the passive majority cheered the invaders and cherished their paroles. That limited and tentative welcome hinged upon a prompt American conquest of the rest of the colony with little damage to private property. When the Americans instead plundered and blundered, the worm turned. Defeated at Stoney Creek on June 6, the American troops fled back to Fort George and Newark in disarray, abandoning most of the Niagara District to the British. A retreating officer saw people "of every age and sex weeping and bewailing their fate" and lamenting that they had "believed the tales [of liberation] we told them too soon."[26]

Drying their tears, most men returned to their militia duty in support of the British advance. Irvine ruefully concluded that a decisive American victory would have "attached to us 18 of 20 of all the inhabitants" in the Niagara District. Instead, "the fatal retreat" plus "the tardiness and want of vigour, decision, and generalship evinced on all occasions, have driven all into the English ranks." The people came to distrust the invaders as unreliable, here today but gone tomorrow, while the British returned to punish those who had helped the enemy.[27]

The volatility of civilian support shocked the Americans, who thought of themselves as beloved liberators. Once sure of Canadian support, Irvine now sang a different tune at Newark:

> Our government cannot be too guarded. Scotch and American Tories can never be converted; their savage allies can never be trusted. . . . Of all the population in this town, there are only 6 persons in any degree friendly to the United States; and four of these are Irishmen. . . . The inhabitants hereabouts are almost altogether very inimical to the Yankees—the men would scalp them, and the women of Newark are loyal enough to eat their hearts and drink their blood. . . . I hope these villains will be put to death and their estates confiscated.

No longer seeing Canadians as liberated friends, the invaders now suspected that most were insidious foes. Of course, this reaction was as excessive as the earlier insistence on a Canadian love for the invaders.[28]

At Newark the Americans turned on the magistrates and paroled militia officers, accusing them of covertly assisting the British. In late June an American officer reported, "The dragoons and riflemen are out every day in scouting parties, and seldom return without prisoners . . . principally Scots and Orangemen." The biggest catch was William Dickson, the Scottish lawyer and magistrate who had shot William Weekes in a duel in 1806. The captors hustled him and twenty-four other captives across the Niagara River and on to a military prison at Greenbush near Albany.[29]

Although resurgent in the Niagara District, the British had only a little more confidence in the civilians within their lines. In August Lieutenant William MacEwen complained,

> The inhabitants are indifferent who gains the day. They are determined to do nothing themselves. Where I am obliged to live, the people would not sell me a fowl nor a potato and even grumble when my men use their dishes.

Resenting that indifference, British soldiers preyed at night upon the gardens, orchards, and hen roosts of the farmers. In September Lieutenant Thomas G. Ridout confessed, "we carry on an extensive robbery of pease, apples, onions, corn, carrots, etc., for we can get nothing but by stealing, excepting milk." Later that month he added, "To-night our dragoon is to make a grand attack upon the onions. The [chicken] nests are kept very nice and clean from the eggs." A sport to bored soldiers, these nocturnal raids threatened to ruin the farmers.[30]

The civilians also suffered from plundering by the Indians allied with the British. In July 1813 an Indian Department superintendent, Colonel William Claus, conceded, "[The Indians] plunder the settlers and return home to deposit what they take from the inhabitants. They destroy every hog and sheep they meet with." Claus complained to the chiefs that the looting was "very hard on these poor people. On the one hand they are injured by the enemy, on the other by us."[31]

The Upper Canadians seemed fickle and selfish to the officers on both sides. But the farmers wondered why they should support either a republic or the empire, when both armies brought them more trouble than protection. Unable to control their native allies or their own soldiers, who looted and burned, the commanders on both sides should have been slower to deride the civilians as unreliable. Through all the changes in military fortune, the people consistently sought to minimize their losses and occasionally to take gains. Sometimes that entailed cooperating with the British, and sometimes that meant hoping for an American victory. Weary of both armies, the civilians longed for one side to win so that both would go away. But both sides misinterpreted that ambivalence as treachery.

WORDS

On July 31, 1813, Isaac Chauncey's squadron returned to York with 250 American troops led by Colonel Winfield Scott. Lacking a garrison, the town's leaders could not resist. Once again the Americans plundered the stores to play Robin Hood by distributing provisions and goods to the common people, who reciprocated by selling veal, eggs, and butter to the soldiers. The invaders also broke open the jail to liberate political prisoners held by the British. But the American return proved brief. After burning some army barracks and storehouses, the invaders sailed away on August 2.[32]

In the wake of that second raid, the embittered magistrates formed a special committee to suppress disaffection. Distrusting the local people, the magistrates bypassed the legal process that required a grand jury to gather testimony and to indict suspects for arrest and trial. "The present crisis demands measures to be taken with the disaffected much stronger than any, that can be warranted by the common operations of the law,"

Reverend John Strachan explained. The plan won support from Strachan's prize protégé, John Beverley Robinson, who had become the acting attorney general. In August and early September Strachan's committee collected affidavits from sixty-four witnesses against thirty-two suspects.[33]

The testimony revealed that disaffection was widespread but thin, lacking in organization and in republican content. At most, some malcontents would make, display, and parade behind an American flag, while expressing a hope that the invaders would "keep the Country and establish their Laws." More often, the disaffected simply predicted that the invaders would and should win the war. Jacob Clock explained "that the King had no right to anything in this Country, that the Americans owned everything here." Samuel Utley insisted that those who served in the militia "fought against their own light and knowledge, that the Americans would conquer the whole of British North America and that they had a right to it." Such men saw no point in fighting on the losing side.[34]

Many common people simply adjusted to the ebb and flow of the fortunes of war. A witness heard David Hill of York declare, "That always when the American fleet was here, he was not a good subject—[but] when our fleet was here he was subject to the King." This flexibility accounted for the swings in support from one side to the other, swings which puzzled and irritated both the American and British officers.[35]

Pragmatic and acquisitive, the country people thought in concrete and personal terms that avoided political abstractions. Often they simply wanted to get even with particular officials who had punished them for evading militia service. Abram Winn longed to "Tar and Feather Ensign Chard and Spencer Patrick for their Loyalty." Loyalists had jailed Gideon Orton for resisting the militia draft, so Orton took enough plunder from York "to pay him four dollars a day for the time he kept out of the way and also for the time he was confined in Gaol for refusing to serve." To justify his plundering, John Lyon declared that "Major Allan of the York Militia had oppressed him." To intimidate the town's militia officers, Lyon left them a note declaring, "I mean to have William Graham's scalp, William Allan, Duncan Cameron, Samuel S. Wilmot and Micah Dyes and George Cutter's scalp before one month in my Still House Hung up."[36]

Attentive to their self-interest, most common people regarded their allegiance as contractual and conditional. Jonathan Stevens declared "that he was not indebted to the king for any thing and that what property he had he bought with his Money that he brought from the States and that Government had not given him one pence and said God Damn them." Punished for refusing to serve in the militia, Andrew Patterson claimed "that when the Americans conquered the Country he would be the better used for it."[37]

Preferring profits to patriotism, many common people readily sold farm produce to the invaders and hauled away plunder from York. John Finch advised a neighbor "to turn to the Americans and they will give you something worth the while . . . but if you continue to serve with the British you will get nothing." When a Loyalist accused Jacob Clock of supplying the Americans, he "replied they were not his Enemies but his Friends, that they supported him and he would support them."[38]

Much of the seditious talk derived from rancorous exchanges in divided communities, where the discontented and the loyal sought to irritate and intimidate one another, particularly when drinking in a tavern. Lyon insisted that all Loyalists "should be beheaded or sent to Greenbush." Edward Philips boasted "that if the Americans came again, he would have all the old Tories hanged." At a tavern, Alfred Barrett offered a toast, "Success to the American Fleet." Later Jeremiah Brown "drank Maddison's health and wished the Americans might always prosper in all their undertakings." But the Loyalists dreaded such tavern chatter as the slippery slope to anarchy and rebellion.[39]

After collecting this testimony, the Strachan committee expected few "convictions from Jurors of whom many are involved in the same guilt and few disposed to enforce that respect for our Government and obedience to our laws which the present moment particularly demands." Indeed, most cases sputtered as the suspects dodged arrest or escaped from custody.[40]

The greatest escape artist was the "notorious Calvin Wood." A Yankee doctor who resided on Yonge Street, Wood stood about five feet ten inches high, possessed a dark complexion, wore a black coat, and was lame in his left foot, but that disability failed to hinder his knack for breaking out. During the first American occupation of York, Wood had informed on caches of hidden British supplies, and had reaped an American reward of seven barrels of flour and some ammunition. During the following summer he harassed at least one Loyalist by cutting and taking away his ripening crop of wheat, and he urged men to evade militia service. To dodge arrest, Wood hid in the woods near Lake Simcoe until early June 1814, when he was taken by a Loyalist captain assisted by Indian trackers. A month later, Wood escaped from his guards while in transit east to Kingston. Quickly retaken, he landed in the Kingston jail, but one morning the jailer found that his prisoners had "broke a large hole through the partition Wall of the Cells . . . and another through the outward Wall (which is very thick) at the back of the Jail without being heard by any one." Somehow, Wood had also broken his heavy leg irons without making a racket. Apparently he made his way across the border to New York.[41]

The Loyalist prosecutors did make an example of Elijah Bentley, a Baptist farmer and preacher. Originally from Rhode Island, Bentley had settled in Markham on Yonge Street, where he led a congregation. A Loyalist deemed Bentley especially "dangerous from [his] great opportunities as a Preacher" to disseminate seditious ideas.[42]

During the first American occupation of York, Bentley had hastened into town to secure paroles for himself and his son. General Dearborn impressed Bentley as "a very conversible man, much more so than any British officer he had met with." The preacher announced that no one in his congregation would bear "arms against persons who were so good to him." Another witness heard Bentley "declare that he had seen more liberty during the few Hours that he was with General Dearborn than he had ever seen in the province—that the men in the American army were allowed to answer their officers back." For once, the lax discipline of the American troops proved an asset to the invasion.[43]

Returning home, Bentley felt emboldened to preach disaffection: "that he had been for sometime in great fear but now he had liberty and would take it and say and think what he pleased for he had been along with General Dearborn." Urging his congregants to seek American paroles, Bentley explained "that he thanked God [because] there was never such freedom for poor people in York as there was since General Dearborn set his foot in it." He concluded "that the Loyalists were done over now and must be very Quiet." Instead, the Loyalists silenced Bentley in March 1814 by convicting and sentencing him to six months in prison. Bentley also had to post a £400 bond for good behavior for five more years. Thereafter he vanishes from the historical record in Upper Canada, which suggests that he returned to the United States.[44]

MARTIAL LAW

In late 1813 and through 1814, the British lowered their demand for militia drafts by bringing in more regulars from Europe to bear the brunt of the combat in Upper Canada. Because the additional regulars strained the colony's food supply, the government needed to allow more militiamen to tend their farms. When drafted, they served in smaller numbers and primarily to guard and to move supplies and to repair roads and forts rather than to fight. In an emergency, however, a British general still had to call out all of the militia in an invaded district—as in Stone's county in November 1813.[45]

The greater reliance on regulars shifted the primary tension between the government and civilians. Increasingly the inhabitants sought to protect their crops and animals from impressment rather than their own bodies from the militia draft. By June 1814 the British had 4,500 regulars and 3,000 Indians on the Niagara Front. Feeding them for a month required 149 tons of flour and 960 head of cattle. That army's oxen and horses consumed another 168 tons of oats or hay per month. To feed the army demanded the entire grain crop produced in the colony. To ensure that local grain became flour rather than whiskey, the government of Upper Canada banned stills. While imported rum and smuggled whiskey mollified the troops, the ban on local stills offended colonists deprived of the profits from distilling.[46]

The army's commissary officers complained bitterly that farmers held their crops back, speculating on a higher future price. Some officers even insisted that the farmers were traitors who sought to help the enemy by starving the British army. The farmers retorted that the commissariat offered skimpy prices and paper notes promising future payment—but then neglected for months and even years to pay cash for the notes. The farmers wondered why they should sell their hard-earned crops at modest prices and for an uncertain payday, when they faced the war-inflated costs of imported goods and farm labor.[47]

The commissary officers had a demanding and thankless job, for they reaped much grief but none of the honor of combat duty. They felt caught between, on the one hand, impatient generals who demanded food immediately, and on the other hand, balky farmers holding out for a better price and prompt payment—or citing religious scruples against helping the military. And often the commissary officers had to scramble for scarce draft animals, wagons, sleighs, and provisions in a countryside plundered by the enemy or by allied Indians. Peter Turquand lamented the strain of his duty in "a country so devastated & impoverished as this and comprising Inhabitants of such various Dispositions, Characters, & Religions."[48]

Commissary officers worked long hours under intense stress. Quartermaster Robert Nichol lamented, "This cursed office, to which for my sins I have been appointed, engrosses *all* my time, and if I don't soon get leave to resign it, I believe I shall go crazy." At least one officer did go crazy. In September 1813 General Rottenburg reported from the Niagara District: "The whole Commissariat, with the exception of

Mr. I. Coffin is laid up with the Fever, and Mr. [Edward] Couche is actually out of his senses."[49]

In November 1813 General Rottenburg issued a martial law proclamation meant to compel the farmers to deliver up forage and provisions. Limited to the districts in the St. Lawrence Valley, the proclamation violated the English common law, which held that martial law could only be invoked in a crisis that required a total suspension of the civil courts throughout the province. But the colonial governors balked at such a sweeping suspension, for merchants needed the civil courts to collect their debts, and they had political clout. Moreover, martial law undercut the ideological foundation of British rule: the reverence for civil law. Britons celebrated the supposed purity and impartiality of their law as superior to the political corruption of America and the arbitrary despotism of France. Consequently, Upper Canada's assembly denounced Rottenburg's proclamation as "arbitrary and unconstitutional and contrary to, and subversive of, the established laws of the land."[50]

In January 1814 Rottenburg's successor, General Gordon Drummond, suspended the unpopular proclamation, to the dismay of the commissary officers. But in April, when provisions ran perilously low at Kingston, Drummond issued his own martial law, limited to acquiring provisions but extended throughout the province. To mollify the inhabitants, Drummond required the commissary officers to get a warrant from a magistrate before taking produce or livestock. Drummond also authorized district boards of magistrates to set the prices paid by the commissariat. Fanning into the countryside, commissary officers demanded hay, flour, grains, and potatoes at the fixed prices and for a paper credit. If farmers balked, the officers employed troops to seize and haul away the crops in impressed wagons.[51]

Cherishing private property rights, some Loyalist magistrates denounced the martial law as unconstitutional because it was unauthorized by the assembly. Samuel Sherwood and Charles Jones financed lawsuits against commissary officers, who were defended by the acting attorney general, John Beverley Robinson. The key case pitted Jacob Empey, a farmer from Cornwall, against Edward Doyle of the commissariat. Deciding against Doyle, a jury awarded Empey £112.10.0 in damages, "considerably beyond the value of the wheat," according to Robinson. But Drummond paid up, for the government could ill afford to sacrifice its claim to uphold the course of justice. Although Robinson recognized that the martial law proclamations were "unconstitutional, however salutary or necessary," he blasted the litigants as "discontented and malignant." In a crisis he expected true Loyalists to overlook legal improprieties for the military good.[52]

ROADS AND BOATS

In addition to the food fight, the civilians and the military clashed over the transportation of troops and their supplies. The colonial regime expected the inhabitants to repair the roads; to provide food and lodging for passing troops; and to submit to the impressment of oxen, horses, carts, wagons, and sleighs. The impressing officer was supposed to secure a warrant from a local magistrate and to offer the farmer a receipt for the property taken. But an officer in a hurry often neglected the legal forms, and farmers could ill afford to lose their work animals and weapons.[53]

Passing soldiers also tore down fences to make fires, and they pilfered from orchards, gardens, henhouses, and pigsties. In March 1814 the York sheriff complained that the local houses were "crammed full of Troops, who not only destroy everything in their way, but carry of[f] whatever they take a liking to." A month later four dragoons forced themselves upon a sick farmer and militia captain in Thurlow, near the Bay of Quinte. Getting drunk on their host's liquor, they "became troublesome in the House & demanded Provisions in the Kitchen." When their bedridden host refused to get up to cook for them, they broke down his bedroom door and "cut Captain Myers' head with the Sword and bruised him and Mrs. Myers also very much with a Club or Stick."[54]

The government exempted religious pacifists—Quakers, Mennonites, and Dunkers—from the militia, but they had to pay annual fines of five pounds per man and had to provide draft animals, wagons, carts, and sleighs on military demand. The Mennonites and Dunkers accepted that compromise, but the Quakers balked at contributing anything that promoted bloodshed. When a man refused to pay his fine or deliver up draft animals, the government jailed him for a month or seized sufficient property—usually livestock—to cover the fine and the costs of the sheriff. About half of the colony's Quakers dwelled north of York along Yonge Street, a major thoroughfare used by the British to move supplies. In harm's way, the Quakers suffered a heavy demand for their animals and frequent conflict with militia officers. Under military pressure, the Yonge Street Meeting looked the other way when some members did haul for the army. But outraged purists rallied around David Willson, who in August 1812 led eighteen families in breaking away to form a new sect called "the Children of Peace." By the end of the war at least a quarter of the Yonge Street Quakers had joined the Children of Peace in search of a spiritual community that would resist demands by the outside world of politics and strife.[55]

On the north shore of Lake Ontario, the Danforth Road became another flash point between soldiers and civilians. The road ran through the Newcastle District, where the settlers were Yankee newcomers from New England—the people most prone to disaffection in Upper Canada. Passing through the district in December 1812, Michael Smith saw about fifty local men "on the main road, with fife and drum, beating for volunteers, crying huzza for Madison." He concluded that the district's inhabitants "were universally in favour of the United States, and if ever another army is landed in Canada, this would be the best place." In December 1813 several Newcastle men rowed across the stormy lake to American-occupied Fort George. Seeking an American invasion, they promised support from three-fourths of their neighbors—but the American commander lacked enough men for an offensive so he advised the residents to return home and remain quiet for a better opportunity in the future. The American support in the Newcastle District remained unrequited, but it also remained unsullied by the American plundering that so disillusioned potential supporters elsewhere.[56]

In the Newcastle District, the arbitrary demands by the British military generated violent frictions with the restive civilians. In March 1813 Major Heathcote escorted a convoy of sleighs laden with supplies. About twenty miles east of York, the major and two lieutenants lodged at a tavern where they noticed "a suspicious person" who seemed to follow them. When he refused to answer their questions, a lieutenant struck him with a horsewhip, but still the suspect would not speak. So the major's soldiers tied the silent man to a post with a rope around his neck. Despite threats to hang him, the suspect remained mute. In the morning, the officers learned that he "was a fool known to be wandering about the country," so they released him, the worse for wear and tear.[57]

One of the whipping officers was Lieutenant Bryan Finan of the Royal Newfoundland Regiment, who in April 1813 retreated through the district with General Sheaffe's troops after their defeat at York. Finan's son recalled, "The majority of the inhabitants of this part of the country evinced great disloyalty as we proceeded, being much gratified with the success of the Americans." Hiding their horses and wagons in the woods, the inhabitants refused to help the troops move their equipment, but merrily warned them to hurry along because the invaders were in hot pursuit—a fiction meant to spook Sheaffe's soldiers.[58]

After the Americans left York, the British reclaimed the Danforth Road, which became the scene of renewed clashes between impatient soldiers and wary civilians. In February 1814 a British lieutenant, F. W. Small, stopped at a blacksmith's shop to impress a sleigh for his troops. When the owner objected, Small ordered a trooper "to draw his Sword and cut off the Arm of Josiah Proctor." A court-martial convicted Small of abusing the civilian but inflicted only a public reprimand.[59]

In March 1814 a farmer with a team of oxen hauled a load of hay along the Danforth Road, where he encountered a British dragoon in a sleigh who "swore that he would have all the road." When the farmer moved aside too slowly, the impatient dragoon leaped out and smacked the man with the butt end of a whip, pummeled him "with his fist, kicked him a number of times and cut open his head and broke one of his ribs." No disaffected colonist, the abused farmer was a lieutenant in the local militia.[60]

Later that year a navy lieutenant raped "an Infant of eleven years of Age." When a local magistrate granted bail to the officer, the outraged "friends of the Child . . . inflicted upon him a severe chastisement." Bothered more by the riot than by the rape, the presiding judge, William Dummer Powell, released the battered lieutenant after he paid a ten-pound fine, which Powell deemed sufficient to "vindicate the impartial administration of Justice." Of course the local people disagreed.[61]

The disaffected struck back by helping prisoners to escape from their British captors when they were marched eastward along the Danforth Road. In late July 1814 a militia guard conducted eight political prisoners to Smith's Creek in the Newcastle District. After a stormy night the sergeant unlocked the prisoners' hut to find half of them gone because sympathizers had removed the boards from the rear of the building. The runaways included the notorious Calvin Wood, who so often escaped from the British clutches.[62]

The Newcastle disaffected also waylaid passing post riders to steal the letters and orders of British commanders. Crossing the lake in boats, the thieves sold the letters to American generals. Occasionally Commodore Chauncey sent a gunboat into a district harbor to gather information from the disaffected and to plunder and burn government storehouses.[63]

The disaffected also built boats to flee across Lake Ontario to the American shore, a twelve-hour trip in calm conditions but a long and perilous ordeal in a storm. "I find there are other Boats building in the

District and disaffected people in different parts raising and threatening their Neighbours," a militia colonel complained. "Those actually gon to the States will no Doubt Give every Information in their Power Respecting our Situation," two magistrates warned. Watching the shore, Loyalist officers shot at departing boats to stop them and then to arrest the refugees. In 1814 the officers seized or destroyed all the boats found along the lakeshore of the Newcastle District to keep people from fleeing.[64]

In the colony as a whole, the government confiscated the land of at least 336 fugitives who had fled to America to avoid militia service in Upper Canada. Many more fugitives were laborers or tenant farmers who had owned no land in the colony. In Norfolk County, for example, the sheriff reported that only thirteen of the forty-eight fugitives had possessed real estate. Extrapolated to the entire province, that ratio suggests that, in addition to the 336 landed absconders, another 1,240 landless men fled from the province. At four dependents per absconding man, the outflow probably amounted to five thousand people.[65]

HANGMAN

In early 1814 General Drummond's victories won him great clout with the assembly, which also became more docile after the defections by three leaders of the opposition: Benajah Mallory, Abraham Markle, and Joseph Willcocks. During the winter session, the assembly dutifully empowered Drummond to suspend the writ of habeas corpus, a measure sought in vain by Brock. The legislature also approved Drummond's law to punish traitors by confiscating their land, with the proceeds to relieve people plundered by the invaders. Another new law provided for the confiscation of property from anyone who had refused the oath of allegiance or had fled from the province. Pleased by the legislative cooperation, Drummond concluded, "by far the greater portion of the Inhabitants are well disposed." But to clinch the shift toward loyalty, Drummond sought to hang some traitors, as a warning to others.[66]

On November 12, 1813, in the London District, Loyalist volunteers had surprised a band of marauders at John Dunham's house. Disaffected Upper Canadians, they plundered homes, rustled cattle, and kidnapped militia officers. After losing three dead in a firefight, sixteen marauders, including Dunham, surrendered to the Loyalists. The little victory thrilled the British generals, who hoped the vivid example of Loyalist zeal would inspire more civilians to resist the enemy and to suppress the disaffected. General Rottenburg insisted that victory had rescued "an extensive district from a numerous and well armed banditti who would soon have left them neither liberty nor property."[67]

Although better described as kidnappers and horse thieves, the prisoners were the best the British could cast as traitors given that the major culprits—Mallory, Markle, and Willcocks—remained at large with the American forces. The attorney general, John Beverley Robinson, explained that the government needed "to overawe the spirit of disaffection in the Province by examples of condign punishment by the laws of the land."[68]

In May 1814 a special court convened at Ancaster, a secure location near the military base at Burlington Heights. For want of a courthouse, the court met in a hotel which had been confiscated from Markle. Three judges presided: Chief Justice Thomas Scott and the associate justices Sir William Campbell and William Dummer Powell. A grand jury indicted seventy men, but only nineteen were in custody for the trials, which began on June 7. Most of the tried men belonged to the London District marauders captured in November. By June 21 one dying man had pled guilty, and the jury had convicted fourteen more of treason.[69]

The convicted included only one significant culprit, Aaron Stevens, a former Indian Department official and a substantial farmer from Newark. Robinson described Stevens as a "man formerly in the confidence of Government, of respectable family and property, convicted of having acted as a spy for the enemy." During the summer of 1813 he had scouted the British post at Burlington Heights "for a large pecuniary reward" from an American general. Witnesses also had seen Stevens bearing arms to defend the enemy camp at Fort George.[70]

The other convicts were petty figures, including Jacob Overholser. Forty years old and illiterate, he had lived in Upper Canada for only four years. Robinson described Overholser as

An ignorant man from Fort Erie of considerable property—a good farmer convicted of having accompanied in arms parties of American Soldiers to the houses of four of his neighbours who were by them made prisoners and sent to Buffalo about 1 Dec[embe]r last. He . . . gave evidence against them charging them with having broken their parole by volunteering in our service after they had been paroled by the enemy. He is not a man of influence or enterprise, and it is thought acted as he did from motives of personal enmity to the persons thus taken away who are not of themselves men of good character.

During the American occupation of Fort Erie, Overholser had turned to their officers for redress against four loutish neighbors who had stolen his horses and threatened to burn his barn. A magistrate described the feud as "nothing but Rancor and ill will Between them and as the times had been Bad enough from the Americans . . . we had better try to be at pease amongst Our Selves." But Overholser's enemies reported him to the British, who convicted him at Ancaster of treason. They needed his conviction to make a point: that no personal feud or local interest could trump the demands of the government for loyal service. Overholser suffered for resisting larcenous neighbors who could claim greater loyalty.[71]

The effective performance of the criminal law required a political balance between enough executions to demonstrate the power of government and enough pardons to impress the people with its mercy. Chief Justice Scott explained, "Example is the chief end of punishment & that the punishment of a few would have an equal, & I even think a more salutary effect in this province than the punishment of many." But he insisted that some from both the Niagara and the London Districts had to be executed as examples that "would strike terror in all."[72]

The Ancaster court sentenced all fifteen convicts to hang but put off the executions until July 20, to permit General Drummond to select a few for a limited pardon that would exile them for life, probably to the penal colony at Botany Bay. Robinson explained, "No person now convicted should be suffered to remain in the Country. The security of those who have disclosed their treasons and been active in their apprehension makes this precaution necessary & just." And, like the executed, the commuted would lose their land to Crown confiscation.[73]

Relying on Robinson's recommendations, Drummond suspended the sentences of seven convicts including Overholser. The general sent them down to Kingston to await their deportation. En route through the Newcastle District, one escaped, but the guards hustled the rest to a crowded, filthy, and cold jail in Kingston, where the typhoid fever killed three of them, including Overholser.[74]

At Burlington Heights on July 20, the British executed eight of the traitors, including Aaron Stevens. The British moved quickly because as Robinson warned, delay would "destroy the effects of the example. Execution should be done while the facts are recent in the memory of the public." The condemned stood in wagons parked beneath a hastily built wooden gallows. Blindfolded, with their arms and legs tied, they wore nooses around their necks. At the fatal moment, horses lurched both wagons forward, leaving the men to dangle and strangle, for the fall was too short to break their necks. Jerking in contortions, their bodies pulled down one beam, which struck at least one man a fatal blow to the skull. After all were dead, the executioners completed their duty to mutilate traitors, by cutting out and burning their entrails, quartering their bodies, and severing their heads for public display on posts.[75]

Drummond concluded that the executions had produced "the most Salutary effects among the people . . . throughout the Province." By employing the civil law to deadly and exemplary effect, the government had established a broad definition of treason that intimidated men prone to resist the draft. After the executions, militia officers more aggressively enforced the laws by tracking down defaulters for heavy fines or for jail if they could not pay. Courts-martial sentenced at least a dozen militiamen to seven years of exile in a penal colony, which they could avoid only by agreeing to serve so long in a British regiment.[76]

The longer the war persisted, the fewer friends the Americans could find in Upper Canada. Their defeats and plundering undercut their credibility as victors and liberators—as did the equivocations of the

Warehouses burned by British troops, *at Sodus, New York, June 1813. From Benson J. Lossing,* The Pictorial Field-Book of the War of 1812 *(New York, 1869), 606.* (Courtesy of the New York State Library.)

American government, which failed explicitly to promise a republican incorporation into the United States. The American ambiguity compounded the ambivalence of most Late Loyalists, who simply wanted to be left alone to work their farms. At the same time the British increased their repression of disaffection, which they severely punished as sedition and treason. Growing numbers of people decided to support the British as their best bet to end the war soon by expelling the invaders who had brought more misery than hope.[77]

U.S. Infantryman, 1813, *by H. McBarron.* (Courtesy of Parks Canada.)

CHAPTER TWELVE

SOLDIERS

We must be careful not to confound Republican Freedom with Military Subordination, things as irreconcilable as opposite Elements—the one being found[ed] in Equality and the other resting on Obedience.

—General James Wilkinson, August 23, 1813[1]

To BECOME PROPER SOLDIERS, men needed to accept subordination to the orders of their officers. Recruits were supposed to compose a machine of unequal but complementary parts. General Wilkinson preached, "preserve this chain of dependence and authority, and the complete machine harmonizes in all its parts; break one link, . . . and confusion and anarchy must ensue." But the republic bred citizens who balked at the regimentation of military life. Colonel Edmund P. Gaines lamented:

> The ordinary operation of civil affairs, in our beloved country, is as deadly hostile to every principle of military discipline, as a complete military government would be to a democracy. . . . Every individual composing [the army] *must* leave at home all of what are considered to be the choicest fruits of republicanism.

Insisting that victory depended upon repeated drill, strict discipline, and immediate obedience, Major Thomas Melville, Jr., asked, "Is there not almost a total absence of these *essentials* in our Army?" Recruits, he argued, had to "be learned to forget *the Citizen* and become *the Soldier*." To turn civilians into soldiers, officers worked to suppress their individuality and their fear by drilling and punishing the men until they would stand and fight as units, for hours if necessary. Daily drills taught companies to march, deploy, load, and fire together, responding promptly and uniformly to orders barked by their officers.[2]

In 1812 few American soldiers had any military experience beyond the charade known as the militia, while most of the British troops were hardened veterans of the demanding war with France, which had raged since 1793 (with one brief interval). Newly concocted, the American regiments lacked the long and proud traditions of their British counterparts. And British and American officers agreed that it took three years of drill to make a proper soldier. Small wonder then that Americans faltered during the first two years of the war. Disciplining troops was hard enough for the British, who came from a stratified society which allotted honor to gentlemen and hardship to commoners. Compared to the more egalitarian Americans, British soldiers more readily accepted orders from their officers.[3]

During the War of 1812 the British and American armies primarily consisted of foot soldiers supplemented by a few mounted "dragoons," who acted primarily as scouts and couriers, and by artillerymen, who managed the iron or brass cannon, which usually fired round shot weighting from three to nine pounds each. Some soldiers had rifles, which imparted a spin to their lead bullets, giving shots greater accuracy at a longer range. But rifles were more expensive, slow to load, prone to jam, and could not attach a bayonet. Because commanders valued reliability more than accuracy, most of the infantry had smoothbore muskets, which limited their accuracy to one hundred yards at best.[4]

To be effective, musket fire had to be in a "volley": a coordinated discharge by at least an entire company, if not a complete regiment. In effect the company functioned as a collective shotgun, compensating for the erratic fire of individual muskets. And a sudden surge of bullets demoralized an enemy far more than did scattered fire. Rather than take careful aim, men were supposed to load and fire as quickly as possible, for victory usually rewarded the side that could discharge more volleys. Well-trained, veteran troops could synchronize their loading and firing to deliver three volleys per minute.[5]

Officers trained their infantry to march in a tight column, under fire, toward an enemy position, and then to deploy into a facing line, three ranks deep. Between and within each rank, the men stood two or three feet apart, close enough to reach out and touch, but with just enough room to wield their muskets. The front two ranks fired while the third rank provided men to fill gaps made by casualties. Once within one hundred yards, the opposing armies exchanged volleys until one side wavered. Then the aggressor could fix bayonets to the muzzles of their muskets and charge forward for hand-to-hand combat to rout the enemy. British generals especially liked the bayonet because it spooked raw American troops.[6]

In combat, soldiers suffered from the thunderous sound and dense, choking smoke of exploding gunpowder, as well as from the brutal kick of a heavy-caliber musket, which bruised and blackened a man's right cheek and shoulder. The pain and confusion quickly eroded the cohesion of Americans thrown into battle with little training. During their attack on Fort George in May 1813, an officer lamented that his troops "became one solid mass of confusion" as "some of our men were firing into the air at an angle of forty-five degrees, others in their confusion did not ram the cartridge half way home, dropped their ramrods on the ground and indeed some rendered their muskets useless during the fight by firing away their rammers."[7]

OFFICERS

In the republic's army, the problems began at the top. Lacking combat experience, most American officers were the lawyers, merchants, and clerks of a commercialized society. "Our army is full of men fresh from lawyers' shops and counting rooms," Peter B. Porter lamented, but he was one of them. In December 1812 Major Thomas Sidney Jesup denounced "the crowd of ignorance & stupidity with which our army abounds." Winfield Scott described most of his fellow officers in 1812 as "imbeciles and ignoramuses." A critic assessed a new officer, Robert Leroy Livingston: "Well known by the name of 'Crazy Bob,' and if throwing Decanters and Glasses were to be the weapons used, he would make a most excellent Lieut. Colonel." Lacking self-discipline, officers struggled to discipline their men.[8]

Serving as officers, former lawyers and store clerks cultivated an exaggerated sense of honor copied from the British army. Many an American officer insisted that he would "devote every thing to the service of his country, except his honor." In this formula, honor trumped duty to the nation and subordination to commanders. A visitor to the army denounced the "excessive vanity" and the "personal hauteur, a supercilious contempt of inferior rank" which bred dissension. Colonel James Burn explained that "bickering over rank and command" prevailed because "self conceit appears to predominate."[9]

Insecure, the army's would-be gentlemen readily insulted others and quickly felt slighted. Most British officers had a keen sense of their rung in a class hierarchy, so they knew when to defer. But the American army was a cockpit of prickly competitors for scarce honor, as almost every officer felt offended by subordination to anyone else. Colonel Isaac A. Coles lamented "that our little army is torn to pieces by dissentions &

broils which disgrace it. Where they have every day opportunities of fighting the enemy, they can surely be under no necessity of fighting each other."[10]

The bitter rivalries of new officers erupted into the newspapers. In this war, combat comprised but the first act of a battle. The second came with a commander's "battle report," an official account submitted to the War Department and published in the newspapers. Of course a commander cast his own conduct in the best possible light and praised favored subordinates. Ambitious, vain, and touchy, American officers carefully parsed battle reports, seeking their names and sufficient applause. Blame infuriated, omission enraged, and tepid praise insulted. The slighted officers vented their wounded pride in letters submitted to the newspapers, where battles raged long after they had been fought in the field. The offended puffed themselves and damned their rivals and any fool general who could not tell the difference.[11]

When armies holed up for the winter, many officers raced to Washington to lobby for promotion. They got "furloughs" to leave from indulgent generals, who thereby advanced their own interests. In December 1813 Governor Tompkins at Albany reported, "The officers have passed thro this place in shoals . . . going to Washington to snort forth their own merits, exploits & claims to promotion." In March 1814 a congressman wrote, "So great has been the resort of epaulettes here that many have inquired who were left with the Troops?" But the congressmen had themselves to blame for promoting their lobbying friends. "One Campaign in the City of Washington is worth *two* on the frontier," one major concluded. By leaving their troops behind for the winter, the furloughed officers lost a golden opportunity to train their men, who resented their own inability to return home.[12]

Measuring honor in their relative rank, officers raged if bypassed for promotion in favor of a rival. Major Charles K. Gardner explained,

> you have no idea of the desire that a small taste of rank excites with one who enters the army at an early day and has been fed by little grades until he becomes voracious. . . . It is not a matter of ambition; but rather of pride, to be equal with your fellow officers on that ground which is alone valued, the footing of honor.

Many a disappointed officer resigned in a huff, citing "a Sacred Regard to my own Honor." One self-impressed young officer insisted: "reflecting that my Commission was given to me during the pleasure of the Government granting it and that reciprocal Justice requires it should

Colonel Isaac A. Coles (*1780–1841*), *engraving by Charles B. J. F. de Saint-Mémin, 1802.* (Courtesy of the National Portrait Gallery, Smithsonian Institution; gift of Mr. and Mrs. Paul Mellon.)

James Craine Bronaugh (*1788–1822*), *oil painting by Ralph Earl.* (Courtesy of the Hermitage: Home of President Andrew Jackson, Nashville, Tenn.)

also be during my own pleasure." Young officers also felt keenly the pressure of peers in their honor culture. Lieutenant Colonel Samuel S. Connor quit after the army elevated some captains at his expense: "Capt. Vischer told me I could not, consistently with the feelings & spirit of an officer, remain in service after seeing Captains put over my head." Often tendered in midcampaign, these abrupt resignations could cripple an army.[13]

The rancor between rival officers also led them to press charges against one another in courts-martial, which were far more abundant in the republic's army than in the empire's. General George Izard lamented, "It is wonderful how much valuable time these Courts Martial engross. I have more than once exerted the Privilege of pardoning in order to empty the Provost Guard-house, but it is rapidly repeopled."[14]

Many feuding officers preferred to test their honor in duels. Although the army's official Rules and Articles of War barred dueling, officers treated with contempt anyone who refused a formal challenge to fight. They even prosecuted insulted officers who refused to issue a challenge. Lieutenant Thomas McMahon was convicted for "suffering himself to be struck with a Sword . . . by an officer of the 16th [Regiment] without noticing the Same." The same court-martial punished Ensign Page for "suffering himself to be called a Damnd. liar and not properly noticing the same as an officer." Indeed, to reduce the number of courts-martial, some generals encouraged officers to settle their disputes by dueling.[15]

Putting honor ahead of nation, the duelists shot at each other instead of at the enemy. In the spring of 1813, to leave New York's legal jurisdiction, two officers crossed the Niagara River to duel on an island, where they were surprised and captured by the British. The duels often crippled or killed the officers whom the army could least afford to lose. At Fort George in September 1813, Lieutenant Smith killed Dr. Shumate, a scarce military surgeon in a camp suffering from epidemics of malaria and dysentery.[16]

In October 1813, in the midst of a pressing campaign, another military surgeon, Dr. James C. Bronaugh, challenged his regimental commander, Colonel Isaac A. Coles, to a duel. A fiery young man from Virginia, Bronaugh blamed Coles for bringing him up before a court-martial on charges of neglecting his medical duties while "taking to his quarters and openly cohabiting with Fanny, a Camp woman" and the wife of a common soldier. Although acquitted, Bronaugh demanded the satisfaction of a duel. When Coles refused, Bronaugh posted a notice in the camp: "I declare to the world, and to the officers of the U.S. army particularly, that Isaac A. Coles, colonel of the 12th regt. of infantry, is a base liar, infamous scoundrel, and coward." No army could survive if subordinates could kill their superiors in duels, so General Wilkinson arrested Bronaugh and sent him back to Sackets Harbor for trial. On the eve of combat, the army lost a desperately needed surgeon because honor mattered most to Dr. Bronaugh.[17]

But most of the army's officers blamed Coles for refusing the doctor's challenge. In a petition in Bronaugh's favor, they expressed incredulity that "this natural and honourable demand was answered by his immediate *arrest*!" A general denounced Coles for publishing his case in a pamphlet: "I pity the man! A couple of fair shots with the Doctor would go farther to justify him before that public, whose opinion he professes to respect, than one hundred pages tho' couched in the language of a Junius and marked by the powers of a Mansfield." For this general, the pistol was mightier than the pen. In early 1814 a court-martial convicted Bronaugh, but the officers of the court urged Wilkinson to pardon him, which he promptly did. At the end of the war the army discharged Coles but retained Bronaugh, deemed a better fit with his fellow officers.[18]

RECRUITS

In addition to suffering from too many bad officers, the army lacked enough good soldiers. In January 1812 Congress authorized an army of 35,000 men, but a year later the nation had raised only 18,500, too few to defend the long seacoast and western frontier much less provide a sufficient force to invade Canada. Recruiting lagged primarily because Congress mandated a low cash bounty for enlistment (sixteen dollars) and monthly pay (five dollars). When a sober laborer could earn ten to twelve dollars per month, why get shot at for half that pay? Cash-starved but land-rich, Congress tried to entice men with the promise of a post-service bounty of 160 acres. But laboring men wanted more cash up front, rather than distant land on a future frontier. An Ohioan assured his U.S. senator that the bounty and pay did not suffice for a man to "turn out and get himself killed." He "wished every member of Congress had 160 acres of land stuffed up his [ass]." Trying to wage war on the cheap, the Republicans miscalculated that a virtuous patriotism would suffice to rally a large and motivated army.[19]

Congress also required regular recruits to serve for five years, a long term that daunted most American men. Proud of their freedom, they disliked submitting to military discipline, which they likened to slavery. Peter B. Porter insisted that his constituents would "not become slaves to the Army for five years." A Federalist congressman argued that no "independent farmer" would "consent to be a mere machine, without any will of his own, and sell himself to be whipped and shot." Noting that only four hundred Kentuckians had enlisted in the regulars, Henry Clay explained, "Such is the structure of our society . . . that I doubt whether many can be engaged for a longer term than six months."[20]

For want of recruits, the Madison administration had to ask state governors to call militiamen into national service. In New England the Federalist governors refused. In New York and Pennsylvania the Republican governors cooperated, but the militia proved badly armed, poorly motivated, and undisciplined. Their training consisted of an annual, single-day muster where drinking trumped the brief drills. When sent to the border, they refused to cross into Canada and then deserted in droves. If forced into combat, they usually threw down their guns to run away in a panic. And militia drafts hurt recruiting for the regular army because many drafted men hired substitutes at ten to fifteen dollars a month, which compared richly to the five dollars per month earned by a regular for harder and longer service.[21]

After the crushing defeats of 1812, the republic needed more and healthier regulars, so Congress raised the private's pay to eight dollars per month (from five dollars) and promised a cash bounty of forty dollars (up from sixteen dollars) as well as 160 acres of land. And Congress gave recruits the option of enlisting for just twelve months, which meant that few would do so for five years. Better pay and a bigger cash bounty did improve recruiting, nearly doubling the army to 34,325 by late 1813, but that number still fell far short of the 55,000 sought.[22]

Meanwhile, during 1813, the British reinforced their army in Canada and began to attack American coastal towns, particularly along Chesapeake Bay. The republic had to divert troops to defend the seaports, absorbing the increase in recruits and leaving too few to conquer Canada. And at the end of the campaign, most of the recent recruits headed home because they had enlisted for only one year. An officer denounced the folly of "recruiting men for twelve months, for before they are disciplined and made to look like soldiers, they are discharged, and thus the bounty and pay, which is so liberal, has been thrown away upon a worthless class of citizens without the least benefit to the nation."[23]

In 1814 the nation had to rebuild the army yet again. Rejecting conscription as political suicide, Congress instead doubled the land bounty to 320 acres and more than tripled the cash bounty to $124. But the new recruits had to commit to serving for either five years or the duration of the war. Desperate for an army, Republicans set aside their fiscal scruples and pushed the nation closer to bankruptcy. The unprecedented bounties enticed about 25,000 new recruits and improved their quality, but they still fell far short of the army's need.[24]

Recruiting suffered because the penurious U.S. Treasury and the disorganized War Department often failed to provide recruiting officers with sufficient funds and clothing to fulfill their promises. At Philadelphia in the spring, William Duane watched recruits march north to the front and remarked, "if we had only Cash in the hands of Recruiting officers, we could have sent 2,000 instead of 700." Potential recruits also balked at the sight of ragged, early recruits shivering and coughing for want of shoes and decent clothes.[25]

The sight of returning veterans also depressed enlistments. Hungry, ragged, limping, and sometimes crippled, their alarming appearance and bitter talk discounted the glory of war. A military surgeon lamented that so many broken-down soldiers were "strolling about the country, subsisting upon the charity of individuals to the no little disgrace of the nation." At Albany, a Republican politician rued "the injury of the recruiting service & the moral effect produced among new troops by the lame & mutilated" returning from the front.[26]

Because armies depend on the poor for recruits, the Americans hampered enlistments by refusing to enlist their poorest people, the African-Americans who comprised a fifth of the nation's population. In 1810 the republic had about 240,000 enslaved and 36,000 free black men of military age, but the Republican government rejected them as recruits. Although many blacks had ably served in Patriot forces during the revolution, thereafter the Republicans rejected black recruits from an emerging conviction that whites would refuse to serve with them. Racial prejudice hampered an American army that desperately needed more men.[27]

The government did accept free blacks into the navy as sailors, but never as officers. When Isaac Chauncey sent some black sailors to serve on Lake Erie, the commander there, Oliver Hazard Perry, complained. An irritated Chauncey replied, "I have yet to learn that the Colour of the skin, or cut and trimmings of the coat, can affect a man's qualifications or usefullness. I have nearly 50 Blacks on board this ship [the *General Pike*], and many of them are amongst my best men." Perry belatedly learned that lesson when the black sailors helped him crush the British warships on his lake in September 1813.[28]

Forbidden to fight for the republic, southern slaves instead looked to the British as liberators. Along Chesapeake Bay, British naval commanders recruited fugitive black men by offering freedom, a twenty-dollar bounty, and the promise of postwar land in a Crown colony. Ordinarily struggling to keep their own men from escaping into America, the naval officers welcomed the turnabout of drawing enslaved Americans into the Royal Navy, where freedom won their loyalty. In 1813–14, the British recruited six hundred Chesapeake runaways as marines. By favoring slavery for southern blacks, the United States lost their military talents to the British.[29]

Within the republic, the leading proponents of black troops were Irish-Americans: William Duane, Nicholas Gray, Thomas Lefferts, and James Mease. Radicals in the United Irish tradition, they were heavily invested in winning the war. With so many Irish immigrants serving in the beleaguered army, their leaders sought to ease their burden by providing black reinforcements. And as radicals and immigrants, they had not yet adopted the full racial prejudices of the republic. In their openness to black potential, this generation of Irish-American leaders represented an alternative to the racism later embraced by white immigrants to escape their own subordination.[30]

SOLDIERS *on a march to* BUFFALO.

Soldiers on a March to Buffalo, *by William Charles, ca. 1815. This cartoon repre-*
sents American regulars helping their camp women cross a stream. (Courtesy of the
William L. Clements Library, University of Michigan.)

Impressed by Duane's arguments, the U.S. secretary of war, John
Armstrong, denounced the restriction on black troops as a blight to the
nation: "We must get over this nonsense . . . if we mean to be what we
ought to be." But Armstrong faced formidable opposition from southern Republicans, including President Madison, who blanched at the
idea of arming free blacks as the slippery slope to slave revolts. A month
later Armstrong lost a power struggle with his great rival in the cabinet,
James Monroe, a slaveholder from Virginia.[31]

In the end the United States failed to enlist an army big enough to
win the war. In the 1810 census, the United States counted 1,120,000
white men of military age (sixteen to forty-five years), but could enlist at
most 62,430 regulars, a paltry 5 percent of the pool. And the real
strength of the army fell far short of that, owing to the midwar expira-
tion of a fifth of those enlistments, the desertion of another tenth, and
the loss of another tenth to combat and disease. The regular army never
exceeded 40,000 men at any point during the war. Many more Ameri-

cans served for a few weeks or months in the militia, but they were virtually useless.[32]

CAMPS

The shorthanded army rushed raw recruits to the front without proper training. In February 1813 a general complained, "the troops are still as ignorant as when they first enlisted." After suffering a defeat, Colonel Robert Purdy conceded that his men "had not been exercised with that rigid discipline so necessary to constitute the soldier. . . . a spirit of subordination was foreign to their views." Badly trained and miserably led, the soldiers reacted as civilians would to the terror of combat.[33]

Defying repeated orders, the men randomly shot their guns at all hours. The firing wasted precious ammunition and threatened to habituate the troops to sudden gunfire that might, in fact, signal an enemy attack. But soldiers delighted in their power to make noise and distraction. In September 1813 General Jacob Brown complained that his standing order "forbidding the discharge of fire arms in or near Camp" was "transgressed daily." Two months later General Wilkinson exploded, "The General is shocked at the continuation of the disorderly, disgraceful, unsoldierly, dangerous practice of firing around the Camp." Despite threatening executions for the practice, Wilkinson concluded, "yet we have a constant firing around." That it drove officers crazy was part of the appeal of random firing, which rendered American camps so loud and their location no secret to the enemy.[34]

Soldiers spent more time marching than fighting, as the rival armies jockeyed for better position. In addition to a musket or rifle, each man lugged a pack, filled with spare clothing and gear, weighing forty to fifty pounds. And their feet suffered in misshapen shoes that unraveled as they slogged through the thick mud of frontier roads and the frigid water of swollen streams. Long, tedious, and exhausting marches drenched men in rain, sleet, or snow. At night they sought relief by building fires. An officer recalled, "We sat around the fires, turning ourselves like a spit all night, the one side freezing and the other roasting." When the enemy lurked nearby, the men could build no fires lest they betray their position. A soldier recalled spending November nights "wet to the skin, with no fire to dry us, freezing cold, and our coats threadbare. The whiz of bullets is not the worst thing about war—burnt powder keeps you warm!"[35]

The American troops spent much of the war in cold and muddy

camps waiting for supplies, reinforcements, and better weather. In November 1813 near Plattsburgh, Private Richard Bishop settled into a new camp in "a very desolate place," a swamp in a forest recently blackened by fire. Made of damp pine, their fires produced more smoke than heat. In one week Bishop's regiment buried fourteen men, the victims of disease. But their officers partied like it was 1799:

> The officers of the Army had a splendid Ball last evening at Skinners Hotel in the village of Plattsburgh. . . . I am still unwell with Rheumatic complaint in one of my shoulders together with a very bad cold. I go to bed this evening in very great pain, if you would call it going to bed to lye down on the cold ground on a few hemlock brush.

In November 1814 Bishop died in a skirmish near the Canadian line, shot "through his Brest." The year before he had anticipated death and hoped to pass "from this world to another, which I hope will be less troublesome and more peaceable."[36]

During the war Sackets Harbor became the nation's primary military base. A snug basin about thirty acres in size, it offered the only decent harbor for ships on the New York shore of Lake Ontario. But it lay perilously close to the main British base at Kingston—a mere thirty-five miles—and dangerously far from the heartland of American men and supplies. So the army had to post thousands of men at Sackets Harbor to defend the naval base from British attack. Supplying them was a nightmare, for only a long and muddy road filled with roots, rocks, and stumps linked the isolated village to the denser and older New York towns to the south in the Mohawk Valley.[37]

The navy and army crowded the little village of sixty houses with thousands of sailors, laborers, shipwrights, and soldiers. A ramshackle array of huts and tents surrounded by earthen walls and studded with wooden blockhouses, Sackets Harbor became a muddy mess from thousands of boots tramping through the rain-drenched clay soil. In the spring of 1813 a general wrote home, "Here I am on the Banks of Lake Ontario, Cooped up in a Dirty little Village, every house, hole & Corner which can give Shelter Crouded, which renders it very unpleasant." Another officer recalled the village as "full of soldiers and of mud. We waded (for when one sinks up to the knees, it is not walking), through the streets to head quarters." In late 1813, a newly arrived officer declared, "Sackets harbor is the damdest hole I ever saw in my life."[38]

Badly fed, miserably housed, and clad in rags, the soldiers made a

Sacketts Harbour on Lake Ontario, *engraving by Baily, from the* Naval Chronicle *(London), 1818.* (Courtesy of the Naval Historical Foundation, U.S. Naval Historical Center.)

sordid appearance, worsened by their heavy drinking to dull their pain. A naval officer, Captain Arthur Sinclair, declared: "Figure to yourself the dirtiest and most slovenly looking blackguards you ever have seen, and you have our army. . . . They fill our ships full of vermin whenever they act as transports for them." Insults between sailors, soldiers, and shipwrights led to riots with fists and clubs, as on May 1, 1814, after a sentry shot a carpenter during the celebration of a ship launching, where "all got drunk as usual."[39]

Crowded with six thousand men, more than ten times the prewar population, the boomtown became an environmental disaster as the men urinated and defecated in open latrines, covered privies, and, despite orders, directly in the streets. In August 1813 Dr. James Tilton reported, "excrementitious matters were scattered every where." Another surgeon, William Ross, declared, "we were enveloped in and respired air surcharged with septic vapour." Rains flushed much of the waste into the harbor, where the ships floated in a stew of water, feces, and urine, but the army's bakery drew its water from the harbor. Dr. Ross lamented the bakery's "proximity to a stagnant part of the lake and the numerous privies which surround it, [so] that the water thereabouts is impregnated with, and contains a diffusion of excrementious matter."[40]

Living in filth, and eating it, the soldiers and sailors became debilitated with disease, particularly dysentery, a painful and often fatal

disease of the bowels. In August 1813 a third of the soldiers were incapacitated. By January 1814 only 500 of the 1,700 soldiers were fit for
duty. A newspaper reported that the village was "interrupted several
times each day with the solemn knell of funerals attended with honors of
war." In April 1813 an officer reported that five hundred soldiers had
been buried at Sackets Harbor during the preceding year. That month
another officer calculated that the army lost from six to ten dead men
every day. Losing track of the fatalities, General Leonard Covington
reported, "We bury hundreds."[41]

But they did not bury them very well. Dr. Tilton complained, "Dead
horses and even human bodies were slightly buried within the lines."
Dr. Ross noted that the corpses "were promiscuously buried not deeper
than two feet" because the topsoil was so thin and the grave diggers
were so weary. At Sackets Harbor the bodies of the dead haunted the living, who struggled to keep up with the mounting losses.[42]

SIGHT AND SOUND

American commanders had to define a stark boundary between their
troops on the one hand and the enemy on the other. That sounds easy
and obvious, but this was an Anglo-American civil war where both sides
spoke English. Without translation, the foes readily understood words
meant to intimidate, cajole, and seduce. During the long lulls between
combat, the rivals sought a psychological edge in communications
between their camps. By projecting confidence, one side tried to demoralize the other, increasing desertion from the foe, which became a key
measure of relative power. Maintaining morale and discipline proved
difficult in a war where soldiers could so easily change sides.[43]

Between battles, the rival armies keenly watched one another, particularly along the Niagara River, where only three hundred yards of water
separated them. To mislead the enemy, each side hid preparations for a
real attack. But when on the defensive, a commander tried to discourage
the enemy by conspicuously shifting around regiments to create false
impressions of new reinforcements and superior numbers. A bustle on
one side always caught the eye, and raised the alarm, on the other.[44]

The rival camps often could hear one another, so the soldiers also
employed sound to compete for a psychological edge. In 1813 an American officer at Black Rock heard "a most interesting rivalry" between
army buglers on the two sides of the river as they "ranged through the
whole catalogue of calls and marches." Collective cheers sought to

demonstrate high morale on one side to deflate the other. At Buffalo on December 1, 1812, when General Smyth failed in his bid to cross the river, the frustrated Americans heard three cheers from the British shore "expressive of ridicule and contempt towards us." Whenever one side fired cannon at the other and scored a hit, their ranks erupted in loud cheering meant to daunt the other. But the receiving side immediately cheered back to signal that the shot had done them no real harm.[45]

Both sides conspicuously celebrated supposed victories elsewhere by hoisting huge flags and firing salutes of cannon. Ostensibly to spare the other side from alarm, the celebrating general would thoughtfully send across a messenger to explain that the cannon would fire blanks as a salute rather than balls in an attack. Of course the primary purpose was to spread demoralizing news in the enemy ranks.[46]

Sometimes both sides claimed victory for the same battle and fired rival salutes—after carefully informing one another. In May 1813 William Henry Harrison's army suffered heavy casualties repelling a British attack on Fort Meigs on the Maumee (or Miami) River. When the news reached the British on the Niagara front, they politely gave their foes notice of a salute "for the success of His Britannic Majesty's Arms on the Banks of the Miami." A day later, the equally polite American commander returned the favor by announcing a cannon salute "on account of the success of the American arms on the borders of the waters of the Miami." A year later a battle reversed the equation as the British captured Oswego but suffered the heavier casualties. Both sides again claimed victory but for opposing reasons.[47]

In a war of persuasion and conversions, commanders struggled to retain their men while enticing deserters from the enemy. Generals measured their fortunes in the ebb and flow of deserters. They felt encouraged by a net gain and discouraged by a reverse flow. "In the course of sixteen days, the enemy have lost sixty-five men by desertion, we barely six," General Wilkinson exulted in September 1813. Whenever deserters from the enemy diminished, commanders became anxious at the evident increased power of the foe and at their own loss of information.[48]

Both armies welcomed defectors as a double boon: they subtracted from the enemy while bolstering the side that provided haven. For the same reason, a commander dreaded defection from his own ranks. An American noted that defection increased on the eve of battle as defectors "believed they would have news to communicate, which would make them welcome" among the enemy. Unable entirely to stop such defectors, this officer advised throwing out a "cock and bull" story as a cover, such "as deserters might carry to the enemy without injury to our plans."[49]

The American army lost more deserters, but they usually fled homeward rather than to the British. The exceptions usually had relatives in Upper Canada, or they were British-born immigrants who had become miserable in an American military camp. Some transients shifted sides several times in the course of the war. Held prisoner at Montreal in early 1814, Benjamin Hodge, Jr., met a British soldier named Morgan, "by birth a Welshman. He was a friend to all nations, but true to none." Morgan began the war as a sailor on board the British warship *Peacock*. Captured by the Americans, he enlisted in their army, but deserted in the fall of 1813 to rejoin the British as a soldier. Later, Hodge learned, Morgan "deserted from the English on the Niagara frontier to join the American army."[50]

Most British deserters fled to the American lines, for the United States allured as a land of cheap whiskey, abundant meat, and good wages. Paid the equivalent of $3.25 per month, a British private could triple his pay by becoming a laborer or a soldier in America. "There is more to be gained there, than here," two ringleaders told their peers to entice them to desert. Colonel Edward Baynes lamented, "The ideal blandishments of the United States, which are most insidiously inculcated into the minds of our Soldiers, is so powerful an incitement, that Corps of the highest established reputation and discipline have not escaped the mortifying disgrace of frequent Desertions." The American general Alexander Macomb reported, "Our pickets are within sight of the enemy's, theirs to prevent desertion & ours to aid those who feel inclined to come over to us." In June 1813 the British sent a naval officer and eight sailors in a boat with a flag of truce to the New York shore of Lake Erie with a message, but no sooner had the boat landed than all of the sailors, save one, deserted.[51]

The flow of British deserters across the lines became so steady that the British exploited it to breach American security. An Irish officer in the British service, James FitzGibbon commanded a predawn raid to surprise the picket guards of American-held Fort George. When challenged by a sentinel, FitzGibbon replied, "Deserters," which seemed plausible given his Irish accent. The sentinel replied, "Pass, deserters," which enabled the attackers to overwhelm the guards. In a fringe benefit for the British, this trick had fatal consequences for some real deserters who were subsequently shot by jumpy American sentinels.[52]

British soldiers could more easily desert when their army invaded the

Storming of Fort Oswego, 1814, *engraving by Captain Steel, 1817.* (Courtesy of the McCord Museum, Montreal, M-923.)

United States. During the first four months of 1814, eighty soldiers (16 percent of the garrison) escaped from the King's Regiment posted at recently captured Fort Niagara on the New York side of the border. Their commander, Colonel Robert Young, felt "disgraced by associating my name with what I formerly and *proudly* designated the King's Regiment . . . My confidence in the regiment is now gone, and its villainous conduct will bring my grey hairs with sorrow to the grave."[53]

In September 1814 Sir George Prevost lost three hundred deserters during his expedition against Plattsburgh. After Prevost withdrew, General Macomb expected no renewed attack because the British commander would "run the risk of losing his whole army . . . by desertion." General Gaines similarly insisted that the enemy could only capture Sackets Harbor in a quick strike, for if bogged down in a prolonged siege, the British "strength would waste away by constant desertions." By attracting British deserters, American prosperity partly compensated for discouraging enlistments in the republic's army.[54]

BOUNDS

While struggling to keep the British at bay, the American commanders also had to fend off their own civilians drawn to the military camps.

Traders hovered about, selling liquor and promoting gambling, corroding the discipline of the troops. Nocturnal pranksters fired guns to awake and alarm the troops. Other opportunists came to gather military information to sell to the British. At Sackets Harbor, a southern officer declared, "The inquisitive, prying unprincipled Yankees about this place are more in the interest of the enemy than I believed it possible for Americans to be."[55]

To turn raw recruits into disciplined soldiers, commanders needed to separate them from the company of citizens. To demarcate the camp as a restricted military zone, commanders drew a boundary one mile beyond and declared martial law to operate within, to the exclusion of the civil law. At Sackets Harbor, the commander ordered,

> The foot patrole will scour the village & *Immediate Environs* & arrest & take up all *disorderly persons*. They will also take up *all persons* lurking about the Camps or Garrisons of this post, or of Suspicious Character & appearance, likewise every *Citizen or Soldier* guilty of discharging *fire arms* or creating false alarums within one mile of the village.

By night and day, guards were supposed to keep the troops in and the citizens out, by requiring passes issued by the commanders for anyone to come or to go. The sentinels had orders to shoot those who ignored a challenge to stop. When a guard killed a passing militiaman at Sackets Harbor, his officer conceded, "The poor fellow died foolishly; but I can not say but that discipline like that is absolutely necessary. There is certainly no other way to govern an army of any kind."[56]

Enforcing the boundary and securing the camp depended upon vigilant guards, particularly at night. But the lot of a sentinel was miserably cold and boring. Throughout the war, American generals complained that their lax guards drank, slept, and built fires, which revealed their position to an enemy. And lazy officers neglected to make the night rounds to check on their guards. When Richard Bishop applied for a pass to go into Plattsburgh, his negligent lieutenant told him simply to ignore the guard and walk on by, which Bishop did "without trouble." At Sackets Harbor, soldiers slipped away from the forts and into the village by bribing the sentinels with alcohol.[57]

Taverns enticed soldiers to break the boundary, but if an officer tried to shut them down, the owners sued, and the American civil courts favored commerce. At Sackets Harbor in 1813, General Lewis complained, "Taverners and Sutlers keep our Soldiers eternally intoxicated, and any officer who attempts to prevent them is sure to be prosecuted and to have a Judgment against him for as heavy a sum as can be given." Harassed by lawsuits, General Gaines concluded, "I shall feel *much relieved* to get once more on the *Shores* of *Canada*"—where the enemy was clearer and could not employ the American civil courts.[58]

The vicinity of a military camp became a muted war zone between soldiers and civilians, particularly in villages where Federalists prevailed. On duty, the soldiers interfered with the smuggling that benefited so many villagers. Off duty, the troops got drunk and rowdy in the streets, and they pilfered from gardens, orchards, and stores. For their part, the soldiers denounced the villagers as "rogues, rascals, pickpockets, knaves, & extortioners," who gouged and cheated their military customers. Sometimes the tensions escalated into an exchange of gunfire and the burning of shops and homes, as with the Buffalo tavern of the insulting Ralph Pomeroy in November 1812.[59]

At Burlington, Vermont, the Federalist majority treated the Republican army as an illegal occupying force that interfered with their liberty to trade with the enemy in nearby Canada. When the army commander arrested two local men for guiding British raiders, the guides protested that "they were free citizens and had a right to go where they pleased." To calm the public furor, General Macomb released both men, who promptly sued his subordinate, Lieutenant Colonel George McFeeley, for false arrest. On the night of May 16, angry soldiers attacked the house of one of the released guides, who fired out of the windows, killing two soldiers. McFeeley added, "this villain's house was burned the next night, and no doubt it was set on fire by some of our soldiers," while their officers looked the other way. This war within the war subsided in June, when Macomb withdrew the troops across Lake Champlain to Plattsburgh, which allowed the Burlington folk to resume trading with the enemy.[60]

In the spring of 1814 the British threatened Oswego, an American munitions depot on Lake Ontario. The local Federalists held a town meeting, which unanimously resolved, "it is not the duty, nor is it advisable for the citizens of this place to attempt resistance" to any "respectable armed British force" if led by a commander who would give "security and indemnity to the lives, persons, and private property of the inhabitants of the said village." When the British did attack, the local militia held back, which forced the American regulars to retreat. The citizens then revealed hidden caches of government property, so the British commander agreed to spare their private property.[61]

At Sackets Harbor the enemy included local civilians as well as British regulars. When the British attacked the post in May 1813, "a

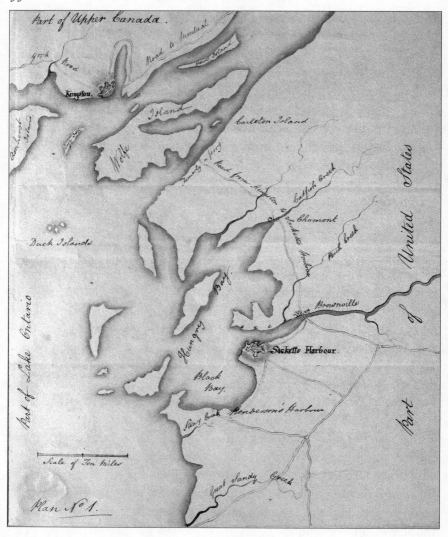

Plan No. 1, *an unsigned sketch prepared by a British spy in 1814. This map depicts the dangerous proximity of Sackets Harbor and Kingston, the principal American and British naval bases on Lake Ontario.* (Courtesy of the Royal Ontario Museum.)

Citizen ran to the British waving a white Handkerchief," to warn them of approaching American reinforcements. After the British retreated, the Americans captured "two Citizens disguised like Savages [who] were in the British Ranks." During the following summer, General Morgan Lewis reported, "Twice has the only Spring which supplies this Village with water been poisoned by quantities of Arsenick thrown into it." After some nocturnal attempts to burn the ships, another officer concluded, "The village is infested by incendiaries." Someone also slipped into a fort to damage the largest cannon with a spike driven into the firing hole.[62]

In July 1813 double disloyalty affected a British bid to surprise Sackets Harbor. As the attack force of Sir James Yeo approached the fortified harbor, British deserters tipped off the Americans. Chauncey prepared a counterattack to surprise the British camp on the shore seven miles to the north, but two disloyal citizens slipped away in a boat to warn Yeo, who prudently withdrew to safety at Kingston. In this dark comedy, neither side could control its own people well enough to surprise the other.[63]

SPIES

Despite the boundary mandated by commanders, American civilians persistently invaded the camps to serve as British spies. Hungry for warning or reassurance, anxious commanders sought news of the other side's numbers, morale, and intentions. Lacking the professional spies of a centralized service, every commander collected disparate information from amateurs, usually traders who crossed the border as smugglers. Loyal to money rather than to a nation, few traders could be trusted to sell their information to just one side. An American general, George Izard, lamented, "The people hitherto employed are, I suspect, as much in the Enemy's Pay as in ours." The civilian spies confirmed, a British general declared, "the long established opinion that the lower class of Americans will do anything for money." Colonel John Harvey described Peter Hogeboom, a petty trader in northern New York, as "*disposable* in any way that may best promote his *personal advantage*, of which it is not the practice of his Nation to lose sight."[64]

In July 1813 the British raided Plattsburgh in northern New York. During the raid, a map fell from the pocket of the British commander. Scooping it up, inhabitants recognized the handwriting of Joel Ackley, a resident. Arrested and questioned, he confessed to having received fifty dollars from the British, with another fifty dollars still due. The Americans jailed Ackley for ten months but discharged him in the spring for want of enough evidence to make a treason charge stick. Unrepentant, Ackley joined the British in Canada and guided another attack on Plattsburgh in September 1814. After the war, he settled in Canada, where he secured £500 from the British in compensation for his services.[65]

Keeping secrets proved impossible in a civil war waged along a porous border where people spoke the same language and had kinship, marital, and trading ties on both sides. On the American bank of the St. Lawrence River, an officer insisted, "One thing is certain, nothing transpires on this Side of the River, but it is immediately known on theirs." At nearby Kingston, General Drummond similarly declared, "It is natural to suppose, that they obtain as good information of our Force here, as we do of their's at Sackett's Harbour." Indeed, the Americans got monthly reports on Kingston from a renegade merchant named William Johnston.[66]

Civilians found it especially easy to spy on American camps for British pay. Under American constitutional law, a court-martial could convict and execute a Briton who spied—but not a citizen, who could only be tried for treason in a civil court with a jury. Treason was almost impossible to prove because the U.S. Constitution narrowly defined it as an overt act of war with at least two witnesses. In 1807 Chief Justice John Marshall declared, "Treason may be machinated in secret, but it can be perpetrated only in the open day and in the eye of the world." That definition precluded spying, which inevitably was "machinated in secret."[67]

Although caught trying to contact the British fleet off the Connecticut shore, Nathaniel G. M. Senter rebuked his American captor: "How can you consider me a *spy* when I am not an enemy, but a countryman of yours . . . for no act of a man can possibly incur the punishment due to a spy, when that man is a citizen." A former law student, Senter concluded, "As for being a traitor, sir, that is incumbent on you *to prove!*" For want of that proof, a judge released Senter, who promptly slipped away to a British warship with his information.[68]

Born in New Jersey, Elijah Clark had lived in Upper Canada for eighteen months when the war began. Never having taken the oath of allegiance to the king, Clark remained an American citizen but one willing to sell his services to General Brock, who sent him across the border to spy on the American troops at Buffalo. Arrested by an army patrol, Clark was court-martialed as a spy, convicted, and sentenced to hang, but President Madison ordered Clark released, on the grounds that no military court could try a civilian.[69]

Widely reported, the Clark decision invited citizens to spy for the British with impunity. At Sackets Harbor in July 1813, General Lewis complained, "Spies eternally march through our Camp in open day and set us at defiance. Arrest one of them, and he immediately pleads his Citizenship, sues you for false imprisonment and recovers heavy damages." General Wilkinson complained of "the ingress & egress of the Emissaries of the Enemy because they are our own Citizens."[70]

William Johnston *(1782–1870), engraving by an unknown artist. From Benson J. Lossing,* The Pictorial Field-Book of the War of 1812 *(New York, 1869), 662.* (Courtesy of the New York State Library.)

Commodore Chauncey sought to make an example of Samuel Stacy, a trader who often visited Sackets Harbor to examine the warships and to ask probing questions. Arresting him on July 1, 1813, Chauncey declared: "It would be very desirable to hang this traitor to his country, as he is considered respectable in the country in which he lives; and I think that it is full time to make an example of some of our countrymen, who are so base and degenerate as to betray their country by becoming the spies and informers of our enemy." But the secretary of war ordered Stacy released because, he explained, "a citizen cannot be considered as a spy." Set free, Stacy promptly crossed the border at Prescott to sell his information to the British.[71]

In Congress in January 1814, Maryland's Robert Wright, an especially partisan Republican, proposed a law to allow the military to try citizens for espionage. Federalists howled in protest. New York's Thomas P. Grosvenor warned that the proposed law would "subject every man in the United States to be dragged before the military tribunals and tried by martial law." Moderate Republicans also balked at the resolution, which died in committee. Not until 1863, during the next (and far bigger) civil war, would Congress make citizens liable to conviction as spies.[72]

In the northern borderland during the War of 1812, the American military apparently executed only one spy, and he was a Briton. An apparent deserter from the British army, William Baker was "found lurking about the encampment of the American Army at Plattsburgh as a Spy." In March 1814 a court-martial convicted and hanged Baker. The *Plattsburgh Republican* observed, "At length, . . . one spy of the hundreds who roam at large over the frontier, has been detected, and sentenced to Death."[73]

Lacking the legal power to punish spying citizens, the Madison administration instead treated immigrants from Great Britain as the chief threat to the republic. Enforcing the Alien Enemies Act of 1812, federal marshals ordered enemy aliens to remove at least forty miles into the interior to prevent them from helping the Royal Navy to attack American ports. Removal posed a severe hardship to artisans and merchants who relied on maritime commerce, but most posed no threat to the republic. Indeed, most were Irishmen caught by a blunt law, for the Alien Enemies Act did little to defend the republic but much to hurt recent immigrants who wanted to become citizens. "Mortified" at being "ranked as an enemy," Thomas Burke declared, "That there may be many persons in the United States who ought to be watched, I have not a doubt, but I believe that few if any of them are Irishmen." An inventor of explosive naval mines (called "torpedoes"), Robert Fulton denounced the suspicion of immigrants: "Indeed, I believe the British have no need to send Spies among us [because] our own citizens, an unfaithful tribe, and our news papers give them every information from the movement of our armies down to an anchored torpedo." In this civil war, loyalty did not neatly follow national origins and identities, which were up for grabs.[74]

ALCOHOL

Attempts to discipline the regular troops also suffered from the abundant alcohol of American life. During the early nineteenth century, Americans drank far more alcohol than did Europeans, for American whiskey was common and cheap owing to the large crops of grain, widespread stills, and low taxes. By getting drunk, men asserted their republican liberty and displayed their masculine prowess. Writing from the Niagara front in early 1813, Baptist Irvine lamented, "To assure sobriety in an [American] army is a great but difficult attainment; for I must confess with chagrin that we are the most tippling race on earth. I believe no nation consumes ardent spirit to half the extent that we do." In addition to corroding discipline, heavy drinking rendered men indifferent to cleanliness and prone to disease.[75]

The military reaped what it sowed by promoting the consumption of alcohol. Recruiters haunted taverns to ply men with free drinks, weakening their resistance. When wives and parents complained of losing a husband or son to a recruiter's bottle, the adjutant general replied that barring the practice "would prevent half the enlistments." Once in the army, men received a daily ration of alcohol to help them cope with their hardships, particularly the cold. An officer noted that unlike food, "we were always sure to find an abundance [of alcohol] every where, laid in with a provident care, as if grog were the staff of life." In fact, it was the staff of army life, for commanders believed that soldiers could better endure hunger than an unsated thirst for alcohol.[76]

Commanders employed or withheld alcohol as carrot or stick to shape the behavior of their soldiers. On the one hand, they gave extra whiskey to celebrate the Fourth of July or an American victory, or to reward soldiers for special duty or good behavior. Coming off nightlong guard duty, sentinels fired at a target. The man with the best shot won a quart of whiskey, the second best got a pint, and the third best secured a half-pint.[77]

On the other hand, commanders punished negligent soldiers by cutting off their alcohol. Found drunk while on guard duty, Cyrus Angell lost fifteen days of whiskey rations and, in a shaming ritual, had "to march from right to left in front of the Brigade, having his arms extended and lashed to a five-foot pole, with a bottle in each hand, one of which is to be empty and the other filled." Losing their alcohol ration was an excruciating punishment for the many soldiers who were alcoholics.[78]

To employ alcohol as carrot or stick, officers had to control the supply, but defiant, craving, and cunning men broke into locked storehouses and boats to steal the liquor, including medical supplies. After the battle of York, the Americans packed up the battered corpse of their dead general, Zebulon Pike, in a cask of rum as a preservative for shipment to Sackets Harbor. "I am ashamed to say that some of our men were inclined to drink the old rum," recalled Ned Myers. When victorious in battle, the American troops broke ranks to rifle the bodies of the dead in search of canteens filled with liquor. When paid, soldiers binged at taverns, stores, and sutlers' tents. One night Richard Bishop wrote in his diary: "the men having a little money soon found the way to the rum cask and from there to their mouths. So ends this day." And when they ran out of money, some soldiers sold their clothing, shoes, and arms for alcohol.[79]

Officers needed to control the modest ration of alcohol, for the army suffered when soldiers drank too much and too freely. At Cleveland, Major Jesup complained, "Soldiers are daily seen drunk in the streets, and even non-commissioned Officers commanding Guards . . . have been found intoxicated and staggering through the Town during their tour of duty." Drunken sentinels imperiled the camp's security against attack. British raiders surprised and captured Fort Schlosser on July 4, 1813, when the entire garrison was too drunk from celebrating independence to post any guards. At Ogdensburg in late 1812, the garrison buried a soldier aptly named Amiel Freeman: "His death was supposed to be occasioned by intemperance." The American freedom to drink had proved fatal to Mr. Freeman.[80]

SUPPLIES

Logistics were of crucial importance for if an army failed to feed and clothe its men properly they would become demoralized and, therefore, prone to defeat and desertion. In December 1812 an American colonel complained:

> My Brave men are in a wretched condition at present. Numbers are barefooted and no clothing to cover their skins from the cold winds of the North. Numbers of them [are] very sickly and several dead. I dread the consequences when I see the way we are clothed and fed.

Although needed by November, winter clothing rarely reached the northern troops before February, "by which time," General Brown lamented, "the constitution of the recruit is broken and destroyed." He concluded, "Owing to this wretched policy, five men have perished by diseases to one who has fallen by the sword."[81]

The northern setting hampered American offensives, for the frontier farms could not feed thousands of troops pushed into the borderland. The climate curtailed both the growing season and the campaign season to just five months, between a late spring and an early winter. The April thaw freed armies to move in boats along the lakes and rivers, but the melt clogged the roads with a thick and paralyzing mud until mid-June, when commanders could begin to move their men and supplies by land. But they had to complete their campaign by December, when the bitter cold and deep snow compelled the troops to hole up in log cabins for the winter. In December 1812 the British general Roger Sheaffe remarked, "The cold weather seems to make the Enemy shrink into nothing." Meanwhile, a thick ice locked up the rivers and lakes. In January 1813 Thomas G. Ridout wrote, "Our Canadian winter has set in very severe, and here I am on the north shore of Lake Ontario, whose great surface is frozen as far as the eye can reach and appears like an immense desert of snow."[82]

The setting favored Canadian defense over an American offensive. To sustain a northern army, the Americans had to transport munitions and provisions from their distant heartland along the Atlantic coast and in the Ohio Valley. New York's Mohawk and Hudson rivers only partially breached the broad and wooded Appalachian Mountains. Interrupted by rapids and portages, obstructed by ice in winter, swollen to floods in the spring, and sometimes falling too low in late summer, the upper reaches of the rivers proved erratic for transportation. But overland travel was far worse, for wagons jolted over the rocks, roots, stumps, and muddy hollows of the frontier roads.[83]

Via the St. Lawrence River and the Great Lakes, the British enjoyed a superior transportation corridor that reached over two thousand miles into the heart of the continent. Although interrupted by ice through a long winter, the northern corridor compensated with a more reliable snow cover for sleighs. In 1814 the American secretary of the navy noted the British advantage in carrying stores "over hard sled roads whilst our roads during the whole winter have been almost impassable." The St. Lawrence River also better suited boat traffic in the warmer months, because it always had plenty of water. Consequently, the British could more easily, cheaply, and quickly move men and supplies from the seaport at Quebec to their Lake Ontario base at Kingston than the Americans could bring goods from New York City to Sackets Harbor. In sum, Upper Canada lay beside the British supply line—in contrast to northern and western New York, which fell on the far side of the difficult Appalachian divide. After the war Madison noted the American struggle "to reach a distant theatre, where the adversary was at home in the midst of all his resources for defence."[84]

To minimize the cost of feeding the army, the American government relied on private contractors who submitted the lowest bid to supply a certain number of rations to a particular military depot. A ration consisted of one and one-quarter pounds of salted beef (or three-quarters of a pound of pork), plus eighteen ounces of bread or flour, and one gill of whiskey. The contractor was also supposed to provide two quarts of salt, four quarts of vinegar, four pounds of soap, and a pound and a half of candles for every hundred rations.[85]

By trying to lock in a low price, the contracting system ignored the seasonal variations in crops, roads, rivers, and mills as well as fluctuations in an army's numbers. The secretary of war, John Armstrong, noted, "In old and well-peopled districts, where corn and cattle are abundant, prices little subject to change, roads safe and unobstructed, and the means of transportation . . . easily procured, the contract plan is the best—because the most economical," but he deemed it folly for the northern borderland, "where the population is thin and poor, supplies scarce and high priced, roads few and bad and much exposed to obstruction." Inevitably everything went wrong, driving up costs beyond the contractors' ability to profit, threatening them with financial ruin. One fatalistic contractor noted, "So it goes, one day one thing and another the next."[86]

Faced with unanticipated costs, some contractors simply defaulted on their contracts, leaving the troops to starve at critical moments. More often, contractors failed to provide the stipulated vinegar, soap, and candles. That neglect threatened the health of the men, for the vinegar contained vitamin C to help stave off scurvy, while the soap promoted cleanliness. Worse still, contractors often substituted additional whiskey, which was cheap, to the dismay of officers already struggling to discipline their troops.[87]

Unscrupulous contractors also cut costs by providing rank meat and rotten flour. According to a military surgeon, some contractors "adulterated [the flour] with plaister of Paris . . . earth, chalk, ashes, Burnt Bones, &c." In Ohio, a post commander considered the rotten beef "such a nuisance in the Fort that yesterday I had it halled out & fire put to it." But a frontier army rarely had any alternative source of supply, so officers usually deemed bad food better than none at all. Compelled to eat carrion, the soldiers suffered from malnutrition and intestinal diseases, particularly dysentery. General Gaines insisted that the army "lost more men by the badness of the provisions, than by the fire of the enemy."[88]

Commanders denounced the contracting system as corrupt and destructive. Winfield Scott insisted, "The interests of the contractor are in precise opposition to those of the troops." After bad flour had sickened his troops, General Brown declared, "we shall never have a great Army until some of our Public Agents Die or get hung." Major Jesup concluded, "It is madness in the extreme to carry on war with such a sys-

tem." In vain, American commanders begged their government to adopt
the British commissariat system, where a specialized military service
dealt directly with farmers to procure sufficient and decent food.[89]

Long supply lines, seasonal swings in weather, frontier underdevel-
opment, and a corrupt contracting system combined to limit the food
that the Americans could accumulate for their northern armies. That
shortfall constrained the size of American forces on the border. In 1812
at Detroit, a soldier reported that savvy Indians "expressed their surprize that Gen. Hull should think of taking the Canadas 'with so many
waggons and so few men!'" But Hull needed many wagons to haul the
bulky provisions for a few men in a campaign held where the local farms
produced so little. On the Canadian front, American armies rarely
exceeded five thousand men, peaking at the seven thousand assembled
by Wilkinson in late 1813. Such modest invasion forces eased the
British challenge in defending Canada.[90]

Spread thin along more than a thousand miles of front, the American
troops often failed even to protect their precious supply depots. Assembled at great cost and with immense difficulty, the stores of flour, pork,
and beef became liabilities whenever the army shifted troops away from
the depots. Frontier citizens rued a poorly guarded depot as a dangerous
invitation to a British raid that would plunder private homes as well as
the public stores. In 1813 such raids devastated Ogdensburg in February, Genesee in June, Plattsburgh in August, and Buffalo and Black
Rock in December. Joseph Ellicott regretted the government depot
near his home: "Had there been no Deposit of this kind, . . . there
would be much less danger of the Enemy making incursions in our territory." Ironically, the government assembled enough food to tempt
British raids but too little to sustain a sufficient army to guard its own
depots—and far too little to conquer Upper Canada.[91]

PUNISHMENT

Desertion surged when the army failed to clothe, feed, and pay the
troops. During the war the army lost at least five thousand men to desertion, about 13 percent of the recruits. By comparison, only 3 percent of
the American troops died in combat and 8 percent died of disease. General Lewis noted, "Deserters have repeatedly assigned as a reason for
their deserting, that they had rather take the chance of being shot for
desertion, than to fall a certain prey to disease."[92]

To discipline wayward soldiers and to discourage desertion, regular
officers resorted to exemplary and brutal punishments. "It is impossible

to command *an army* stripped of the power of punishing offenders,"
General Brown explained.[93]

The British army relied on flogging with a special whip known as a
cat-o'-nine-tails: nine knotted cords fixed to a wooden handle. The culprit was marched to the parade ground, stripped to the waist, and tied
spread-eagle to a frame. Supervised by the drum major, drummers
inflicted 25 strokes each in a rotation; 50 lashes sufficed to bloody a
back, but most sentences mandated 300 strokes. A young officer, John
Le Couteur, recalled watching his first flogging in Canada:

> The lash lacerated his back speedily and the blood flowed freely. He
> stood close in front of me, the inward groan, at each lash, from being
> stifled, went sufficiently to my heart, but, soon after, the Drummer,
> in swinging his Cat of Nine Tails, switched a quantity of his blood
> over my Face and Belts. I fainted away like a Sick girl, to my own
> great horror and Confusion, but it was not unnatural after all. The
> Officers laughed at me, but the men did not.

If the prisoner seemed about to die, the attending surgeon could halt a
flogging, but that merely suspended the remaining strokes until a future
day after his back had healed just enough for another round. Officers
believed that only the fear of pain could restrain men from the lower
orders, considered closer to brutes than to gentlemen.[94]

In 1812 Congress abolished flogging in the U.S. Army in hopes of
increasing enlistments. Denied the whip, American officers invented
new rituals of shaming which required the entire camp to watch. One
officer fined seven deserters just two dollars each and sentenced them
"to ride on each others' backs thro camp." More commonly, convicts
were paraded through the camp while musicians played "The Rogue's
March." To increase the disgrace, some had their coats turned inside
out, had half of their heads shaved, and donned a dunce cap or a plac-
ard around the neck labeled TORY or naming their crime. To add a little
pain, some were tied sitting on a sharp rail or had to stand barefoot on
stakes, while the music played and their comrades jeered. After a brief
but public punishment, the wayward could be welcomed back into
service.[95]

But many commanders adopted a closer substitute to flogging
known as "cobbing." Instead of whipping the bare back, cobbing
employed a wooden stick to strike a man's exposed buttocks. Caught
sleeping at his sentry post, James Givens was "sentenced to receive ten
cobs on his bear posteriors, well laid on, with a paddle, four inches wide

and one half of an inch thick, bored full of holes." To the British, cobbing seemed characteristically American, a hypocritical evasion to preserve a hollow claim to moral superiority over their flogging enemy.[96]

Soldiers hated cobbing as degrading to their manhood. Arrested for getting drunk while on guard duty, Private Dennis Baker "said that if Lt. Hoffman paddled him, he would kill him and desert." So Baker got a double paddling, once for neglecting his duty and a second for threatening his lieutenant. A few days later, Baker's company had to watch as Hoffman compelled two drunken soldiers named Jenkinson and Mitchell "to fight it out." When Jenkinson got the upper hand, Baker bellowed, " 'well done Jenkinson'—upon which Lieutenant Hoffman struck him over the head with a pole and broke it." Jenkinson, Baker, and Hoffman anticipated the Three Stooges.[97]

Shaming and cobbing failed to deter desertion, so commanders increasingly resorted to executions. General Gaines sought "the awful but indispensable examples to check the monstrous crimes of Desertion in our army." The condemned had their hands tied behind their backs and were, a young soldier recalled, "dressed in white robes with white caps upon their heads, and a red target fastened over the heart." While muffled drums played a solemn "death march," the victims and their guards marched through the ranks to coffins placed in front of fresh graves. Forced to kneel on their coffins, they heard a last prayer from a chaplain, while officers loaded the dozen guns of the firing squad, one with a blank to try to salve the conscience of them all. Once the victims were blindfolded, the presiding officer ordered the squad to fire from a distance of five paces. If anyone survived the eleven bullets, a sergeant fired a point-blank shot to the head, "scattering brains in every direction," one witness recalled. Thrust into their coffins, the dead were cast into the graves and covered with earth.[98]

Sometimes the commander scared the condemned nearly to death by having the entire ritual performed but with blanks loaded into all of the guns. Such convicts often fainted and had to be revived. With a dramatic flourish, the general then issued his pardon while vowing that a repeat offense would warrant no future mercy. Repeated too often, the charades lost their impact on jaded troops, so generals increasingly had to complete the executions. From just 3 in 1812, U.S. Army executions soared to at least 32 in 1813 and to 146 in 1814. The army shot or hanged another 24 in just the first six weeks of 1815, making for a grand total of 205. By comparison, Lord Wellington, a stickler for discipline, condemned only 118 men to die in his larger British army over a five-year period. Instead, Wellington punished men with brutal floggings of up to one thousand lashes. Lacking that option, American commanders had to shoot or hang deserters to get the attention of their troops. By banning flogging, Congress unwittingly increased military executions.[99]

The executions made a powerful impression. William Hodge recalled watching four deserters die at Buffalo: "An awful thing it was to stand near by and see a young man in full vigor of life thus put out of existence." Some exasperated generals ordered death by hanging rather than by the more honorable firing squad. At Sackets Harbor, Jarvis Hanks saw the botched hanging of a deserter, where the fall failed to break his neck, so he slowly choked to death: "We were compelled to remain upon the ground until life was extinct, a period of twenty or thirty minutes."[100]

Short on soldiers, the republic could ill afford to destroy the health and lives of so many men. General Brown sadly concluded, "Perhaps in no country is it so difficult to procure men as in ours, and yet I believe there never was a Govt. that took less pains to preserve the soldiers when once obtained." Brown added: "we are so humane, there is so

Scenes at La Prairie 1812, 13. This execution of a British soldier by a firing squad took place near Montreal on November 2, 1813. The victim kneels on his coffin before his grave. Note his hair standing on end in terror. While a chaplain reads a prayer for malefactors, the assembled troops watch the grim spectacle. Four more culprits await their turn behind the dying man. (Courtesy of the Library and Archives Canada, RG 8, I, 1203:5.)

much of the milk of human kindness in the Nation that the Soldier cannot be flogged and properly corrected for his *offences*, but he may perish with Cold or Hunger or expire in your Infamous Hospitals for the want of the necessary supplies and the proper attendance."[101]

Brown insisted that the American army had it backward in paying men so much cash while spending so little on their shelter, clothing, food, and medical care. Suffering from exposure, hunger, and sickness, the troops sought relief by spending their money to get drunk. The general favored shifting to the British model, which promoted greater discipline by a mix of paternalism for the deserving and flogging for the wayward: "Give a Bounty that will command the men you want and put on the Stripes, Shute, and Hang for desertion. Pay as little as possible *during service*—feed well—render the soldiers at all times to be well clad."[102]

The war trapped Americans between their republican ideals and their military needs. Republicans invaded Canada to save the republic, but to win the war they needed a regular army with a coercive discipline enforced by a hierarchy of command. Such an army appealed to few white Americans, who cherished their liberty and equality. And racism barred black recruits. So the army lacked enough recruits. And the troops blundered in combat because they were badly supplied and poorly trained by amateur officers preoccupied with quarrels over their rank and honor. Thousands of suffering troops deserted, and news of their hardships, defeats, and executions further depressed enlistments. Too few Americans would forsake the liberty of citizens to accept the subordination of soldiers. And such an undermanned and demoralized army would falter when sent to invade Canada.

John Binns (*1772–1860*), *engraving by T. B. Welch. From John Binns,* Recollections of the Life of John Binns (*Philadelphia: Parry & McMillan, 1854*). (Courtesy of the American Antiquarian Society.)

CHAPTER THIRTEEN

PRISONERS

*On the question [of] who are our citizens and who are British subjects,
we are now at issue. Our seamen, our soldiers are not her subjects.*

—*The National Intelligencer,* February 4, 1813[1]

IN OCTOBER 1812 Winfield Scott arrived at Montreal as a British prisoner. He and his fellow captives were paraded through the streets by "a large escort of troops" with a band playing "The Rogue's March" and "Yankee Doodle," while a crowd jeered. Shocked by capture, disarmed, stripped of their outer clothes by Indians, unshaved and unwashed, hungry, and prodded by guards, the prisoners invited contempt. The display culminated with a presentation to Sir George Prevost at the government house, where the band played "God Save the King" while the guards compelled the prisoners to remove their hats in homage. Infuriated, Scott denounced Prevost as a turncoat: "being of an American family," he "behaved like a renegade."[2]

Stung by defeat in the American Revolution, the British relished their chance to humble the Americans as merely lucky once. By displaying humiliated prisoners, the British also discredited the invaders in the eyes of Canadians. A spectator declared, "Both men and officers are as shabby looking a set as ever you set eyes on, and reminded me of Falstaff's men very forcibly." Another Canadian disdained the ragged and slouching captives, who contrasted with the "well-organized and appointed troops that escorted them."[3] As intended, the Canadians felt more confident in victory, and more resolved to fight after watching their invaders displayed and disgraced as prisoners.

Histories usually emphasize battles and treat prisoners as a mere byproduct. In this war, however, the management of prisoners became pivotal to a conflict waged over the contested boundary between the king's subject and the republic's citizen.

To score political points, both sides sought to manipulate the triangular relationship of prisoners, guards, and watching civilians. To impress their civilians, both sides tried alternately to humiliate and to convert prisoners: to make citizens of subjects or the reverse. In that process, the British relied more on the push of prison misery than did the Americans, who usually counted on the pull of their more prosperous society. Although all prisoners were up for grabs, the struggle primarily focused on Irish-Americans, former subjects who claimed the right to fight against the empire as the republic's citizens.

REVENGE

Irish-Americans welcomed the war as a chance to smite the British. Recalling the United Irish martyrs of 1798, a New York immigrant exhorted, "Erin, avenge your murdered sons." In mid-June 1812, on the eve of war, the Royal Navy seized and impressed thirty Irish immigrants from an American merchant ship, the *Alexander*. By taking them when within sight of their land of liberty, the navy reiterated the British position that the migrants remained the king's subjects. New York City's Irish-American newspaper, the *Shamrock*, erupted: "Merciful God! When will the thirst of Britain for slavery and blood be quenched, or is it insatiable? Shall a day of retribution ever arrive?"[4]

Thrilled by the declaration of war, Irish-Americans predicted that the liberation of Canada would send shock waves through the British empire, producing a republican revolution to liberate Ireland. The *Shamrock* insisted, "Ireland will be rescued from British bondage on the plains of CANADA." On July 4, Irishmen in Philadelphia offered this toast: "May the Canadian Beaver, soon liberated by the warlike genius of the Republican Eagle, prove the precursor of freedom, to the chained wolf dog of Ireland." Irish-American editors and politicians promoted enlistment in the American army, navy, and privateers. Ned Myers recalled serving with an Irish-born boatswain: "His religion was to hate an Englishman."[5]

As in other American wars, the military relied heavily on immigrant recruits, which in 1812 meant the Irish. Along with the zeal to fight Britain, relative poverty added to the allure of the bounties for army enlistment or the prize money of naval or privateer service. A study of enlistments reveals that immigrants comprised at least 13 percent of the American regular troops—more than their 11 percent share of the overall population. And 53 percent of those immigrant soldiers came from Ireland, and another 16 percent from elsewhere in the British Isles. The real percentage of Irish recruits was higher, for they had a powerful incentive to deny Irish birth in recruiting records lest that imperil their lives if captured by the British.[6]

The Irish-American officers included such veterans of the 1798 rebellion as Nicholas Gray, the army's inspector general, and Alexander Denniston, who commanded the Twenty-seventh Infantry, primarily composed of Irish recruits from New York City. Gray aptly described Denniston as "a Gentleman who has fought and beaten the Enemies of America in his native Country and now doubly are [his] enemies."[7]

Britons regarded their former subjects as essential to the American forces. A British writer declared the runaways to be "the most formidable enemies the British will have to contend with in the new world." Indeed, British officers *perceived* Irish renegades as their primary foes. Mocking that British belief, American troops hollered at their attackers: "Come over you rascals, we're British deserters and Irish rebels."[8]

Shocked by American naval victories in 1812, the British credited runaways among the victorious crews. The British diplomat, Thomas Barclay, insisted that former Britons comprised two-thirds of the sailors on American warships: "It is an abuse of words to call the crews of the U.S. Ships American. They are British crews commanded by American officers." They fought so hard and well, Barclay insisted, from a desperate fear of capture and execution as deserters. "The naval engagements which have taken place may with truth be termed actions between British Seamen in different Ships," he concluded. Although Barclay exaggerated the proportion of the British-born in the American crews, he aptly expressed the British *conviction* that runaway subjects imperiled the empire.[9]

In Upper Canada, the British feared for the loyalty of their own troops because most were Irish. After the suppressed rebellion of 1798, Ireland had become a prime recruiting ground for the British army. Pushed by poverty, recruits sought food, clothing, pay, and a way out of Ireland. In July 1812 all three of the British regiments in Upper Canada—the Forty-first, the Forty-ninth, and the Royal Newfoundland Fencibles—had been recruited primarily in Ireland or from Irish immigrants in Newfoundland. The Forty-first foot included dozens of captured rebels of 1798, who had agreed to enlist to avoid the gallows. Former rebels faced one another in Canada during the War of 1812. Guarded by the Forty-first, an American prisoner noted, "They appeared to be very sociable, generally of the Irish descent." In 1813 most of the reinforcements sent to Upper Canada also came from Ireland. They included the Eighty-ninth foot, described by a military surgeon as "a fine, jovial, unsophisticated set of 'wild tremendous Irishmen,'" and the One Hundredth foot, nicknamed the "Irish Heroes."[10]

Given that Irish predominance in the ranks, the British commanders in Canada feared the corrosive example set by the Irish in the American forces. To control their own troops, the British felt compelled to take a hard line against any subjects captured while bearing American arms. The secretary of Lower Canada, Herman Witsius Ryland, denounced any leniency as "holding out to the army at large the Prospect of impunity for every Man who shall desert the standard of his Country." Colonel Baynes insisted on "the *incontrovertible right* of Great Britain to her Subjects, wherever she found them & to consider as traitors all those born in her dominions found in arms against her, no matter what might have been their term of residence in, the extent of their engagements to, or the nature of the Laws of the adopted Country."[11]

Making it a high priority to recover and punish former subjects, the British closely vetted their prisoners. Noting the Irishmen on both sides in the war, Benjamin Hodge, Jr., recorded an anecdotal exchange between an Irish Loyalist in the British army, "John Bull," and an imprisoned Irish-American, "Brother Jonathan":

> JOHN BULL: Aye my Horry & you are an Irishman.
> BROTHER JONATHAN: And surely I am not.
> JOHN BULL: And by glory surely you are.
> BROTHER JONATHAN: And by glory surely I am no Irishman.
> JOHN BULL: Where was you born?
> BROTHER JONATHAN: In Pennsylvania, in America.
> JOHN BULL: And do they make Irishmen in Pennsylvania?
> BROTHER JONATHAN: And truly they do, we have a rapid machine
> there that turns out Irishmen by the dozens.

Of course the real machine was naturalization, whic̲h̲ ̲ ̲ ̲ ̲ ̲ ̲rishmen into Americans by the dozens, particularl̲y̲ ̲ ̲ ̲ ̲

The British gave captured subjects ̲ ̲ ̲ ̲ ̲ ̲ ̲ ̲ ̲ ̲their military or face trial and execution as tra̲ ̲ ̲ ̲ ̲ ̲ ̲ ̲ ̲ ̲nlist- ing, they could "atone for their past delin̲ ̲ ̲ ̲ ̲ ̲ ̲ ̲ ̲ ̲that he spurned offers by captured subjects "to ̲ ̲ ̲ ̲ ̲ ̲ ̲ ̲ ̲ ̲rn- ing their arms against their recent employe̲ ̲ ̲ ̲ ̲ ̲ ̲ ̲ ̲o- paganda, refuted by his actual practice. Des̲ ̲ ̲ ̲ ̲ ̲ ̲British preferred conversions to executions.[13]

Most of the accused subjects were Irish by birth. On November 1, 1812, at the Montreal jail, a British major compiled a list of thirty-nine suspects captured in the American service. Almost all (thirty-two of thirty-nine) confessed to be Irish or were "supposed to be Irish." The seven exceptions came from England (three), Canada (two), Wales (one), and the Isle of Man (one). The Irish prominence was no surprise, given that most American immigrants came from Ireland. And, unlike the English and the Scots in America, the Irish were eager to fight for the republic and against the empire. In addition, their strong accents and distinctive manners rendered them marked men. Barclay noted, "It may occur that an American may be mistaken for an Englishman and vice versa; but Scotch and Irish features and dialect are too obvious ever to be mistaken."[14]

The British culling of prisoners began with the capture of Michilimackinac in July 1812. Per the surrender terms, the fifty-seven captured Americans were supposed to be sent home on parole, but the British commander, Captain Charles Roberts, seized nearly half of them as British subjects. Three were British deserters and twenty-one were French Canadians. Over the protests of the American commander, Roberts enlisted at least twenty into his own shorthanded force. A month later, General Procter similarly culled the American regulars captured at Detroit, claiming twenty-five as confessed subjects. They included Henry Barker, an American by birth who had served in the British army but deserted in 1806 and escaped to Boston, where he had enlisted in the U.S. Army in 1809.[15]

In early 1813 Procter sent Dr. William McDowell Scott of Detroit east to prison in Montreal. The British considered the Irish-born Scott a traitor, although he had immigrated to the United States in 1796 and become a naturalized citizen and a magistrate and federal marshal. During the summer of 1812, Scott had commanded an American militia company, earning the hatred of the British. A friend feared that his captors would "make his life so wretched and miserable that Death itself would be a welcome messenger." From prison Scott smuggled out a letter: "British born Subjects are Shamefully treated & not used as Citizens at all."[16]

British courts-martial made lethal examples of captives proven to have deserted from the royal forces. On August 30, 1812, Peter B. Porter reported, "Yesterday a number of men were shot at Fort George in view of our troops." On December 28, 1812, at Fort George, another British firing squad killed an Irish deserter from the Forty-ninth Regiment, who, according to General Sheaffe, had "confessed his guilt, acknowledging that he had given to the Enemy all the aid in his power, and had probably caused the Death of one or more of his old comrades. For all which, he declared his penitence and sorrow." Probably hoping for a last-minute reprieve, this deserter had made the finest of confessions.[17]

After winning the battle at Stoney Creek on June 6, 1813, the British made examples of two captured American soldiers who had been British deserters. James Gready had fled to the Americans in March, but Terence Hunt had deserted ten years before and had since lived in the United States. Therefore, Hunt's death made a political point, demonstrating to the troops, in Prevost's words, "that no length of residence or service in a foreign country can absolve them from their allegiance to their King or secure them from the just punishment which sooner or later must attend their desertion of his cause."[18]

British naval commanders also hung former subjects as deserters, Admiral John Borlase Warren explained, "to impress on their minds the heinousness of taking up Arms against their Sovereign and Country." The British even scoured for former subjects during raids on the American coast. On May 3, 1813, Admiral Warren seized and plundered Havre de Grace, in Maryland at the head of Chesapeake Bay. The local militia broke and ran, save for John O'Neill, a defiant old man who fought 150 attackers until wounded and captured. A naturalized citizen, O'Neill hated the British as "the oppressors of the human race, and particularly of my native country, Ireland." The victors threatened to hang O'Neill as a traitor, although he was defending his own home and had resided in the United States for fifteen years.[19]

But Warren balked for fear of making a martyr of a respectable property owner. On May 6 the admiral released O'Neill on parole and then implausibly assured the Americans, "I was not informed of this man being an Irishman, or he would certainly have been detained, to account to his sovereign and country for being in arms against the British colors." Thereby Warren could deny that he had compromised his nation's policy of punishing any former subject found in arms against the king. O'Neill became a hero to Republicans, particularly the Irish-born, who raised funds to rebuild his home.[20]

RETALIATION

On November 20, 1812, on a prison ship at Quebec, British officers assembled the Americans captured at Queenston a month before. The officers pulled aside twenty-three prisoners, deemed Irish by look and speech. One asserted, "we were born in the British dominions, though we are all citizens of the United States, and have our wives and children there." But Prevost denounced them as "Traitors . . . guilty of the basest

& most unnatural crime that can disgrace human nature, raising their parricide arms against the country which gave them birth."[21]

Prevost had vowed "to punish every man . . . found in arms against the British King contrary to his native allegiance." But he did not want to punish them himself. Rather than try them by court-martial in Canada, he sent them to England for civil trial as traitors. In July 1813 one of them, Henry Kelly, slipped out a letter: "They used every tyrani-cal means to make us Enter in the [British] Service. They have done so much as bring us to the Gangway and read their articles of war and Pun-ish [us] in the most Tyranical manner." But, he exclaimed, "we are poss-est of that Spirit of Patriotism for our adopted Country that the Lash of the Tyrants cannot alter."[22]

In January 1813 their former commander, Winfield Scott, had returned on parole to the United States, where he publicized the plight of the twenty-three. Scott denounced the British for persecuting men "for having borne arms against a power, which, by its multiplied oppres-sions had driven them from their native homes to seek shelter in a for-eign land." In October 1812 the British Prince Regent had issued a proclamation that threatened to execute as traitors any former subjects captured while bearing arms for the Americans. Combined with Scott's news of the Quebec arrests, the proclamation exposed the key issue of the war.[23]

When Federalists applauded the Prince Regent's proclamation, anx-ious Irish-American leaders sought reassurance from Congress and the president. In Philadelphia in early January, the editor John Binns con-vened a protest meeting, which adopted a petition signed by 1,875 nat-uralized citizens. Widely published, the petition demanded retaliation for every American soldier or sailor treated as a traitor by the British. At Philadelphia alone, the petition noted, five hundred Irishmen had enlisted in the army, although they had "never been naturalized." But the petitioners insisted that "every man who fights the battles of the country is entitled to its protection whether he be, or be not, a citizen." Otherwise, they warned, immigrants would balk at enlisting, which would diminish the recruits so desperately needed by the republic. A writer in the *National Intelligencer* agreed: "On the question who are our citizens and who are British subjects, we are now at issue. Our seamen, our soldiers are not her subjects."[24]

The fate of the twenty-three Irish-American soldiers became the central controversy in a war fought over the distinction between a sub-ject and a citizen. By convicting and hanging them, the British could bolster their insistence that any natural-born subject owed allegiance for life, no matter where he went or what nation naturalized him. There would be precious little left to fight for, if the United States tamely accepted a British right to hang any former subject captured in the American service.

On March 3, 1813, Congress authorized the president to retaliate against British prisoners for any violence committed against imprisoned Americans. But retaliation was more easily threatened than exercised by a nation that had lost many more prisoners than it had taken during the first year of the war. In the spring, however, the Madison administration concluded that the tide of war was shifting after Dearborn's victory at York. In mid-May the secretary of war directed Dearborn to confine twenty-three captured Britons as hostages for the safekeeping and exchange of the twenty-three American soldiers sent to England for trial. Half of the British hostages (twelve of the twenty-three) were also Irish, for their regiments had been recruited in Ireland. In this dimension of the civil war, the Americans held Irish from the British service hostage for the fate of Irish-Americans confined as traitors by the British.[25]

The American retaliation infuriated British officials, who resented any attempt to dictate to them by a rogue republic with pretensions to moral superiority. The British insisted that the anarchic Americans neither understood international law nor would abide by it. Lord Bathurst raged that the retaliation impugned and meddled with the operation of British justice over British people. Prevost agreed that the retaliation violated "the Constitutional Principle of every other independent Nation adopted and acted upon for ages, before the American Government or People had a name." Defenders of tradition, the British battled the radical innovations of the upstart republic.[26]

To teach the Americans a lesson, Bathurst ordered Prevost to confine forty-six imprisoned Americans as hostages for the twenty-three held by the enemy. The British threatened to execute two for every hostage killed by the Americans. And, if the Americans executed anyone, Bathurst threatened "to prosecute the war with unmitigated severity against all cities, towns and villages belonging to the United States."[27]

Upon receiving Bathurst's order in October, Prevost confined forty-six Americans, including twenty officers. In response, President Madison ordered forty-six more British officers set aside as hostages for the fate of the additional forty-six confined by the British. In December Prevost accordingly confined every American officer in his possession as hostages for the Americans' forty-six.[28]

The crisis became more tangled when the Americans learned that in mid-September Prevost had sent another fifty-nine soldiers to England as accused traitors. Captured in June at Beaver Dams, they went to England via Halifax, where the admiral added 101 sailors to the shipment of "traitorous Irishmen, who had been fighting against their king and *country*." Another prisoner reported, " 'We fled from our native land,' said these unfortunate men, 'to avoid the tyranny and oppression of our British task-masters, and the same tyrannical hand has seized us here and sent us back to be tried, and perhaps executed as rebels.' "[29]

Outraged by the additional transfers, American officials designated another 160 prisoners as hostages. Of course the British admiral retaliated by adding to his hostages, raising the total at Halifax to 248. On December 19, Barclay predicted, "If the System is pursued, in Six Months every British Prisoner in these States will be thus confined and double the number of Americans."[30]

With each escalation, the two nations crept closer to the brink of a cascading bloodbath that would be triggered should the British convict and execute any of the original twenty-three. In that impending confrontation, the British felt confident because, Barclay explained, "there are at least six times as many American Prisoners to His Majesty as there are British Prisoners in these States." American defeats had given the British more prisoners and more leverage.[31]

By exploiting the controversy, the British sought to intensify the political division in the United States. Barclay publicly challenged the American "Government to determine whether it will continue its claims to protect His Majesty's subjects found on the high seas, or in His Majesty's dominions, in arms against their sovereign, at the expense of the ease, comfort, and perhaps lives of its native citizens [held prisoner], or restore them to freedom by abandoning a doctrine not acknowledged by any European Power." Barclay urged native-born Americans to blame immigrants for an unnecessary war that threatened to culminate in mass executions. The Federalists agreed that the protection of naturalized citizens should end at the border, leaving those on the high seas and in other lands fair game for British seizure. Congressman Zebulon Shipherd warned that retaliations would "doom our country to everlasting hostilities" with an empire that would not, and could not, concede a fundamental right to control its own subjects.[32]

Of course Republicans denounced as neocolonialism any British right to seize any naturalized citizen found on the high seas or in an invading army. The Republicans insisted that any new citizen should "be protected whilst fighting under our banners beyond our territorial limits." They also accused the British of a double standard, for British law allowed foreign seamen to become British subjects by serving on a warship for just two years. And, in Canada, American emigrants had to take the oath of allegiance and defend the colony with their lives.[33]

EXCHANGE

The escalating hostage taking undermined the exchange of all prisoners. In 1812 Prevost had adopted a generous policy for paroling his many prisoners—except for the former subjects among them. Paroled prisoners could not serve until exchanged for Britons held by the Americans. Under this arrangement, Winfield Scott had been repatriated, along with the other American-born prisoners taken at Queenston. Of course the Americans lagged in the exchanges for want of prisoners in their hands. Prevost could live with this American deficit so long as his paroled surplus did not return to the fight.[34]

Prevost's system of immediate paroles for future exchange required both sides to keep careful records and to trust each other. In 1813 that trust broke down under the pressures of an increasingly bitter war, for the British soured on the Americans as acting in bad faith. Allegedly, they kept prisoners despite failing to account for the generous British parole of two hundred captured officers and three thousand soldiers during the previous year. Barclay warned that the conniving Americans understood nothing but force: "It is sound Policy not to Parole any more Prisoners. . . . The best method to make the Americans tired of the War will be by keeping their relations and friends [as] prisoners." In mid-1813 Prevost stopped paroling American prisoners until the United States could settle its deficit.[35]

In January 1814 the American commissary general for prisoners, John Mason, reported that the United States held 1,700 British prisoners—both soldiers and sailors—compared to 4,300 Americans in British hands. The American deficit primarily derived from their defeats on the northern front, but the disorganized and penurious national government also lacked the ability to keep track of the prisoners taken by its forces. And the government struggled to keep its prisoners from escaping. "It is mortifying in the extreme to see in so many instances that the Government cannot hold safe their Prisoners," Mason lamented. Lacking national prisons, the government relied on state penitentiaries and local jails. Poorly built and laxly guarded, the jails leaked prisoners.[36]

Some officers escaped to the British lines in Canada, usually with the assistance of disaffected citizens. In Federalist-dominated Massachusetts, James Prince, the United States marshal, noted that "nothing will have a greater tendency to engender acts of insubordination" by prisoners "than a frequent intercourse and connection with the Citizens." Prince foolishly placed ten hostage British officers in the county jail at Worcester, a heavily Federalist town. On the night of January 12, 1814, nine escaped, with the help of local Federalists, who had smuggled in a pistol. Prince's posse retook five of the escapees, but four got away across Vermont to Canada.[37]

On the other side of the ledger, the British inflated their own prisoner numbers by counting Americans impressed before the war and then confined in 1812. American officials insisted that the impressed should have been released to return home, rather than held as prisoners of war. But the British were not about to swell the number of sailors available to serve on American warships and privateers. And the British dismissed as fraudulent any documents presented by the sailors to prove their citizenship. The American agent in London, Reuben G. Beasley, bitterly complained, "It is insulting to talk any longer of evidence when it is manifest that none that could be produced would be found satisfactory, when [the British] refuse even to examine the cases, and when the very language the victims speak is considered prima facie evidence against them." In October 1814 impressed sailors amounted to at least 2,100 men, or 15 percent of the prisoners held by the British.[38]

The American prisoner deficit also reflected the republic's reliance on privately owned warships—known as privateers—to compensate for its small navy. Preying on British merchant ships in distant waters, the privateers devoted their scarce space to captured cargoes, which were more valuable than prisoners, who cost money to feed. The privateers released most of their captives on parole at the nearest port, usually neutral and far from the United States. Contemptuous of privateers as little better than pirates, the British refused to recognize any prisoners "paroled at sea" in their accounting of the balance. Only men landed and held at a French or American port could count, which eliminated two-thirds of the 6,500 captives taken by privateers in 1812–13, thereby inflating the American deficit.[39]

To increase the republic's prisoners, in March 1814 Congress offered a one-hundred-dollar bounty for every captive brought to the United States by a privateer. Congressman Alexander McKim explained that the bounty sought "to get as many prisoners of war as we could, to balance accounts with the enemy, and enable us to redeem our fellow-citizens from captivity." During the ensuing year, however, the new law produced only 704 new prisoners, for privateers still preferred to bring in captured cargo rather than people.[40]

But the prisoner bounty law outraged the British as inviting the despised privateers to act as kidnappers. And the British meant to keep the leverage afforded by their surplus stock of prisoners. In retaliation, the British raided the coast of Chesapeake Bay to grab citizens, whether acting in the militia or not, and sent them to the prison at Halifax. An American official predicted, "In this way their Prison will be Constantly Crouded, and given to us as a reason for sending them to England."[41]

At Quebec in late 1813, Prevost could not afford to feed his prisoners through the winter, but he would not parole them to return home. Instead, he shipped them to Halifax in Nova Scotia, where they strained the capacity of the naval prison at Melville Island, so the admiral shipped them on to England. The British insisted that they acted humanely by exporting prisoners to better food and housing in England, but they followed a punitive pattern, sending away men who had tried to escape or otherwise made trouble. They also sought to reduce privateers by shipping their sailors to England rather than the sailors taken from merchant ships. The British counted on the dread of shipment to discourage Americans from enlisting in their army and navy, and privateers.[42]

Shipment to England terrified imprisoned Americans and outraged their government. Captives dreaded this voyage as the worst form of captivity: stuffed into the dark and verminous holds of wooden ships bucking the stormy waves for over a month. A prisoner wrote, "Imagine to yourself, Christian reader! *Two hundred and fifty* men crammed into a place too small to contain one hundred with comfort, stifling for want of air, pushing and crowding each other . . . to push forward to the grated hatchway to respire a little fresh air." On board the transports, the British reduced the already spare ration allotted to a prisoner, for they reasoned that an immobile man needed fewer calories. Moreover, exchange became more difficult and less likely on the other side of the Atlantic.[43]

In 1814, as imprisoned Americans accumulated in England, a resolution of the war seemed far more difficult and remote. Initially, the British sent their American prisoners to fourteen hulks (former warships) moored in the Medway River at Chatham. During the summer, however, they shifted most to England's largest prison at Dartmoor in Devon. By December Dartmoor housed 5,300 American prisoners, about three-quarters of all those held by the British.[44]

Dartmoor made a daunting impression as "the most dreadful prison in all England." Fifteen miles from the channel, the prison lay on a barren mountain above a treeless moor cloaked in fog, or swept by cold winds and driving rains. Two stone walls fourteen feet high circled an inner stockade of tall iron stakes. Within this triple barrier lay a compound of seven stone prisons, each three stories tall, 180 feet long, and 40 wide, with gray slate roofs. Within each prison the men slept stacked in hammocks within open galleries. Although dank, cold, and depressing, Dartmoor was bigger, less crowded, and better managed than other prisons. The chief plight of the prisoners was the tedium and suspense of prolonged captivity. Day after dreary day, Dartmoor seemed to become their eternal fate and their early grave.[45]

AGENTS

To help the captives, both nations appointed agents to reside near the leading prisoner depots. They supplied clothing and sundries to the prisoners and negotiated with prison officials to arrange exchanges and to resolve disputes over conditions and treatment. With the withdrawal of other diplomats for the duration of the war, the prisoner agents became the only official representatives of one belligerent in the domain of the other. Initially, each government welcomed and politely treated the prisoner agents of the other. During the summer of 1813, however, the retaliation crisis soured those relationships. Distrust ripened as each side treated the other's agents as spies and liars. By the end of the war, both sides had marginalized the agents or driven them away.[46]

In late 1812 Thomas Barclay became Britain's agent general for prisoners in the United States. Born in New York Ciy as the son of an Anglican clergyman, Barclay graduated from King's College (now Columbia) and studied law with John Jay. At the outbreak of the American Revolution, Barclay remained loyal to the empire and commanded a Loyalist regiment. At the end of the war he fled to Nova Scotia, where he served in the assembly. In 1799 Barclay returned to New York City as the British consul general, developing close business and personal ties with Federalist merchants. During the new war, as an American Loyalist with a network of Federalist friends, Barclay especially alarmed Republican officials.[47]

Suspecting Barclay as a spy, the administration distrusted his residence at New York City, the nation's premier seaport and naval base. Indeed, Barclay was sending information in coded letters to Prevost. In early 1814 Mason ordered Barclay to remove to Bladensburg, Maryland. Near the national capital, the new location enabled Mason more easily to meet with Barclay and to keep an eye on him. But their relationship blew up in August 1814, when a British invasion force swept through Bladensburg to attack Washington. Slow to honor Mason's order to remove westward, Barclay instead conveyed information to the advancing British commander. That fall, Mason and Monroe angrily deported Barclay to England, depriving the British of an agent in the United States.[48]

Playing tit for tat, the British tightened their restrictions on the American agents for prisoners: John Mitchell at Halifax, Robert Gardner at Quebec, and Reuben G. Beasley in England. The new restrictions kept them away from the prisoners and censored or blocked their letters. In addition to preventing spying, the British sought to increase their own power over prisoners by isolating the agents. Frustrated, Gardner resigned in May 1814, while the British ousted Mitchell in December in retaliation for Barclay's deportation.[49]

The restrictions sowed resentment by the prisoners, who blamed their agents' absence on their supposed indifference. In England, Beasley faced the greatest discontent. The prisoners raged that he never replied to their messages, but the British barred him from doing so except through the Transport Board, which often kept his letters. And whenever prisoners complained of their treatment, the British guards insisted that Beasley was profiting from their distress. At Dartmoor, a prisoner committee denounced Beasley as "a trafficker in the misery of his countrymen." The Dartmoor prisoners made an effigy of Beasley in a frilly shirt and a cravat, "a pretty genteel, haughty looking, gentleman-agent." They tried the effigy for "depriving many hundreds of your countrymen of their lives, by the most wanton and most cruel deaths, by nakedness, starvation, and exposure to pestilence." A raucous throng convicted, hanged, and burned the effigy in the prison yard.[50]

Beasley was a flawed character cast in a tragedy. Proud and insecure, he dreaded making some mistake that would compromise his nation's diplomatic position. And he saw little point in hearing complaints from the prisoners, when he could do so little to redress them. He rarely visited the prisons, owing both to British restrictions and to his own wariness of humiliation. After visiting Chatham, he left to the "hooting and hisses of his countrymen, as he passed over the side of the ship." Beasley tried to remain philosophical: "Confinement naturally inclines to discontent, and, as it answers the purpose of the enemy, . . . I have had more than my share of complaints."[51]

RIGOR

Most of what the Americans considered harsh treatment derived from the professional rigidity of British officers. John Mitchell explained that at Halifax, "Here our Prisoners are treated well but with great *exactness*."

Hierarchical and bureaucratic, the British military officers were sticklers for regulations. During their long war with France, they had developed a precise system for controlling prisoners and reducing their costs. And the British officers saw no need to afford the Americans better treatment than the French got. To administer prisoners and prisons, the British relied on the Transport Board of the Royal Navy, an especially unbending set of military bureaucrats who disdained Americans as pushy and whiny. Mitchell sighed, "of all men, Officers of the British Navy are the least pleasant to transact Business with."[52]

The chief bone of contention became the rations provided to the prisoners by the British. In May 1813 agents for both nations agreed to a prisoner cartel, which stipulated "sound and wholesome provisions, consisting of one pound of beef, or twelve ounces of pork, one pound of wheaten bread, and a quarter of a pint of pease, or six ounces of rice, or a pound of potatoes per day to each man." But the Transport Board rejected the agreement, clinging to its stingier regulations established to feed French prisoners. Five days a week, the American prisoners got only half a pound of beef or pork, half to two-thirds of what the cartel had stipulated. Twice a week, they got fish instead of meat. Every day, the British afforded more bread, but it was hard biscuit instead of wheaten bread. The British prison ration nearly matched the calories of the cartel ration but did so with more carbohydrates and less protein.[53]

The Transport Board reasoned "that if British and French Prisoners in England and France could live on the usual allowance, no reason could be assigned why British and American Prisoners . . . should have more." In fact, most American men were taller than the English and the French, for Americans grew up on a diet richer in protein, thanks to the relative abundance of their agricultural society. A captive insisted that an American needed "a third more solid flesh meat than would satisfy a potato-eating Irishman, an oat-feeding Scotchman, or an half-starved English manufacturer," for a laboring "American eats three times the quantity of animal food that falls to the share of the same class of people in England."[54]

The deprivation was cultural as well as physical. Priding themselves on their consumption of meat, Americans felt starved and humiliated when stinted. "To young men so brought up and nourished, a British captivity on board their horrid transports, and even on board their prison-ships, is worse than death," insisted a prisoner. Often the British fed prisoners a Scottish oatmeal gruel called burgoo, which was healthier than the salted meat craved by the Americans, but a "mess more repellant to a Yankee's stomach could not well be contrived."[55]

American men took a similar pride in their consumption of alcohol, but the British had enough trouble with the Americans without allowing them to drink. Begging the British to relent, Mitchell explained, "Spirit from habit has become almost a Necessary to that class of People." Dependent on alcohol, many experienced the torments of the damned when cut off. A prisoner lamented that the "formerly intemperate . . . felt the loss of their beloved stimulants, and their spirits sunk, and they had rather lie down and rot, and die, than exert themselves."[56]

The prisons crowded with unhappy men promoted diseases, particularly during the summer at Quebec and Chatham. The most common affliction was "the itch," from wearing ragged old clothes and rarely bathing. Although painful, the itch rarely killed. Some prisoners did die of typhoid fever, pneumonia, dysentery, and smallpox, but at a lower rate than in American army camps. For the British enforced a stricter cleanliness, and their hospitals were better run, warmer, and cleaner than their American counterparts. In this regard British exactness benefited the prisoners.[57]

The prisoners also lacked warm clothes to cope with the dank cold. Per the prisoner cartel, each nation was supposed to clothe its own people held as prisoners by the enemy. Alas, the captive Americans suffered from the same logistical, contracting, and financial problems that so afflicted their army. Striving to minimize expenditures, the American officials naively hoped that exchanges would promptly bring most of the prisoners home before they needed warmer clothing. "The United States allows absolute necessarys but nothing more," Mitchell assured the grumbling prisoners at Halifax.[58]

The agents also accused the prisoners of selling any new clothes to guards in return for money to gamble with. Mitchell noted, "It is truly surprising that, altho they are so badly of[f] for Cloaths, yet they scarcely are furnished before they commence a Sale of them and more espetially among the Soldiers." A prisoner agreed, "I never saw a set of more ragged, dirty men in my life; and yet they were disposed to sell their last rag to get money to game with." A "passion that rages in proportion to the degrees of misery, until it becomes a species of insanity," gambling provided scarce excitement to bored men. Staking and losing hammocks and blankets, some men slept in rags on the cold stone floors of their prisons.[59]

The British jailers exploited the rigorous conditions to pressure their prisoners to defect and enlist in the service of the Crown. Recruiting officers haunted the prisons, offering pay, fresh air, more food, and daily alcohol and tobacco: powerful enticements to long-imprisoned men. By converting an American into a British soldier or sailor, a recruiter won a small reversal of the revolution and a little restoration of the colonial relationship. British officers denied ever enlisting a "true born Citizen," but they exercised a very broad and creative definition of the subject, encouraging all sorts of prisoners to declare themselves British. At Quebec, Gardner reported, "We have lost many by Inlistment in the British Army who previously declare themselves not to be American Citizens."[60]

As the British accumulated a large stock of prisoners serving long stints in crowded prisons, the apparently hopeless conditions weakened resistance to British enticement. At Quebec, the captive General Winchester reported that delayed exchanges enabled the enemy to "recruit to his army and navy by continual enlistments from those unfortunate men crowded and half famished on board unhealthy ships—constantly pressed by an artful noncommissioned officer to abandon the cause of their country." In London, Beasley urged renewed exchanges as "the only way to keep them out of the British Navy & Merchant men, many being disposed to enter rather than remain confined in prison on scanty allowance."[61]

Hiding the enlistments from American agents, the British officers obscured the numbers enticed. From prisoner informants, Beasley calculated that 176 captives in England had entered the British service from July 1813 through March 1814. He considered his report incomplete because the British had removed so many enlisted captives "from the prison in the night, after the others have retired to rest."[62]

To endure their captivity and resist temptation by their captors, the defiant majority developed a fierce pride in their republic. Prisoners and guards exchanged taunts and boasts meant to affirm, or to break, American defiance. At Chatham, a prisoner wrote in his journal,

> Tenders are daily passing down the river, filled with seamen and marines, bound to America. As they pass by us, they play *Yankee Doodle*, and cry out to us that they are bound to America, to flog the Yankees. We holloa to them in return, and tell them what they will meet there, and predict to them their fate.

British guards boasted that they would "shortly reduce the United States to colonies of Great Britain," adding that "although we were yet prisoners of war, they considered us their subjects." In the intimate confines of the prisons, guards and captives reenacted the struggle to achieve, or to repress, American independence.[63]

Denied newspapers, the prisoners got their news from new arrivals or from the guards, who gleefully reported catastrophic defeats beyond even those actually suffered by American forces. "Sometimes we are told that Baltimore is burnt; and then that New-York is taken; and we have been positively assured that old New-England has declared for the British," a prisoner noted. But the captives could intuit an American victory, when "the keepers treated them with much greater severity" or just fell silent about events.[64]

On the Fourth of July the captives provoked their captors by displaying makeshift American flags, singing "Yankee Doodle," and loudly cheering for liberty and union. The loudest prisoner harangued the guards by celebrating American naval victories and bashing the British for their Indian alliance:

Bloody villains! Detestable associates! Linked together by fear, and leagued with savages by necessity, to murder a Christian people, for the alleged crime of fighting over again the battle of independence. Beware, bloody nations of Britons and savage Indians, of the recoiling vengeance of a brave people.

Drawn together from disparate states, the diverse prisoners created a national identity by treating the British guards as their common enemy. "Captivity under British prison keepers and British captains of transport men of war, are the proper colleges for teaching the love of our republican government and strong attachment to its administration," recalled one captive.[65]

This polarization created a new sense of difference between otherwise similar peoples who spoke a common language. A prisoner noted,

The God of nature has ordained that nations should be separated by a difference of language, religion, customs and manners, for wise purposes; but where two great nations like the English and American have the same language, institutions and manners, he . . . allowed the devil to inspire one with a portion of his own infernal spirit of cruelty, in order to effect a separation and keep apart two people, superficially resembling each other.

By defining the British as "a hard-hearted, cruel and barbarous race" of captors, their prisoners made themselves into Americans.[66]

That prison nationalism also expressed a white supremacy. White prisoners insisted that the ultimate "British cruelty" was to treat them as if they had the dark skins of an inferior race. In asserting a national distinction from the British, white Americans also insisted on their racial distinction from African-Americans in the same prisons. At Dartmoor, the white majority imposed a segregation that limited the black 15 percent to one barracks known as Block Four.[67]

Excluded from the committee government elected by whites, the blacks relied on the rule of Richard Crafus, known as King Dick. Born in Maryland, King Dick had served on a privateer until captured by the British in March 1814. A stout man of twenty-three years, King Dick was six feet three inches in height, towering over other sailors, white and black. "He is by far the largest, and I suspect the strongest man in the prison," recalled another prisoner.[68]

His charisma, intelligence, and strength won the allegiance of the black prisoners and the grudging respect of the whites. Wearing a bearskin cap and wielding a large club, King Dick patrolled his barracks to suppress any disorder. A shrewd entrepreneur, he monopolized illicit beer sales and levied taxes on petty trade within Block Four, and he took a cut from all games of chance. A powerful and skilled boxer, he taught that sweet science to others, white and black, for a fee. He also sold tickets to plays, employing costumes and props bought from departing French prisoners. The performances included *Romeo and Juliet* and *Othello*. On Sundays he sponsored fiery preaching by a black Methodist.[69]

The respect of white prisoners for King Dick had an edge that cut at the rest of his race. Observers cast him as the unique despot needed to control the larcenous disorder of other blacks. Allegedly incapable of a republic, they could only be ruled by a king. Of course, this story obscured the role of blacks in choosing his leadership, for African-American communities had a tradition of annually electing a king. By simplifying King Dick's authority as mere bullying, the white accounts denied the republican nation to black Americans.[70]

SEDUCTION

As a rule, the Americans treated their prisoners well. In 1813, Barclay conceded: "The British Prisoners have been liberally fed hitherto by the United States, and the humane treatment of the Marshals in each state towards them is universally acknowledged." An American insisted that a captured Briton "finds friends among his Enemys" and "fares better & enjoys greater liberty than when in his own Country, and thus it is no wonder that the . . . English Prisoner wishes to tarry with his foe."

Another prisoner concluded, "An American in England pines to get home, while an Englishman and an Irishman longs to become an American citizen."[71]

To save costs, American jailers often allowed their prisoners to work for wages and to lodge with their employers. In labor-scarce America, farmers and manufacturers eagerly hired prisoners, who welcomed the good pay and better fare of civilian life in the republic. Consequently, many later balked at exchanges that would return them to British military service. In Ohio, a marshal reported that the "Farmers will rather secrete them for the sake of having them to work on their farms and some from an Idea of humanity would assist them in making their escape." Unlike their officers, common prisoners rarely escaped except when they feared being sent back to the British army or Royal Navy. John Mason warned, "According to the constant habit of the British soldiers when about to be exchanged, every effort to escape is to be expected."[72]

Jailers also colluded with recruiting officers to entice prisoners to join the American army, navy, or privateers. Although officially barred, the practice flourished in the many dispersed forts and jails that received new prisoners. Shorthanded commanders and cooperative marshals often accepted a captive's story that he was, in fact, a deserter rather than a prisoner.[73]

The American enticement of prisoners infuriated the British commanders, who fought the war to preserve control over their subjects. In March 1813 Admiral Warren protested that so many captured Britains were "seduced from the allegiance they owe their Country, that not half the number taken in any Vessel have been as yet returned." In mid-1813, the British adopted a man-for-man exchange policy, which pressured Americans to treat captured Britons as enemies rather than as potential brethren. In British prisons, impatient Americans exhorted their government to tighten control over its captives to increase the numbers delivered up for exchange. In response, Mason ordered marshals to cease helping prisoners escape into America, for "every British Prisoner suffered to escape is a man lost to us in the account of exchange . . . and thus may protract the confinement of an American Prisoner." Therefore, "that sort of humanity towards the British Prisoners, by an officer of Government would be direct cruelty on our part to the American Prisoners."[74]

By taking more prisoners and imposing a man-for-man exchange policy, the British compelled their enemy to abandon a radical position which had sought to liberate Britons by enticing them to become Americans. Eager for freedom, captured Americans embraced the British distinction between native-born and naturalized citizens. The American-born held at Halifax asserted a "birth right" for priority in release and denounced being "Subjects of Retaliation" to screen "British Subjects [who] have Emigrated from their Native Country since the War." British pressure increased the nativism of the American-born, who increasingly rejected solidarity with captured Britons.[75]

A pivotal episode occurred in the harbor of Salem, Massachusetts, in November 1813. The U.S. marshal loaded a cartel vessel, the *Analosten*, with seventy imprisoned Britons for delivery to Halifax. Preferring to remain in America, the prisoners seized control of the ship, subduing the guards and officers. But an alarm spread among the local citizens, and the crew of a privateer. They stormed the cartel ship, subdued the prisoners, and sent them in irons to Halifax. Rejecting sympathy for the imprisoned Britons, the local citizens and privateersmen insisted that they alone were Americans. They sought to repatriate more of their countrymen held in Halifax as hostages for the return of "British sailors." The Salem riot starkly contrasted with prewar riots when common Americans had defended British deserters from recapture by their officers.[76]

Despite the man-for-man exchange policy, some American officers wanted to have their cake and eat it too. By treating prisoners well but compelling their exchange, these officers hoped to entice them subsequently to return to America as deserters, who could be welcomed and enlisted. At Sackets Harbor, an American officer reported that when prisoners sought "to enlist in the service of the States, I told them it was necessary to exchange them for our own men the British held," but "when exchanged it would be in their power to desert to this country and that they would be treated with the same kindness and hospitality." The officer hoped that the exchanged prisoners would spread that word to their peers at Kingston, adding to the flow of deserters to America.[77]

Thomas Melville, Jr., was born in 1776, the son of a merchant who participated in the Boston Tea Party and the uncle of the novelist Herman Melville. Well-educated and ambitious, as a young man he became a merchant in Europe, where he married a Frenchwoman. When his trading ventures failed, Melville returned to the United States in 1811. Settling in Pittsfield, in western Massachusetts, Melville became a genteel farmer noted for his "amiable & pleasing manners" as well as his "great industry and judgment." A Republican, he won a major's commission in the army and a convenient posting in Pittsfield as a commissary for a cantonment of new recruits.[78]

In 1813 Melville proposed to transform his cantonment into a military prison, where he would concentrate all of the prisoners then scattered in the district and county jails of New York and New England. Poorly guarded, these dispersed jails leaked prisoners, often with the collusion of local Federalists. A healthy location in the hills about thirty miles east of Albany, Pittsfield lay in Berkshire County, where most of the people were Republicans who would support Melville.[79]

The War Department approved Melville's plan. Located a quarter mile beyond the village center, the Pittsfield prison consisted of two wooden barracks, each two hundred feet long, thirty feet wide, and two stories tall, and both surrounded by a plank stockade, a dozen feet high. Outside the wall stood a stables, a hospital, a kitchen house, a smaller barracks for guards, and an officers' quarters for Melville and his assistants. This prison housed enlisted prisoners, while paroled officers lodged in private homes in the adjoining town of Cheshire. Pittsfield became the republic's premier prison, holding 1,327 inmates by January 1815.[80]

In a war replete with incompetence, Melville stood out as systematic and shrewd. He planned to win the war by winning the hearts and minds of the prisoners at his model prison:

> By the System I had adopted relative to the Prisoners, the seeds of discontent for the British service were so completely sown, their taste for our habits & customs so deeply rooted, their confidence in myself & my immediate officers so unbounded, that it would have been ... dangerous for the enemy to have brought into action any one of the Corps, or Regiments, who had had Prisoners at this depot—for they would not have fought with any Spirit against Am[erica]n troops and would prefer being made Prisoners to standing to their Colors. ... Their discontent for the British Service & their predilection for this Country was a constant theme among the British officers at this Depot.

Melville's prisoners were the best fed and best clothed of any prison on either side. When they lacked for anything, he spent his own money and counted on his government for compensation. Melville allowed his prisoners to work in local farms and woolen factories, where they made two or three dollars a day plus room and board, the equivalent of a month's pay for a British private. British agents and officers extolled Melville as "a Gentleman and a man of feelings" who treated prisoners generously. No other keeper in the war won such praise.[81]

In August 1814 William Hamilton Merritt, an Upper Canadian,

William H. Winder *(1775–1824)*, *engraving by an unknown artist. From Benson J. Lossing,* The Pictorial Field-Book of the War of 1812 *(New York, 1869), 918.* (Courtesy of the New York State Library.)

Colonel Edward Baynes, *painting by an unknown artist. From John Richardson,* Richardson's War of 1812 with Notes and a Life of the Author *(Toronto: Historical Publishing, 1902), 26.* (Courtesy of the New York State Library.)

became a paroled prisoner at Cheshire. Merritt reported, "we are allowed every indulgence, we can expect in our situation." The paroled officers ate so well, he reported, that "[we] are getting the Gout. Every evening or two [we] have a Dance among ourselves." Free to move about the town, the officers rode horses and played cricket, quoits, billiards, football, and whist. They also flew kites, went fishing, attended sermons, read books and newspapers, and debated politics with "a real democrat and a little demon," the daughter of Merritt's landlord. On August 31 he reported: "Our old routine—eating, drinking, rambling, with the addition of a horse-race, which ended the day." On September 12: "carousing all night," but the next morning he was "quite unwell." No American officer held by the British fared so well.[82]

Another British officer recognized what Melville was up to. Exchanged and returned to Canada, Captain Robert R. Loring warned his superiors of "the ruinous System of Temptation to which our Prisoners are exposed." He explained that "the general liberty given them to be at large, for the purpose of working, throws out so strong a temptation to the Men to remain in the States that unless an exchange speedily takes place, not half the Number of Men can reasonably be expected to return."[83]

The exceptions were captured militiamen, who longed to return to their families in Upper Canada. In January 1814 twelve prisoners escaped with the help of their "relations or friends in this part of the Country." Melville offered rewards for the runaway "British soldiers," but only one was born in the empire (in Canada). The rest were Late Loyalists from New Hampshire (five), Vermont (two), New York (two), Connecticut (one), and New Jersey (one). Former citizens, they sought to resume their lives as subjects in Canada. Meanwhile, Melville worked at turning British-born prisoners into deserters to America. Such were the inversions of a civil war meant to divide citizens from subjects in a porous borderland of shifting identities.[84]

WINDER

To undermine the American "retaliating system," the British counted on their American officers held as hostages to bring political pressure on their government. As local notables, the officers could rally influential friends and family to lobby the administration to relent. At Quebec, the most influential hostage was General William Winder. An accomplished lawyer but a novice officer, Winder had blundered into captivity at Stoney Creek in June 1813. At home in Maryland he left a wife, five young children, and deteriorating business affairs. Eager to stay alive and get home, he agreed with Prevost that a belligerent had every right to punish former subjects captured in the service of the enemy. If paroled to return home, Winder promised to lobby his government to abandon "the horrible & barbarous form of retaliation." Winder conceded that he held an "interest, perhaps fatal . . . on this subject." But the Irish-American soldiers held in British prisons had an equally fatal but opposing interest.[85]

Prevost paroled Winder to visit home and to consult his government in Washington. Although not yet exchanged (and so still a British prisoner), Winder returned to Canada in April 1814 with a commission from the Madison administration to negotiate an end to the hostage crisis. Rejecting Winder's own views, Monroe instructed him "not to relinquish the ground taken by the United States in relation to the 23 Prisoners sent to England." Of course, Winder was compromised by his long captivity, which would resume if the talks failed. Prevost compounded that pressure by insisting that, absent an agreement, he would send all of his prisoners across the Atlantic to England. In that event Winder feared that the British would entice more of the long-suffering prisoners to forsake their country and enlist in the British service.[86]

At Montreal, Winder dealt with Prevost's chief aide, the canny Edward Baynes. As instructed, Winder began by calling for the release of the original twenty-three held by the British. Expecting this, Baynes pounced, declaring the American position "inadmissible in principle." As he explained:

It would be wasting time to enter into any further discussion on this subject. Great Britain has successfully maintained her national rights unsullied, for twenty years, against the whole world combined; it is not to be supposed, that it is reserved for the United States to stop the course of justice and to dictate to England what procedure she shall observe towards her own natural-born subjects in her own Courts of Civil Judicature, arrested in her own territories in the commission of acts of treason and rebellion.

Abruptly canceling the talks, Baynes announced that Winder reverted to his status as a prisoner and hostage. As Baynes expected, Winder folded. Dreading to "linger out a tedious, protracted confinement finally to be terminated by an inglorious death," he agreed to omit the original twenty-three from the discussions. And, when pressed by Baynes, the desperate Winder falsely and foolishly insisted that he had been empowered to make a final and binding agreement because his government had relinquished any right to review and ratify. Game, set, and match to Baynes and Prevost.[87]

On April 25 Baynes and Winder concluded and signed a prisoner convention that bound the Americans to release all of their prisoners taken from Prevost's command *except* for the twenty-three men kept at Greenbush as hostages. In return, Prevost would release all of his prisoners *except* for forty-six hostages retained as counters for the twenty-three held by the Americans. The convention left the font of the crisis, the original twenty-three Irish-Americans, in British hands and subject to British law.[88]

Madison disliked the convention as a betrayal by Winder of his instructions. But it became more palatable in June, when the Madison administration got reassuring news from England. In March 1814 a high-ranking British official had privately assured Beasley that the twenty-three would not be tried. Lacking the evidence to convict, the

British feared losing an important trial that would set a dangerous legal precedent. Although the British refused to make any public announcement, they quietly shifted the twenty-three into a regular captivity with other prisoners of war.[89]

By shipping them across the Atlantic for trial, Prevost had separated the twenty-three from the essential witnesses: army officers who remained in Canada to fight the war. An irritated Lord Bathurst instructed Prevost, with similar prisoners in the future, to "take on the Spot the necessary Measures for their Disposal, and not send them to this country." He was to try traitors by court-martial in Canada, "and after Conviction, execute them without delay."[90]

Encouraged by Beasley's report, Madison sought revisions to Winder's convention by sending a veteran diplomat, Tobias Lear, north to negotiate with Baynes. Signed on July 16, 1814, the revised deal restored the twenty-three Greenbush and forty-six Quebec hostages to the status of ordinary prisoners so that they could be exchanged. Lear and Baynes left the fate of the original twenty-three held in England to peace negotiators. Limited to soldiers taken in Canada, the prisoner

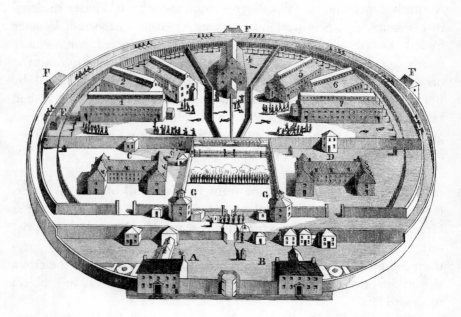

Dartmoor Prison in 1815, *engraving. The numbered buildings are the barracks for the prisoners. C represents the hospital and D the barracks for the guards. F and G indicate guard posts. The commandant, Captain Shortland, lived at B. From Benson J. Lossing,* The Pictorial Field-Book of the War of 1812 *(New York, 1869), 1068. (Courtesy of the New York Library.)*

convention did not free the thousands captured by the Royal Navy at sea or along the American coast. And even on the Canadian front, the Winder-Lear-Baynes convention produced only a short-lived improvement in prisoner relations because of a troubling American delay in returning the Britons held in Kentucky.[91]

In early 1814 most of the survivors from General Henry Procter's army were prisoners in Frankfort, Kentucky. In July their American guards marched them north across Ohio toward Lake Erie. In late August they reached the Sandusky shore, where they waited for American ships to ferry them across Lake Erie for release. But an American general, Jacob Brown, ordered the navy to stall to prevent the exchanged men from reinforcing the British on the Niagara Peninsula. During the delay the prisoners succumbed to malaria borne by the mosquitoes around their swampy camp. The prisoners also wasted away from hunger. The guards shot one desperate man who broke out to plunder a nearby potato patch. Forty men escaped, apparently to enlist as American soldiers with the collusion of their guards.[92]

Not until late September, after Brown had broken the siege of Fort Erie, did the American ships begin to carry the shattered prisoners across the lake. On the north shore, a British officer described the arriving prisoners as "some dead, others dying, and one-half of them unable to help themselves in any manner whatever." A military surgeon predicted that only one in twenty would fully recover his health. Charging the American government with "premeditated" murder, he concluded, "Far more generous and manly would it have been to have put at once an end to the existence of these Prisoners than thus expose them insidiously to slow but inevitable destruction." While Melville's Pittsfield represented the war's best treatment of prisoners, the stall at Sandusky was the war's worst. An enraged Prevost canceled further exchanges, including the return of his last forty-six hostages.[93]

The treatment of prisoners was pivotal to a war fought over the boundary between subject and citizen as well as over the border between Canada and the United States. But historians of the war devote their attention to battles rather than to prisons. That neglect leads one historian to declare: "The lot of those captured was much happier, as both nations treated their prisoners with scrupulous respect." True of Pittsfield, but few thought so at Frankfort, Sandusky, Greenbush, Quebec, Halifax, Chatham, or Dartmoor. In fact, both sides manipulated captives to make and to unmake citizens and subjects.[94]

Major General Jacob Jennings Brown *(1775–1828), oil painting by John Wesley Jarvis.* (Courtesy of the Corcoran Gallery of Art, Washington, D.C.)

CHAPTER FOURTEEN

HONOR

You have behaved nobly. You have rescued the military character of
your country from the odium brought upon it by fools and rascals.

—John Armstrong to Jacob Brown, August 7, 1814[1]

BORN A QUAKER, Jacob Brown had an odd background for a general.
Raised in eastern Pennsylvania, he attended the University of Pennsylvania, graduating in 1790 when only fifteen. After teaching school, sur-
veying land, and writing newspaper essays, Brown moved north to the
New York frontier near Sackets Harbor in 1799. Pragmatic, opportunistic, shrewd, and ambitious, he developed the town of Brownville,
erecting a sawmill, gristmill, and store to attract settlers. Prospering as
a land speculator, he reaped the political rewards of an American town
builder: state appointments as a magistrate and militia captain in newly
organized Jefferson County. And he married Pamelia Williams, the sister of Nathan Williams, a successful lawyer, banker, and Republican
congressman.[2]

Initially a Federalist, Brown made a timely conversion to support the
election of Daniel D. Tompkins as governor in 1807 and 1810. Grateful
for Republican majorities in Jefferson County, Tompkins promoted
Brown to militia colonel in 1809 and to general in 1811.[3]

As a frontier capitalist and Republican politician, Brown resembled
Peter B. Porter of Black Rock. Both men feared war's destructive impact
on their vulnerable properties near the border with Canada. But if there
must be a war, they longed for an aggressive and powerful offensive that
could quickly conquer Canada. Developing a new ambition, Brown
angled for, and secured, a brigadier general's command in the regular
army in mid-1813. In early 1814 the secretary of war promoted Brown
to major general, while sidelining Wilkinson and other senior generals.
Armstrong looked to a younger generation of officers to lead and
reform the faltering army on the northern frontier.[4]

Longing to erase the disgrace of past defeats, Brown vowed that his
troops would fight to "gain a name in arms worthy of our selves or the

General Winfield Scott (1786–1866), engraving by an unidentified artist, ca. 1815.
(Courtesy of the National Portrait Gallery, Smithsonian Institution, NPG. 79.6.)

gallant nation in whose name we fight." Matching the British in combat
became his definition of victory: "Let us meet our present gallant
and accomplished Foe, Reg[ular] to Reg[ular]," for only then could
Americans "be proud of our Men and Nation." Brown substituted an
intangible—the restoration of honor—for the tangible conquest of
Canada. Unlike previous commanders, Brown expressed no republican
zeal for liberating the Canadians. Nor did he share the obsession with
Indians that had hampered so many other generals. Instead, he sought
to impress British commanders by beating them at their own game.[5]

For the campaign of 1814, the conquest of Canada receded as a
viable American goal. Because the British had crushed Napoleon in
Europe, they could send massive reinforcements to North America.
Meanwhile, the United States struggled to raise enough men to cope
with the increased British attacks along the American coast. Rather than
attack the British strongholds at Montreal and Kingston, Madison's cabinet shifted its troops westward to attack the Niagara District, where the
British forces were weaker. By winning some easy victories, the troops
might improve American prospects in the pending peace negotiations.

And that campaign would please the powerful governor of New York, Daniel D. Tompkins, who demanded the recovery of Fort Niagara and the protection of Buffalo from renewed attack. But such a modest campaign could never conquer Canada.[6]

REGULARS AND VOLUNTEERS

Brown gathered his troops at Buffalo, where the inhabitants had begun to rebuild their burned homes. An officer described Buffalo as "a wide, desolate expanse, with only two small houses visible; a few rude sheds and shanties; a soiled tent, here and there," and with many sentinels "keeping guard over as many irregular piles of loose stores and camp-equipage." One colonel despaired of proving his honor in such a setting: "I would rather distinguish myself, if I can, under view of my fellow citizens, than here in the wilderness, where nobody cares much about the army."[7]

A shrewd judge of talent, Brown relied on Winfield Scott to train the troops. More politician than general, Brown needed Scott's expertise to prepare the disciplined army needed to retrieve American honor by standing up to British regulars. A veteran captain noted, "General Brown is a very industrious officer, but I consider General Scott as the life & soul of that army. . . . General Brown knows how to profit by the services of those intelligent men who know *how* to fight." Scott possessed an ego to match his formidable will, intelligence, and appearance. Six feet, five inches tall, he towered over others, and presented broad shoulders, a powerful chest, and a handsomely chiseled face. One awed contemporary described Scott as "the God of War." Born and raised in Virginia, Scott had studied law, which bored him, so he secured a captain's commission in the artillery in 1808. Driven by ambition, he carefully studied military literature to master the arts of command and drill. Impressing his superiors (save for Wilkinson), Scott advanced rapidly to become the army's youngest brigadier general in early 1814, when he was just twenty-eight years old.[8]

With Brown's support, Scott demanded far more of the men than had any previous American commander. Imposing daily drills of seven to ten hours, with weekly parades and inspections, Scott sought to turn civilians into soldiers "broken into habits of subordination." One captain marveled, "General Scott drills & damns, drills & damns, drills & damns, & drills again." And he stemmed desertion by shooting five culprits—just as any good British commander would do.[9]

The troops fell into line because Scott both terrified and thrilled them. He understood that men would take pride in drilling, if they could see progress and if he looked after their well-being. Bullying contractors, Scott procured better food and uniforms than American soldiers were used to. To improve their health, he enforced strict sanitation and hygiene, including bathing three times a week with soap in Lake Erie. His men avoided the dysentery that had afflicted every previous American military camp. Attentive to every detail, Scott regulated haircuts, knapsack contents, and the proper mode of saluting "with scrupulous exactness." Scott and Brown also benefited from the previous military disasters, which persuaded many recruits that their survival in combat depended on mastering discipline. And their officers were a conscientious lot because most of their negligent peers had resigned after the last campaign. Two years earlier, the generals would have had more recalcitrant men and less dedicated officers.[10]

In just three months, Scott produced a military miracle: an American army proud of its progress in discipline. One soldier marveled, "constant exercise, wholesome provisions, and strict discipline soon made our regiment have another appearance." Another boasted that "the regular troops are the best in appearance ever in the service of the United States, greatly improving in discipline and very healthy." Even Buffalo's Federalist newspaper praised the soldiers' health and good behavior.[11]

But Peter B. Porter, western New York's preeminent Republican, bristled at Scott's contempt for volunteers. Porter vowed to raise and train a brigade "to assert its equal rights and privileges with the regular troops, and not be what an inferior militia force always will be, the tools and drudges of the regular troops." Unlike regulars, the volunteers would serve for only six months and would elect their own officers except for the brigade commander, Porter, and his second-in-command, John Swift. The men would receive eight dollars per month, equipment, arms, and rations, but they had to provide their own clothing. The recruiting proved disappointing, because men could make more as farm laborers. William B. Rochester assured Porter, "Appeals to patriotism are unavailing, and all are aware that the [volunteer] plan holds out no temptations to cupidity." By early July, Porter had recruited and organized only one thousand volunteers, less than half of what he had sought.[12]

To make up for Porter's shortfall in New York volunteers, Brown assigned to him a regiment of five hundred Pennsylvania volunteers commanded by Colonel James Fenton. Porter also took charge of the sixty Canadian Volunteers led by Lieutenant Colonel Joseph Willcocks. Better still, Brown entrusted to Porter five hundred Haudenosaunee warriors, primarily from Buffalo Creek. Porter coveted the warriors to reassure his volunteers, who dreaded facing alone the Indian allies of the British.[13]

Brown led a bifurcated army—half regulars and half volunteers and Indians—with clashing standards of discipline. To vindicate American honor, Brown exhorted his men to protect civilian property in Upper Canada: "Profligate men who follow the army for plunder must not expect that they will escape the vengeance of the gallant spirits who are struggling to exalt the national character. Any plunderer shall be punished with death who may be found violating this order." Brown also reassured Armstrong, "All private property, ever has been, and ever will be, by me, respected. No such man as Dr. Chapin, will I hope accompany an army that I have the honor to command." But Porter's brigade included many men very much like Cyrenius Chapin. Resenting the destruction of the Niagara frontier towns in December, they regarded plunder as a just revenge against the Canadian "Tories." The burning zeal of the volunteers worked at cross-purposes with Brown's pursuit of honor by a professional army. While the volunteers meant to fight the revolution anew, Brown sought to win the respect of British officers.[14]

On the sunny morning of May 15, the fruit trees were in full bloom at Dover, a prosperous town on the Canadian shore of Lake Erie. A teenage girl, Amelia Ryerse, heard dogs barking: "When I looked up, I saw the hill-side and fields, as far as the eye could reach, covered with American soldiers." Lieutenant Colonel John B. Campbell and seven hundred Pennsylvania volunteers had crossed Lake Erie from Presque Isle in eight ships. Ryerse reported, "Two men stepped from the ranks, selected some large chips, and came into the room where we were standing, and took coals from the hearth without speaking a word." In vain, her mother protested to Campbell. "Very soon we saw columns of dark smoke arise from every building, and of what had been a prosperous homestead, at noon there remained only smouldering ruins." The volunteers burned three flour mills, three distilleries, twelve barns, and twenty houses. Shooting the horses, cattle, and pigs, they left the corpses to rot.[15]

To justify the destruction, Campbell denounced Dover's leaders as "old revolutionary Tories, who had been very active not only in oppressing our friends in Canada, but in aiding all in their powers the burning and plundering [of] Buffalo." Campbell explained, "I determined to make them feel the effects of that conduct [which] they had pursued towards others." An especially zealous republican, Campbell favored a civil war to liberate the Upper Canadians: "we must penetrate to the

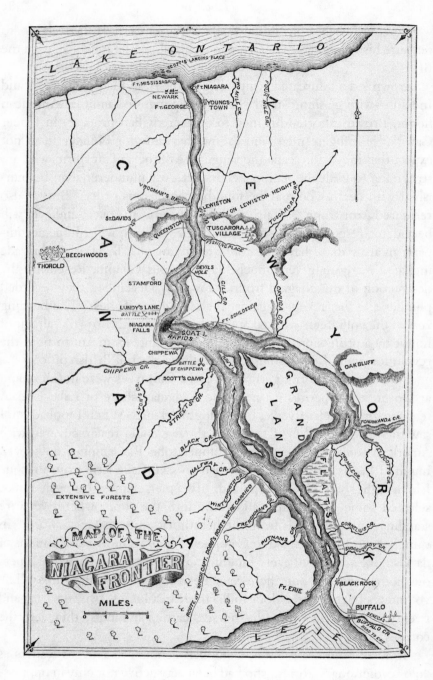

Map of the Niagara Frontier, *1814. Brown began his invasion by crossing from Black Rock to Fort Erie, at the outlet of Lake Erie into the Niagara River. He then moved north, beside the river to Chippawa, where the British had dug in to protect a bridge. Engraving from Benson J. Lossing,* The Pictorial Field-Book of the War of 1812 *(New York, 1869), 382.* (Courtesy of the New York State Library.)

interior, give confidence to the people, and establish a rallying point for the disaffected, of which description there are great numbers in the upper province."[16]

But the burning of Dover contradicted Brown's drive to vindicate the honor of American officers by winning British respect. Brown conveyed regrets to the British commander and ordered a court-martial to investigate Campbell's conduct. Unwilling to cashier a popular officer, the court only mildly rebuked Campbell for burning private homes, while approving his destruction of the flour mills. The court even expressed "admiration [for] his kind and amiable treatment of the women and children." After this slap on the wrist, Campbell was reinstated and promoted to colonel in time to join Brown's invasion of the Niagara District.[17]

BATTLE

On the night of July 2–3, Brown and his troops crossed the Niagara River to attack Fort Erie. On the eve of battle, Brown explained his goals to Major Thomas Sidney Jesup, who recalled, "If we could do nothing else, we might at least strike such a blow as to restore the tarnished military character of the country, which, in his estimation, was an object worth the sacrifice of the whole force he commanded." Jesup avidly supported Brown's vision: "Every one was anxious of an opportunity to remove the disgrace which former disasters and defeats had attached to our arms and to our military character." So the officers resolved, as "a point of honor to go into action with sashes and epaulettes and to wear [them] throughout the campaign." By calling dangerous attention to the officers, the bright red sashes and golden epaulets displayed their courage to the British. For that conspicuous pride, many would pay dearly, but such was the value of honor, and the fear of disgrace, to the young officers of Brown's army. Some of that attitude filtered down the ranks, for a sergeant informed his father "that, if I continue to live, I shall live victorious and, if I die, my Death will be glorious."[18]

Before dawn on July 3, the invaders landed unopposed on the Canadian shore. The one mishap was characteristic. Determined to be the first ashore, Scott prematurely leaped out of the lead boat in the dense fog. Finding the water too deep, he "had to swim for his life . . . encumbered with sword, epaulets, cloak and high boots." The attire of military honor nearly sank Scott to an inglorious death. But his brigade splashed ashore and surrounded Fort Erie, so the British commander quickly surrendered his 137 men. The victors marched into the fort while their fifers and drummers played "Yankee Doodle."[19]

With General Gordon Drummond away at York, General Phineas Riall commanded the British force on the Niagara front. To block the American advance down the Niagara River, Riall had 1,350 regulars, 350 warriors, and 200 militia in a strong position along Chippawa Creek, where British cannon guarded the lone bridge. But rather than remain snugly within his trenches, Riall crossed the creek to seek battle with the Americans, whom he underestimated. Victories had bred a British contempt for Americans as easily frightened because so badly led.[20]

Brown sent Porter's volunteers and Indians into the woods to the west to drive away the British-allied warriors led by John Norton. Overwhelmed by superior numbers, Norton's men fled. Porter recalled "scenes of frightful havoc & slaughter" in the woods as the slower enemy "suffered themselves to be cut down by the tomahawk, or, turning upon their pursuers, fought hand-to-hand to the last."[21]

After covering three-quarters of a mile, Porter had to halt when Riall's main force crossed the river and opened fire. Porter's volunteers broke and ran, which confirmed Riall in his illusion that he confronted the usual raw American troops given to confusion and panic. But Brown sent Scott's regular brigade forward to rescue Porter's men. Despite heavy British artillery fire, Scott neatly turned his advancing column into a line, parallel to the British. The two armies advanced to within one hundred yards in an open field, where they exchanged volleys to deadly effect. To Riall's shock, the British line crumpled first, as his men broke ranks to fall back, forcing Riall to withdraw across the Chippawa to the safety of his trenches. For the first time in this war, the British in Canada faced a regular army that had to be taken seriously, a sobering development. A British officer conceded, "that their Troops are far superior to every thing they have ever brought into the Country during the present War."[22]

Both armies paid dearly. The British regulars suffered 456 casualties, a quarter of the attacking force, and Riall did not know the number of dead and wounded Indian allies. Brown reported 295 casualties, primarily in Scott's brigade, which bore the brunt of the fighting. That night, an American captain reported that "the groans of the living was Shocking." In the field hospital, "there was not a room in the house but what they had a man on the Table amphetating." On the British side, Captain William Hamilton Merritt spent a "very unpleasant night" among "many officers lying wounded, groaning with pain."[23]

Despite their losses, the Americans exulted in the victory, but the volunteers and regulars differed in their grounds for celebration. Porter regarded Chippawa as "the first decisive advantage gained" over the British-allied Indians, "who had been the terror of our troops in the west during all the preceding stages of the war, and had kept the camps of Gen. Dearborn, Gen. Lewis & Gen. Boyd in a perpetual panic during the campaign of 1813." The regular officers instead dwelled on the new discipline of their soldiers. Seeing nearby Niagara Falls, Brown declared, "I can fancy nothing to equal it, but the noble contest of gallant men on the field of Battle, struggling for their nation's glory & their own." Colonel Charles K. Gardner declared Chippawa "the most important action ever fought by American troops" for giving "an assurance of strength to our Country, which she never had any proof of before." Eager to forget two years of shameful defeats, Republicans celebrated Chippawa as the greatest of victories.[24]

But the officers squabbled over their proper share in the public credit for that glory. In his hastily prepared but widely published report, Brown extolled Scott by name and then broadly praised "every officer and every man" of his brigade. This was not enough for the subordinate officers, who needed to see their names in print. Feeling dishonored, Major Henry Leavenworth protested to Scott: "My feelings are injured, my understanding insulted and my Country abused. The consequence is I have lost that confidence which every soldier ought and must have in his commanding General to enable him to do his duty." Taking offense on behalf of his officers, the touchy Scott tendered his resignation. Unable to spare him, Brown talked Scott down by writing a fuller report to praise more officers, including Leavenworth. In their prickly zeal for individual honor, the officers demonstrated that the professionalism of the American army remained a work in progress.[25]

REVENGE

Eager for British applause, the victors earnestly solicited praise from their prisoners. Writing home, an American sergeant gushed that a captured British officer declared that his regiment had never before retreated or suffered such heavy losses. An American lieutenant declared that Chippawa marked "the beginning of a new era, in the mutual confidence and esteem of the opposing forces. . . . The result of this battle then was to awaken a far more generous intimacy between the two services, if not between the two Nations, than had ever existed before."[26]

The lieutenant conveyed an important but partial truth. At parleys after Chippawa, British officers treated their American counterparts with a new respect that intoxicated them. But the good feelings did not include the irregulars on both sides, who continued to wage a brutal civil war. At the end of the battle, the Buffalo Creek warriors cut the throats of the wounded enemy and scalped their heads. When Porter protested, an interpreter for the warriors replied "that we ought to recollect that these were very hard times." On the British side, the Indians abused captured volunteers, including Lieutenant Colonel Bull, whom they tomahawked and scalped. Another captured volunteer, Samuel White, insisted that Riall encouraged the Indian atrocities to dissuade other volunteers from crossing into Canada. And while the regular officers, British and American, were exchanging new pleasantries, the British were preparing to hang eight Upper Canadians as traitors at Ancaster.[27]

After the defeat at Chippawa, most of Riall's Indian allies bolted, depriving him of the scouts and warriors needed to protect his wooded flank to the west. On July 8, Brown turned that flank by finding a logging road through the woods to build a bridge across the upper reaches of Chippawa Creek. Riall abruptly withdrew north along the Niagara River to Fort George. Rather than trust another American occupation, hundreds of civilian refugees followed the retreating British troops.[28]

On July 9, Brown's troops advanced to Queenston, seven miles south of Fort George. To scout the countryside and gather forage for the army's horses, Brown relied on the volunteers, especially Joseph Willcocks's Canadians, but they ignored Brown's orders against destroying or plundering private property. Disgusted civilians fed information to the Loyalist militia and to Captain Merritt's dragoons, who were "daily skirmishing and driving in [United] States' parties, who were plundering every house they could get at; they even plundered women of everything they had." An American regular officer complained, "The whole population is [now] against us; not a foraging party but is fired on, and not infrequently returns with missing numbers." The Loyalist militia also ambushed the American supply wagons hauling provisions north along the Niagara Road to the camp at Queenston.[29]

Gone were the British laments of a disaffected populace and an ineffectual militia. A British lieutenant colonel reported, "The Canadian Militia harassed the enemy in a very manly and spirited style. They merit my most favorable opinion." Riall boasted "that almost the whole body of Militia is in Arms & seems actuated with the most determined spirit of Hostility to the Enemy." The executions near Ancaster had marginalized or intimidated the disaffected, while the renewed American plundering infuriated most of the people.[30]

In a vicious spiral, the American plundering fed a Canadian resistance, which the volunteers regarded as treachery by Tories. Porter assured Brown that the volunteers were "the victims of your own generous policy of suffering the inhabitants, who profess neutrality, to remain unmolested." But the inhabitants did not feel "unmolested." Indeed, plundered women became especially effective spies for the British. Porter reported that the enemy "were advised of all our movements and positions by the women who were thronging around us on our march . . . professing friendship." The volunteers also resented the execution of Lieutenant Colonel Bull and the assassination of their second-in-command, General John Swift. On July 12, Swift had accepted the surrender of a Loyalist, but before he could be disarmed, the prisoner had raised his musket and shot the general "through the breast."[31]

To arrest "Tories" suspected of recent ambushes, Porter sent mounted volunteers to St. Davids, a prosperous settlement at a crossroads four miles west of Queenston. He gave that command to Lieutenant Colonel Isaac W. Stone, a tavern keeper and mill owner from western New York. After a skirmish, the volunteers seized and plundered the village and then burned down fourteen homes, two shops, and a gristmill.[32]

Like the torching of Dover, the destruction of St. Davids threatened Brown's drive to earn British respect. Because a court-martial had failed to punish Campbell for burning Dover, Brown dispensed with any trial for Stone, instead summarily dismissing him from the army the next day. A fellow volunteer officer protested that, because Stone "is tumbled headlong among the gaping Multitude in disgrace, without a Trial, he finds those rights trampled upon which he is sheding his Blood to defend." Committed to a republican crusade to punish Tories, the volunteers resented Brown's emphasis on the strict obedience to the arbitrary authority of the regular command. The volunteers were not fighting for British respect.[33]

Brown also tried to control the Indians, who were so fearsome in battle but so alienating to civilians. In addition to stealing horses from farmers, they seized a British depot containing fifty barrels of alcohol. When the army quartermaster confiscated the alcohol, the disgusted Indians returned home on June 20, despite Brown's and Porter's pleas to stay. The Buffalo Creek chiefs also reached an understanding with their Grand River kin: both would withdraw from a civil war where the Haudenosaunee killed one another.[34]

RETREAT

To capture Fort George and Fort Niagara, which jointly controlled the mouth of the Niagara River, Brown needed help from Isaac Chauncey, the American naval commander on Lake Ontario. By sailing southwest from Sackets Harbor to the Niagara River, Chauncey could interrupt the British supply line that sustained Riall. American command of the lake would also shorten Brown's supply line, breaking his vulnerable dependence on the Niagara Road. And Brown counted on Chauncey to bring the heavy artillery needed to batter the British forts. Day after day, Brown's scouts scanned the lake in vain for any sign of Chauncey's fleet. Instead, British vessels kept bringing supplies and men to reinforce Riall.[35]

After two years of botched campaigns, Chauncey was fed up with subordinating his fleet to the orders of generals. In November 1813 Wilkinson's wild-goose chase down the St. Lawrence River had been the last straw for the commodore. Never again would he expose his precious naval base to British attack by withdrawing his fleet to help some general attack a distant fort. Chauncey would only support an assault on the nearby British naval base at Kingston and only when his fleet was good and ready. Chauncey had his own powerful sense of honor to defend: "In the expected Contest next Summer, the Naval reputation of the Nation, as well as my own, will be at stake." Smoking out Yeo's fleet for a battle on the lake would advance Chauncey's honor far more than would serving as Brown's errand boy.[36]

Chauncey had become monomaniacal about building a massive fleet on Lake Ontario. Even the U.S. secretary of the navy complained that "one fourth of our naval force [is] employed for the defence of a wilderness, while our Atlantic frontier—our flourishing Cities, towns & villages, cultivated farms, rising manufactories, public works & edifices are deprived of the services and protection" of a navy. But Madison supported Chauncey's program, so coastal warships were shut down and their crews sent to Sackets Harbor to man the swelling lake fleet.[37]

By letter, Chauncey informed Brown that he would not sail west to the Niagara front unless led there in pursuit of Yeo's fleet. If Brown wanted a coordinated attack on the British, he should return to Sackets Harbor for an offensive against Kingston. Claiming "a higher destiny— we are intended to seek and to fight the enemy's fleet," Chauncey refused to render his ships "a convenience in the transportation of provisions and stores for the use of the army, and an agreeable appendage to attend its marches and counter-marches."[38]

By early July 1814 newly built warships gave lake supremacy to the Americans, but their fleet remained idle because malaria left Chauncey bedridden. Determined to enjoy the honor of defeating Yeo, Chauncey refused to let a subordinate lead the fleet onto the lake and into combat. Knowing Brown's needs, the army officers at Sackets Harbor denounced Chauncey as selfish: "There was a fine opportunity of fighting and winning the long wished for battle, but lost because the only man in the fleet who was not ready was the commanding officer." By infecting Chauncey, one mosquito's bite had paralyzed the fleet at the campaign's critical moment. But it was Chauncey's ego that enabled that bite to freeze a fleet and to stymie an army.[39]

While waiting in vain for Chauncey's fleet, Brown maneuvered around Fort George, trying to draw the British out of their entrenchments for a new battle. When that failed, Brown fell back to Chippawa on July 24. There he drew supplies from Buffalo to prepare for a strike into the interior against the British base at Burlington Heights. But on the morning of July 25, he learned that the British were advancing south in search of battle. Chauncey's negligence had enabled Drummond to sail across the lake with reinforcements from Kingston. Given "the decided Naval Superiority of the Enemy," Drummond considered his unmolested crossing "a most extraordinary circumstance."[40]

That afternoon, Brown sent Scott north with 1,200 regulars to seek the advancing British. At about 7:15 p.m. Scott reached Lundy's Lane to find 2,800 British troops, far more than he had bargained on. Scott's messenger raced south to Brown to urge the rest of their army to hasten forward. Despite the strong British position on a low hill, their superior numbers, and the dimming daylight, Scott attacked without waiting for Brown and reinforcements. Scott shared Isaac Brock's conviction that aggression worked a double advantage by breeding confidence in the attackers and doubts in the attacked. Courageous but foolhardy, the attack impressed the British but shattered Scott's brigade, for the Americans were cut down by a withering fire.[41]

At about 9:00 p.m., Brown arrived with fresh troops to renew the attack despite the darkness, compounded by a dense cloud of gunpowder smoke. As regiments jockeyed for position in the darkness and smoke, friendly fire took a toll on both armies, and many men became prisoners by blundering into the wrong side. John Le Couteur, a British lieutenant, noted, "from going in among the enemy in the Dark, and from speaking the same language, once separated, we could not distinguish friends from foe." In the second round of battle, the Americans swept the British from the crest of the hill and captured their cannon, but Drummond was every bit as determined and stubborn as Brown. Three British counterattacks convulsed the hill in hand-to-hand combat with bayonets and clubbed muskets.[42]

At midnight the British desisted, leaving the hill to the Americans, who were exhausted and shattered by six hours of combat. Many were dying from thirst, their lungs choked with gunpowder smoke, and they were nearly out of ammunition. Because bullets had pierced Brown's thigh and shattered Scott's shoulder, command fell to General Eleazar W. Ripley, who withdrew the survivors three miles to their camp, where they could rest and draw food, water, and ammunition.[43]

Misery also reigned among the British survivors, who shivered through the cold and damp night, so different from the hot, dry day of fighting. Le Couteur recalled, "I assure you, I never passed so awful a night as that of the action. The stillness of the evening after the firing ceased, the Groans of the dying and wounded . . . A Soldier's life is very horrid sometimes." Sent out to relieve the wounded, Le Couteur found an American officer, Captain Abraham Hull, the twenty-eight-year-old son of the disgraced General Hull. Serving in Scott's brigade, young Hull had been cut down while trying to retrieve his family's honor. Le Couteur comforted the dying young man with brandy, water, and conversation. Noting the nearby Indians "scalping and plundering," Le Couteur offered to take in charge Hull's "watch, rings and anything He wished sent to his family." Hull declined, and when Le Couteur returned in the morning, he found "a beautiful Corpse, stripped stark naked—amongst a host of friends and foes."[44]

On the morning of July 26, the British reclaimed the contested hill. Ripley dared not attack for fear that another battle would destroy the remains of his army. Instead, he ordered a retreat southward, which disgusted Brown, who wanted the tokens of victory—control of the battlefield and the British cannon—at any cost. Instead, Drummond could claim victory, so Brown blasted Ripley for robbing him of it.[45]

But retreat seemed the right call to the men in the ranks. A Pennsylvania volunteer, Alexander McMullen, noted the "slow and melancholy steps" of his company, "the shattered remains of only twenty-five out of the hundred that had left Franklin County [Pennsylvania]" in the spring. McMullen counted forty-two wagons laden with the groaning wounded. Shell-shocked, he "lay down in front of a house in despair, not caring what became of me," until an officer goaded him back into the marching ranks. That night the rain fell in torrents on men without tents: "This of all nights I had ever spent was the most dreadful."[46]

The grim battle cost the Americans 853 casualties (171 dead, 572 wounded, and 110 captured or deserted). The dead included Colonel John B. Campbell of Dover infamy. The British suffered fewer dead (84) and wounded (559) but lost more prisoners (169), including General Riall, who had stumbled into an American unit in the darkness. In pursuit of honor, Brown and Scott had sacrificed a third of the precious little army that they had organized and disciplined during the spring.[47]

The British secured the bloodiest battlefield of the war (to date). An American surgeon remarked, "such a scene of carnage I never beheld . . . red coats and blue and grey were promiscuously intermingled, in many places three deep, and around the hill . . . the carcasses of 60 or 70 horses disfigured the scene." Too worn out to bury so many dead, the British troops heaped the corpses onto gathered fence rails and fallen trees to make a human bonfire. When an Indian cast a severely wounded American into the fire, an outraged British soldier shot the warrior and added him to the fire. The new respect for American regulars led Britons to treat Indians with greater disdain.[48]

The British surgeons struggled to cope with hundreds of wounded from both sides. There was no sanitation when barns and barracks served as field hospitals. One sleepless surgeon, William Dunlop, recalled, "The weather was intensely hot, the flies were in myriads, and lighting on the wounds, deposited their eggs, so that maggots were bred in a few hours, producing dreadful irritation, so that long before I could go round dressing the patients' [wounds], it was necessary to begin again." He hastily amputated dozens of limbs that might have been saved had there been more surgeons to attend fewer wounded. Dunlop lamented the plight "of an Army Surgeon after a battle—worn out and fatigued in body and mind, surrounded by suffering, pain and misery, much of which he knows it is not in his power to heal or even to assuage." The surgeons had no anesthetic except alcohol, and they did not clean their saws between amputations, each of which took about ten excruciating minutes to complete.[49]

The American officers sought meaning and nobility in the sacrifice of so many good men. Ripley celebrated the officers who "died on the field where a soldier should pant to perish, gallantly leading and animating their men." Colonel Gardner added: "Our victory may be counted among the most glorious of late years, in Europe or America. It is prominently so, if the glory of an action is commensurate with its being bloody." But in a more candid moment, Gardner recalled "the slaughter of the last fruitless affair."[50]

SIEGE

Instead of halting at Chippawa Creek, which offered a strong defensive position, Ripley kept retreating to Fort Erie, which he also wanted to abandon by withdrawing across the river to Buffalo, but Brown refused to give up the last foothold won by his campaign. Distrusting Ripley as gloomy, Brown summoned General Gaines from Sackets Harbor to take command at Fort Erie. Brown and Scott then withdrew to recover from their wounds.[51]

On August 2, Drummond pushed his troops forward to Fort Erie, which he found strengthened by the desperate Americans during the weeklong interval after the battle. They had extended the earthworks southwestward along the lakeshore, to Snake Hill, which they also fortified and mounted with cannon. To increase the vulnerability of attackers, the defenders cleared away the trees and brush from three hundred yards in front of their lines. They used the wood to construct an abatis—a tangle of sharpened stakes and brush—along the ditch in front of their earthworks. But the fruits of Brown's invasion had been reduced to one fort just 800 yards long by 250 yards wide. "Our position is a wretched one," Porter lamented, "closely surrounded by woods which are occupied by the enemy." Backed by the lake, the defenders could not retreat by land, leaving them no margin for error or defeat.[52]

To cut the fort's supply line, Drummond sent Colonel John Tucker and six hundred men across the Niagara River to attack Buffalo. They landed safely but fell into an ambush set by 240 riflemen at Conjocta Creek. After suffering a dozen killed and seventeen wounded, the attackers crumbled, so Tucker withdrew across the river to the Canadian shore. Infuriated by the setback, Drummond showed his darker side, humiliating the defeated troops in a general order that reiterated an inflexible standard for combat: "Crouching ducking, or laying down when advancing under fire are bad habits and must be corrected." He insisted upon "the duty of all officers to punish with death on the spot any man under their command who may be found guilty of misbehavior before the enemy." The draconian order added to the unease that many officers felt toward their increasingly testy commander.[53]

Drummond settled down to a siege, building earthen batteries to shelter cannon to bombard Fort Erie. The cannon opened fire on August 7, but made little impact because they were set too far from their target. On August 14 a lucky British shot did hit and ignited a small ammunition magazine in the fort. Although the explosion killed no one and created no structural damage, the bright flash and loud sound ignited British cheering and persuaded Drummond that his cannon had, at last, weakened the enemy.[54]

That night he ordered an attack designed also to discipline his troops, for Drummond remained irked by their losing behavior at Conjocta Creek. Enforcing old-school tactics, he ordered the men to remove the flints from their muskets, so that they could not fire prematurely, which would warn the Americans. Once within the fort, they could rely on their bayonets—"that valuable weapon" so dear to a disciplinarian like Drummond. But he remained safely in the camp, while he entrusted command of the three assault columns to his nephew Lieutenant Colonel William Drummond, Colonel Hercules Scott, and Lieutenant Colonel Victor Fischer.[55]

General Drummond's three-pronged attack was too complex for the inevitable confusion of darkness. And the 2,500 attackers were too few to overwhelm the 2,200 Americans holding a strong fort and well led by General Gaines. Coordination broke down as the three columns stumbled about in the dark and tripped over stumps en route to their attacks. To get over the walls, the British brought scaling ladders, but they proved too short. Stalled at the wall around Snake Hill, Fischer's men were shot down "like so many sheep" by the aroused Americans. Lacking flints, the attackers could not fire back.[56]

The central and eastern columns hit the main fort. Despite suffering heavy casualties, Colonel Drummond's troops broke into the northeast bastion and killed the American gunners. But the attack stalled as the Americans sealed off the bastion and blasted the intruders. The defenders could hear Colonel Drummond bellow, "*Give the d[amne]d Yankees no quarter!*" Setting the example, he shot a wounded Irish-American artillery officer, Patrick McDonogh, as he tried to surrender. To the Americans' delight, a bullet then struck Colonel Drummond through the heart.[57]

An American lieutenant recalled, "suddenly, every sound was hushed by the sense of an unnatural tremor beneath our feet, like the first heave of an earthquake." An instant later, "the centre of the bastion burst up, with a terrific explosion; and a jet of flame, mingled with fragments of timber, earth, stone and bodies," rose over a hundred feet in the air before falling "in a shower of ruins." The ammunition magazine beneath the bastion had ignited. Another American recalled seeing Britons flying into the air, "their cartridge boxes filled with fixed ammunition ignited and spangled out in every direction."[58]

Lieutenant Le Couteur was knocked unconscious and blown back twenty feet. Coming to his senses, he saw scores of men "roasted, man-

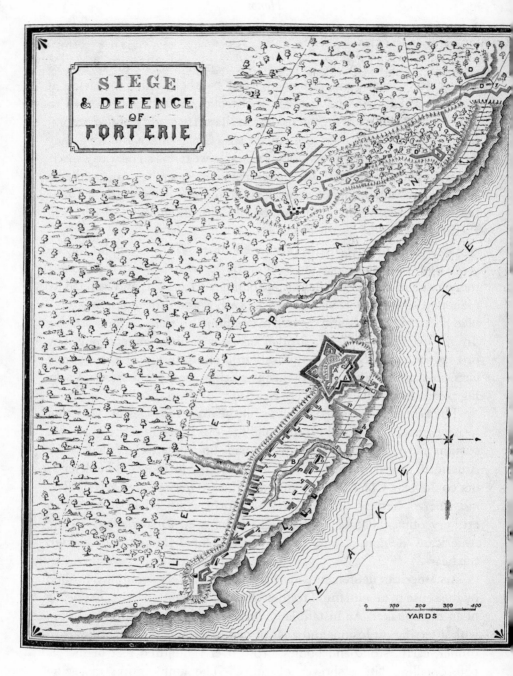

Siege & Defence of Fort Erie, *engraving. In August 1814, American troops defended the star-shaped fort (at A) and a line of entrenchments extending southwest to Snake Hill. General Drummond's British forces erected entrenched batteries to the north at* D. *From Benson J. Lossing,* The Pictorial Field-Book of the War of 1812 *(New York, 1869), 839. (Courtesy of the New York State Library.)*

gled, burned, wounded, black [and] hideous to view." To steady himself, Le Couteur placed a hand on his captain's back: "I found my hand in a mass of blood and brains—it was sickening." Le Couteur joined the other survivors in running for their lives away from the deadly fort. Dunlop recalled fleeing "along the road at the top of my speed, with a running accompaniment of grape[shot], cannister and musketry whistling about my ears, and tearing the ground at my feet."[59]

The Americans lost only 62 casualties, but the British suffered 905 (including 221 dead) out of the 2,500 in the assault. After the battle, an American soldier found "legs, arms and heads lying in confusion, separated by the concussions from the trunks to which they had long been attached." Another American concluded, "I never before witnessed such a scene of carnage & havoc among human beings."[60]

Embarrassed by the losses, General Drummond blamed his men and posed as their victim in his report to Prevost: "The agony of mind I suffer, from the present disgraceful, and unfortunate conduct of the Troops, committed to my superintendence, wounds me to the Soul!" In fact the men had been betrayed by Drummond's folly in ordering a premature and complicated assault by insufficient numbers with short ladders and without flints. By evading responsibility and blasting his men, Drummond undermined their morale. After the battle, British desertion surged, primarily from the disgraced De Watteville regiment.[61]

The cause of the fatal explosion invited varying speculations, which revealed how the two sides perceived the war's meaning. The British insisted that one of their deserters had set off a mine, or that he had given his cap and red coat to an American soldier, who slipped among the attackers to set a fuse. These stories reflected the British insistence that their deserters had provoked and sustained the war. But Americans favored an explanation that gave just deserts to British arrogance: after being shot by Colonel Drummond, Patrick McDonogh had crawled into the powder magazine and ignited it. Other soldiers believed that one of them had ignited the explosion for a reward from General Gaines: a large cash payment and immediate discharge from the army. That fantasy was the fondest wish of men weary of war.[62]

SORTIE

In the no-man's-land between Fort Erie and the British lines, both forces posted picket guards of riflemen or light infantry. Both sides raided the pickets of their enemy. In that nasty fighting, the Americans relied on Willcocks and his Canadian Volunteers. Although few in number, they won high praise from Porter, Brown, and Ripley for their enterprise and bravery. A New York volunteer officer declared, "Of Col. Willcocks I take pleasure in announcing that in every movement he behaved worthy of a hero and a patriot. Calm and unruffled, he rushed on in defence of our country's rights until he fell entwined with the laurels of glory." On September 5 he died, shot through the chest while charging an enemy's picket. The Irish-American newspaper the *Shamrock* mourned the loss of an "ardent friend of human rights." Reinventing his past in Ireland, the obituary claimed that Willcocks had been a "member of the Society of *United Irishmen*."[63]

Britons and Loyalists exulted in the death of their ultimate traitor. Three days after the skirmish, an excited Colonel John Harvey reported: "The affair of the 5th was more important than was thought at the time." The British were especially delighted that Willcocks had died from a bullet fired by a loyal Canadian of the Glengarry Light Infantry. Although American officers had admired Willcocks, his death favored their shift away from a civil war for a republican Canada and to a crusade for national honor, which depended upon a respect that the British would never have granted to "that Arch Rebel."[64]

Persisting in his siege, Drummond brought in more ammunition, cannon, and 1,200 men—more than compensating for his losses. He praised Commodore Yeo "for his prompt acquiescence" in sending them forward, conduct so very different from Chauncey's indifference to Brown's needs. Drummond's men built a new battery, closer to the enemy lines and more effective. On August 25 a British shell burst through the roof of General Gaines's office and exploded, shattering his desk "& enveloping the Genl. in Smoke, blaze & some dust." Staggering out of the ruins, Gaines was "Miserably bruised & losing much Blood" from five wounds. Command reverted to the pessimistic Mr. Ripley, who again pressed for an evacuation: "Nothing saves this wreck of a gallant army from perfect annihilation but crossing to our own shore."[65]

Instead, the convalescing Brown took command at Fort Erie on September 2. Desperate for reinforcements, Brown pressed Governor Tompkins to rally four thousand militia and send them to Buffalo, where he hoped to persuade them to cross the border to bolster Fort Erie. Given his preference for regulars, turning to militia was a tough pill for Brown to swallow. And Ripley mocked the effort as futile: "No Military man who has known the Conduct of the Militia of this frontier, even on their own ground, should hold a post & hazard an army on this side [of] the straits by relying on them."[66]

But Brown found an eager and able ally in Porter, who felt renewed when the regulars needed a rescue by New York militia. In a published call for volunteers, he warned of the savage menace that would erupt into western New York, "the moment that the army, its only barrier, shall be broken down." Porter appealed to the interests of farmers as patriarchs: "That army destroyed, and your fruitful fields, your stately edifices, and your fair possessions are laid waste. Your women and children will feel the weight of the tomahawk."[67]

In early September three thousand militia volunteers came to Buffalo. A friend assured Porter, "The Militia have continually . . . been flocking in by companies & passing on and . . . they continue in high spirits & full of fight." But most intended only to defend Buffalo, rather than cross into Canada. To sway them, Porter doled out flattering speeches, generous whiskey, and patriotic music. A festive parade through the streets drew in volunteers, who cheered themselves and jeered those who hung back, gathering strength until about half of the militia agreed to march into the waiting boats on September 9 and 10.[68]

Meanwhile, day after day of pouring rain dispirited the British troops in Drummond's low-lying camp of leaky huts. He lamented, "[Our] Camp literally resembles a Lake in the midst of a thick wood." A British sergeant complained that his men were "obliged to cut down trees to sleep upon to keep us from drowning." Because food and fodder ran short, Drummond had to put his troops and their horses on short rations. Lacking enough gunpowder and cannonballs, Drummond also reduced the fire by his cannon. But mosquitoes increased their attacks, spreading debilitating ague and fever among the British troops. On September 16 Drummond reluctantly decided to withdraw. A day later, while his men began to remove their cannon, Brown's troops erupted from Fort Erie.[69]

With his own army in desperate straits, Brown resorted to a sortie. Asserting that his troops "would prefer to die in the blaze of their own glory, than live dishonoured by Captivity or Defeat," Brown resolved "to make one grand effort to save the suffering remains of a force that appeared to be neglected by a Country for which it had devoted itself." Ripley opposed the attack as suicidal, but Brown cared little for Ripley's opinion and gave command of the sortie to Porter.[70]

Porter's troops surprised and overwhelmed two British batteries, disabling the cannon and blowing up their ammunition magazines. When the British counterattacked, Brown ordered his men to withdraw back to the fort. Both Drummond and Brown claimed victory, Brown with better cause because the British suffered heavier casualties, including the loss of at least 316 prisoners. And the sortie further demoralized the

British troops, while it thrilled the Americans. On September 21, under torrents of rain, Drummond withdrew his army north to Chippawa, where they dug in.[71]

Brown took a special pride in the volunteers, who fought well in the sortie: "The militia of New York have redeemed their character—they behaved gallantly." Politically, "their good conduct cannot but have the happiest effect upon the nation," for they had atoned for their embarrassing failures in 1812 and 1813. Brown credited Porter, who fought as hard as he played: "He *drinks*, and I mourn over him, for I love him as a soldier and respect him as a man of talents devoted to the interest and glory of his country." After a rocky start in the spring, Brown and Porter had become close collaborators by summer's end. And the volunteers had won a share with the regulars in the honor of the campaign. Republicans needed the good news from Fort Erie to compensate for a recent humiliation at Washington, D.C., which the British had captured on August 24. Taking revenge for York, Dover, and St. Davids, the British burned the U.S. Capitol and the White House.[72]

MEANDER

In early October, the Americans gained a decisive advantage on the Niagara front with the arrival of General George Izard and 3,500 regulars. In August, the secretary of war, John Armstrong, had ordered Izard to march his army from Lake Champlain to the Niagara front, but the distance was great and their progress slow. Leaving Plattsburgh on August 29, Izard's army did not reach the Niagara River until October 10. At a critical moment in the war, that force was lost to the troop-scarce nation for forty precious days, able neither to defend Plattsburgh nor to attack at Niagara. The slow, erratic, and wasteful march was another great folly in a war replete with them. Citizens mocked Izard as "our meandering General," but Armstrong deserved a third of the blame, for ordering the march, and Chauncey warranted another third for delays in ferrying the troops across Lake Ontario.[73]

In vain Izard had warned Armstrong that a march west would expose Plattsburgh to an impending British attack. Indeed, two days after Izard left, Sir George Prevost pushed south, crossing the border with ten thousand men, the largest British army assembled during the war. To defend Plattsburgh, General Alexander Macomb had only 1,500 regulars, and most were convalescents and raw recruits. But on September 11, the American flotilla of Thomas Macdonough crushed the British naval attack by four warships led by Captain George Downie. Discouraged by Downie's defeat and death, Prevost canceled his land attack, although his troops were poised to crush Macomb. Retreating in disorder, Prevost abandoned valuable military stores and lost three hundred deserters.[74]

At Plattsburgh the Americans dodged a catastrophe because caution froze Prevost, as at Sackets Harbor in 1813. But this time Prevost faced powerful critics, his subordinate generals, who were used to Wellington's aggressive and victorious style in Europe. Yeo also blamed Prevost for pressuring Captain Downie to attack prematurely. Prevost's military critics found political allies in Canada's militant Anglophones, who resented his generous treatment of the French Canadians. A vicious letter-writing campaign by the critics spilled into the previously docile Canadian press. Some writers revived the canard that Prevost was a closet traitor because his parents were Americans and "true republicans." Dismayed by the infighting, the imperial lords would recall Prevost and Yeo to England in the spring.[75]

Meanwhile, on the Niagara front, Izard outranked Brown and assumed command of their joint force of 6,300, twice Drummond's number. On October 14, Izard moved north to face the British lines on the Chippawa Creek, but he quickly soured on the attempt as futile and ordered a retreat. Izard disdained the Niagara front as a foolish place to wage war because "so distant from our Sources of Supply" and "thinly settled and incapable of affording subsistence for an army even of the smallest size." Izard preferred a campaign in the St. Lawrence Valley, where an invasion could sever the British supply line between Montreal and Upper Canada. In effect, Izard faulted Brown for adopting a strategic folly in pursuit of merely tactical honor. But Brown seethed at the retreat, for he longed to conclude the campaign with a clear victory over the British at Chippawa. After forty days of marching, Izard had maneuvered for another ten before calling the whole campaign off.[76]

Izard removed most of his troops across the river to Black Rock and Buffalo, where they built huts for the winter. Porter discharged the volunteers, who headed home. Brown and two thousand men returned to Sackets Harbor to defend Chauncey's fleet, not the happiest of assignments for a general who despised the commodore. Brown predicted, "Chauncey will, I suppose, build a few more Ships and fight as usual another Campaign at a profit of from thirty to fifty thousand Dollars." Feuding, Chauncey and Brown avoided each other, no easy accomplishment in a village as small as Sackets Harbor. "We of course have had no *intercourse*," Brown noted.[77]

On the last day of October, as Izard withdrew from Upper Canada, a

British firing squad executed John McMillan, convicted of deserting from the militia to join the Americans. During the sortie from Fort Erie on September 17, McMillan had been captured while serving with Willcocks's Canadian Volunteers. His death represented the demise of organized disaffection in Upper Canada: a collateral damage from the failed Niagara campaign. In the wake of Willcocks's death, the Canadian Volunteers crumbled, as the two majors, Abraham Markle and Benajah Mallory, bitterly fought to command a dwindling force.[78]

Initially, Izard kept a garrison at Fort Erie as the lone trophy of the American invasion and as a bargaining chip for the peace negotiations under way in Europe. But he soon worried that the garrison would be locked up and isolated by the winter ice, useless to the Americans and vulnerable to British attack. So Izard removed the garrison on November 5 and blew up the fort. "The explosion was tremendous, and worth seeing," an officer noted. "Snake Hill is now a mound of sand, so completely have they blown up the works," a British engineer reported.[79]

After the withdrawal, the British celebrated victory, for the Americans had no territory in the Niagara District to show for their long, bloody, and expensive campaign. Captain Merritt exulted, "The campaign has ended as usual, unfavourable to the United States arms; as they are not in possession of a foot of land in Canada." Drummond boasted that he had compelled the enemy to "return in disgrace to his own shores." The imperial lords rewarded Drummond for his victory with a knighthood in January and promotion in April to replace Prevost in overall command in Canada.[80]

Irritated by the British boasts, Brown and his officers insisted that they had won a glorious, if intangible, goal: the honor due to a courageous and disciplined army. A captain declared, "The business on the Niagara has been glorious! And highly honorable to our arms. These Europeans affected to despise us; a few such scenes will teach them to respect us." Republicans liked to boast that their army had triumphed over the hitherto victorious veterans of Wellington's army.[81]

The Niagara campaign seemed glorious when compared to the follies of the previous two years, for multiple defeats had set the bar low for Brown in 1814. With the conquest of Canada receding as a war aim, American officers could define success as simply matching the British in combat. Major Jesup observed, "The organization of the army is so extremely imperfect that if we avoid disgrace, our country should consider us victorious." Writing to Brown, Armstrong concluded: "You have behaved nobly. You have rescued the military character of your country from the odium brought upon it by fools and rascals."[82]

But that honor and respect had not come cheap. On the Niagara front in 1814, over one thousand Americans had died of combat wounds or camp fevers; and many more suffered crippling injuries. Near the end of the campaign, General James Miller reflected that in Brown's army "every major, save one, every lieutenant-colonel, every colonel that was here when I came and has remained here, has been killed or wounded, and I am now the only general officer out of seven that has escaped." With their lives or their limbs, they paid for the honor won by exposing themselves to enemy fire while dressed in gold epaulets and scarlet sashes.[83]

After the battle of Lundy's Lane, the British surgeon Dunlop treated a mortally wounded American volunteer, a farmer in his late fifties. A musket ball had shattered his thigh. His wife, "a respectable elderly looking woman," came under a flag of truce to visit the military hospital, "where she found her husband lying on a truss of straw, writhing in agony, for his sufferings were dreadful." She sat on the ground, "and taking her husband's head on her lap, continued long, moaning and sobbing, while the tears flowed fast down her face." Then, "looking wildly around," she exclaimed, " 'O that the King and President were both here this moment to see the misery their quarrels lead to. They surely would never go to war without a cause that they could give as a reason to God at the last day, for thus destroying the creatures that He hath made in his own image.' " She saw little honor in her husband's death.[84]

Seeing the campaign as honorable also required looking away from the burning and plundering inflicted by American troops, primarily the volunteers, on the civilians of the Niagara District. That destruction completed their alienation from their American kin. Drummond exulted that the militia had fought hard and well against the invaders. In a war that depended on winning the hearts and minds of an occupied people, the Niagara campaign deepened the American defeat.[85]

Izard had vowed to "spare no pains to protect the wretched people from being plundered" by vigorously punishing all culprits. Such promises had been made and broken before. Indeed, Izard prosecuted only one man for plundering in Canada. A wagon master rather than a soldier, he was charged with the minor offense of buying a stolen horse and reselling it to an officer. Discharged from the army, the wagon master had to refund the officer's payment—the mildest of penalties. And neither the horse-stealing soldier nor the horse-buying officer suffered a court-martial.[86]

The campaign's glory also seemed flimsy to the troops left at Buffalo for the winter. An officer grumbled, "we have nothing here—neither eating, drinking f[uc]k[in]g, fighting, nor fidling—neither society [n]or wilderness enough to make us Social." Stewing in his misery, the officer concluded, "Of our late movements, of our Generals &c., &c., I say nothing. I durst not blame them, but be d[amne]d if I praise them."[87]

While extolling his campaign in public, Brown privately doubted that it had accomplished anything tangible: "a few brave men have met the enemy and triumphed over a superior number of troops hitherto esteemed the best in the world, but the general execution of the plan of campaign has been disgraceful." He despised Madison as a weak leader, but insisted that the rot ran to the core of the republic: "We have been a

General George Izard (1776–1828), *oil painting by Charles Bird King, 1813.* (Courtesy of the Arkansas Arts Center Foundation.)

puffing, money-getting People almost destitute of National feeling or honor, and I have no doubt but that ten years more of War would have rendered us perfectly contemptible."[88]

Far from improving the American chances for victory in 1815, the Niagara campaign had wasted the nation's finest troops in futile battles. And through the winter Armstrong, Monroe, Brown, Chauncey, Izard, Scott, and Ripley squabbled over credit for the tactical successes and blame for the strategic failure. The campaign had also depleted the national treasury, which verged on bankruptcy. Most of the troops had not been paid since April, and the army had run out of funds to buy them winter clothing.[89]

But the Americans subsequently crafted a mirage of military victory by winning at the peace negotiations what had eluded them on the battlefield. Brown contributed to that treaty by claiming honor as the war's goal, a substitute for the earlier bid to conquer Canada to extort maritime concessions from the British. By insisting that they had won honor, Americans could make a peace that extricated them from a military stalemate. Ultimately a successful peace would clinch their claims to have won a war for honor on the Niagara front in 1814.[90]

The Peace of Ghent, 1814, and Triumph of America, *engraving by Chataignier.
Published in Philadelphia after the war, this allegory celebrates the peace treaty as
securing a glorious victory for the United States. The shield of Minerva, the goddess of
wisdom, records the names of the American treaty commissioners. The obelisk lists
American war heroes. And the pedestal below names the short list of American victories. An American Hercules, with a club, tramples on Neptune's trident, a symbol of
the Royal Navy, and on a prostrate British flag. An American eagle soars overhead.
From Benson J. Lossing,* The Pictorial Field-Book of the War of 1812 *(New York,
1869), 1066. (Courtesy of the New York State Library.)*

CHAPTER FIFTEEN

PEACE

*It is to me an Enigma that I cannot solve that our Country, the first in
Wealth, in power, in arms, the mistress of the World, . . . should make
concession after concession and with a cautious and measured policy
truckle to a nation . . . of no character.*

—British lieutenant colonel Robert McDouall, 1815[1]

IN 1812, WILLIAM HAMILTON MERRITT, eighteen years old, was in
love with Catherine Prendergast. She agreed to marry him, but the war
interfered. Although born in the United States, Merritt felt honor-
bound to defend his new home, at St. Catharines in the Niagara District. But the Prendergast family fled from the war, moving back to New
York State, separating the young lovers. In dismay Merritt blasted "this
unnatural, unjust and Distructive War," which he blamed on the United
States as the invading aggressor. He also denounced his uncle William
for fleeing to New York rather than staying to fight: "I am grieved
beyond utterance at his Conduct. His ignorance has ruined him forever.
There is something shocking in the Idea of a man's leaving his country."
Like so many families in Upper Canada, the civil war divided the Mer-
ritts of St. Catharines.[2]

In January 1814 Catherine Prendergast wrote to urge Merritt to
resign his commission and join her in New York. Her entreaty pitted
their love against his ambition. In reply Merritt reasoned that surely she
"would detest the man who deserts his Country," which for Merritt was
Canada and not the United States. "You accuse me of Ambition," he
added. "If I have any, you are the cause of it." Determined to provide
well for his future family, Merritt had latched his ambition to the British
regime in Canada. So he bristled when Catherine teasingly linked Great
Britain to the piratical Algiers as "the two most *despotic* governments of
Earth." In an earnest reply, Merritt rejected "comparing one of the most
magnanimous Governments in the world to a gang of Pirates."[3]

In July 1814, at the battle of Lundy's Lane, American troops captured Merritt and sent him east to Cheshire in Massachusetts as a pris-

William Hamilton Merritt (*1793–1862*), *engraving. From Benson J. Lossing,* The Pictorial Field-Book of the War of 1812 (*New York, 1869*), *602.* (Courtesy of the New York State Library.)

oner. Once again she wrote, begging Merritt to break parole and desert from his service by coming to her. And once again he declared that he could never "desert so just & honorable a Cause."[4]

Irritated by Merritt's priorities, Catherine abruptly replied in January 1815 to declare the engagement doomed by the endless war:

> Situated as we now are, it would be folly to suppose we ever shall meet, at least for a number of years & so uncertain is human life & indeed every thing in this world, that to be anticipating events so far off is what I never can endure with any satisfaction. . . . Knowing you will experience more happiness in your present or what will soon be your pursuits than you would in any other situation, I resign you to them with prayers that the happiness you desire & so truly deserve will shortly be yours. All the consolation I have at present is that by my exertions this unfortunate atachment will wear out like every thing else after a while.

Received at Cheshire on February 9, her letter devastated Merritt.[5]

But there was a happy ending. Within a week surprising news arrived from Europe that British and American negotiators had made a peace treaty to end the war. In March the prisoners at Cheshire won their release, and Merritt hurried west to marry Catherine at her home in Mayville, New York. In the spring the couple moved across the border to live at St. Catharines. In the nick of time, the news of peace had saved their engagement. Ultimately, Merritt won his war by adding Catherine to the honor, status, and property that he had secured by defending Upper Canada.[6]

GHENT

In June 1812 a *combination* of three causes had impelled the Republican Congress to declare war: the British Orders in Council which empowered the Royal Navy to interfere with American maritime commerce; the impressment of sailors from American ships; and the British alliance with native peoples dwelling within the American border. When the British promptly rescinded the Orders in Council, the Americans kept fighting a war for frontier expansion and for sailors' rights. The thorny issue of impressment derived from the fundamental clash between the American concept of the citizen by choice and the British notion of the permanent subject by birth. A Federalist merchant explained:

> The principal subject of dispute is drawn to this point. The American Government alleges that a subject of G[reat] B[ritain] may expatriate himself & that after becoming a citizen of the U. S., by our laws of naturalization, he is free to navigate our ships & that to impress him from thence is on the part of G. B. a violation of our neutral rights & an infringement of our Sovereignty. While G. B. maintains the doctrine that no man can abandon his natural allegiance to his King & that, whenever his services are required by his Monarch, the latter has a right to them & therefore so long as we continue to entice their seamen from them & suffer them to enter our merchant service, they will continue to take them from us whenever they catch them on the ocean.

The Republicans relied on naturalized citizens, primarily Irish-Americans, as voters, sailors, and soldiers. But the British desperately needed the same men to wage global war against Napoleon. Viscount Castlereagh assured an American diplomat that "as England was fight-

ing the battles of the world, as well as for her own existence as an independent Nation, she required the services of all her subjects."[7]

In a supposed compromise, President Madison and Secretary of State
James Monroe proposed that the British cease taking sailors from American ships in return for an American law barring former Britons from
serving on those ships. The British dismissed that offer as hollow, for
they regarded sailors as cheats, American documents as fraudulent, and
the republic as too weak to enforce its laws. The British trusted nothing
but the forcible regulation of American ships and sailors by the Royal
Navy. But that British position infuriated Republicans as reducing their
commerce and people to a neocolonial subordination on the high seas.[8]

In late 1813 the Madison administration accepted a British offer
of negotiations. Aside from Jonathan Russell, the five American peace
commissioners were prominent politicians representing the key regions
of the loose union. Foreign-born Gallatin had long resided in Pennsylvania before serving as Jefferson's and Madison's secretary of the
treasury. Well-educated and socially smooth, Gallatin made the best
diplomat. A president's son, John Quincy Adams was a former Federalist from Massachusetts. Delaware's James A. Bayard was a great political
rarity: a moderate Federalist willing to cooperate with the Republicans.
Henry Clay was a savvy Republican politician who represented Kentucky and western interests. Their disparate backgrounds and goals led
to fierce quarrels, particularly between the austere and thin-skinned
Adams and the hard-drinking and card-playing Clay. But they carefully
kept their disputes hidden from the British.[9]

The three British commissioners were lesser talents, for the imperial
lords had assigned their top diplomats to more important European
negotiations at Vienna. To hold a hard line on maritime issues, the
British commission included William Adams, an admiralty lawyer, and
Lord James Gambier, a veteran naval officer who had led a controversial
attack on neutral Denmark in 1807. The youngest and most active
British negotiator was Henry Goulburn, an undersecretary in the Colonial Office charged with protecting Britain's interests in Canada.
Regarding the war as "unprovoked aggression on the Part of the United
States," Goulburn sought to humiliate the Americans by compelling
major concessions.[10]

Despite the faltering American prospects in the war, Monroe saddled
the American commissioners with unrealistic instructions. They were to
seek an end to British impressment: "This degrading practice must
cease; our flag must protect the crew; or the United States, cannot con-

sider themselves an independent Nation." Monroe also wanted to press the British to surrender Canada to the United States: the height of cheek given the American failure to conquer more than a sliver of land on the east bank of the Detroit River. Indeed, the British had taken more American land, including Michilimackinac and Fort Niagara. But Monroe expected the commissioners to persuade the British that they would inevitably lose Canada to a future American war or to a Canadian revolution. So why not avoid that costly bother by giving up Canada right away?[11]

Already scant, American leverage shrank with the collapse of Napoleon's regime in the spring of 1814. That collapse freed up thousands of British troops for service in North America. No longer obliged to remain on the defensive in Canada, the reinforced British armies could invade the United States from multiple directions: attacking northern New York, eastern Maine, the Chesapeake shores, and even New Orleans. Giddy with victory over mighty Napoleon, the British public longed to punish and humble the Americans as aggressors who had indirectly assisted the hated French emperor.[12]

Sobered by the surging British power and resolve, Madison's cabinet lowered its expectations in June. Abandoning the acquisition of Canada and a stop to impressment, the cabinet authorized the negotiators to make a treaty that simply ended the war, restoring the prewar boundaries. The Madison administration hoped that Napoleon's defeat would enable the British to shrink the Royal Navy, dispensing with thousands of sailors and suspending the practice of impressing from American ships.[13]

While the Americans reduced their demands, however, the British increased theirs. In addition to restricting American fishing rights in Canadian waters, the British sought border adjustments meant to improve Canada's security from a future invasion. They coveted eastern Maine, Fort Niagara, and Michilimackinac as well as a broad Indian buffer zone to include most of the American land between the Ohio River and the Great Lakes.[14]

By promising such a buffer zone, British commanders had persuaded their Indian allies to attack the Americans. Having pledged their honor to the Indians, the British commanders pressed their superiors in London to stand by their promises, for they could not defend Canada without native allies. Montreal's powerful fur trade firms also lobbied for the buffer zone to keep their American competitors away from the Great Lakes.[15]

In early August the negotiations opened at Ghent, near Brussels, with the British commissioners arguing that American aggression required more secure boundaries for Canada. Adams lamely replied "that the American Government never had declared the intention of conquering Canada." To refute Adams, the British commissioners cited the proclamations issued in 1812 by Generals Hull and Smyth offering liberation to Canadians. The American commissioners weakly responded that the United States government had never authorized the proclamations, but the British countered that the Madison administration had also never disavowed them. Once again, the British concluded that sophistry and chicanery characterized a republic.[16]

In the heated debate over the proposed Indian buffer zone, the British cast the natives as sovereign allies who had earned British protection against greedy American settlers, speculators, and officials. But the American commissioners bristled at any intrusion on their national sovereignty. Clay denounced "the absurdity" of Britain acting as a guardian "for savage tribes, scattered over our acknowledged territory." The Americans regarded the Indians as a few roaming hunters hoarding fertile lands better owned and worked by American farmers. Adams insisted, "To condemn vast regions of territory to perpetual barrenness and solitude, that a few hundred savages might find wild beasts to hunt upon it, was a species of game law that a nation descended from Britons would never endure." And no treaty could restrain the swelling tide of American settlement: "It was opposing a feather to a torrent." Goulburn responded, "I had, till I came here, no idea of the fixed determination which prevails in the breast of every American to extirpate the Indians and appropriate their territory." He concluded that there would be no peace unless the British abandoned their Indian allies to American domination and dispossession.[17]

RUIN

In October shocking news of the British demands reached the United States. The New England Federalists defended the British terms as the just American deserts for waging an unjust war. But Republicans denounced the terms as meant to ruin the republican union by blocking westward expansion. Monroe blasted "the object of the British Government, by striking at the principal sources of our prosperity, to diminish the importance, if not to destroy the political existence of the United States." A tenuous coalition of restive states, the union could survive no major concession that would alienate a region—say by imposing an Indian buffer zone at the expense of the western states. Monroe assured

Congress, "The United States must relinquish no right, or perish in the struggle. There is no intermediate ground to rest on." Any major concession, he reasoned, would unravel the union and consign the fragments to British domination.[18]

In late 1814 national dissolution seemed plausible because Royal Navy commanders were already pressuring vulnerable American coastal communities to drop out of the war. Unlike most of Massachusetts, the island of Nantucket had a Republican majority, but the people faced starvation from a British naval blockade. In August the islanders accepted a separate peace from Admiral Alexander Cochrane, who lifted the blockade in return for their declaration of neutrality, including a cessation of paying taxes to the United States. At Dartmoor Prison, the British released the prisoners from Nantucket as if they belonged to a distinct and neutral nation. After occupying eastern Maine, the British compelled the inhabitants to take an oath of neutrality. They went further at Eastport, imposing an oath of allegiance, for they claimed that island town as properly a British possession.[19]

Defection from the war threatened to spread throughout New England, as Federalists urged their states to seize control of their own defense or even to make a separate peace with the British. In November 1814 the Federalist governor of Massachusetts, Caleb Strong, sent a secret emissary to Nova Scotia to seek military protection from the British. While Nova Scotia's governor forwarded Strong's proposal to London, a convention of New England Federalists met in Hartford, Connecticut. The convention's secret proceedings encouraged speculation that the delegates would secede from the union and ally with the British, which would provoke civil war within the union.[20]

The Madison administration sent Colonel Thomas Sidney Jesup to Hartford, ostensibly to raise recruits but primarily to keep an eye on the convention. If the delegates did seek secession, Jesup was supposed to secure the national arsenal at Springfield, Massachusetts, and rally local Republicans to defend the union. To support Jesup, Monroe shifted one thousand troops from the Niagara front east to Greenbush near the Massachusetts line. "We should be prepared for all events," Jesup agreed.[21]

But the Federalist delegates were cautious men who settled for half measures. They proposed that the New England states assume their own defense and keep most of their federal tax revenues. They also demanded seven constitutional amendments meant to reduce the political rights of immigrants and the political power of Virginia in the union. In particular, the delegates sought to ban naturalized citizens from holding political office. By presenting these demands to the Republican-controlled Congress, the Federalists could only expect rejection, but that process would buy time to see what the winter and spring would bring. If the war worsened, Congress's rejection of the demands might rankle the public in New England enough to embolden the Federalists to pursue a separate peace and secession in June 1815, when the delegates planned to meet again.[22]

While threatened by unrest in New England, the national government was also in disarray at Washington. In late August the British had swept into the city to burn the government buildings, including the White House and Capitol. The cabinet was in upheaval, for the president had ousted the secretary of war, John Armstrong, as a scapegoat for the British victory. Thereafter Monroe did double duty as head of both the Departments of War and of State. The cabinet suffered another blow when the able but exasperated secretary of the navy, William Jones, announced his resignation effective December 1. And the secretary of the treasury abruptly quit because he was unable to cope with the nation's fiscal crisis.[23]

In December a new secretary of the treasury, Alexander J. Dallas, grimly reported that the government needed $56 million to fund the war in 1815, but he warned that taxes would yield only $15.1 million. Only loans could bridge that gap, but investors had lost confidence in the administration as the war seemed futile and endless. And the nation lacked hard money because American smugglers had exported so much to buy British manufactured goods. For want of cash, the nation's banking system verged on collapse, denying the government the means to shift funds to the military frontiers. In late 1814 a belated attempt to create a new national bank crumbled in bickering between the administration and Congress.[24]

Never good, the military supply system withered as the government failed to pay its officers, troops, and contractors. At Detroit in early 1815 the commander reported, "we are in a wretched situation here—not a dollar in the whole Military department." Unpaid for more than a year, the Detroit troops threatened to mutiny and to go home. Unpaid for seventeen months, Thomas Melville, Jr., had to borrow $5,000 on his own credit to sustain the military prison at Pittsfield. Unless quickly reimbursed by the government, Melville faced financial ruin.[25]

To conquer Canada, Monroe estimated that the nation needed 100,000 regulars, but the army had only 40,000 at the end of 1814. And the financial crisis undercut both retention and expansion of that force, for without money the government could pay neither the rewards to recover deserters nor the large bounties to buy recruits. News of the unpaid troops at the front also depressed recruiting. In desperation, Monroe proposed conscription, but Congress refused for fear of violent public resistance, particularly in New England. With conscription dead, the nation would again have to rely on bounties, which it could no longer afford to pay.[26]

The government seemed on the verge of collapse. Recalling the darkest days of the revolution, an army officer insisted that "a war to try Men's Souls . . . can alone save this Government & this Nation from disunion & disgrace." To survive, the republic needed a miracle, which it got at Ghent. A surprising peace would save more than just the engagement of William Hamilton Merritt and Catherine Prendergast.[27]

NEWS

In October at Ghent, both teams of commissioners played for time, while awaiting good war news from North America to strengthen their hand and to weaken their rival's. On October 3, to rattle the Americans, Goulburn sent an oh-so-polite note to Clay: "If you find Brussels as little interesting as I have done, you will not be sorry to have the occupation of reading the latest Newspapers which I have received." Those British newspapers conveyed the grim news that the British had captured Washington in late August. Clay reported, "I tremble, indeed, whenever I take up a late News paper. Hope alone sustains me." At month's end, he read the consoling news that Baltimore had repulsed a British attack and that Prevost had retreated from Plattsburgh.[28]

Meanwhile, the British commissioners learned of a potential diplomatic rupture at Vienna that threatened to renew war in Europe. Given that possibility, the imperial lords wanted out of the annoying and distracting war with the pesky republic. Doubting that the British could win a decisive victory in North America during the next campaign, the Duke of Wellington advised making a quick peace. Sobered by the new developments, Lord Liverpool directed the British peace commissioners to recognize "the inconvenience of the continuance of the war." The U.S. commissioners benefited from the secondary status of North America for an empire preoccupied with Europe.[29]

The British negotiators abandoned their provocative Indian buffer zone, proposing instead a treaty article restoring their native allies "to all the rights, privileges, and territories which they enjoyed in the year 1811." The American commissioners accepted that vague language because it would do nothing to protect the Indians in the future. A

British official later conceded that the Americans could fulfill the article merely by allowing the Indians "to return to their former Situation for a week or a month." Gallatin explained to Monroe: "I really think that there is nothing but [the] nominal in the Indian article as adopted. . . . You know that there was no alternative between breaking off the negotiations & accepting the article." By settling for the hollow article, the British again abandoned their Indian allies, as in 1783 and 1794.[30]

On the other hand, the British rejected an American proposal to bar the employment of Indians in any future war. British policy sought to protect Indians just enough to retain them as allies. The British also rebuffed an American proposal to safeguard the person or property of any Canadian who had assisted the invaders. The peace treaty would protect neither the disaffected in Canada nor the Indians within the United States.[31]

The second key breakthrough came in late November, when the British agreed to restore the prewar boundary and to permit American forts and warships on the Great Lakes. In exchange for occupied Amherstburg and Sandwich on the Canadian bank of the Detroit River, the Americans would recover Michilimackinac, Fort Niagara, and eastern Maine—save for Eastport, whose fate the commissioners left to a postwar boundary commission. At British insistence, the Americans also agreed that Congress had to ratify or reject the treaty as a package, without amendment, for congressional tinkering had irritated the British in past treaty negotiations. Hostilities would not cease until both governments had ratified the treaty.[32]

Eager to make peace before an expensive new campaign would begin in the spring, the commissioners signed the treaty on December 24. In their haste they set aside the maritime issues that had provoked the war. In the short term, those issues had become moot because, with Napoleon defeated, the Royal Navy no longer needed to interfere with the crews and cargoes of neutral nations. But the issues could revive whenever the British resumed fighting the French. The treaty also referred difficult boundary disputes to postwar commissions, mutually chosen. And the treaty left to subsequent diplomacy the American right to dry fish on Canadian shores and the British claim to navigate the Mississippi River.[33]

Both Americans and Britons thought that the incomplete treaty offered a temporary truce rather than a lasting peace. Clay tepidly defended the treaty as making the best of the nation's bad situation. The terms were "undoubtedly not such as our Country expected at the commencement of the War. Judged of, however, by the actual condition of things, so far as it is known to us, they cannot be pronounced very unfavorable. We lose no territory, I think no honor."[34]

Parliament quickly ratified the treaty, and Viscount Castlereagh celebrated "being released from the millstone of an American war." British manufacturers and export merchants welcomed the reopening of the lucrative American market and the lifting of the menace by American privateers to British shipping. But Canadian merchants and officials felt betrayed by a restoration of the confining border that threatened to suppress the Indians and to facilitate a future American attack. On balance, British public opinion disliked the terms as too soft on the Americans, but the British also balked at the high taxes needed to prolong the war.[35]

In early 1815 news traveled slowly across the Atlantic, at the creeping pace of a sailing ship buffeted by head winds and winter gales. On February 11, six weeks after the signing at Ghent, an official copy of the treaty reached New York City and then passed overland to the national capital two days later. Madison promptly sent the treaty to the Senate with his endorsement, and the Senate unanimously approved on February 16. The next day, the war formally ended when Monroe exchanged ratified copies of the treaty with a newly arrived British diplomat, Anthony St. John Baker.[36]

Reports of peace reached Upper Canada and northern New York in late February. Recent enemies, the officers of both sides could now exchange friendly visits. At Kingston on February 25 Lieutenant John Le Couteur reported, "Several American officers came over from Sackets Harbour with the news. We received them very well, gave them a dinner, and made our Band play 'Yankee Doodle' on drinking the President's health, which gave them great pleasure." The officers of both sides could indulge in a professional solidarity as military men, no longer divided by national and ideological enmity. Le Couteur celebrated the end of "a hot and unnatural war between kindred people. Thank God!"[37]

A stunning and pleasant surprise, the treaty saved the republic from division, doubts, and financial ruin. Welcoming "the heartily cheering intelligence," a Philadelphia merchant, Thomas Cope, confided, "a continuation of the war must have ended in our political dissolution." Giddy with relief, Americans celebrated with parades, fireworks, illuminations, toasts, and ringing bells. "The public manifestations of joy are almost unbounded," Cope noted. In Salem, Massachusetts, a Federalist noted, "Our Town was frantic with joy at the news of Peace. It has come just in season to save our Country from destruction."[38]

Noting the treaty's silence on the causes of the war, most Federalists detected another national disgrace that, they hoped, would at last discredit the Republican party. But one savvy Federalist aptly predicted that the Republicans would downplay the failed invasion of Canada and, instead, portray "a war on our part of pure self defence against the designs of the British to reduce us again to subjection." Indeed, Madison extolled the treaty as "an event which is highly honorable to the nation, and terminates, with peculiar felicity, a campaign signalized by the most brilliant successes." A Federalist complained, "it is attempted to make us believe that all the objects of the war have been obtained, when every thing, for which it was declared has been abandoned."[39]

Having failed to conquer Canada or compel British maritime concessions, the Republicans redefined national survival as victory. Monroe assured the Senate that "our Union has gained strength, our troops honor, and the nation character, by the contest." He concluded, "By the war we have acquired a character and a rank among other nations, which we did not enjoy before." By emphasizing honor rather than territory as the measure of victory, Republicans took their cue from General Jacob Brown, who had developed that theme during his 1814 campaign on the Niagara front. In return, the Republican spin on the peace treaty imparted a rosier glow in memory to Brown's futile campaign.[40]

In early February the myth of the glorious war got a boost with the arrival, on the East Coast, of dramatic news that American troops had won a sensational victory near New Orleans. On January 8, in the war's most lopsided battle, General Andrew Jackson's army had routed six thousand British regulars. At a cost of only thirty minutes and seventy-one casualties, the Americans had killed 290 Britons, wounded 1,262, and captured 484. Before dying in the battle, the overconfident British commander had marched his men across open ground in a frontal assault on entrenched Americans who merely had to blast away at the exposed attackers.[41]

The battle of New Orleans nicely fit the cherished stereotype of bungling Britons unsuited for war in North America, so it became celebrated in American story and song. In fact, the battle was exceptional. Most of the war had been fought in the northern borderland, where Britons and their Indians had been more resourceful and victorious. And at New Orleans the victory primarily belonged to the artillery of the regular army rather than to the celebrated riflemen from the frontier.[42]

A different legend dismisses the battle as inconsequential because it was waged two weeks after the signing of the peace treaty. In fact, the peace did not become official until the exchange of ratifications on February 17, more than a month after the battle of New Orleans. And the battle had an enormous impact on a generation of British officers and officials, who balked at again invading the United States. New Orleans confirmed the lesson of Saratoga and Yorktown from the previous war: that invaders risked destruction within the United States. Thereafter, British restraint gave the Americans a free hand to dispossess Indians. The victory at New Orleans had enduring and massive consequences.[43]

At Dartmoor, news of Jackson's triumph thrilled the American prisoners because it humbled their jailers:

> Nothing now is thought of or talked of, but *New Orleans* and *Jackson*, and *Jackson* and *New Orleans*. We already perceive that we are treated with more respect, and our country spoken of in honorable terms. The language now is—we are all one of the same people. You have all English blood in your veins, and it is no wonder that you fight bravely.

An enormous psychological victory for the Americans, the battle of New Orleans helped to reconcile the British to the peace treaty. In effect, the victory enabled the United States to turn the ambiguous treaty into an advantage in subsequent dealings with the British.[44]

In mid-February news of the great victory merged with the ratification of peace to shape the American memory of the war. Because most Americans learned of New Orleans shortly before hearing of the peace treaty, they believed that their one big victory on land had forced the British to abandon the war. The news from New Orleans and Ghent also coincided with the arrival in Washington of a delegation of New England Federalists bearing the demands of the Hartford Convention. Unlucky in their timing, the delegates were roundly mocked by Republicans as defeatist fools and crypto-traitors. Ignored by Congress and the president, the delegates returned home in a disgrace inflicted by the unanticipated events at New Orleans and Ghent. Thereafter, the Hartford Convention became a synonym for treason, hurled at the Federalists during every election.[45]

Most voters preferred the comforting myth of a glorious war confirmed by an honorable peace, so the Federalists crumbled at the polls, even in New England. In the election of 1816 James Monroe easily won the presidency, and the Federalists lost a third of their seats in Congress, and they would lose half of the rest two years later. "Never was there a more glorious opportunity," Joseph Story boasted, "for the Republican party to place themselves permanently in power."[46]

Hartford Convention Candidate. *A piece of Republican electoral propaganda, this engraving depicts a Federalist candidate as a black devil wearing a monarch's crown and brandishing a flaming torch. Lady Liberty and the American eagle support the Republican candidate, who champions the People's Rights. From Benson J. Lossing,* The Pictorial Field-Book of the War of 1812 *(New York, 1869), 1015.* (Courtesy of the New York State Library.)

HOME

Eager to cut expenditures, Congress cut the size and pay of the army to prewar levels: ten thousand men with privates paid a mere five dollars a month. In March Congress reduced the officers to 674, down from 3,495 in January. During the spring General Jacob Brown chaired the board that reviewed the officers to determine who could stay and who should go. Although Brown claimed that merit alone decided, he favored those who had served and supported him. Two-thirds of his subordinates in the Niagara campaign made the grade, while almost all of the other officers had to make do with three months of severance pay. Brown was a superb political infighter who took care of his protégés by nurturing a hero's reputation.[47]

The Canadian Volunteers could not go home again. Joseph Willcocks was dead, and only a handful of officers and twenty-three enlisted men served to the end in June 1815. To their dismay, Congress refused to compensate them in cash for their property losses, preferring grants of undeveloped, frontier lands—and only to those who had been born in the United States. Accused of embezzlement, Benajah Mallory left the service under a cloud, which darkened in 1816 when he was accused of fraud in issuing certificates for bounty land to men who had never served in the regiment. Settling in Lockport, New York, he landed in the state prison for theft in 1829. Andrew Westbrook moved to Michigan, where he became a county commissioner and supervisor of highways. Increasingly eccentric, he expected neighbors to call him Baron Von Steuben. In Upper Canada he became the dark protagonist of John Richardson's postwar novel *Westbrook, the Outlaw; or the Avenging Wolf.* Abraham Markle helped to found Terre Haute, Indiana, where he rebuilt his fortunes as a miller, land speculator, and innkeeper. The sign of his "Eagle and the Lion" inn featured an American eagle tearing the eyes out of a forlorn British lion. More at home in America, Markle delighted in horse racing, drinking, moneymaking, and lawsuits.[48]

The war could not truly end until both sides repatriated thousands of prisoners. But the American captors struggled to force their British prisoners to return to their military service after experiencing better conditions in the United States. The American commissary general for prisoners, John Mason, instructed a federal marshal, "From the disposition to escape which has been manifested by the B[ritish] Pr[isoner]s in our hands & their great unwillingness to return to their own country, it will be absolutely necessary to have a sufficient guard provided for their security on board the cartel to prevent their rising on the crew & running away with the vessel." Despite Mason's orders, federal marshals struggled to control prisoners eager to remain in America. In April at Baltimore, a magistrate reported that nineteen of the twenty-six held in the jail had escaped when informed that they would be sent home.[49]

In Britain, the captive Americans longed to go home. At Dartmoor, a prisoner vividly recalled the news of the peace treaty:

> After a momentary stupor, acclamations of joy burst forth from every mouth. It flew like wild fire through the prison; and "Peace! Peace! Peace!" echoed throughout these dreary regions. . . . Some screamed, holloed, danced, sung, and capered, like so many Frenchmen.

But none would be released until after word arrived, in late March, that the United States had ratified the treaty. Even then, the logistical challenge of shipping home the Dartmoor prisoners kept them locked up into the spring. To bring home the six thousand Americans held in England would require twenty-four ships. Alas, in the spring of 1815, few vessels were available in England for charter, and only at exorbitant rates, because of the surging demand for ships to carry British manufactured goods to the reopened American market. Impatient for release, the Dartmoor prisoners treated their guards with increasing contempt, which brought the prison to the brink of an eruption.[50]

The explosion began with the American pastime on April 6, when some bored prisoners were playing ball in a prison yard. A powerful batter smote the ball over the wall. When the guards ignored appeals to toss the ball back, angry prisoners began to dig at the wall, dislodging a large stone to make a hole to get to their ball. Fearing a mass breakout, the guards rang the alarm bell. The ringing attracted an unruly throng of prisoners, who hooted at the guards and hurled sods and stones. Fed up, Captain Thomas Shortland ordered his troops to fire into the air to disperse the prisoners. Then he sent his guards, armed with bayonets, to drive the prisoners into their barracks to be locked up for the night. Drawn from the Somerset militia, the guards were newly arrived, inexperienced, and easily rattled. Losing control, they shot and lunged in ten minutes of fury that subdued the prisoners but left seven dead and thirty-two wounded.[51]

Angry prisoners blamed Shortland for "the Dartmoor Massacre," deemed a replica of the Boston Massacre that had helped to spark the American Revolution. But the British and American governments wanted to avoid renewed war, so they quickly appointed commissioners to investigate. Their report sought to soothe American public opinion by describing the bloodshed as a tragic accident provoked by unruly prisoners. While charging the soldiers with an overreaction, the commissioners cleared Shortland of responsibility and recommended that no one be punished. By offering compensation to the families of the dead men, the prince regent tried to smooth over the crisis, but it persisted in lurid and popular accounts published by prisoners in American newspapers and books.[52]

The "Dartmoor Massacre" lit a fire under the American consul, Reuben G. Beasley, to find the vessels needed to take the prisoners home. Eager to avoid more bloody trouble, the British agreed to bear half the cost and to loan transport ships. The releases began on April 20, but persisted into August, as twenty-four voyages gradually carried 5,978 men to America. En route, many prisoners mutinied to seize control of the ships, redirecting them away from the destination chosen by Beasley—Norfolk, Virginia—to New York City or Boston, which brought them closer to their homes.[53]

Boarded at Plymouth on June 30, 1815, the *Santa Maria* carried the

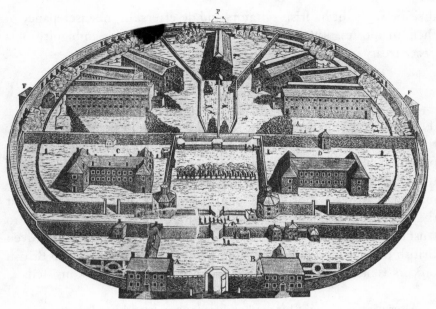

Massacre of the American Prisoners of War at Dartmoor, *1815, engraving by George C. Smith. From Benjamin Waterhouse, ed.,* A Journal of a Young Man of Massachusetts *(Boston: Row & Hooper, 1816).* (Courtesy of the New York State Library.)

surviving twenty of the original twenty-three Irish-American soldiers threatened with execution as traitors by the British. These prisoners also seized their vessel, redirecting it to Boston, where they landed on August 9, ending their long nightmare. In his memoirs General Winfield Scott later insisted that he had met the liberated men upon arrival in New York City on July 9. Wishful thinking, that story conveyed his sense that their safe return had vindicated his efforts on their behalf. And he wanted to recall the war as an American victory that had compelled the British to recognize the soldiers as naturalized citizens rather than runaway subjects.[54]

The Marquis of Tweeddale, a British general, also nurtured a memory that placed Irish-Americans at the center of the war—but with a different spin. In March 1815 he visited the United States. On board a sloop on Lake Champlain, a boatload of Irish deserters from the British army rowed up to insult him. To Tweeddale's delight, the sloop's American-born crew "came on deck and threatened to throw them into the Lake. They called them . . . cowardly deserters daring to insult officers in a friendly country." In this memory, Tweeddale interpreted the peace as a reconciliation of Americans and Britons, who rejected the division wrought by Irish agitators and deserters. In the discrepancy of their memories, Tweeddale and Scott registered the ambiguity of a peace treaty mute to the causes of the war.[55]

IRON FRONTIER

The British commanders in the Great Lakes country tried to reconcile the Indians to peace terms that fell far short of what they had been promised. The natives would not recover the country north and west of the Ohio River, nor would the British retain the key fort at Michilimackinac. Instead, the Indians had to settle for a vague promise that they would be restored to their possessions of 1811, and they had to trust in their bitter enemies, the Americans, to keep that promise. Given British presents and hollow promises, angry chiefs rebuked the British officers as liars and deceivers. The Lakota chief Little Crow insisted:

> After we have fought for you, endured many hardships, lost some of our people and awakened the vengeance of our powerful neighbours, you make peace for yourselves, leaving us to obtain such terms as we can. You no longer need our service; you offer us these goods to pay us for having deserted us. But no, we will not take them; we hold them and yourselves in equal contempt.

But most Indians were too impoverished by war to join Little Crow in rejecting the presents of consolation.[56]

The British army officers resented having to break their own pledges made throughout the war. At Michilimackinac, Lieutenant Colonel Robert McDouall wondered how the world's most powerful empire could grant such generous terms to the crass and defeated republic:

> It is to me an Enigma that I cannot solve that our Country, the first in Wealth, in power, in arms, the mistress of the World, swaying the destinies of Europe that she has delivered, . . . that a country exalted to the utmost pinnacle of human greatness should make concession after concession and with a cautious and measured policy truckle to a nation . . . of no character.

During the spring of 1815 McDouall delayed returning Michilimackinac to the Americans in the hope that his home government would reconsider the peace treaty. The delay aggravated Americans, for the fortified island was the strategic pivot of Indian trade and relations deep within the continent. Without that fort, the Americans could not persuade Indians that further resistance was futile.[57]

To pressure the British, the American government clung to Amherstburg, which the British were especially keen to recover so that they could repatriate the Indian refugees clustered at Burlington Heights, where they strained supplies and plundered civilians. At last, in late May, General Drummond ordered McDouall to surrender Michilimackinac as soon as he had built a new fort on nearby Drummond Island. Informed of that order, the Americans transferred Amherstburg to a British garrison on July 1. Seventeen days later, American troops took possession of Michilimackinac.[58]

Bloody memories and bitter feelings persisted after the exchange of occupied posts. In the Detroit Valley, John McDonnell ran afoul of the new British commander and his Indian allies. Born in Scotland, McDonnell had moved to Upper Canada as a boy, and he later became a merchant's clerk at Amherstburg. In 1810 he moved across the river to Detroit, where he served as an American officer when the war broke out. When Hull surrendered in 1812, Indians plundered McDonnell's home and store. During the British occupation, he spent large sums to ransom American prisoners taken by the Indians. After the Americans recovered Detroit and seized Amherstburg in 1813, McDonnell commanded a volunteer company that raided into Upper Canada.[59]

In June 1815 McDonnell visited British-held Sandwich, where he was arrested and jailed as a traitor by Lieutenant Colonel Reginald James. A British officer explained, "To assist a fellow of that kind that took up Arms against his Country & raised a Corps to fight against us would be damnation. I hope our Government will keep a good look out to give the rascal what he deserves—a Rope." James told McDonnell, "Don't you know it is as much as I can do to prevent your life from being taken by the Indians," who wanted revenge for a warrior killed by McDonnell's men during the war. By bribing a sentinel, McDonnell broke out of the military guardhouse. For three days and nights he hid in the woods, dodging British and Indian search parties, before he could escape across the river to Detroit. But the British confiscated McDonnell's property at Amherstburg.[60]

A parallel episode unfolded at Michilimackinac after the Americans resumed control and sought to purge British influence. The new commanders, Lieutenant Colonel Talbot Chambers and Major William H. Puthuff, were staunch republicans who despised the British for their Indian alliance. In 1815 they especially wanted to get rid of Elizabeth Mitchell, an Ojibwa woman and trader who had married the British military surgeon, Dr. David Mitchell. In July he removed with the British garrison to Drummond Island, but she stayed behind at Michilimackinac to continue trading with Indians for furs. Distrusting her influence, the American officers canceled her license to sell liquor, barred her from meeting with visiting Indians, and encouraged soldiers to plunder her garden and cornfield. When McDouall protested, Chambers and Puthuff replied that they would heed no meddling by a British officer. In October Puthuff prepared to arrest Elizabeth Mitchell, but she escaped at night in a canoe to Drummond Island.[61]

Her ouster from Michilimackinac and that of McDonnell from Amherstburg offer mirror images. Reclaiming those posts from occupation, both the British and the Americans purged people distrusted as traitors and spies. But they did so in service to contrasting notions of the proper place of Indians in the restored society. At Amherstburg, the British commander permitted Indians to plunder, evict, and threaten men who had fought against them. By contrast, at Michilimackinac, the Americans ousted an Indian woman with British ties. Where the British relied on native peoples as allies, the Americans sought to subordinate and isolate them from British influence.

Although the Americans lost the northern war to conquer Canada, they won the western war to subdue Indian resistance. In 1813, at the battle of the Thames, they had killed Tecumseh, their most formidable Indian adversary and the chief proponent of native unity and resistance. On the southern frontier in 1814, Andrew Jackson had employed superior numbers to crush the Creeks, who lived in present-day Alabama. He had then forced them to surrender more than 20 million acres of land—over half of their domain. Although the Treaty of Ghent committed the Americans to restore Indians to their prewar lands, the Creeks recovered nothing.[62]

To the north, in the Great Lakes country, American officers held treaty councils with most of the native nations during the summer of 1815. Many Indians attended to get the presents and provisions customary at councils, for their villages and crops had been devastated or neglected during the war, reducing many to starvation. Held at Spring Wells, near Detroit, and at Portage des Sioux, on the Mississippi River, the councils adhered to the letter, if not the spirit, of the Treaty of Ghent by granting peace and presents to Indians without compelling new land concessions. But the commissioners did pressure the Indians to ratify disputed land cessions made before the war.[63]

At Spring Wells, the American commissioners clung to a controversial prewar cession of two million acres in southeastern Michigan. The

U.S. government needed that land for a surge in settlement meant to improve Detroit's security from British and Indian attack in the future. The new settlers would provide a larger militia and fill the dangerous gap between Detroit and Ohio: a domain of swamps and forests exploited by Indian warriors to ambush American supply convoys during the war. The U.S. secretary of war explained, "It is an object of the first importance to the nation, with a view to any future war which may occur with the British Empire, that the settlements of the state of Ohio should be connected with those in the Michigan Territory, with the least possible delay."[64]

At the peace councils the American commissioners boasted of their new military power, and they denigrated the British as weak and defeated. Citing Andrew Jackson's great victory at New Orleans, the commissioners argued that the Indians must look only to the American president, and not to the British king, as their great father, as the sole font of presents and advice. Invoking the terrible name of the "Merciless Jackson . . . as the Instrument of Vengeance," the commissioners warned that natives faced destruction if they resisted the Americans in the vain hope of British help.[65]

The American chatter offended the British officers along the border. How dare such upstarts impugn the might of an empire that had crushed Napoleon? And what had the Americans done during the war to merit their boasts of new power? The American canards menaced Canadian security, for they might persuade Indians to forsake the cross-border alliance that the British counted on if war resumed. At Drummond Island, an indignant McDouall assured visiting Ottawa that the hated American "Big Knives" sought "to frighten you with words where their Arms [had] failed . . . They often boasted they would drive us from the Canadas, but in every attempt to do so, they failed with great loss."[66]

At the American treaty councils, the commissioners also announced plans to construct new forts on the Mississippi River and along the western shore of Lake Michigan. "This is the time," an American Indian agent explained, "to expel the British entirely from the Indian country. Such another opportunity may never again present itself." By demonstrating American domination, the new forts would refute British claims that the Indians remained sovereign peoples. During the summer of 1816, American troops rebuilt Fort Dearborn, at the mouth of the Chicago River, and constructed new forts near Prairie du Chien, on the upper Mississippi, and at the mouth of the Fox River on Green Bay.[67]

The garrisons enforced a new law passed by Congress banning all foreigners from trading with Indians within the American border.

When a British diplomat complained, John Quincy Adams retorted, "A bitter experience of thirty years had proved that all the Indian Wars in which we had been involved, had been kindled by the pestilential breath of British agents and Traders." By imposing an American trade monopoly within the border, the government tried to exclude British influence from the Indian country. Delighted by the new law and new forts, the governor of the Michigan Territory, Lewis Cass, exulted, "A very few years more will present an iron frontier which [will] laugh to scorn the combined efforts of British & Indians."[68]

To resist the new forts and trade restrictions, the Indian chiefs sought military help from their British allies. In the Great Lakes country, the British officers empathized with the Indians, casting the new forts as a violation of the pledge in the peace treaty to restore natives to their 1811 situation. McDouall feared that "the whole of the Western Indians" would be "completely hemmed in, thoroughly in the power of the Americans, & their assistance [to Britain] in any future war *hopeless*." And once Canada lost its protective screen of Indian allies, "the hordes of Ohio and Kentucky eager for plunder and revenge could . . . sweep the defenceless upper Province like a Pestilence. *I think the present Crisis presents too strong a temptation for such a Government*," by which he meant the volatile republic. Canada's new governor-general, Sir Gordon Drummond, expressed a painful sense of dilemma:

> Many of our faithful allies will apply for succour in their distress. If it is refused them, we force them into the power of their bitterest Enemies. If it is granted them, we inevitably bring on another Rupture between ourselves and the United States.

Damned if he did and damned if he did not, Drummond had to obey his restraining orders from London, which he enforced on his subordinates in the Indian country. When the native chiefs demanded help against the new American forts, a British agent snapped, "I have my Great Father's orders to obey and all the Indians in the universe will not make me deviate from them."[69]

RIVER

In 1815–16 a cold war persisted along the Detroit River, as American officials and settlers confronted the British and their Indian allies in three ways. First, by restricting the movement of Indians, the Americans asserted their sovereignty at the expense of native nations. Second, the

Michilimackinac, on Lake Huron, *engraving by Richard Dillon, 1813. The British fort occupies the hill in the background, overlooking the traders' village in the foreground, beside the island's harbor.* (Courtesy of the McCord Museum, McGill University, Montreal.)

Americans promoted the desertion of British soldiers and sailors, weakening British military power on the border. Third, the Americans challenged British attempts to inspect lake vessels for deserters, compelling diplomats to confront an issue sidestepped in the Treaty of Ghent. In all three confrontations, the people and officials of Detroit acted with "aggravating and vexatious tenacity," in the words of one British officer.[70]

A deft politician, Governor Cass made the most of the popular animus in Michigan toward the British and their Indian allies. During their wartime occupation of that territory, the British had tolerated an Indian plundering which had impoverished and embittered the settlers. After the war, Cass denounced the British for continuing to provide provisions, presents, and flattering speeches at Amherstburg and Drummond Island to thousands of Indians visiting from the American side of the border. The British sought to maintain, at a low level, an alliance for full mobilization in the event of another war with the Americans. Welcoming Indians, Lieutenant Colonel James promised, "Your Great Father . . . will place you on his pillow at night that he may remember you early in the morning."[71]

Dreading the British hospitality as a menacing interference with American sovereignty over the natives, Cass sought to "prevent the Indians from crossing to the British without our knowledge & consent." While working to keep American Indians within that boundary, Cass also tried to keep out the Indians who had remained with the British during the war. He accused the Kickapoo and the Sauk of crossing over to kill the cattle and to steal the horses of American settlers. But he ignored Indian complaints that Americans breached the border to steal the horses of natives and to shoot at them when they fished in the river at night from lighted canoes.[72]

On October 4, five Kickapoo paddled to Grosse Island, on the American side of the channel. They claimed that they came to hunt squirrels, but the local farmers accused them of shooting cattle and hogs. A patrol of ten American soldiers and an officer ordered the Indians to return to the British shore. As the hunters paddled away, a soldier shot a hunter named Akockis in the back. Taken ashore at Amherstburg, he died the next day.[73]

The killing angered Lieutenant Colonel James, who protested to Cass. Posing as the leader of a cross-border native alliance, James insisted that the peace treaty had restored not just the Indian lands of 1811 but the British interest and influence in the Indian country within the United States. He claimed that the Indians looked to the British "for a fulfillment of that solemn agreement, which insures to them free and unmolested Ingress and Egress through all parts of America." To his superiors, James warned that Cass sought "to cut off all communication between Great Britain and the Western Indians," which would compel them "to become allies of America, and if they do, Canada is lost." Eager to keep the peace, but on British terms, James urged Cass to surrender the soldier for a murder trial in Canada. Otherwise, James threatened that the Indians would take a bloody revenge against the American settlements.[74]

In a bristling reply, Cass rejected James's concern and jurisdiction. Scorning both British advice and Indian threats, the governor vowed that American magistrates would investigate and adjudicate the death. Cass lectured James that "a British officer has consequently no right to require, nor ought an American officer to give, an explanation upon the subject." Rejecting the mixed and overlapping sovereignties of an Indian borderland, Cass insisted on a strict boundary that separated the British from Indians under American rule:

> The Jurisdiction of the United States and of Great Britain within their Territorial Limits is exclusive. . . . We do not acknowledge in principle, nor shall we ever admit in practice, the right of any foreign authorities to interfere in any arrangement or discussion between us and the Indians living within our Territory. Any other principle would render the Sovereignty of the United States merely nominal and, by giving to the agents of another Government the Right of Interfering, would lay the foundation for continuous disputes.

Rather than turn to the British for mediation, complaining Indians must seek redress only from American officials. But a hasty American investigation cleared the murdering soldier on the alleged grounds that he had shot in self-defense, although Akockis had taken the fatal bullet in his back.[75]

While Cass sought to close the border to Indian movement, he kept it open for British deserters fleeing to Michigan. Here too he pushed to win on the river a diplomatic goal unfulfilled at Ghent, where the British had again rejected an American offer to extradite deserters in return for a ban on impressment. To pressure the British to reconsider, American officials tacitly welcomed a postwar surge of deserters across the border.[76]

During the spring of 1815, hundreds of British soldiers escaped into America before the high command could send their regiments back to Europe. At least 145 fled in April and another 295 in May, followed by 140 in June, when most of the troops in Canada were put onto ships to return home. A British diplomat complained that "several Sergeants of the most unblemished characters, without a single grievance to complain of, had absconded with many of their men." Lamenting "the disgraceful Desertion that prevails throughout the army," General Frederick P. Robinson concluded, "Neither the Army nor Navy can place confidence in any one under the rank of a commissioned officer."[77]

The deserters poured across the Niagara, St. Lawrence, and Detroit Rivers, usually in stolen boats or canoes. Often they carried other stolen goods to sell to conniving Americans who offered encouragement, haven, alcohol, and employment. In September 1815 James worried, "The System of desertion and robbery is now carried on to such an extent as to alarm and shake the force intended for the defence of this

Country." When Cass refused to return the deserters, James accused the tricky Americans of acting "under the most subtill cloak of punctilio . . . In fact, Sir, nothing can equal the duplicitous transactions carried on in this Quarter."[78]

On the night of September 3–4, 1815, eight sailors deserted from the British schooner *Confiance* anchored in the Detroit River. They robbed the trunks of several officers before stealing a boat and rowing to the American shore, where they found a tavern and got drunk. The following night, Lieutenant Alexander Vidal pursued with twelve loyal sailors. Landing at Grosse Pointe on the American side, Vidal found one drunken deserter named Thomas Rymer and forced him into a canoe, which returned to the *Confiance*. Searching for the other deserters, Vidal ran into an American militia patrol, which arrested him. Vidal's superior officer, Commodore Edward Owen, appealed to Cass for Vidal's release and the return of the remaining deserters and their loot. Owen hoped for an informal, local resolution to subdue "those irritable feelings which it is so desirable shall be forgotten."[79]

Instead, Cass exploited "those irritable feelings" to score propaganda and political points at the British expense. He failed to seek and return the stolen boat and other goods, and he retained Vidal for trial. Indeed, Cass demanded that Owen return Rymer, the deserter taken from American soil. With equal duplicity, Owen replied that the British could not return Rymer because he had repented of his desertion: "It would be extraordinary, indeed, were I to expose the Loyalty of any subject of His Majesty to be assailed by all the Arts which Interest or prejudice can possibly invent."[80]

As with Akockis, the Americans brazened out a victory in the Vidal case. On October 9, a jury convicted him of provoking a riot and of disturbing the peace, and the judge levied a hefty fine: $631.48. The British military paid the fine, which released Vidal to return to the *Confiance*. With the legal point made by the conviction, President Madison pardoned Vidal and remitted his fine, but the British had to desist from pursuing their deserters across the border.[81]

In search of deserters, British naval officers did continue to stop and inspect American vessels on Lake Erie and in the Detroit River. During the summer of 1816, in the most heated case, the British warship *Tecumseth*, named for the great Indian chief, stopped and boarded an American merchant schooner, the *Union*. The names nicely represented a confrontation that pitted the British–Indian alliance against the United States. Seizing upon the episode, Cass pressed the British to cease meddling with American ships: "From the tone and temper of public sentiment, if this practice is continued, I am confident it will terminate in blood."[82]

In 1816 Cass's pressure paid off, as the imperial lords backed down, choosing peace at the expense of Indian and Canadian interests. When push came to shove, the imperial government favored economic interests at home, which wanted to keep open the American market for British manufactures. Eager also to avoid the high costs of another war, the imperial lords directed James and Owen to cease their testy exchanges with Cass over political issues best left to diplomats. Lord Bathurst instructed Canada's officers to treat Americans and their ships in a manner "strictly Conformable to the Relations of Amity and Friendship so happily subsisting between the two Nations."[83]

To complete the British retreat within their border, they accepted an American proposal to demilitarize the Great Lakes. In the Rush-Bagot agreement of April 1817, both sides reduced their naval forces on the Great Lakes to a bare minimum: no more than one small warship each on Lake Ontario and two per nation for the upper Great Lakes. And no lake ship could mount more than a single cannon. Lowering tensions and saving money, both nations disarmed and sold (or laid up) almost all of their warships on the lakes.[84]

The imperial government accepted the new American control over the lands and natives within their border, as well as over their own merchant ships on the rivers and lakes. Obeying orders, Britain's frontier officers stopped boarding American vessels on the lakes, which set a precedent also followed by the Royal Navy operating in the Atlantic. Unable to defeat impressment during the war or at Ghent, the Americans instead prevailed by pressing postwar confrontations along the Detroit River. By abandoning impressment and leaving the Indians to their American fate, the British gave the United States a belated victory in the War of 1812.[85]

VICTORY

All too soon, the British forgot that the Indians had helped to save Canada from the American invasions in 1812 and 1813. By intimidating American troops, the warriors had done more to foil the invaders than had the Canadian militia, but a postwar myth glorified the militia and degraded the Indians. Difficult allies, they had irritated British commanders by coming and going as they chose and by consuming great quantities of presents and provisions. British officers also felt uneasy about their own complicity in the native mode of war. Embarrassed by

American propaganda, the British officers sought to distance themselves from allies increasingly disdained as savages. Lieutenant Le Couteur insisted, "The Mohawks of whom we have all heard so much, are mostly cowards, thieves, and dirty."[86]

Upper Canadian farmers denounced the Indians as plunderers. Initially encouraged by British officers to intimidate the disaffected, the plundering became indiscriminate in 1813 and 1814 as Indian refugees from the west crowded into the Niagara District. Some exasperated farmers lashed back. In November 1814, ten vigilantes surprised and butchered three sleeping Indians camped near Stoney Creek. A fourth native suffered wounds but escaped to identify the attackers. The leading vigilante, Samuel Green, claimed that he had been "Dispoiled of Every thing by the Indians in the presence of Capt. Norton of the Indian Department." A magistrate arrested Green and two brothers, casting them into the York jail, but the magistrates released them without a trial in late 1815. Their legal impunity measured the declining clout of natives in Upper Canada.[87]

On both sides of the border, the war had deepened the division between the Buffalo Creek and the Grand River Haudenosaunee, who had fought and killed one another, particularly at the battle of Chippawa in July 1814. To make their own peace, the Grand River and Buffalo Creek chiefs met in council at Fort George in August 1815. But they failed to resolve the schism between their rival council fires as each group of chiefs claimed to represent the true Haudenosaunee confederacy of ancient tradition.[88]

The split made it easier for the British and the Americans to press the divided Haudenosaunee to cede more lands in New York and Upper Canada. In New York, the Ogden Land Company claimed an insidious "preemption right" to buy the remaining native lands. To procure those lands, the company had to push the Indians to move west. Politically powerful, the company relied on Peter B. Porter and Governor Daniel D. Tompkins to pressure the Haudenosaunee. During the war, Porter had gained great influence with the natives by supplying, paying, and leading their warriors in the Niagara campaigns of 1813 and 1814. Eager to accelerate economic development in western New York, Tompkins and Porter wanted to extinguish native title to their remaining lands.[89]

In Upper Canada the Haudenosaunee and the Mississauga faced similar pressures to surrender their lands. From 75,000 in 1815, the settler population doubled to 150,000 in 1824, overwhelming the eight thousand natives in the colony. Between 1815 and 1824 the government secured nearly 7.4 million acres in a series of one-sided land cession treaties. By the mid-1820s, most of the colony's natives were restricted to reserves that resembled the American reservations.[90]

During the 1820s British policy also undermined the warrior culture that had previously defended Upper Canada. The lieutenant governor, Sir Peregrine Maitland, pressured the natives to embrace the Christian faith and morality and to practice the European mode of agriculture, rather than their traditional mix of hunting, fishing, gathering, and horticulture. As Christian farmers, Indian men seemed less threatening than as armed and roaming hunters and warriors. In 1821 a visiting American missionary met with Maitland, who "expressed in strong terms his approbation of what was doing in the U. States, for the benefit of our Indians; rejoiced very sincerely in our success, and manifested his readiness to co-operate with us ... for the accomplishment of the great and common object in view, the complete civilization of the Indians." Prior to the war, no British lieutenant governor would have endorsed the American policy that sought to restrict, dispossess, and transform Indians. But after the war Upper Canada's Indian policy converged with the American model. That convergence made it easier for the British to forsake their alliance with the Indians within the American border.[91]

Superficially, the war seems to have been an inconsequential draw, for the peace treaty changed neither Canada's boundary nor British policies. But that limited view diminishes the war to a simple struggle between two nations, the British and the Americans. And the superficial view abruptly stops with ratification of the Treaty of Ghent. A wider and deeper perspective reveals an ultimate American victory that secured continental predominance. For, in addition to fighting the British to the north, the Americans had attacked Indians to the west in a struggle that began before the declaration of war and persisted after the peace treaty.[92]

During 1815–16, the Americans exploited the ambiguous peace treaty to consolidate their dominion over the natives within their boundary. By pushing new settlements into Michigan, building new forts, barring British traders, and restricting Indian movement across the border, the Americans gradually isolated the natives from their British allies. A British officer attested that the Americans sought "the total extinction of all British influence amongst those Indians from whom they had suffered so much during the war." He noted the "anxiety which the American Government evinced from the moment the Peace was signed in effecting this separation." The Americans forced the British to choose between alliance with the Indians and peace with the republic. By choosing peace, the British accepted the Americans' continental power.[93]

Before the war, Americans had felt tormented by the insecurity and instability of their risky experiment in a republic on a continental scale. Both Federalists and Republicans had dreaded a fatal synergy between domestic and foreign enemies. While Federalists expected the Republicans to betray the republic to France, the Republicans dreaded that the Federalists would help British invaders. In 1815 those fears dissolved with the dramatic conjunction of the peace treaty, the victory at New Orleans, and the disgrace of the Federalist convention at Hartford. The triumphant Republicans felt more confident that republican union would endure. Gallatin celebrated the new nationalism: "The people . . . are more American; they feel and act more as a nation; and I hope that the permanency of the Union is thereby better secured."[94]

No single cause accounts fully for the repeated failures of the American invasion of Canada during the war. Instead, those defeats derived from a linked set of follies. The bid to conquer failed, in part, because the Republicans had no clear idea of what they would do with Canada, a confusion which undercut their appeal to the Upper Canadians. During the war, the Canadians steadily lost their little faith as the Americans took plunder and lost battles. The invaders did more looting than winning in Canada because most Americans balked at the discipline of military life and because too few officers inspired confidence in their men. The United States also failed to recruit and to supply an army sufficient to overcome the environmental challenge of waging war in a northern borderland of immense forests, vast lakes, and stark seasonal swings in the weather. When thrust into combat in that environment, too many soldiers panicked as they fought their own vivid nightmares of Indians cast as bloodthirsty savages. And the republic's leaders dispersed their limited forces to fight in marginal areas instead of concentrating their men to strike at Canada's core on the St. Lawrence River. The republic's bitter internal divisions also promoted spying for, and smuggling with, the British, which further compromised the armies of invasion.

Although the British had fewer men (until 1814) and felt disappointed in their support within Upper Canada, they repeatedly repelled attacks because of the multiple, systemic failures of the republic. Those interacting failures generally derived from a fundamental division within the United States. In 1800–1801, the Republicans had triumphed electorally by deriding as aristocratic the Federalist bid to construct a national government with the "energy" to levy taxes and to build an army and navy. Thereafter, embittered Federalists became obstructionists when the republic went to war without an adequate military or sufficient revenue, for they hoped that defeats would disabuse the voters of their illusions. But most of the voters ultimately preferred to make scapegoats of the Federalists for the failures of the war, while crediting the Republicans for winning the peace.

So a war that had exposed the republic's weaknesses became, in memory, a war that had proven its strengths. Only a few Republicans wished to look back in sorrow. In 1816 John Quincy Adams soberly (but privately) wrote to this father, "my country men . . . look too intently to their Triumphs & turn their eyes too lightly away from their disasters." He felt that Americans were "rather more proud than they have reason [to be] of the War."[95]

But illusions often prove paradoxically valuable. The new confidence in the republic enabled Americans to accept the persistence of British Canada as innocuous. After 1815–16 the northern border also seemed more secure as the British reduced their support for the native peoples within the United States. The ultimate legacy of the war was that the empire and the republic would share the continent along a more clearly defined border more generous to the Americans and more confining to the British—but most ominous to the Indians.

Sacket's Harbour, L. Ontario, U.S. Naval Station, *pen-and-ink drawing by John J. Bigsby, 1819. After the war the American navy mothballed its Lake Erie fleet, covering them with pitched wooden roofs. The largest warship, the massive U.S.S.* New Orleans, *received an entire warehouse, at the right. The elaborate and expensive shelters conveyed the American expectation that the war might soon resume on the Great Lakes.* (Courtesy of Library and Archives Canada.)

The Right Reverend Alexander Macdonell, *oil painting by an unknown artist. A military chaplain in the Glengarry Light Infantry, he later became the Catholic bishop of Kingston.* (Courtesy of Library and Archives Canada, C-11059.)

CHAPTER SIXTEEN

ALIENS

There are thousands, aye tens of thousands of Englishmen, Scotchmen, and above all, of Irishmen, now in the United States, who only wait till the standard be planted in Lower Canada, to throw their strength and numbers to the side of democracy.

—William Lyon Mackenzie, 1837[1]

A STOUT AND FIERY MAN, Alexander Macdonell combined a staunch Loyalism with his devout Catholicism. Born in 1762 at Glengarry in the Scottish Highlands, Macdonell studied for the priesthood and became a chaplain in the British army. Ambitious and energetic, he helped to recruit and organize a regiment of fellow Catholics from the Highlands. In 1798 they fought against the rebellion in Ireland, impressing their British commanders. But in 1802, during a brief interlude of European peace, the British government disbanded the Glengarry regiment to cut costs. In 1804, seeking a new challenge, Macdonell immigrated to Glengarry, a county in Upper Canada. He joined Catholic Highlanders who had moved there during the 1780s as Loyalist refugees from New York, where they had settled a decade before. As the Catholic vicar general (and later as bishop) for Upper Canada, Macdonell tirelessly organized congregations and built new chapels.[2]

Before the war, Macdonell lobbied the government to subsidize the transportation of more Highlanders to Upper Canada to form "a strong barrier against the contagion of Republican principles so rapidly diffusing among the people of this Province by the industry of the settlers from the United States." His former commander in Ireland, General Peter Hunter, supported Macdonell's plan, but the home government balked, bending to the political opposition from Highlands landlords, who wanted to keep their tenants at home. In early 1812 Generals Brock and Prevost did approve Macdonell's proposal to revive the Glengarry Regiment in Canada. Macdonell became the fighting chaplain, who excommunicated any men who held back in battle. But most of the

Glengarries fought hard and well through the war, bolstering his political clout.[3]

At war's end Macdonell again called on the government to subsidize Scots immigration to bolster Upper Canada's security against the American "Contagion of democracy." By failing to do so before the war, "the place which those loyal emigrants would have occupied in the Province is now filled with the worst description of settlers from the United States." Worse still, by discouraging Scots and Irish immigration to Canada, the government had unwittingly diverted them to the United States. And they left Britain, in Macdonell's words,

> under an irritation of mind, which in their new adopted Country, became an irreconcilable and riveted antipathy towards the British Government, and hence the reason we have seen so many of them stand foremost in the front ranks of the American Army in every attempt that has been made during the war to overrun these provinces.

By strengthening the United States, that emigration of discontent had menaced Canada, which had also been compromised within by newcomers from America.[4]

Father Macdonell sought to reverse the double tide of migration that had threatened the British empire in North America: of Irish and Scots to strengthen the United States, and of Americans to weaken Upper Canada. By sponsoring immigration to Canada and away from the United States, the empire could form "a strong population of loyal subjects and . . . such a formidable barrier as would baffle all the efforts of an invading enemy." Endowed with grateful and loyal subjects, the colony would no longer need to gamble on former citizens as settlers.[5]

Many British officers and officials agreed with Macdonell. Colonel Edward Baynes blamed the difficulties of the war on "the American Interloper industriously undermining the fidelity of his Neighbours by disseminating democracy, affording intelligence to the Enemy, and frequently concluding his career by going over to him." John Strachan also wanted to replace the Americans with Britons, diverted from migrating to the United States, for "to lose good subjects is a serious evil to the empire."[6]

Baynes, Macdonell, and Strachan renounced John Graves Simcoe's vision of Upper Canada as a haven for discontented Americans. Simcoe had treated Americans as subjects who could—and should—return to the empire. By inviting them to settle in Upper Canada, he tried to undermine the republic and to bolster the empire. But he drew into the colony a motley population distrusted by later colonial officials. William Dummer Powell concluded that Simcoe's "head was filled with vast utopian projects among which the least rational, and ultimately the most ruinous to the Colony, was to restore the old British Colonies to the Empire and a Persuasion that he was to be the Instrument."[7]

After the War of 1812, Britons recast Upper Canada as a defensive bastion rather than as a forward base for recovering the lost thirteen colonies. As a defensive outpost, Upper Canada needed a more strictly defined border with the republic, so the colony began to discourage citizens from coming in to settle. Rejecting Simcoe's vision, the British hardened the standards for qualifying as a loyal subject in a more defensive Upper Canada perched next to an enduring republic. Few Americans were welcome, and they faced a longer and more difficult naturalization as subjects.[8]

RUINS

At war's end in Upper Canada, the retreating invaders left behind a wasteland of plundered farms and burned mills and villages. During the summer of 1815 an American woman visited the Niagara District to find "not a house or barn but what was burnt or the inside destroyed . . . It presented such a sight that I felt ashamed of my own countrymen." Two years later, another American toured the London District, where he felt "struck with the devastations which had been made by the late war: beautiful farms, formerly in high cultivation, now laid waste; houses entirely evacuated and forsaken." In 1819 John Goldie reported, "the Americans carried on the war in this part of the country more like Savages than civilised Beings. They carried off all that they could seize, even the household furniture, burnt a great number of private houses, and cut down most of the fruit trees."[9]

The plundering and burning embittered Upper Canadians. Goldie reported, "Many of the Inhabitants here hate the Yankies as the Devil, and wish to have another opportunity of shooting a few of them." An innkeeper, William Forsyth, "complained that the U.S. Army had robbed his house of every moveable article & even the baby linen of his infant in the cradle was taken." As a consequence, he expressed "a thorough detestation of the Americans & felt strongly the blessings of British protection." Forsyth even disinherited his eldest son for having joined the American forces during the war. In 1820 an Irishman visited the Canadian side of the St. Lawrence and marveled: "A stranger as he goes thro' the country w[oul]d really suppose on hearing the hostile feelings that exist between the Canadians & their neighbours on the opposite side of the river, that a war was raging between them." And so it was in bitter memory.[10]

Hatred of the invaders generated a new patriotism in Upper Canada. In the Niagara District in 1816 the Englishman Francis Hall lodged at a tavern run by a widow: "Her son had served in the militia, in token of which he was most obstreperously loyal, both in speech and song, during the whole evening." Hall wished for less patriotism and more sleep. John Beverley Robinson noted that, although waged by the Americans "for the purpose of subjugating the Canadas," the war "had the effect of binding them, as well as Nova Scotia and New Brunswick, much more strongly to the Crown." The people developed a new, shared identity that transcended their parochial localisms.[11]

In memory, the war became a great transforming divide in Upper Canadians' sense of themselves. A visitor remarked, "The last American war forms an important era in the history of Upper Canada, and as such, it is continually referred to by the people, who, when alluding to the time at which any circumstance occurred, say that it happened before or after the war." Geography as well as time became more divided. Formerly negligible in local minds, the border became a powerful divide separating recent enemies committed to rival governments. "The line of separation" between the colony and the republic "was more distinctly drawn," declared the Kingston newspaper.[12]

That sharper boundary divided the churches in Upper Canada from those in the United States. Before the war, the colonists had favored the evangelical Methodists, Presbyterians, and Baptists, rather than the Anglican church sponsored by the government. The evangelicals had relied on itinerant preachers sent by American-based associations to the alarm of British officers. In 1814 General Drummond complained, "Previous to the war, itinerant fanatics, enthusiastic in political as well as in religious matters, were in the habit of coming hither from the United States, and from the scarcity of regular clergymen in the country, were always cordially received by the people, amongst whom they succeeded but too well in disseminating their noxious principles." The war interrupted the flow of American preachers into Upper Canada, and the British ousted some for showing republican sympathies. After the war the British discouraged their return and pressured the Upper Canadian churches to seek replacements from England and Scotland. A Presbyterian explained, "We must be British or the cry is raised against us."[13]

With the severing of American ties, the Canadian churches downplayed evangelical modes of worship and church organization. The Methodists remained the preeminent denomination by becoming more respectable in their style and more vociferously loyal in their politics. Reducing passionate outbursts, the postwar Methodists favored a more austere style of preaching and of conversion. Forsaking the voluntarist and localist approach of the Americans, the Upper Canadian churches sought greater centralization and hierarchy, deeming both as more compatible with Canada's government. Strachan denounced any effort "to separate religion from the State, with which it ought ever to be firmly united, since one of its greatest objects is to give stability to good Government." The orderly worship in Upper Canada contrasted with the evangelical fervor that persisted on the American side of the border.[14]

FAMILY COMPACT

The postwar reaction against all things American empowered Loyalists led by Strachan. Conspicuous loyalty during the war became a litmus test for land grants and for elective or appointive office. In 1816 the voters elected Loyalists or their sons to the assembly—to the virtual exclusion of the Late Loyalists, who dwindled to just three members. Four-fifths of the members had held a military commission during the war.[15]

Strachan insisted that the war had purified Upper Canada as the land of true Loyalists by distinguishing "our friends from our foes, and rid[ding] us of all those traitors and false friends whom a short sighted and mistaken policy had introduced among us." To preserve their purified colony, Loyalists barred the return of wartime refugees, who had fled across the border to evade militia service. In the Johnstown District, a magistrate denounced them as "the most dangerous and contaminating class of Aliens." To discourage their return, the district magistrates confiscated their land and prosecuted them as militia deserters.[16]

Maintaining that purity required constant vigilance by Strachan and his protégés, who made a fetish of their Loyalist zeal. Forming an oligarchy known as "the Family Compact," Strachan's friends and clients dominated the province's assembly, legislative council, executive council, and district magistracies. Although few were related, they behaved like a tight-knit family by helping each other to acquire lands, offices, and contracts. Exulting in his patronage, Strachan declared, "The power of rewarding modest worth is perhaps the sweetest blessing that attends rank and authority, for our Great Master tells us it is more blessed to give than to receive." He especially favored his former students. A critic concluded, "Magistrates, members of parliament, and militia officers, besides the attorney and solicitor general, had sprung up in the school of Cornwall, and were all zealous in the cause of their master."[17]

Strachan's leading protégé was John Beverley Robinson, the son of a Virginia Loyalist who had served in Simcoe's Queen's Rangers and of the Loyalist daughter of an Anglican clergyman. Seven years old when his father died in 1798, Robinson found a surrogate father a year later, when he joined Strachan's school at Cornwall. During the next eight years Robinson absorbed his mentor's passion for elitism and empire and his contempt for the "Democratic levelling principle" of the republic. Robinson learned to advance in society by cultivating elite patrons rather than by seeking common popularity.[18]

In 1812 Robinson fought as a gentleman volunteer in Brock's great victory at Detroit. Those who had aided Brock at that dark hour enjoyed great acclaim and patronage thereafter in postwar Upper Canada. In 1813 Robinson became the colony's acting attorney general, although only twenty-one years old and not yet admitted to the bar. A year later he impressed General Drummond by prosecuting the Ancaster traitors. After the war the government made him the permanent attorney general, and in 1820 Robinson won election to the assembly. Zealous, able, and energetic, Robinson guided the administration of Sir Peregrine Maitland, who served as lieutenant governor from 1818 to 1828.[19]

Called "Tories," the members of the Family Compact celebrated the British empire as the grandest, freest, and richest in history. The Tories defended elite rule from a conviction that human inequality reflected "the universal order of nature, from the Divinity, downwards, to the communities of the meanest insects." They denounced any dissent as inviting anarchy and another invasion by the Americans, who promoted the alluring fraud of republicanism. To survive beside such dangerous neighbors, Canadians had to unite under a strong government led by the Tories, who treated all opposition as disloyalty to Britain.[20]

Contrary to Tory charges, their critics were not closet republicans seeking annexation to the United States. Instead, the reformers were British patriots who argued that a corrupt colonial elite had perverted the beloved mixed constitution, thereby betraying the king's loyal subjects in Upper Canada. In the Tory harping on loyalty, the reformers heard corrupt self-interest. John Matthews declared, "Loyalty, loyalty is all the cry now a-days, but . . . you will find that it is loyalty to the Attorney General which is meant, because he is able to give away a great many good things."[21]

Although committed to the empire and the mixed constitution, the reformers envied the commercial development on the American side of the border. Compared to the dynamic United States, Upper Canada seemed a sleepy rural backwater. From the western shore of the Niagara River, John Howison looked across to New York: "There, bustle, improvement, and animation fill every street; here dulness, decay, and apathy discourage enterprise and repress exertion." Pining for more business, reformers blamed the stagnation on the stodgy distrust by a corrupt elite for entrepreneurial enterprise. Tories, however, feared that adopting an American-style economy would prepare the people for a republican revolution. A Tory insisted, "I dislike this continual harping about the State of New York. . . . Let our uniform standard be regulated by that of the land of our fathers—Old England."[22]

More loyal than the king, the Tories distrusted even the imperial government as poorly informed about Canada and too soft on the Americans and on discontented colonists. According to the Tories, during the war the imperial lords had weakened Canada by imposing Prevost's defensive leadership. And they had squandered Brock's and Drummond's victories by foolishly granting a generous peace to the defeated Americans. Then those rulers had withdrawn most of the British troops from Canada with an indecent haste and had abandoned the Indians living within the American boundary. The Tories suspected that the imperial lords bore watching nearly as much as the "powerful and treacherous" Americans.[23]

GOURLAY

Reversing Simcoe's land policy, the British refused to grant Crown land in Canada to newcomers from America. In September 1815 the government barred magistrates from even administering the oath of allegiance to Americans, who needed that oath to qualify for a Crown land grant. The new policy slowed, but did not stop, the migration of Americans into Upper Canada, for immigrants could still rent farms or work for wages. But Americans increasingly turned westward, finding an alternative destination in Michigan, newly opened to settlement by the postwar suppression of Indian resistance.[24]

In 1815 the restrictive policy was popular with Canadians seething over the plundering and burning by American troops. But the policy lost support a year later, when an economic depression afflicted Upper

Canada. As produce prices fell, the farmers lost credit with the merchants, who resorted to lawsuits and foreclosures to collect on overdue debts. A bitterly cold year deepened the depression by inflicting early and late frosts, which devastated crops and starved the cattle. And the revenue-strapped government could not fulfill promises to fund the pay long overdue to militiamen and to compensate farmers for their war-ravaged property.[25]

To boost the economy, reformers proposed reviving the flow of Americans into Upper Canada. The reformers endorsed Simcoe's confidence that Upper Canada could serve as a redeeming haven for Americans discontented with the republic. A reformer declared, "Americans ought to be considered as strong sheep returning to the fold, and instead of driving them off, we ought to hail with rejoicing their return, receive them with open arms, and order the fatted calf to be killed and make merry." Deriding the Tory suspicion of the newcomers, John Matthews insisted "that the King had thousands more of good and excellent subjects than many of his friends were willing to allow him."[26]

Defying the government ban, the leading Niagara District magistrate, William Dickson, continued to issue the oath of allegiance to newcomers from America. No radical, Dickson had shot William Weekes for insulting the government in 1806 and, during the war, had been imprisoned by the Americans for resisting their occupation of Newark. But the postwar Dickson was also a land speculator who needed American customers to buy and develop his 94,000 acres of forest. To stem his rogue actions, the lieutenant governor revoked Dickson's authority to issue the oaths of allegiance and dissolved the assembly when it prepared resolutions against the government's land and immigration policies.[27]

Later in 1817 Robert Gourlay arrived from Scotland to reinforce the opposition in Upper Canada. Thirty-nine years old, he was a restless agitator and schemer who acknowledged his "peculiar opinions," claiming, "I am quite a radical, but I am one of my own sort." A farmer's son, he had obtained a university education, which he applied in pushing to improve the conditions, education, and rights of Britain's rural poor. Getting nowhere in Britain, he immigrated to Canada, settling in the Niagara District, where his wife had inherited land from her uncle, and where she also had two well-connected cousins, Thomas Clark and William Dickson, both legislative councillors. Eager to sell land to Americans, they encouraged Gourlay to gather and publish agricultural information meant to nudge reforms from the grudging government.[28]

Gourlay circulated a questionnaire to magistrates and entrepreneurs in the country towns. Most of the responses came from the Niagara, Gore, and London Districts in the colony's western half, heavily settled by Americans. Their reports blamed rural stagnation on the lack of postwar settlers from America and on the large tracts of wild land kept as Crown and Clergy Reserves. Meant to provide a rental revenue to the government and for the Anglican clergy, the reserves locked up two-sevenths of the colony's land. Most remained undeveloped because settlers balked at renting land, preferring to own their farms. Kingston's report declared, "Such lands remain like a putrid carcass, an injury and a nuisance to all around." Bearing an extra burden for local taxes and road work, settlers resented the undeveloped reserves in their midst.[29]

Gourlay proposed selling the reserves to American farmers and employing the revenue to compensate the militia and the civilians who had suffered from the war. Rebuffed by the government, he blamed the "system of paltry patronage and ruinous favouritism" by "the vile, loathsome and lazy vermin of Little York," led by a "monstrous little fool of a parson." Although short, Strachan was nobody's fool, as he would soon prove to Gourlay.[30]

Seeking a confrontation, Gourlay called for a convention of delegates to petition the Crown for "a radical change of system in the government of Upper Canada." That proposal outraged the Tories, who blamed the revolution in the thirteen colonies on direct appeals that had stirred up the common people. The Tories distrusted civil society: any private groups, outside of government, that tried to mobilize public opinion. Embarrassed by Gourlay's confrontational turn, his patrons, Clark and Dickson, broke with him and discouraged the convention, which assembled only fourteen delegates. In January 1819 Dickson arranged for Gourlay's arrest, which led to his expulsion from the colony on a charge of sedition in August. Financially ruined, Gourlay returned to Scotland. In Upper Canada, the restrictions on American immigration stood; the Crown and Clergy Reserves persisted; and Clark and Dickson had to subordinate their land speculating to Tory policy.[31]

BIDWELL

Like all Americans of his generation, Barnabas Bidwell was a "natural-born subject" until rendered a citizen by the revolution. The son of a Congregational minister, Bidwell was born in 1763. He graduated from Yale in 1785, became a lawyer, and settled in Berkshire County in western Massachusetts. Initially a Federalist, he shrewdly became a Republican on the eve of the electoral revolution of 1801, winning a seat in the state senate and, four years later, in Congress.[32]

His campaign literature celebrated the republic and derided the British constitution, which Bidwell accused the Federalists of favoring. The state election of 1805 was, he insisted, "between elective and hereditary government," for the Federalists meant to increase "taxes, loans, armies, establishments and patronage, till, under a republican form," the government "shall acquire an aristocratic or monarchical energy." By electing Republicans, the citizens could keep their government weak and inexpensive: a winning formula for elections if not for the coming war.[33]

Although new to Congress, Bidwell impressed Thomas Jefferson, who relied on him to push the president's agenda in the House of Representatives. In 1806 a Federalist congressman reported that Bidwell had become "J[efferson]'s right hand man." The Federalist added, "Mr. Bidwell is as smooth as the ocean unruffled by the slightest breeze," for his "talents are considerable and in smoothness and hypocrisy he is not lacking."[34]

But his political career suddenly crashed and burned in 1810, when the Federalists discovered that Bidwell had mismanaged his post as the treasurer for Berkshire County. Unable to account for about $331 in missing funds, he panicked and fled across the border into Upper Canada. By overreacting to his enemies, Bidwell damned himself in public opinion. And by fleeing to Canada, he moved under the British constitution that he had so flamboyantly denounced for electoral gain. His was the fastest and strangest political downfall of that generation.[35]

Settling at Ernestown near Kingston, Bidwell made his living by conducting a small private academy. His arrival aroused British suspicions, for Bidwell had been Jefferson's right-hand man, and he came at a time of increasing tensions between the republic and the empire. Loyalists howled that Bidwell would poison young minds with democracy and kleptocracy. When the war began, British officials suspected that he was acting as an American spy. To avoid expulsion, Bidwell reluctantly took the oath of allegiance to the king.[36]

During the war Bidwell kept a low profile, but thereafter he became an active reformer who supported Gourlay. In 1821 Bidwell narrowly won a seat in the assembly. Denouncing "the old vagabond" as "scum," Robinson declared, "It positively made me sick to hear of old Bidwell's [election] return." The canny attorney general sent an investigator to Berkshire County to procure a certified proof that, as an American treasurer and congressman, Bidwell had taken an oath renouncing allegiance to the king.[37]

Presented with that evidence, the assembly debated whether Bidwell merited his seat. The Tories insisted that he remained an American-born alien "incapable of being elected to serve in the Parliament of this Province." Here the Tories toyed with political gunpowder, for their argument would disenfranchise the immigrants from the United States, who comprised most of the men in the colony. If he and others like him were expelled, Bidwell warned, "more than half the inhabitants of this province would lose the elective franchise."[38]

Bidwell cited Simcoe's proclamation of 1792, which had invited Americans to resume their status as subjects by immigrating and taking the oath of allegiance as he had done. Bidwell concluded that he "was born a B[ritish] subject—he was so still, the oath in the states to the contrary." A Tory privately conceded, "I do not think Bidwell ought to have a seat, but at the same time, it must be confessed that Simcoe's proclamation has given some room for Emigrants from the States to hold undisturbed possession of the rights & privileges of other subjects."[39]

By just a single vote, the Tories ousted Bidwell from the assembly on the vague grounds that he was morally unfit. Robinson explained that the goal was to "dispose of old Barney one way or the other." To seal the deal, the assembly also passed a law to disqualify from their ranks anyone who had ever renounced his allegiance to the Crown by holding a political office in the United States.[40]

Renewing the battle, the reformers enlisted Marshall Spring Bidwell to run for his father's vacant seat. Born in 1798 in Massachusetts, young Bidwell was eleven when he fled with his father to Upper Canada. Lacking any record of crimes or political service in the republic, he had won admission to the colony's bar and had taken the oath of allegiance. In 1824 the assembly seated young Bidwell, overruling a Tory sheriff who had declared him disqualified by his American birth.[41]

Later that year, however, an English court decision threatened to oust Bidwell and to disenfranchise most Upper Canadians. The Court of King's Bench ruled that the residents of the United States had become aliens in 1783 and that none of their offspring could subsequently claim the rights of subjects merely by returning to the empire. As aliens, they could not vote, hold office, or own land unless naturalized by legal or parliamentary process, which was longer and less certain than simply taking the oath of allegiance upon arrival in a colony.[42]

By discrediting Simcoe's dream of reconciling Americans to the empire, the war had hardened national differences, which came to seem enduring. No longer could the British plausibly treat Americans as once and potential subjects. Instead, a British court declared that they had become as alien as the French or Spanish. In effect, the ruling reflected a belated acceptance of American independence. At last the British recognized that Americans were foreigners who would not, and should not, return to the empire. But if a victory for American independence, the ruling was a blow to the Americans who lived in Upper Canada.[43]

Reaching Upper Canada in early 1825, the news aroused a furor by casting a cloud on the political and property rights of the American-born majority. That uncertainty threatened to embroil the entire colony in legal and economic chaos—and potential rebellion. While eager to avert that crisis, the Tories also hoped to exploit it. They favored a "Naturalization Act," written by Robinson, to restore property but not political rights to the American-born. The Tories preferred to let the immigrants remain in the colony as farmers but without any right to vote or to serve in the assembly.[44]

Such sweeping disenfranchisement promised to destroy the reform movement by assuring Tory domination in the assembly. Matthews charged that the Tories meant to "divide and govern," with the "Scotch, English, and Irish pitted against the Americans," so that "by setting these parties against each other, the most intolerant becomes the most powerful." As if to prove that point, Robinson declared that he "would suffer death before he would consent to a measure that would confer the rights of a subject on men who, but a few years ago, had *invaded our country—ransacked our villages—burnt our houses—and murdered our wives and children*." In Robinson's mind, the war still raged.[45]

Rejecting the Naturalization Act, the reformers in the assembly instead passed a simple "Declaratory Act"—which asserted that the people remained British subjects by descent even if American citizens by birth. But the Tories controlled the executive and legislative councils, which rejected the assembly's act. The political deadlock plunged the colony into an uproar of angry recriminations in public meetings. Unfortunately for the Tories, their Naturalization Act set an unintended precedent that threatened to compromise a key diplomatic position of the imperial government: that neither a subject nor a citizen could abjure his birth status by naturalization.[46]

In 1827 the imperial government mandated a new provincial law closer to the reformers' Declaratory Act than to the Naturalization Act of the Tories. Drafted by Marshall Spring Bidwell, the new law affirmed the subject status of any colonist who had moved into Upper Canada before 1820 or who had subsequently taken the oath of allegiance, received a land grant, or held office in the colony. By those generous rules, almost every adult male resident qualified. And subsequent arrivals could be naturalized after completing seven years of continuous residence.[47]

Although the reformers had won the battle, they were on the verge of losing the electoral war. The alien issue polarized politics in Upper Canada, as the reformers and Tories organized rival parties to coordinate their electioneering. The politicization benefited from a growing population, the proliferation of newspapers and civic associations, and improved roads and waterways. Fewer Upper Canadians lived in isolation from political news and debate. In 1828 a reformer declared, "It had been difficult to awaken the people from their slumber, but they had at last been roused to save their liberties." But the Tories built their own popular following among the growing number of immigrants from Britain, who transformed the demography of Upper Canada during the late 1820s and early 1830s.[48]

TRANSITION

To Alexander Macdonell's delight, postwar policy subsidized increased immigration to Canada from Britain, and especially from Scotland, deemed a hive of loyalty. In 1815 Lord Bathurst explained that the government wanted to divert "to the British Colonies that part of the Population of the United Kingdom which would otherwise emigrate to the United States." The imperial government sponsored settlement by British soldiers demobilized in Canada and by families from Scotland and Ireland. Initially, every emigrant family received free passage, farm tools, six months of rations, and one hundred acres of Canadian land. A Tory insisted that former malcontents in Ireland became, in Canada, "grateful to the government to whom they owe all the advantages they enjoy [and] they are the most loyal and devoted of his Majesty's subjects."[49]

In 1820 the government abandoned the subsidies for emigration, but the program had sufficed to start a self-sustaining chain migration, as the early migrants wrote home to encourage kin and friends to follow. Between 1815 and 1842 the colony attracted 78,000 Irish, 41,000 English and Welsh, and 40,000 Scots. During that period, the 159,000 emigrants from Britain outnumbered the 32,000 from America by

nearly five to one. Thanks to the British immigration, and to the growing number born in the colony, the American-born share of the population fell to 7 percent by 1842. A majority in 1812, the American-born
had become a small minority thirty years later.[50]

Some of the immigrants from Britain gravitated to the reform party.
They included William Lyon Mackenzie, a fiery Scots journalist who
arrived in 1820. But most of the newcomers were poor folk with little
political experience. Cultivated by the Tories, they came to see the
reformers as Yankee republicans bent on overthrowing British rule in
Canada. The most zealous new Tories were Protestant Irish who
imported their Orange Order, an association of Loyalist vigilantes. The
antithesis of the secular and radical United Irishmen, the Orange Order
reflected the polarization along religious lines that afflicted Ireland
after the failed rebellion of 1798. Dedicated to fighting Catholics in Ireland, the order focused their Canadian attacks on supposed republicans
from America. Bearing clubs, the Orangemen attacked the meetings of
reformers.[51]

In early 1836 the impulsive Sir Francis Bond Head arrived from
England as the new lieutenant governor. Head insisted that he had "to
contend on the soil of America with Democracy, and that if I did not
overpower it, it would overpower me." During the summer of 1836
Head forcefully led the Tory campaign in the most heated and violent
election in the colony's history. Wooing the immigrants from Britain,
Head declared a "moral war . . . between those who were for British
institutions, against those who were for soiling the empire by the introduction of democracy." In a political coup, Head persuaded the Orangemen to cooperate with the provincial Catholics led by their fiery bishop,
Macdonell, in shared hatred for American republicanism. This strange
alliance swung the election for the Tories, who routed the reformers,
capturing two-thirds of the seats in the assembly. The victors especially
exulted in ousting Mackenzie and Bidwell.[52]

The electoral triumph inflated the lieutenant governor's already formidable ego. Vindictive in victory, Head dismissed from local office
anyone who had helped the reformers in the election. He also
responded slowly and clumsily to an economic depression that afflicted
both Canada and the United States in 1837. Meanwhile, a crackdown
on French Canadian radicals in Lower Canada provoked a serious
rebellion there. Head sent all of Upper Canada's regulars eastward to
reinforce the crackdown. In the wake of his big electoral victory, Head
felt secure in his Anglophone colony.[53]

Exploiting the removal of the regulars, Mackenzie began to plot a revolution during the summer and fall of 1837. In early December he rallied five hundred supporters on Yonge Street north of Toronto (as York had been renamed) for an armed march on the capital. While Mackenzie hoped to create a republic, most of his followers expected only an armed but bloodless demonstration meant to intimidate Head into making some concessions. The gap between his plans and their expectations proved fatal to the so-called rebellion. On the outskirts of Toronto, Tory guards fired on the marchers, who broke and fled, leaving three dead. Lacking firearms, most had carried only pikes, pitchforks, and clubs. A few rallied at Montgomery's Tavern for a final skirmish with at least one thousand attacking Tories, commanded by James FitzGibbon, the Irish Loyalist hero of the battle at Beaver Dams during the war. FitzGibbon routed the rebels and burned the tavern. To the west, in the London District, about three hundred armed radicals had mustered, but they scattered upon learning of Mackenzie's debacle. In the spring, the government hanged two of the captured rebels as traitors and as examples; a third died in his cold, damp prison.[54]

Having bungled his ill-conceived uprising, Mackenzie fled across the Niagara River to western New York, where he found far less support than he had bargained on. During the summer of 1837, Mackenzie had assured his Canadian supporters: "There are thousands, aye tens of thousands of Englishmen, Scotchmen, and above all, of Irishmen, now in the United States" who would support rebellion in Canada. But, to Mackenzie's dismay, the American government opposed his rebellion, as did almost all local leaders along the frontier, including Peter B. Porter. Burned by the War of 1812, Porter wanted no part in a sequel.[55]

Along the Niagara River, Mackenzie rallied a few hundred armed Americans, primarily unemployed men enticed by a promised reward in Canadian land. During 1838 they raided across the Detroit, Niagara, and St. Lawrence Rivers to plunder and burn, but they were soon routed by larger numbers of loyal militia. The victors hanged or shot about a score of the raiders and shipped another seventy-eight to the penal colony on Tasmania in the South Pacific. Worse than useless, the raids justified the Tory repression of all reformers. The peaceable Marshall Spring Bidwell fled to the United States in fear of Orange Order vengeance. The moderate reformers cursed Mackenzie for his reckless folly as well as the Tories for their harsh response.[56]

The border raids appalled the American president, Martin Van Buren, who meant to avoid war with the empire. In Congress he found strong support from the former war hawks, Henry Clay and John C. Calhoun. And almost all of the American newspapers disavowed the cross-border raids. To restore order, the president sent two thousand troops commanded by a war hero, General Winfield Scott, to the New York border. In 1814 Scott had led an invasion of the Niagara District; twenty-four years later, he worked to protect British Canada from American raiders. Arrested for violating American neutrality laws, Mackenzie was convicted in June 1839. After serving eleven months in prison, he felt betrayed by the republic.[57]

As a fiasco, the Upper Canadian rebellion demonstrated that the War of 1812 had decisively divided the continent between the republic and the empire. The great majority of Upper Canadians, reformers as well as Tories, supported their government against the rebels and the raiders. By failing so miserably as a revolutionary, Mackenzie was the exception who proved the rule of a conservative consensus in postwar Upper Canada. Two varieties of loyalty prevailed in the colony: Toryism and moderate reform, neither of them republican.[58]

Most Americans, including their national leaders, had balked at a renewed war. By jailing instead of supporting Mackenzie, the Americans conceded that they could live beside the British as neighbors. No longer did the survival of the republic seem to hinge on driving the empire from the continent. Throughout the nineteenth century, some blowhards in the press and Congress periodically declared an American destiny to absorb British Canada—deemed an unnatural intrusion on a republican continent. That bombast surged during occasional border disputes, but invariably the nation's leaders compromised with the British to avert a new war. By preferring inaction and compromise, the Americans assured Canada's persistence as a British domain.[59]

Head declared victory: "The struggle on this continent between Monarchy and Democracy has been a problem which Upper Canada has just solved." But the expensive suppression of the rebellion appalled the imperial lords, who recalled Head to England. Seeking a reconciliation between Tories and reformers, the government mandated a union of Upper and Lower Canada in 1840. That union would give Anglophones a majority in the Canadian legislature. Eight years later, the imperial Parliament instituted the "responsible government" long sought by the reformers. This introduced a parliamentary system where the executive council answered to the elected assembly rather than to the appointed governor. And in 1867 Canada obtained domestic autonomy and a transcontinental confederation that included new western provinces as well as the old maritime colonies. Confederation consolidated the partition of English-speaking America between the United

States and Canada. Simcoe's vision of reuniting North America under the empire was dead, but Canada had endured and expanded.[60]

PRIOR TO THE WAR OF 1812, Upper Canada and the United States had been incompletely separated by the American Revolution. Although that revolution had generated a powerful ideological divide between the republic and the empire, Americans remained the majority on both sides of the border. Their political convictions still seemed in play to the ideologues of republic and empire, who either hoped or feared that the Americans would embrace or reject the republicanism of the revolution. Ideological division within a cultural and demographic overlap made for

The Rival Candidates, *watercolor by F. H. Consitt, 1828. During a heated election in Upper Canada, the rival parties sought to control the polling places by force of numbers. The conservative candidate, Morris, relies on fellow Scots immigrants, including some wearing kilts.* (Courtesy of the William Morris Collection, Queen's University Archives, 2139 [box 3].)

a dangerously unstable compound, which led to a civil war for North America in 1812.

By producing a military stalemate, the war led to a sharper distinction between Upper Canada and the United States. The destruction wrought by the invaders alienated most of the American colonists from their brethren in the republic, and the postwar surge in Scots and Irish immigrants generated the colony's new majority. In postwar Upper Canada, the people and their culture became more committed to the mixed constitution and to the union of the empire.

The postwar culture generated distinct, national histories on both sides of the border. To bolster patriotism within, the historians made foils of the people on the other side of a newly significant border. Those histories subtly distorted the war by imposing on the past the nationalism spawned *after* that conflict and *because* of it. By writing of the Americans fighting the British as distinct nations, each united, the patriotic historians obscured the civil war waged for the future of the empire and of the continent, a civil war that had divided Americans, Indians, and the Irish during a lingering age of revolution.

Notes

Abbreviations

AAS	American Antiquarian Society (Worcester, Mass.)
AC	[United States] *Annals of Congress. Debates and Proceedings in the Congress of the United States, 1789–1825.* 42 vols. Washington, D.C., 1834–56. Scholarly convention abbreviates this compilation as the *Annals of Congress (AC)*
ANB	John A. Garraty and Mark C. Carnes, eds., *American National Biography*, 24 vols. (New York: Oxford University Press, 1999)
AO	Archives of Ontario (Toronto)
ASP-FR	[United States] *American State Papers: Foreign Relations*
ASP-MA	[United States] *American State Papers: Military Affairs*
BECHS	Buffalo and Erie County Historical Society (Buffalo, N.Y.)
BFP	Baldwin Family Papers
CFP	Campbell Family Papers
CJIP	Charles Jared Ingersoll Papers
CKGP	Charles K. Gardner Papers
DCB	*Dictionary of Canadian Biography*
DHCNF	E. A. Cruikshank, ed., *Documentary History of the Campaigns upon the Niagara Frontier in 1812–1814*, 9 vols. (Welland, Ont.: Tribune Press, 1896–1908)
DHCNF-1814	E. A. Cruikshank, ed., *Documentary History of the Campaign on the Niagara Frontier in 1814*, 2 vols. (Niagara-on-the-Lake, Ont.: Lundy's Lane Historical Society, 1896)
DMP	Duncan McArthur Papers
DP-JRP	David Parish–Joseph Rosseel Papers
DPL	David Parish Letterbooks
DPP	Daniel Parker Papers
DRIC	E. A. Cruikshank, ed., *Documents Relating to the Invasion of Canada and the Surrender of Detroit, 1812* (Ottawa: Government Printing Bureau, 1912)
EEPFP	Ellicott-Evans-Peacock Family Papers
FFP	Ford Family Papers

GP   Goodyear Papers

HCH   Historic Cherry Hill (Albany, N.Y.)

HDP   Henry Dearborn Papers

HL   Huntington Library (San Marino, Calif.)

HLCP   Holland Land Company Papers

HP   Hodge Papers

HSP   Historical Society of Pennsylvania (Philadelphia)

IHS   Indiana Historical Society (Indianapolis)

JBP   Jacob Brown Papers

JEWP   John E. Wool Papers

JMP   John Mitchell Papers

JSP   Joel Stone Papers

LAC   Library and Archives Canada (Ottawa)

LAHS   Lennox and Addington Historical Society (Nappanee, Ont.)

LC   Library of Congress (Washington, D.C.)

MeHS   Maine Historical Society (Portland)

MFP   Macaulay Family Papers

MHS   Massachusetts Historical Society (Boston)

MPHS, *MHC*   Michigan Pioneer Historical Society, *Michigan Historical Collections* (Lansing: Wynkoop, Hallenbeck, Crawford, 1886–1912)

NHSP   Norfolk Historical Society Papers

NWP   Nathan Williams Papers

NYHS   New-York Historical Society (New York City)

NYPL   New York Public Library (New York City)

NYSL   New York State Library (Albany)

OCHS   Oneida County Historical Society (Utica, N.Y.)

PBPP   Peter B. Porter Papers

PFP   Peter Force Papers

PJM-PS   J. C. A. Stagg et al., eds., *The Papers of James Madison: Presidential Series*, 6 vols. to date (Charlottesville: University of Virginia Press, 1984–)

QUA   Queens University Archives (Kingston, Ont.)

RBP   Richard Bishop Papers

RFP   Rochester Family Papers

SBD   William Wood, ed., *Select British Documents of the Canadian War of 1812*, 3 vols. (Toronto: Champlain Society, 1920–28)

SC-PL-DU   Special Collections, Perkins Library, Duke University (Durham, N.C.)

SC-RRL-UR   Special Collections, Rush Rhees Library, University of Rochester (N.Y.)

SC-SLU   Special Collections, St. Lawrence University (Canton, N.Y.)

SoVRP   Solomon Van Rensselaer Papers

StVRP   Stephen Van Rensselaer Papers

SULSC: Syracuse University Library Special Collections (Syracuse, N.Y.)

TJP-AMS	Thomas Jefferson Papers, American Memory Series (online), Library of Congress
TRL	Toronto Reference Library
TSJP	Thomas Sidney Jesup Papers
USNA	United States National Archives (Washington, D.C.)
VHS	Virginia Historical Society (Richmond)
VRMP	Van Rensselaer Manor Papers
WBP	William Bell Papers
WHHP	William Henry Harrison Papers
WHMP	William Hamilton Merritt Papers

RECORD GROUPS IN THE ARCHIVES OF ONTARIO (AO)

F 24	Cartwright Family Papers
F 46	Peter Russell Papers
F 983	John Strachan Papers
RG 1, A-I-1	Crown Lands, Letters Received by the Surveyor General
RG 1, A-I-6	Crown Lands, Letters Received by the Surveyor General
RG 4–1	Office of the Attorney General, Pre-Confederation Records

RECORD GROUPS IN THE LIBRARY AND ARCHIVES, CANADA (LAC)

MG 11	Colonial Office 42: Correspondence from Colonial Governors
MG 13	War Office 17, Monthly Returns of Troops in Canada
MG 16	Foreign Office 5: Consuls in the United States
MG 19, E 1	Earl of Selkirk Papers
MG 21	Sir Frederick Haldimand Papers
MG 23, H-I-1, ser. 4	John Graves Simcoe Papers, Wolford Transcripts
MG 23, H-I-3	Jarvis Family Papers
MG 23, H-I-4	William Dummer Powell Papers
MG 23, H-II-1	McDonald-Stone Family Papers
MG 23, H-II-7	Peter Russell Papers
RG 1, E3	Upper Canada Executive Council, State Submissions
RG 4, A 1	Lower Canada, Civil Secretary, Correspondence Received
RG 5, A 1	Upper Canada, Civil Secretary, Correspondence Received
RG 8	British Military Records
RG 9, B 1	Upper Canada, Adjutant General, Correspondence
RG 10	Indian Affairs

RECORD GROUPS IN THE UNITED STATES NATIONAL ARCHIVES (USNA)

RG 45, M 125	United States Navy, Letters Received from Captains
RG 45, Ser. RE, RN 1812–15	United States Navy, Correspondence regarding Prisoners

RG 59, M 179	Department of State, Miscellaneous Letters Received
RG 59, M 588	Department of State, War of 1812 Papers
RG 59, T 168	Department of State, Dispatches from Consuls at London
RG 75, M 15	Office of the Secretary of War, Indian Affairs, Letters Sent
RG 94, #127	Records of the Adjutant General, War of 1812 Prisoners
RG 94, M 566	Records of the Adjutant General, Letters Received
RG 98	Records of U.S. Army Commands, 1784–1812
RG 107, M 6	Secretary of War, Letters Sent
RG 107, M 221	Secretary of War, Letters Received, Registered Series
RG 107, M 222	Secretary of War, Letters Received, Unregistered Series

Introduction

1. "An American Farmer," [Philadelphia] *Aurora*, June 18, 1813.

2. Cooper, ed., *Ned Myers*, 43 ("we caught").

3. Cooper, ed., *Ned Myers*, 80–81 and 91 ("America").

4. For Myers's prewar travails with press-gangs, see Cooper, ed., *Ned Myers*, 17–18, 25–27, and 35–38.

5. Cooper, ed., *Ned Myers*, 80–95. For confirmation of his service on the transport *Regulus*, see George Glasgow to Francis Kempt, Sept. 17, 1813, RG 94, ser. 127, box 20, folder 1, USNA.

6. Hinderaker, *Elusive Empires*, 260–61; Kettner, *American Citizenship*, 173.

7. Bushman, *King and People*, 211–52; Morgan, *Inventing the People*, 239–306; G. Wood, *Radicalism*, 3–8 and 229–369.

8. Jasanoff, "Other Side of Revolution," 207–8. The American Revolution generated a higher proportion of political refugees than did the French Revolution. Jasanoff calculates that one in forty colonists became a refugee compared to one in two hundred French during their revolutionary upheaval.

9. Jonathan Russell to James Monroe, Feb. 3, 1812, in Manning, ed., *Diplomatic Correspondence*, 1:609; "The Enemy Within" and "The Old Congress," [Philadelphia] *Aurora*, June 10 and 12, 1812.

10. Graves, ed., *Merry Hearts*, 133 ("pleasanter Sport" and "Indeed, Lieutenant"), 134–35 ("Strange"), and 147 ("The rascals"). Le Couteur identified the friendly American as an artillery officer from Virginia. Was it Winfield Scott, then at Fort George?

11. Beall, "Journal," 789 and 790 ("was amused" and "sign of the harp").

12. Beall, "Journal," 804; Couture, *War and Society*, 105 and 145.

13. Graves, ed., *Merry Hearts*, 147, 246n31; Klinck and Talman, eds., *Tiger Dunlop's Upper Canada*, 44 ("he discovered" and "the virulence").

14. Beall, "Journal," 804 ("depend"); Daniel McFarland to Daniel Millikin, Mar. 30, 1812 ("hellish project"), in Crombie, ed., "Papers of Daniel McFarland," 103; Shepard, *Autobiography*, 72 ("between the two parties").

15. Augustus Foster to James Monroe, June 1, 1812 ("similarity"), MG 16, 86:174, reel B-1999, LAC. For the mutual importance of commerce, see Perkins, *Prologue to War*, 24–30.

16. "An American Farmer," [Philadelphia] *Aurora*, June 18, 1813 ("the people").

17. Colley, *Captives*, 4–12 (C. W. Pasley quoted on 10: "an oak").

18. For critiques of conventional military history, see Shy, "Ian Steele as Military Historian," 18–29; Keegan, *Face of Battle*, 27–46. For valuable overviews I have relied on Hickey, *War of 1812*; Hitsman, *Incredible War*; Latimer, *1812*; J. C. A. Stagg, *Madison's War*; and Stanley, *War of 1812*. Hitsman, Latimer, and Stanley operate within the Anglo-Canadian tradition of narrating the war, while Hickey and Stagg primarily interpret events through American eyes. For a new approach to the war's military history (an approach which pays greater attention to the social context of the war), see Graves, *Field of Glory*; Graves, *Right and Glory*; Malcomson, *Capital in Flames*; Malcomson, *Lords of the Lake*; Malcomson, *Very Brilliant Affair*; and Sheppard, *Plunder*.

19. For the fluid uncertainties of postrevolutionary North America, see Onuf, "Expanding Union," 50–80; and A. Taylor, "Land and Liberty," 81–108.

Chapter One: Loyalists

1. Lord Dorchester to Lord Sydney, Oct. 14, 1788 ("daily expectation"), MG 11, 51:203, LAC.

2. John Graves Simcoe to Henry Dundas, June 30, 1791, and Aug. 12, 1791, in Cruikshank, ed., *Correspondence of Simcoe*, 1:29–30 and 150; Craig, *Upper Canada*, 36–38 and 66–84; Hitsman, *Safeguarding Canada*, 53–54.

3. Craig, *Upper Canada*, 15–19.

4. Fryer and Dracott, *John Graves Simcoe*, 111 and 116; John Graves Simcoe to Evan Nepean, Dec. 3, 1789 ("to consecrate"), in Cruikshank, ed., *Correspondence of Simcoe*, 1:7–8.

5. Hughes, *Journal*, 141–42; [Anonymous], "Canadian Letters," 90–99; Edgar, ed., *Ten Years*, 38; Fryer and Dracott, *John Graves Simcoe*, 136.

6. Conway, *War, State, and Society*, 241–42; A. L. Burt, *Old Province*, 1:160–81; Neatby, *Quebec*, 133–41; Lawson, *Imperial Challenge*, 126–45; Milobar, "Conservative Ideology," 47; Harlow, *Founding*, 2:694–98.

7. Conway, *War, State, and Society*, 241–42.

8. Conway, *War, State, and Society*, 243–45; Bushman, *King and People*, 176–210; R. M. Brown, "Back Country Rebellions," 73–98; Countryman, "Indians," 342–62.

9. Burt, *Old Province*, 1:185–86; Neatby, *Quebec*, 133–42; "Declaration of Independence," in R. D. Brown, ed., *Major Problems*, 171 ("For abolishing").

10. Creighton, *Empire*, 62; Harlow, *Founding*, 2:714–16; Burt, *Old Province*, 1:182–224; Lanctot, *Canada*, 108–36; C. Moore, *Loyalists*, 63–64; McDowell, *Ireland in the Age of Imperialism and Revolution*, 239–40.

11. R. C. Stuart, *United States Expansionism*, 17.

12. [Anonymous], "Canadian Letters," 90, 92, and 105 ("In winter"); Hughes, *Journal*, 140 ("By the first"); Innis, ed., *Mrs. Simcoe's Diary*, 51–52, 54 ("How happy"), and 55–56.

13. Hughes, *Journal*, 140; Edgar, ed., *Ten Years*, 38; Robert Nichol to John Askin, Aug. 26, 1804 ("The first"), in Quaife, ed., *John Askin Papers*, 2:429; Innis, ed., *Mrs. Simcoe's Diary*, 56–57 ("I do not like").

14. William Osgoode to John Graves Simcoe, Feb. 25, 1794, and Richard Cartwright to Davison & Co., Nov. 4, 1797, MG 23 H I 1, ser. 4 (Simcoe Transcripts), 5:27 and 56, LAC; Innis, ed., *Mrs. Simcoe's Diary*, 11 and 81; [Anonymous], "Canadian Letters," 138 ("A Londoner"); Hughes, *Journal*, 140.

15. Richard Cartwright to Davison & Co., Nov. 4, 1797 ("Communications"),

MG 23 H I 1, ser. 4 (Simcoe Transcripts), 5:56, LAC; William Osgoode to John King, June 17, 1799 ("Remember"), in Colgate, ed., "Letters," 157; Frederick Haldimand to Lord North, Nov. 18, 1783, MG 11, 46:25, LAC.

16. Fryer and Dracott, *John Graves Simcoe*, 137–42; [Anonymous], "Canadian Letters," 102–5; F. Hall, *Travels*, 42–43; Maude, *Visit to the Falls*, 231.

17. [Anonymous], "Canadian Letters," 105–7 ("middle sized"); Grew, *Journal*, 98–100; Bigelow, *Journal*, 86–103; Reed, ed., "John Strachan's Journey," 216 ("Every house").

18. [Anonymous], "Canadian Letters," 113–14; Bigelow, *Journal*, 79–81; Weld, *Travels*, 2:66; Innis, ed., *Mrs. Simcoe's Diary*, 66–67.

19. Howison, *Sketches of Upper Canada*, 21 ("diminutive," "profusion," and "piles"); P. Campbell, *Travels*, 123–27; Talman, ed., *Loyalist Narratives*, 113; Innis, ed., *Mrs. Simcoe's Diary*, 67 and 72–73 ("the pleasure").

20. Countryman, *People in Revolution*, 127–28, 139–41, 146–47, and 178–79. Cruikshank, "King's Royal Regiment of New York," 193; Lender and Martin, eds., *Citizen-Soldier*, 59.

21. Colley, *Britons*, 11–54; Milobar, "Conservative Ideology," 45–46; Mills, *Idea of Loyalty*, 15–16; Potter, *Liberty We Seek*, viii–ix, 10–16, 54–55, 107, 153–57, and 172–80; McConville, *King's Three Faces*, 2–9.

22. Graymont, *Iroquois*, 104–254; Cruikshank, "King's Royal Regiment of New York," 276–80; Brown and Senior, *Victorious in Defeat*, 24–27; Morris, *Peacemakers*, 351–85.

23. Morris, *Peacemakers*, 263–70, and 301–3; Ritcheson, *Aftermath*, 4–5; R. C. Stuart, *United States Expansionism*, 22–24; Neatby, *Quebec*, 208–9; Watson, *Reign*, 249; C. Stuart, "Lord Shelburne," 245 (Shelburne quoted, "If we").

24. C. Moore, *Loyalists*, 109–12; Albany resolutions, May 19, 1783 ("never to be"), MG 21, 21,763:121, reel A-681, LAC; Zeichner, "Loyalist Problem," 289–95; Cruikshank, "King's Royal Regiment of New York," 293–97; Brown and Senior, *Victorious in Defeat*, 25 (includes George Clinton quote: "rather roast"), 29.

25. Cruikshank, ed., "Records of Niagara, 1784–7," 15–16, 37, 80–81, and 95; C. Moore, "Disposition to Settle," 53–79; Gentilcore and Wood, "Military Colony," 32; Gates, *Land Policies*, 11–15; Siebert, "Loyalists and Six Nations," 91–92.

26. Gates, *Land Policies*, 11–15; C. Moore, "Disposition to Settle," 68–71; Cometti, ed., *American Journals*, 298–301; Lord Dorchester to Lord Sydney, Oct. 14, 1788 ("on all occasions"), MG 11, 51:203, LAC.

27. Lord Sydney to Henry Hope, Aug. 22, 1785 ("Sufferers"), MG 11, 48:36, LAC; Phineas Bond to Lord Carmathen, June 28, 1788, and Bond to Evan Nepean, Nov. 16, 1788, in Bond, "Letters," 568 and 584–86; Cruikshank, ed., "Records of Niagara, 1784–7," 126–28. For population growth, see McCalla, *Planting the Province*, 249. For increased American taxes, see Holton, " 'From the Labour of Others,' " 275–76.

28. Burt, *Old Province*, 1:378–81; A. Taylor, " 'Hungry Year,' " 145–81; Pauley, "Fighting the Hessian Fly," 377–400.

29. Lord Grenville to Lord Dorchester, Oct. 20, 1789 ("the minds"), in Shortt and Doughty, eds., *Documents*, 970; Rogers, *History of the Town of Paris*, 21; Prince Edward quoted in Guillet, *Early Life*, 213 ("My father").

30. Hunter, *Quebec to Carolina*, 111; D. W. Smith, *Short Topographical Description*, 15; Weld, *Travels*, 2:65–67; Ogden, *Tour*, 60; P. Campbell, *Travels*, 139–41; [Anonymous], "Canadian Letters," 120–21; Innis, ed., *Mrs. Simcoe's Diary*, 71.

31. Heriot, *Travels*, 142–44; P. White, ed., *Lord Selkirk's Diary*, 186; Innis, ed., *Mrs. Simcoe's Diary*, 71 and 74; William Bentinck, "Travel Journal," 17–19, MG 24 H I, LAC; Hughes, *Journal*, 150; [Newark] *Canada Constellation*, Dec. 7, 1799.

32. P. White, ed., *Lord Selkirk's Diary*, 145 and 296; O'Brien, *Speedy Justice*, 71; William Bentinck, "Travel Journal," 17–19, MG 24 H I, LAC; P. Campbell, *Travels*, 143–44 ("Let us"); Maude, *Visit to the Falls*, 173–74 ("great Snake"); Innis, ed., *Mrs. Simcoe's Diary*, 74 and 157.

33. Cometti, ed., *American Journals*, 119–20; Lindley, "Account," 578 ("a strong"); Hunter, *Quebec to Carolina*, 100; [Anonymous], "Canadian Letters," 125–26; Dunnigan, "Military Life at Niagara," 73; Weld, *Travels*, 2:89–90 and 94; Innis, ed., *Mrs. Simcoe's Diary*, 75–76.

34. Dunnigan, "Military Life at Niagara," 92–93; [Anonymous] "Canadian Letters," 129; P. Campbell, *Travels*, 180–83; Innis, ed., *Mrs. Simcoe's Diary*, 83–84, 86 ("pleasant society"), and 87 ("The worst").

35. Roland, "Health, Disease, and Treatment," 236–40; P. White, ed., *Lord Selkirk's Diary*, 178; [Anonymous], "Canadian Letters," 131–32 ("ague and fever"); Boulton, *Sketch*, 11; Riddell, ed., *La Rochefoucault-Liancourt's Travels*, 55; Weld, *Travels*, 2:91–92.

36. B. Wilson, *Enterprises*, 4–6 and 91–94; P. Campbell, *Travels*, 155–56; William Hartshorne, Diary, June 1, 1793, NYPL.

37. D. W. Smith, *Short Topographical Description*, 30–32; Hughes, *Journal*, 151; Schultz, *Travels*, 74; [Anonymous], "Canadian Letters," 153–55; Riddell, ed., *La Rochefoucault-Liancourt's Travels*, 23; Innis, ed., *Mrs. Simcoe's Diary*, 76–77 ("The fall").

38. Graymont, *Iroquois*, 259–91; John Butler, Return of the Six Nation Indians and Confederates, June 24, 1783, RG 10, Ser. A6, 15:74, LAC; Ketchum, *History of Buffalo*, 1:359–67.

39. Captain John Deserontyon to Daniel Claus, Jan. 8, 1784, MG 19 F 1 (Claus Family Papers), 24:15, LAC; Allan MacLean to Frederick Haldimand, May 18, 1783 ("a free People"), MG 21, 21, 763:118, LAC; Calloway, *Crown and Calumet*, 8–9.

40. Lord Sydney to Lord Dorchester, Apr. 5, 1787, MG 11, 50:37, LAC; Patrick Murray to John Graves Simcoe, Dec. 23, 1791 ("We are"), MG 23, H I 1, 3d ser. (Simcoe Transcripts), 1:367, LAC; Wright, *Britain and the American Frontier*, 2.

41. R. White, *Middle Ground*, 413–17, 433–43, and 447–48. Calloway, *Crown and Calumet*, 9–14; Hinderaker, *Elusive Empires*, 189 and 268–70; A. Taylor, *Divided Ground*, 111–17.

42. Allen, *His Majesty's Indian Allies*, 56–57; Wright, *Britain and the American Frontier*, 69–72; François de Barbe-Marbois to Comte de Vergennes, Sept. 30 and Oct. 30, 1784, in Giunta, ed., *Emerging Nation*, 2:451 and 482–83.

43. Allen, *His Majesty's Indian Allies*, 56–57; Wright, *Britain and the American Frontier*, 20–26, 36, and 42–43; Ritcheson, *Aftermath*, 33–37 and 59–69; Lord Sydney to Henry Hope, Apr. 6, 1788, in Cruikshank, ed., "Records of Niagara, 1784–7," 88.

44. James Monroe to Thomas Jefferson, Nov. 1, 1784, in S. M. Hamilton, ed., *Writings of Monroe*, 1:43–44; John Jay to John Adams, Oct. 14, 1785 ("Our foederal"), in Giunta, ed., *Emerging Nation*, 2:863; R. C. Stuart, *United States Expansionism*, 7 and 37–38.

45. James Monroe to Thomas Jefferson, Nov. 1, 1784, in Hamilton, ed., *Writings of Monroe*, 1:43–44; John Adams to John Jay, Oct. 15, and Dec. 3, 1785 ("they rely"), in Giunta, ed., *Emerging Nation*, 2:864–65 and 940–41; Calloway, *Crown and Calumet*, 17.

46. Riddell, ed., *La Rochefoucault-Liancourt's Travels*, 16–17; Grew, *Journal*, 77–78; Lindley, "Account of a Journey," 583–84, 593–94, 610, and 613; William Hartshorne, Diary, June 10, 1793, NYPL; Howison, *Sketches*, 199–200; Boulton, *Sketch*, 62.

47. Hughes, *Journal*, 155–62; William Hartshorne, Diary, June 10–12, 1793, NYPL; Riddell, *William Dummer Powell*, 73–74; J. Moore, "Journal," 639, 643; Coventry, *Memoirs*, 1:882; Lindley, "Account of a Journey," 584, 594, and 596 ("All is well"); Gray, ed., "From Fairfield to Schonbrun," 71 ("thoughtless") and 73.

48. Colley, *Britons*, 144–45; Gould, *Persistence of Empire*, 182 and 208–14; Gould, "American Independence," 122.

49. John Adams to Robert R. Livingston, June 23, 1783 ("British Ministry"), in Giunta, ed., *Emerging Nation*, 2:169–70; Gould, "American Independence," 134–36; Milobar, "Conservative Ideology," 48; Bayly, *Imperial Meridian*, 7–10.

50. O'Connell, *Irish Politics*, 25–30; McDowell, *Ireland*, 240–46; Morley, *Irish Opinion*, 137–43 and 168–69; Curtin, *United Irishmen*, 17–19; "Address to the People of Ireland," quoted in Baseler, "*Asylum*," 140 ("a safe"); Whelan, "The Green Atlantic," 216–24.

51. O'Connell, *Irish Politics*, 22–23; Morley, *Irish Opinion*, 332; Wickwire and Wickwire, *Cornwallis*, 214–15; Durey, *Transatlantic Radicals*, 80–87; Watson, *Reign*, 242–46 and 388–90; Morris, *Peacemakers*, 283.

52. Hinde, *Castlereagh*, 19–21; D. Wilson, *United Irishmen*, 16–17; McDowell, "Ireland in 1800," 695–96.

53. John Adams to Robert R. Livingston, July 17, 1783, in Giunta, ed., *Emerging Nation*, 2:195; Watson, *Reign*, 253–56; McCusker, "British Mercantilist Policies," 337–62; Rodger, "Sea-Power and Empire, 1688–1793," 169–83.

54. Graham, *British Policy and Canada*, 56–59, 65, and 71 (Sir Guy Carleton quoted: "firm hold"); Ritcheson, *Aftermath*, 6; Milobar, "Conservative Ideology," 57–58; Board of Trade report quoted in Harlow, *Founding*, 2:259 ("no right").

55. Ritcheson, *Aftermath*, 5–6, 12, 18–20, 31–45, 50–56, and 63–69; Graham, *British Policy and Canada*, 62–71; Harlow, *Founding*, 2:254–58.

56. Wright, *Britain and the American Frontier*, 31–32.

57. William Smith, Jr., to Lord Dorchester, Feb. 5, 1790, in Shortt and Doughty, eds., *Documents*, 1018–19; McConville, *King's Three Faces*, 227 and 229n18; Upton, *Loyal Whig*, 104–33, 199, and 204; Harlow, *Founding*, 2:747–48.

58. Upton, *Loyal Whig*, 136–142 (Smith to Carleton, July 15, 1783, quoted on 141: "on the Eve"); Upton, ed., *Diary*, 1:276.

59. Henry Lee to George Washington, Nov. 11, 1786, and Edward Carrington to Edmund Randolph, Dec. 8, 1786, in P. H. Smith, ed., *Letters of Delegates*, 24:26 and 43–45; John Jay to Thomas Jefferson, Dec. 14, 1786, in Manning, ed., *Diplomatic Correspondence*, 1:32; Samuel Osgood to John Adams, Nov. 14, 1786, in Giunta, ed., *Emerging Nation*, 3:367–68; Szatmary, *Shays' Rebellion*, 108–9 and 118.

60. Lord Dorchester to Lord Sydney, June 9, 1788, and July 10, 1788, and Lord Grenville to Lord Dorchester, Oct. 20, 1789 ("It appears"), MG 11, 59:116 and 234, LAC; Harlow, *Founding*, 2:596–603; Graham, *British Policy and Canada*, 118–28 and 131–32; Wright, *Britain and the American Frontier*, 44.

61. Reuter, " 'Petty Spy' or Effective Diplomat," 472–73; Boyd, *Number* 7, 8–9; Upton, *Loyal Whig*, 201.

62. Boyd, *Number* 7, 6–10; R. H. Brown, *Redeeming*, 3–5; [Beckwith], "Enclosure A," in Lord Dorchester to Lord Sydney, Apr. 10, 1787, MG 11, 50:95, LAC.

63. [Beckwith], "Enclosure A," in Lord Dorchester to Lord Sydney, Apr. 10, 1787 ("At this moment" and "from experience"), MG 11, 50:95–97, LAC; Reuter, " 'Petty Spy' or Effective Diplomat," 477–79; Peter Allaire to Sir George Yonge, Mar. 7, 1787, in Giunta, ed., *Emerging Nation,* 3:445. For Alexander Hamilton's flirtation with monarchy, see also Syrett et al., eds., *Papers of Hamilton,* 26:198n4 and 324n3.

64. Lord Sydney to Lord Dorchester, Sept. 14, 1787, MG 11, 51:44, LAC.

65. [Beckwith], "Enclosure A," in Lord Dorchester to Lord Sydney, Apr. 10, 1787, MG 11, 50: 95, LAC; Rakove, *Original Meanings,* 23–56; Wood, *Creation,* 430–564.

66. [George Beckwith], enclosure in Lord Dorchester to Lord Sydney, Oct. 14, 1788 ("of energy"), MG 11, 41:109, LAC.

67. Neatby, *Quebec,* 87–141, 172, and 181–92; Lanctot, *Canada,* 17–18.

68. Upton, *Loyal Whig,* 150 and 167; Greenwood, *Legacies of Fear,* 8–9; Colley, *Britons,* 11–54; Milobar, "Conservative Ideology," 52; Harlow, *Founding,* 2:725–26.

69. William Smith, Jr., to Lord Dorchester, Feb. 5, 1790, and Lord Grenville to Dorchester, June 5, 1790, in Shortt and Doughty, eds., *Documents,* 1018–19 and 1027; Greenwood, *Legacies of Fear,* 10–11; Upton, *Loyal Whig,* 142, 154–88; G. P. Browne, "Guy Carleton, 1st Baron Dorchester," *DCB,* 5:148–49; Harlow, *Founding,* 2:731–32 and 747–48.

70. Hugh Finlay to Evan Nepean, Apr. 4 and July 30, 1788, MG 11, vol. 61, LAC; Henry Hope to Lord Dorchester, May 1, 1787, MG 11, 40:374, LAC; Adam Mabane to Frederick Haldimand, June 27 and July 27, 1789, and Gabriel Christie to Frederick Haldimand, Oct. 19, 1789 ("Ruin"), MG 21, reel A-670, LAC; Hugh Finlay to Evan Nepean, Feb. 13, 1787 ("barrier"), MG 11, 41:276, LAC. A partisan of the British party, Finlay summarized an argument that he disagreed with.

71. Lord Dorchester to Lord Sydney, June 13, 1787, MG 11, 50:107, LAC; Upton, *Loyal Whig,* 161–66, 177, and 189–92; Lord Grenville to Lord Dorchester, Oct. 20, 1789, in Shortt and Doughty, eds., *Documents,* 970; Milobar, "Conservative Ideology," 45 and 61–63; Harlow, *Founding,* 2:751–52; Greenwood, *Legacies of Fear,* 35–38.

72. Craig, *Upper Canada,* 15–19; Upton, *Loyal Whig,* 202; "Discussion of Petitions and Counter Petitions," and William W. Grenville to Lord Dorchester, Oct. 20, 1789, in Shortt and Doughty, eds., *Documents,* 976 and 987–88.

73. Harlow, *Founding,* 2:760–62; Mason, "American Loyalist Diaspora," 244; "Discussion of Petitions and Counter Petitions," in Shortt and Doughty, eds., *Documents,* 983–86 (982: "the constitution" and 983: "no care"); Lord Thurlow to W. W. Grenville, Sept. 10, 1789, in Cruikshank, ed., *Correspondence of Simcoe,* 1:4–5.

74. Lord Dorchester to William W. Grenville, Feb. 8, 1790, in Shortt and Doughty, eds., *Documents,* 1004.

75. Young, *Democratic Republicans,* 237.

76. Bushman, *King and People,* 118–25, 137–38, 155–62, and 165–75; Potter, *Liberty We Seek,* 172; Upper Canada Civil Establishments for 1794 and 1795, in Cruikshank, ed., *Correspondence of Simcoe,* 3:250, and 4:167; McCalla, *Planting the Province,* 17–19 and 352n27.

77. Shortt and Doughty, eds., *Documents,* 985–86; "An Act for Laying and Collecting of Assessments and Rates," *Upper Canada Gazette,* July 25, 1793; John Graves Simcoe to Henry Dundas, Aug. 2, 1794, and the Upper Canada Civil Establishments for 1794 and 1795, in Cruikshank, ed., *Correspondence of Simcoe,* 3:1–2, 3:250, and 4:167; McCalla, *Planting the Province,* 17–19, 352n27, and 352n28. For the provincial revenue

in 1808, see Francis Gore to Sir James H. Craig, Jan. 5, 1808, in Brymner, ed., "Note B: Anticipation," 35.

78. [Anonymous], "Canadian Letters," 126; M. Smith, *Geographical View*, 60; John Askin to James McGill, Oct. 7, 1805, in Quaife, ed., *John Askin Papers*, 2:484; American emigrant quoted in Maude, *Visit to the Falls*, 60. For New York's tax rate on land, see Young, *Democratic Republicans*, 27 and 61.

79. Gates, *Land Policies*, 24–25 and 303; Lord Grenville to Lord Dorchester, Oct. 20, 1789 ("if it"), in Shortt and Doughty, eds., *Documents*, 970.

80. "Discussion of Petitions and Counter Petitions," in Shortt and Doughty, eds., *Documents*, 983–87.

81. Bushman, *King and People*, 85–86; Morgan, *Inventing the People*, 239–62; Greenwood and Wright, "Parliamentary Privilege," 412–15; "Discussion of Petitions and Counter Petitions," in Shortt and Doughty, eds., *Documents*, 984–86.

82. Burt, *Old Province*, 2:116–58; Upton, *Loyal Whig*, 150–51 and 167; Craig, *Upper Canada*, 17–19; Lord Grenville to Lord Dorchester, Oct. 20, 1789, in Shortt and Doughty, eds., *Documents*, 987–89; Greenwood, *Legacies of Fear*, 43–44.

83. Greenwood, *Legacies of Fear*, 45; Craig, *Upper Canada*, 17–19; "Discussion of Petitions and Counter Petitions," in Shortt and Doughty, eds., *Documents*, 977.

84. William Osgoode to John Graves Simcoe, "Secret & Confidential," n.d. but c. 1793 ("Grain is"), and Simcoe to Lord Dorchester, June 15, 1794 ("indispensably necessary"), in Cruikshank, ed., *Correspondence of Simcoe*, 2:124 and 3:109; Gates, *Land Policies*, 35–36; Johnson, *Becoming Prominent*, 79.

85. Garner, *Franchise and Politics*, 82–90; "List of the Poll and Candidates for the County of Leeds," June 21, 1804, MG 24, B 7 (Charles Jones Papers), 1:275, LAC.

86. James, "First Legislators," 93–119; Romney, *Mr. Attorney*, 21. For the republican innovations, see Morgan, *Inventing the People*, 239–62; Wood, *Creation*, 162–96.

87. John Graves Simcoe to Peter Russell, July 17, 1791 ("The persons"), quoted in Gates, *Land Policies*, 36; Simcoe to Henry Dundas, Nov. 4, 1792, and Sept. 16, 1793, and to the Duke of Portland, Dec. 20, 1794, in Cruikshank, ed., *Correspondence of Simcoe*, 1:249, 2:53, and 3:237; Errington, *Lion*, 29–32; Craig, *Upper Canada*, 31.

88. David W. Smith to John Askin, July 26, 1792 ("I beg"), and Aug. 14 ("Let the peasants"), 1792, in Cruikshank, ed., *Correspondence of Simcoe*, 1:182 and 196.

89. David W. Smith to John Askin, Oct. 2, 1792 ("We cannot"), in Cruikshank, ed., *Correspondence of Simcoe*, 1:231–32.

90. Riddell, ed., *La Rochefoucault-Liancourt's Travels*, 51 ("Where no taxes").

91. Wood, *Radicalism*, 287–305. For the reactionary nature of the postwar empire, see Bayly, *Imperial Meridian*, 1–15; Gould, "American Independence," 107–41.

92. Young, *Democratic Republicans*, 17–22; Varga, "Election Procedures and Practices," 249–77; Countryman, *People in Revolution*, 76–79 and 166–69; Spafford, *Gazetteer*, 25–28.

93. Lord Thurlow to W. W. Grenville, Sept. 10, 1789, in Cruikshank, ed., *Correspondence of Simcoe*, 1:4–5 ("have given"); Milobar, "Conservative Ideology," 64.

Chapter Two: Simcoe

1. William Dummer Powell, "First Days in Upper Canada," 1044, MG 23 H-I-4, LAC.

2. John Graves Simcoe to Joseph Banks, Jan. 8, 1791 ("I am one"), Simcoe to Henry Dundas, Aug. 12 and Aug. 26, 1791 ("It is in"), Simcoe to Alured Clarke,

Apr. 5, 1793, and Simcoe to the Duke of Portland, Jan. 22, 1795, in Cruikshank, ed., *Correspondence of Simcoe*, 1:17, 1:43, 1:52–53, 1:310, and 3:265; Craig, *Upper Canada*, 120–22; S. R. Mealing, "John Graves Simcoe," *DCB*, 5:755.

3. John Graves Simcoe to Evan Nepean, Dec. 3, 1789, in Cruikshank, ed., *Correspondence of Simcoe*, 1:7; Riddell, *Simcoe*, 17–21 and 31–35 (Captain Simcoe's maxims); Mealing, "John Graves Simcoe," *DCB*, 5:754; Simcoe, *Simcoe's Military Journal*, iii–iv; [Anonymous], "Canadian Letters," 140 ("a man of some reading").

4. Mealing, "John Graves Simcoe,"*DCB*, 5:754; Riddell, *Simcoe*, 55–58 and 63; Simcoe, *Military Journal*, ii–iii, 1–3, 8, and 26.

5. Simcoe to the Duke of Portland, Dec. 20, 1794, in Cruikshank, ed., *Correspondence of Simcoe*, 3:233; Simcoe, "Remarks," 18–19 ("fined, whipt").

6. Riddell, *Simcoe*, 58–59; Simcoe, *Military Journal*, 62; Willcox, ed., *American Rebellion*, 147–48.

7. Simcoe, *Military Journal*, 32 and 84–85; Kaplan, "Hidden War," 123–29; Van Doren, *Secret History*, 283–390; Riddell, *Simcoe*, 64 and 70n10.

8. Simcoe, *Military Journal*, 146–49; Riddell, *Simcoe*, 64–66.

9. Mealing, "John Graves Simcoe," *DCB*, 5:754; Innis, ed., *Mrs. Simcoe's Diary*, 3–4; Riddell, ed., *La Rochefoucault-Liancourt's Travels*, 25–26 and 38; [Anonymous], "Canadian Letters," 139.

10. Riddell, ed., *La Rochefoucault-Liancourt's Travels*, 37 ("The hatred").

11. Simcoe, "Remarks," 17–19, 27, 29, 33, and 43–46 ("let all"); Riddell, *Simcoe*, 91.

12. Charles Stevenson to John Graves Simcoe, May 8, 1792 ("inclined"), and Simcoe to Henry Dundas, Nov. 4, 1792 ("same manner"), in Cruikshank, ed., *Correspondence of Simcoe*, 1:156 and 246. Dundas rebuked Simcoe and Stevenson for considering such a plot. See Dundas to Simcoe, Oct. 2, 1793, in Cruikshank, ed., *Correspondence of Simcoe*, 2:79–82.

13. John Graves Simcoe to Evan Nepean, Dec. 3, 1789, Simcoe to Henry Dundas, June 30, 1791, Simcoe to Alexander Grant, Dec. 1, 1791, Simcoe to Lord Dorchester, Mar. 3, 1794, and Simcoe to the Duke of Portland, Dec. 21, 1794, and June 18, 1796, all in Cruikshank, ed., *Correspondence of Simcoe*, 1:7, 1:27, 1:86, 2:176, 3:235, and 4:302.

14. John Graves Simcoe to Joseph Banks, Jan. 8, 1791, in Cruikshank, ed., *Correspondence of Simcoe*, 1:18; Simcoe to Lord Grenville, undated, c. 1791, in Simcoe Papers, reel MS-1797, AO; MacLeod, "Fortress Ontario or Forlorn Hope?," 155.

15. John Graves Simcoe to Sir Joseph Banks, Jan. 8, 1791, Simcoe to Henry Dundas, June 30, 1791, Simcoe to James Bland Burgess, Aug. 21, 1792, and Simcoe to the Lords of Trade, Sept. 1, 1794, in Cruikshank, ed., *Correspondence of Simcoe*, 1:18, 1:28, 1:205, and 3:60; Peter Russell to Simcoe, Aug. 16, 1791, in Simcoe Papers, reel MS-1797, AO.

16. John Graves Simcoe to Henry Dundas, June 30, 1791 ("utmost Attention"), and Nov. 4, 1792, and Simcoe to Lord Dorchester, Mar. 3, 1794, in Cruikshank, ed., *Correspondence of Simcoe*, 1:27, and 1:250, and 2:176.

17. John Graves Simcoe to Henry Dundas, Dec. 7, 1791, and Apr. 28, 1792, and E. B. Littlehales, Journal, Mar. 2, 1793, in Cruikshank, ed., *Correspondence of Simcoe*, 1:18, 144, and 293; Simcoe to James Bland Burgess, Sept. 23, 1793, in Jackman, ed., "Two Simcoe Letters," 42; William Dummer Powell, memorandum, May 27, 1801, RG 5, A 1, 2:604, reel C-4502, LAC; Brant quoted by Lord Selkirk in P. White, ed., *Lord Selkirk's Diary*, 153 ("great deal").

18. [Anonymous], "Canadian Letters," 143–46; Craig, *Upper Canada*, 31; John Graves Simcoe to Henry Dundas, Sept. 16, 1793, in Cruikshank, ed., *Correspondence of*

Simcoe, 2:53; Winks, *Blacks in Canada*, 96–99. In 1798, after Simcoe left the colony, the provincial assembly passed a bill to revive the importation of slaves into the province, but the legislative council and Simcoe's administrator, Peter Russell, blocked the bill. See Couture, *Study*, 65.

19. Craig, *Upper Canada*, 35–38; McCalla, *Planting the Province*, 249; Ellis, "Rise of the Empire State," 5–6; Macauley, *Natural, Statistical and Civil History*, 1:417–18.

20. Robert Hamilton to Peter Russell, Nov. 1, 1798 ("The Trade"), F 46 (Russell Papers), reel MS-75/5, AO; Richard Cartwright to Peter Hunter, Aug. 23, 1799, in Cartwright, ed., *Life and Letters*, 96; Wood, *Making Ontario*, 22–28; McCalla, *Planting the Province*, 15–17; Creighton, *Empire*, 116–23.

21. Simcoe to Henry Dundas, Aug. 12, 1791, and Nov. 23, 1792, in Cruikshank, ed., *Correspondence of Simcoe*, 1:50–51 and 264; F. Landon, *Western Ontario*, 6.

22. Richard Cartwright to Peter Hunter, Aug. 23, 1799, in Cartwright, ed., *Life and Letters*, 96.

23. John Graves Simcoe to Henry Dundas, June 30, 1791, in Cruikshank, ed., *Correspondence of Simcoe*, 1:27.

24. Simcoe, "Proclamation," Feb. 7, 1792, in Cruikshank, ed., *Correspondence of Simcoe*, 1:108; Gates, *Land Policies*, 28; Cruikshank, "Petitions for Grants of Land, 1792–1796," 17; John Munro to John Graves Simcoe, Mar. 14, 1792 ("the pleasure"), Simcoe Letterbook for 1792–1793, Manuscript #558, HL; Innis, ed., *Mrs. Simcoe's Diary*, 81; Craig, *Upper Canada*, 67 and 70–71. For land prices in the United States, see Ellis, *Landlords and Farmers*, 25; Evans, *Holland Land Company*, 45; Rohrbough, *Land Office Business*, 10.

25. For skepticism regarding the Late Loyalists, see Brown and Senior, *Victorious in Defeat*, 51; Errington, *Lion*, 40 and 47; Sheppard, *Plunder*, 19.

26. W. Brown, "Loyalists and Non-Participants," 126–27; Van Doren, *Secret History*, 66–112; P. H. Smith, *Loyalists and Redcoats*, 77–86.

27. For the York and Northumberland connection, see Burkholder, *Brief History*, 21–22; Sider, "Early Years of Tunkers," 121–24; C. Johnston, "Outline of Early Settlement," 55–57; Cruikshank, ed, "Petitions for Grants of Land, . . . 1796–1799," 141–42; John E. Eshelman, "A Brief History and Genealogical Record of the Yonge Street Quaker Pioneer Families Migrating from Pennsylvania to Upper Canada, 1800–1825," MU 2101, AO. For the Rankin plot, see Van Doren, *Secret History*, 130–34, 221–23, 404–16; Simcoe, *Military Journal*, 85–86; Willcox, ed., *American Rebellion*, 518, 523, 535, and 555.

28. Simcoe to George Yonge, June 17, 1792 ("I have"), and Simcoe to Henry Dundas, June 21, 1792, in Cruikshank, ed., *Correspondence of Simcoe*, 1:166 and 172; "Governor Simcoe's Conversation with Pierce Duff, June 1793 at Niagara," in Timothy Pickering Papers, 59:190, MHS; Riddell, ed., *La Rochefoucault-Liancourt's Travels*, 38–39 ("no hillock").

29. Lord Dorchester to the Seven Nations, Feb. 10, 1794, Dorchester to John Graves Simcoe, Feb. 17, 1794, Dorchester to Henry Dundas, Feb. 24, 1794, Simcoe to Dorchester, Apr. 29, 1794, and July 10, 1794, and John Jay to George Washington, July 21, 1794, in Cruikshank, ed., *Correspondence of Simcoe*, 2:149–50, 154, 160, 220, 315, and 333; Wright, *Britain and the American Frontier*, 87–88; Werner, "War Scare and Politics," 324–34.

30. John Graves Simcoe to Lord Dorchester, July 23, 1794 ("Upper Canada"), Simcoe to Henry Dundas, Aug. 5, 1794, Simcoe to Dorchester, Aug. 16, 1794, Simcoe, Diary, Sept. 27, 1794, and Robert Newman to unknown, Oct. 2, 1794 (Simcoe quoted:

"destroy the mob"), in Cruikshank, ed., *Correspondence of Simcoe*, 2:336, 2:353, 2:382–83, 3:98, and 3:114; MacLeod, "Fortress Ontario," 158 and 161–67.

31. John Graves Simcoe to the Duke of Portland, Oct. 23, 1794, in Cruikshank, ed., *Correspondence of Simcoe*, 3:144; MacLeod, "Fortress Ontario," 169–78. For Simcoe's animus from 1783, see Simcoe, *Military Journal*, 148–49; and Riddell, *Simcoe*, 65–66.

32. Simcoe, *Military Journal*, 36–37, 69, and 147; John Graves Simcoe to Henry Dundas, June 20, 1794, in Cruikshank, ed., *Correspondence of Simcoe*, 2:286–87.

33. John Jay to George Washington, July 21, 1794, in H. Johnston, ed., *Correspondence of John Jay*, 4:33–34; Wright, *Britain and the American Frontier*, 92–95; Henry Dundas to John Graves Simcoe, July 4, 1794, and Duke of Portland to Simcoe, Sept. 5, 1794, in Cruikshank, ed., *Correspondence of Simcoe*, 2:300 and 3:39.

34. John Graves Simcoe to the Duke of Portland, Nov. 10, 1794, Portland to Simcoe, Nov. 19, 1794, Simcoe to Portland, Dec. 20, 1794, May 20, 1795, and Oct. 30, 1795, in Cruikshank, ed., *Correspondence of Simcoe*, 3:176, 3:184, 3:230–32, 4:14, and 4:118; MacLeod, "Fortress Ontario," 168.

35. William Jarvis to Samuel Peters, Nov. 10, 1795 ("peevish"), John Graves Simcoe to Duke of Portland, Dec. 1, 1795, in Cruikshank, ed., *Correspondence of Simcoe*, 4:139 and 152; John White to Peter Russell, June 30, 1796 ("footballs"), Russell Papers, box 2 (1796–98), Baldwin Room, TRL.

36. John Graves Simcoe to Duke of Portland, May 20, 1795, Lord Dorchester to Simcoe, July 31, 1795, and May 26, 1796, Simcoe to Richard England, June 1, 1796, and Joseph Chew to Alexander McKee, Aug. 11, 1796, in Cruikshank, ed., *Correspondence of Simcoe*, 4:14, 55, 275, 285, and 345; John Stuart to William White, Oct. 1, 1796 ("Foresight"), in Cruikshank, ed., *Correspondence of Peter Russell*, 1:52.

37. Thomas Merritt to Nehemiah Merritt, July 16, 1800 ("astonished"), in Talman, ed., *Loyalist Narratives*, 286; Cruikshank, ed., "Petitions for Grants of Land," 17; McCalla, *Planting the Province*, 15; M. Smith, *Geographical View*, 51. For want of a census or any surviving and comprehensive register of the newcomers, the pace and scale of immigration defy precise calculation.

38. Simon Desjardins et al., "Castorland Journal," Oct. 9, 1793, translated by Franklin B. Hough, typescript, AAS; Coventry, *Memoirs*, 1:780; Ogden, *Tour*, 66; Higgins, *Life of Gould*, 24–25; Wood, *Making Ontario*, 23–27. In 1796 the colony's surveyor general, David W. Smith, collected data on 250 male immigrants who obtained land between November 6, 1794, and December 31, 1795. Nearly three-quarters (71 percent) came from the United States, with the British Isles (22 percent) accounting for most of the rest. The Americans primarily came from New Jersey (*n* = 54), New York (50), and Pennsylvania (29). Smaller numbers originated in New England (9) or the southern states (13). The numbers do not all add up to 250 because of missing data for some variables: in 21 cases for origin; 21 cases for age; and in 45 cases for occupational status. The calculations exclude the cases that do not provide data for that variable. The British immigrants came from Ireland (27), Scotland (12), and England (12). Another 16 immigrants came from Germany (8), Bermuda (1), Nova Scotia (1), Lower Canada (5), and Spain (1). See David W. Smith, Report, Jan. 30, 1796, RG 1, A-II-1, 1:33, reel MS-3696, AO.

39. John Graves Simcoe to Henry Dundas, Feb. 23, 1794, in Cruikshank, ed., *Correspondence of Simcoe*, 2:162; Riddell, ed., *La Rochefoucault-Liancourt's Travels*, 60; D. W. Smith, *Short Topographical Description*, 34–35.

40. Alexander Macdonell to John Graves Simcoe, Oct. 5, 1791 ("silver-tongued"), RG 1, A-I-6, reel MS-563/1, AO; William Dummer Powell, "First Days in Upper

Canada," 1044 ("base"), MG 23 H-I-4, LAC; Richard Cartwright to Peter Hunter, Aug. 23, 1799, in Cartwright, ed., *Life and Letters*, 96–97; Thomas Talbot to John Sullivan, Oct. 27, 1802 ("Those"), in Cruikshank, ed., "Early History of the London District," 207; Maude, *Visit to the Falls*, 60 ("a nest"); Errington, *Lion*, 51; Garner, *The Franchise*, 86.

41. Benjamin Mortimer, Journal, May 13, 1798 ("has invited"), in Gray, ed., "From Bethlehem to Fairfield," 116; William Bentinck, Journal, Apr. 26, 1800 ("Five hundred"), MG 24 H-I, LAC; Budka, ed., "Journey to Niagara," 105 ("Thus having"); Richard Cartwright to Peter Hunter, Aug. 23, 1799, in Cartwright, ed., *Life and Letters*, 96; M. Smith, *Geographical View*, iii ("in order"), 211–12; Ellicott, "Extracts," 125.

42. Ogden, *Tour*, 34 ("The object"); John Stuart to Jacob Mountain, Apr. 23, 1795, and Aug. 23, 1795, in Preston, ed., *Kingston*, 300 and 305; Johnson, *Becoming Prominent*, 24 and 30.

43. Gates, *Land Policies*, 30–31; Jacob Watson to John Graves Simcoe, n.d. but c. Feb. 1794, in Cruikshank, ed., *Correspondence of Simcoe*, 5:81–82; Silvester Tiffany to Jedediah Morse, Nov. 20, 1796, and Tiffany to Samuel Allen, May 1, 1796, Misc. Coll., NYHS; Kline, ed., *Correspondence of Burr*, 1:222n1; Robert Liston quoted in Parmet and Hecht, *Aaron Burr*, 113 ("high-flying").

44. M. Smith, *Geographical View*, iii; Francis Gore to William Windham, Oct. 1, 1806, in Brymner, ed., *Report on Canadian Archives, 1892*, 37.

45. Peter Hunter to Lord Hobart, Apr. 25, 1804 ("principally settled"), MG 11, 334:34, reel B-288, LAC; P. White, ed., *Lord Selkirk's Diary*, 156 ("lowest order"); Boulton, *Sketch*, 7; Richard Cartwright to Hunter, Aug. 23, 1799, in Cartwright, ed., *Life and Letters*, 96; David W. Smith, Report, Jan. 30, 1796, RG 1, A-II-1, 1:33, reel MS-3696, AO. Of the 250 immigrants assessed in Smith's report, 137 were in their teens or twenties, 59 in their thirties, and only 44 were older men. A register survives of male newcomers taking the oath of allegiance between 1794 and 1800 in the Home District, the center of government and settlement in the colony. Of the 719 names on the register, 171 (24 percent) made a mark instead of signing, an illiteracy rate about three times higher than usually prevailed in the northern American states during the 1790s. See Upper Canada, Oaths of Allegiance, Home District, 1794–1800, RG 1, E11, vol. 16, LAC. For the second, smaller register, see Robert Kerr, Register, Feb. 23, 1793, RG 1, E 11, vol. 11, LAC. By "relatively poor," I do not mean that they were beggars utterly without means, merely that they came from the lower class of agriculturalists: those who possessed farm tools and some livestock but few consumer goods and little or no credit. On the oath register, 35 of the names were subscribed by other men in lists from a common settlement, so they have been excluded from the calculations. If we assume that they were illiterate and include them, then the illiterate proportion rises to 206 of 754 (27 percent).

46. Mortimer, Journal, May 13, 1798, in Gray, ed., "From Bethlehem," 60.

47. McCalla, *Planting the Province*, 24–25; P. Campbell, *Travels*, 121–22; [Anonymous], "Canadian Letters," 88–89 and 113–16; Richard Cartwright to Isaac Todd, Oct. 21, 1792, in Cruikshank, ed., *Correspondence of Simcoe*, 1:239.

48. P. Campbell, *Travels*, 136; Bigelow, *Journal*, 66; Mortimer, Journal, May 19, 1798 ("no stores"), in Gray, ed., "From Bethlehem," 125; Russell to Hugh Hovell Farmer, Mar. 2, 1795 ("best Country"), MG 23, H-II-7, 2:7, reel A-128, LAC.

49. Gates, *Land Policies*, 1–80; Riddell, ed., *La Rochefoucault-Liancourt's Travels*, 53 and 71–72; John Elmsley to Peter Russell, Nov. 26, 1797 ("Who will work"), in Cruikshank, ed., *Correspondence of Russell*, 2:25–26.

50. Gray, ed., "From Bethlehem," 121 and 125; P. Campbell, *Travels*, 136; John McGill to James Green, May 23, 1797, in Cruikshank, ed., *Correspondence of Russell*, 1:176–77. For civil society, see McNairn, *Capacity to Judge*, 9–17; Wilton, *Popular Politics*, 11–12.

51. Robert Lochiel Fraser, III, "Benajah Mallory," *DCB*, 8:606–8; Muir, "Burford's First Settler," 492–95; Riddell, "Benajah Mallory," 573–75.

52. Burkholder, *Brief History*, 21–22; Sider, "Early Years of Tunkers," 121–24; Reaman, *Trail of the Black Walnut*, 65 and 102; C. Johnston, "Outline of Early Settlement," 55–57; Richard Cartwright to Isaac Brock, Feb. 26, 1812 ("The Country"), F 24, 4:344, reel MS-44, AO; Melish, *Travels*, 2:318–19 and 336; John E. Eshelman, "A Brief History and Genealogical Record of the Yonge Street Quaker Pioneer Families Migrating from Pennsylvania to Upper Canada, 1800–1825," MU 2101, AO; Dorland, *Society of Friends*, 52–53 and 92–94; Sherk, "Pennsylvania Germans," 100–101; Healey, *From Quaker*, 39–40, 58–60, and 65. For the revolutionary alienation of the pacifist denominations, see W. Brown, "Loyalists," 126–27; Riordan, *Many Identities*, 43–81.

53. Charles Stevenson to John Graves Simcoe, Mar. 27, 1792, Simcoe to Phineas Bond, May 7, 1792, and Simcoe to Henry Dundas, Aug. 20, 1792, in Cruikshank, ed., *Correspondence of Simcoe*, 1:124, 151–54, and 198; Epp, *Mennonites*, 51–61 and 97–103; Wallace, ed., "Captain Miles Macdonnell's Journal," 176 ("They were").

54. Riordan, *Many Identities*, 83–130; Schrauwers, "Politics of Schism," 38; Healey, *From Quaker*, 3–4; Peter Lossing to unknown, Jan. 26, 1811 ("pleasing in theory"), RG 5, A 1, 13:5192, reel C-4507, LAC; Jacob Burckholder, petition, n.d. but c. 1794, RG 1, A-I-1, 50:526, reel MS-626/1, AO.

55. Christopher Beswick to James Green, Jan. 10, 1805 ("have not forgot"), RG 5, A 1, 4:1281, reel C-4503, LAC; F. Landon, *Western Ontario*, 19–20. For the majoritarian, republican threat to minority communities posed by the American Revolution, see Nelson, *American Tory*, 90–91; Mancke, "Another British America," 5 and 17.

56. Hansen and Brebner, *Mingling*, 83–85; C. Johnston, "An Outline," 55–57; Colley, *Captives*, 234–38; Countryman, "Indians," 342–62; Frederick Haldimand to Lord North, Nov. 27, 1783, MG 11, 46:41, reel B-37, LAC.

57. P. White, ed., *Lord Selkirk's Diary*, 173 and 198; Gray, ed., "From Bethlehem," 112, 121, and 125; Higgins, *Life of Gould*, 24–25; Reaman, *Trail of the Black Walnut*, 65 and 102; Wise, *God's Peculiar Peoples*, 190; Errington, *Lion*, 14–15; Healey, *From Quaker*, 31–32 and 38.

58. John Graves Simcoe to Henry Dundas, June 30, 1791, Aug. 12, 1791, and Nov. 6, 1792, and Jacob Mountain to Dundas, Sept. 15, 1794 ("would prove"), in Cruikshank, ed., *Correspondence of Simcoe*, 1:31–33, 1:43, 1:252, and 3:91; William Dummer Powell, Oct. n.d., 1797 ("religious Establishments"), in Cruikshank, ed., *Correspondence of Russell*, 1:311.

59. Healey, *From Quaker*, 10–11; Fahey, *In His Name*, 1–7, 116, and 118 (includes John Strachan: "will of God").

60. John Stuart to Charles Inglis, July 5, 1791, and Jacob Mountain to Henry Dundas, Sept. 15, 1794, in Preston, ed., *Kingston*, 176 and 292; Rawlyk, *Canada Fire*, 104; Fahey, *In His Name*, 9; Richard Cartwright to John Graves Simcoe, Oct. 12, 1792, in Cruikshank, ed., *Correspondence of Simcoe*, 1:235; Adamson, "God's Continent Divided," 433.

61. John Stuart to Jacob Mountain, Apr. 23 and Aug. 23, 1795, in Preston, ed., *Kingston*, 300 and 305–6.

62. McCartney, "Sectarian Strife," 69–72; Grant, *Profusion of Spires*, 22; Dorland, *History of the Society of Friends*, 63 and 79–83; Epp, *Mennonites in Canada*, 56–61; Sider, "Early Years of Tunkers," 123–24; Alexander Macdonell, petition, June 20, 1792 ("great churches"), MG 23, H-I-1, ser. 3, 2:136, LAC; Healey, *From Quaker*, 41–42.

63. Hannah Jarvis to Samuel Peters, Mar. 4, 1810 ("a Veil"), MG 23, H-I-3, 2:186, LAC; Christie, "In These Times," 11–19; Adamson, "God's Continent Divided," 417 and 445–46; Jacob Mountain to Henry Dundas, Sept. 15, 1794 ("dissolve"), in Preston, ed., *Kingston*, 292.

64. Ivison and Rosser, *Baptists*, 121–22; Rawlyk, *Canada Fire*, 112 and 148–55; Moir, "Early Methodism," 54.

65. Amelia Harris, "Historical Memoranda," in Talman, ed., *Loyalist Narratives*, 143 ("the class"); Playter, *History of Methodism in Canada*, 42–48 and 98; Rawlyk, *Canada Fire*, 102 and 121–22; French, *Parsons & Politics*, 41–46.

66. John Stuart to Charles Inglis, Mar. 5, 1790, and Jacob Mountain to Henry Dundas, Sept. 15, 1794 in Preston, ed., *Kingston*, 157 and 292; Richard Cartwright to Isaac Brock, Feb. 26, 1812 ("The Country"), F 24, 4:344, reel MS-44, AO; Adamson, "God's Continent Divided," 433; French, *Parsons & Politics*, 41–45 and 70; Ivison and Rosser, *Baptists*, 80. Between 1790 and 1812 the New York Methodist Conference sent seventy-six missionaries to Upper Canada; all but seven were of American birth.

67. John Stuart to Charles Inglis, Mar. 5, 1790, and Court of Quarter Sessions Proceedings, Apr. 14, 1790, in Preston, ed., *Kingston*, 157–58 and 159–60; Playter, *History of Methodism in Canada*, 17; Sissons, "Martyrdom," 12–13.

68. Johnson, *Becoming Prominent*, 26, 50, 59, 92–103, and 148.

69. John Elmsley to Peter Russell, Nov. 26, 1797 ("the weakest"), in Cruikshank, ed., *Correspondence of Russell*, 2:33; Playter, *History of Methodism in Canada*, 56; Ivison and Rosser, *Baptists*, 122–25; Fahey, *In His Name*, 9.

70. Hinderaker, *Elusive Empires*, 260–61; Baseler, "*Asylum*," 254–55; P. J. Smith, "Civic Humanism versus Liberalism," 114.

71. Armstrong, *Handbook*, 158–59 and 198.

72. Johnson, *Becoming Prominent*, 60–65; Armstrong, *Handbook*, 158–59; B. Wilson, *Enterprises*, 117–18; Wylie, "Instruments," 14–19; Romney, *Mr. Attorney*, 37.

73. David McGregor Rogers, Memorandum, Mar. 5, 1808 ("An American"), F 533 (Rogers Family Papers), reel MS-522, AO; Johnson, *Becoming Prominent*, 60–65, 79, 84, and 148; M. M. Smith, *Geographical View*, 69.

74. Charles Stevenson to Henry Dundas, July 31, 1793 ("that he had said"), and E. B. Littlehales to D. Short, Dec. 30, 1794, in Cruikshank, ed., *Correspondence of Simcoe*, 1:410 and 3:243; Executive Council Minutes, July 6, 1798 ("preferring"), in Cruikshank, ed., *Correspondence of Russell*, 2:206.

75. Wright, "Sedition in Upper Canada," 7; William Demont, "To the Public," *Upper Canada Gazette*, May 11, 1799.

76. E. Howe, "Recollections of a Pioneer Printer," 378 ("No mails"); James Green to Thomas Scott, Jan. 16, 1804, RG 4-1, box 1, folder 1804–1810, AO; Peter Hunter to Lord Hobart, Apr. 25, 1804 ("did not produce"), MG 11, 334:33, reel B-288, LAC; Titus Geer Simons, affidavit, Feb. 2, 1807, in Brymner, ed., "Political State," 78; Thomas Welch to William Halton, Dec. 12, 1808, RG 5, A 1, 8:3522, reel C-4503, LAC.

77. Robert Hamilton to John Graves Simcoe, Aug. 16, 1794 ("to associate"), in Cruikshank, ed., *Correspondence of Simcoe*, 2:385; *Canada Constellation*, Sept. 6, 1799; Isaac James et al., petition, Mar. 5, 1808, RG 5, A-1, 7:2917–18, LAC.

78. Executive Council Minutes, Sept. 17, 1799, MG 11, 332:87, reel B-287, LAC; Robert Short to David W. Smith, Oct. 7, 1797 ("to render"), RG 1, A-I-6, reel 563/2, AO; Wilton, *Popular Politics*, 9; McNairn, *Capacity to Judge*, 92–93.

79. Errington, *Lion*, 51; Major William Graham to David W. Smith, Mar. 29, 1802 ("They use"), MG 11, 332:44, reel B-287, LAC; *Upper Canada Gazette*, July 6, 1799. Graham referred to Webster, *American Selection of Lessons*, see especially 115–40.

80. David W. Smith to the Executive Council, Aug. 14, 1798 ("May Loyalty"), RG 1, A-II-1, 1:314, reel MS-3696, AO; Richard Cartwright to Henry Allcock, Mar. 17, 1807, in Cartwright, ed., *Life and Letters*, 134; Melish, *Travels*, 2:338 ("There is").

81. John Graves Simcoe to Alured Clarke, May 31, 1793 ("a Government"), in Cruikshank, ed., *Correspondence of Simcoe*, 1:343; McNairn, *Capacity to Judge*, 139, 159, and 179.

82. McNairn, *Capacity to Judge*, 139, 159, and 179; Ogden, *Tour*, 50 ("carefully guarded").

83. John Elmsley to Peter Russell, Nov. 26, 1797, in Cruikshank, ed., *Correspondence of Russell*, 2:28; Simcoe to Alured Clarke, May 31, 1793, Simcoe to the Duke of Portland, Dec. 20, 1794, and Simcoe to John King, Feb. 16, 1795, in Cruikshank, ed., *Correspondence of Simcoe*, 3:233 and 298; Riddell, ed., *La Rochefoucault-Liancourt's Travels*, 75 ("As to"). For New York State newspapers in 1795, see Lathem, *Chronological Tables*, 31–35.

84. Wallace, "First Journalists," 372–81; Riddell, ed., *La Rochefoucault-Liancourt's Travels*, 57–58 ("abstract").

85. E. B. Littlehales to William [*sic:* Gideon] Tiffany, Apr. 19, 1795 ("Good sense" and "a libel"), in Cruikshank, ed., *Correspondence of Simcoe*, 3:346; Court of King's Bench, rough term-books, Apr. 24 and July 19, 1797, RG 22, ser. 126, AO; Daniel J. Brock, "Gideon Tiffany," *DCB*, 8:887; John Elmsley to David W. Smith, Feb. 25, 1798 ("finest thing"), and Executive Council Minutes, Apr. 25, 1798, in Cruikshank, ed., *Correspondence of Russell*, 2:104 and 144; John White to Peter Russell, Apr. 23, 1798 ("I think"), and Silvester Tiffany to Russell, Apr. 30, 1798, in Russell Papers, box 2, Baldwin Room, TRL.

86. For Gideon Tiffany's singing, see Henry Weishuhn to Peter Russell, Mar. 13, 1799 ("God Save"), in Russell Papers, box 3, Baldwin Room, TRL; Douglas G. Lochhead, "Silvester Tiffany," *DCB*, 5:814–15; "To the Public," *Niagara Herald*, Aug. 1, 1801.

87. P. Campbell, *Travels*, 19–20 ("get lands"); Errington, *Lion*, 14–15, 18, and 22–23; Clarke, *Land, Power, and Economics*, 91.

88. Sheppard, *Plunder*, 17–18, 35; Erastus Granger to Henry Dearborn, Sept. 14, 1807, TJP-AMS, LC; Douglas, *Medical Topography*, 4 ("The settlers"); William Dummer Powell, "First Days in Upper Canada," 1044 ("His head"), MG 23 H-I-4, LAC.

89. John Graves Simcoe to the Duke of Portland, n.d. but c. 1799 ("had every one"), in Simcoe Papers, MG 23, H-I-1, ser. 4, 4:5, LAC; Mealing, "John Graves Simcoe," *DCB*, 5:758–59; Riddell, *Simcoe*, 310–15.

Chapter Three: United Irishmen

1. John Richardson to Herman W. Ryland, Feb. 22, 1802 ("unaccountable"), RG 4 A 1, 76:23768, reel C-3013, LAC.

2. Margaret Wright to Alexander McNish, May 27, 1808, in K. A. Miller et al., eds., *Irish Immigrants*, 48.

3. Tillyard, *Citizen Lord*, 113–14; McDowell, "Age of the United Irishmen," 363; Curtin, *United Irishmen*, 21–22; Scots judge quoted in E. P. Thompson, *Making*, 124 ("British constitution"); Watson, *Reign*, 302 (William Windham quoted: "hurricane"), 356–57 and 359.

4. Watson, *Reign*, 358–59; E. P. Thompson, *Making*, 17–22, 149–57, and 182–83.

5. Watson, *Reign*, 359–60; Philips, *William Duane*, 39–46; Durey, *Transatlantic Radicals*, 35–36; E. P. Thompson, *Making*, 140–49, 163–68, and 175–77.

6. O'Connell, *Irish Politics*, 17–20.

7. O'Connell, *Irish Politics*, 16–17; Wickwire and Wickwire, *Cornwallis*, 209–13; Watson, *Reign*, 387–88; McDowell, "Ireland in 1800," 686.

8. McDowell, "Age of the United Irishmen," 291–301 and 351; Durey, *Transatlantic Radicals*, 93–102; Curtin, *United Irishmen*, 25–31; K. A. Miller et al., eds., *Irish Immigrants*, 610–11; United Irish toast quoted in Whelan, "The Green Atlantic," 224 ("A fourth").

9. Curtin, *United Irishmen*, 2–4; McDowell, "Age of the United Irishmen," 352–53; Durey, *Transatlantic Radicals*, 116.

10. Greenwood, *Legacies of Fear*, 4, 6–7, 76–80, 83–85, and 96–102.

11. Greenwood, *Legacies of Fear*, 89–92 (Robert Prescott quoted on 90: "Sensation"), 101–2 and 105–9; Zeisberger, *Diary*, 2:462.

12. Greenwood, *Legacies of Fear*, 84 and 93; Graffagnino, " 'Twenty Thousand Muskets,' " 421–22.

13. Ira Allen to the French Directory, n.d. but June 1796, in Duffy, ed., *Ethan Allen*, 2:473–74; Graffagnino, " 'Twenty Thousand Muskets,' " 417–21; Greenwood, *Legacies of Fear*, 83–84.

14. Palmer, *Age of the Democratic Revolution*, 3–20; A. Taylor, " 'To Man Their Rights,' " 231–57.

15. Wilbur, *Ira Allen*, 2:68; J. A. Graham, *Descriptive Sketch*, ix–x, xiv–xv, and 5–7; "Extract from sundry letters," Sept. 1, 1801 ("very needy"), RG 4 A 1, 74:23280–88, LAC; Truman Squier to Samuel Peters, Nov. 18, 1795, in Cameron, ed., *Papers*, 122; Perrin, " 'So Good Bye, You Jackall,' " 97–101 ("You have" and "Good Bye").

16. Graham, *Descriptive Sketch*, 2–3 ("kindred inhabitants"), 5 ("I have"), and 10–11.

17. John A. Graham to Charles Delacroix, Aug. 19, 1796, in Cameron, ed., *Papers of Samuel Peters*, 131; Graham, *Descriptive Sketch*, xvi–xvii and 144–45 ("sincerely hope"); Duke of Portland to Robert Prescott, Jan. 20, 1797, in Brymner, ed., "Note D: French Republican Designs," 63; Wilbur, *Ira Allen*, 2:141; Timothy Pickering to Rufus King, June 16, 1797, in Manning, ed., *Diplomatic Correspondence*, 1:109–10; Ira Allen, "Proposed Plan to Revolutionize British America," in Duffy, ed., *Ethan Allen*, 2:783–84; Graffagnino, " 'Twenty Thousand Muskets,' " 423–27.

18. T. Pennoyer to Thomas Dunn, Aug. 25, 1797, in Manning, *Diplomatic Correspondence*, 1:498–99; Greenwood, *Legacies of Fear*, 139–47; Wilbur, *Ira Allen*, 2:323–24.

19. Greenwood, *Legacies of Fear*, 124–26, 150–53, 164–66, and 170; "Quebec," *Albany Centinel*, Aug. 11 and 22, 1797; Timothy Pickering to Rufus King, June 20, 1797, in Manning, ed., *Diplomatic Correspondence*, 1:111.

20. Walter Corish Devereux to John Corish Devereux, Apr. 1, 1798, in K. A. Miller et al., eds., *Irish Immigrants*, 41–43; Wickwire and Wickwire, *Cornwallis*, 217–20; Durey, *Transatlantic Radicals*, 106–8, 122–24, and 128–29; Watson, *Reign*, 397–98; McDowell, "Age of the United Irishmen," 354; Curtin, *United Irishmen*, 258; Tillyard, *Citizen Lord*, 272–93.

21. Wells, *Insurrection*, 131 and 139–42; McDowell, "Age of the United Irishmen," 349–50, 355–60; Watson, *Reign*, 397–99; Curtin, *United Irishmen*, 261–80; Wickwire and Wickwire, *Cornwallis*, 221–26; Bartlett, "Clemency and Compensation," 101–3.

22. Hinde, *Castlereagh*, 67; Curtin, *United Irishmen*, 281; Wickwire and Wickwire, *Cornwallis*, 228–29; Durey, "Marquess Cornwallis," 129–37 and 143 (Cornwallis quoted: "wretched business"); Durey, *Transatlantic Radicals*, 130–32; Bartlett, "Clemency," 99–100 and 102–7.

23. Curtin, *United Irishmen*, 280–81; Hinde, *Castlereagh*, 65–67; Durey, "United Irishmen," 96–105; Bric, "Evolution of the 'New Politics,' " 158; Ernst, *Rufus King*, 261–64 (263: Rufus King to Duke of Portland, Sept. 13, 1798, quoted: "I certainly"); Lord Castlereagh to William Wickham, Oct. 29, 1798 ("the majority"), quoted in Geoghegan, *Robert Emmet*, 93; D. Wilson, *United Irishmen*, 58–60; K. A. Miller et al., eds., *Irish Immigrants*, 6–11.

24. Bradburn, *Citizenship Revolution*, 233–34; Grabbe, "European Immigration," 191–97; Carter, " 'Wild Irishman,' " 332–33 and 339–41; Purvis, "Patterns," 114–19; D. Wilson, *United Irishmen*, 2–5; Carter, " 'Wild Irishman,' " 343; K. A. Miller et al., eds., *Irish Immigrants*, 585–86.

25. Irish immigrant quoted in McDowell, *Ireland*, 134 ("the lowest"); Quinn, *Irish in New Jersey*, 54; D. Wilson, *United Irishmen*, 34 and 177; Durey, *Transatlantic Radicals*, 8; Binns, *Recollections*, 226–28.

26. Buel, *Securing the Revolution*, ix–xii and 91–92; J. Howe, "Republican Thought," 147–51.

27. Thomas Jefferson to Francis Hopkinson, Mar. 13, 1789, in Boyd et al., eds., *Papers of Thomas Jefferson*, 14:650; Jefferson to William B. Giles, Dec. 31, 1795 ("honest men and rogues"), and Jefferson to William Duane, Mar. 28, 1811 ("the republicans"), quoted in Onuf, *Jefferson's Empire*, 88 and 97; Buel, *Securing the Revolution*, 91–92; J. Howe, "Republican Thought," 147–65.

28. Elkins and McKitrick, *Age of Federalism*, 19–29; Freeman, "Corruption," 91.

29. Onuf, *Jefferson's Empire*, 53–56, 83, and 95.

30. Wood, *Creation*, 476–80; Fischer, *Revolution*, 1–17 and 250–51; Wood, "Interests," 69–109; Appleby, *Capitalism*, 51–53, 70–78, and 90–94.

31. Ben-Atar and Oberg, "Introduction," 9–11; Egerton, "Empire of Liberty," 309–30.

32. Perkins, *First Rapprochement*, 12–14; Elkins and McKitrick, *Age of Federalism*, 303–30; Sharp, *American Politics*, 69–91; Bradburn, *Citizenship Revolution*, 16–17.

33. Ritcheson, *Aftermath*, 331–52; Perkins, *First Rapprochement*, 92–98 and 101–13; DeConde, *Quasi-War*, 117–21; Egerton, "Empire of Liberty," 310-22; R. C. Stuart, *United States Expansionism*, 39–40.

34. Bradburn, *Citizenship Revolution*, 224–27; Bric, "Irish Immigrant," 163–68; Whelan, "Green Atlantic," 225–28 (228 quotes the American United Irish oath: "attainment"); Uriah Tracy to Oliver Wolcott, Aug. 7, 1800 ("United Irishmen"), quoted in D. Wilson, *United Irishmen*, 1. Under Pennsylvania's state constitution of 1790, any freeman who had resided in the state for two years and had paid taxes within the previous six months could vote; this included many who had not yet been naturalized as citizens. See Carter, " 'Wild Irishman,' " 337.

35. Bradburn, *Citizenship Revolution*, 148–67; Whelan, "Green Atlantic," 225–26; Ernst, *Rufus King*, 261–62; William Cobbett quoted in D. Wilson, *United Irishmen*, 45 ("tyger"); Cobbett quoted in Phillips, *William Duane*, 61 ("Hyena"); Carter, " 'Wild Irishman,' " 335 and 345.

36. Bradburn, *Citizenship Revolution*, 162–66; J. M. Smith, *Freedom's Fetters*, 22–34, 51–56, 61–62, 66–67, 90–91, and 163–65; Miller, *Crisis in Freedom*, 47–48, 67–70, 163–65, and 189; Bric, "Evolution of the 'New Politics,' " 153–54; Kettner, *American Citizenship*, 244–45; Robert Goodloe Harper, speech, June 19, 1798 ("The time"), *AC*, 5th Congress, 2d Session, 1991–92.

37. Whelan, "Green Atlantic," 226; Miller, *Crisis in Freedom*, 67–70, 75–76, and 81–85; Pasley, "Tyranny of Printers," 118–24; J. M. Smith, *Freedom's Fetters*, 94–95 and 419–21.

38. Pickering quoted in Bric, "Evolution of the New Politics," 153 ("Irish villains"); Syndergaard, " 'Wild Irishmen,' " 19–22; Pasley, "Tyranny of Printers," 125 and 176–78; Phillips, *William Duane*, 1–30.

39. Phillips, *William Duane*, 14–60 and 83; Pasley, "Tyranny of Printers," 179 (John Shore quoted: "attempting") and 180–81.

40. Pasley, "Tyranny of Printers," 126, 131, 153–55, 167–74, and 181–89 (188: *Connecticut Courant*, Aug. 18, 1800, quoted: "every important subject"); J. M. Smith, *Freedom's Fetters*, 204, 278, and 288.

41. *Gazette of the United States*, May 16, 1799 ("not an American" and "Jails and dungeons"); Phillips, *William Duane*, 61–80; J. M. Smith, *Freedom's Fetters*, 278–79.

42. Robert Liston to Peter Russell, May 6, 1799, and May 23, 1799, and "Plutarch," in [Philadelphia] *Aurora*, July 13 and 17, 1799; "Grand Discovery," [Niagara] *Canada Constellation*, Aug. 23, 1799; [Philadelphia] *Aurora*, Oct. 22, 1799; William Duane to unknown, Apr. 17, 1800, in Ford, ed., "Letters of William Duane," 260; "Mr. Swayze's Defence," *Niagara Herald*, Mar. 28, 1801; B. G. Wilson, "Isaac Swayze," *DCB*, 6:746–47; Phillips, *William Duane*, 77–84; J. M. Smith, *Freedom's Fetters*, 282–86.

43. Lewis, " 'What Is to Become,' " 8–11, 14–20, and 21; Onuf, *Jefferson's Empire*, 82 and 100–102; Pasley, "1800 as a Revolution," 122–23; DeConde, *Quasi-War*, 187–99, 215–22, and 253–88; Freeman, "Corruption," 91.

44. Bradburn, *Citizenship Revolution*, 281–82; Lewis, " 'What Is to Become,' " 3; Onuf, *Jefferson's Empire*, 80–81, 85, and 93; Pasley, "1800 as a Revolution," 122–25; Kettner, *American Citizenship*, 245–46; Carter, " 'Wild Irishman,' " 336; Baseler, *"Asylum,"* 301.

45. Thomas Barclay to Lord Hawkesbury, Aug. 3, 1801 ("immense" and "every conveyance"), in Rives, ed., *Correspondence*, 129–30; Robert McArthur to John McArthur, Nov. 4, 1802, in K. A. Miller et al., eds., *Irish Immigrants*, 600; Grabbe, "European Immigration," 197–202; Neel, *Phineas Bond*, 149–51.

46. D. Wilson, *United Irishmen*, 64–67; Ernst, *Rufus King*, 261 and 302–4; K. A. Miller et al., eds., *Irish Immigrants*, 614–16; Harrison, ed., *Philadelphia Merchant*, 232.

47. Wickwire and Wickwire, *Cornwallis*, 230–33 and 238–51; Watson, *Reign*, 399–402; McDowell, "Age of the United Irishmen," 362–72; Curtin, *United Irishmen*, 284–89; K. A. Miller et al., eds., *Irish Immigrants*, 603–4; Whelan, "Green Altantic," 230–31.

48. Peter Hunter to Legislative Council and House of Assembly, May 30, 1801 ("British Nations"), MG 11, 327:41, reel B-285, LAC; F. G. Halpenny and J. Hamelin, "Peter Hunter," *DCB*, 5:439; O'Brien, *Speedy Justice*, 22; Cruikshank, "Memoir of Hunter," 20.

49. Armitage, "Greater Britain," 427–45; Richards, "Scotland and the Atlantic Empire," 67–114; Creighton, *Empire*, 22–27; McFarland, "Scotland and the 1798 Rebellion," 568–69.

50. Peter Russell to William Osgoode, July 22, 1802, F46, reel MS-75/5, AO; Richard Cartwright to James McGill, July 12, 1800, and Cartwright, Memorandum, 1801, in Cartwright, ed., *Life and Letters*, 89 and 126; Hannah Jarvis to Samuel Peters, Nov. 6, 1801, in Young, ed., "Letters from the Secretary," 57; William Jarvis to Peters, Jan. 23, 1802, and H. Jarvis to Peters, Sept. 28, 1805 ("For my part"), MG 23 H-I-3, 2:132 and 157, LAC; F. G. Halpenny and J. Hamelin, "Peter Hunter," *DCB*, 5:439–40; Cruikshank, "Memoir of Hunter," 5–32; Gates, *Land Policies*, 67–74; O'Brien, *Speedy Justice*, 22–24.

51. W. N. T. Wylie, "Thomas Scott," *DCB*, 6:698–99; William Osgoode to Peter Russell, Jan. 21, 1801 ("no man" and "Combinations"), F 46, reel MS-75/5, AO; William Birdseye Peters to Samuel Peters, June 5, 1801, MG 23, H-I-3, 6:286, LAC; Romney, *Mr. Attorney*, 50.

52. [Anonymous], "Canadian Letters," 164; Richard Cartwright to Messrs. Davison & Co., Nov. 4, 1797, and Cartwright to Peter Hunter, Oct. 24, 1801, in Cartwright, ed., *Life and Letters*, 76–77 and 79–80; Heriot, *Travels*, 165–67; B. Wilson, *Enterprises*, 58–67 and 105–10.

53. Greenwood, "John Richardson," *DCB*, 6:639–40.

54. Greenwood, "John Richardson," *DCB*, 6:640–41.

55. Wilbur, *Ira Allen*, 2:70 and 319–20; General Burton to Major Green, July 15, 1801, in *SBD*, 1:135; Graham, *Descriptive Sketch*, 79, 86–87, 139, and 159; Greenwood, *Legacies of Fear*, 172–74.

56. Jonathan Sewell to Robert S. Milnes, Sept. 3, 1801, Sewell to H. W. Ryland, Sept. 7, 1801, and John Richardson to Ryland, Sept. 14 and Sept. 17, 1801, RG 4 A 1, 74:23298, 23308, 23327, and 23328, reel C-3013, LAC; Milnes to John King, Sept. 16, 1801, MG 11, 117:249, reel B-70, LAC; Wilbur, *Ira Allen*, 2:329–32 (Nicholas Palmer quoted on 332: "a wire").

57. Anonymous to John Richardson, undated, Richardson to H. W. Ryland, Nov. 16, 1801, Ryland to Executive Council, Nov. 24, 1801, Executive Council Minutes, Dec. 10, 1801, Richardson to Ryland, Dec. 14, 1801, and Mar. 22, 1802, RG 4 A 1, 74:23288, 74:23294, 75:23491, 75:23516, and 75:23872, reel C-3013, LAC; Wilbur, *Ira Allen*, 327–28.

58. For treasure seeking, see A. Taylor, "Supernatural Economy," 6–34. For Rogers, see *New-Jersey Journal*, Nov. 11, 1789, Oct. 19, 1791, and June 14, 1814; [Anonymous], *Account . . . of Ransford Rogers* (for the quotation, see 9: "descended"). For Graham, see Wilbur, *Ira Allen*, 2:321–28.

59. John Richardson to Herman W. Ryland, Feb. 22, 1802 ("Truly"), RG 4 A 1, 76:23768, reel C-3013, LAC. For the "garrison mentality," see Greenwood, *Legacies of Fear*, 3–11.

60. John Richardson to Herman W. Ryland, Sept. 21 ("generally speaking"), and Oct. 1, 1801, RG 4 A 1, 74:23346 and 23376, reel C-3013, LAC; John Richardson to Herman W. Ryland, June 9, June 13, and Aug. 8, 1803, RG 4 A 1, 80:24989, 80:25003, and 81:25282, reel C-3014, LAC; Bigelow, *Journal*, 103 ("antipathy").

61. John Elmsley to Peter Hunter, Feb. 1, 1802, and Elmsley to Hunter, Apr. 14, 1802 ("1 & 2 Millions"), Elmsley Letterbook (1800–1802), Baldwin Room, TRL. For a fuller discussion of this plot, see A. Taylor, "Northern Revolution," 383–409.

62. Willcocks quoted in G. H. Patterson, "Whiggery," 25 ("the people"); Errington, *Lion*, 63; Israel Chapin, Jr., to Joseph Lyman, May 28, 1801, Butler Library, Columbia University; Asa Danforth, Jr., to Timothy Green, Feb. 17, 1801 ("observed"), Danforth File, Misc. Coll., NYHS.

63. E. B. Littlehales (for Simcoe) to Jacob Watson, Jan. 20, 1795 ("You must"), RG 1, A-I-1, 52:1044, reel MS-626/1, AO; Executive Council Minutes, July 3, 1797, and Peter Russell to Robert Prescott, Feb. 4, 1799, in Cruikshank, ed., *Correspondence of Russell*, 1:205–6 and 3:95; Gates, *Land Policies*, 41.

64. John Elmsley to Peter Russell, Dec. 5, 1797, in RG 1, E3, 12:77, reel C-1189, LAC; Elmsley to Russell, Nov. 26, 1797 ("Article of Commerce"), and Elmsley to David W. Smith, Feb. 25, 1798 ("strong arm"), in Cruikshank, ed., *Correspondence of Russell*, 2:26 and 103.

65. John Elmsley to David W. Smith, Feb. 18, 1798 ("Can lands"), in Cruikshank, ed., *Correspondence of Russell*, 2:84.

66. Asa Danforth, Jr., to Timothy Green, Mar. 5, 1797, and Mar. 19, 1800, Green Family Papers, box 1, SULSC; Cruikshank, ed., "Petitions . . . Second Series," 153–54, 155, and 157; William Chewett to the Executive Council, Dec. 6, 1799, RG 1, A-II-1, 1:523, reel MS-3696/1, AO; *Upper Canada Gazette*, Dec. 14, 1799; John Elmsley to Peter Hunter, Jan. 15, 1801, Elmsley Letterbook (1800–1802), Baldwin Room, TRL; Gates, "Roads, Rivals, and Rebellion," 235–42.

67. Asa Danforth, Jr., to Richard Cockrell, Jan. 4, 1801, and Danforth to Richard Cockrell, July 20, 1801, RG 5, A1, 2:557 and 660, reel C-4502, LAC; Danforth to Timothy Green, Feb. 17, 1801 ("oppinion"), Danforth File, Misc. Coll., NYHS; Danforth to Green, Mar. 13, 1801 ("It has been"), ms. #15411, NYSL; A. Taylor, "Northern Revolution," 390–91 and 406n18.

68. John Elmsley to Peter Hunter, Apr. 6, 1801, Elmsley Letterbook (1800–1802), Baldwin Room, TRL; Asa Danforth, Jr., to Ebenezer Allan, Jan. 6, 1802, and Danforth to Elisha Beaman, Mar. 2, 1802, RG 5 A 1, 2:687 and 708, reel C-4502, LAC; Judd, *Hatch and Brood of Time*, 98–101 and 121–32; Douglas G. Lockhead, "Silvester Tiffany," *DCB*, 5:815–16; Daniel J. Brock, "Ebenezer Allan," *DCB*, 5:13; Brock, "Gideon Tiffany," *DCB*, 8:887; Gates, "Roads, Rivals, and Rebellion," 235–37.

69. Asa Danforth, Jr., to Ebenezer Allan, Jan. 6, 1802, and Danforth to Elisha Beaman, Mar. 2, 1802, RG 5 A 1, 2:687 and 708, reel C-4502, LAC.

70. Richard Cockrell to David W. Smith, July 10, 1802, and Asa Danforth, Jr., to Richard Cockrell, June 26, 1802, RG 5 A 1, 2:758 and 759, reel C-4502, LAC; Peter Russell to William Osgoode, July 22, 1802 ("a tissue"), F 46, reel MS-75/5, AO; Perkins, *First Rapprochement*, 171.

71. Gates, "Roads, Rivals, and Rebellion," 250–51; Judd, *Hatch and Brood*, 135; Lockhead, "Silvester Tiffany," *DCB*, 5:815–16; Wallace, "First Journalists," 379.

72. Asa Danforth, Jr., to Timothy Green, Feb. 17, 1802, Danforth File, Misc. Coll., NYHS; McCalla, *Planting the Province*, 13–29 and 250.

73. Asa Danforth, Jr., to Timothy Green, Feb. 17, 1801, Danforth File, Misc. Coll., NYHS; Isenberg, *Fallen Founder*, 223–50; Perkins, *First Rapprochement*, 129–32.

74. Assemblyman quoted in Hannah Jarvis to Samuel Peters, Feb. 18, 1801 ("silk caps"), in Young, ed., "Letters from the Secretary," 56; Alexander Grant to John Askin, Oct. 24, 1805, and Feb. 24, 1806 ("vomiting"), in Quaife, ed., *John Askin Papers*, 2:486 and 506; Grant to Lord Castlereagh, Mar. 14, 1806, in Brymner, ed., "Political State," 32–33; C. Whitfield, "Alexander Grant," *DCB*, 5:363–67; Romney, *Mr. Attorney*, 40.

75. Robert Thorpe to Edward Cooke, Jan. 24, 1806 ("the reins"), Thorpe to Lord Castlereagh, Mar. 4, 1806, Thorpe to Cooke, Mar. 5, 1806, Thorpe to Adam Gordon, Apr. 2, 1806, and Thorpe to Gordon, July 14, 1806, in Brymner, ed., "Political State," 39, 40, 44, 46, and 49; Guest, "First Political Party," 279; Errington, *Lion*, 49–50;

McKenna, *Life of Propriety*, 66–67; Romney, *Mr. Attorney*, 44; G. H. Patterson, "Robert Thorpe," *DCB*, 7:864–65.

76. Alexander Macdonell to Lord Selkirk, Dec. 17, 1806 ("Revolutionary genius"), and Jan. 27, 1807 ("like a mole"), MG 19, E 1, 54:14338 and 14395, reel C-14, LAC; Guest, "First Political Party," 287–88.

77. Joseph Willcocks, "Diary," in Middleton and Landon, eds., *Province of Ontario*, 2:1316–19; William Weekes, "Address," Jan. 26, 1805, in Firth, ed., *Town of York*, 171–72; Guest, "First Political Party," 277–78; G. H. Patterson, "William Weekes," *DCB*, 5:844–45.

78. Willcocks quoted in Riddell, "Joseph Willcocks," 477 ("attachment"), 490n5; E. H. Jones, "Joseph Willcocks," *DCB*, 5:854.

79. Willcocks quoted in Riddell, "Joseph Willcocks," 477 ("most pleasant"); Joseph Willcocks, "Diary," in Middleton and Landon, eds., *Province of Ontario*, 2:1252–1301; E. H. Jones, "Joseph Willcocks," *DCB*, 5:854.

80. Willcocks quoted in Riddell, "Joseph Willcocks," 477 ("Beauty") and 478 ("Mr. Russell"); Willcocks, "Diary," in Middleton and Landon, eds., *Province of Ontario*, 2:1279, 1281, 1292, 1303, and 1314–15 ("a great deal"); E. G. Firth, "Elizabeth Russell," *DCB*, 6:669–70.

81. Joseph Willcocks, "Diary," in Middleton and Landon, eds., *Province of Ontario*, 2:1316–18; E. H. Jones, "Joseph Willcocks," *DCB*, 5:855–56 (Willcocks quoted: "the officers"); Riddell, "Joseph Willcocks," 478–79.

82. Home District Address to Francis Gore, n.d. but c. Oct. 1806, in Brymner, ed., "Political State," 52; G. H. Patterson, "Whiggery," 30–31; Mills, *Idea of Loyalty*, 24–25. For the tradition, see Bushman, *King and People*, 36–63; McConville, *King's Three Faces*, 7–10.

83. E. H. Jones, "Joseph Willcocks," *DCB*, 5:855–56; Robert Thorpe to Edward Cooke, Jan. 24, 1806 ("Nothing"), and Thorpe to Sir George Shee, Dec. 1, 1806 ("This Shopkeeper Aristocracy"), in Brymner, ed., "Political State," 39 and 57–58; G. H. Patterson, "Whiggery," 29–30.

84. Peter Lossing to William Halton, Jan. 26, 1811 ("insidious"), in Cruikshank, ed., "Early History of the London District," 245; Guest, "First Political Party," 278–84; J. K. Johnson, *Becoming Prominent*, 26, 50, 59, 92–103, 121–26, and 148; McNairn, *Capacity to Judge*, 179–80; G. H. Patterson, "Whiggery," 25–44; Wilton, *Popular Politics*, 10–11.

85. S. R. Mealing, "Francis Gore," *DCB*, 8:336; Gore to George Watson, Oct. 4, 1807 ("I have"), in Brymner, ed., "Political State," 113.

86. Robert Thorpe to Sir George Shee, Dec. 1, 1806 ("imperious"), Francis Gore to William Windham, Oct. 29, 1806 ("most respectable People"), and William Halton, notes, Oct. 31, 1806 ("plain English"), in Brymner, ed., "Political State," 57, 61, and 69–71; [Cartwright], *Letters*, 68; Guest, "First Political Party," 282–83.

87. Robert Hamilton and Joseph Edwards to Lt. Gov. Gore, Oct. 10, 1806 ("Gothic Barbarian"), in Cruikshank, ed., "Records of Niagara, 1805–1811," 33; Robert Thorpe to Joseph Willcocks, Oct. 15, 1806, in Brymner, ed., "Political State," 82; Alexander Macdonell to Lord Selkirk, Dec. 17, 1806, MG 19, E 1, 54:14388–91, reel C-14, LAC; Guest, "First Political Party," 284–85; G. H. Patterson, "William Weekes," *DCB*, 5:845.

88. Francis Gore to Viscount Castlereagh, Sept. 4, 1809, and Samuel Thompson to Robert Thorpe, Dec. 24, 1806, MG 11, 349:90 and 350:262, reel B-294, LAC; Gore

to William Windham, Mar. 13, 1807, and Thomas G. Gough to the Electors of York, Durham, and Simcoe Counties, Jan. 8, 1807 ("the standard of Discord"), William Willcocks et al., resolutions, Jan. 13, 1807, and Robert Thorpe to Francis Gore, n.d. but c. Nov. 1806, in Brymner, ed., "Political State," 62, 68, 69, and 93; Guest, "First Political Party," 284–89; Firth, ed., *Town of York*, 173–74; [Cartwright], *Letters*, 55; Curtin, *United Irishmen*, 269.

89. Richard Cartwright to Henry Allcock, Mar. 14, 1807, in Cartwright, ed., *Life and Letters*, 131–34; Francis Gore to William Windham, Mar. 13, 1807 ("Courts of Justice," "strictures," and "peculiar duty"), Executive Council Minutes, July 4, 1807, and Robert Thorpe to Sir George Shee, Mar. 12, 1807, and Gore to George Watson, Oct. 4, 1807, in Brymner, ed., "Political State," 61–64, 82, 97–98, and 114; Guest, "First Political Party," 291–92.

90. George Richard Ferguson, affidavit, Feb. 12, 1807 ("would carry"), Joseph Cheniquy, affidavit, Feb. 12, 1807, John Richardson, affidavit, Feb. 14, 1807, and Francis Gore to William Windham, Apr. 23, 1807, in Brymner, ed., "Political State," 76, 79, and 80; Guest, "First Political Party," 289; E. H. Jones, "Joseph Willcocks," *DCB*, 5:856.

91. Francis Gore to William Windham, Mar. 13, 1807, Lord Castlereagh to Gore, June 19, 1807, Gore to George Watson, July 29, 1807, Thorpe to Shee, July 12, 1807, Gore to George Watson, July 29, 1807 ("it now rests"), Gore to Castlereagh, Aug. 21, 1807, and Gore to Castlereagh, Nov. 14, 1807, in Brymner, ed., "Political State," 61–64, 81, 87, 88, 102, and 120; G. H. Patterson, "Robert Thorpe," *DCB*, 7:864–65.

92. E. H. Jones, "Joseph Willcocks," *DCB*, 5:858–59; "Fidelitas" to John McGill, June 17, 1807 (*"to revolutionize"*), John Powell to Francis Gore, Aug. 13, 1807, and Gore to George Watson, July 29, 1807, in Brymner, eds., "Political State," 85, 86, and 104; Guest, "First Political Party," 290–91; O'Donnell, *Robert Emmet*, 58–60.

93. Robert Addison to Robert Thorpe, July 1, 1807, and *Upper Canada Guardian*, Aug. 6, Aug. 27, and Sept. 3, 1807, in MG 11, 350:217, 225, 226–27, and 231, reel B-294, LAC; "Old Woman," "Editor," and "Editor," *Upper Canada Guardian*, Dec. 30, 1809 ("only man" and "Some have sucked"), June 9, 1810, and June 23, 1810 ("the middle"), enclosed in Francis Gore to Earl of Liverpool, Aug. 9, 1810, MG 11, 350:235, 243, and 248, reel B-294, LAC; McNairn, *Capacity to Judge*, 159; Riddell, "Joseph Willcocks," 480–81 and 485–86.

94. Joseph Willcocks, address, *Upper Canada Guardian*, Dec. 25, 1807, reprinted in "Two Informations," in [New York] *American Citizen*, Jan. 18, 1808; Francis Gore to George Watson, Oct. 4, 1807, in Brymner, ed., "Political State," 113.

Chapter Four: Deserters

1. Adams to Edmund Jennings, June 11, 1780, in R. J. Taylor et al., eds., *Adams Papers*, 9:408.

2. Tucker and Reuter, *Injured Honor*, 1–14; Perkins, *Prologue to War*, 141; Cray, "Remembering," 454–58; Dye, *Fatal Cruise*, 59–67.

3. Tucker and Reuter, *Injured Honor*, 4–17 and 76 (Admiral Berkeley quoted: "the conduct"); Cray, "Remembering," 453–54; Dye, *Fatal Cruise*, 57–58.

4. Cray, "Remembering," 453–54 and 464; Perkins, *Prologue to War*, 142; Dye, *Fatal Cruise*, 48–50.

5. Tucker and Reuter, *Injured Honor*, 71–75; Cray, "Remembering," 465 (Ratford quoted: "the land"); Horsman, *Causes of the War*, 102; Dye, *Fatal Cruise*, 50.

6. Cray, "Remembering," 465; Dye, *Fatal Cruise*, 66 and 69–70.

7. Baseler, *"Asylum,"* 254; Kettner, *American Citizenship*, 50 and 55; Lewis, *Social History of the Navy*, 435; Zimmerman, *Impressment*, 21.

8. Baseler, *"Asylum,"* 254–55; Bradburn, *Citizenship Revolution*, 10–13; Hinderaker, *Elusive Empires*, 260–61; Kettner, *American Citizenship*, 173, 246–47, and 270.

9. Colley, *Captives*, 4–12; Zimmerman, *Impressment*, 23–24; Thomas Barclay to Richard Barclay, Mar. 10, 1807 ("owes"), MG 16, 53:186, reel B-1872, LAC.

10. N. A. M. Rodger, "Mutiny or Subversion?," 559–60.

11. Lavery, *Nelson's Navy*, 113, 117–22, and 128; Lewis, *Social History of the Navy*, 92–101.

12. Tucker and Reuter, *Injured Honor*, 33; Perkins, *Prologue to War*, 28–29, 86, and 90n41.

13. Lewis, *Social History of the Navy*, 436–37; Zimmerman, *Impressment*, 18; Tucker and Reuter, *Injured Honor*, 33 and 47.

14. Phineas Bond to Viscount Harwick, Mar. 1, 1807, MG 16, 53:43, reel B-1872, LAC; Perkins, *Prologue to War*, 93–95; H. Adams, *Administrations of Jefferson*, 667–68.

15. McKee, "Foreign Seamen," 386–88 and 393 (Captain John Rodgers quoted: "We never hear"). For a lumping of the sailors as "Englishmen," see Perkins, *Prologue to War*, 90.

16. Captain Mowat to Robert Liston, Mar. 27, 1797 ("my duty"), quoted in Tucker and Reuter, *Injured Honor*, 62; Lavery, *Nelson's Navy*, 125–26.

17. Gilje, *Liberty on the Waterfront*, 158; Horsman, *Causes of the War*, 26–27; Perkins, *Prologue to War*, 87–88.

18. McKee, "Foreign Seamen," 390–91; Cray, "Remembering," 452; S. Newman, "Reading the Bodies," 59–82.

19. Horsman, *Causes of the War*, 21; Tucker and Reuter, *Injured Honor*, 34–35; Cray, "Remembering," 461; Dye, "Early American Merchant Seafarers," 331–33; Thomas Barclay to Richard Barclay, Mar. 10, 1807 ("for every real American"), MG 16, 53:186, reel B-1872, LAC; Gould, "Making of an Atlantic State System," 254–55.

20. Tucker and Reuter, *Injured Honor*, 48, 119 (Captain Stephen Decatur quoted: "well known"); Perkins, *Prologue to War*, 91–93.

21. Cooper, ed., *Ned Myers*, 2–14, 16–17 ("mixed character"), and 31 ("great vortex"); A. Taylor, *William Cooper's Town*, 342–45.

22. Cooper, ed., *Ned Myers*, 17–18 (all quotations).

23. Cooper, ed., *Ned Myers*, 25–27 ("poor fellow" and "my foot") and 37–38 ("a party" and "showed fight").

24. Whitfield, *Tommy Atkins*, 59 ("Nowhere else"); John Richardson to Herman W. Ryland, Feb. 9, 1804 ("so few"), RG 4, A 1, 83:25688, reel C-3014, LAC. In 1800 the British force in Canada amounted to 2,224 men; 696 were posted in Upper Canada, with the rest in Lower Canada. See State of the Forces in Upper and Lower Canada, Dec. 1, 1800, RG 8, 1029:108A, reel C-3523, LAC.

25. Isaac Brock to James Green, Oct. 26, 1803 ("fine lads"), and June 12, 1804 ("vexed"), RG 8, 513:98 and 145, reel C-3045, LAC; P. White, ed., *Lord Selkirk's Diary*, 297; Whitfield, *Tommy Atkins*, 59–60; Graves, *Field of Glory*, 176–78; Couture, *Study*, 72.

26. John Vincent to James Green, Mar. 20, 1803, RG 8, 254:110, reel C-2851, LAC; Peter Hunter to William Henry Clinton, Feb. 7, 1804 ("composed"), and Isaac Brock to Adjutant General, Mar. 17, 1807, RG 8, 1240:335 and 1214:187, reel C-3524, LAC. Brock concluded that 458 of the 469 men in the 100th Regiment came from Ire-

land. He considered them potentially troublesome, although they "were principally raised in the North of Ireland and are mostly all Protestants." To British officers of the early nineteenth century, the troublesome Irish identity trumped the distinction between Protestant and Catholic which looms so (excessively) large in American history writing about that period.

27. Whitfield, *Tommy Atkins*, 60–61; James Green for Peter Hunter to Lt. Shackleton, May 11, 1802 ("Irishmen"), RG 8, 1210:29, reel C-3524, LAC.

28. Peter Hunter to Duke of Portland, Oct. 27, 1800 ("Frontier Posts"), and Hunter to Lord Hobart, Apr. 25, 1804, MG 11, 326:236, reel B-285, and 334:35, reel B-288, LAC; Richard Cartwright to John Strachan, Mar. 17, 1804, in Cartwright, ed., *Life and Letters*, 129.

29. Richard Cartwright to John Strachan, Mar. 17, 1804, in Cartwright, ed., *Life and Letters*, 129; Peter Hunter to Lord Hobart, Apr. 25, 1804, MG 11, 334:35, reel B-288, LAC; Thomas Carnie to Major Green, Sept. 13–14, 1803, in Preston, ed., *Kingston*, 250–51; Peter Hunter to William Henry Clinton, Feb. 7, 1804 ("composed"), RG 8, 1211:334–35, reel C-3524, LAC.

30. James Green to Roger Sheaffe, June 4, 1803 ("such a manner"), and Green to John Vincent, Sept. 19, 1803, RG 8, 1211:83 and 183, reel C-3524, LAC; Bunn, "Narrative," 412–13 ("the savages").

31. John Askin to David W. Smith, Oct. 15, 1800, in Quaife, ed., *John Askin Papers*, 2:316; Detroit Court of Sessions, proceedings, Oct. 17, 1800, RG 5, A 1, 2:574–75, reel C-4502, LAC; "Niagara," *Niagara Herald*, Sept. 19, 1801; James Madison to Peter Hunter, May 5, 1801, in Manning, ed., *Diplomatic Correspondence*, 1:153; Hunter to Madison, Aug. 29, 1801, and James Green to John McDonnell, Sept. 6, 1801, in RG 8, 1209:285 and 292, reel C-3523, LAC; Holt MacKenzie to Green, Sept. 8, 1801, in Preston, ed., *Kingston*, 247.

32. John McDonnell, advertisement, *Niagara Herald*, Oct. 10, 1801.

33. Hector McLean to James Green, Oct. 26, 1800, MPHS, *MHC*, 15:25–26.

34. John Gentle, untitled essay, [Philadelphia] *Aurora*, Nov. 10, 1806 ("Murder!" and "rushed"), reprinted in Farmer, *History of Detroit*, 183–84; Alexander Campbell to [James Green], Jan. 5, 1806, James Abbott and William M. Scott to Stanley Griswold, Dec. 14, 1805 ("blow them"), and Griswold to James Madison, Dec. 21, 1805, in MPHS, *MHC*, 15:30, 31:548, and 31:552; Gilpin, *Territory of Michigan*, 50–51; Woodford, *Mr. Jefferson's Disciple*, 82–84.

35. Thomas Sherwood and Henry Arnold, "Examination of Evidences," May 2, 1809, MG 11, 349:50, reel B-294, LAC; Strum, " 'A Most Cruel Murder,' " 293–95.

36. Francis Gore to David Montague Erskine, June 17, 1809, MG 11, 349:60, reel B-294, LAC; Strum, " 'A Most Cruel Murder,' " 295–98.

37. Perkins, *Prologue to War*, 2–5; Horsman, *Causes of the War*, 30–39; Tucker and Reuter, *Injured Honor*, 49; Stagg, *Madison's War*, 18–19.

38. Augustus J. Foster to Elizabeth Foster, Feb. 1, 1806 ("The two greatest"), quoted in Perkins, *Prologue to War*, 73.

39. Alexander Henry to John Askin, Apr. 25, 1806 ("the Devil"), in Quaife, ed., *John Askin Papers*, 2:515; "New York," *American Citizen*, July 1, 1806; Thomas Barclay to Richard Barclay, Mar. 10, 1807 ("contending"), MG 15, 53:186, reel B-1872, LAC.

40. Lewis, *Social History of the Navy*, 434–35; Zimmerman, *Impressment*, 19–20; Horsman, *Causes of the War*, 30 (Lord Harrowby quoted: "Pretension"); Perkins, *Prologue to War*, 192.

41. Tucker and Reuter, *Injured Honor*, 208; H. Adams, *Administrations of Jefferson*,

665–67; David M. Erskine to George Canning, Oct. 5, 1807 ("highly grating"), in Perkins, *Prologue to War*, 75; Phineas Bond to Canning, Dec. 1, 1807, MG 16, 53:151, reel B-1872, LAC.

42. John Howe to Francis Feeling, Sept. 19, 1807, and Augustus Foster to James Monroe, June 1, 1812, MG 16, 55:316, reel B-1873, and 86:174, reel B-1999, LAC; Perkins, *Prologue to War*, 7–10, 74–75, and 107; Tucker and Reuter, *Injured Honor*, 52, 65, and 72; Horsman, *Causes of the War*, 84 and 87 (Lord Grenville quoted: "a *Mob Government*").

43. Tucker and Reuter, *Injured Honor*, 65 and 72.

44. Tucker and Reuter, *Injured Honor*, 101–3; Malone, *Jefferson*, 422–23; Cray, "Remembering," 455; Thomas Barclay to George Canning, July 2, 1807 ("lower Class"), MG 16, 53:204, reel B-1872, LAC; Davis, ed., *Jeffersonian America*, 293 ("ringleader").

45. Horsman, *Causes of the War*, 103–6; Tucker and Reuter, *Injured Honor*, 105 (Admiral Berkeley quoted: "to run up"), 114; George Cranfield Berkeley to James Barry, Sept. 14, 1807 ("wretched Outcasts"), Gratz Coll., case 4, box 36, HSP.

46. Perkins, *Prologue to War*, 50–51; Horsman, *Causes of the War*, 107–8; Skelton, *American Profession*, 7–8; Jacobs, *Tarnished Warrior*, 247.

47. Phineas Bond to Thomas Dunn, July 6, 1807, RG 8, 666:12, reel C-3171, LAC; Perkins, *Prologue to War*, 39–41; Henry Dearborn quoted in Tucker and Reuter, *Injured Honor*, 107–8 ("those in the North"); Albert Gallatin to Thomas Jefferson, July 25, 1807 ("none"), in H. Adams, ed., *Writings of Gallatin*, 1:345–48.

48. Dye, "Physical and Social Profiles," 223; Murrin, "Jeffersonian Triumph," 3–4.

49. Cruikshank, "Chesapeake Crisis," 282 and 300; Francis Gore to unknown, n.d. ("old"), in Cartwright, ed., *Life and Letters*, 135; Isaac Brock to Adjutant General, Mar. 18, 1807, and July 1, 1807, RG 8, 1214:197, reel C-3525, LAC.

50. John Warren to Aeneas Shaw, Apr. 22, 1808, and Ralfe Clench to Shaw, May 25, 1808, in RG 9, I-B-1, box 1, folder for 1808, LAC; John Bethune, Jr., to John Macauley, May 13, 1810, MFP, reel MS-78, AO; Peter Drummond to William Halton, Sept. 10, 1807, Alexander Chisholm to Francis Gore, Dec. 5, 1807, and Samuel Ryerse to Shaw, Dec. 24, 1807, in RG 9, I-B-1, box 1, folder for 1807, LAC; Alleyne Hampden Pye to Isaac Brock, Aug. 14, 1807, in Preston, ed., *Kingston*, 253; Thomas Welch to William Halton, Nov. 11, 1807 ("internal Enemies"), Thomas Welch Papers, NHSC, 1058, reel M-274, LAC.

51. Isaac Brock to Alleyne Hampden Pye, Aug. 1, 1807, and Brock to Gordon, Sept. 6, 1807, RG 8, 1214:347 and 372, reel C-3525, LAC; James H. Craig to Francis Gore, Dec. 6, 1807, and Gore to Craig, Jan. 5, 1808 ("carefully concealed"), in Brymner, ed., "Note B: Anticipation," 30–32 and 35–37.

52. Francis Gore to James Craig, Jan. 5, 1808 ("connexion"), in Brymner, ed., "Note B: Anticipation," 35–37; Gore to Viscount Castlereagh, Mar. 21, 1808, MG 11, 348:30, reel B-293, LAC; Joseph Willcocks to Daniel Cozens, July 24, 1807 ("thunderstruck"), MG 11, 350:220, reel B-294, LAC.

53. Wright, "Sedition in Upper Canada," 27–28; Francis Gore to unknown, n.d. but Mar. 1809, in Cartwright, ed., *Life and Letters*, 135–36; Edgar, ed., *Ten Years*, 31; William Dummer Powell to Francis Gore, Oct. 3, 1809 ("almost every"), and "A Friend to Justice," *Upper Canada Guardian*, Apr. 21, 1810, enclosed in Francis Gore to Earl of Liverpool, Aug. 9, 1810, MG 11, 349:166, and 350:238, reel B-294, LAC; Gore quoted in E. H. Jones, "Joseph Willcocks," *DCB*, 5:856 ("relished").

54. Richard Cartwright to John Strachan, Mar. 18, 1809, F 24 (Cartwright Family

Papers), Cartwright Letterbooks, 4:297, reel MS-44, LAC; Fraser, "Politics at the Head of the Lake," 18; Johnson, *Becoming Prominent*, 121–26; John Strachan to James Brown, Oct. 9, 1808 ("ignorant clowns"), in A. Smith, "John Strachan," 170–72.

55. Malone, *Jefferson*, 57; *Quebec Gazette*, Sept. 3, 1807, and M. Hunter to Prince Edward, Sept. 4, 1807, in Cruikshank, ed., "Records of Niagara, 1805–1811," 40; Major General Skerrett quoted in Cruikshank, *Political Adventures*, 16 ("Thomas Addis Emmett"); Francis Gore to George Watson, Oct. 4, 1807, MG 11, 347:222, reel B-293, LAC; G. W. L. Nicholson, "John Skerrett," *DCB*, 5:761.

56. George Cranfield Berkeley to Francis Gore, Aug. 17, 1807 ("every information"), MG 11, 347:5, reel B-293, LAC; Nevins, ed., *Diary of John Quincy Adams*, 53 ("to conquer"); Cruikshank, "Chesapeake Crisis," 287.

57. Tucker and Reuter, *Injured Honor*, 126–27; Cray, "Remembering," 466; James Monroe to James Madison, Oct. 10, 1807, in S. M. Hamilton, ed., *Writings of Monroe*, 10.

58. Parker, ed., "Secret Reports," 78–81, 86, 96, 102, and 343; Phineas Bond to George Canning, Aug. 2, 1807 ("Consequences"), and Thomas Barclay to Canning, Aug. 5, 1807, MG 16, 53:109 and 210, reel B-1872, LAC.

59. James Monroe to James Madison, Oct. 10, 1807, in S. M. Hamilton, ed., *Writings of Monroe*, 14; Tucker and Reuter, *Injured Honor*, 114–15 and 129–37; Perkins, *Prologue to War*, 190–96.

60. Tucker and Reuter, *Injured Honor*, 135–36; Horsman, *Causes of the War*, 109–10 and 117–22; Perkins, *Prologue to War*, 184–204.

61. Nevins, ed., *Diary of John Quincy Adams*, 48; Tucker and Reuter, *Injured Honor*, 208–9; Erney, *Henry Dearborn*, 216. A frigate, mounting forty-four cannon, cost at least $300,000 to build and equip, comparable to the cost of twenty-five gunboats. See Perkins, *Prologue to War*, 51.

62. Perkins, *Prologue to War*, 148–56; Stagg, *Madison's War*, 20–22; Horsman, *Causes of the War*, 99; Tucker and Hendrickson, *Empire of Liberty*, 19 and 204–11.

63. Perkins, *Prologue to War*, 24 and 149–56 (151: John Quincy Adams quoted: "nations"); John Russell to Nathan Williams, Jan. 21, 1808, NWP, Box 2, OCHS.

64. Perkins, *Prologue to War*, 26–30, 166–70, and 204–5; Horsman, *Causes of the War*, 125–38; Tucker and Reuter, *Injured Honor*, 119–22; McKee, "Foreign Seamen," 392; John Howe to Sir George Prevost, June 7, 1808, in Parker, ed., "Secret Reports," 89.

65. John Howe to Sir George Prevost, May 5, 1808, and June 22, 1808, in Parker, ed., "Secret Reports," 78 and 94; Perkins, *Prologue to War*, 157–59; Irwin, *Daniel D. Tompkins*, 65–69.

66. Daniel D. Tompkins to Albert Gallatin, Dec. 1, 1808, in Hastings, ed., *Papers of Tompkins*, 2:165–66; Hough, *History of Jefferson County*, 458; R. C. Stuart, *United States Expansionism*, 46–53; John Richardson to Herman W. Ryland, June 20, 1808, in Cruikshank, ed., "Records of Niagara, 1805–1811," 62; Skelton, *American Profession*, 82; Perkins, *Prologue to War*, 160–64 (161: Gallatin quoted, "I had rather"); Tucker and Hendrickson, *Empire of Liberty*, 224–25.

67. Nevins, ed., *Diary of John Quincy Adams*, 56; Malone, *Jefferson*, 563–65, 571–74, and 594–97; Irwin, *Daniel D. Tompkins*, 65–69; Stagg, *Madison's War*, 22–28.

68. Republican campaign broadside, Apr. 1807 ("Every Shot's"), in Irwin, *Daniel D. Tompkins*, illustration facing 131.

69. Malone, *Jefferson*, 613–15; H. Adams, *Administrations of Jefferson*, 1123–25.

70. Tucker and Hendrickson, *Empire of Liberty*, 179 and 212.

71. Perkins, *Prologue to War*, 182; Tucker and Hendrickson, *Empire of Liberty*, 222–28.

72. "From the North Carolina Minerva," [New York] *American Citizen*, July 16, 1808; *New-York Evening Post*, Feb. 23, 1809; Alexander Henry to John Askin, Mar. 16, 1809, in Quaife, ed., *John Askin Papers*, 2:625; [Anonymous], "Diary . . . by a British Subject of a Journey from New York City," 49 ("Thomas Jefferson"), Diary Collection, NYPL.

73. Hendrickson, *Peace Pact*, 258–59; Stagg, *Madison's War*, 125; Elijah Brush to Henry Dearborn, Apr. 8, 1808, in Carter, ed., *Territorial Papers*, 10:214; "The Citizens of the First Congressional District of Pennsylvania," [Washington, D.C.] *National Intelligencer*, May 26, 1812 ("without foreign"); John A. Harper, speech, Jan. 4, 1812 ("We are" and "more power"), *AC*, 12th Congress, 1st Session, 653–54. For British and American national expenditures, see Bradburn, *Citizenship Revolution*, 1.

74. Onuf, "Expanding Union," 64–67; Onuf, *Jefferson's Empire*, 107–8 (107: Jefferson quoted: "strongest Government"), 117–21.

75. John Henry to Herman Witsius Ryland, Nov. 16, 1807 ("that crazy coalition"), and June 5, 1808, in Cruikshank, *Political Adventures*, 9 and 33; Jonathan Russell to James Monroe, Feb. 3, 1812, in Manning, ed., *Diplomatic Correspondence*, 1:609–10; Thomas Talbot to George Prevost, n.d. but c. 1811, MPHS, *MHC*, 15:10.

76. John Elmsley to David W. Smith, Feb. 28, 1798, in Cruikshank, ed., *Correspondence of Russell*, 2:106; John Howe to Sir George Prevost, May 5, 1808, and June 22, 1808, in Parker, ed., "Secret Reports," 78 and 94; P. White, ed., *Lord Selkirk's Diary*, 130; Augustus Foster quoted in Horsman, *Causes of the War*, 49 ("Province of Maine").

77. Weld, *Travels*, 1:413; Robert Nichol to John Askin, Oct. 15, 1802 ("The Heats"), in Quaife, ed., *John Askin Papers*, 2:384; P. White, ed., *Lord Selkirk's Diary*, 123–24; John Howe to Sir George Prevost, May 31, 1808, and n.d. but c. Jan. 1809 ("servile means"), in Parker, ed., "Secret Reports," 84–85 and 345; George H. Rose to George Canning, Jan. 17, 1808 ("one Sailor"), MG 16, 56:92, reel B-1873, LAC.

78. John Howe to Sir George Prevost, June 7, 1808 ("perpetual source"), Aug. 5, 1808, and n.d. but c. Jan. 1809 ("The enmity"), in Parker, ed., "Secret Reports," 85, 97, and 345; [John Howe], "Answers to Questions on Affairs in the United States," in Brymner, ed., "Note B: Anticipation," 50; Davis, ed., *Jeffersonian America*, 57, 159 ("Irishmen"), and 270 ("motley set").

79. Strachan, *Discourse on the Character*, 22–23 ("Liberty"); Gould, "Making of an Atlantic State System," 253–54; Davis, ed., *Jeffersonian America*, 57.

80. Augustus Foster to James Monroe, June 1, 1812 ("similarity"), MG 16, 86:174, reel B-1999, LAC; Perkins, *Prologue to War*, 24–30.

81. Hinderaker, *Elusive Empires*, 260–61; Kettner, *American Citizenship*, 173.

Chapter Five: Blood

1. Holmden, ed., "Baron de Gaugreben's Memoir," 58.

2. William Hull to William Eustis, Mar. 6, 1812 ("The British"), in *DRIC*, 22; Allen, *His Majesty's Indian Allies*, 120–22.

3. Allen, "His Majesty's Indian Allies," 3–5; Horsman, "British Indian Policy," 51–52.

4. Horsman, "British Indian Policy," 51–58; Allen, "His Majesty's Indian Allies," 6–10 (10: Matthew Elliott quoted: "keep your eyes"); Francis Gore to Viscount

Castlereagh, Oct. 7, 1807, MG 11, 347:3, reel B-293, LAC; Horsman, *Causes of the War,* 204–6.

5. Perkins, *Prologue to War,* 285–86; Horsman, *Expansion,* 154 and 167; [Philadelphia] *Aurora,* Jan. 11, June 5, and June 17, 1812.

6. Edward Thornton to Sir Robert S. Milnes, Feb. 25, 1802, RG 7, G 18, LAC.

7. Horsman, *Expansion,* 104–9; R. White, *Middle Ground,* 473–74; A. Taylor, *Divided Ground,* 37–38 and 60–61.

8. Horsman, *Expansion,* 109–14 and 142–57; R. White, *Middle Ground,* 474 and 496–16; Stagg, *Madison's War,* 177–82; Henry Dearborn to William Hull, July 22, 1806, and Hull to William Eustis, July 12, 1810, in Carter, ed., *Territorial Papers,* 10:63–64 and 314–16.

9. Stagg, *Madison's War,* 184–88; Perkins, *Prologue to War,* 282–84; Brant, *James Madison: The President,* 190, 384–85 and 388; Hickey, *War of 1812,* 25; Walker, *Journal,* 43–45.

10. [Lexington, Ky.], *Reporter,* Dec. 10, 1811 ("The blood"), quoted in Hickey, *War of 1812,* 26; "An American," [Philadelphia] *Aurora,* June 16, 1812 ("certain hell" and "demolish").

11. James Madison, Message to Congress, Nov. 5, 1811 ("trampling"), in *PJM-PS,* 4:1–5; [Philadelphia], *Aurora,* Mar. 10, 1807 ("Will you"); John C. Calhoun, speech, May 6, 1812, in *AC,* 12th Congress, 1st Session, 1399; Stagg, *Madison's War,* 71–79; Pratt, *Expansionists,* 42–50; Horsman, *Causes of the War,* 179; Perkins, *Prologue to War,* 249–59, 367.

12. Hickey, *War of 1812,* 29–30; Perkins, *Prologue to War,* 46–49, 223, and 350–51.

13. Henry Clay, speech, Feb. 22, 1810 ("extinguish"), quoted in Horsman, *Causes of the War,* 182; Clay, speech in Congress, Dec. 31, 1811, in Hopkins et al., eds., *Papers of Clay,* 1:606–8; "Report on Relations with Great Britain," Nov. 29, 1811, in Meriwether et al., eds., *Papers of Calhoun,* 1:66–68 ("We must"); Peter B. Porter, speech, Dec. 6, 1811, *AC,* 12th Congress, 1st Session, 417; Perkins, *Prologue to War,* 241, 266–67, 343–47, and 435; Pratt, *Expansionists,* 50; Stagg, *Madison's War,* 84; Hickey, *Don't Give Up the Ship!,* 40–41; Watts, *Republic Reborn,* 263–74.

14. Brant, *James Madison: The President,* 390–96; R. H. Brown, *Republic in Peril,* 55–57 and 89–90; Perkins, *Prologue to War,* 360–62; Malcomson, *Lords of the Lake,* 15; Hickey, *War of 1812,* 34; Hitsman, *Safeguarding Canada,* 84–85; Graves, *Field of Glory,* 15.

15. Josiah Quincy, speeches, Jan. 25, 1812, and Mar. 3, 1812, *AC,* 12th Congress, 1st Session, 957; Josiah Quincy quoted in Hickey, *War of 1812,* 54 ("How will war").

16. Stagg, *Madison's War,* 54–56; James Madison to Thomas Jefferson, Apr. 24, 1812, and May 25, 1812, in *PJM-PS,* 4:346, and 415–16; Henry Clay to unknown, June 18, 1812 ("The one"), in Hopkins et al., eds., *Papers of Clay,* 1:674.

17. Albert Gallatin to Thomas Jefferson, Mar. 10, 1812, in H. Adams, ed., *Writings of Gallatin,* 1:517; Henry Clay to James Morrison, Dec. 21, 1811, in Hopkins et al., eds., *Papers of Clay,* 1:600; John A. Harper to William Plumer, Feb. 6, 1812, and Feb. 17, 1812, in Egan, ed., "Path to War," 156 and 158; James A. Bayard quoted in Malcomson, *Lords of the Lake,* 14 ("float"); Perkins, *Prologue to War,* 362–66; Stagg, *Madison's War,* 88–90.

18. Mortimer, "The Ohio Frontier in 1812," 206 ("headache," and "end of the world"); Abijah Bigelow to Hannah Bigelow, Jan. 1, 1812 ("shock" and "hope"), and Feb. 8, 1812, in Brigham, ed., "Letters of Abijah Bigelow," 323–24 and 328; Crawford, ed., "Lydia Bacon's Journal," 385; John C. Calhoun to James MacBride, Feb. 16, 1812

("How unusual"), in Meriwether et al., eds., *Papers of Calhoun*, 1:90–91; Thomas P. Cope, Diary, Feb. 18, 1812 ("strange comet"), in Harrison, ed., *Philadelphia Merchant*, 268; Walker, *Journal*, 38.

19. Cruikshank, *Political Adventures*, 1–2; Greenwood, "John Henry," *DCB*, 8:387–88.

20. John Henry to Herman W. Ryland, Oct. 5, 1807, Ryland to Henry, Oct. 11, 1807, Henry to Ryland, Nov. 16, 1807 ("good management"), and Ryland to Henry, Jan. 26, 1809, in Cruikshank, *Political Adventures*, 4–5, 6, 9, and 41; Henry to Ryland, Mar. 2, Mar. 6, Mar. 10, Mar. 18, Apr. 14, 1808 , and Sir James H. Craig to Viscount Castlereagh, May 5, 1808, in Brymner, ed., "Note B: Anticipation," 38–46.

21. Greenwood, "John Henry," *DCB*, 8:388–89. John A. Harper to William Plumer, Mar. 11, 1812, in Egan, ed., "Path to War," 161; Cruikshank, *Political Adventures*, 41, 67–85, and 88 (Henry quoted: "produce"); *PJM-PS*, 4:117n1; Stagg, *Madison's War*, 93–94.

22. John A. Harper to William Plumer, Mar. 11, 1812 ("The federalists"), in Egan, ed., "Path to War," 159; Greenwood, *Legacies of Fear*, 228–29; Parker, ed., "Secret Reports," 80; Perkins, *Prologue to War*, 370–72. For dismissal of the Henry revelations, see Stagg, *Madison's War*, 97–98; Hickey, *War of 1812*, 38–39.

23. John C. Calhoun to Robert Cresswell, Mar. 10, 1812 ("Such is the conduct"), and "Report on the Causes and Reasons for War," June 3, 1812, in Meriwether et al., eds., *Papers of Calhoun*, 1:92–93 and 117–18; Pratt, *Expansionists*, 54; Thomas Jefferson to Tadeusz Kosciusko, June 28, 1812, in Lipscomb and Bergh, eds., *Writings of Jefferson*, 6:67. See also [Philadelphia] *Aurora*, Mar. 25, 1812; Henry Clay, speech in Congress, Apr. 1, 1812, in Hopkins et al., eds., *Papers of Clay*, 1:642.

24. John C. Fredriksen, "Peter Buell Porter," *ANB*, 17:707–9; Hauptman, *Conspiracy of Interests*, 121–24; Erastus Granger to William Eustis, Aug. 14, 1812, RG 107, M 222, reel 5, USNA; W. Campbell, ed., *Life and Writings*, 141.

25. Peter B. Porter, speech, Dec. 6, 1811, *AC*, 12th Congress, 1st Session, 416; Perkins, *Prologue to War*, 375; Stagg, "Between Black Rock," 385–90; Porter to William Eustis, Apr. 19, 1812 ("act of madness"), RG 47, M 221, reel 47, USNA; Augustus J. Foster to Lord Castlereagh, Apr. 21, 1812, in *DHCNF*, 1:54; Davis, ed., *Jeffersonian America*, 94 ("after being for war").

26. Elbert Anderson, Jr., to David Parker, June 24, 1812, DPP, box 2, HSP; Erastus Granger to William Eustis, Aug. 14, 1812, RG 107, M222, reel 5, USNA; Stagg, "Between Black Rock," 396 and 403; Perkins, *Prologue to War*, 407; Melish, *Travels*, 2:328 and 337.

27. James Harrison to Albert Gallatin, Dec. 19, 1811 ("Comparatively"), RG 107, M 221, reel 44, USNA.

28. John Binns to Jonathan Roberts, May 5, 1812 ("The honor"), quoted in Hickey, *War of 1812*, 27; John McKim, Jr., to Henry Clay, May 13, 1812 , in Hopkins et al., eds., *Papers of Clay*, 1:654; Thomas Webb to Daniel Parker, May 19, 1812 ("our Doom"), DPP, box 2, HSP; James Monroe to John Taylor, June 13, 1812, in S. M. Hamilton, ed., *Writings of Monroe*, 1:205–6.

29. [Washington, D.C.] *National Intelligencer*, Apr. 14, 1812, in Hopkins et al., eds., *Papers of Clay*, 1:645–47; James Madison quoted in Pratt, *Expansionists*, 155 ("he knew"); Robert Wright quoted in Hickey, *War of 1812*, 47 ("get married"); John C. Calhoun, speech, May 6, 1812 ("So far"), in Meriwether et al., eds., *Papers of Calhoun*, 1:104.

30. John C. Calhoun, "Report on the Causes and Reasons for War," June 3, 1812,

in Meriwether et al., eds., *Papers of Calhoun*, 1:116; Hickey, *Don't Give Up the Ship!*, 42; Perkins, *Prologue to War*, 403–15; R. H. Brown, *Republic in Peril*, 44–47, 131, and 143–45; Stagg, *Madison's War*, 110–14; Horsman, *Causes of the War*, 224.

31. John Randolph, speech, Dec. 16, 1811 ("Agrarian cupidity"), *AC*, 12th Congress, 1st Session, 533; Hacker, "Western Land Hunger," 365–95; Abijah Bigelow to Hannah Bigelow, June 26, 1812, in Scotti, ed., "Additions to the Letters," 248. For historians who emphasize the Orders in Council, see Hickey, *Don't Give Up the Ship!*, 36–40; Perkins, *Prologue to War*, 288 and 427; Horsman, *Causes of the War*, 171–75, 223–29, and 267 ("conquest of Canada"); R. H. Brown, *Republic in Peril*, 35–39 and 72–82.

32. For the British suspension of the Orders in Council, see R. H. Brown, *Republic in Peril*, 36–38; Stagg, *Madison's War*, 118–19 and 421; Perkins, *Prologue to War*, 337–40.

33. Caledonia meeting resolutions, Sept. 23, 1812 ("British spoiliations"), [Batavia, N.Y.] *Republican Advocate*, Oct. 3, 1812. See also "True Answers," [Canandaigua, N.Y.] *Ontario Messenger*, Dec. 15, 1812.

34. [Philadelphia] *Aurora*, Feb. 13, 15, 22, 26, 27, Mar. 10, 11, 12, 17, 18, 19, 23, 28, Apr. 8, 9, 18, 22, May 2, 16, 18, June 15 and 18, 1812; John C. Calhoun, "Report on the Causes and Reasons for War," June 3, 1812 ("Our Citizens"), in Meriwether et al., eds., *Papers of Calhoun*, 1:116; Stagg, *Madison's War*, 110–11.

35. "Report on Relations with Great Britain," Nov. 29, 1811 ("enslaves"), in Meriwether et al., eds., *Papers of Calhoun*, 1:67; Waterhouse, ed., *Journal*, 78 ("muster the crew") and 93; "True Answers," [Canandaigua, N.Y.] *Ontario Messenger*, Dec. 15, 1812 ("the restoration"); "Honor Calls for War," [Philadelphia] *Aurora*, June 19, 1812.

36. "The Goal" and "Honor Calls for War," [Philadelphia] *Aurora*, Apr. 28 and June 19, 1812; Waterhouse, ed., *Journal*, 188 ("stripped"); Richard M. Johnson, speech, Dec. 11, 1811 ("Who could"), *AC*, 12th Congress, 1st Session, 465.

37. Skelton, *American Profession*, 268–69; "An Act Making Further Provision for the Army of the United States," May 16, 1812, U.S. Congress, *Public Statutes*, 2:735; "Worthy the attention of the Patriot and Soldier," *Buffalo Gazette*, Aug. 11, 1812 ("*body*"). Despite the political sympathy expressed for impressed sailors, Congress implicitly assigned them to a lower caste than soldiers by declining to ban flogging in the navy.

38. Cogswell, *An Oration*, 5–6 ("hordes"); Fredericksburgh Republican meeting, Jan. 1, 1812 ("infernal engines"), and Andrew Brown et al., to William Eustis, May 9, 1812, in *PJM-PS*, 4:173 and 371; "What do we Want of Canada?" [Batavia, N.Y.] *Republican Advocate*, June 6, 1812; Irwin, *Daniel D. Tompkins*, 77.

39. Irwin, *Daniel D. Tompkins*, 77; "From the Ontario Repository," *Geneva* [N.Y.] *Gazette*, Apr. 28, 1812 ("Of what avail"); Felix Grundy, speech, Dec. 9, 1811 ("We shall drive"), *AC*, 12th Congress, 1st Session, 426.

40. "An American," [Philadelphia] *Aurora*, June 16, 1812; Allan McLane to Peter B. Porter, Feb. 28, 1812, PBPP, reel 2, BECHS; Thomas Jefferson to James Madison, June 29, 1812, in *PJM-PS*, 4:519.

41. Speeches by Peter B. Porter, Dec. 6, 1811, Richard M. Johnson, Dec. 11, 1811 ("I should not wish"), and John A. Harper, Jan. 4, 1812 ("Author of Nature"), *AC*, 12th Congress, 1st Session, 416, 456, and 657; Henry Clay, speech, Jan. 11, 1812, in Hopkins et al., eds., *Papers of Clay*, 1:615; "What do we want of Canada?" and "The Conquest of Canada," [Batavia, N.Y.] *Republican Advocate*, June 6 and Aug. 8, 1812; Stagg, *Madison's War*, 30–40.

42. Anonymous to James Madison, June 9, 1812, in *PJM-PS*, 4:464; Stagg, ed., "Between Black Rock," 421–22; James A. Bayard to Andrew Bayard, May 2, 1812 ("No

Proposition"), in Donnan, ed., "Papers of Bayard," 196–97; Gideon Granger to John Todd, Dec. 26, 1811 ("doubtless"), Granger Papers, LC; Pratt, *Expansionists*, 146–47.

43. Stagg, ed., "Between Black Rock," 419; John A. Harper to William Plumer, May 13, 1812 ("an address"), in Egan, ed., "Path to War," 174; *AC*, 12th Congress, 1st Session, 322–24.

44. *AC*, 12th Congress, 1st Session, 325–26; R. H. Brown, *Republic in Peril*, 126–28; Augustus Foster to Lord Castlereagh, July 10, 1812, RG 59, M 588, reel 7, USNA; Pratt, *Expansionists*, 151–52; Stagg, *Madison's War*, 4–6; Stagg, ed., "Between Black Rock," 399.

45. Hickey, *Don't Give up the Ship!*, 38; R. H. Brown, *Republic in Peril*, 125; Stagg, *Madison's War*, 4; James Monroe quoted in Perkins, *Prologue to War*, 416 ("difficult").

46. Hull, proclamation, July 13, 1812, in *SBD*, 1:355–56 ("Raise not"); Hull to Eustis, July 13, 1812, in *DRIC*, 58; Eustis to Hull, June 24, 1812, and Aug. 1, 1812, in MPHS, *MHC*, 40:397 and 428; Alexander Smyth, "To the Soldiers of the Army of the Centre," Nov. 17, 1812 ("The time"), in Severance, ed., "The Case of Alexander Smyth," 227.

47. Elisha R. Potter, speech to Congress, Jan. 21, 1814 ("the object of this war"), *AC*, 13th Congress, 2d Session, 1106.

48. Malcolmson, *Very Brilliant Affair*, 14–16; Henry Clay, speech, Feb. 22, 1810 ("the militia"), *AC*, 11th Congress, 2d Session, 580; Stagg, *Madison's War*, 523; Thomas Jefferson to William Duane, Aug. 4, 1812 ("the acquisition"), TJP-AMS, LC.

49. Hickey, *Don't Give Up the Ship!*, 7; Graves, *Field of Glory*, 170–71 and 319–20; Cookson, *British Armed Nation*, 5–6.

50. Albert Gallatin to James Madison, Dec. 17, 1811, in *PJM-PS*, 5:70; Richard M. Johnson, speech, Dec. 11, 1811, and John A. Harper, speech, Jan. 4, 1812 ("they must"), *AC*, 12th Congress, 1st Session, House, 458 and 652; W. Campbell, ed., *Life and Writings*, 126 ("great majority"); Erastus Granger to Henry Dearborn, Sept. 14, 1807 ("very large majority"), TJP-AMS, LC; Melish, *Travels*, 2:338 and 383; Schultz, *Travels*, 50, 55, and 59.

51. F. Landon, *Western Ontario*, 23; "Old Woman," *Upper Canada Guardian*, Dec. 30, 1809, MG 11, 350:235, reel B-294, LAC; "Upper Canada Guardian," [Batavia, N.Y.] *Republican Advocate*, Dec. 28, 1811. For the bias against Americans as magistrates or militia officers, see M. Smith, *Geographical View*, 69; Johnson, *Becoming Prominent*, 60–65, 79, 84, and 148. For resentment of the Crown and Clergy Reserves, see Anonymous Resolutions, Dec. 3, 1807, RG 5, A 1, 6:2709; Gourlay, ed., *Statistical Account*, 275, 305, 313, and 319.

52. Erastus Granger to Henry Dearborn, Sept. 14, 1807, TJP-AMS, LC; "Advantages to be derived from the Conquest of Canada," [Batavia, N.Y.] *Republican Advocate*, Aug. 8, 1812; William Hull, proclamation, July 13, 1812 ("wealth"), in *SBD*, 1:355–56.

53. Cruikshank, ed., "Early History of the London District," 208; Thomas Talbot to John Sullivan, Oct. 27, 1802 ("growing tendency"), MG 11, 330:201, LAC; [Talbot] to Sir George Prevost, c. 1811 ("industrious Settlers"), in MPHS, *MHC*, 15:17.

54. Cruikshank, ed., "Early History of the London District," 179, 183–86, 192, 245–54, and 256–57; Thomas Talbot to Simon Zelotes Watson, Mar. 2, 1811 ("His Majesty"), and Francis Gore to Talbot, Mar. 16, 1811 ("Do not let"), in Coyne, ed., *Talbot Papers*, 107 and 110.

55. Cruikshank, ed., "Early History of the London District," 186–88 and 254–56; Thomas Talbot to Simon Zelotes Watson, Mar. 12, 1811, Talbot to Major Halton, Mar. 14, 1811 (quotes Watson: "neither the Governor"), and Watson to Talbot, Mar.

22, 1811 ("decide"), in Coyne, ed., *Talbot Papers*, 107–8, 108–9, and 111–12; Hamil, *Lake Erie Baron*, 69–71.

56. Donald Macpherson to Noah Freer, July 5, 1812, RG 8, 676:119, reel C-3172, LAC; Klinck and Ross, eds., *Tiger Dunlop's Upper Canada*, 14–16 ("good," "shot," and "I found"); Weld, *Travels*, 2:174; Johnson Butler to Aeneas Shaw, Oct. 29, 1811, RG 9, I-B-1, 1:473, LAC; Strachan, *Sermon Preached at York*, 21.

57. [Barnabas Bidwell], "Sketches of Upper Canada," in Gourlay, ed., *Statistical Account*, 1:204, 223, and 249 ("Politics"); M. Smith, *Geographical View*, 67–70; Peter L. Chambers, "The War in Canada," MG 40 G 4, File 2, LAC; Erastus Granger to Henry Dearborn, Sept. 14, 1807, TJP-AMS, LC; Cruikshank, *Fight in the Beechwoods*, 7.

58. William Graham to James Brock, Mar. 7, 1812, RG 5, A1, 14:6049, reel C-4507, LAC; Cruikshank, "Notes on the Early Settlement of Burford," 388; Isaac Brock to George Prevost, July 12, 1812, in *DHCNF*, 1:123; Erastus Granger to Henry Dearborn, Sept. 14, 1807 ("not to calculate"), TJP-AMS, LC; William Hamilton Merritt, affidavit, July 23, 1812 ("Whither"), RG 8, 688:143, reel C-3231, LAC.

59. "Falkland" and "An Elector of the County of Frontenac," *Kingston Gazette*, Feb. 11 and Mar. 17, 1812; William Campbell, Charge to the Western District, Sept. 10, 1812 ("Is there"), in MPHS, *MHC*, 22:633–35. The author of "Falkland" was Richard Cartwright. See A. Gray to Sir George Prevost, Jan. 29, 1812, in *SBD*, 1:252.

60. "Falkland" and "A Loyalist," *Kingston Gazette*, Feb. 11, 18 ("composed"), and May 12 ("Our wives"), 1812; Beall, "Journal," 804; "A Canadian," *Montreal Gazette*, Jan. 13, 1812.

61. [Anonymous], "The Last War in Canada," 277; Thomas G. Ridout to Betsey Ridout, Jan. 5, 1813 ("inducement"), in Edgar, ed., *Ten Years*, 169; *Upper Canada Gazette*, Oct. 24, 1812, in *DHCNF*, 2:127; "A Loyalist's Son," *Kingston Gazette*, Nov. 7, 1812; Darnell, *Journal*, 74n ("only coming" and "killed at Queenstown"); Gourlay, ed., *Statistical Account*, 1:379–80.

62. "Montreal," *Montreal Gazette*, Jan. 27, 1812; Isaac Brock, Proclamation, July 22, 1812 ("Are you prepared"), in *DHCNF*, 1:136–38.

Chapter Six: Invasions

1. Fairchild, ed., *Journal*, 12 ("The crown").

2. Joseph Ellicott to Paul Busti, Feb. 26, 1813 ("From the Manner"), HLCP, reel 12, BECHS.

3. Joseph Ellicott, Journal, June 25, 1812, in Severance, ed., "Joseph Ellicott's Letter Books," 150; Peter B. Porter to William Eustis, June 28, 1812, RG 107, M 221, reel 47, USNA; Daniel D. Tompkins to DeWitt Clinton, June 29, 1812, in Hastings, ed., *Papers of Tompkins*, 2:646; Cruikshank, "Sketch of the Public Life," 21–22; [Philadelphia] *Aurora*, July 11, 1812.

4. Peter B. Porter to William Eustis, June 28, 1812, RG 107, M 221, reel 47, USNA; Amos Hall to Daniel D. Tompkins, June 28, 1812, in *DHCNF*, 1:78; Ellicott to Paul Busti, July 7, 1812, Ellicott Letterbook, vol. 2, EEPFP, BECHS.

5. Albert Gallatin to James Madison, Dec. 17, 1811, in *PJM-PS*, 4:70; Joseph Ellicott, Journal, June 25, 1812, in Severance, ed., "Joseph Ellicott's Letter Books," 150; Daniel D. Tompkins to DeWitt Clinton, June 29, 1812, in Hastings, ed., *Papers of Tompkins*, 2:646; Porter, *John Jacob Astor*, 249–60.

6. Daniel D. Tompkins to DeWitt Clinton, June 29, 1812, and Tompkins to J. R. Mullany, July 1, 1812, in Hastings, ed., *Papers of Tompkins*, 2:646 and 652. Another

Astor emissary rode north from Albany to tip off his fur trade partners in Montreal. See Forsyth, Richardson, & Co., to H. W. Ryland, June 24, 1812, in *DHCNF,* 1:73; Porter, *John Jacob Astor,* 262. For accusations against Gallatin, see Thomas Sidney Jesup to unknown, Feb. 12, 1813, TSJP, 1:127, LC; Gallatin, Memorandum, c. 1815, H. Adams, ed., *Writings of Gallatin,* 1:678–79.

7. Richardson, *Richardson's War,* 116 ("exceedingly affable"); Charles Askin to John Askin, Oct. 15, 1811, in Quaife, ed., *John Askin Papers,* 2:698–99 ("General Brock"); Malcolmson, *Very Brilliant Affair,* 33–34; C. P. Stacey, "Isaac Brock," *DCB,* 5:114.

8. Malcolmson, *Very Brilliant Affair,* 33–35; C. P. Stacey, "Isaac Brock," *DCB,* 5:109–12.

9. Isaac Brock to George Prevost, Dec. 3, 1811 ("act with"), MG 11, 352:55b, reel B-295, LAC; William H. Merritt, "Journal," in *SBD,* 3, part 2:545 ("peculiar faculty"); Brock to Prevost, Feb. 12, 1812, in *DHCNF,* 1:38–39.

10. William H. Merritt, "Journal," in *SBD,* 3, part 2:546–47; Isaac Brock to George Prevost, Dec. 2, 1811 ("to animate"), Dec. 24, 1811, and July 12, 1812 ("cool calculators"), and Brock to Edward Baynes, July 29, 1812 ("Most of the people"), in *DHCNF,* 1:21–24, 26, 123, and 153; C. P. Stacey, "Isaac Brock," *DCB,* 5:112.

11. Hitsman, *Safeguarding Canada,* 79 and 83–84 (Prevost quoted: "final defence"); Malcomson, *Very Brilliant Affair,* 36; Allen, *His Majesty's Indian Allies,* 119.

12. Sheppard, *Plunder,* 41–42; [Bidwell], "Sketches of Upper Canada," in Gourlay, ed., *Statistical Account,* 1:229–30. For the potential strength of 13,000 (including officers, drummers, and sergeants), see Aeneas Shaw, "Annual Return of the Militia of Upper Canada," June 4, 1810, RG 9, I-B-1, box 1, LAC.

13. Couture, *Study,* 10–11, 37–46, and 56; Sheppard, *Plunder,* 41–42; Isaac Brock to Earl of Liverpool, May 25, 1812, in *DHCNF,* 1:27–28; Brock to George Prevost, May 16, 1812, RG 8, 656:112, reel C-3172, LAC.

14. Isaac Brock to George Prevost, Feb. 25, 1812, in *DHCNF,* 1:43; Sheppard, *Plunder,* 41–42; M. Smith, *Geographical View,* 83 ("Had this act").

15. Isaac Brock to George Prevost, Dec. 2, 1811, Prevost to Brock, Dec. 24, 1811, Brock to Prevost, Feb. 25, 1812 ("inert"), and Prevost to Brock, Mar. 31, 1812, in *DHCNF,* 1:22–23, 27, 43–44, and 51; Allen, *His Majesty's Indian Allies,* 118–22.

16. Peter Burroughs, "Sir George Prevost," *DCB,* 5:693–95; W. B. Turner, *British Generals,* 25.

17. Jean-Pierre Wallot, "James Henry Craig," and Burroughs, "Sir George Prevost," *DCB,* 5:205–8 and 694–95; Greenwood, *Legacies of Fear,* 213–23; W. B. Turner, *British Generals,* 27–29.

18. Fecteau, Greenwood, and Wallot, "Sir James Craig's 'Reign of Terror,'" 351–53; James McGill et al. to Sir George Prevost, July 1, 1812 ("declared"), and David Ross to John Taylor, July 9, 1812, RG 4, A 1, 121:38758, and 122:39046, reel C-3200, LAC.

19. Cecil Bisshopp to Kate Bisshopp, Oct. 19, 1812 ("alacrity"), MG 24, F 4, LAC; George Prevost to Earl of Bathurst, Oct. 17, 1812, in *DHCNF,* 1:135; Daniel D. Tompkins to Alexander Macomb, July 12, 1812, in Hastings, ed., *Papers of Tompkins,* 3:26.

20. George Prevost to the Earl of Liverpool, July 15, 1812 ("to avoid"), in MPHS, *MHC,* 25:317; Horsman, "British Indian Policy," 62–64; Allen, *His Majesty's Indian Allies,* 118–22; Hitsman, *Safeguarding Canada,* 90–91; Graves, *Field of Glory,* 13–16.

21. W. H. Merritt, "Journal," in *SBD,* 3, part 2:545; George Ridout to Thomas G. Ridout, June 27, 1812, in Edgar, ed., *Ten Years,* 131.

22. Allen, *His Majesty's Indian Allies,* 123–30; Antal, *Wampum Denied,* 46–47;

Matthew Irwin to John Mason, Oct. 16, 1812 ("discharged"), in Carter, ed., *Territorial Papers*, 10:413; John Askin, Jr., to John Askin, Sr., July 19, 1812, and Porter Hanks to William Hull, Aug. 4, 1812, in MPHS, *MHC*, 32:482 and 40:430–32.

23. Peter L. Chambers, "The War in Canada," MG 40 G 4, File 2, LAC; John Johnston to William Eustis, Aug. 6, 1812 ("no calculating"), RG 107, M 221, reel 46, USNA; Allen, *His Majesty's Indian Allies*, 130; Malcomson, *Very Brilliant Affair*, 76.

24. Augustus Woodward, public meeting resolves, Dec. 8, 1811 ("whole territory"), in MPHS, *MHC*, 40:349–50; William Woodbridge to Juliana Trumbull Woodbridge, Jan. 18, 1815 ("my great terror"), in Quaife, ed., "From Marietta to Detroit," 149–50; Dunnigan, "Fortress Detroit," 175–81; Gilpin, *Territory of Michigan*, 11–21 and 39; Antal, *Wampum Denied*, 7–10.

25. Peter Audrain to Albert Gallatin, July 6, 1808, and William Hull to William Eustis, July 20, 1810, in Carter, ed., *Territorial Papers*, 10:230 and 319; Augustus Woodward to James Madison, July 18, 1807, in MPHS, *MHC*, 22:505–6; Robert Lucas to James Foster, Nov. 4, 1812 ("ignorant French"), in Parish, ed., *Robert Lucas Journal*, 89–90.

26. Wilbur, *Ira Allen*, 2:78; M. Campbell, *Revolutionary Services*, 268–69; General Burton to Major Green, July 15, 1801, in *SBD*, 1:135.

27. Gilpin, *Territory of Michigan*, 7–8; Woodford, *Mr. Jefferson's Disciple*, 12, 53–55, and 102; William Hull to James Madison, Apr. 30, 1806 ("surrounded"), in MPHS, *MHC*, 31:559; Hull to William Eustis, Dec. 23, 1809, in Carter, ed., *Territorial Papers*, 10:303.

28. Augustus B. Woodward to the bench, Nov. 5, 1806, in MPHS, *MHC*, 31:567; Stanley Griswold to Jared Mansfield, Jan. 7, 1808 ("Assassination"), and Woodward to William Hull, July 23, 1810, in Carter, ed., *Territorial Papers*, 10:173 and 324; Peter Audrain to Woodward, Mar. 19, 1808 ("got gay"), and Apr. 8, 1808 ("unhappy place"), in MPHS, *MHC*, 12:449 and 36:219.

29. William Hull to William Eustis, Dec. 17, 1811, in MPHS, *MHC*, 40:359. For the conventional wisdom, see John Armstrong to William Eustis, Jan. 2, 1812, in *DHCNF*, 1:33–34; Henry Dearborn to James Madison, Apr. 6, 1812, in *PJM-PS*, 4:298–99.

30. William Hull to William Eustis, Mar. 6, 1812 ("probably induce"), in *DRIC*, 19–22.

31. William Hull to William Eustis, Mar. 6, 1812 ("should obtain"), in *DRIC*, 19–22; Stagg, *Madison's War*, 191–93 and 301n3; Pratt, *Expansionists*, 168 and 171.

32. Stagg, "Between Black Rock," 397–98; Stagg, *Madison's War*, 506–7; Irwin, *Daniel D. Tompkins*, 155–56; Stacey, "American Plan," 348–59.

33. Jonathan Russell to James Monroe, Feb. 3, 1812, in Manning, ed., *Diplomatic Correspondence*, 1:609; William Pope to James Madison, July 30, 1812, in *PJM-PS*, 5:99.

34. William Hull to William Eustis, Mar. 6, 1812, in *DRIC*, 19; William Hull, speech, May 25, 1812, in [Anonymous], *Capitulation*, 9.

35. James Miller to William Eustis, June 12, 1812, and William Hull to Eustis, June 18, 1812, in MPHS, *MHC*, 40:390 and 393; Hull to Eustis, June 24, 1812, in *DRIC*, 36; Antal, *Wampum Denied*, 35; "General Hull," [Philadelphia] *Aurora*, Oct. 6, 1812 ("If an army").

36. Beall, "Journal," 787; Crawford, ed., "Lydia Bacon's Journal," 65–67; M. C. Dixon to R. H. Bruyeres, July 8, 1812, in *DRIC*, 48; Lewis Bond, Journal, 3, LC; Antal, *Wampum Denied*, 35–36.

37. William Hull to William Eustis, July 13, 1812, in *DRIC*, 57; James Taylor to Eustis, July 14, 1812 ("their homes"), and Hull, statement, Mar. 16, 1814, in MPHS, *MHC*, 40:412 and 598–99; [Anonymous], *Capitulation*, 27, 30–31 ("army of Cannibals"), and 35; Beall, "Journal," 787; Antal, *Wampum Denied*, 40–43.

38. William Hull, proclamation, July 13, 1812, in *SBD*, 1:355–56.

39. William Hull, proclamation, July 13, 1812, in *SBD*, 1:356–57.

40. Thomas B. St. George to Isaac Brock, July 15, 1812, and James Taylor to William Eustis, July 14, 1812, in MPHS, *MHC*, 15:104 and 40:412–14; Henry Procter to Isaac Brock, July 26, 1812, in *SBD*, 1:414; [Anonymous], *Capitulation*, 31–35; Lewis Bond, Journal, 4 ("Genl. Hull"), LC.

41. Daniel Brock, "Ebenezer Allan," *DCB*, 5:13–14; D. R. Beasley, "Andrew Westbrook," *DCB*, 6:808; Sabathy-Judd, ed., *Moravians*, 484 ("to destroy").

42. Thomas Talbot to Brock, July 27, 1812, Henry Bostwick to Peter L. Chambers, July 27, 1812, and Chambers to Christopher Myers, July 31, 1812, in *DRIC*, 93, 94–95, and 114–15; William H. Merritt, "Journal," in *SBD*, 3, part 2:551–52; Brock to Prevost, Aug. 17, 1812 ("The disaffected"), MG 11, 352:125, reel B-295, LAC; M. Smith, *Geographical View*, 85 ("an end").

43. "Buffalo," in [Batavia, N.Y.] *Republican Advocate*, July 18, 1812; Buttrick, *Voyages*, 25 ("Waggons" and "Bad"); M. Smith, *Human Sorrow and Divine Comfort*, 4–5.

44. *Buffalo Gazette*, Aug. 11, 1812, in *DHCNF*, 1:170 and 205; Buttrick, *Voyages*, 52; M. Smith, *Geographical View*, 84 ("Had not").

45. Charles Askin, Journal, July 24–30, 1812, in Quaife, ed., *John Askin Papers*, 2:711–13; Isaac Brock to George Prevost, July 26, 1812, in *DHCNF*, 1:144; Thomas Talbot to Brock, July 27, 1812, in *DRIC*, 94; Brock to Earl of Liverpool, Aug. 29, 1812, MG 11, 352:105, reel B-295, LAC.

46. Isaac Brock to George Prevost, July 26 ("impending"), July 28, and July 29, 1812, and Brock to Edward Baynes, July 29, 1812 ("situation"), in *DHCNF*, 1:146, 149, 151, and 152; Brock to the Executive Council, Aug. 3, 1812, MG 11, 352:109, reel B-295, LAC; Brock to Edward Baynes, Aug. 4, 1812 ("name of heaven"), in *SBD*, 1:408.

47. William Hull to Thomas B. St. George, July 16, 1812, and St. George to Hull, July 16, 1812, in MPHS, *MHC*, 25:319 and 320; James Taylor to John Armstrong, Apr. 15, 1814, RG 107, M 221, reel 57, USNA; Walker, *Journal*, 55; [Anonymous], *Capitulation*, 34–35, 38, and 73; Antal, *Wampum Denied*, 45; Couture, *War and Society*, 126–27; Farmer, *History of Detroit*, 278.

48. William Hull to William Eustis, July 22, 1812, and Hull, court-martial testimony, Mar. 14, 1814, in MPHS, *MHC*, 40:422 and 600–609 ("The army"); Cruikshank, "General Hull's Invasion," 236–39.

49. William Hull to William Eustis, July 21, 1812, in MPHS, *MHC*, 40:420–21; [Peter L. Chambers], "The War in Canada," MG 40, G 4, File 2, LAC; [Anonymous], *Capitulation*, 44; Parish, ed., *Robert Lucas Journal*, 34 and 40–42 ("mistery"); Walker, *Journal*, 54 ("Such skirmishing"); Antal, *Wampum Denied*, 47 (Lewis Cass quoted: "Instead") and 50–51.

50. Lewis Bond, Journal, 7 ("Panic Struck"), LC; William Hull, court-martial statements, Mar. 14, and Mar. 15, 1814, in MPHS, *MHC*, 40:600, 606 ("My officers"), and 648; [Anonymous] to [Anonymous], July 28, 1812 ("They replied"), and Peter L. Chambers to Christopher Myers, July 31, 1812, in *DRIC*, 76 and 115.

51. Beall, "Journal," 802 ("British officers"), 805; Antal, *Wampum Denied*, 50–51.

52. Cruikshank, ed., "General Hull's Invasion," 245 and 252–54; William Hull to William Eustis, Aug. 4, 1812, in MPHS, *MHC*, 25:327–28; Hull to Eustis,

Aug. 8, 1812, and Henry Procter to Isaac Brock, Aug. 11, 1812, in *DRIC*, 126–27 and 135–36.

53. William Hull to William Eustis, Aug. 8, 1812, Henry Procter to Isaac Brock, Aug. 11, 1812, and Lewis Cass to Return J. Meigs, Aug. 12, 1812 ("We have"), in *DRIC*, 126–27, 135–36, and 137; Hull, statement, Mar. 14, 1814 ("Civil War"), in MPHS, *MHC*, 40:635; Parish, ed., *Robert Lucas Journal*, 52, 57, and 59–60 ("imbesile"); Antal, *Wampum Denied*, 83.

54. J. B. Glegg to Edward Baynes, Aug. 5, 1812, in *SBD*, 1:413; John McDonald to Duncan Cameron, Aug. 10, 1812 ("It has rained"), in *DRIC*, 130–31; Parish, ed., *Robert Lucas Journal*, 55 ("Such Confusion").

55. [Peter L. Chambers], "The War in Canada," MG 40, G 4, File 2, LAC; Isaac Brock to George Prevost, Aug. 17, 1812, MG 11, 352:125, reel B-295, LAC; Antal, *Wampum Denied*, 78; Couture, *War and Society*, 140.

56. Isaac Brock to George Prevost, Aug. 17, 1812, MG 11, 352:125, reel B-295, LAC; William McKay, Journal, Aug. 15, 1812 ("We are told"), MG 24, G 10, LAC; Parish, ed., *Robert Lucas Journal*, 60 ("now reduced"); Couture, *War and Society*, 140. For the numbers in Brock's force, see "Prize Pay List," n.d., in *DRIC*, 148.

57. William McKay, Journal, Aug. 15, 1812, MG 24, G 10, LAC; Crawford, ed., "Lydia Bacon's Journal," 70–71 ("bombs"); Richardson, *Richardson's War*, 54 ("Scattering"); Quaife, ed., "Chronicles," 108–10; John Whistler to William Eustis, Oct. 6, 1812, and William Hull, court-martial statement, Mar. 15, 1814, in MPHS, *MHC*, 40:490 and 715–20; Antal, *Wampum Denied*, 93 and 96–97 (Major Snelling quoted: "His lips").

58. Isaac Brock to William Hull, Aug. 15, 1812 ("war of extermination"), in *DRIC*, 144; William Hull, court-martial statement, Mar. 14, 1814 ("bleeding"), and Mar. 15, 1814, in MPHS, *MHC*, 40:641 and 715.

59. Cruikshank, ed., "General Hull's Invasion of Canada," 281; Quaife, ed., "Chronicles," 107–8 ("some covered," "he was standing," and "terrific din"); Antal, *Wampum Denied*, 94–95.

60. William Hull, court-martial testimony, Mar. 14, 1814 ("this moment" and "A Savage"), and Mar. 15, 1814, in MPHS, *MHC*, 40:640, 641, 648, and 699; Antal, *Wampum Denied*, 95–97; Lewis Cass to William Eustis, Sept. 10, 1812, in Richardson, *Richardson's War*, 79–80.

61. William McKay, Journal, Aug. 16, 1812 ("We saw the best"), and Aug. 17, 1812 ("to obtain"), MG 24, G 10, LAC; [Peter L. Chambers], "The War in Canada," 11, MG 40, G 4, File 2, LAC; Walker, *Journal*, 66–67 ("*Treachery*"); Byfield, "Common Soldier's Account," 6; Augustus B. Woodward to James Monroe, Dec. 23, 1813 ("friends"), in MPHS, *MHC*, 36:315; Parish, ed., *Robert Lucas Journal*, 65–67; Fairchild, ed., *Journal*, 18–19 ("hollowing").

62. Isaac Brock to George Prevost, Aug. 17, 1812, MG 11, 352:125, reel B-295, LAC.; Quaife, ed., "Chronicles," 111; [Anonymous], *Capitulation*, 76 ("kisses"); Antal, *Wampum Denied*, 98–99.

63. William Hull to William Eustis, Aug. 26, 1812, in MPHS, *MHC*, 40:468; Isaac Brock to George Prevost, Aug. 16, 1812, in *SBD*, 1:463–64; William McKay, Journal, Aug. 16, 1812 ("dirty"), MG 24, G 10, LAC; Charles Askin, Journal, Aug. 16, 1812 ("poorest looking"), in Quaife, ed., *John Askin Papers*, 2:720; Robert Nichol, "General Return of Prisoners," Aug. 16, 1812, in *DRIC*, 153.

64. Andrew W. Cochran to his mother, Sept. 13, 1812 ("I believe"), in *DRIC*, 213–

14; Edward Baynes to Isaac Brock, Sept. 10, 1812, and George Prevost to Earl Bathurst, Sept. 22, 1812, in *DHCNF*, 1:249 and 290.

65. Edward Baynes for George Prevost to Isaac Brock, July 4, 1812 ("extreme moderation"), in *DHCNF*, 6:100; George Prevost to Isaac Brock, Sept. 30, 1812, in Cruikshank, ed., "Records of Niagara, . . . 1812," 37–38; Antal, *Wampum Denied*, 122.

66. T. C. Pothier to George Prevost, Sept. 8, 1812 ("without them"), in *DRIC*, 217; Robert Dickson to Prevost, Dec. 23, 1812, in Esarey, ed., *Messages and Letters*, 2:252; Antal, *Wampum Denied*, 119 and 128–29 (Brock quoted: "The enemy").

67. Isaac Brock to George Prevost, Sept. 18 and Sept. 28, 1812, in *DHCNF*, 1:277 and 299; Henry Procter to Edward Baynes, Jan. 31, 1813 ("Our Influence"), in MPHS, *MHC*, 15:233; Antal, *Wampum Denied*, 103–4, 111, 122–24, and 148.

68. Quaife, ed., "Chronicles," 91–92 ("Spectators"); Henry Procter to Isaac Brock, Sept. 16 and 30, 1812, in *SBD*, 1:523 and 524; Procter to Roger H. Sheaffe, Nov. 28, 1812, RG 59, M 588, reel 7, USNA.

69. Edward Dewar to Henry Procter, Aug. 28, 1812, in *DRIC*, 173; Dewar to Robert McDouall, Oct. 19, 1812, in MPHS, *MHC*, 15:170–71.

70. Edward Dewar to Henry Procter, Aug. 28, 1812 ("ran their swords"), in *DRIC*, 173–74; Couture, *War and Society*, 156–57; Antal, *Wampum Denied*, 113.

71. Peter L. Chambers to Henry Procter, Aug. 24, 1812, in *DRIC*, 175; Charles Askin, Journal, Aug. 18 and 20, 1812, in Quaife, ed., *John Askin Papers*, 2:721–24; Procter to Isaac Brock, Oct. 3, 1812, in MPHS, *MHC*, 15:155; Couture, *War and Society*, 149; Procter to Major Reynolds, Dec. 23, 1812, RG 59, M 588, reel 7, USNA.

72. Peter L. Chambers to Henry Procter, Aug. 24, 1812, and Procter to Isaac Brock, Aug. 26, 1812, in *DRIC*, 176 and 180–81; Lewis Bond, Journal, 22, LC.

73. Roger H. Sheaffe (for Brock) to Henry Procter, Sept. 1, 1812, in *DRIC*, 209; Sheaffe (for Brock) to Procter, Sept. 24, 1812 ("a hundred fold"), RG 59, M 588, reel 7, USNA; Procter to Sheaffe, Oct. 1, 1812, RG 8, 688:107, reel C-3231, LAC.

74. George Wythe Mumford to William Preston, Aug. 15, 1812 ("I have no news"), Preston Family Papers, VHS; Charles Humphrey to Charles K. Gardner, Sept. 23, 1812, CKGP, box 2, NYSL; Jacob Brown to Nathan Williams, Sept. 1, 1812 ("Do you not"), JBP, box 1, OCHS; Brown to Daniel D. Tompkins, Aug. 26, 1812 ("I will never"), and Sept. 7, 1812, RG 98, Third Military District, # 19, USNA.

75. John G. Jackson to William Eustis, RG 107, M 221, reel 46, USNA; Robert Johnson to James Madison, Sept. 3, 1812 ("The Idea"), in *PJM-PS*, 5:261; Samuel Dana to Daniel Parker, Sept. 6, 1812, DPP, box 2, HSP.

76. Robert Lucas to William Eustis, Oct. 10, 1812, RG 107, M 221, reel 46, USNA; Parish, ed., *Robert Lucas Journal*, 57–58 and 61; [Anonymous], *Capitulation*, 62 and 65–68 ("red and blue stripes"); Daniel Parker, "Minutes for the Trial of General Hull," DPP, box 22, HSP.

77. Daniel Parker, "Minutes for the Trial of General Hull," DPP, box 22, HSP; David Jones to James Madison, Aug. 25, 1812, in *PJM-PS*, 5:197; John C. Fredriksen, ed., "Letters of Captain John Scott," 67; [Anonymous], *Capitulation*, 34; "Extract of a letter," [Philadelphia] *Aurora*, Sept. 14, 1812.

78. Daniel Springer to Thomas Talbot, Sept. 10, 1812, in Coyne, ed., *Talbot Papers*, 156; Cruikshank, ed., "General Hull's Invasion," 278 and 287; Cruikshank, "Study of Disaffection," 25; Romney and Wright, "State Trials," 383; William H. Merritt, "Journal," in *SBD*, 3, part 2:551–52; Daniel J. Brock, "Ebenezer Allan," *DCB*, 5:14. Owing to incomplete records, the fate of the four tried for treason remains unknown.

79. William Campbell, Charge, Sept. 10, 1812 ("recent rescue"), in MPHS, *MHC*, 22:630; R. J. Morgan and Robert Lochiel Fraser, "Sir William Campbell," *DCB*, 5:113–19.

80. Warner, ed., "The Bold Canadian," 303 ("Those Yankees"); Isaac Brock, General Order, Aug. 16, 1812, in *DRIC*, 148–50.

81. "Address to the Inhabitants of Upper Canada," *Buffalo Gazette*, Mar. 20, 1813, reprinted in *DHCNF*, 5:119–21; M. Smith, *Geographical View*, 88–89 ("scarcely believe"); John McDonnell, Militia General Order, Sept. 21, 1812, RG 9, I-B-1, box 2, folder 1812 miscellaneous, LAC; "List of Civil Prisoners at Fort George," Sept. 8, 1812, RG 8, 688:36, reel C-3231, LAC; Cruikshank, "Study of Disaffection," 27.

82. [Baptist Irvine] to the editors, Dec. 22, 1812, in *Baltimore Whig*, Jan. 20, 1813; Charles G. Boerstler to James Monroe, Feb. 2, 1813 ("Some Indians"), RG 107, M 221, reel 50, USNA; M. Smith, *Human Sorrow*, 5–6 ("the Indians felt") and 6–7 ("pull off").

83. John Askin, Jr., to Duncan Cameron, June 3, 1813 ("Those scoundrels"), and James B. Dennis to John Vincent, June 8, 1813 ("to effect"), in *DHCNF*, 5:297 and 6:59; [Anonymous], "The Last War in Canada," 431 ("by threatening"); M. Smith, *Human Sorrow*, 6.

84. M. Smith, *Geographical View*, 89 ("The people"), 94–96; Isaac Brock to [unnamed brothers], Sept. 3, 1812, in *DHCNF*, 1:234; John Strachan to George Prevost, Oct. 1812 ("infinite service"), in Spragge, ed., *John Strachan Letterbook*, 13.

85. W. D. Jones, ed., "British View," 484–85 (Henry Goulburn quoted: "It was impossible"); Reuben G. Beasley to James Monroe, Oct. 13, 1812 ("This disaster"), RG 59, T168, reel 10, USNA.

86. Fredriksen, ed., "Letters of Captain John Scott," 58.

Chapter Seven: Crossings

1. Sir Andrew Francis Barnard to George Cooke, Nov. 8, 1808 ("not likely"), ms. #13489, NYSL.

2. John Lovett to Abraham Van Vechten, Aug. 28, 1812 ("I saw"), in Bonney, ed., *Legacy*, 1:221.

3. John Lovett to Abraham Van Vechten, Aug. 28, 1812 ("Between"), SoVRP, sub-ser. 18, HCH; Aug. 31, 1812 ("Now use"), Gratz Coll., box 34, HSP.

4. Peter B. Porter to Daniel D. Tompkins, Aug. 30, 1812, in *DHCNF*, 1:223; Philetus Swift to Stephen Van Rensselaer, Aug. 26, 1812, SoVRP, sub-ser. 17, HCH; Lovett to Abraham Van Vechten, Aug. 26, 1812 ("war-hawks"), Gratz Coll., box 34, HSP.

5. Stephen Van Rensselaer to Roger H. Sheaffe, Aug. 25, 1812, RG 8, vol. 688A: 233, reel C-3231, LAC; Amos Hall to Van Rensselaer, Aug. 25, 1812, in SoVRP, sub-ser. 17, HCH; John Lovett to Joseph Alexander, Aug. 26, 1812, SoVRP, sub-ser. 18, HCH; Bonney, ed., *Legacy*, 1:288; Solomon Van Rensselaer to the Editors, Jan. 1813 ("high spirits," "*Belligerent*," and "*Scoundrel*"), SoVRP, sub-ser. 3.3, HCH.

6. "An American Farmer," [Philadelphia] *Aurora*, June 18, 1813.

7. "The Enemy Within," "The Old Congress," and "An Old American," [Philadelphia], *Aurora*, June 10, June 12, and July 26, 1812; [Baltimore] *American*, July 16, 1812 ("two parties"); Hickey, *War of 1812*, 55; Cope, ed., *Philadelphia Merchant*, 273 ("refractory"); Thomas Jefferson to James Madison, June 29, 1812, in *PJM-PS*, 4:519.

8. Gilje, *Rioting in America*, 61; Hickey, *War of 1812*, 56; *Niles' Register*, Sept. 19, 1812 ("head-quarters").

9. Pasley, "*Tyranny of Printers*," 241–44; Hickey, *War of 1812*, 57.

10. [Baltimore] *Federal Republican*, June 1, 1812 ("dictators"); Philip Lewis quoted in Hickey, *War of 1812*, 59 ("Temple of Infamy"); Gilje, *Rioting in America*, 60.

11. Gilje, *Rioting in America*, 61–62; Hickey, *War of 1812*, 60–63 (includes Thomas Wilson quoted: "civil authority"); Pasley, "*Tyranny of Printers*," 246–47.

12. Gilje, *Rioting in America*, 62–63; Hickey, *War of 1812*, 64–66 (includes quotations).

13. Hickey, *War of 1812*, 66–68 (juror quoted: "the affray").

14. "From the Baltimore Whig," "Vox Populi, Vox Dei Est," and "The Old Soldier," [Philadelphia] *Aurora*, Aug. 1, 1812, Oct. 21, 1812 ("any reasonable man"), and Dec. 23, 1812; Hickey, *War of 1812*, 69 (*Maryland Republican* quoted: "must abide"), and 70–71.

15. Hickey, *War of 1812*, 65, 68–69 (Boston town meeting quoted: "a prelude"), and 70; Pasley, "*Tyranny of Printers*," 247; "New York Convention," *Buffalo Gazette*, Oct. 6, 1812 ("republican" and "by exasperating").

16. L. M. Parker to Daniel Parker, June 22, 1812, DPP, box 2, HSP; Cope, ed., *Philadelphia Merchant*, 273; Rufus King quoted in Ernst, *Rufus King*, 318 ("Things"); Hickey, *War of 1812*, 53–54.

17. James Monroe to John Taylor, Nov. 19, 1810, in S. M. Hamilton, ed., *Writings of Monroe*, 5:156; Thomas Jefferson to William Duane, Apr. 30, 1811 ("our *party*"), quoted in Stagg, *Madison's War*, 61; R. H. Brown, *Republic in Peril*, 160–66.

18. W. Scott, *Memoirs*, 30–36; Daniel D. Tompkins to John Smith, Feb. 22, 1812, to William Eustis, Mar. 4, 1812, and to General Paulding, Apr. 3, 1812, in Hastings, ed., *Papers of Tompkins*, 2:491, 515, and 522; Elbridge Gerry to James Madison, Dec. 27, 1811 ("would retard"), and Henry Dearborn to Madison, Mar. 21, 1812, in *PJM-PS*, 4:93 and 258; Brant, *James Madison: The President*, 438–40; Richard Rush quoted in Stagg, *Madison's War*, 166–67 ("enemies").

19. Erney, *Henry Dearborn*, 41–44, 230, 244, and 260–62; Stagg, *Madison's War*, 165; Dolly Madison to Anna Payne Cutts, Mar. 20, 1812 ("Genl. Dearborn"), *PJM-PS*, 4:258n1.

20. Elbridge Gerry to Henry Dearborn, Sept. 2, 1811 ("secession" and "kill them"), quoted in Stagg, *Madison's War*, 254; Gerry to James Madison, May 19, 1812 ("By a war"), and Dearborn to Madison, June 12, 1812, in *PJM-PS*, 4:397–98 and 473–74; Erney, *Henry Dearborn*, 271–75 (Dearborn quoted: "effect"); William Eustis to Henry Dearborn, June 9, 1812 ("The blow"), HDP, box 1, MHS.

21. Hickey, *War of 1812*, 259–60; *PJM-PS*, 5:13n1.

22. Morgan Lewis to James Madison, Aug. 21, 1812 ("We have"), *PJM-PS*, 5:175; Malcomson, *Very Brilliant Affair*, 92.

23. Edward Baynes to George Prevost, Aug. 12, 1812 ("greatest contempt"), RG 8 (British Military), 677:27, reel C-3172, LAC; Malcomson, *Very Brilliant Affair*, 84–91; Hitsman, *Safeguarding Canada*, 92.

24. Stephen Van Rensselaer to Henry Dearborn, Sept. 5, 1812, in *DHCNF*, 1:238–39; Van Rensselaer to Roger H. Sheaffe, Sept. 4, 1812, in Bonney, ed., *Legacy*, 1:226; Stagg, *Madison's War*, 245; Erney, *Henry Dearborn*, 304.

25. Malcomson, *Very Brilliant Affair*, 62–64; Daniel D. Tompkins to Stephen Van Rensselaer, July 13, 1812, in Hastings, ed., *Papers of Tompkins*, 3:27–28.

26. Lovett to Abraham Van Vechten, Aug. 5, 1812 ("the deformed"), ms. #3538,

NYSL; Solomon Van Rensselaer to Harriot Van Rensselaer, Sept. 1, 1812 ("If nothing"), SoVRP, sub-ser. 3.2.1, HCH; Malcomson, *Very Brilliant Affair*, 68–69.

27. John Lovett to Abraham Van Vechten, July 30, 1812 ("the order" and "as quiet"), and Aug. 5, 1812 ("fond"), ms #3537 and #3538, NYSL; Lovett to Joseph Alexander, Aug. 17, 1812, in Bonney, ed., *Legacy*, 1:209.

28. Stephen Van Rensselaer, General Orders, Aug. 22, 1812, SoVRP, sub-ser. 3.2, HCH; John R. Fenwick to Stephen Van Rensselaer, Oct. 9, 1812 ("Our Guardroom"), SoVRP, sub-ser. 17, HCH; Malcomson, *Very Brilliant Affair*, 82–83; John Lovett to Joseph Alexander, Sept. 22, 1812, in Bonney, ed., *Legacy*, 1:236–37; Couture, *Study*, 78.

29. Brock, District Orders, July 2, 1812, Van Rensselaer to Brock, Sept. 20, 1812, and Van Rensselaer to Henry Dearborn, Sept. 27, 1812, in *DHCNF*, 1:92, 283, and 298; Isaac Brock to Stephen Van Rensselaer, Sept. 17, 1812, SoVRP, sub-ser. 17, HCH.

30. John Lovett to Joseph Alexander, Aug. 26, 1812, SoVRP, sub-ser. 18, HCH.

31. Thomas Evans to Isaac Brock, Aug. 19, 1812 ("familiar conversation"), in *SBD*, 1:598–99.

32. Peter B. Porter to Daniel D. Tompkins, Aug. 30, 1812, in *DHCNF*, 1:224–25; John Lovett, "Statement of the Affair at Queenston," 1813, StVRP, folder 4, NYHS; John C. Spencer to Tompkins, Sept. 5, 1812 ("General Van Rensselaer," "confidence," "precious couple," and "The soldiers"), Misc. Mss., Tompkins file, NYHS; Solomon Van Rensselaer to Morgan Lewis, Sept. 11, 1812 ("a traitor"), in Bonney, ed., *Legacy*, 1:231.

33. John Lovett to Joseph Alexander, Sept. 2, 1812, SoVRP, sub-ser. 18, HCH; Lovett, "Statement of the Affair at Queenston," 1813 ("Distrust"), StVRP, folder 4, NYHS; Lovett to Stephen Van Rensselaer, Nov. 6, 1812 ("I know"), VRMP, box 77, NYSL.

34. John Lovett to Joseph Alexander, Sept. 22, 1812 ("most tremendous"), and Oct. 6, 1812 ("We are"), SoVRP, sub-ser. 18, HCH; Lovett to Abraham Van Vechten, Sept. 24, 1812 ("We eat"), ms. #3541, NYSL.

35. Stephen Van Rensselaer to Henry Dearborn, Sept. 22, 1812, SoVRP, sub-ser. 17, HCH; John Lovett to Abraham Van Vechten, Sept. 24, 1812 ("no one dares"), ms. #3541, NYSL; Isaac Brock to George Prevost, Sept. 28, 1812 ("perfect health"), in *DHCNF*, 1:299; John R. Fenwick to Henry Dearborn, Oct. 8, 1812, Joseph M. Toner Papers, box 264, LC.

36. Mary Murray, "Journal of a Tour from New York to Niagara," June 21, 1808, NYHS; Charles Prentice, "Journal to Upper Canada," Oct. 10–11, 1807, TRL; Patrick McDonogh to his sister, Oct. 16, 1812 ("very poor country"), in *DHCNF*, 4:10; Malcomson, *Very Brilliant Affair*, 10.

37. Solomon Van Rensselaer to Abraham Van Vechten, Sept. 5, 1812, John Lovett to Van Vechten, Sept. 8, 1812, and Van Rensselaer to Morgan Lewis, Sept. 11, 1812, in Bonney, ed., *Legacy*, 1:227, 229, and 231; Malcomson, *Very Brilliant Affair*, 108; Augustus Porter to Peter B. Porter, July 13, 1812, in *DHCNF*, 1:126; P. B. Porter to James Monroe, Jan. 26, 1813, RG 107, M 221, reel 55, USNA; John C. Spencer to Daniel Parker, July 15, 1813, DPP, box 23, HSP.

38. Henry Dearborn to Stephen Van Rensselaer, Sept. 26, 1812 ("*At all events*"), in *DHCNF*, 1:295–96; Daniel D. Tompkins to Peter B. Porter, Sept. 9, 1812, and Tompkins to Van Rensselaer, Sept. 9, 1812, in Hastings, ed., *Papers of Tompkins*, 3:105–7 and 108–10; Stagg, *Madison's War*, 241–42; Erney, *Henry Dearborn*, 287–91.

39. John C. Fredriksen, "Alexander Smyth," *ANB*, 20:325–26; Malcomson, *Very Brilliant Affair*, 109–14; Bonney, *Legacy*, 1:239–42; Quimby, *U.S. Army*, 1:64–65.

40. Stephen Van Rensselaer to William Eustis, Oct. 14, 1812, in *DHCNF*, 4:79–81; Quimby, *U.S. Army*, 1:66–68.

41. John Lovett to Abraham Van Vechten, Aug. 26, 1812, and Solomon Van Rensselaer to Van Vechten, Sept. 5, 1812 ("blustering"), Gratz Coll., box 34 and box 35, HSP.

42. John Lovett to Joseph Alexander, Oct. 14, 1812, in Bonney, ed., *Legacy*, 1:266; Winfield Scott to William Eustis, Dec. 29, 1812, RG 107, M 221, reel 57, USNA; Malcomson, *Very Brilliant Affair*, 158–73; Quimby, *U.S. Army*, 1:69–70; Scott, *Memoirs*, 56–58.

43. John Lovett to Joseph Alexander, Oct. 14, 1812, in Bonney, ed., *Legacy*, 1:266–67; Quimby, *U.S. Army*, 1:69–71; Stanley, *War of 1812*, 126–27.

44. Stephen Van Rensselaer to William Eustis, Oct. 14, 1812, in Bonney, ed., *Legacy*, 1:257; anonymous soldier to father, Oct. 17, 1812 ("the sight"), in [Philadelphia] *Aurora*, Oct. 29, 1812; John Chrystie to Thomas H. Cushing, Feb. 22, 1813, in *DHCNF*, 4:96–99; Malcomson, *Very Brilliant Affair*, 165–68.

45. Thompson Mead to Daniel D. Tompkins, Nov. 9, 1812, RG 98, Third Military District, #19, USNA; Solomon Van Rensselaer, General Orders, n.d. but c. Oct. 12, 1813 ("expiate their crime"), SoVRP, sub-ser. 3.3.2, HCH; O'Reilly, ed., "Hero of Fort Erie," 75–76; Stephen Van Rensselaer to William Eustis, Oct. 14, 1812, in Bonney, ed., *Legacy*, 1:257.

46. Malcomson, *Very Brilliant Affair*, 172 (Jared Wilson quoted: "I thought hell") and 183–94; Stanley, *War of 1812*, 128–31; [Peter L. Chambers], "The War in Canada," 17 ("The Indians"), MG 40, G 4, file 2, LAC; Scott, *Memoirs*, 60–62; M. Smith, *Geographical View*, 91–92.

47. Roger H. Sheaffe to Stephen Van Rensselaer, Oct. 13, 1812, and Van Rensselaer to Sheaffe, Oct. 14, 1812, in SoVRP, sub-ser. 17, HCH; Sheaffe to George Prevost, Oct. 17 and Nov. 8, 1812, in Sheaffe, "Documents," 284–85 and 305; "Extract of a Letter," [Philadelphia] *Aurora*, Nov. 3, 1812 ("even the Irishmen").

48. Stephen Van Rensselaer to Henry Dearborn, Oct. 20, 1812, in *DHCNF*, 4:143; Van Rensselaer to Roger H. Sheaffe, Oct. 16, 1812, Sheaffe to Van Rensselaer, Oct. 16, 1812 ("Allow me"), and John Lovett to Joseph Alexander, Oct. 25, 1812, in SoVRP, sub-ser. 17 and 18, HCH; Charles Askin to John Askin, Dec. 14, 1812 ("General Van Ranselair"), in Quaife, ed., *John Askin Papers*, 2:740.

49. "New York Convention," Sept. 17–18, 1812 ("the employment"), in *Buffalo Gazette*, Oct. 6, 1812; *Buffalo Gazette*, Oct. 27, 1812; Washington Benevolent Society to John Lovett and Solomon Van Rensselaer, Dec. 1, 1812, SoVRP, sub-ser. 3.2, HCH; John Lovett, "Statement of the Affair at Queenston," 1813, StVRP, folder 4, NYHS; Malcomson, *Very Brilliant Affair*, 201.

50. John Burkholder, affidavit, Oct. 31, 1812, in *SBD*, 1:640–42; [Canandaigua, N.Y.] *Ontario Messenger*, Nov. 10, 1812; [Philadelphia] *Aurora*, Nov. 14, 1812; Joseph Ellicott to Paul Busti, Mar. 23, 1813 ("a good"), and Mar. 25, 1813, HLCP, reel 12, BECHS.

51. Henry Dearborn to Alexander Smyth, Oct. 21, 1812 ("pass into"), in *DHCNF*, 4:151; Dearborn to Smyth, Oct. 28, 1812, and Smyth to Dearborn, Oct. 30, 1812, in *ASP-MA*, 1:495.

52. Alexander Smyth to William Eustis, Oct. 20, 1812, in *DHCNF*, 4:140; William King to Smyth, Oct. 5, 1812 ("mere militia" and "on which shoulder"), Smyth to

Henry Dearborn, Oct. 24, 1812, Thomas Parker to Smyth, Oct. 30, 1812, J. W. Livingston to Smyth, Nov. 4, 1812, and Smyth to Dearborn, Nov. 9, 1812, in *ASP-MA*, 1:491, 494, 495, 496, and 497.

53. Thomas Parker to Alexander Smyth, Oct. 30, 1812, and Smyth to Henry Dearborn, Oct. 30, 1812, in *ASP-MA*, 1:495.

54. Alexander Smyth, "To the Men of New York" and "To the Soldiers," in Severance, ed., "The Case of Alexander Smyth," 226 ("In a few days") and 228 ("spoils" and "You have seen").

55. [Canandaigua, N.Y.] *Ontario Messenger*, Nov. 24, 1812, and Dec. 1, 1812 ("The friends"); Porter, "To the Public," *Buffalo Gazette*, Dec. 14, 1812; John C. Spencer to Daniel Parker, July 15, 1813, DPP, box 23, HSP.

56. Alexander Smyth to Henry Dearborn, Nov. 9, 1812, in *ASP-MA*, 1:497; [Manlius, N.Y.] *Times*, Nov. 17, 1812 ("In fine"), in *DHCNF*, 4:219; Joseph H. Dwight to E. Hoyt, Nov. 18, 1812 ("Greenland"), JEWP, box 7, NYSL.

57. Archer, ed., "Journal of Major Roach," 139; Alexander Smyth to Henry Dearborn, Nov. 9, 1812, David Campbell to Smyth, Nov. 27, 1812 ("forcibly struck"), Isaac A. Coles, troop return, Dec. 5, 1812, and George McFeely to Smyth, Dec. 1, 1812, in *ASP-MA*, 1:497, 500–501, 506, and 507; David Harvey, affidavit, Dec. 5, 1812, in *DHCNF*, 4:249.

58. Joseph Ellicott to Paul Busti, Feb. 5, 1813 ("The fact is"), EEPFP, Letterbook II, BECHS; Hodge, "William Hodge Papers," 227; Jasper Parrish, petition to Congress, Nov. 15, 1819, Jasper Parrish Papers, box 1, BECHS.

59. James Aigin, "Reminiscences," BECHS; "Extract of a Letter," Nov. 10, 1812, [Philadelphia] *Aurora*, Dec. 12, 1812; *Geneva* [N.Y.] *Gazette*, Sept. 16, 1812; *Buffalo Gazette*, Aug. 11, Sept. 15, and Oct. 6, 1812; Ketchum, *History of Buffalo*, 2:237; "Baptist Irvine to S. Barnes, Nov. 27, 1812 (Pomeroy quoted: "every volunteer"), [Philadelphia] *Aurora*, Dec. 17, 1812; Abel M. Grosvenor to his brother, Nov. 25, 1812 ("kill all"), in *DHCNF*, 4:238; Isaac A. Coles to Thomas Jefferson, Dec. 30, 1812, TJP-AMS, LC; "Disgraceful Outrage," *Geneva* [N.Y.] *Gazette*, Dec. 9, 1812; Ketchum, *History of Buffalo*, 2:237–38.

60. Baptist Irvine to S. Barnes, Nov. 27, 1812; [Philadelphia] *Aurora*, Dec. 17, 1812; Abel M. Grosvenor to his brother, Nov. 25, 1812, and Bill Sherman, affidavit, Dec. 3, 1812 ("fighting enough"), in *DHCNF*, 4:238 and 247; James Aigin, "Reminiscences" ("The Excitement"), BECHS; Isaac A. Coles to Thomas Jefferson, Dec. 30, 1812 ("threatened"), TJP-AMS, LC; Ketchum, *History of Buffalo*, 2:238–39 ("Old Blow-Hard"); Graves, *Field of Glory*, 37.

61. Alexander Smyth, general order, Nov. 25, 1812, and Nov. 27, 1812 ("Friends"), in *ASP-MA*, 1:500–501.

62. Peter B. Porter, "To the Public," *Buffalo Gazette*, Dec. 15, 1812; Alexander Smyth to Cecil Bisshopp, Nov. 28, 1812, in *ASP-MA*, 1:502; Severance, ed., "Case of Alexander Smyth," 233; Smyth to Henry Dearborn, Dec. 4, 1812, HDP, box 1, MHS; Isaac A. Coles to Thomas Jefferson, Dec. 30, 1812, TJP-AMS, LC.

63. Peter B. Porter, "To the Public," *Buffalo Gazette*, Dec. 15, 1812; Smyth quoted in Severance, ed., "Case of Alexander Smyth," 233–34 ("Hearts of War!"); Isaac A. Coles to Thomas Jefferson, Dec. 30, 1812 ("Nothing"), TJP-AMS, LC; David Campbell, "Confidential," n.d. ("The General"), CFP, box 2, SC-PL-DU.

64. Alexander Smyth to George McClure et al., Dec. 3, 1812, in *DHCNF*, 4:269–72; Cyrenius Chapin, "Counter Statement," *Buffalo Gazette*, Dec. 29, 1812.

65. Peter B. Porter, "To the Public," Dec. 14, 1812 ("4,000 men"), in *Buffalo*

Gazette, Dec. 15, 1812; Isaac A. Coles, to Thomas Jefferson, Dec. 30, 1812 ("a few barrels" and "damned Tory"), TJP-AMS, LC; "Disaster upon Disaster," *Utica Patriot,* Dec. 15, 1812 ("a coward"); "From the Pennsylvania Republican," [Philadelphia] *Aurora,* Dec. 25, 1812 ("worse than Hull"); David Campbell, "Confidential," n.d. ("I have never seen"), CFP, box 2, SC-PL-DU.

66. Cyrenius Chapin to Solomon Van Rensselaer, Dec. 13, 1812, in Bonney, ed., *Legacy,* 1:284; William H. Winder and Samuel Angus, "Duel," Dec. 13, 1812 ("gentleman and officer"), in Severance, ed., "Case of Alexander Smyth," 242; "General Smyth & General Porter," [Philadelphia] *Aurora,* Feb. 2, 1813.

67. Peter B. Porter, "To the Public," Dec. 14, 1812, in *Buffalo Gazette,* Dec. 15, 1812; Alexander Smyth to the Editors of the *National Intelligencer,* Jan. 28, 1813, in Severance, ed., "Case of Alexander Smyth," 244–46 ("too Indolent").

68. "Gen. Smyth," [Canandaigua, N.Y.] *Ontario Messenger,* Dec. 15, 1812;"Extract of a Letter," *New York Statesman,* Feb. 2, 1813 (*"demi-brute"*), in *DHCNF,* 5:40; Smyth to John Armstrong, Feb. 3, 1813, in *ASP-MA,* 1:508; Ketchum, *History of Buffalo,* 2:370–71; John Campbell to David Campbell, Jan. 31, 1813 ("Your general"), CFP, box 2, SC–PL–DU; Irwin, *Daniel D. Tompkins,* 159; Stagg, *Madison's War,* 251.

69. John Lovett to Joseph Alexander, Oct. 8, 1812 (*"Rascal"*), and Solomon Van Rensselaer to *The Columbian,* n.d. but c. Jan. 1813, in Bonney, ed., *Legacy,* 1:243 and 296–97; Augustus Porter to Peter B. Porter, Feb. 3, 1813 ("I beg"), in *DHCNF,* 5:56.

70. Harold Smyth, inspection report, Dec. 8, 1812, in *ASP-MA,* 1:507; David Harvey, affidavit, Dec. 5, 1812 ("rascality" and "preference"), and Patrick McDonogh to his parents, Dec. 12, 1812, in *DHCNF,* 4:249 and 5:19.

71. William Wadsworth to Stephen Van Rensselaer, Dec. 30, 1812, ms. #124, NYSL; Daniel Hudson, "Remarks," *Geneva* [N.Y.] *Gazette,* Jan. 13, 1813; Joseph Ellicott to Paul Busti, Jan. 18, 1812 ("the most sickly"), in Ellicott, "Extracts," 151; Joseph Lovett to Harmanus Bleecker, Feb. 6, 1813 ("eat like wolves"), in GP, box 2, BECHS; *Buffalo Gazette,* Feb. 2, 1813 (*"Buffalo Fever"*).

72. *Buffalo Gazette,* Dec. 15, 1812; "Cassandra, No. 1," *New-York Evening Post,* Jan. 13, 1813; Mann, *Medical Sketches,* 44 and 142–43; Major Samuel Stewart to Judge Childs, Jan. 7, 1813, [Philadelphia] *Aurora,* Feb. 4, 1813; [Baptist Irvine] to the editors, Feb. 14, 1813 (*"judgments"* and "disasters"), in *Baltimore Whig,* Feb. 17, 1813.

73. [Baptist Irvine] to the editors, Feb. 14, 1813 ("the plan"), *Baltimore Whig,* Feb. 17, 1813; Samuel H. Moore to the editors of the *Baltimore Patriot,* [Philadelphia] *Aurora for the Country,* Oct. 18, 1813 ("without the consent" and "the disloyal"); Morris S. Miller et al., "To the Electors of the Western District," Apr. 14, 1813 ("the late violent"), Broadside #1593, NYSL.

74. Hickey, *War of 1812,* 103–5; Stagg, *Madison's War,* 252.

75. John Lovett to Joseph Alexander, June 12, 1813, SoVRP, sub-ser. 18, HCH; Solomon Van Rensselaer to Stephen Van Rensselaer, May 11, 1813 ("The die" and "Canada"), HDP, Box 1, MHS. For the New York election returns see the *Albany Register,* June 8, 1813. In the entire state, Tompkins secured 43,329 votes, compared to 39,720 for Van Rensselaer. Tompkins won most of his majority—a 3,609-vote advantage—in the western region, including Niagara County, which voted 542 for Tompkins and just 238 for Van Rensselaer.

76. Roger Hale Sheaffe to George Prevost, Dec. 4, 1812, in Sheaffe, "Documents," 318; Charles Askin to John Askin, Dec. 11, 1812, in Quaife, ed., *John Askin Papers,* 2:738; "York," *Kingston Gazette,* Dec. 19, 1812; [Baptist Irvine] to the editors, Dec. 22, 1813 ("taunts and sarcasms"), in *Baltimore Whig,* Jan. 20, 1813.

77. Roger H. Sheaffe to George Prevost, Oct. 13, Nov. 3, and Nov. 13, 1812, in Sheaffe, "Documents," 277, 300, and 313; Couture, *Study*, 100; M. Smith, *Geographical View*, 92–94; Isaac A. Coles to Thomas Jefferson, Dec. 30, 1812, TJP-AMS, LC.

78. Henry Clay, speech to Congress, Jan. 9, 1813, in Hopkins et al., eds., *Papers of Clay*, 1:770–73; Joseph B. Hawkins to John Armstrong, Feb. 14, 1813, RG 107, M 221, reel 53, USNA; Phineas Reed to William Eustis, Nov. 4, 1812 ("to drive"), RG 107, M 221, reel 48, USNA; Horsman, "On to Canada," 16–19.

79. John Armstrong to Henry Dearborn, Mar. 29, 1813 ("first step" and "state of prostration"), in *DHCNF*, 5:140; Hickey, *War of 1812*, 105–7; Stagg, *Madison's War*, 282–84; Skeen, *John Armstrong*, 129 and 135–37.

Chapter Eight: Scalps

1. John Askin to William Dummer Powell, Jan. 25, 1813, in *DHCNF*, 5:50.

2. Malcomson, ed., *Sailors of 1812*, 29–31 ("to surrender," "that the woods," and "armed to the teeth"); Edward B. Brenton to Noah Freer, May 30, 1813, RG 8, 1707:227, reel C-3840, LAC. The surrendering officer was Lieutenant Colonel Thomas Aspinwall of the Ninth U.S. Infantry.

3. Malcomson, ed., *Sailors of 1812*, 31 ("The dread"); Wright, *Human Life*, 44 and 112 ("allowed to grow up").

4. John Askin, Jr., to John Askin, Sept. 8, 1807 ("The Americans"), in Quaife, ed., *John Askin Papers*, 2:572; Solomon Sibley to Thomas Worthington, Feb. 26, 1812 ("war with England"), quoted in Antal, *Wampum Denied*, 25; Mortimer, "Ohio Frontier in 1812," 205, 213–14 ("each other"), and 216 ("not an Indian"). For the development of the American horror of Indian violence, see Silver, *Our Savage Neighbors*, 39–94.

5. Hamilton, ed., "Guy Johnson's Opinions," 322; Richardson, *Richardson's War*, 34; Silver, *Our Savage Neighbors*, 50–51.

6. Walker, *Journal*, 41–42 ("shockingly"); Amos Spafford to William Eustis, Apr. 21, 1812, RG 107, M 221, reel 48, USNA; Silver, *Our Savage Neighbors*, 41–45, 53–58, and 69–71; Benn, *Iroquois*, 78 and 84; Lewis Bond, "Journal," 42, LC.

7. Detroit public meeting resolves, Dec. 8, 1811 ("tenderest infant"), in MPHS, *MHC*, 40:347. This chapter explores the American fear of Indians; it does *not* attempt a close and balanced examination of native diversity and the full range of the complex Indian cultures. For fuller attention to a broader range of Haudenosaunee culture, see A. Taylor, *Divided Ground*.

8. R. White, *The Middle Ground*, 343–50, 368–78, and 383–96; Whelan, "Green Atlantic," 235; Silver, *Our Savage Neighbors*, 60–64 and 360n83.

9. Charles McNeill to Thankfull McNeill, July 14, 1812 ("It was said"), Manuscript #16997, NYSL; Darnell, *Journal*, 16–17 ("seemed to shake"); James Wilkinson to Morgan Lewis, July 6, 1813 ("more anxiety"), Lewis Papers, Box 3, Folder 3, NYHS; Silver, *Our Savage Neighbors*, 79–90; R. White, *Middle Ground*, 368–78 and 383–96.

10. Anonymous midshipman to J. Jones, Aug. 13, 1813 ("been surrounded" and "shockingly butchered"), in Dudley, ed., *Naval War*, 2:536–57.

11. William H. Merritt, Journal, July 8, 1813 ("The poor devils"), in *DHCNF*, 6:210.

12. Graves, ed., *Merry Hearts*, 127–29 ("a poor unfortunate" and "Rescue Him"); Benn, *Iroquois*, 120.

13. Francis de Rottenburg, Nov. 1, 1813, in *SBD*, 2:330; Robert McDouall to Henry Procter, June 14, 1813 ("Our Indians"), Gratz Coll., box 36, HSP; Charles Askin to John Askin, July 8, 1813, in Quaife, ed., *John Askin Papers*, 2:766.

14. Thomas Wilson to James Madison, Oct. 17, 1812, RG 107, M 221, reel 49, USNA; "The Old Soldier," "The Indian Tribes," and "The Savage Tomahawk," [Philadelphia] *Aurora*, Nov. 24, 1812, Feb. 9, 1813, and Mar. 24, 1813 ("hand of vengeance"); *Baltimore Whig*, May 27, 1813 ("Hang"); Crombie, ed., "Papers of Major Daniel McFarland," 104–5.

15. James Madison, speech to Congress, Nov. 4, 1812, in *PJM-PS*, 5:428; Henry Clay and James Madison quoted in Antal, *Wampum Denied*, 155 ("Canada innocent?") and 201 ("eager to glut").

16. "The Savage Allies of England," "The War," "Map of the Seat of War," and "An American Farmer," [Philadelphia] *Aurora*, Aug. 31, Sept. 19, and Oct. 16, 1812 ("country where"), and June 29, 1813; Henry Dearborn to Stephen Van Rensselaer, Oct. 4, 1812, in *DHCNF*, 2:31; William Henry Harrison, General Orders, Jan. 2, 1813 ("Let an account"), in Esarey, ed., *Messages and Letters*, 2:290.

17. Edward Baynes to George Prevost, Aug. 12, 1812, RG 8, 677:22, reel C-3172, LAC; Francis de Rottenburg to Henry Dearborn, July 15, 1813, CKGP, box 4, NYSL; John Vincent to William Henry Harrison, Nov. 10, 1813, in Esarey, ed., *Messages and Letters*, 2:599.

18. Thomas Evans to Isaac Brock, Oct. 15, 1812, in *SBD*, 1:619–20; Henry Procter to Roger H. Sheaffe, Feb. 1, 1813, RG 59, M 588, reel 7, USNA; James Commins to Mr. Davidson, Aug. 23, 1815 ("These Kentucky men"), in Lord, ed., "War of 1812," 206; "From the *National Intelligencer*," [Philadelphia] *Aurora*, Mar. 4, 1812 ("as a justification").

19. John Ketcham, "Reminiscences," and Isaac L. Baker to James Winchester, Feb. 25, 1813, in Esarey, ed., *Messages and Letters*, 2:283 ("first month's service") and 371; Darnell, *Journal*, 28; Fredriksen, ed., "Chronicle of Valor," 256 ("two Indian scalps").

20. John Strachan to William Wilberforce, Nov. 1, 1812, in Spragge, ed., *John Strachan Letterbook*, 23; Black Bird, speech, July 15, 1813 ("Big Knives"), in *DHCNF*, 6:242; Henry Procter to Roger H. Sheaffe, Feb. 1, 1813, RG 59, M 588, reel 7, USNA.

21. Beall, "Journal," 803; Parish, ed., *Robert Lucas Journal*, 36, 43–44; Walker, *Journal*, 69; William H. Merritt, "Journal," in *SBD*, 3:549–50; [Peter L. Chambers], "The War in Canada," MG 40, G 4, file 2, LAC; Antal, *Wampum Denied*, 35 and 50.

22. Henry Procter to Major Reynolds, Dec. 23, 1812, and Jan. 4, 1813, RG 59, M 588, reel 7, USNA; Isaac Day to William Henry Harrison, Jan. 12, 1813 ("Five hundred"), and James Winchester to Harrison, Jan. 17, 1813, in Esarey, ed., *Messages and Letters*, 2:307–8 and 314.

23. James Winchester to Harrison, Jan. 17, 1813, and Harrison to James Monroe, Jan. 26, 1813, in Esarey, ed., *Messages and Letters*, 2:314 and 337; John Allen quoted in Antal, *Wampum Denied*, 162 ("Can we"); Couture, *War and Society*, 166; Atherton, *Narrative*, 32–33.

24. Atherton, *Narrative*, 42 ("the thundering"), 52; Darnell, *Journal*, 52–55; Antal, *Wampum Denied*, 170–71; Hitsman, *Incredible War*, 126.

25. Darnell, *Journal*, 71–72; Henry Procter, quoted in Antal, *Wampum Denied*, 175 ("band of banditti"); Joseph Ellicott to Paul Busti, Feb. 19, 1813, HLCP, reel 12, BECHS.

26. Medard Labbadi, affidavit, Feb. 11, 1813, and Isaac L. Baker to James Winchester, Feb. 25, 1813 ("with sculls"), in Esarey, ed., *Messages and Letters*, 2:361–62 and

371–74; Charles G. Boerstler to James Monroe, Feb. 11, 1813 ("We are afraid"), RG 107, M 221, reel 50, USNA; affidavits by Joseph Robert, Feb. 4, 1813, and Alexis Labadie, Feb. 6, 1813 ("The hogs"), in *ASP-MA*, 1:368 and 369; [Peter L. Chambers], "The War in Canada" ("fierce glare"), MG 40, G 4, File 2, LAC; Darnell, *Journal*, 59–62; Antal, *Wampum Denied*, 174–77.

27. Couture, *War and Society*, 175–76.

28. MPHS, *MHC*, 12:463n102.

29. Robert Richardson to John Askin, Feb. 7, 1813 ("Be assured"), in Quaife, ed., *John Askin Papers*, 2:750; "Shocking Barbarity!," [New York], *Shamrock*, Feb. 27, 1813; "Spirit and Manner in Which the War is Waged by the Enemy," July 31, 1813, in *ASP-MA*, 1:339–40; Antal, *Wampum Denied*, 200–2; Latimer, *1812*, 120.

30. Thomas Barclay to John Mason, Sept. 7, 1813, and Mason to Barclay, Oct. 5, 1813 ("on the Raisin River"), in *ASP-FR*, 1:674; John Strachan to Francis de Rottenburg, Sept. 6, 1813, in Spragge, ed., *John Strachan Letterbook*, 45.

31. Green Clay, address, Apr. 7, 1813 ("Should we encounter"), in Richardson, *Richardson's War*, 175; Richard M. Johnson, "A Call for the Mounted Regiment," May 11, 1813, RG 107, M 221, reel 54, USNA; Antal, *Wampum Denied*, 182 and 211–12.

32. Decius Wadsworth to James Monroe, Jan. 8, 1813, RG 107, M 222, reel 9, USNA; John Armstrong to U.S. Cabinet, Feb. 8, 1813, and Armstrong to Henry Dearborn, Feb. 10, 1813, in *DHCNF*, 5:63 and 66; Stagg, *Madison's War*, 284–87.

33. Henry Dearborn to John Armstrong, Mar. 9 and Apr. 28, 1813, and William Dummer Powell, "An Account of the Capture of York," in *DHCNF*, 5:101, 166–67, and 175–76; Malcomson, *Capital in Flames*, 160–64, 167–69, and 190–98.

34. Fredriksen, ed., " 'Poor But Honest Sodger,' " 139; P. Finan, "Onlooker's View," in Gellner, ed., *Recollections*, 91; Miller, ed., *Beaumont's Formative Years*, 46 ("fellow creatures" and "Oh Dear!"); Malcomson, *Capital in Flames*, 199–200, 215–19, and 225–26.

35. Hitsman, *Incredible War*, 140; William Chewett et al., memorandum, May 8, 1813, in *DHCNF*, 5:192–96; Malcomson, *Capital in Flames*, 228–230.

36. Terms of Capitulation, Apr. 27, 1813, in Firth, ed., *Town of York*, 296; William Dummer Powell to Henry Dearborn, Apr. 29, 1813, and Chewett et al., memorandum, May 8, 1813, in *DHCNF*, 5:172 and 192–99; John Strachan, diary, Apr. 27–28, 1813 ("a deception"), in Henderson, ed., *John Strachan*, 40–41.

37. William Allan to Roger H. Sheaffe, May 2, 1813 ("Few houses"), and William Chewett et al., memorandum, May 8, 1813 ("great degree"), in *DHCNF*, 5:178 and 199–200; Penelope Beikie to John Macdonell, May 5, 1813, Isaac Chauncey to William Dummer Powell, Nov. 14, 1813, and John Beikie to Miles Macdonnell, Mar. 19, 1814 ("Those who"), in Firth, ed., *Town of York*, 300, 322–23, and 329; Benn, *Battle of York*, 50–51. Chauncey later collected and returned some of the books pillaged from the library.

38. Arthur Sinclair to John H. Cocke, July 4, 1813 ("Some of them"), in Malcomson, ed., *Sailors of 1812*, 47; John Strachan, diary, Apr. 30, 1813, and May 1, 1813 ("confesses"), in Henderson, ed., *John Strachan*, 41–42; Strachan to Dr. James Brown, June 14, 1813, and William Dummer Powell, memorandum, Oct. 3, 1815, in Firth, ed., *Town of York*, 296 and 301.

39. Henry Dearborn to John Armstrong, May 3, 1813 ("suspended"), RG 107, M 221, reel 52, USNA; Fredriksen, ed., " 'Poor But Honest Sodger,' " 139; [Baltimore] *Weekly Register*, May 22, 1813; Isaac Chauncey to William Jones, June 4, 1813, in *ASP-MA*, 1:375; [Philadelphia] *Aurora*, May 20, 1813; "Capital Affair," *Geneva* [N.Y.]

Gazette, Sept. 15, 1813; "British Humanity," [Canandaigua, N.Y.] *Ontario Messenger*, July 13, 1813; Malcomson, *Capital in Flames*, 248–49 and 290–91. For the plausible explanation of the scalp, see [Barnabas Bidwell], "Sketches of Upper Canada," in Gourlay, ed., *Statistical Account*, 1:90–92.

40. [Baptist Irvine] to the Editors, May 7, 1813, in *Baltimore Whig*, May 25, 1813; John Armstrong to Henry Dearborn, May 15, 1813, in *DHCNF,* 6:3.

41. John Harvey to Edward Baynes, May 25, 1813, and John Vincent to George Prevost, May 28, 1813, in *SBD*, 2:102 and 103–7; Fredriksen, ed., "Chronicle of Valor," 260–65; Quimby, *U.S. Army*, 1:230–33.

42. [Anonymous], "First Campaign," 204; Winfield Scott to Charles K. Gardner, June 4, 1813 ("no General"), CKGP, box 2, NYSL; Morgan Lewis, "The Battle of Fort George," Lewis Papers, Box 3, Folder 3, NYHS; John Harvey, "Journal of a Staff Officer," 25 ("This display"), Reel MS-842, AO; Quimby, *U.S. Army*, 1:233–34; Cooper, ed., *Ned Myers*, 57–59.

43. [Anonymous], "First Campaign," 201, 205 ("many log cabins" and "They found"); Lt. Col. Holcroft to Major Gibson, June 20, 1813, RG 94, # 127, box 19, folder 1, USNA; Morgan Lewis to Daniel Parker, Sept. 17, 1813 ("every house"), RG 94, # 127, box 1, folder 3, USNA.

44. Morris, *Sword of the Border*, 40–42; Hitsman, *Incredible War*, 146; Quimby, *U.S. Army*, 1:235–36.

45. Jacob Brown to Daniel D. Tompkins, June 1, 1813, in *DHCNF,* 5:286–87; George Prevost to Earl Bathurst, June 1, 1813, in *SBD*, 2:130–34; Malcomson, *Lords*, 135–39; Quimby, *U.S. Army*, 1:237–41; Lord, ed., "War of 1812," 204; Klinck and Ross, eds., *Tiger Dunlop's Upper Canada*, 31; Graves, ed., *Merry Hearts*, 117.

46. Stanley, *War of 1812*, 185–86; Malcomson, *Lords*, 135–36 and 143; Richard Smith to Franklin Wharton, June 11, 1813, in Dudley, ed., *Naval War*, 2:479; Isaac Chauncey to William Jones, June 2, 1813, MG 24, F 13, LAC.

47. Malcomson, *Lords*, 129, 140, and 146–47; Isaac Chauncey to William Jones, June 11, 1813 ("more mature"), MG 24, F 13, LAC; Stanley, *War of 1812*, 185–86.

48. Jacob Brown to Daniel D. Tompkins, in *DHCNF,* 5:286–87; Morris, *Sword of the Border*, 49–55; Major Herkimer et al. to John Armstrong, July 1, 1813, RG 107, M222, reel 8, USNA.

49. Edward Baynes, June 4, 1813, and John Harvey to Baynes, June 6, in *SBD*, 2:137 and 139–41; Quimby, *U.S. Army*, 1:241–46; Stanley, *War of 1812*, 186–90.

50. Charles Askin to John Askin, June 8, 1813, in Quaife, ed., *John Askin Papers*, 2:757; M. W. Thompson, ed., "Billy Green, 'the Scout,' " 175 ("we yelled"); Shepard, *Autobiography*, 55–56 ("Indians!" and "The British"); Fredriksen, ed., "Memoirs of Ephraim Shaler," 419 ("surrounded"); James FitzGibbon to James Somerville, June 7, 1813, James Burn to Henry Dearborn, June 7, 1813, John Chandler to Dearborn, June 18, 1813, and Anonymous to *United States Gazette*, June 22, 1813, in *DHCNF,* 6:12–15, 24–25, 26–28, and 50–51; James Burn to Charles J. Ingersoll, July 1, 1813, CJIP, box 1, HSP; Joseph Hawley Dwight, "Journal of an Ensign,", General Coll., box 93, OCHS.

51. William H. Merritt, "Memoir," in *DHCNF,* 6:46; Thomas Evans to John Vincent, June 8, 1813, and Vincent to Sir George Prevost, June 9, 1813, in *SBD*, 2:145 and 149; James Burn to Charles J. Ingersoll, July 1, 1813, CJIP, box 1, HSP; Fredriksen, ed., "Chronicle of Valor," 266; Robert McDouall to Henry Procter, June 9, 1813 ("to carry terror"), RG 59, M 588, reel 7, USNA; Quimby, *U.S. Army*, 1:246–47.

52. [Anonymous], "First Campaign," 176 ("Had a map"); Thomas Evans to John Harvey, June 10, 1813, in *SBD*, 2:155; Stanley, *War of 1812*, 190–91.

53. John Harvey, "Journal of a Staff Officer," 34 ("most important"), reel MS-842, AO; [Anonymous], "First Campaign," 286 ("Misery"); Henry Dearborn to Armstrong, June 23, 1813 ("Incessant rains"), RG 107, M 221, reel 52, USNA; officer quoted in Graves, *Field of Glory*, 35 ("durty"); Mann, *Medical Sketches*, 63–67 and 91–93.

54. Ambrose Spencer to John Armstrong, Feb. 20, 1813, quoted in Stagg, *Madison's War*, 333; Peter B. Porter to Armstrong, July 27, 1813 ("two stately"), in *DHCNF*, 6:284.

55. William B. Skelton, "John Parker Boyd," *ANB*, 3:311; Scott, *Memoirs*, 93–94 ("respectable"); Morgan Lewis to Armstrong, July 5, 1813 ("Bully"), RG 107, M222, reel 8, USNA.

56. John Harvey to Edward Baynes, June 11, 1813, J. B. Glegg, Return of the Troops, June 13, 1813, and Morgan Lewis to John Armstrong, June 14, 1813, in *DHCNF*, 6:67, 73, and 74; Henry Dearborn to Armstrong, June 20, 1813, RG 107, M 221, reel 52, USNA; [Anonymous], "First Campaign," 176 ("the limits"), and 259.

57. Ketchum, *History of Buffalo*, 2:156–60; Valenti, "Cyrenius Chapin," 1–25; Cyrenius Chapin to Henry Dearborn, June 2, 1813, CKGP, box 2, NYSL; *Buffalo Gazette*, June 22, 1813, in *DHCNF*, 6:109; James Aigin, "Reminiscences," ("Forty Thieves"), BECHS.

58. McKenzie, *James FitzGibbon*, 10–24; Cruikshank, *Fight in the Beechwoods*, 6–7.

59. Cruikshank, *Fight in the Beechwoods*, 6–7; William H. Merritt, "Memoir," in *DHCNF*, 6:98–99 ("Irish Greens" and "Bloody Boys"); Cruikshank, ed., "Records of Niagara . . . January to July 1813," 49.

60. Charles G. Boerstler, "Narrative," in *DHCNF*, 6:130–31; James C. Bronaugh to David Campbell, July 24, 1813, CFP, box 2, SC-PL-DU; Quimby, *U.S. Army*, 248–49; Cruikshank, *Fight in the Beechwoods*, 11–14.

61. Boerstler, *Battle*, 1; William Johnson Kerr to William Claus, Dec. 8, 1815, in *DHCNF*, 6:121–22; Willoughby Morgan to David Campbell, July 18, 1813, CFP, box 2, SC-PL-DU; Quimby, *U.S. Army*, 1:248–49.

62. Cruikshank, *Fight in the Beechwoods*, 11–15; Boerstler, *Battle*, 1; William Johnson Kerr to William Claus, Dec. 8, 1815, in *DHCNF*, 6:121–22; Laura Secord, "Memoir," Feb. 18, 1861, in *SBD*, 2:164–65; Moir, "Early Record," 310–13.

63. Charles G. Boerstler, "Narrative," in *DHCNF*, 6:132–33; Quimby, *U.S. Army*, 1:249–50.

64. James FitzGibbon to P. V. Van Haren, June 24, 1813, Cecil Bisshopp to John Vincent, June 24, 1813, FitzGibbon to William Johnson Kerr, Mar. 30, 1818 ("Not a shot"), and Charles G. Boerstler, "Narrative," in *DHCNF*, 6:111, 112, 120, and 133–35 ("general massacre"); Charles Askin to John Askin, July 8, 1813, in Quaife, ed., *John Askin Papers*, 2:763–65; Graves, ed., *Merry Hearts*, 126–27 ("badly wounded"); Boerstler quoted in Stanley, *War of 1812*, 196 ("For God's sake"); Klinck and Talman, eds., *Journal of Norton*, 333.

65. [Anonymous], "First Campaign," 182–83; Charles J. Ingersoll to Alexander J. Dallas, July 6, 1813 ("climax"), CJIP, box 2, HSP; Stagg, *Madison's War*, 335; James Burn to Ingersoll, July 16, 1813 ("old buck"), in Fredriksen, ed., "Colonel James Burn," 307; Winfield Scott to Charles K. Gardner, July 16, 1813, CKGP, box 2, NYSL.

66. Cyrenius Chapin to Henry Dearborn, July 13, 1813, in Ketchum, *History of Buffalo*, 2:372; John Walworth to Jonas Simonds, July 14, 1813, MG 24, F 16, one folder, LAC; [Anonymous], "First Campaign," 262–63 ("sort of triumph" and "gallant"); Boerstler, *Battle*, 1.

67. John Armstrong to Morgan Lewis, July 9, 1813, and Armstrong to James Wilkinson, Aug. 8, 1813, in *DHCNF,* 6:212 and 322; Fredriksen, ed., "Colonel James Burn," 307 and 322; [Anonymous], "First Campaign," 259; Willoughby Morgan to David Campbell, July 18, 1813 ("immolated"), CFP, box 2, SC-PL-DU; Graves, *Field of Glory,* 37.

68. Anonymous to the editors, June 30, 1813, in *New-York Evening Post,* July 13, 1813, Francis de Rottenburg to Edward Baynes, July 14, 1813, Rottenburg to Prevost, July 20 1813, ("daily engaged"), and Peter B. Porter to John Armstrong, July 27, 1813 ("This army"), in *DHCNF,* 6:167–68, 233, 282, and 283; John Norton to Henry Goulburn, Jan. 29, 1816 ("so far intimidated"), in Cruikshank, ed., "Account of the Operations," 45.

69. "Extract—Dated Fort George, Upper Canada, July 9, 1813," [Philadelphia] *Aurora for the Country,* July 22, 1813; "Extract of a Letter, dated Fort George, Upper Canada, July 16," *New-York Evening Post,* July 28, 1813; James Burn to Nathan Williams, July 14, 1813, NWP, box 1, OCHS; Burn to Charles J. Ingersoll, July 16, 1813, CJIP, box 1, HSP; [Anonymous], "First Campaign," 337–38 ("utterly stripped" and "war of extermination"); Willoughby Morgan to David Campbell, July 18, 1813, and July 20, 1813, CFP, box 2, SC-PL-DU; [Baptist Irvine] to his friend in Baltimore, July 12, 1813, in *Baltimore Whig,* July 27, 1813.

70. John P. Boyd to Peter B. Porter, July 19, 1813, PBPP, reel 2, BECHS; Boyd to Porter, July 21, 1813, in *DHCNF,* 6:261; Willoughby Morgan to David Campbell, July 20 and July 27, 1813 ("We have forborne"), CFP, box 2, SC-PL-DU.

71. John Norton to James Craig, Aug. 10, 1808, in Cruikshank, ed., "Records of Niagara, 1805–1811," 64–65; Benn, *Iroquois,* 18–26; A. Taylor, *Divided Ground,* 297–324.

72. William Eustis to Erastus Granger, June 19, 1812, in Snyder, ed., *Red and White,* 55; Red Jacket, speech, in *Buffalo Gazette,* Aug. 4, 1812 ("If we sit still"), in *DHCNF,* 1:165; Benn, *Iroquois,* 63–64; Peter B. Porter to Eustis, June 28, 1812, RG 107, M 221, reel 47, USNA.

73. Klinck and Talman, eds., *Journal of Norton,* 336; M. Smith, *Geographical View,* 100 ("unite"); Peter B. Porter to Henry Dearborn, July 11 and July 13, 1813, and Francis de Rottenburg to Edward Baynes, July 14, 1813, in *DHCNF,* 6:216, 224–25, and 233; Thomas Clark to John Harvey, July 12, 1813, in *SBD,* 2:176; Porter, "Account of the Battle of Black Rock," PBPP, Reel 4, image 436, BECHS; James Aigin, "Reminiscences," ("drinking" and "good time"), Misc. Mss., BECHS.

74. Peter B. Porter to Henry Dearborn, July 11 and July 13, 1813, and Erastus Granger to John Armstrong, Aug. 9, 1813, in *DHCNF,* 6:216, 224–25, and 326–27; Thomas Clark to John Harvey, July 12, 1813, in *SBD,* 2:176; Porter, "Account of the Battle of Black Rock," PBPP, Reel 4, image 436 ("appalling"), BECHS; James Aigin, "Reminiscences," ("The River"), BECHS; "Our Indians," [Canandaigua, N.Y.] *Ontario Messenger,* July 27, 1813; *Aurora for the Country,* July 31 and Aug. 7, 1813.

75. Peter B. Porter to John P. Boyd, Aug. 5, 1813, Erastus Granger to Boyd, Aug. 6, 1813 ("now committed"), and Boyd to Porter, Aug. 8, 1813, in *DHCNF,* 6:311, 315, and 322; Cruikshank, "Blockade of Fort George," 54.

76. John P. Boyd to Peter B. Porter, Aug. 8, 1813, Anonymous letter, Aug. 17, 1813, in *Niles Weekly Register,* Aug. 28, 1813, Boyd to Porter, Aug. 17, 1813, Charles Askin to John Askin, Aug. 17, 1813, and Boyd to John Armstrong, Aug. 18, 1813, in *DHCNF,* 6:322, and 7:27, 7:28, 7:30, 7:32, and 7:36; [Anonymous], "First Campaign," 260–61; Scott, *Memoirs,* 97 ("closely pinioned"); Anonymous officer quoted in Cruik-

shank, "Blockade of Fort George," 60 ("Sundry scalps"); Benn, *Iroquois*, 137–39; Klinck and Talman, *Journal of Norton*, 338–40.

77. Charles Askin to John Askin, Aug. 17, 1813, in *DHCNF*, 7:32; Robert Livingston, petition, c. July 24, 1815, in MPHS, *MHC*, 16:167–69 and 726n; Cruikshank, "Blockade of Fort George," 58–60.

78. [Anonymous], "First Campaign," 262 ("that a man"); Robert Livingston, petition, c. July 24, 1815 ("greatest inhumanity"), in MPHS, *MHC*, 16:169; Francis de Rottenburg to John P. Boyd, Aug. 23, 1813, and Boyd to Rottenburg, Aug. 25, 1813, RG 107, M 221, reel 50, USNA.

79. Charles Askin to John Askin, Aug. 17, 1813, and Aug. 20, 1813, in *DHCNF*, 7:32 and 33; William Claus to unknown, Dec. 4, 1813, in Cruikshank, ed., "Account of the Operations," 34; John Harvey, "Journal of a Staff Officer," 43–44, AO.

80. [Canandaigua, N.Y.] *Ontario Repository*, Sept. 3, 1813, in *DHCNF*, 7:94; Joseph Hawley Dwight, "Journal of an Ensign," Aug. 18, 1813 ("Indians"), War of 1812 File, OCHS; Klinck and Talman, eds., *Journal of Norton*, 340.

81. John Boyd, general order, Aug. 1, 1813 ("Should the enemy"), in George Howard, Orderly Book #191, Reel 18 of "Early American Orderly Books, 1748–1817," NYHS.

82. John Harvey to Phineas Riall, July 23, 1814 ("your flanks"), in *DHCNF-1814*, 1:83.

83. James Madison quoted in Stagg, *Madison's War*, 502n5.

Chapter Nine: Flames

1. Joseph Ellicott to Simeon De Witt, Dec. 30, 1813, HLCP, reel 12, BECHS.

2. John Strachan, autobiography, in Henderson, ed., *John Strachan*, 2 ("The day"); G. M. Craig, "John Strachan," *DCB*, 9:751–52.

3. G. M. Craig, "John Strachan," *DCB*, 9:752; John Strachan to James Brown, Aug. 25, 1799, and Strachan, Travel Journal, Nov. 14, 1799 ("most of the causes"), in Henderson, ed., *John Strachan*, 13 and 14; Thomas G. Ridout to Thomas Ridout, June 16, 1807 ("Mr. Strachan"), in Edgar, ed., *Ten Years*, 25–26.

4. Thomas G. Ridout to Thomas Ridout, June 16, 1807, and George Ridout to T. G. Ridout, Oct. 19, 1811, in Edgar, ed., *Ten Years*, 22 and 64; John Strachan to Marquis Wellesley, Nov. 1, 1812 ("to prevent"), in Spragge, ed., *Strachan Letterbook*, viii and 29; A. Smith, "John Strachan," 162–63, 169, and 170–71 (Strachan quoted: "my pupils").

5. John Strachan to James Brown, Oct. 27, 1803 ("Plenty" and "little or no"), and Oct. 9, 1808 ("new nation"), in A. Smith, "John Strachan," 166–67 and 170–72.

6. A. Smith, "John Strachan," 168–69; John Strachan to Solomon Jones, July 30, 1812, and Oct. 6, 1812, Solomon Jones Papers, reel MS-520, AO; Strachan to Jacob Mountain, Oct. 1, 1812, Strachan to James McGill, Nov. 1812, and Strachan to Marquis Wellesley, Nov. 1, 1812, in Spragge, ed., *Strachan Letterbook*, 13, 14, and 25–26; Strachan, *Discourse*, 22–23, 44 ("You have"), and 77.

7. John Strachan to Jacob Mountain, Oct. 1, 1812, Strachan to James McGill, Nov. 1812 ("The people"), and Strachan to Marquis Wellesley, Nov. 1, 1812, in Spragge, ed., *Strachan Letterbook*, 13, 14, and 25–26.

8. C. M. Whitfield and W. B. Turner, "Roger Hale Sheaffe," *DCB*, 8:793; Malcomson, *Very Brilliant Affair*, 95–96; W. B. Turner, *British Generals*, 85–87.

9. Scott, *Memoirs*, 66–67; Lord, ed., "War of 1812," 201; C. M. Whitfield and W. B. Turner, "Roger Hale Sheaffe," *DCB*, 8:793; Turner, *British Generals*, 88 and 91–92; Malcomson, *Very Brilliant Affair*, 198–201.

10. Allan MacLean to Roger H. Sheaffe, Mar. 3, 1813, and George Prevost to Earl Bathurst, Apr. 21, 1813, in *DHCNF*, 5:98 and 159; Thomas Evans to William Dummer Powell, Jan. 6, 1813, J. B. Glegg to unknown, Jan. 10, 1813 ("irresistible"), George Prevost to Earl Bathurst, Feb. 27, 1813, and Mar. 19, 1813, in *DHCNF*, 5:29, 32–34, 82, and 126–27; Malcomson, *Capital in Flames*, 41–42, 67–69, and 73–80; W. B. Turner, *British Generals*, 90–93; Fraser, "Politics at the Head of the Lake," 20.

11. William Chewett et al., Memorandum, May 8, 1813 ("the disgrace"), William Dummer Powell, "Narrative," and John McGilivray to Simon McTavish, June 7, 1813, in *DHCNF*, 5:192–202, 5:205, and 6:18–22; John Strachan to James McGill, Nov. 1812, and Strachan to John Richardson, May 10, 1813, in Spragge, ed., *Strachan Letterbook*, 26–27, and 37; Benn, *Battle of York*, 38 and 56–57; Malcomson, *Capital in Flames*, 260–61; W. B. Turner, *British Generals*, 95–97 and 99–100.

12. George Prevost, General Order, June 18, 1813, in *SBD*, 2:157; Prevost to Earl Bathurst, June 24, 1813, in *DHCNF*, 6:139; Malcomson, *Capital in Flames*, 279–81.

13. *Upper Canada Guardian*, June 9, 1812, in *SBD*, 1:191–93; Joseph Willcocks to John McDonell, Sept. 1, 1812, in C. Johnston, ed., *Valley of the Six Nations*, 196–97; William H. Merrit to Catherine Prendergast, Feb. 1813 ("You will be surprised"), in *DHCNF*, 5:97; E. H. Jones, "Joseph Willcocks," *DCB*, 5:857–58; Malcomson, *Very Brilliant Affair*, 13 and 98. Hard-liners sought to sabotage Willcocks's rehabilitation by accusing him of sedition, but the alleged words were implausible and more than a year old, so nothing came of the prosecution. See Cruikshank, "Study of Disaffection," 26–27; Romney and Wright, "State Trials," 382–83.

14. *Quebec Gazette*, July 28, 1813, reprinted in Cruikshank, ed., "Records of Niagara . . . January to July 1813," 53; Abraham Markle to Roger H. Sheaffe, June 18, 1813 ("without my Protection"), RG 5, A 1, 16:6510, reel C-4508, LAC; Robert Lochiel Fraser, "Abraham Markle," *DCB*, 6:488–89; Fraser, "Politics at the Head of the Lake," 18–22.

15. Henry Dearborn to Joseph Willcocks, July 10, 1813, RG 107, M 221, reel 50, USNA; E. H. Jones, "Joseph Willcocks," *DCB*, 5:858. For a more cynical take on Willcocks's defection, see Sheppard, *Plunder*, 84–86 and 163.

16. Henry Dearborn to Joseph Willcocks, July 10, 1813, and Joseph Willcocks to John P. Boyd, July 19, 1813 ("Corps of Volunteers"), RG 107, M 221, reel 50, USNA.

17. [Baptist Irvine], "Latest from the Army," June 9, 1813 ("number of Yankees"), in *Baltimore Whig*, June 17, 1813; Stray, "Canadian Volunteers Burn," 222–25.

18. John P. Boyd to John Armstrong, Aug. 17, 1813 ("Canadian Volunteers"), in *DHCNF*, 7:30; [Anonymous], "First Campaign of an A.D.C.," 177 and 260 ("local feuds"); Cruikshank, ed., *Fight in the Beechwoods*, 9.

19. Fredriksen, ed., "Chronicle of Valor," 266–67; Mann, *Medical Sketches*, 204; George Prevost to Earl Bathurst, Aug. 25, 1813, in *SBD*, 2:185–86; Prevost to James L. Yeo, Sept. 19, 1813 ("a situation"), in *DHCNF*, 7:148; Graves, *Field of Glory*, 34–35; Cruikshank, "Blockade of Fort George," 52.

20. [Anonymous], "First Campaign," 330 ("lying alongside"), 333; Graves, ed., *Merry Hearts*, 133, 135, and 147–48 ("coward"); Graves, *Field of Glory*, 42–43 and 51–52.

21. William Claus, Journal, in C. Johnston, ed., *Valley of the Six Nations*, 217;

George Prevost to Earl Bathurst, Sept. 15, 1813, in *DHCNF,* 7:131; Edward Baynes to Henry Procter, Sept. 18, 1813 ("would have lost"), in Esarey, ed., *Messages and Letters,* 2:582–83.

22. Francis de Rottenburg to Henry Procter, Aug. 6, 1813 ("bed of roses"), RG 59, M 588, reel 7, USNA; Rottenburg to Edward Baynes, July 14, 1813, MacEwen to his wife, July 26, 1813, Rottenburg to George Prevost, Sept. 17, 1813 ("procrastination"), and Sept. 28, 1813 ("crippled"), in *DHCNF,* 6:233, 6:279, and 7:141.

23. Quimby, *U.S. Army,* 1:183–88; Skeen, *John Armstrong,* 151–53; William Jones to Isaac Chauncey, Apr. 8, 1813 ("Naval barrier"), in Dudley, ed., *Naval War,* 2:433.

24. Lewis Bond, "Journal," 44, LC; Henry Procter to Roger H. Sheaffe, Feb. 1, 1813 ("that Depot"), Feb. 4, 1813, and Feb. 21, 1813, RG 59, M 588, reel 7, USNA; Augustus Woodward to James Monroe, Mar. 22, 1813, in Carter, ed., *Territorial Papers,* 10:433–36; Antal, *Wampum Denied,* 191–92 and 307–8 (British officer quoted: "As we are now").

25. Lewis Bond, Journal, 40 ("encreased fury") and 57, LC; George Meldrum to John Askin, Mar. 29, 1814 ("all my pigs"), in Quaife, ed., *John Askin Papers,* 2:778; Couture, *War and Society,* 205–7.

26. [Peter L. Chambers], "The War in Canada," 48 ("degrading truth"), MG 40, G 4, file 2, LAC; Henry Procter to George Prevost, Aug. 9, 1813, in *SBD,* 2:44–45; Antal, *Wampum Denied,* 254–67; Hitsman, *Incredible War,* 166–68.

27. George Prevost to Henry Procter, Aug. 22, 1813 ("clamour"), Gratz Coll., box 36, HSP; Procter to Robert McDouall, June 10, 1813, in *DHCNF,* 6:64; Procter to Prevost, July 11, and 13, 1813, in *SBD,* 2:254 and 256–57.

28. Henry Procter to Roger H. Sheaffe, Apr. 13, 1813, RG 8, 688E:42, reel C-3232, LAC; Robert H. Barclay to James L. Yeo, Sept. 1, 1813, and Procter to Noah Freer, Sept. 6, 1813, in Dudley, ed., *Naval War,* 2:551 and 552; Robert Gilmore to Edward Couche, Aug. 6, 1813, in *DHCNF,* 6:317; Malcomson, *Lords,* 128.

29. George Prevost to Henry Procter, Aug. 22, 1813, Gratz Coll., box 36, HSP; Procter to Prevost, Aug. 26, 1813, and Robert H. Barclay to James L. Yeo, Sept. 1, 1813, in Dudley, ed., *Naval War,* 2:550 and 552; Barclay to Yeo, Sept. 6, 1813 ("the Risk"), in *SBD,* 2:293; Antal, *Wampum Denied,* 275–83; Quimby, *U.S. Army,* 1:260–65.

30. Robert H. Barclay to James L. Yeo, Sept. 12, 1813, in Dudley, *Naval War,* 2:555–56; Richardson, *Richardson's War,* 286–87; Lewis Bond, Journal, 60–62 ("Servility"), LC; Quimby, *U.S. Army,* 1:266–68; Antal, *Wampum Denied,* 285–89.

31. Henry Procter to Francis de Rottenburg, Sept. 12, 1813, in *SBD,* 2:272; Antal, *Wampum Denied,* 297–309 and 318; Quimby, *U.S. Army,* 1:272–73; Couture, *War and Society,* 214–16.

32. Walker, *Journal,* 124–29; William Henry Harrison to John Armstrong, Sept. 27 and 30, 1813 in Esarey, ed., *Messages and Letters,* 2:550–51 and 555; Lewis Bond, "Journal," 65–66 ("joyful acclamations"), LC; Lewis Cass to William Woodbridge, Nov. 9, 1813 ("to pillage"), in MPHS, *MHC,* 32:561.

33. Couture, *War and Society,* 217–21; Antal, *Wampum Denied,* 316–20; Quimby, *U.S. Army,* 1:274–76; Simon Z. Watson, certificate, Oct. 14, 1813, WHHP, 9:393, IHS.

34. John Schnall, report, Oct. 8, 1813 ("We heard"), in Sabathy-Judd, ed., *Moravians,* 515; Nicholas Cornwall and Michael Gordon, affidavit, Oct. 23, 1813, RG 9, I-B-1, box 2, LAC; Thomas McCrae, diary, Oct. 8, 1813, in *DHCNF,* 7:203; Andrew Kemp quoted in Antal, *Wampum Denied,* 326 ("They robbed" and "Who cares").

35. Thomas McCrae, diary, Sept. 30, 1813, in *DHCNF,* 7:180; Antal, *Wampum Denied,* 331–39; Quimby, *U.S. Army,* 1:277–81.

36. Antal, *Wampum Denied*, 340–49; Henry Procter to Francis de Rottenburg, Oct. 23, 1813, in *SBD*, 2:323–26; Richardson, *Richardson's War*, 209–20; Quimby, *U.S. Army*, 1:282–84.

37. William Henry Harrison to John Armstrong, Oct. 9, 1813, in Esarey, *Messages and Letters*, 2:565; Richardson, *Richardson's War*, 212; Walker, *Journal*, 138–40; Antal, *Wampum Denied*, 346 and 355–56; Klinck and Talman, eds., *Journal of Norton*, 343.

38. Sabathy-Judd, ed., *Moravians*, 505–7 and 511–15 (all quotations); Antal, *Wampum Denied*, 346 and 355–56.

39. William Henry Harrison to John Armstrong, Sept. 30, 1813, and Oct. 10, 1813, and Indian Armistice, Oct. 14, 1813, in Esarey, ed., *Messages and Letters*, 2:555–56, 573–74, and 577; Duncan McArthur to John Armstrong, Oct. 6, 1813 ("It is certain"), in MPHS, *MHC*, 40:535–36; Quimby, *U.S. Army*, 1:286 and 290; Antal, *Wampum Denied*, 356.

40. R. White, *Middle Ground*, 516–17.

41. Francis de Rottenburg to Sir George Prevost, Sept. 30, 1813, Oct. 3, 1813, and J. B. Glegg to William Dummer Powell, Oct. 8, 1813, and Rottenburg to Prevost, Oct. 16, 1813, in *DHCNF*, 7:179–80, 7:192, 7:204, and 8:68–69; William H. Merritt, "Journal of Events," in *SBD*, 3, part 2:594.

42. For the retreat, see Thomas G. Ridout to Thomas Ridout, Oct. 14 and 16, 1813, in Edgar, ed., *Ten Years*, 237 and 238; John Vincent to Francis de Rottenburg, Oct. 9 and 11, 1813, and J. B. Glegg to William Dummer Powell, Oct. 14, 1813, in *DHCNF*, 7:222, 8:50, and 8:59; Vincent to Rottenburg, Nov. 15, 1813, in *SBD*, 2:333–37. For the Indian refugees, see Vincent to Rottenburg, Oct. 18, 1813, and William Claus, "Return of the Six Nations," Oct. 26, 1813, in *DHCNF*, 8:78 and 97; Matthew Elliott to Claus, Oct. 24, 1813, and Claus, Journal, Dec. 4, 1813, in Cruikshank, ed., "Account of the Operations," 40 and 42; Benn, *Iroquois*, 145.

43. R. H. Bruyeres to George Prevost, Oct. 11, 1813, RG 8, 387:138, reel C-2936, LAC; Thomas G. Ridout to Thomas Ridout, Oct. 2, 1813, in Edgar, ed., *Ten Years*, 228; J. B. Glegg to John Strachan, Oct. 11, 1813 ("Our prospects"), Strachan Papers, reel MS-35, AO; William H. Merritt, "Journal of Events," in *SBD*, 3, part 2:603 ("our great men"); Robert Lochiel Fraser, "Benajah Mallory," *DCB*, 8:608–9; Fraser, "Abraham Markle," *DCB*, 6:489–90.

44. John Vincent to Francis de Rottenburg, Oct. 18, 1813, Rottenburg to Vincent, Oct. 23, 1813, Rottenburg to George Prevost, Oct. 30, 1813, Rottenburg to the Adjutant General, Nov. 2, 1813, Robert Nichol to Earl Bathurst, Sept. 24, 1817, and Vincent to Rottenburg, Dec. 13, 1813, in *DHCNF*, 8:78, 88, 102, 125, 247, and 274; Vincent to Rottenburg, Oct. 18, 1813 ("Grand River Indians"), in MPHS, *MHC*, 15:419; Rottenburg to Vincent, Nov. 1, 1813, in *SBD*, 2:331; Klinck and Talman, eds., *Journal of Norton*, 343.

45. Winfield Scott to James Wilkinson, Oct. 11, 1813, in *ASP-MA*, 1:482; Quimby, *U.S. Army*, 1:349–50; George McClure, "Narrative," in McMaster, *Steuben County*, 118–46.

46. George McClure, "To the Men of New York," Dec. 24, 1812 ("blustering"), in [Philadelphia] *Democratic Press*, Jan. 4, 1813.

47. George McClure, address to his brigade, Sept. 10, 1813 ("the rights" and "Without discipline") and Oct. 5, 1813 ("Let us wipe"), and McClure, General Order, Oct. 10, 1813, in *DHCNF*, 7:113, 7:186, and 8:45; McClure, *Causes*, 31–32.

48. George McClure, "To the Soldiers of the Brigade of Detached Militia," Oct. 5, 1813 (all quotations), in *DHCNF*, 7:184–85.

49. George McClure, General Order, Oct. 10, 1813, in *DHCNF,* 8:45–46; McClure, *Causes,* 33–34.

50. William B. Rochester to Nathaniel Rochester, Oct. 15, 1813 ("completely raw" and "flour"), RFP, SC-RRL-UR; John C. Spencer to Daniel D. Tompkins, Oct. 16, 1813 ("wholly defenceless"), in *DHCNF,* 8:64–65; McClure to John Armstrong, Oct. 23, 1813 ("such protection" and "universal"), RG 107, M 221, reel 55, USNA.

51. William B. Rochester to Nathaniel Rochester, Oct. 15 and 19, 1813, RFP, SC-RRL-UR; George McClure, "Proclamation to the Inhabitants of Upper Canada," Oct. 16, 1813, in *DHCNF,* 8:66; McClure, *Causes,* 34.

52. William Henry Harrison to John Armstrong, Oct. 22 and 24, 1813, and Harrison to Robert Brent, Oct. 31, 1813, WHHP, reel 9, IHS; McClure, *Causes,* 13–14 and 37–38; George McClure to Tompkins, n.d. but c. Nov. 10, 1813 ("the conquest"), and McClure, "To the Public," in *DHCNF,* 8:164–65 and 9:49; Quimby, *U.S. Army,* 1:351.

53. William B. Rochester to Nathaniel Rochester, Nov. 1, 8, and 21, 1813, RFP, SC-RRL-UR; William Henry Harrison to John Armstrong, Nov. 8, 1813, in Esarey, ed., *Messages and Letters,* 2:597; Harrison to Isaac Chauncey, Nov. 15, 1813, WHHP, reel 9, IHS; McClure to Harrison, Nov. 15, 1813, in *ASP-MA,* 1:485; Harrison to Armstrong, Nov. 16, 1813, RG 107, M 221, reel 53, USNA; McClure, *Causes,* 13–14 ("commenced") and 45–46.

54. George McClure to Armstrong, Nov. 21 and Dec. 6, 1813, RG 107, M 221, reels 53 and 55, USNA; McClure, General Order, Nov. 30, 1813, in *DHCNF,* 8:244–45; McClure, *Causes,* 47 ("confidence"); William H. Merritt, "Journal," in *SBD,* 3, part 2:603.

55. William B. Rochester to Nathaniel Rochester, Nov. 25, 1813, RFP, SC-RRL-UR; George McClure to John Armstrong, Dec. 10, 1813 ("best and most"), in *ASP-MA,* 1:486; "From the Western Frontier," *Geneva* [N.Y.] *Gazette,* Dec. 29, 1813; McClure, *Causes,* 15–17 and 50n.

56. McClure, *Causes,* 27–29 ("But, says a militia man"); George McClure to John Armstrong, Dec. 25, 1813 ("In spite"), in *ASP-MA,* 1:487.

57. George McClure to Daniel D. Tompkins, Dec. 10, 1813, and John Murray to John Vincent, Dec. 12, 1813, in *DHCNF,* 8:264 and 270; McClure, *Causes,* 17–19; Quimby, *U.S. Army,* 1:355; Hitsman, *Incredible War,* 193.

58. Joseph Willcocks to Armstrong, Nov. 22, 1813 ("excellent officer" and "declare"), RG 107, M 222, reel 9, USNA; George McClure to John Armstrong, Dec. 15, 1813 ("much indebted"), in *DHCNF,* 8:280; McClure, *Causes,* 48.

59. E. D. Wood, Orders, Nov. 4, 1813, RG 98, # 52 (Orderly Book of a Rifle Detachment, 9th Military District), vol. 439, USNA; William H. Merritt, "Journal," in *SBD,* 3, part 2:598 ("whole management"); William Henry Harrison to General Clarke [*sic:* McClure], Nov. 15, 1813 ("make use"), in Esarey, ed., *Messages and Letters,* 2:602–3.

60. George McClure to John Armstrong, Dec. 10, 1813, in *ASP-MA,* 1:486; McClure to Daniel D. Tompkins, Dec. 10, 1813, in *DHCNF,* 8:264; McClure to Armstrong, Dec. 15, 1813, and Dec. 25, 1813, RG 107, M 221, reel 55, USNA; Stray, "Canadian Volunteers Burn Old Niagara," 229–31; Cruikshank, "Study of Disaffection," 48–49.

61. *Ontario Repository,* Dec. 21, 1813, in *DHCNF,* 8:268; William H. Merritt, "Journal," in *SBD,* 3, part 2:605; George McClure to John Armstrong, Dec. 15, 1813 ("our friends"), McClure, "Address to the Inhabitant," and McClure to Daniel D. Tompkins, Dec. 20, 1813, in *DHCNF,* 8:280, 9:8, and 9:26; McClure, *Causes,* 63.

62. John Murray to John Vincent, Dec. 12, 1813 ("delivered") and Sir George Prevost, General Order, Dec. 21, 1813, in *DHCNF,* 8:270 and 9:32.

63. Gordon Drummond to George Prevost, Dec. 18, 1813, in *SBD,* 2:486–87; W. B. Turner, *British Generals,* 115–18.

64. Gordon Drummond to George Prevost, Dec. 20, 1813, in *SBD,* 2:490; [Montreal] *Canadian Courant,* Dec. 28, 1813, in *DHCNF,* 8:16; John Harvey to John Murray, Dec. 17, 1813 ("strictest discipline" and "profoundest silence"), and Lt. Driscoll, "The Capture of Fort Niagara," in *DHCNF,* 9:3 and 18–19.

65. Lt. Driscoll, "The Capture of Fort Niagara" ("trumps," "bayonets," and "grim silence"), in *DHCNF,* 9:18–19; Quimby, *U.S. Army,* 1:357.

66. George Ferguson quoted in Graves, ed., *Field of Glory,* 307 ("supposing"); Robert Lee, affidavit, Jan. 18, 1814, and Lt. Driscoll, "The Capture of Fort Niagara" ("exasperated men"), in *DHCNF,* 9:17 and 19–20; Gordon Drummond to George Prevost, Dec. 18, 1813, and Dec. 20, 1813 ("how irresistible"), in *SBD,* 2:487 and 490–91; Klinck and Talman, eds., *Journal of Norton,* 346.

67. Gordon Drummond to George Prevost, Dec. 18, 1813, and Dec. 20, 1813, in *SBD,* 2:487 and 490–91; Daniel D. Tompkins to John Armstrong, Dec. 24, 1813 ("greatest importance"), in Hastings, ed., *Papers of Tompkins,* 3:407; Stanley, *War of 1812,* 220–21.

68. Heitman, ed., *Historical Register,* 628; Gordon Drummond to George Prevost, Dec. 22, 1813 ("Nothing"), in *SBD,* 2:501; George McClure to John Armstrong, Dec. 25, 1813, and Lewis Cass to Armstrong, Jan. 12, 1814, in *ASP-MA,* 1:487; McClure, *Causes,* 24–26; Court Martial of Richard T. Murphy, Sept. 25, 1812, SoVRP, 3.3, HCH.

69. McClure, *Causes,* 60; Quimby, *U.S. Army,* 1:357. Exchanged by the British in May, 1814, Leonard was never tried by the army. Instead, he was simply dismissed. See George Izard to John Armstrong, May 17, 1814, RG 107, M 221, reel 54, USNA; C. K. Gardner to Samuel D. Harris, June 30, 1814, Harris Papers, BECHS.

70. Charles Askin, diary, Dec. 19, 1813 ("as soon"), in Quaife, ed., *John Askin Papers,* 2:775–76; William P. Bennett to James Wilkinson, Jan. 1, 1814, in *Geneva* [N.Y.] *Gazette,* Jan. 12, 1814; Jonas Harrison to Samuel H. Smith, Dec. 24, 1813 ("some not more"), in Jonas Harrison Letterbook, BECHS.

71. [Montreal] *Canadian Courant,* Dec. 28, 1813, in *DHCNF,* 9:16; Charles Askin, diary, Dec. 19, 1813 ("as soon" and "Indians"), in Quaife, ed., *John Askin Papers,* 2:775–76; William P. Bennett to James Wilkinson, Jan. 1, 1814, in *Geneva* [N.Y.] *Gazette,* Jan. 12, 1814; Gordon Drummond to George Prevost, Dec. 20 and 22, 1813, in *SBD,* 2:492–93 and 504–5; Stanley, *War of 1812,* 221.

72. *Albany Argus,* Dec. 26, 1813, in *DHCNF,* 9:55; Jonas Harrison to Richard Rush, Dec. 31, 1813 ("with their heads"), Jonas Harrison Letterbook, BECHS. For the Federalist response, see Amos Hall to Daniel D. Tompkins, Dec. 26, 1813, and Hall to McClure, Dec. 29, 1813, in Hall, "Militia Service of 1812–1814," 30.

73. Erastus Granger to George McClure, Dec. 11, 1813, in Snyder, ed., *Red and White,* 72–73; McClure, "Address to the Inhabitants," Dec. 18, 1813 ("The enemy"), Timothy Hopkins to Daniel D. Tompkins, Dec. 20, 1813, and McClure to Tompkins, Dec. 20, 1813, in *DHCNF,* 9:8, 24, and 25–26; McClure, *Causes,* 24.

74. George McClure to Daniel D. Tompkins, Dec. 20, 1813 ("greater rascal"), McClure to Erastus Granger, Dec. 25, 1813 ("Shoot him"), and John C. Spencer to Tompkins, Dec. 26, 1813, in *DHCNF,* 9:26, 46, and 52; McClure to John Armstrong, Dec. 25, 1813, in *ASP-MA,* 1:487; McClure, *Causes,* 27–29.

75. John C. Spencer to Daniel D. Tompkins, Dec. 26, 1813 ("incompetent"), George McClure to Erastus Granger, Dec. 28, 1813, and James Wadsworth to Tompkins, Jan. 6, 1814, in *DHCNF*, 9:53, 61, and 97; McClure, *Causes*, 27 ("Each had"), 29–30; McClure quoted in affidavit by Asa Ransom, Mar. 14, 1814 ("they may), in Ketchum, *History of Buffalo*, 2:408.

76. Amos Hall to Daniel D. Tompkins, Dec. 29, 1813, in Hall, "Militia Service of 1812–1814," 34; Hall, General Order, Dec. 29, 1813, and Hall to Tompkins, Jan. 6, 1814 ("irregular troops"), in *DHCNF*, 9:65–66 and 92–93.

77. Amos Hall to Daniel D. Tompkins, Dec. 30, 1813, Phineas Riall to Gordon Drummond, Jan. 1, 1814, and Hall to Tompkins, Jan. 6, 1814, and John G. Camp to the editor of the *Buffalo Gazette*, Jan. 29, 1814, in *DHCNF*, 9:66, 70–71, 93–95, and 156–57; Hodge, "William Hodge Papers," 215-17 ("savage yells," "general stampede," and "flock of sheep"); Brayman, ed., "Pioneer Patriot," 364 ("bursting shells"); D. Riddle, "Destruction of Buffalo, 1813," GP, box 2, BECHS.

78. James Aigin, "Reminiscences," ("Every Man," "As we went out," and "long Black hair"), BECHS; Cyrenius Chapin, "To the Public, No. II," *Buffalo Gazette*, June 21, 1814 ("all was confusion"); Klinck and Talman, eds., *Journal of Norton*, 347; Hodge, "William Hodge Papers," 223.

79. Phineas Riall to Gordon Drummond, Jan. 1, 1814, and "Good and Glorious News," *Kingston Gazette*, Jan. 5, 1814, and Seth Grosvenor to [Daniel D. Tompkins], Apr. 3, 1814, in *DHCNF*, 9:70–71, 77, and 280–81; Gordon Drummond to George Prevost, Dec. 30, 1813, in *SBD*, 2:511–12; Benjamin Hodge, Jr., "An Account" ("a friend"), HP, box 6, HL; Quimby, *U.S. Army*, 1:360.

80. D. Riddle, "Destruction of Buffalo, 1813," GP, box 2, BECHS; Myron Holley et al., to DeWitt Clinton, Jan. 8, 1814 ("mothers"), and Anthony Lamb to Daniel D. Tompkins, Jan. 20, 1814, in Ketchum, *History of Buffalo*, 2:388 and 398; Joseph Ellicott, report, June 1, 1814, in Bingham, ed., *Reports of Joseph Ellicott*, 2:126.

81. John Haddock to Daniel Haddock, Jan. 15, 1815 ("gained"), Misc. Mss., BECHS.

82. James Wadsworth to Daniel D. Tompkins, Jan. 6, 1814, Gordon Drummond to George Prevost, Jan. 9, 1814, and Amos Hall, General Order, Jan. 20, 1814, in *DHCNF*, 9:97, 104–5, and 134; Joseph Ellicott to Simeon De Witt, Dec. 30, 1813 ("Every thing"), HLCP, reel 12, BECHS.

83. George McClure to John Armstrong, Dec. 22, 1813, in *ASP-MA*, 1:487; Amos Hall to Daniel D. Tompkins, Jan. 13, 1814, and Hall, General Order, Feb. 21, 1814, in Hall, "Militia Service of 1812–1814," 40–41; George Hosmer to [Joseph Willcocks], Jan. 15, 1814, in *DHCNF*, 9:118; Benajah Mallory to Joseph Willcocks, Feb. 7, 1814 ("Genl. McClure"), Canadian Volunteers Records, 1813–1815, reel M-7480, LAC; Graves, "The Canadian Volunteers," 115.

84. Peter B. Porter to John Armstrong, Feb. 4, 1814 ("This corps"), RG 107, M 222, reel 13, USNA; Armstrong to Joseph Willcocks, Apr. 19, 1814, RG 107, M 221, reel 62, USNA; Willcocks to Armstrong, Feb. 18, 1814, and July 1, 1814, Canadian Volunteer Records, reel M-7480, LAC.

85. [Canandaigua, N.Y.] *Ontario Repository*, Jan. 4, 1814 ("horrid character"), in *DHCNF*, 9:80; John Armstrong to William Henry Harrison, Dec. 29, 1813 ("These settlements"), and Jan. 1, 1814, in Esarey, ed., *Messages and Letters*, 2:613–14 and 616; Skeen, *John Armstrong*, 173–74; Harrison to Armstrong, Jan. 23, 1814, WHHP, 9:635, IHS.

86. Gould, "Making of an Atlantic State System," 241–65; George Prevost, Proclamation, Jan. 12, 1814 ("this departure" and "full measure"), and Earl Bathurst to Prevost, Mar. 5, 1814, in *DHCNF,* 9:112–14 and 213; Gordon Drummond to Prevost, Jan. 19, 1814, in *SBD,* 2:514.

87. Donald Fraser to John Harvey, Dec. 22, 1813, and James Wilkinson to George Prevost, Jan. 28, 1814, in *DHCNF,* 9:38 and 153; Nathaniel Macon, "Spirit and Manner in Which the War is Waged," July 31, 1813, in *ASP-MA,* 1:339–40; James Monroe to Alexander Cochrane, Sept. 6, 1814, in Manning, ed., *Diplomatic Correspondence,* 1:624–25.

88. John Armstrong to James Wilkinson, Jan. 6, 1814, RG 107, M 222, reel 14, USNA; Wilkinson to George Prevost, Jan. 28, 1814, in *DHCNF,* 9:153; James Monroe to Alexander Cochrane, Sept. 6, 1814, and Monroe to William W. Bibb, Feb. 28, 1815, in Manning, ed., *Diplomatic Correspondence,* 1:624–25 and 628; "Brilliant Exploit," *New-York Evening Post,* Jan. 6, 1814.

89. James Wilkinson to Peter B. Porter, Sept. 18, 1813 ("patriotism" and "enemy's property"), in *DHCNF,* 7:143; George Prevost to Wilkinson, Feb. 10, 1814, MPHS, *MHC,* 25:574–75.

90. "Buffalo Destroyed!" and "Address to Fellow-Citizens of the Western District," *Utica Patriot,* Jan. 4, and Mar. 8, 1814; Daniel D. Tompkins to the State Legislature, Jan. 25, 1813 ("Many of"), and reply from the State Senate, Jan. 25, 1814, Assembly reply to Daniel D. Tompkins, Jan. 25, 1814, in Hastings, ed., *Papers of Tompkins,* 3:428–29, 433, and 433–34; "Genesee County Nomination," *Buffalo Gazette,* Apr. 13, 1814 ("Where was" and "would rebuke"), BECHS.

91. Irwin, *Daniel D. Tompkins,* 178–79; "Utica," *Utica Patriot,* May 10, 1814. In Niagara County the Republican state senate slate of four candidates averaged 378 votes (63 percent), compared to 223 (37 percent) for the four Federalists. In Genesee County the Republicans won an average of 1,247 votes (67 percent), compared to 617 (33 percent) for the Federalists. See Philip Lampi, "America Votes," AAS.

92. Duncan McArthur, General Orders, Sept. 30, 1813, Oct. 3 and Oct. 6, 1813, RG 98, Orderly Book of a Rifle Detachment, 1813–1815, Ninth Military District, USNA; Charles Gratiot, troop strength report, Dec. 1, 1813, Anthony Butler to John Armstrong, Jan. 23, 1814 ("none"), and Feb. 3, 1814, and Alfred Brunson to Armstrong, Jan. 25, 1814, RG 107, M 221, reel 51, USNA; Lewis Cass to John Armstrong, Nov. 28, 1813, in MPHS, *MHC,* 40:543–44; Lewis Bond, Journal, 81, LC; Brunson, *Western Pioneer,* 144–45; Farmer, *History of Detroit,* 283–84.

93. Lewis Cass to John Armstrong, Oct. 21, 1813, and Oct. 28, 1813 ("whole resources"), and Dec. 11, 1813, and Cass, troop strength return, Dec. 1, 1813, in MPHS, *MHC,* 40:537–38, 541–42, 547, and 555; William Henry Harrison, order, Oct. 26, 1813, WHHP, 9:459, IHS; George Croghan to Harrison, May 22, 1814, and May 27, 1814, DMP, 9:1565 and 1594, LC; William A. Gano to William Henry Harrison, Jan. 17, 1814, Jan. 25 and Jan. 27, 1814 ("I would hang"), in *DHCNF,* 9:128–29, 145, and 152.

94. William Henry Harrison to John Armstrong, Oct. 10, 1813, in Esarey, ed., *Messages and Letters,* 2:575; Anthony Butler to Armstrong, Jan. 2 and 23, 1814, and Feb. 3, 1814, RG 107, M 221, reel 51, USNA; Thomas McCrae, diary, Jan. 7, 11, and 12, 1814, in *DHCNF,* 9:109–10; Couture, *War and Society,* 220–22.

95. William Henry Harrison to John Armstrong, Oct. 10, 1813, in Esarey, ed., *Messages and Letters,* 2:575; Lewis Cass to Armstrong, Oct. 21, 1813 ("For the peace"),

and Dec. 17, 1813, in MPHS, *MHC*, 40:538–39 and 553; Thomas McCrae, diary, Dec. 20, 22, and 24, 1813, and Henry Medcalf to Henry Bostwick, Dec. 25, 1813, in *DHCNF*, 9:21 and 44–45; Anthony Butler to John Armstrong, Jan. 23, 1814 ("sufficient severity"), RG 107, M 221, reel 51, USNA.

96. Lewis Bond, Journal, 83, LC; Andrew H. Holmes, "To the People of the New Settlement," Apr. 18, 1814 ("Did you" and "one scene"), *Montreal Gazette*, June 21, 1814; Gordon Drummond to George Prevost, May 27, 1814, in *SBD*, 2, part 1:92; Couture, *War and Society*, 222.

97. Gordon Drummond to George Prevost, Dec. 22, 1813, in *SBD*, 2:502–3; Drummond to Prevost, Jan. 21, 1814, and Prevost to Drummond, Jan. 29, 1814, in *DHCNF*, 9:137–40 and 154.

98. Anthony Butler to John Armstrong, Jan. 23, 1814, and Butler to William Henry Harrison, Apr. 3, 1814, RG 107, M 221, reels 51 and 53, USNA; Lewis Bond, Journal, 84 ("the confusion"), LC; Gordon Drummond to George Prevost, Feb. 3, 1814, Feb. 8, 1814, Feb. 19, 1814, and Mar. 5, 1814, in *DHCNF*, 9:163, 192, and 208; Couture, *War and Society*, 227–28.

99. Anthony Butler to John Armstrong, Feb. 3, 1814, RG 107, M 221, reel 51, USNA; Thomas McCrae diary, Feb.2, and 12–14, 1814, Gordon Drummond to Noah Freer, Feb. 14, 1814, Leslie Patterson to Thomas Talbot, Feb. 26, 1814, Drummond to George Prevost, Mar. 5, 1814, and *National Advocate*, Mar. 31, 1814 ("rather than"), in *DHCNF*, 9:144, 175–76, 179, 206, 210, and 241–42; D. R. Beasley, "Andrew Westbrook," *DCB*, 6:809; F. Landon, *Western Ontario*, 44; Couture, *War and Society*, 224–26.

100. George Prevost to Gordon Drummond, Mar. 19, 1814 ("incendiary system"), RG 5, 19:8136, reel C-4543, LAC; Andrew H. Holmes to Anthony Butler, Mar. 10, 1814 ("shot to pieces"), RG 107, M 221, reel 51, USNA; Alexander Stewart to Phineas Riall, Mar. 5, 1814, in *SBD*, 2:347–50; Quimby, *U.S. Army*, 2:730–33.

101. John Armstrong to James Madison, Apr. 30, 1814, in *DHCNF*, 9:320; George Prevost to Gordon Drummond, Jan. 8, 1814 ("I consider"), and James Madison, notes, June 7, 1814, in Dudley, ed., *Naval War*, 3:379 and 497; William Henry Harrison and Lewis Cass to Armstrong, July 17, 1814, and Duncan McArthur to Armstrong, Aug. 31, 1814 ("nothing can"), RG 107, M 221, reels 62 and 64, USNA.

102. George Croghan to Duncan McArthur, July 13, 1814, DMP, 12:2286, LC; Arthur Sinclair to William Jones, July 22, 1814, in Dudley, ed., *Naval War*, 3:564; Robert McDouall to George Prevost, Aug. 14, 1814, in MPHS, *MHC*, 25:592–93; Quimby, *U.S. Army*, 2:744–48.

103. George Croghan to Duncan McArthur, Aug. 23, 1814, DMP, 14:2684, LC; Quimby, *U.S. Army*, 2:748–50; Gough, *Fighting Sail*, 105–16; Arthur Sinclair to William Jones, Nov. 11, 1814 ("*hearts* and *livers*"), in Dudley, ed., *Naval War*, 3:649.

104. Lewis Cass to John Armstrong, Aug. 13, 1814 ("the catastrophe"), and Aug. 20, 1814, RG 107, M 221, reel 60, USNA; Cass to Duncan McArthur, Sept. 11, 1814, and John Miller to McArthur, Sept. 16, 1814, DMP, 15:2900 and 16:2956, LC; McArthur to James Monroe, Sept. 26, 1814, RG 107, M 222, reel 12, USNA; William Faux quoted in *DRIC*, 31n1 ("dirty"); Andrew Cayton, "Duncan McArthur," *ANB*, 14:814–15.

105. Duncan McArthur to John Armstrong, July 31, 1814, Armstrong to McArthur, Aug. 2, 1814, and Aug. 7, 1814, McArthur to James Monroe, Sept. 10, 1814, William Walker to McArthur, Oct. 3, 1814, and McArthur to Isaac Shelby, Oct. 15, 1814, DMP, 13:2497, 14:2532, 15:2862, 15:2890, 17:3238, and 18:3394, LC; McArthur to Monroe, Nov. 18, 1814, in *DHCNF*, 11:308; Quimby, *U.S. Army*, 2:750–57.

106. Peter L. Chambers to William Smelt, Nov. 9, 1814, Chambers to Louis de Watteville, Nov. 10, 1814, Watteville to John Harvey, Nov. 10, 1814, Duncan McArthur to James Monroe, Nov. 18, 1814, and George Prevost to Earl Bathurst, Nov. 21, 1814, in *DHCNF*, 11:299, 301, 303, 308–12, and 462; Quimby, *U.S. Army*, 2:757–58.

107. Lewis Cass to John Armstrong, Aug. 13, 1814, RG 107, M 221, reel 60, USNA; John Miller to Duncan McArthur, Sept. 2, 1814, Cass to McArthur, Sept. 11, 1814, Miller to McArthur, Sept. 16, 1814, Harris H. Hickman to C. S. Todd, Nov. 24, 1814, McArthur to Thomas Worthington, Dec. 13, 1814, Miller to McArthur, Dec. 31, 1814, and McArthur to Cass, Jan. 22, 1815 ("When I left"), DMP, 15:2805, 15:2904, 15:2956, 19:3787, 20:3901, 21:3998, and 22:4247, LC; John Miller, proclamation, Sept. 26, 1814, in *SBD*, 3, part 1:296–97; Miller, proclamation, Nov. 5, 1814, in *DHCNF*, 11:292–93; William Woodbridge to Juliana Trumbull Woodbridge, Jan. 18, 1815, and Jan. 23, 1815 ("The country"), in Quaife, ed., "From Marietta to Detroit," 151 and 152.

108. Lewis Cass to James Monroe, Sept. 4, 1814 ("It appears" and "a desert"), in Carter, ed., *Territorial Papers*, 10:482–83; C. S. Todd to S. Thrasher, Nov. 25, 1814, and Anthony Butler to Duncan McArthur, Feb. 12, 1815 ("blood letting"), and Feb. 19, 1815, DMP, 20:3791, 23:4451, and 23:4509, LC.

109. Duncan McArthur to James Monroe, Oct. 10, 1814, RG 107, M 221, reel 66, USNA; McArthur to William Woodbridge, Nov. 17, 1814 ("leaving nothing"), in MPHS, *MHC*, 32:564; McArthur to Monroe, Nov. 18, 1814, in *DHCNF*, 11:311; McArthur to Monroe, Feb. 6, 1815 ("Some of these people" and "most dangerous"), in Carter, ed., *Territorial Papers*, 10:503–4; Atherton, *Narrative*, 68–69.

110. For the new British confidence in their support in western Upper Canada, see Robert Nichol to Colley Foster, Oct. 4, 1814, RG 9, I-B-1, box 2, misc. folder, LAC; Reginald James to John Harvey, Nov. 21, 1814, in MPHS, *MHC*, 15:679.

Chapter Ten: Northern Lights

1. Nathan Ford to David Ford, July 5, 1813, FFP, reel MS-7695, AO.

2. Stacey, "American Plan," 348–49; Klinck and Ross, eds., *Tiger Dunlop's Upper Canada*, 24 ("If they had done so"); [Anonymous], "The Last War in Canada," 433; Burt, *United States*, 325–26. For American officers who advised concentrating on the St. Lawrence, see E. P. Gaines to G. W. Campbell, Jan. 31, 1814, David Jones to Armstrong, May 25, 1814, Gaines to John Armstrong, Dec. 30, 1813, and Joseph Totten to George Izard, July 11, 1814, RG 107, M 221, reels 53, 54, 61, and 62, USNA.

3. [Anonymous], "The Last War in Canada," 433 ("private interests"); H. Landon, "British Sympathizers," 131–32; Walters and Walters, "American Career," 149–66; Walters and Walters, "David Parish," 146–51.

4. Hough, *History of St. Lawrence*, 589–93 (593: "a terror"); Curry, ed., "Letter from Ogdensburg," 208; Nathan Ford to David Ford, May 9, 1807 ("wild Irishmen"), FFP, reel MS-7695, AO; Hough, *History of St. Lawrence*, 609; D. Noon to Peter B. Porter, May 20, 1812, in *DHCNF*, 1:64.

5. Nathan Ford to David Ford, May 4, 1808, and May 30, 1810, FFP, reel MS-7695, AO; Joseph Rosseel to David Parish, May 16 and 22, 1812, DP-JRP, box 16, SC-SLU; David A. Ogden to William Short, June 20, 1811 ("would regret"), in Pratt, *Expansionists*, 175.

6. Spafford, *Gazetteer*, 263; Walters and Walters, "David Parish," 156–57; John

Lovett to Joseph Alexander, July 20, 1812 in Bonney, ed., *Legacy*, 1:197; Jacob Brown to Daniel D. Tompkins, June 26, 1812, in Hough, *History of Jefferson County*, 580.

7. H. Landon, "British Sympathizers," 132–33; Hough, *History of St. Lawrence*, 619.

8. Andrew Gray to George Prevost, Jan. 13, 1812, RG 8, 676:83, reel C-3171, LAC; Nathan Ford to David Ford, June 28, 1812, FFP, reel MS-7695, AO; James Reid to John Strachan, July 11, 1812, John Strachan Papers, reel MS-35, AO; border sign quoted in Stagg, *Madison's War*, 234 ("scratch"); David Ford, "To the Editor," *New-York Evening Post*, Jan. 12, 1814.

9. Lemmon, *Frustrated Patriots*, 65–68; Inspection Return, June 30, 1814 ("a brave, intrepid"), quoted in Fredriksen, *Green Coats*, 55n175; Arthur Sinclair to John Hartwell Cocke, July 4, 1813 ("little better"), in Malcomson, ed., *Sailors of 1812*, 45–47.

10. Akenson, *Irish in Ontario*, 66–68; Elizabeth M. Morgan, "Joel Stone," *DCB*, 6:738–39; Joel Stone to Benoni Wiltse, July 13, 1813, RG 9, I-B-1, box 2, LAC; Benjamin Forsyth to William Eustis, Oct. 24, 1812 ("a tory" and "remained since"), RG 107, M 221, reel 44, USNA.

11. Benjamin Forsyth to William Eustis, Oct. 24, 1812, RG 107, M 221, reel 44, USNA; "Kingston," *Kingston Gazette*, Sept. 26, 1812; Joel Stone to Gordon Drummond, Nov. 23, 1814, RG 9, I-B-1, box 3, LAC; Fredriksen, *Green Coats*, 29; Quimby, *U.S. Army*, 1:63–64.

12. Benjamin Forsyth to Henry Dearborn, Feb. 8, 1813, RG 107, M 221, reel 52, USNA; Thomas Pearson to Francis de Rottenburg, Feb. 7, 1813, in *SBD*, 2:134–14; Graves, *Field of Glory*, 117–18; Fredriksen, *Green Coats*, 28; William Thompson to his brother, Feb. 26, 1813 ("idiot"), ms. #17618, NYSL.

13. John Strachan to Solomon Jones, Oct. 6, 1812 ("marauding parties"), Solomon Jones Papers, reel MS-520, AO; Joseph Rosseel to David Parish, Feb. 20, 1813 ("poor farmers' sons"), DP-JRP, box 19, SC-SLU; "Ogdensburgh," *Ogdensburgh Palladium*, Feb. 3, 1813 ("Deserters from Canada"); "War Events at Ogdensburgh," *Buffalo Gazette*, Mar. 2, 1813.

14. John Ross to David Parish, Feb. 20, 1813, and Joseph Rosseel to Parish, Feb. 20, 1813 ("send his Indians," "Nothing," and "that the british commander"), DP-JRP, box 19, SC-SLU.

15. [Anonymous], "Last War in Canada," 435–37; Benjamin Forsyth to Alexander Macomb, Feb. 22, 1813, and George Macdonell to Edward Baynes, Feb. 22, 1813, in *DHCNF*, 5:74; Graves, *Field of Glory*, 118–19; Quimby, *U.S. Army*, 1:215–17.

16. George Macdonell to Edward Baynes, Feb. 22, 1813, in *DHCNF*, 5:74; Joseph Rosseel to David Parish, Feb. 26, 1813, DP-JRP, box 19, SC-SLU; Hough, *History of St. Lawrence*, 630 ("by swarms") and 634; Nathan Ford to David Ford, Feb. 27, 1813 ("Many families"), FFP, reel MS-7695, AO.

17. *New-York Evening Post*, Mar. 2, 1813 ("for the distress"), and Mar. 15, 1813; D. Parish to Stephen Van Rensselaer, Dec. 1, 1813 ("as long as"), VRMP, box 77, NYSL; D. Parish to Rosseel, Mar. 2, 1813 ("have represented"), to Nathan Ford, Mar. 17, 1813, and to John Parish, Mar. 20, 1813, DPL, 4:200, 211, and 240, reel 2, NYHS.

18. John Jacob Astor to Albert Gallatin, Feb. 14, 1813, Gallatin Papers, reel 8, NYHS; Stephen Van Rensselaer to David Parish, Mar. 26, 1813 ("want of funds"), StVRP, Folder 4, NYHS; Parish to Joseph Rosseel, Apr. 7, 1813, and Sept. 16, 1813, DP-JRP, boxes 20 and 22, SC-SLU; Parish to Nathan Ford, Mar. 17, 1813, DPL, 4:212, reel 2, NYHS; Hickey, *War of 1812*, 122 (includes Gallatin quotation: "We have"); Walters and Walters, "American Career," 160–61.

19. David Ford to Nathan Ford, Apr. 20, 1813, and N. Ford to D. Ford, May 16, 1813, FFP, reel MS-7695, AO; David Parish to John Parish, Mar. 20, 1813, and Apr. 9, 1813, and D. Parish to Joseph Rosseel, Apr. 7, 1813, DPL, 4:243, reel 2, NYHS.

20. John Ross to D. Parish, May 13, 1813 ("fiddles"), DP-JRP, box 21, SC-SLU.

21. David Parish to Joseph Rosseel, Apr. 7, 1813, Rosseel to Parish, Apr. 30, 1813, Parish to Rosseel, May 5, 1813, George Macdonell to John Ross, Sept. 4, 1813, DP-JRP, box 22, SC-SLU; Parish to Thomas Pearson, Aug. 10, 1813, RG 8, 14:173, reel C-2610, LAC; Parish to Isaac Todd, Aug. 10, 1813 ("this foolish"), DPL, 4:372, reel 2, NYHS.

22. John Ross, "Postscript," Feb. 27, reprinted from the *Albany Register* in the [Philadelphia] *Democratic Press*, Mar. 10, 1813 ("promised protection"); Joseph Rosseel to David Parish, Mar. 5, 1813 ("We are entirely" and "a System"), and Ross to Parish, Mar. 6, 1813, DP-JRP, box 20, SC-SLU; Nathan Ford to David Ford, Mar. 10, 1813 ("feel safer"), FFP, reel MS-7695, AO.

23. Joseph Rosseel to Louisa Miller Rosseel, Mar. 2, 1813 ("The british officers"), and John Ross to David Parish, Mar. 6, 1813, Mar. 13, 1813 ("quiet as lambs"), Mar. 20 and 27, 1813 ("frequent communications"), DP-JRP, box 20, SC-SLU; Nathan Ford to David Ford, Apr. 2, 1813, FFP, reel MS-7695, AO.

24. Nathan Ford to David Ford, Mar. 5, 1813, Mar. 10, 1813, and Mar. 27, 1813, FFP, reel MS-7695, AO; Ford, "To the People of the County of St. Lawrence," *New-York Evening Post*, Apr. 8, 1813 ("if forbearance"); Thomas Pearson to Edward Baynes, June 30, 1813 ("name"), and [Ford] to Pearson, June 27, 1813, RG 5, 17:7405 and 7408, reel C-4543, LAC.

25. Nathan Ford to David Ford, Mar. 10, 1813, and Apr. 2, 1813 ("Tory hole"), FFP, reel MS-7695, AO; John Ross to David Parish, Apr. 24, 1813, DP-JRP, box 20, SC-SLU; Ford, "A Note to Gen. Dearborn," *New-York Evening Post*, Mar. 22, 1813 ("I care not"); "Latest from the Lakes," [Philadelphia] *Democratic Press*, May 13, 1813 ("treason").

26. Joseph Rosseel to David Parish, Mar. 5, 1813 ("total distruction"), and Mar. 19, 1813, and John Ross to Parish, Mar. 20 and 27, 1813, and Rosseel to Parish, Apr. 24, 1813, DP-JRP, box 20, SC-SLU; Nathan Ford to David Ford, Mar. 5, 1813 ("every passion"), and Mar. 10, 1813, FFP, reel MS-7695, AO.

27. Nathan Ford to David Ford, Mar. 27 and May 20, 1813, FFP, reel Ms-7695, AO; Joseph Rosseel to David Parish, Feb. 26, 1813, John Ross to Parish, Mar. 6, 1813, Parish to Rosseel, Mar. 10, 1813, Ross to Parish, Mar. 20, 1813, and Mar. 27, 1813, and Rosseel to Parish, Apr. 24, 1813, DP-JRP, box 20, SC-SLU; "Ogdensburgh," *New-York Evening Post*, Mar. 15, 1813.

28. For the smuggling, see Nathan Ford to David Ford, Aug. 4, 1813, FFP, reel MS-7695, AO; David Parish to Isaac Todd, Aug. 10, 1813, DPL, 4:372, reel 2, NYHS; John Ross to Parish, Sept. 3 and 24, 1813, and Oct. 9, 1814 ("prudent"), DP-JRP, box 28, SC-SLU; H. Landon, "British Sympathizers," 131–35. For the forwarding of British general orders, see N. Ford to D. Ford, Jan. 7, 1814, FFP, reel MS-7695, AO. For the new press, see William Gilkison to Robert Loring, Apr. 7, 1814, RG 5, 14:8183, reel C-4543, LAC.

29. Thomas B. Benedict to Morgan Lewis, July 21, 1813, RG 107, M 222, reel 7, USNA; Ross to Parish, Oct. 9, 1814 ("great importance" and "curry favour"), DP-JRP, box 28, SC-SLU; John Ross to David Parish, Mar. 27, 1813 ("minutely informed"), DP-JRP, box 20, SC-SLU; Thomas Pearson to George Prevost, Aug. 9, 1813, in *SBD*, 2:430–32.

30. John Ross to David Parish, May 27, 1813, and Joseph Rosseel to Parish, June 17, 1813, DP-JRP, box 21, SC-SLU; Nathan Ford to David Ford, May 28, 1813, FFP, reel MS-7695, AO; "From the *Ogdensburgh Palladium*," *New-York Evening Post*, June 7, 1813; Hough, *History of St. Lawrence*, 635.

31. Peter Sailly to Zebulon Pike, Feb. 10, 1813, Pike to John Armstrong, Feb. 15, 1813 ("commanding officers"), Alexander Richards to Henry Dearborn, Mar. 16, 1813 ("a speedy stop"), and Richards to Pike, Mar. 21, 1813, RG 107, M 221, reel 55, USNA.

32. Zebulon Pike, "Proclamation," [Canandaigua, N.Y.] *Ontario Messenger*, Feb. 9, 1813; Pike to Alexander Richards, Mar. 23, 1813, Pike to Loring Austin, Mar. 25, 1813, Austin to Pike, Apr. 8, 1813, Apr. 9, 1813, and Apr. 10, 1813 ("legal patronage"), Pike Papers, OCHS; Nathan Ford to David Ford, Apr. 16, 1813 ("little funny" and "determined"), FFP, reel MS-7695, AO; Pike to John Armstrong, Apr. 14, 1813, RG 107, M 221, reel 55, USNA; David Parish to Nathan Ford, Apr. 28, 1813, DPL, 4:286, reel 2, NYHS.

33. Nathan Ford to David Ford, May 1, 1813, FFP, reel MS-7695, AO; John Ross to David Parish, Sept. 30, 1813, DP-JRP, box 22, SC-SLU.

34. *Buffalo Gazette*, Aug. 10, 1813, in *DHCNF*, 6:288–89; Joseph Rosseel to David Parish, May 1, 1813, and July 22, 1813, DP-JRP, box 21, SC-SLU; Rosseel to Parish, Nov. 5, 1813, DP-JRP, box 24, SC-SLU; Nathan Ford to David Ford, July 15, 1813, Aug. 4, 1813, and Aug. 13, 1813, FFP, reel MS-7695, AO.

35. [Anonymous], "First Campaign," 441; Jacob Brown to Nathan Williams, Sept. 2, 1813 ("marked" and "no common Man"), JBP, 1:125, OCHS; Mathew Hughes to his parents, Sept. 9, 1813 ("general joy"), in [Anonymous], *Sketch of the Life*, 37; Rufus McIntire to John Holmes, Sept. 11, 1813 ("Gen. Wilkerson"), War of 1812 Coll., box 1, AAS.

36. Skelton, *American Profession*, 51; H. Adams, *Administrations of Jefferson*, 579; Isenberg, *Fallen Founder*, 347–49; Malone, *Jefferson*, 216–18.

37. Paul David Nelson, "James Wilkinson," *ANB*, 23:400–401; Graves, *Field of Glory*, 27.

38. Paul David Nelson, "James Wilkinson," *ANB*, 23:401; Skelton, *American Profession*, 51 (includes Anthony Wayne quotation: "that worst of all bad men").

39. Major John Fuller to Patty Fuller, July 28, 1809, in Skelton, *American Profession*, 51; Ellery, ed., *Memoirs of Swift*, 107; Jacobs, *Tarnished Warrior*, 226–27; Gideon Granger quoted in Malone, *Jefferson*, 222 ("one of the most").

40. Paul David Nelson, "James Wilkinson," *ANB*, 23:401; Skelton, *American Profession*, 80–81; Jacobs, *Tarnished Warrior*, 227 (Edward Hempstead quotation: "petty tyrant"), 245–52, and 264; H. Adams, *Administrations of Jefferson*, 750–51: Isenberg, *Fallen Founder*, 288–90.

41. Paul David Nelson, "James Wilkinson," *ANB*, 23:401; Jacobs, *Tarnished Warrior*, 238–39; Skelton, *American Profession*, 80–81; Isenberg, *Fallen Founder*, 287 and 361–65; Malone, *Jefferson*, 328–29 and 361–67.

42. T. D. Johnson, *Winfield Scott*, 14–17; Jacobs, *Tarnished Warrior*, 252–57.

43. T. D. Johnson, *Winfield Scott*, 13–17 (includes Scott quote: "as disgraceful"); Scott, *Memoirs*, 36–39; Jacobs, *Tarnished Warrior*, 261–62; Graves, *Field of Glory*, 27–28.

44. James Wilkinson to Aaron Greeley, July 26, 1810, Rogers Family Papers, MS-522, AO; Ellery, ed., *Memoirs of Swift*, 96–97 ("many very queer transactions") and 106–7; Jacobs, *Tarnished Warrior*, 263–75; Graves, *Field of Glory*, 27–28.

45. John M. Taylor to John Armstrong, Mar. 22, 1813, RG 45, RN 1812–15, box

599, folder 5, USNA; Isaac Shelby to William Henry Harrison, Apr. 4, 1813, in Esarey, ed., *Messages and Letters*, 2:414–15; *Baltimore Whig*, June 18 and 25, 1813; "Philadelphia," [New York] *Shamrock*, Mar. 27, 1813; William Duane to Thomas Jefferson, Feb. 14, 1813 ("the man"), in Ford, ed., "Letters of William Duane," 360.

46. Jacobs, *Tarnished Warrior*, 280–81; Skeen, *John Armstrong*, 158; Hickey, *War of 1812*, 144.

47. Jacobs, *Tarnished Warrior*, 283–85; Graves, *Field of Glory*, 28–43.

48. Graves, *Field of Glory*, 31–33, 46 (Wilkinson's general order quoted: "He will cherish").

49. Council of War, Aug. 26, 1813, in Wilkinson, *Memoirs*, 3:497; John Armstrong to James Wilkinson, Sept. 18, 1813, in *ASP-MA*, 1:468; Armstrong, Journal, Oct. 4, 1813, in *DHCNF*, 7:197; Graves, *Field of Glory*, 61–65.

50. John Armstrong to James Wilkinson, Mar. 12, 1813 ("If our cards"), quoted in Skeen, *John Armstrong*, 158; Graves, *Field of Glory*, 76.

51. James Tilton to Armstrong, Feb. 18, 1814, RG 107, M 221, reel 57, USNA; [Anonymous], "First Campaign," 91; Ellery, ed., *Memoirs of Swift*, 116; Graves, *Field of Glory*, 78–79, 122–23, 132, and 139; Stagg, *Madison's War*, 345.

52. "Letter from Ogdensburgh," *New-York Evening Post*, Nov. 25, 1813 ("moving Hospital"); James Wilkinson to Wade Hampton, Nov. 6, 1813 ("our artillery"), in *DHCNF*, 8:141; Graves, *Field of Glory*, 61, 82–83, 115–16, 122–23, and 126–30.

53. *National Intelligencer*, Nov. 3, 1813 ("in ten days"); Thomas Jefferson to Thomas Mann Randolph, Nov. 14, 1813 ("rejoicing"), TJP-AMS, LC; Nathan Ford to David Ford, Sept. 2, 1813, Oct. 22, 1813 ("weak"), Nov. 5, 1813 ("pattent"), and Dec. 17, 1813, FFP, reel MS-7695, AO.

54. Quimby, *U.S. Army*, 1:337–38; Graves, *Field of Glory*, 130–34; Nathan Ford, "To General James Wilkinson," Nov. 10, 1813 ("your wish" and "I am now"), *New-York Evening Post*, Dec. 3, 1813; Ellery, ed., *Memoirs of Swift*, 116 ("dignified"), 136; Nathan Ford to David Ford, Nov. 17, 1813, FFP, reel MS-7695, AO.

55. Jacob Brown to Ambrose Spencer, Dec. 17, 1813, Gratz Coll., box 32, HSP; James Wilkinson, General Order, Nov. 4, 1813 ("It will be the pride"), RG 98, #47 (Orderly Book, Second Brigade), USNA; Graves, *Field of Glory*, 124, 142, 151, and 192; John Strachan to the Lord Bishop, Sept. 15, 1816, in Spragge, ed., *Strachan Letterbook*, 89; John Harvey to James Wilkinson, Nov. 14, 1813 ("that system"), and John Walback (for Wilkinson) to John Harvey, Nov. 14, 1813, in RG 107, M 222, reel 9, USNA.

56. William Clay Cumming to his father, Nov. 20, 1813 ("We were marched"), in Fredriksen, ed., "Georgia Officer," 682; [Joseph Hawley Dwight], "Journal of an Ensign," General Coll., box 93, OCHS; Graves, *Field of Glory*, 134, 147–48, 159, 185–98, and 261.

57. Joseph Morrison to Francis de Rottenburg, Nov. 12, 1813, in *SBD*, 2:441–43; Klinck and Ross, eds., *Tiger Dunlop's Upper Canada*, 12–13; Graves, *Field of Glory*, 223–33, 261–63, and 268; Quimby, *U.S. Army*, 1:342–44.

58. Nathan Ford to David Ford, Dec. 17, 1813 ("Never was there"), FFP, reel MS-7695, AO; Jacob Brown to Nathan Williams, Dec. 11, 1813 ("I would prefer"), JBP, 1:126, OCHS.

59. Sylvanus Thayer, "Report of Hampton's Campaign," n.d., RG 107, M 221, reel 57, USNA; Graves, *Field of Glory*, 94–98; Quimby, *U.S. Army*, 1:327.

60. Sylvanus Thayer, "Report of Hampton's Campaign," n.d., RG 107, M 221, reel 57, USNA; Graves, *Field of Glory*, 98–99; Quimby, *U.S. Army*, 1:328–29.

61. Sylvanus Thayer, "Report of Hampton's Campaign," n.d., RG 107, M 221, reel 57, USNA; Graves, *Field of Glory*, 99–105; Quimby, *U.S. Army*, 1:329–30.

62. Sylvanus Thayer, "Report of Hampton's Campaign," n.d. (all quotations), RG 107, M 221, reel 57, USNA; Graves, *Field of Glory*, 105–8.

63. Sylvanus Thayer, "Report of Hampton's Campaign," n.d., RG 107, M 221, reel 57, USNA; Wade Hampton to John Armstrong, Nov. 1 and 12, 1813, RG 107, M 221, reel 53, USNA; James Wilkinson to Armstrong, Nov. 16, 1813, in *DHCNF*, 8:209; Graves, *Field of Glory*, 98–112, 271, 280, and 296; Quimby, *U.S. Army*, 1:323–31 and 345–46.

64. James Wilkinson, General Order, Nov. 13, 1813, and Wilkinson to John Armstrong, Nov. 24, 1813, in *DHCNF*, 8:175 and 230; Graves, *Field of Glory*, 286.

65. Elbert Anderson, Jr., to John Armstrong, Jan. 14, 1814, and James Tilton to Armstrong, Feb. 18, 1814, RG 107, M 221, reels 50 and 57, USNA; James Wilkinson to Armstrong, Jan. 16, 1814, RG 107, M 222, reel 14, USNA; Fredriksen, ed., " 'Poor But Honest Sodger,' " 148 and 160n56; Mann, *Medical Sketches*, 125–26.

66. James Wilkinson to Armstrong, Jan. 16, 1814 ("recover"), and Armstrong to Wilkinson, Jan. 20, 1814, in *DHCNF*, 9:127–28; Wilkinson to Armstrong, Feb. 12, 1814, RG 107, M 221, reel 58, USNA; Fredriksen, ed., "Chronicle of Valor," 270–72 ("This morning").

67. "Extract of a Letter from Ogdensburgh," *New-York Evening Post*, Nov. 25, 1813; Nathan Ford to David Ford, Nov. 13 and 17, 1813 ("Our wounded"), Nov. 27, 1813, and Dec. 17, 1813 ("stringing along"), FFP, reel MS-7695, AO; Joseph Rosseel to David Parish, Nov. 13, 1813, DP-JRP, box 24, SC-SLU.

68. "Query" and "Calumny Exposed," reprinted from the *National Intelligencer* in *Aurora for the Country*, Dec. 24, 1813, and Jan. 4, 1814; George M. Troup, speech to Congress, Jan. 8, 1814 ("hoisted"), *AC*, 13th Congress, 2d Session, 881.

69. "The First Step" and "His Honor Judge Ford," *New-York Evening Post*, Jan. 31, 1814, and Apr. 4, 1814; Nathan Ford to David Ford, Feb. 16, 1814, Jacob Arnold to D. Ford, Feb. 17, 1814, and N. Ford to D. Ford, June 5, 1814, FFP, reel MS-7695, AO; James Curry, affidavit, June 29, 1814, RG 107, M 221, reel 61, USNA.

70. Charles K. Gardner to Henry Atkinson, Jan. 19, 1814 ("an Imposter"), CKGP, box 1, NYSL; Jacob Brown to Ambrose Spencer, Dec. 17, 1813, Gratz Coll., box 32, HSP; Brown to Nathan Williams, Dec. 28, 1813 ("James Wilkinson"), JBP, 1:127, OCHS.

71. George M. Bisby to James P. Preston, Apr. 15, 1814 ("His talent"), Preston Family Papers, Section 4, VHS; Graves, *Field of Glory*, 293–99; Jacobs, *Tarnished Warrior*, 304–6; Quimby, *U.S. Army*, 2:481–84.

72. Wilkinson, *Memoirs*, 3:16–21 and 458; Jacobs, *Tarnished Warrior*, 306–14; Quimby, *U.S. Army*, 2:484.

73. George Izard to John Armstrong, July 31, 1814 ("From the St. Lawrence"), in *DHCNF*, 10:114–15; Joseph Hawkins to James Monroe, Jan. 4, 1815 ("as much impossible"), RG 107, M 221, reel 62, USNA; Thomas G. Ridout to Thomas Ridout, Nov. 20, 1813, and May 15, 1814, in Edgar, ed., *Ten Years*, 255–56 and 281.

74. Thomas G. Ridout to Thomas Ridout, Jan. 19, 1814 ("The country"), in Edgar, ed., *Ten Years*, 269; George Prevost to Earl Bathurst, Aug. 27, 1814 ("In fact"), in *DHCNF*, 10:180; Monthly Return of Rank and File, June 25, 1812, and Mar. 25, 1814, in MG 13, 1516:66 and 1518:39, reel B-1570, LAC.

75. Thomas A. Smith to Abimael Y. Nicoll, Nov. 30, 1813, WHHP, reel 9, IHS; William D. Cheever to James Monroe, Dec. 17, 1814 ("scarcity"), RG 107, M 221,

reel 61, USNA; Elisha Jenkins to James Monroe, Dec. 3, 1814 ("drain our country"), RG 107, M 222, reel 12, USNA.

76. John Chandler to James Monroe, Nov. 21, 1814 ("Our citizens"), RG 107, M 221, reel 60, USNA; Elisha Jenkins to James Monroe, Dec. 3, 1814, RG 107, M 222, reel 12, USNA.

77. Thomas G. Ridout to Thomas Ridout, June 19, 1814 ("contracted with"), in Edgar, ed., *Ten Years*, 282; Klinck and Ross, eds., *Tiger Dunlop's Upper Canada*, 22–23 ("Well, Colonel"). Ridout and Dunlop may describe the same Yankee smuggler.

78. James Wilkinson to John Armstrong, Feb. 19, 1814, and Mar. 13, 1814, RG 107, M 221, reel 58, USNA; George Izard to John Armstrong, June 29, 1814, RG 107, M 221, reel 62, USNA; Fredriksen, *Green Coats*, 52.

79. Moses Mooers quoted in Fredriksen, *Green Coats*, 53n170 ("He was"); George Izard to John Armstrong, June 29, 1814 ("the gallant"), July 3, 1814 ("many Instances"), and July 19, 1814, RG 107, M 221, reel 62, USNA; William H. Merritt, "Journal," in *DHCNF,* 6:174 ("When I heard"). Forsyth remains commemorated by Forsyth Street in downtown Manhattan and Forsyth County in North Carolina. See Fredriksen, *Green Coats*, 53.

Chapter Eleven: Traitors

1. William Graves to John Armstrong, Mar. 24, 1814, RG 107, M 222, reel 11, USNA.

2. Akenson, *Irish in Ontario*, 66–77; Elizabeth M. Morgan, "Joel Stone," *DCB*, 6:738–39.

3. Anonymous to Joel Stone, July 14, 1812, and Joel Dunbar, affidavit, Jan. 18, 1813, MG 23, H-II-1, 2:800 and 849, LAC; Nathaniel Coffin to Joel Stone, Sept. 24, 1814, JSP, box 1, QUA; Thomas Pearson to Colley Foster, Feb. 7, 1814 ("disaffected"), quoted in Akenson, *Irish in Ontario*, 122.

4. Asahel Geralds to Reuben Sherwood, May 18, 1814 ("to speculate"), RG 5, A 1, 20:8370, reel C-4543, LAC; Solomon Jones et al. to Edward McMahon, Sept. 14, 1814, and Ann Catharine Johnston to Gordon Drummond, Nov. 21, 1814, RG 5, A 1, 16:6954 and 6973, reel C-4508, LAC; Joel Stone to Richard Cartwright, Aug. 17, 1814 ("treasonable"), MG 23, H-II-1, 2:916, LAC.

5. Joel Stone to Benoni Wiltse, July 13, 1813 ("vain enough"), RG 9, I-B-1, box 2, Leeds folder, LAC; Stone to Gordon Drummond, Nov. 23, 1814 ("surrounded"), RG 9, I-B-1, box 3, Leeds folder, LAC.

6. William Knot to Joel Stone, July 14, 1812, and Metty Douglas to Robert Lethbridge, Oct. 13, 1812 ("I am a poor"), MG 23, H-II-1, 2:797 and 830, LAC; John Gilbert, Jr., et al. to Gordon Drummond, Jan. 17, 1814 ("Tyranical conduct" and "judging that"), RG 9, I-B-1, box 3, Leeds Folder, LAC; Akenson, *Irish in Ontario*, 97–98, 104–5, 114–15, and 129–30.

7. Benoni Wiltse to Joel Stone, Apr. 13, 1813 ("Certain Calamity"), JSP, reel MS-519 (1), AO; Wiltse to Gordon Drummond, May 26, 1814, and Dec. 24, 1814 ("his impolitick"), RG 9, I-B-1, box 3, Leeds folder, LAC.

8. Militia returns of Joshua Adams, Joseph Benedict, Peter Bresse, William Jones, Duncan Livingston, John Schofield, and Joseph Wiltse, June 4, 1814, JSP, reel MS-519, AO. For land holdings by deserters, see also the returns by Adams, Benedict, Bresse, Schofield, Jones, and Wiltse, June 4 and 24, 1814, RG 9, I-B-1, box 3, Leeds folder, LAC; returns by Duncan Livingston and John Schofield, Dec. 26–27, 1814,

JSP, reel MS-519, AO. For the motives of deserters, see the testimony in court-martial of Isaac Hogeboom, James Brown, and Lyman Maxon, Feb. 3, 1814 ("to see" and "considered"), RG 9, I-B-1, box 2, misc. folder, LAC. John Strachan reported, "In the County of Leeds nearly three hundred Militia deserted to the Enemy." See Strachan to unknown, June 22, 1818, Strachan Papers, reel MS-35 (10), AO.

9. Affidavits by Daniel McNiel, David S. Baldwin, and John McNiel, all Sept. 24, 1814, RG 9, I-B-1, box 3, Leeds folder, LAC; John Landries court-martial, Jan. 10, 1815, and Uriah Kelsey court-martial, Jan. 10, 1815, RG 9, I-B-1, box 4, Leeds folder, LAC. For another deserter who felt misled by his officers, see Robert Lochiel Fraser III, "Joseph Seely," *DCB*, 5:747–49.

10. Joel Stone to Benoni Wiltse, July 13, 1813, RG 9, I-B-1, box 2, Leeds folder, LAC; Wiltse to Stone, July 19, 1813, and Stone to Noah Freer, Sept. 21, 1813, MG 23, H-II-1, 2:866 and 880, LAC; Stone to Gordon Drummond, Jan. 27, 1814 ("the Elderly"), RG 5, A 1, 16:6710, reel C-4508, LAC; Stone to Nathaniel Coffin, Mar. 27, 1814, and Stone to Colley Foster, Dec. 30, 1814, RG 9, I-B-1, box 3, Leeds folder, LAC.

11. Joel Stone to Gordon Drummond, Jan. 27, 1814, RG 5, A 1, 16:6710, reel C-4508, LAC; Benoni Wiltse to Drummond, May 26, 1814 ("such as Remaind"), and Court Martial, Apr. 4, 1814, RG 9, I-B-1, box 3, Leeds folder, LAC. For the strength of Stone's regiment, the Second Leeds, see General Annual Return, Mar. 24, 1814, RG 9, I-B-2, vol. 1, LAC.

12. Joel Stone to Robert Loring, Mar. 13, 1814, JSP, box 1, QUA; Stone testimony, Benoni Wiltse court-martial, Apr. 4, 1814 ("I had got a flea"), and Rachel Wiltse to Gordon Drummond, Dec. 24, 1814 ("their aged"), RG 9, I-B-1, box 3, Leeds folder, LAC.

13. Joel Stone to Nathaniel Coffin, June 7, 1814 ("he so escaped" and "have his life"), and Oct. 27, 1814 ("obstinate man" and "Tantalize"), RG 9, I-B-1, box 3, Leeds folder, LAC.

14. Joel Stone to Nathaniel Coffin, Oct. 27, 1814, RG 9, I-B-1, box 3, Leeds folder, LAC; Isaac Simpson court-martial testimony, Jan. 10, 1815 ("length" and "presumption"), and Colley Foster (for Gordon Drummond), Militia General Order, Feb. 14, 1815 ("directly"), RG 9, I-B-1, box 4, Leeds folder, LAC.

15. Joel Stone to Gordon Drummond, Nov. 23, 1814, RG 9, I-B-1, box 3, Leeds folder, LAC; Nathaniel Coffin to Stone, Nov. 19, 1814, Stone to Drummond, n.d. but c. Apr. 1815, and Stone to Coffin, Apr. 15, 1815 ("Age and Infirm[ities]"), JSP, box 1, QUA; Akenson, *Irish in Ontario*, 132–33.

16. Joel Stone to Nathaniel Coffin, Apr. 15, 1815 ("every exertion"), RG 9, I-B-1, box 4, Leeds folder, LAC; Stone to Coffin, Apr. 15, 1815 ("there is a certain," and "too prevelant"), JSP, box 1, QUA.

17. Erastus Granger to Henry Dearborn, Sept. 14, 1807, TJP-AMS, LC; Cruikshank, "Study of Disaffection," 27–28; Akenson, *Irish in Ontario*, 97–98 and 104–5.

18. Roger H. Sheaffe, proclamation, Nov. 9, 1812, *Buffalo Gazette*, Jan. 5 and 26, 1813, and George Prevost to Roger H. Sheaffe, Mar. 27, 1813, in *DHCNF*, 2:188, 4:336, 5:52, and 5:134–35; Alexander McMillan et al. to Roger H. Sheaffe, n.d. but c. Dec. 1812 ("charge of nursing"), RG 9, I-B-1, box 2, misc. folder, LAC; Couture, *Study*, 48.

19. Thomas Pearson to Aeneas Shaw, Jan. 18, 1813 ("the constant"), RG 9, I-B-1, box 2, misc. folder, LAC; Prevost to Earl Bathurst, May 26, 1813 ("growing discontent"), and [Baptist Irvine], untitled, *Baltimore Whig*, June 5, 1813, in *DHCNF*, 5:243

and 269; Fredriksen, ed., " 'Poor But Honest Sodger,' " 155; M. Smith, *Geographical View*, 93.

20. Simeon Washburn to Richard Cartwright, June 24, 1814 ("The Truth"), RG 9, I-B-1, box 3, Prince Edward County folder, LAC; John Chisholm to Richard Beasley, Jan. 16, 1813, Beasley to Aeneas Shaw, Jan. 24, 1813 ("by his actions" and "skulking"), and Beasely, "Return of the 2nd Regiment of York Militia," Mar. 25, 1813, RG 9, I-B-1, box 2, York folder, LAC.

21. John Conradt, affidavit, June 1, 1815 ("was determined"), RG 5, A 1, 23:9948, reel C-4545, LAC; Cruikshank, ed., "County of Norfolk," 23–24; Pinckney Mabee quoted in Sheppard, *Plunder*, 92 ("take away"); Quaife, ed., "Chronicles," 158.

22. Sheppard, *Plunder*, 79–81; Malcomson, *Capital in Flames*, 251–52. Relying primarily on the testimony of Dr. William Beaumont, Sheppard advances the high figure of 1,700 paroles. Donald Graves discounts that number because Dearborn's staff recorded the names of only 1,193 paroled militiamen from the victories at *both* York and Fort George. See Hitsman, *Incredible War*, 334n37. But the American record keeping regarding paroles and prisoners was notoriously negligent and incomplete. For a British officer's testimony that the inhabitants "voluntarily flocked in" to take paroles, see John Harvey, "Journal," 12–15, reel MS-842, AO.

23. William Dummer Powell to John Vincent, May 1, 1813 ("wretches"), William Chewett et al., memorandum, May 8, 1813 ("great number"), and Powell, "Narrative," in *DHCNF*, 5:174, 199–200, and 204; P. Finan, "Onlooker's View," 93 and 98.

24. John Vincent to Sir George Prevost, May 19, 1813 ("With respect"), in *SBD*, 2:100–101; Cruikshank, "John Beverley Robinson," 195; Lt. Col. De Boucherville to George Prevost, June 13, 1813 ("The disaffection"), in *DHCNF*, 6:70–71.

25. [Baptist Irvine], "Extract of a Letter," May 30, 1813 ("Our friends"), in *Baltimore Whig*, June 10, 1813; Henry Dearborn to John Armstrong, June 3, 1813 ("large majority"), in *DHCNF*, 6:55; James Preston to Armstrong Irvine, May [*sic:* June] 2, 1813, ms. #14120, NYSL.

26. [Canandaigua, N.Y.] *Ontario Messenger*, July 6, 1813; Fredriksen, ed., *Surgeon*, 38; anonymous to the editor, June 22, 1813 ("of every age"), in *DHCNF*, 6:51; [Anonymous], "First Campaign of an A.D.C.," 280; Stagg, *Madison's War*, 336.

27. [Baptist Irvine], "Fort Niagara, June 30," in *Baltimore Whig*, July 6, 1813 ("attached to us").

28. [Baptist Irvine], "Latest from the Army," June 9, 1813 ("Our government"), and "An Eye for Eye—and a Tooth for a Tooth," *Baltimore Whig*, June 18, 1813, and July 1, 1813.

29. Morgan Lewis to John Armstrong, July 5, 1813, RG 107, M 222, reel 8, USNA; Baptist Irvine to John P. Boyd, Sept. 20, 1813, and Boyd to Thomas Melville, Jr., Sept. 21, 1813, RG 94, #127, box 9, folder 2, USNA; William Dickson to Thomas William Moore, Aug. 14, 1813, in Dickson, "Correspondence," 1–4; Green, "John De Cou," 99–102; American officer to editor of the *Albany Argus*, June 23, 1813 ("The dragoons"), in *DHCNF*, 6:71.

30. Francis de Rottenburg, District General Order, July 29, 1813, and William MacEwen to his wife, Aug. 13, 1813 ("The inhabitants"), in *DHCNF*, 6:291 and 7:14; Thomas G. Ridout to Thomas Ridout, Sept. 4, 1813 ("we carry"), and T. G. Ridout to T. Ridout, Sept. 21, 1813 ("To-night"), in Edgar, ed., *Ten Years*, 212 and 227.

31. William H. Merritt, "Journal," in *DHCNF*, 6:211; William Claus to John Johnson, July 11, 1813 ("plunder the settlers"), and Claus, speech, July 25, 1813 ("very hard"), in *DHCNF*, 6:215–16 and 275; Cruikshank, "Blockade of Fort George," 34.

32. Malcomson, *Capital in Flames*, 309–12. For the assistance given to the invaders, see the affidavits by Duncan Cameron, Aug. 16, 1813, William Knott, Aug. 17, 1813, Jacob Anderson, Aug. 18, 1813, James Degeer, Aug. 19, 1813, Luke Stoutenburgh, Aug. 19, 1813, and John Daniel, Aug. 21, 1813, RG 5, A 1, 16:6554, 6563, 6590, 6601, 6603, and 6617, reel C-4508, LAC.

33. William Allan to Edward Baynes, Aug. 3, 1813, and John Strachan, Aug. 14, 1813 ("present crisis"), in *SBD*, 2:195 and 200; John B. Robinson to Francis de Rottenburg, Aug. 30, 1813, RG 5, A 1, 16:6532, reel C4508, LAC; Romney and Wright, "State Trials," 1:385.

34. Affidavits by Allan McNabb, Aug. 7, 1813, George Cutter, Aug. 16, 1813, Edward Sanders, Aug. 16, 1813 ("fought against"), Stillwell Willson, Aug. 17, 1813, Elias Anderson, Aug. 18, 1813 ("that the King"), Jacob Anderson, Aug. 18, 1813, James Lymburner, Aug. 23, 1813 ("keep the Country"), and Henry Mulholland, Aug. 24, 1813, RG 5, A 1, 16:6536, 6537, 6557, 6585, 6561, 6590, 6640, and 6646, reel C-4508, LAC.

35. Affidavits by Edward Sanders, Aug. 16, 1813, Norman Millikin, Aug. 23, 1813 ("always when"), and John Young, Aug. 23, 1813, RG 5, A 1, 16:6537, 6634, and 6638, reel C-4508, LAC. For the political culture of common people in Upper Canada, see Akenson, *Irish in Ontario*, 97–98, 104–5, and 114–17.

36. Affidavits by George Cutter, Aug. 16, 1813, William Lee, Aug. 16, 1813 ("Major Allan"), Edward Sanders, Aug. 16, 1813 ("to pay him"), and Christopher Ventry, July 2, 1814 (Winn quoted: "Tar and Feather"), in RG 5, 16:6537, 6546, 6557, and 6900, reel C-4508, LAC; John Lyon, undated note ("I mean to have"), quoted in Malcomson, *Capital in Flames*, 311–12.

37. Joel Stone, warrant, Aug. 6, 1812 ("not indebted"), MG 23, H-II-1 (McDonald-Stone Family Papers), 2:806, LAC; affidavit by Edward Sanders, Aug. 16, 1813 ("when the Americans"), RG 5, A 1, 16:6537, reel C-4508, LAC.

38. Affidavits by Jacob Anderson, Aug. 18, 1813 ("replied"), William Wells, Aug. 20, 1813, and Stephen Whitney, Aug. 20, 1813, RG 5, A 1, 16:6590, 6609, and 6611, reel C-4508, LAC.

39. Affidavits by George Cutter, Aug. 16, 1813 ("beheaded" and "Success"), William Darius Forrest, Aug. 16, 1813, Philip Haines, Aug. 17, 1813, George Sisler, Aug. 18, 1813, Elias Anderson, Aug. 18, 1813, George Reid, Aug. 18, 1813, George Anderson, Aug. 18, 1813 ("if the Americans"), Jacob Anderson, Aug. 18, 1813, Weston Stevens, Aug. 19, 1813, and Thomas Johnson, Aug. 23, 1813, RG 5, A 1, 16:6537, 6542, 6567, 6575, 6583, 6585, 6587, 6590, 6605, and 6634, reel C-4508, LAC.

40. Thomas Ridout et al. to Francis de Rottenburg, Aug. 16, 1813 ("convictions"), and Sept. 29, 1813, RG 5, A 1, 16:6664 and 6667, reel C-4508, LAC.

41. Affidavits by Samuel Haight, Sept. 1, 1813, William Huff, Sept. 7, 1813, and James McCarty, Sept. 7, 1813, RG 5, A 1, 16:6656, 6658, and 6660, reel C-4508, LAC; John B. Robinson to Colley Foster, June 13, 1815 ("broke"), and Thomas Ridout to Robert R. Loring, June 17, 1814 ("notorious"), RG 5, A 1, 20:8464 and 8477, reel C-4543, LAC; John Beikie, reward notice, Aug. 2, 1814, RG 5, A 1, 20:8733, reel C-4544, LAC; Richard Cartwright to Foster, Aug. 7, 1814, RG 9, I-B-1, box 2, misc. folder, LAC; Riddell, "Ancaster 'Bloody Assize,' " 114.

42. Affidavit by John Riddel, Aug. 31, 1813 ("dangerous"), RG 5, A 1, 16:6654, reel C-4508, LAC; Robert Lochiel Fraser III, "Elijah Bentley," *DCB*, 5:65; Ivison and Rosser, *Baptists*, 101–2 and 124–25.

43. Affidavits by James W. Sharrard, Aug. 23, 1813 ("very conversible"), Elijah Jor-

dan, Aug. 23, 1813, Ephraim Palmer, Aug. 23, 1813 ("declare"), and John Riddel, Aug. 31, 1813, RG 5, A 1, 16:6628, and 6630, reel C-4508, LAC.

44. Affidavits by Robert Graham, Aug. 18, 1813 ("thanked God"), Thomas Kennedy, Aug. 21 1813 ("that the Loyalists"), John Daniel, Aug. 21, 1813, Betsey Osborn, Aug. 21, 1813 ("in great fear"), and Thomas Johnson, Aug. 23, 1813, RG 5, 16:6569, 6615, 6617, 6622, and 6634, reel C-4508, LAC; Fraser, "Bentley," *DCB*, 5:66; Romney and Wright, "State Trials," 386.

45. Gordon Drummond, Militia General Orders, Oct. 10, 1814, RG 9, I-B-1, box 2, misc. folder, LAC; Sheppard, *Plunder*, 95, 280n96; F. Landon, *Western Ontario*, 40.

46. Gordon Drummond to Earl Bathurst, Mar. 20, 1814, MG 11, 355:20, reel B-295, LAC; Thomas Ridout to Thomas G. Ridout, July 10, 1814, in Edgar, ed., *Ten Years*, 289; Gordon Drummond, proclamation, Mar. 14, 1814, in *DHCNF*, 9:235. For the monthly demand in the Niagara and Home Districts, see Sheppard, *Plunder*, 113–14.

47. William H. Robinson to Prevost, Mar. 15, 1814, Edward Couche to Robert R. Loring, July 6, 1814, and Couche to Edward McMahon, Dec. 30, 1814, RG 5, 19:8143, reel C-4543, and 20:8616 and 21:9164, reel C-4544, LAC; William Dummer Powell to George Prevost, June 28, 1813, in *DHCNF*, 6:157–58.

48. Edward Couche to William H. Robinson, Sept. 27, 1813, Robinson to Prevost, Oct. 6, 1813, Couche to Robinson, Feb. 4, 1814, and Peter Turquand to Couche, Jan. 8, 1815 ("a country"), RG 8, 117:138, 117:145, 118:36, and 119:11, reel C-2682, LAC.

49. Robert Nichol to Thomas Talbot, Dec. 18, 1812 ("cursed office"), *DHCNF*, 4:327; Francis de Rottenburg to George Prevost, Sept. 28, 1813 ("whole Commissariat"), in MPHS, *MHC*, 15:395.

50. Francis de Rottenburg, proclamation, Nov. 22, 1813, and House of Assembly, resolution, Feb. 19, 1814 ("arbitrary"), in *DHCNF*, 8:226 and 227; Romney and Wright, "State Trials," 385–86, 397, 401n33, and 401n34.

51. Gordon Drummond, proclamations, Jan. 25, 1814, and Apr. 12, 1814, and Drummond to Earl Bathurst, July 3, 1814, in *DHCNF*, 8:226, 9:292, and 10:24; Drummond to George Prevost, Mar. 14, 1814, in *SBD*, 3, part 1:94.

52. Samuel Sherwood to David Jones, Feb. 10, 1814, Edward Robinson to Robert R. Loring, June 2, 1814 ("unconstitutional" and "discontented"), and Edward Couche to Robert R. Loring, June 7, 1814, RG 5, A 1, 19:8165, 20:8414, and 20:8440, reel C-4543, LAC; Robinson to Loring, May 31, 1815 ("considerably beyond"), RG 5, A 1, 23:9945, Reel C-4555, LAC; Brode, *Robinson*, 19–20.

53. Daniel Jones to Gordon Drummond, Apr. 12, 1814, and Andrew Kennedy to Robert R. Loring, Apr. 22, 1814, RG 5, A 1, 19:8205 and 8230, reel C-4543, LAC; Drummond, militia general order, Apr. 6, 1814, WBP, 2:1042, LAHS.

54. Gordon Drummond to George Prevost, Mar. 14, 1814, *DHCNF*, 9:236–37; John Beikie to Miles Macdonnell, Mar. 19, 1814 ("crammed"), in Firth, ed., *Town of York*, 329–30; James McNabb to Richard Cartwright, Apr. 7, 1814 ("cut Captain"), RG 5, A 1, 19:8186, reel C-4543, LAC; Sheppard, *Plunder*, 119–20.

55. William Graham to Aeneas Shaw, May 18, 1812, RG 9, I-B-1, box 2, York Folder, LAC; Epp, *Mennonites*, 97–102 and 104; Dorland, *Society of Friends*, 104–8 and 310–12; Healey, *From Quaker*, 45–47, 103–4, and 117; Schrauwers, "Politics of Schism," 31 and 42–50.

56. Finan, "Onlooker's View," 79–81; M. Smith, *Geographical View*, 93 ("main road" and "universally"); John Strachan to unknown, June 22, 1818, Strachan Papers, reel MS-35 (10), AO; John Peters to Nathaniel Coffin, Apr. 15, 1814, RG 9, I-B-1, box

3, Northumberland folder, LAC. For the December 1813 visit to Fort George, see McClure, *Causes*, 23.

57. Finan, "Onlooker's View," 79–81; John Strachan to unknown, June 22, 1818, Strachan Papers, reel MS-35 (10), AO; William W. Baldwin to C. B. Wyatt, Apr. 6, 1813, in Murray, ed., "Recovered Letter," 53–54 ("suspicious" and "a fool"). Convicted of assault, the major had to pay a forty-pound fine and the two lieutenants twenty pounds each.

58. P. Finan, "Onlooker's View," 93, 98 ("The majority"), 103; William W. Baldwin to C. B. Wyatt, Apr. 6, 1813, in Murray, ed., "Recovered Letter," 53.

59. Harry Calvert to George Prevost, July 26, 1814 ("to draw"), RG 8, 166:88, reel C-2774, LAC.

60. Elisha Jones, affidavit, Mar. 11, 1814 ("swore" and "with his fist"), RG 5, A 1, 19:7972, reel C-4543, LAC.

61. William Dummer Powell to Gordon Drummond, Sept. 12, 1814 (all quotations), RG 5, A 1, 21:8799, reel C-4544, LAC.

62. Aeneas Shaw to David M. Rogers, Jan. 13, 1814, RG 9, I-B-1, box 3, Northumberland Folder, LAC; John Ferguson to Nathaniel Coffin, Apr. 26, 1814, RG 9, I-B-1, box 3, Lenox Folder, LAC; John Beikie to Thomas Scott, Aug. 1814, and John B. Robinson to Edward McMahon, Sept. 10, 1814, RG 5, A 1, 20:8732 and 21:8791, reel C-4544, LAC; John Montgomery court-martial, Aug. 27, 1814, RG 9, I-B-1, box 3, York Folder, LAC; Richard Cartwright to Colley Foster, Aug. 7, 1814, RG 9, I-B-1, box 2, misc. folder, LAC.

63. John Peters to Nathaniel Coffin, Apr. 15, 1814, and Sept. 1, 1814, and John Burn to William W. Baldwin, n.d., RG 9, I-B-1, box 3, Northumberland folder, and Durham folder, LAC; Robert P. Wilkins to Robert R. Loring, July 2, 1814, RG 5, A 1, 20:8580, reel C-4544, LAC; Samuel Brown to Nathan Williams, Sept. 8, 1814, and W. H. Tisdale to Williams, Sept. 3, 1814, NWP, boxes 1 and 3, OCHS; S. White, *History of the American Troops*, 32.

64. John Peters to George Prevost, May 25, 1813 ("I find"), David M. Rogers to Robert R. Loring, Apr. 27, 1814, and Elias Jones to Loring, May 26, 1814, RG 5, A 1, 17:7325, 19:8243, and 20:8387, reel C-4543, LAC; Ebenezer Washburn and Stephen Conger to Richard Cartwright, Apr. 8, 1814 ("Those actually gon"), RG 9, I-B-1, box 2, misc. folder, LAC; John Peters to Nathaniel Coffin, Apr. 15, 1814, RG 9, I-B-1, box 3, Northumberland folder, LAC; Rogers to Loring, July 2, 1814, RG 5, A 1, 16:6913, reel C-4508, LAC.

65. Cruikshank, "Study of Disaffection," 54–63; George C. Salmon, return of Norfolk County, June 1814, RG 5, A 1, 16:6899, reel C-4508, LAC; Romney and Wright, "State Trials," 388 and 396; Cruikshank, "John Beverley Robinson," 196–97 and 203–4.

66. Gordon Drummond, speech to the legislature, Feb. 15, 1814, and Drummond to Earl Bathurst, May 20, 1814 ("by far"), MG 11, 355:18 and 20, reel B-295, LAC; W. B. Turner, *British Generals*, 117–19; Stanley, *War of 1812*, 301–2.

67. Henry Bostwick to J. B. Glegg, Nov. 14, 1813, *Buffalo Gazette*, Nov. 23, 1813, and Francis de Rottenburg, general order, Nov. 25, 1813 ("extensive"), in Cruikshank, *DHCNF*, 8:181, 225, and 233–34; "Study of Disaffection," 39.

68. John Beverley Robinson to Gordon Drummond, Mar. 25, 1814 ("to overawe"), RG 4-1, box 1, AO; Robinson to Robert Loring, Apr. 4, 1814, RG 5, A 1, 16:6761, reel C-4508, LAC; Cruikshank, "County of Norfolk," 26.

69. Thomas Scott to Gordon Drummond, June 28, 1814, RG 5, A 1, 16:6859, reel

C-4508, LAC; Cruikshank, "John Beverley Robinson," 210–11; Romney and Wright, "State Trials," 390; Riddell, "Ancaster 'Bloody Assize,' " 109–13; Fraser, "Politics at the Head of the Lake," 25.

70. John B. Robinson to Robert R. Loring, June 18, 1814 ("man formerly"), and Thomas Scott to Gordon Drummond, June 28, 1814, RG 5, A 1, 16:6846, and 6859, reel C-4508, LAC; Riddell, "Ancaster 'Bloody Assize,' " 111 and 123; Cruikshank, "Blockade of Fort George," 75.

71. John B. Robinson to Robert R. Loring, June 18, 1814 ("An ignorant"), Thomas Moore to Gordon Drummond, June 28, 1814 ("nothing but Rancor"), and William Dummer Powell to Thomas Scott, July 2, 1814, RG 5, A 1, 16:6846, 6872, and 6902, reel C-4508, LAC; Romney and Wright, "State Trials," 392; Fraser, "Jacob Overholser," *DCB*, 5:642–44.

72. Thomas Scott to Gordon Drummond, July 5, 1814, RG 5, A 1, 16:6932, reel C-4508, LAC; Scott to Drummond, July 8, 1814 ("would strike"), MG 11, 355:112, reel B-295, LAC.

73. John B. Robinson to Robert R. Loring, June 18, 1814 ("No person"), and Thomas Scott to Gordon Drummond, June 28, 1814, RG 5, A 1, 16:6846, and 6859, reel C-4508, LAC.

74. Gordon Drummond to Thomas Scott, July 9, 1814, RG 4–1, box 1, AO; Charles Stuart to Edward McMahon, July 28, 1815, RG 5, A 1, 23:10221, reel C-4545, LAC; Riddell, "Ancaster 'Bloody Assize,' " 114. The other commuted men were Isaac Petit, Garrett Neill, and John Johnston. Neill and Petit also died of the typhus fever.

75. John B. Robinson to Robert R. Loring, June 18, 1814 ("destroy"), RG 5, A 1, 16:6846, reel C-4508, LAC; John Harvey to Hercules Scott, July 6, 1814, MG 24, F 15, LAC; Gordon Drummond to Thomas Scott, July 9, 1814, RG 4–1, box 1, AO; Thomas Scott to Gordon Drummond, July 14, 1814, RG 5, A 1, 16:6942, reel C-4508, LAC; Sheppard, *Plunder*, 168–69; *Buffalo Gazette*, Aug. 30, 1814.

76. Gordon Drummond, proclamation, July 25, 1814, RG 9, I-B-1, box 2, misc. folder, LAC; Drummond to Earl Bathurst, Nov. 20, 1814 ("most Salutary"), MG 11, 355:124, reel B-295, LAC. For stricter enforcement of the militia laws, see William Chewett to Colley Foster, June 3, 1814, RG 9, I-B-1, box 3, York folder, LAC; Chewett to Nathaniel Coffin, Jan. 1, 1815, RG 9, I-B-1, box 4, York folder, LAC; Thomas Dickson to Foster, Mar. 9, 1815, RG 9, I-B-1, box 4, Lincoln folder, LAC; Couture, *Study*, 109; Sheppard, *Plunder*, 91.

77. The decline in even tepid support for the invaders resembled the decay of Loyalism during the American Revolution. See Shy, *A People Numerous and Armed*, 195–224.

Chapter Twelve: Soldiers

1. James Wilkinson, General Order, Aug. 23, 1813, in George Howard, orderly book #191, Early American Orderly Books, 1748–1817, reel 18, NYHS.

2. James Wilkinson, general orders, Aug. 23, 1814 ("preserve"), and Aug. 24, 1813, in Wilkinson, *Memoirs*, 3:499–500 and 501; Edmund P. Gaines to Thomas H. Cushing, Jan. 20, 1813 ("ordinary operation"), in [Philadelphia] *Aurora*, Mar. 16, 1813; Thomas Melville to [Daniel Parker], Mar. 4, 1814 ("total absence" and "learned to forget"), RG 94, #127, box 2, folder 3, USNA; Graves, *Field of Glory*, 174.

3. Fredriksen, ed., "Letters of Captain John Scott," 77; Malcomson, *Very Brilliant Affair*, 103; Graves, *Field of Glory*, 164–66, 170–73, 178, and 319–20.

4. Graves, *Field of Glory*, 163 and 169; Malcomson, *Very Brilliant Affair*, 101–6.

5. Graves, *Field of Glory*, 163, 167, and 231; Graves, *Right and Glory*, 30–34; Malcomson, *Very Brilliant Affair*, 101.

6. Graves, *Field of Glory*, 168 and 203–4.

7. Fredriksen, ed., "Chronicle of Valor," 262–63 ("became" and "some"); [Anonymous], "First Campaign," 76.

8. Anonymous to James Madison, Apr. 14, 1812 ("Well known"), in *PJM-PS*, 4:320; Sylvanus Thayer, "Report of Hampton's Campaign," n.d., RG 107, M 221, reel 57, USNA; Thomas Sidney Jesup to James Taylor, Dec. 28, 1812 ("the crowd of ignorance"), TSJP, 1:118, LC; W. Scott, *Memoirs*, 30–31 and 35–36 ("imbeciles"); Peter B. Porter to John Armstrong, July 27, 1813 ("Our army"), in *DHCNF*, 6:283; "Court Martial," *Buffalo Gazette*, Sept. 15, 1812; Fredriksen, ed., "New Hampshire Volunteer," 161 and 177; Skelton, "High Army Leadership," 255–59 and 263.

9. John C. Spencer to Peter B. Porter, Dec. 26, 1812 ("devote"), PBPP, reel 2, BECHS; William Duane to John Armstrong, July 29, 1812, RG 107, M 221, reel 52, USNA; "Extract of a Letter," [Philadelphia] *Aurora for the Country*, July 10, 1813 ("personal hauteur"); James Burn to Charles J. Ingersoll, July 16, 1813 ("self conceit"), in Fredriksen, ed., "Colonel James Burn," 308.

10. Skelton, *American Profession*, 53–54; Isaac A. Coles to David Campbell, July 4, 1813 ("our little army"), CFP, box 2, SC-PL-DU.

11. C. S. Todd to Isaac Watkins, Nov. 21, 1814, DMP, 19:3738, LC; John Walworth to Jonas Simonds, May 13, 1813, MG 24, F 16 (Simonds fonds), one folder, LAC; "The Army," [Philadelphia] *Democratic Press*, Jan. 9, 1813; Peter B. Porter to Henry Dearborn, Sept. 20, 1813, Misc. Coll., LC; Thomas H. Cushing, general order, Nov. 27, 1812, in MPHS, *MHC*, 31:310; Wilkinson, *Memoirs*, 3:499.

12. Daniel D. Tompkins to John Armstrong, Dec. 24, 1813 ("The officers have passed"), in Hastings, ed., *Papers of Tompkins*, 3:405–6; Jonathan Fisk to Charles K. Gardner, Mar. 17, 1814 ("So great"), CKGP, box 4, NYSL; Roger Jones to Jacob Brown, Dec. 22, 1814 ("One Campaign"), RG 107, M 221, reel 63, USNA; Fredriksen, ed., " 'Poor But Honest Sodger,' " 134; [Baptist Irvine], "Fort Niagara" and "Extract to the Editors," *Baltimore Whig*, Jan. 20, 1813, and Apr. 25, 1813; George Izard to James Monroe, Sept. 28, 1814, in *DHCNF-1814*, 2:234.

13. Charles K. Gardner to Captain Romaine, Apr. 13, 1813 ("you have no idea"), CKGP, box 1, NYSL; O'Reilly, ed., "Hero of Fort Erie," 83, and 88; Thomas Parker to John Armstrong, Apr. 20, 1813 ("Sacred Regard"), RG 107, M 221, reel 55, USNA; Isaac Clark to Armstrong, Apr. 15, 1813, RG 107, M 221, reel 51, USNA; Henry Leavenworth to Henry Dearborn, June 10, 1813 ("reflecting"), C. E. French Coll., MHS; Samuel S. Conner to Henry Dearborn, July 26, 1814 ("Capt. Vischer"), Gratz Coll., box 32, HSP.

14. Fredriksen, ed., "Letters of Captain John Scott," 77–78; James Burn to Charles J. Ingersoll, Aug. 12, 1813, in Fredriksen, ed., "Colonel James Burn," 311; George Izard to James Monroe, July 19, 1814 ("It is wonderful"), and Nov. 17, 1814, RG 107, M 221, reel 62, USNA; John Breck to Henry A. S. Dearborn, Nov. 26, 1814, C. E. French Coll., MHS.

15. Morgan Lewis to John Armstrong, Aug. 3, 1813, RG 107, M 221, reel 54, USNA; Thomas McMahon, court-martial, Dec. 17, 1814 ("struck with a Sword"), and Ensign Page, court-martial, Jan. 6, 1815 ("Damnd. liar"), Orderly Book of a Rifle Detachment, 9th Military District, RG 98, Entry 52, vol. 439, USNA; Henry Atkinson

to Armstrong, June 24, 1814, RG 107, M 221, reel 59, USNA; Skelton, *American Profession*, 55–56.

16. For the captured duelists, see John Vincent to Roger H. Sheaffe, Apr. 15, 1813, John Clark, "Memoir," and *Buffalo Gazette*, Apr. 20, 1813, in *DHCNF*, 5:154, 155, and 157. For the death of Dr. Shumate, see "From Fort George," *Geneva* [N.Y.] *Gazette*, Sept. 15, 1813; [Anonymous], "First Campaign," 333; Joseph Hawley Dwight, "Journal of an Ensign," General Coll., box 93, OCHS.

17. Isaac A. Coles to David Campbell, Jan. 25, 1813, Willoughby Morgan to Campbell, Feb. 4, 1813 ("Fanny"), and Morgan to Campbell, May 15, 1813, CFP, box 2, SC-PL-DU; James C. Bronaugh to Coles, Oct. 25, 1813, Bronaugh, notice, Oct. 25, 1813 ("I declare"), TJP-AMS, LC; James Wilkinson to John Armstrong, Oct. 28, 1813, RG 107, M 222, reel 9, USNA; Coles, *To the Public*, 10–29. For Bronaugh, see also Moser et al., eds., *Papers of Andrew Jackson*, 4:63n3 and 5:219–20n2. For Coles, see *PJM-PS*, 1:49n1; Stagg, *Madison's War*, 334, 335n114.

18. Thomas Sangster et al., to the United States Senate, Dec. 11, 1813 ("natural and honourable"), in Coles, *To the Public*, 39; James C. Bronaugh to Thomas Jefferson, July 5, 1814, TJP-AMS, LC; Daniel Parker, general order, Jan. 25, 1815, TJP-AMS, LC; General Tucker to David Campbell, July 26, 1814 ("I pity"), CFP, box 3, SC-PL-DU; Lewis Burwell Willis to James P. Preston, Aug. 16, 1814, Preston Family Papers, section 9, VHS; Coles, *To the Public*, 47–48.

19. William Eustis to Joseph Anderson, June 6 and 8, 1812, in *ASP-MA*, 1:319; Hezekiah Huntington to James Madison, Aug. 31, 1812, William Plumer to Madison, Sept. 23, 1812, and Henry Dearborn to Madison, Sept. 30, 1812, in *PJM-PS*, 5:228, 351–52, and 365; Dearborn to John Armstrong, Jan. 5, 1813, RG 107, M 221, reel 52, USNA; Stagg, *Madison's War*, 162–63 (J. H. Campbell quoted: "turn out"), 170, and 276. During the summer of 1812, road workers in western New York could earn twelve dollars per month plus room, board, and whiskey. See *Buffalo Gazette*, Aug. 12, 1812.

20. Peter B. Porter, speech, Feb. 18, 1812, *AC*, 12th Congress, 1st Session, 1058–69; Elisha R. Potter, speech, Jan. 21, 1814 ("independent farmer"), *AC*, 13th Congress, 2nd Session, 1100; Pratt, *Expansionists*, 156 and 60 (Henry Clay quoted: "Such is the structure"); James Monroe to John Taylor, June 13, 1812, in S. M. Hamilton, ed., *Writings of Monroe*, 5:207–8.

21. Thomas Acheson to James Madison, Aug. 25, 1812, Henry Dearborn to Madison, Sept. 30, 1812, and Albert Gallatin to Madison, Jan. 7, 1813, in *PJM-PS*, 5:192, 365, and 557; Samuel Huntington to James Monroe, Jan. 14, 1813, RG 107, M 221, reel 53, USNA; Lewis Cass to William Eustis, Nov. 6, 1812, in MPHS, *MHC*, 40:499–500; Kutolowski and Kutolowski, "Commissions and Canvasses," 5–38.

22. James Madison to James Monroe, Sept. 21, 1812, in *PJM-PS*, 5:344; Henry Dearborn to William Eustis, Nov. 8, 1812, RG 107, M 221, reel 43, USNA; James Monroe to George W. Campbell, Dec. 23, 1812, in S. M. Hamilton, ed., *Writings of Monroe*, 5:230–35; Hickey, *War of 1812*, 111; Stagg, "Enlisted Men," 622; Stagg, *Madison's War*, 275–81 and 637n3; Skeen, *Citizen Soldiers*, 21–23.

23. Thomas A. Smith to John Armstrong, Jan. 16, 1814, RG 107, M 221, reel 57, USNA; Arthur Sinclair to John H. Cocke, July 4, 1813, in Malcomson, ed., *Sailors of 1812*, 40; Graves, *Field of Glory*, 20; Skeen, *John Armstrong*, 134.

24. Skeen, *John Armstrong*, 134–35; Hickey, *War of 1812*, 76–77 and 164–65; Stagg, *Madison's War*, 366–68; Stagg, "Enlisted Men," 621–23, 625, 633, and 639–40.

The army paid the cash bounty in three installments, fifty dollars at enlistment, fifty dollars once mustered in a regiment, and twenty-four at discharge from the service.

25. Orsamus C. Merrill to John Armstrong, Feb. 13, 1814, and Melancton Smith to James Monroe, Nov. 14, 1814, RG 107, M 221, reels 55 and 66, USNA; William Duane to Daniel Parker, May 27, 1814 ("if we had only Cash"), and Aug. 31, 1814, DPP, Box 3, HSP; Stagg, *Madison's War,* 155 and 171–74; Lemmon, *Frustrated Patriots,* 51–52; Fredriksen, ed., "New Hampshire Volunteer," 160; Fredriksen, ed., "Chronicle of Valor," 246.

26. Mann, *Medical Sketches,* 272 ("strolling"); Fredriksen, ed., "New Hampshire Volunteer," 177–78; James Wilkinson to John Armstrong, Dec. 24, 1813, RG 107, M 222, reel 9, USNA; Elisha Jenkins to Armstrong, Apr. 23, 1814 ("the injury"), RG 107, M 221, reel 54, USNA.

27. Berlin, *Many Thousands Gone,* 369–75; Nash and Soderlund, *Freedom by Degrees,* 167–93; Newman, *Freedom's Prophet,* 54–127; Foner, *Blacks and the Military,* 3–22. For historians who emphasize the prosperity of white America as undermining a regular army, see Anderson, *People's Army,* 53–58 and 238; Martin and Lender, *Respectable Army,* 90–91. The 1810 census counted 1,200,000 slaves and 180,000 free blacks in total; calculating military-age men as a fifth of those totals yields 240,000 enslaved and 36,000 free black men as potential recruits.

28. Oliver Hazard Perry to Isaac Chauncey, July 27, 1813, and Chauncey to Perry, July 30, 1813, in Dudley, ed., *Naval War,* 2:530; E. McDonell to Thomas Sydney Beckwith, February. 4, 1815, in *SBD,* 3, part 1:512; Foner, *Blacks and the Military,* 22; Bolster, *Black Jacks,* 68–101.

29. Bartlett and Smith, " 'Species of Milito-Nautico-Guerilla Warfare,' " 187–89; Morris, *Cockburn and the British Navy,* 98–99; Foner, *Blacks and the Military,* 23.

30. William Duane to Thomas Jefferson, Aug. 11, 1813, in Ford, ed., "Letters of William Duane," 373–74; Duane to John Armstrong, July 12, 1814, and July 29, 1814, Duane, "Memoir on the Formation of Military Corps of Coloured Men," Aug. 25, 1814, and Nicholas Gray to James Monroe, Oct. 1, 1814, RG 107, M 221, reel 61, USNA; James Mease to Armstrong, Aug. 2 and 8, 1814, RG 107, M 221, reel 64, USNA; RG 107, M 221, Thomas Lefferts to Armstrong, Sept. 6, 1814, RG 107, M 221, reel 63, USNA. Duane is miscast as an early racist in Nash and Soderlund, *Freedom by Degrees,* 136. For the development of racial prejudice by Irish-Americans see Ignatiev, *How the Irish Became White.*

31. John Armstrong to William Duane, July 15, 1814 ("We must"), in Duane, "Selections from the Duane Papers," 63. Citing an Armstrong letter of August 6, 1814, J. C. A. Stagg concludes, "Not until 1814 did the War unequivocally endorse the enlistment of blacks." See Stagg, "Enlisted Men," 628. But this overstates by implying that the government's support for black troops ever became "unequivocal," for Armstrong could not commit the administration and was on his way out, effectively ousted on August 27. The spotty subsequent enlistments of blacks were at the local initiative of a few recruiting officers. For Armstrong's downfall, see Skeen, *John Armstrong,* 137–43, 161, and 198–204.

32. [Baptist Irvine], "Extract to the Editors," *Baltimore Whig,* Apr. 25, 1813; Stagg, "Enlisted Men," 621.

33. Samuel Nye to Daniel Parker, Sept. 2, 1812, DPP, box 2, HSP; Morgan Lewis to John Armstrong, Feb. 8, 1813 ("the troops"), and C. Van De Venter to John Armstrong, Mar. 15, 1813, RG 107, M 221, reels 54 and 58, USNA; Robert Purdy, statement, c. Nov. 4, 1813 ("had not been"), in *DHCNF,* 8:129–33.

34. Darnell, *Journal*, 40; William Henry Harrison, Aug. 30, 1813, and Sept. 25, 1813, DMP, 3:562, and 4:588, LC; Alexander Macomb, general order, Mar. 11, 1813, and Zebulon Pike, general order, Apr. 8, 1813, RG 98, Entry 42, 340:80 and 110, USNA; Jacob Brown, general order, Sept. 8, 1813 ("transgressed"), and James Wilkinson, general order, Nov. 4, 1813 ("The General"), RG 98, Entry 47, USNA.

35. Richard Bishop, diary, Nov. 2, 9, 11, and 19, 1813, RBP, box 1, NYSL; Fredriksen, ed., "Chronicle of Valor," 268 ("We sat"); Hanks, "Memoir," in Graves, ed., *Soldiers of 1814*, 27; Fredriksen, ed., "New Hampshire Volunteer," 171 ("wet to the skin").

36. Richard Bishop, diary, Nov. 19, 1813 ("very desolate"), and Nov. 26, 1813 ("The officers"), and R. Bishop to Abigail Bishop, Oct. 1, 1813 ("from this world"), R. Bishop to Azel Hatch and A. Bishop, Feb. 11, 1814, and Rufus Green to A. Bishop, Nov. 9, 1814 ("his Brest"), RBP, box 1, NYSL.

37. F. Hall, *Travels*, 105–6; Crombie, ed., "Papers of McFarland," 112; Elbert Anderson, Jr., to John Armstrong, Apr. 21, and 26, 1813, RG 107, M 221, reel 50, USNA; Malcomson, *Lords*, 10 and 18–19.

38. John Chandler to Ebenezer T. Warren, Apr. 14, 1813 ("Here I am"), Vaughan Family Papers, 6:5, MeHS; [Anonymous], "First Campaign," 88 ("full of soldiers"); James McDonald to Duncan McArthur, Nov. 28, 1813 ("damdest hole"), DMP, 4:622, LC; Crombie, ed., "Papers of McFarland," 114–15; Fredriksen, ed., "Observations," 322.

39. Arthur Sinclair to John H. Cocke, July 4, 1813 ("Figure"), in Malcomson, ed., *Sailors of 1812*, 45; Crombie, ed., "Papers of McFarland," 112 ("drunk as usual"); Isaac Chauncey to William Jones, May 2, 1814, in Dudley, ed., *Naval War*, 3:458; Skeen, *John Armstrong*, 156.

40. Malcomson, *Lords*, 57, 72, 91, and 251–52; James Tilton to John Armstrong, Feb. 18, 1814 ("excrementitious matters"), RG 107, M 221, reel 57, USNA; William M. Ross, report, Sept. 18, 1813 ("enveloped" and "proximity"), in Wilkinson, *Memoirs*, 3:514 and 516; Morgan Lewis to Gertrude Livingston Lewis, Aug. 9, 1813, in *DHCNF*, 6:328–29.

41. Morgan Lewis to John Armstrong, July 20, 1813, and Aug. 15, 1813, RG 107, M 221, reel 54, USNA; Wilkinson, *Memoirs*, 3:347 and 505; Isaac Chauncey to William Jones, July 21, 1813, and Dec. 19, 1813, in Dudley, ed., *Naval War*, 2:524; James Tilton to John Armstrong, Feb. 18, 1814, RG 107, M 221, reel 57, USNA; Crombie, ed., "Papers of McFarland," 114–15; *Ontario Repository*, July 26, 1814 ("interrupted") and Leonard Covington quoted ("We bury"), in Graves, *Field of Glory*, 48.

42. James Tilton to John Armstrong, Feb. 18, 1814 ("Dead horses"), RG 107, M 221, reel 57, USNA; William M. Ross, report, Sept. 1813 ("promiscuously buried"), and Ross to Edmund P. Gaines, June 15, 1814, in Wilkinson, *Memoirs*, 3:514.

43. John Harvey, "Journal of a Staff Officer," 34, reel MS-842, AO.

44. *Buffalo Gazette*, Mar. 16, 1813, in *DHCNF*, 5:115; Jacob Porter Norton to his father, Oct. 6, 1814, in Porter, ed., "Jacob Porter Norton," 52; Fredriksen, ed., "Chronicle of Valor," 250.

45. [Anonymous], "First Campaign," 162 ("interesting rivalry"); Fredriksen, ed., *Surgeon of the Lakes*, 19 ("expressive"); Horton, ed., "Original Narrative," 26.

46. John Lovett to Abraham Van Vechten, Aug. 25, 1812, Gratz Coll., box 34, HSP; Lovett to Joseph Alexander, Oct. 6, 1812, SoVRP, 3:18, HCH; *Buffalo Gazette*, Mar. 9, 1813, and *New York Statesman*, Mar. 29, 1813, in *DHCNF*, 5:101 and 133–34; [Anonymous], "First Campaign," 438; Fredriksen, ed., "Chronicle of Valor," 258–59.

47. John B. Glegg to Winfield Scott, May 16, 1813 ("for the success"), and Scott to

Glegg, May 18, 1813, CKGP, box 4, NYSL; John Walworth to Jonas Simonds, May 19, 1813, MG 24, F 16 (Simonds fonds), LAC; [Anonymous], "First Campaign," 438. For rival claims after the attack on Oswego, see George Prevost, general order, May 12, 1814, and Jacob Brown, General Order, May 12, 1814, in *DHCNF,* 9:345 and 346.

48. James Wilkinson to John Armstrong, Sept. 16, 1813 ("In the course"), in *DHCNF,* 7:134.

49. Isaac Chauncey to William Jones, Mar. 8, 1813, MG 24 F 13 (Chauncey fonds), folder 1, LAC; [Anonymous], "First Campaign," 261, 437 ("believed"), and 443 ("cock and bull" and "without injury"); Henry Dearborn to John Armstrong, Mar. 25, 1813, William Quin, deposition, Sept. 4, 1813, and John B. Glegg, memorandum book, Sept. 2–Oct. 4, 1813, in *DHCNF,* 5:133, 7:97–98, and 7:191; Cruikshank, "Blockade of Fort George," 52. For the American policy on enlisting deserters, see John Mason to Robert Young, Nov. 21, 1814, and Mason to W. C. Hobbs, Dec. 31, 1814, RG 45, RV 464, box 609, folders 3 and 4, USNA.

50. William Quin, deposition, Sept. 4, 1813, and Francis Brown, deposition, Sept. 4, 1813, in *DHCNF,* 7: 97–98; Benjamin Hodge, Jr., "An Account," HP, Box 6, HL; Stephen Barber, statement, c. Nov. 12, 1813, in *DHCNF,* 8:159.

51. J. T. Tachereau, general order, June 8, 1813 ("more to be gained"), in *SBD,* 3, part 2:697; Cruikshank, "Blockade of Fort George," 47–52; Isaac Chauncey to William Jones, Mar. 26, 1814, in Dudley, ed., *Naval War,* 3:410; Edward Baynes to George Prevost, June 18, 1814 ("The ideal"), MG 11, 355:404, reel B-295, LAC; James Yeo to John Wilson Croker, July 16, 1813, in *DHCNF,* 6:245; Richard Dennis to John Armstrong, Dec. 6, 1813, RG 107, M 221, reel 52, USNA; Alexander Macomb to James Monroe, Sept. 26, 1814 ("Our pickets"), RG 107, M 221, reel 65, USNA; William Peacock to Joseph Ellicott, July 2, 1813, HLCP, reel 8, BECHS; Whitfield, *Tommy Atkins,* 59–61.

52. Cruikshank, "Blockade of Fort George," 62 ("Pass deserters"); Thomas G. Ridout to George Ridout, Sept. 16, 1813, in Edgar, ed., *Ten Years,* 226.

53. Lieutenant Glassell to David Campbell, Mar. 2, 1814, CFP, box 3, SC-PL-DU; Robert Young to Phineas Riall, Mar. 14 and 17, 1814 ("disgraced by associating"), Riall to Drummond, Mar. 15 and 17, 1814, and Drummond to George Prevost, Apr. 13, 1814, in *DHCNF,* 9:237, 238, 239–40, 240–41, and 294; Graves, *Field of Glory,* 311–12.

54. Edmund P. Gaines to John Armstrong, Apr. 13, 1814 ("waste away"), RG 107, M 221, reel 53; Alexander Macomb to James Monroe, Sept. 26, 1814 ("run the risk"), RG 107, M 221, reel 65, USNA; "Deserters," and "Extract of a letter to the Editors, dated Albany 4th October," [New York] *Shamrock,* Oct. 1, 1814, and Oct. 8, 1814 ("streets of Albany"). Prevost reported only 200 deserters, but Plattsburgh's American commander, Alexander Macomb, reported receiving 300, a more plausible number. The *Shamrock* put the number at 600.

55. James McDonald to Nancy McArthur, Jan. 15, 1814, DMP, 4:692, LC; Thomas A. Smith to James Wilkinson, Jan. 9, 1814 ("The inquisitive"), in Fredriksen, *Green Coats,* 47; Alexander Macomb to James Monroe, Feb. 9, 1815, RG 107, M 221, reel 64, USNA.

56. Henry Dearborn, division order, May 12, 1813, RG 107, M 222, reel 8, USNA; John Michael O'Connor, general order, July 1, 1813 ("foot patrole"), O'Connor Papers, box 2, NYHS; James Wilkinson, general order, Aug. 26, 1813, RG 98, Entry 47, USNA; Wilkinson to John Armstrong, Jan. 30, 1814, RG 107, M 221, reel

58, USNA; Thomas A. Smith, order, Feb. 1, 1814, RG 98, Entry 52, vol. 439, USNA; John Miller, order, Mar. 23, 1814, James Preston/James Paxton order book, PFP, 13D:141, LC; Solomon Beardsley to Jay Hathaway, Oct. 18, 1812 ("poor fellow"), Joshua Hathaway Papers, box 1, folder 2, NYSL.

57. Richard Bishop, diary, Nov. 11, 1813 ("without trouble"), RBP, box 1, NYSL; Jacob Brown, court-martial, Sept. 22, 1813, Second Brigade Orderly Book, Sackets Harbor, RG 98, Entry 47, USNA.

58. John M. O'Connor, order, July 1, 1813, CKGP, box 4, NYSL; Morgan Lewis to John Armstrong, July 5, 1813 ("Taverners"), RG 107, M 222, reel 8, USNA; Edmund P. Gaines to Jacob Brown, July 14, 1814 (*much relieved*), in Edmund Kirby, orderly book, GP, box 2, BECHS.

59. D. Porter, ed., "Jacob Porter Norton," 53 ("rogues") and 56; Orderly Book of a Rifle Detachment, Ninth Military District, Dec. 20, 1814, Dec. 23, 1814, and Feb. 6, 1815, RG 98, vol. 439, USNA.

60. Robert Elliott to David Jones, June 6, 1814, RG 107, M 221, reel 63, USNA; Fredriksen, ed., "Chronicle of Valor," 280–81 ("were free citizens" and "villain's house"); George McFeeley and Joseph Wallace, "Cantonment, Burlington," and George Robinson to Samuel Mills, May 28, 1814, [Burlington] *Northern Sentinel*, May 27, 1814, and June 3, 1814.

61. Eli Parsons and Samuel B. Beach, "Resolutions," Apr. 18, 1814 ("not the duty"), *Utica Patriot*, June 21, 1814; George Mitchell to Jacob Brown, May 8, 1814, in Dudley, ed., *Naval War*, 3:475.

62. Morgan Lewis to John Armstrong, July 5, 1813 ("Arsenick"), RG 107, M 222, reel 8, USNA; Jonathan Conner to Charles K. Gardner, June 7, 1813 ("incendiaries"), War of 1812 Coll., box 1, folder 1, AAS; "Latest from the Lakes," [Philadelphia] *Democratic Press*, May 13, 1813.

63. George Prevost to Earl Bathurst, July 3, 1813, in *DHCNF*, 6:176; Isaac Chauncey to William Jones, July 3, 1813, MG 24 F 13 (Chauncey fonds), folder 1, LAC; Morgan Lewis to John Armstrong, July 5, 1813, RG 107, M 222, reel 8, USNA; Rufus McIntire to John Holmes, War of 1812 Coll., box 1, folder 2, AAS; James Richardson, "Memoirs," in Malcomson, ed., *Sailors of 1812*, 35–36 and 41–43.

64. John Harvey, "Journal," 4, reel MS-842, AO; Caleb Nichols to John Armstrong, June 16, 1814, RG 107, M 221, reel 65, USNA; Armstrong to Jacob Brown, Aug. 16, 1814, in Edmund Kirby, orderly book, GP, box 2, BECHS; Thomas G. Ridout to Thomas Ridout, Feb. 9, 1814, in Edgar, ed., *Ten Years*, 274; George Izard to John Armstrong, May 24, 1814 ("The people"), RG 107, M 221, reel 62, USNA; Preston, ed., "Journals of General Robinson," 353 ("long established opinion"); Amos Hall, general order, Jan. 21, 1814, in *DHCNF*, 9:136; John Harvey to Edward Baynes, July 23, 1813 (*disposable*), and Peter Hogeboom to Francis de Rottenburg, July 23, 1813, in Dudley, ed., *Naval War*, 2:521 and 523.

65. Roger H. Sheaffe to Edward B. Brenton, Aug. 19, 1813, Thomas Brisbane, certificate, Apr. 6, 1815, Thomas Woodward and Peter B. Bidle, certificate, Mar. 19, 1816, and Earl of Bathurst to Gordon Drummond, June 19, 1816, in *SBD*, 3, part 2:855–59; "Burlington, August 20," *New-York Evening Post*, Aug. 25, 1813; *Plattsburgh Republican*, Oct. 29, 1814.

66. Thomas B. Benedict to Morgan Lewis, July 21, 1813 ("One thing"), RG 107, M 222, reel 7, USNA; Alexander Macomb to James Monroe, Jan. 6, 1815, RG 107, M 221, reel 64, USNA; Gordon Drummond to George Prevost, July 11, 1814 ("It is natural"), in *SBD*, 3, part 1: 125; Edmund P. Gaines to John Armstrong, Apr. 14, 1814,

and April 22, 1814, RG 107, M 221, reel 53; William M. Crane to Isaac Chauncey, Jan. 6, 1814, and Jacob Brown to John Armstrong, May 1, 1814, RG 107, M221, reel 51, USNA; Brown to Nathan Williams, May 13, 1814, JBP, 1:140, OCHS; Graves, *Field of Glory*, 126; J. K. Johnson, "William Johnston," *DCB*, 9:414–15.

67. Senter, *Vindication*, 44; Marshall quoted in Isenberg, *Fallen Founder*, 336 ("Treason"); William Jones to Edmund P. Kennedy, July 13, 1814, in Dudley, ed., *Naval War*, 3:545; Hitsman, "Spying at Sackets Harbor, 1813," 121–22.

68. Senter, *Vindication*, 41 ("How can you" and "As for being").

69. Senter, *Vindication*, 41 and 60; Elijah Clark, court-martial, Aug. 5–8, 1812, in Amos Hall, Letterbook, GP, Box 1, BECHS; *Buffalo Gazette*, July 28, 1812, Amos Hall, general order, Dec. 2, 1812, and *Buffalo Gazette*, Dec. 8, 1812, in *DHCNF*, 1:151, 4:266, and 4:293; William Eustis to Amos Hall, Oct. 20, 1812, RG 107, M 6, reel 6, USNA.

70. Alexander Macomb to John Armstrong, June 10, 1813, RG 107, M 221, reel 55, USNA; Morgan Lewis to Armstrong, July 5, 1813 ("Spies"), RG 107, M 222, reel 8, USNA; James Wilkinson to Armstrong, Jan. 30, 1814 ("ingress & egress"), RG 107, M 221, reel 58, USNA; Crombie, ed., "Papers of Major Daniel McFarland," 115. For coverage of the Clark case, see *New-York Evening Post*, Jan. 2, 1813; [Philadelphia] *Poulson's Daily Advertiser*, Jan. 4 and 5, 1813; [Boston] *Repertory*, Jan. 8, 1813; [Providence] *Rhode Island American*, Jan. 8, 1813; *Baltimore Patriot*, Jan. 11, 1813; [New Haven] *Connecticut Journal*, Jan. 11, 1813; [Washington, D.C.] *Federal Republican*, Jan. 18, 1813.

71. Isaac Chauncey to William Jones, July 4, 1813 ("It would be very"), and John Armstrong to Joseph Anderson, July 26, 1813 ("on the ground"), in *ASP-MA*, 1:384; Thomas B. Benedict to Morgan Lewis, July 10, 1813, RG 107, M 222, reel 7, USNA; Jones to Chauncey, July 14, 1813, in Dudley, ed., *Naval War*, 2:501 and 521n1; Hitsman, "Spying at Sackets Harbor," 120–22. For Stacey's home, see Joseph Totten to George Izard, July 11, 1814, RG 107, M 221, reel 62, USNA.

72. Speeches by Robert Wright, Daniel Webster, George M. Troup, Alexander Hanson, and Thomas P. Grosvenor, Jan. 8, 1814 ("subject every man"), *AC*, 13th Congress, 2nd Session, 881–87; Hickey, *War of 1812*, 165; Hitsman, "Spying at Sackets Harbor," 122; D. Henderson, *Congress*, 112.

73. William Baker, court-martial, Mar. 25, 1814 ("found lurking"), Gratz Coll., box 35, USNA; "A Spy Detected," *Plattsburgh Republican*, Mar. 26, 1814 ("At length"); "Plattsburgh, March 28," [Exeter, N.H.] *Constitutionalist*, Apr. 5, 1814. For the failure of the federal courts to convict accused traitors during the war, see D. Henderson, *Congress*, 111–13.

74. James Monroe to William Duane, Dec. 2, 1813, RG 45, RN 1812–1815, box 599, folders 3 and 6, and box 601, folders 1 and 2, USNA; D. Henderson, *Congress*, 99–103; Hickey, *War of 1812*, 175–76. "Alien-Law," [New York] *Shamrock*, July 4, 1812; James Wilson and Daniel McMillan to James Madison, Aug. 28, 1812 in *PJM-PS*, 5:214–16; Thomas Burke quoted in D. Wilson, *United Irishmen*, 87 ("That there may be"); Robert Fulton to John Mason, Dec. 16, 1813 ("I believe") RG 45, RN 1812–1815, box 601, folder 2, USNA.

75. Rorabaugh, *Alcoholic Republic*, 5–21; [Baptist Irvine], "A Voice in the Wilderness," *Baltimore Whig*, Feb. 5, 1813 ("To assure"); Mann, *Medical Sketches*, 36–37 and 124.

76. Alexander Smyth to George McFeely, June 29, 1812 ("would prevent"), quoted in Stagg, *Madison's War*, 170; William Linnard to William Eustis, Dec. 7, 1811, RG

107, M 221, reel 46, USNA; [Anonymous], "First Campaign," 27 ("staff of life"); Alexander Smyth to James Thomas, Nov. 30, 1812, in *ASP-MA*, 1:502.

77. Winfield Scott, general order, July 3, 1813, in George Howard, orderly book #191, Early American Orderly Books, reel 18, NYHS; Cromwell Pearce, general order, Feb. 16, 1815, PFP, 8D:141, USNA; [Anonymous], *Capitulation*, 63; Stephen Van Rensselaer, general order, Aug. 19, 1812, SoVRP, 3rd ser., HCH; Malcomson, *Very Brilliant Affair*, 82.

78. Amos Hall, order, n.d. but 1814, in A. Hall, "Militia Service," 55–56; George Izard, order, Mar. 17, 1814, James Preston/James Paxton Order Book, PFP, 8D:141, LC.

79. Brunson, *Western Pioneer*, 144; James Winchester, general orders, Oct. 9 and 28, 1812, in MPHS, *MHC*, 31:264–65 and 282; Arthur Sinclair to Duncan McArthur, Nov. 11, 1814, DMP, 19:3646, USNA; Fredriksen, ed., "Chronicle of Valor," 245; Richard Bishop, diary, Nov. 1, 1813 ("the men"), Nov. 25, 1813, and Dec. 6, 1813, RBP, box 1, NYSL; [Baptist Irvine], "A Voice in the Wilderness," *Baltimore Whig*, Feb. 5, 1813; Cooper, ed., *Ned Myers*, 51 ("I am ashamed") and 54–55. Myers misidentified the general's corpse as that of the British commander, Isaac Brock.

80. Moses Porter, Detachment Orders, Mar. 11, 1813, RG 107, M 221, reel 50, USNA; Lord, ed., "War of 1812," 209; Thomas Sidney Jesup, order, Aug. 2, 1813 ("Soldiers"), TSJP, 1:175, LC; Reuben King, orderly book, Dec. 21, 1812 ("His death"), NYSL. For Fort Schlosser, see Henry Dearborn to John Armstrong, July 6, 1813, RG 107, M 221, reel 52, USNA; Cruikshank, "Blockade of Fort George," 35.

81. Samuel Wells to Eustis, Dec. 21, 1812 ("Brave men"), RG 107, M 221, reel 58, USNA; Atherton, *Narrative*, 14–15; Darnell, *Journal*, 36–40; Lewis to John Armstrong, May 13, 1813, and July 13, 1813, RG 107, M 221, reel 54, USNA; James Tilton to Armstrong, Feb. 18, 1814, RG 107, M 221, reel 57, USNA; Jacob Brown to Monroe, Nov. 29, 1814 ("by which time" and "wretched policy"), RG 107, M 221, reel 59, USNA.

82. Frederick de Gaugreben to Col. Rowley, Nov. 10, 1815, in Holmden, ed., "Gaugreben's Memoir," 61; Jesse Moore et al. to Simon Snyder, Sept. 3, 1812, RG 107, M 221, reel 48, USNA; Thomas Worthington to John Armstrong, Aug. 11, 1814, RG 107, M 221, reel 67, USNA; Graves, *Field of Glory*, 11; Roger H. Sheaffe to John B. Glegg, Dec. 9, 1812 ("The cold weather"), RG 8, 688B:172, reel C-3231, LAC; Thomas G. Ridout to Betsey Ridout, Jan. 5, 1813 ("Our Canadian winter"), in Edgar, ed., *Ten Years*, 166–67.

83. Peter B. Porter to James Monroe, Jan. 26, 1813, RG 107, M 221, reel 55, USNA; Frederick de Gaugreben, to Col. Rowley, Nov. 10, 1815, in Holmden, ed., "Gaugreben's Memoir," 61; H. Adams, *Administrations of Jefferson*, 6–7, 14; Lincoln, "Journal of a Treaty," 120–22; Coventry, *Memoirs*, 1:593.

84. William Jones to John Armstrong, Apr. 18, 1814 ("hard sled roads"), RG 107, M 221, reel 54, USNA; Creighton, *Empire*, 3–7; Madison quoted in Stagg, *Madison's War*, 502n5 ("to reach"); Frederick de Gaugreben to Col. Rowley, Nov. 10, 1815, in Holmden, ed., "Gaugreben's Memoir," 61.

85. "War Dept," [Canandaigua, N.Y.] *Ontario Messenger*, Dec. 22, 1812; Skeen, *John Armstrong*, 130–31.

86. John Armstrong to William Eustis, Jan. 2, 1812 ("In old" and "population is thin"), and Augustus Porter to Peter B. Porter, June 16, 1813 ("So it goes"), in *DHCNF*, 1:32 and 6:88.

87. Morgan Lewis to John Armstrong, Feb. 8, 1813, RG 107, M 221, reel 54, USNA; Winfield Scott, "Observations," and John R. Fenwick to James Monroe, Dec. 23, 1814, in *ASP-MA*, 1:599 and 601.

88. John Watts to Eustis, Sept. 18, 1812 ("adulterated"), RG 107, M 221, reel 49, USNA; William Henry Harrison to Duncan McArthur, Sept. 1, 1813, and C. Scott to McArthur, June 16, 1814 ("a nuisance"), DMP, 3:567 and 10:1842, LC; Fredriksen, ed., "Pennsylvania Volunteers," 131, 137, and 140; Duncan McArthur to William Eustis, Sept. 21, 1812, RG 107, M 221, reel 47, USNA; Morgan Lewis to John Armstrong, July 5, 1814 ("condemnation"), RG 107, M 221, reel 63, USNA; Edmund P. Gaines to James Monroe, n.d. but c. Dec. 1814 ("lost more men"), and John R. Fenwick to Monroe, Dec. 23, 1814, in *ASP-MA*, 1:601.

89. James Monroe to George M. Troup, Dec. 23, 1814, Winfield Scott, "Observations," and John R. Fenwick to James Monroe, Dec. 23, 1814, in *ASP-MA*, 1:599, 600 ("The interests"), and 601; Jacob Brown to Nathan Williams, Dec. 11, 1813 ("we shall never"), JBP, 1:126, OCHS; Thomas Sidney Jesup to unknown, Sept. 8, 1814 ("madness"), TSJP, 1:220, LC; John Miller to Duncan McArthur, Dec. 31, 1814, DMP, 21:3998, LC; McArthur to Monroe, Jan. 11, 1815, RG 107, M 221, reel 64, USNA.

90. Walker, *Journal*, 49 ("expressed their surprize").

91. Henry Dearborn to John Armstrong, Feb. 18, 1813, RG 107, M 222, reel 7, USNA; Thomas Jesup to Armstrong, Apr. 11, 1813, RG 107, M 221, reel 54, USNA; Joseph Ellicott to Archibald S. Clarke, Mar. 7, 1814 ("Had there been"), HLCP, reel 12, BECHS; "Plattsburgh, Aug. 4," *Buffalo Gazette*, Aug. 17, 1813.

92. Phineas Reed to William Eustis, Nov. 4, 1812, RG 107, M 221, reel 58, USNA; Morgan Lewis to John Armstrong, Apr. 27, 1813, and July 13, 1813 ("Deserters"), RG 107, M 221, reel 54, USNA; William Quin, deposition, Sept. 4, 1813, in *DHCNF*, 7:97–98. For the desertion rate, see Stagg, "Enlisted Men," 624.

93. Jacob Brown to John Armstrong, Feb. 24, 1814 ("impossible to command"), RG 107, M 221, reel 51, USNA; Whitfield, *Tommy Atkins*, 73–76; Hare, "Military Punishments," 225–39.

94. Whitfield, *Tommy Atkins*, 76, 91–97; Hare, "Military Punishments," 236–37; Graves, ed., *Merry Hearts*, 80 ("The lash").

95. Hare, "Military Punishments," 230–36; Fredriksen, ed., "Pennsylvania Volunteeers," 146 ("to ride on"); Darnell, *Journal*, 38; Benjamin Seigley, court-martial, June 30, 1814, Archibald Howard, court martial, Oct. 14, 1814, DMP, 18:3384, LC; Fredriksen, ed., "New Hampshire Volunteer," 162; A. Hall, "Militia Service," 55–56; Skeen, *Citizen Soldiers*, 47.

96. James Winchester, general order, Oct. 28, 1812 ("sentenced"), Nov. 5, 1812, MPHS, *MHC*, 31:281 and 285; McLellan and McLellan, eds., "Garrison Orders," 83 and 85; Fredriksen, ed., "New Hampshire Volunteer,"164; Hare, "Military Punishments," 238.

97. Walker, *Journal*, 6; Dennis Baker, court martial, June 29, 1814 (all quotations), DMP, 11:1991, LC.

98. James Bankhead, order, Oct. 27, 1812, in *DHCNF*, 4:179; Morgan Lewis to John Armstrong, July 13, 1813, RG 107, M 221, reel 54, USNA; Edmund P. Gaines, order, July 8, 1814 ("the awful"), in Henry Wendell, orderly book, NYSL; Hanks, "Memoir," in Graves, ed., *Soldiers of 1814*, 31 ("dressed in white"); Hodge, "William Hodge Papers," 253; Brunson, *Western Pioneer*, 131–32; Fredriksen, ed., "New Hampshire Volunteer," 164–65 and 172; James Aigin, "Reminiscences" ("scattering brains"), Misc. Mss., BECHS; Hare, "Military Punishments," 238–39.

99. Hodge, "William Hodge Papers," 253; O'Reilly, "Hero of Fort Erie," 72; Darnell, *Journal*, 26–28; James Wilkinson, order, Aug. 29, 1813, Second Brigade Orderly Book, RG 98, Entry 47, USNA; Richard Bishop, diary, Oct. 19, 1813, RBP, box 1, NYSL; Atherton, *Narrative*, 17; Graves, *Field of Glory*, 180; Hare, "Military Punishments," 238. The numbers come from Hare's study, which relied on the official records of general courts-martial from the office of the judge advocate general. Incomplete, these records understate the number of executions. Hare reports only one reprieve (and four executions) in 1812, but other sources cited above report many more halted executions during the first year of the war.

100. *Buffalo Gazette*, June 7, 1814; James Aigin, "Reminiscences," Misc. Mss., BECHS; Hodge, "William Hodge Papers," 253 ("An awful thing"); Morgan Lewis to John Armstrong, July 20, 1813, RG 107, M 221, reel 54, USNA; Hanks, "Memoir," in Graves, ed., *Soldiers of 1814*, 25 ("We were compelled").

101. Jacob Brown to Nathan Williams, Dec. 11, 1813, Dec. 28, 1813 ("so humane"), and May 10, 1814, JBP, 1:126, 127, and 138, OCHS; Brown to James Monroe, Nov. 29, 1814 ("Perhaps in no country"), RG 107, M 221, reel 59, USNA.

102. John Watts to William Eustis, Sept. 18, 1812, RG 107, M 221, reel 49, USNA; Jacob Brown to John Armstrong, Mar. 4, 1814 ("Give a Bounty"), RG 107, M 222, reel 10, USNA; Brown to James Monroe, Nov. 29, 1814, RG 107, M 221, reel 59, USNA.

Chapter Thirteen: Prisoners

1. "Ghost of Montgomery," [Philadelphia] *Aurora*, Feb. 4, 1813.

2. "A Magnanimous Enemy," [Philadelphia] *Aurora*, Nov. 5, 1812; [Winfield Scott], "Journal of an American Officer," [Philadelphia] *Aurora*, Jan. 13, 1813 ("large escort"); W. Scott, *Memoirs*, 71 ("a renegade"). For other Montreal parades of prisoners, see Cooper, ed., *Ned Myers*, 82; Crawford, ed., "Lydia Bacon's Journal," 75; Benjamin Hodge, Jr., "An Account," HP, box 6, folder HG 72A, HL; Atherton, *Narrative*, 115, 118 and 125; Waterhouse, ed., *Journal*, 15; Finan, "Onlooker's View," 50.

3. Richardson, *Richardson's War*, 140; George Ridout to Thomas G. Ridout, Oct. 21, 1812, in Edgar, ed., *Ten Years*, 159; Andrew William Cochran to his mother, Sept. 13, 1812 ("Falstaff's men"), in *SBD*, 1:521; Finan, "Onlooker's View," 50 ("well-organized").

4. "The Impressment" and "Military," in [New York] *Shamrock*, June 20 ("When will"), and July 18, 1812 ("Erin"); D. Wilson, *United Irishmen*, 79–83.

5. "Summary," "Amicus," "Summary," "Extract of a Letter from a Gentleman in this City," "Fourth of July," "Military," untitled, and "Sons of Hibernia," [New York] *Shamrock*, Jan. 11 and 18, 1812, June 27, 1812, July 4 and 11, 1812, Sept. 19 and 26 ("will be rescued"), 1812; Michael Fortune, toast, July 4, 1812 ("Canadian Beaver"), in [Philadelphia] *Aurora*, July 17, 1812; "Attention!," [Philadelphia] *Aurora*, Sept. 19, 1812; "Military" and "General orders,"[New York]; D. Wilson, *United Irishmen*, 76–79; Cooper, ed., *Ned Myers*, 70 ("His religion").

6. "Summary," [New York] *Shamrock*, Oct. 10, 1812. For the Irish proportion of the recruits, see Stagg, "Enlisted Men," 626 and 628. Thomas Barclay insisted, "When British Seamen enter into their Service, they are instructed by the recruiting party to conceal the real place of their nativity, and instead to name some place within these states, as the place of their Birth." See Barclay to William Hamilton, May 25, 1813, MG 16, 95:7, reel B-2002, LAC.

7. Durey, "Marquess Cornwallis," 132–33; [New York] *Shamrock*, Sept. 26, 1812;

Nicholas Gray to Peter B. Porter, Jan. 4, 1815 ("a Gentleman"), PBPP, reel 3, BECHS; [United States], *The Army Register* (Philadelphia, 1814), 37; Charles Humphrey to Charles K. Gardner, Sept. 13, 1814, CKGP, box 2, NYSL.

8. James Commins to Mr. Davidson, Aug. 23, 1815, in Lord, ed., "War of 1812," 202; "Irish Magazine," [New York City], *The War*, July 11, 1812 ("most formidable"); John Harvey, "Journal," 8, reel MS-842, AO; Roger H. Sheaffe to Henry Procter, Mar. 22, 1813, RG 59, M 588, reel 7, USNA; Cecil Bisshopp to Catherine Bisshopp, Mar. 21, 1813, MG 24, F 4 (Bisshopp fonds), one folder, LAC; Graves, ed., *Merry Hearts*, 189 ("Come over").

9. Andrew Allen, Jr., to unknown, Jan. 24, 1813, MG 16, 95:38, reel B-2002, LAC; W. S. Skinner to John Borlase Warren, Apr. 15, 1813, MG 16, 100:37, reel B-2003, LAC; Thomas Barclay to William Hamilton, May 25, 1813 ("The naval engagements"), MG 16, 45:7, reel B-2002, LAC; Barclay to Lord Castlereagh Sept. 30, 1813 ("abuse of words"), in Rives, ed., *Correspondence of Barclay*, 337.

10. Graves, *Field of Glory*, 177; George Prevost, troop strength report, July 25, 1812, MG 13, 1516:81, reel B-1570, LAC; Durey, "Marquess Cornwallis," 144; Darnell, *Journal*, 71 ("very sociable"). For the Irish origins of the Forty-first and Forty-ninth Regiments, see also Peter Hunter to William Henry Clinton, Feb. 7, 1804, and Isaac Brock to the Adjutant General, Mar. 17, 1807, RG 8, 1211:335 and 1214:187, reel C-3524, LAC; Fredriksen, ed., "Chronicle of Valor," 265. William McGillivray to unknown, June 7, 1813, in MPHS, *MHC*, 25:463; Graves, *Field of Glory*, 177; Klinck and Ross, *Tiger Dunlop's Upper Canada*, 19 ("fine, jovial"); Hitsman, *Incredible War*, 194; Stanley, *War of 1812*, 219–20. Brock reported that 458 of the 469 men in the Forty-ninth Regiment came from Ireland.

11. Herman Witsius Ryland to Thomas Amyot, Nov. 17, 1812 ("holding out"), MG 24, B 3 (Ryland fonds), 3:511, reel H-2955; Earl of Bathurst to George Prevost, May 13, 1813, in MPHS, *MHC*, 15:288; Edward Baynes quoted in Thomas Melville, Jr., to John Mason, Jan. 28, 1814 (*"incontrovertible right"*), RG 94, ser. 127, box 14, folder 3, USNA.

12. Roger H. Sheaffe to George Prevost, Dec. 16, 1812, in Sheaffe, "Documents," 322n1; Benjamin Hodge, Jr., "An Account," Apr. 25, 1814, and Aug. 24, 1814 ("John Bull"), HP, box 6, folder 72A, HL.

13. Earl Bathurst to Sir George Prevost, May 13, 1813 ("atone"), in MPHS, *MHC*, 15:288; George Prevost, general order, Dec. 12, 1813 ("to expiate"), in *SBD*, 3, part 2:826–27. Prevost's claim has misled at least one accomplished historian. See Hickey, *War of 1812*, 178. For the actual policy of pardoning prisoners who confessed and converted, see Edward Baynes (for Prevost) to George Glasgow, Nov. 3, 1812, in MPHS, *MHC*, 25:400.

14. C. D. Shekleton, "Return of British Subjects Serving in the Army of the United States, Prisoners of War," Nov. 1, 1812, RG 8, 689:141, reel C-3232, LAC; Thomas Barclay to William Hamilton, May 25, 1813 ("It may occur"), MG 16, 45:7, reel B-2002, LAC.

15. Articles of capitulation, July 17, 1812, and Roberts to John B. Glegg, July 29, 1812, in *DRIC*, 63 and 100; Roberts to Hanks, July 19, 1812, Hanks to Roberts, July 19, 1812, and Roberts to Hanks, July 22, 1812, in MPHS, *MHC*, 40:443–45; Roberts to Roger H. Sheaffe, Oct. 12, 1812, in MPHS, *MHC*, 15:166; Sheaffe to Roberts, Nov. 6, 1812, GP, box 1, folder 2, BECHS; Dunnigan, "Michigan Fencibles," 279–81. For Detroit's captives, see Patrick McAnnally et al., court-martial, Aug. 19, 1812, in MPHS, *MHC*, 32:529–30; Henry Procter to Isaac Brock, Aug. 26, 1812, and Roger H.

Sheaffe to Procter, Sept. 1, 1812, in *SBD*, 1:494–95 and 516; Procter to Brock, Sept. 9, 1812, and Christopher Myers, "Return of Prisoners of War," Dec. 4, 1812, in MPHS, *MHC*, 15:145 and 195. For Barker, see A. Walker, *Journal*, 73.

16. Christopher Myers to Henry Procter, Mar. 3, 1813, RG 59, M 588, reel 7, USNA; Elijah Brush to James Monroe, June 8, 1813 ("make his life"), RG 94, ser. 127, box 12, folder 1, USNA; James Taylor to John Mason, July 20, 1813, RG 94, box 19, folder 1, USNA; William M. Scott to Peter B. Porter, Aug. 31, 1813 ("British born"), PBPP, reel 2, BECHS; Scott to Robert Gardner, Oct. 8, 1813, in *SBD*, 3, part 2:816–17. In early 1814 the British exchanged Scott for some Upper Canadian civilians arrested by General Dearborn. See John Mason to Thomas Melville, Jr., Nov. 30, 1813, in *ASP-FR*, 1st ser., 1:681; Melville to Mason, Dec. 8, 1813, RG 94, ser. 127, box 9, folder 2, USNA; Edward Baynes to Melville, Jan. 31, 1814, RG 94, ser. 127, box 2, folder 3, USNA.

17. Peter B. Porter to Daniel D. Tompkins, Aug. 30, 1812 ("Yesterday"), in *DHCNF*, 2:224; Roger H. Sheaffe to George Prevost, Dec. 16, 1812, and Dec. 29, 1812 ("confessed"), in Sheaffe, "Documents," 322 and 326.

18. John Vincent to George Prevost, June 22, 1813, and Francis de Rottenburg to E. B. Brenton, July 9, 1813, RG 8, 165:136 and 141, reel C-2773, LAC; Edward Baynes, general order, June 29, 1813, in *DHCNF*, 6:161–62.

19. John Mitchell to James Monroe, June 17, 1813, RG 94, ser. 127, box 20, folder 2, USNA; John Talbot to Mitchell, Aug. 6, 1813, RG 94, ser. 127, box 3, folder 1, USNA; Mitchell to Monroe, Jan. 25, 1813, and William Miller to Mitchell, Aug. 26, 1813, and Nov. 29, 1813, JMP, 1:189, 1:355, and 3:454, LC; John Borlase Warren to John W. Croker, July 22, 1813, and Oct. 27, 1813 ("to impress"), in Dudley, ed., *Naval War*, 2:192; Hawthorne, ed., *Yarn*, 162–63; Dye, *Fatal Cruise*, 289–90; Henry Miller to John Borlase Warren, May 8, 1813, in [New York] *Shamrock*, May 22, 1813; John O'Neill to Thomas Leiper et al., June 8, 1813 ("the oppressors"), in Binns, *Recollections*, 221; "The Case of O'Neale," [Philadelphia] *Aurora*, May 11 and 17, 1813.

20. Henry Miller to John Borlase Warren, May 8, 1813, and Warren to Miller, May 10, 1813 ("not informed"), in [New York] *Shamrock*, May 22, 1813; Binns, *Recollections*, 220–21; "The Case of O'Neale," [Philadelphia] *Aurora*, May 11 and 17, 1813; John O'Neill to John Mason, Aug. 30, 1813, RG 45, ser. RE 1812–15, box 590, USNA.

21. Henry Dearborn to James Monroe, Jan. 1, 1813, RG 107, M 221, reel 52, USNA; "Journal of an American Officer," [Philadelphia] *Aurora*, Jan. 13, 1813; Winfield Scott to James Monroe, Jan. 30, 1813, and Henry Kelly to Reuben G. Beasley, Feb. 6, 1813, *ASP-FR*, 1st ser., 1:634–35; George Prevost, general order, Oct. 27, 1813 ("Traitors"), *SBD*, 3, part 2:819–20; W. Scott, *Memoirs*, 72.

22. Winfield Scott to James Monroe, Jan. 30, 1813 ("to punish"), in *ASP-FR*, 1st ser., 1:634; George Prevost, general order, Dec. 12, 1813 ("infamous" and "outcast"), in *SBD*, 3, part 2:826–27; Henry Kelly to unknown, July 2, 1813 ("They used" and "we are possest"), RG 94, M 2019, one reel, USNA.

23. Malcomson, *Very Brilliant Affair*, 196; [Winfield Scott], "Journal of an American Officer," [Philadelphia] *Aurora*, Jan. 13, 1813 ("having borne arms"); Scott to James Monroe, Jan. 30, 1813, in *ASP-FR*, 1st ser., 1:634; W. Scott, *Memoirs*, 73–74; Scott to John Armstrong, Feb. 9, 1813, RG 107, M 221, reel 57, USNA; [New York] *Shamrock*, Dec. 26, 1812, and Jan. 2, 1813; D. Wilson, *United Irishmen*, 86; *PJM-PS*, 5:547n1.

24. John Binns et al. to James Madison, Jan. 2, 1813, in *PJM-PS*, 5:545–47; *Balti-*

more Whig, Jan. 5, 1813; [Philadelphia] *Democratic Press,* Feb. 22, 1813 ("who fights the battles"); "Ghost of Montgomery," *National Intelligencer,* reprinted in [Philadelphia] *Aurora,* Feb. 4, 1813 ("On the question"); "The Memorial" and "Important to Irishmen," [New York] *Shamrock,* Mar. 6, 1813.

25. W. Scott, *Memoirs,* 73–74; D. Wilson, *United Irishmen,* 86; *PJM-PS,* 5:547n1 and 547n4; Meriwether et al., eds., *Papers of Calhoun,* 1:167–68; "Mr. Binns," [Philadelphia] *Democratic Press,* Feb. 13, 1813; John Armstrong to Henry Dearborn, May 15, 1813, in *ASP-FR,* 1st ser., 1:635; Dearborn to George Prevost, May 31, 1813, *DHCNF,* 5:288. For the Irish origins of twelve of the hostages, see, David Curtis, memorandum, Aug. 12, 1814, RG 94, ser. 127, box 18, folder 1, USNA. Most of the hostages had been captured at Fort George and belonged to the Eighth or Forty-ninth foot. In addition to the twelve from Ireland, nine came from England and two from Canada.

26. Lord Bathurst to George Prevost, Aug. 12, 1813, in *DHCNF,* 7:11–12; Thomas Barclay to John Mason, Nov. 30, 1813, in *ASP-FR,* 1st ser., 1:661; Prevost to James Wilkinson, Dec. 11, 1813 ("Constitutional Principle"), in MPHS, *MHC,* 25:559.

27. Earl Bathurst to George Prevost, Aug. 12, 1813 ("to prosecute"), in *DHCNF,* 7:11–12; Edward Griffith to Transport Board, Sept. 1, 1813, in MPHS, *MHC,* 25:521.

28. George Prevost to James Wilkinson, Oct. 17, 1813, Prevost to Thomas Barclay, Oct. 27, 1813, and Prevost to Wilkinson, Dec. 11, 1813, in *ASP-FR,* 1st ser., 1:635–38; Mason to John Armstrong, Nov. 29, 1813, RG 107, M 221, reel 55, USNA; Wilkinson to Prevost, Dec. 3, 1813, and Prevost, general order, Dec. 12, 1813, in *SBD,* 3, part 2:822–23 and 826–27.

29. John Mason to James Prince, Sept. 28, 1813, and Thomas Barclay to Mason, Oct. 1, 1813, in *ASP-FR,* 1st ser., 1:655 and 656–58; Waterhouse, ed., *Journal,* 40 (William Miller quoted: "traitorous Irishmen") and 42 ("We fled").

30. John Mason to James Prince, Sept. 28, 1813, Thomas Barclay to Mason, Oct. 1, 1813, and Mason to Thomas Steele, Oct. 12, 1813, in *ASP-FR,* 1st ser., 1:655, 656–58, and 659; John Mitchell to William Miller, Dec. 12, 1813, and Miller to Mitchell, Dec. 15, 1813, RG 94, ser. 127, box 7, folder 3, USNA; Barclay to George Prevost, Dec. 19, 1813 ("If the System"), in *SBD,* 3, part 2:829.

31. Thomas Barclay to John Mason, Sept. 17, 1813 ("six times"), RG 94, ser. 127, box 10, Folder 2, USNA; Thomas Jefferson to William Duane, Sept. 18, 1813, in Duane, "Selections," 65.

32. Thomas Barclay to John Mason, Sept. 27, 1813 ("Government"), in *ASP-FR,* 1st ser., 1:654; John Lovett, speech, Dec. 21, 1813, Robert H. Gouldsborough, speech, Feb. 1, 1814, and Zebulon Shipherd, speech, Feb. 18, 1814 ("doom our country"), *AC,* 13th Congress, 2d Session, 802, 1205, and 1508; "Retaliation," *Geneva* [N.Y.] *Gazette,* Mar. 23, 1814.

33. Waterhouse, ed., *Journal,* 43; John C. Calhoun, speech, Feb. 2, 1814 ("be protected"), in Meriwether et al., eds., *Papers of Calhoun,* 1:202–3; Henry Clay, speech, Jan. 9, 1813, in Hopkins et al., eds., *Papers of Clay,* 1:766–67; Augustus B. Woodward to Henry Procter, Jan. 29, 1813, in MPHS, *MHC,* 36:277–78; Binns, *Recollections,* 219; James Madison, "Great Britain-Naturalization," Apr. 16, 1814, in *ASP-FR,* 1st ser., 1:631.

34. Robert McDouall and Henry Dearborn, prisoner cartel, Nov. 12, 1812, RG 5, 15:6487, Reel C-4508, LAC; Prevost, ratification, Nov. 24, 1812, in MPHS, *MHC,* 25:406–7.

35. Earl Bathurst to George Prevost, Dec. 9, 1812, and Prevost to Bathurst,

Dec. 10, 1812, in MPHS, *MHC*, 25:413 and 414; Prevost, general order, Feb. 8, 1813, in *SBD*, 3, part 2:790–92; Henry Dearborn to John Armstrong, Apr. 3, 1813, RG 107, M 221, reel 52, USNA; Bathurst to Prevost, May 12, 1813, in MPHS, *MHC*, 15:287; Prevost to Bathurst, June 24, 1813, and Thomas Barclay to Prevost, July 20, 1813 ("sound Policy"), in *DHCNF*, 6:138 and 259; Barclay to Prevost, Sept. 24, 1813, in MPHS, *MHC*, 15:389; Barclay to John Mason, Oct. 8, 1813, RG 94, ser. 127, box 21A, folder 1, USNA; Alexander McLeay to Reuben G. Beasley, Aug. 13, 1813, RG 94, ser. 127, box 17, folder 3, USNA.

36. John Mitchell to James Monroe, Apr. 16, 1813, JMP, 2:242, LC; Thomas Barclay to the Transport Board, June 5, 1813, in Rives, ed., *Correspondence of Barclay*, 334; James Taylor to John Mason, June 23, 1813, and Mason to John Gaillard, Jan. 12, 1814, RG 45, ser. RE 1812–15, boxes 589 and 591, USNA; Mason to unknown, May 30, 1814 ("mortifying"), RG 45, ser. 464, box 606, folder 3B, USNA; Dietz, "Prisoner of War," 9–11, 17–18, 22–23, and 144–46.

37. James Prince to Thomas Melville, Jr., Aug. 18, 1813 ("nothing"), RG 94, ser. 127, box 11A, folder 1, USNA; Prince to John Mason, Dec. 4, 1813, RG 94, ser. 127, box 1, folder 4, USNA; Thomas Barclay to Mason, Dec. 21, 1814, in *SBD*, 3, part 2:834–35; Mason to Barclay, Dec. 29, 1813, in *ASP-FR*, 1st ser., 1:640; Waters, "Episode," 500–503; *Salem Gazette*, Jan. 25, 1814; [Worcester, Mass.] *National Aegis*, Jan. 26 and Feb. 2, 1814.

38. John Mitchell to John Mason, May 14, 1814, RG 45, ser. RE 1812–15, box 591, USNA; Reuben G. Beasley to Viscount Castlereagh, Oct. 12, 1812, RG 59, T-168, reel 10, USNA; Mitchell to James Monroe, Dec. 5, 1812, RG 94, ser. 127, box 13, folder 4, USNA; Beasley to Monroe, June 10, 1813 ("insulting"), and July 5, 1813, RG 94, ser. 127, box 7, folder 2, USNA; Alexander McLeay to Beasley, Oct. 20, 1813, RG 94, ser. 127, box 2, folder 2, USNA; Dietz, "Prisoner of War," 250–52. For the numbers of impressed sailors among all American prisoners, see Dye, "American Maritime Prisoners of War," 301–2; Fabel, "Self-Help in Dartmoor," 174.

39. John Mason to John Gaillard, Jan. 12, 1814, and Mason to Lemuel Taylor, June 8, 1814, RG 45, ser. RE 1812–15, boxes 591, and 592, USNA; Harry Calvert, General Order, Mar. 4, 1814, RG 8, 692:128, reel C-3233, LAC; Dye, "American Maritime Prisoners of War," 301–2.

40. John Mason to John Gaillard, Jan. 12, 1814, RG 45, ser. RE 1812–15, box 591, USNA; Alexander McKim, speech, Mar. 5, 1814 ("to get as many"), *AC*, 13th Congress, 2d Session, 1805; Hickey, *War of 1812*, 124 and 165; Dietz, "Prisoner of War," 350–52.

41. Alexander Cochrane to Thomas Barclay, July 31, 1814, RG 94, ser. 127, box 11, folder 2, USNA; John S. Skinner to John Mason, Aug. 12, 1814, and Mason to Cochrane, Sept. 2, 1814, RG 45, ser. RE 1812–15, box 592, folders 3 and 4, USNA; John Mitchell to Mason, Sept. 22, 1814 ("In this way"), and Jan. 30, 1815, RG 94, ser. 127, box 3, folder 1, USNA; Robert Barrie to Mason, Nov. 15, 1814, RG 45, ser. RE 1812–15, box 597, folder 3, USNA.

42. George Prevost to Thomas Barclay, Oct. 27, 1813, Barclay to John Mason, Oct. 4, 1813, and William Miller to John Mitchell, Oct. 17, 1813, in *ASP-FR*, 1st ser., 1:637, 659, and 660; T. L. Coote to Robert Gardner, Oct. 28, 1813, RG 94, ser. 127, box 19, folder 6, USNA; Edward Griffith to the Transport Board, Sept. 1, 1813, in MPHS, *MHC*, 25:521; Griffith to Barclay, Dec. 16, 1813, RG 94, ser. 127, box 6, folder 1, USNA; Mitchell to James Monroe, Nov. 9, 1813, and Mitchell to John

Mason, Nov. 30, 1813, RG 94, ser. 127, box 3, folder 1, and box 7, folder 3, USNA; Miller to Barclay, Nov. 24, 1813, RG 94, ser. 127, box 6, folder 1, USNA; Mason to Reuben G. Beasley, Jan. 9, 1814, RG 45, ser. 464, box 606, folder 3A, USNA.

43. John Mason to Thomas Barclay, Sept. 29, 1813, and Reuben G. Beasley to the Transport Board, Feb. 19, 1814, *ASP-FR*, 1st ser., 1:655 and 727; John Mitchell to William Miller, Oct. 18, 1813, RG 94, ser. 127, box 3, folder 1, USNA; David Cummings to John Mason, Oct. 31, 1814, RG 45, ser. RE 1812–15, box 592, folder 4, USNA; Waterhouse, ed., *Journal*, 37–45, 54–55 ("Imagine"), and 88–91.

44. Reuben G. Beasley to Mason, Aug. 26, 1813, RG 45, ser. RE 1812–15, box 590, USNA; Beasley to John Mason, May 6, 1814, and July 11, 1814, RG 94, ser. 127, box 9, folder 4, USNA; Beasley to Mason, Dec. 31, 1814, RG 94, ser. 127, box 9, folder 4, USNA; Andrews, *Prisoners' Memoirs*, 16, 139, and 149; Waterhouse, ed., *Journal*, 57–63 and 133; Dye, "American Maritime Prisoners," 305–6; Dye, "Physical and Social Profiles," 220–28; Fabel, "Self-Help in Dartmoor," 165; Waterhouse, ed., *Journal*, 162.

45. Andrews, *Prisoners' Memoirs*, 17–19; Waterhouse, ed., *Journal*, 172–76 and 185; Hawthorne, ed., *Yarn*, 167–70; Fabel, "Self-Help in Dartmoor," 166 and 187; Bolster, *Black Jacks*, 104; Dye, *Fatal Cruise*, 292.

46. John Mason to John Mitchell, n.d. but c. 1813, JMP, 3:492, LC; Robert Gardner to Edward Baynes, Oct. 4, 1813, RG 94, ser. 127, box 21, folder 1, USNA.

47. Thomas Barclay to William Hamilton, Apr. 15, 1813, MG 16, 95:3, reel B-2002, LAC; Barclay to Transport Board, June 22, 1813, in Rives, ed., *Correspondence of Barclay*, 95–96 and 335–36; Judith Tulloch, "Thomas Henry Barclay," *DCB*, 6:33–35; Dietz, "Prisoner of War," 137–39; John Mason to Barclay, Jan. 19, 1814, RG 94, ser. 127, box 17, folder 1, USNA; Barclay to Mason, Jan. 25, 1814, RG 94, ser. 127, box 6, folder 1, USNA; Rives, ed., *Correspondence of Barclay*, 312–15; Dye, "American Maritime Prisoners," 303.

48. John Mason to Thomas Barclay, Oct. 5, 1813, and James Monroe to Barclay, Dec. 28, 1813, and Feb. 2, 1814, in Rives, ed., *Correspondence of Barclay*, 338–39, 341, and 343; Barclay to Prevost, Aug. 31, 1813, and Sept. 25, 1813, in MPHS, *MHC*, 15:367 and 391; Mason to Barclay, Aug. 31, 1814, and Barclay to Mason, Sept. 2, 1814, RG 94, ser. 127, box 10, folder 2, USNA; Mason to James Monroe, Sept. 8, 1814, and Mason to Reuben G. Beasley, Oct. 11, 1814, RG 45, ser. 464, RV, 1812–15, box 609, folder 2a, USNA; Dye, "American Maritime Prisoners," 303.

49. John Mitchell to John Mason, Dec. 18, 1813, RG 94, box 7, folder 3, USNA; Mitchell to Mason, July 23, 1814, RG 94, ser. 127, box 3, folder 1, USNA; Edward Griffith to John Cochet, Nov. 13, 1814, and Cochet to Mitchell, Nov. 14, 1814, JMP, 4:658 and 660, LC; Thomas Barclay to George Prevost, Sept. 20, 1813, RG 8, 1712:54, reel C-3840, LAC; Robert Gardner to Daniel Parker, Aug. 11, 1813, RG 454, ser. RP 1812–15, box 605, folder 2, USNA; Gardner to Mason, Mar. 25, 1814, RG 94, ser. 127, box 9, folder 2, USNA; Gardner to George Prevost, May 6, 1814, RG 8, 693:1, reel C-3223, LAC.

50. Atherton, *Narrative*, 120–21; Benjamin Hodge, Jr., "An Account," Apr. 21, 1814, HP, box 6, folder 72A, HL; John O'Brien to John Mason, May 6, 1813, and William Scribner et al., to James Madison, June 8, 1813, RG 45, ser. 464, RP 1812–15, box 605, folder 2, USNA; Neil C. Lemon et al., to James Monroe, Sept. 29, 1814 ("trafficker"), RG 45, ser. 464, RV 1812–15, box 566, folder 6, USNA; Andrews, *Prisoners' Memoirs*, 27–28, 50, and 157–58 ("depriving"); Waterhouse, ed., *Journal*, 72–73 and 214–15 ("pretty genteel"); Alexander McLeay to Reuben G. Beasley, Mar. 6, 1813,

RG 94, ser. 127, box 7, folder 2, USNA; Beasley to John Mason, Mar. 24, 1814, RG 94, ser. 127, box 9, folder 4, USNA; Dye, "American Maritime Prisoners," 300–301.

51. Neil C. Lemon et al., to James Monroe, Sept. 29, 1814, RG 45, ser. 464, RV 1812–15, box 566, folder 6, USNA; Dye, "American Maritime Prisoners," 300–301; Waterhouse, ed., *Journal*, 72–73 ("hooting"); Reuben G. Beasley to James Monroe, Mar. 25, 1813 ("Confinement"), RG 94, ser. 127, box 2, folder 1, USNA; Beasley to John Mason, Feb. 15, 1815, and May 2, 1815, RG 94, ser. 127, box 9, folder 4, USNA.

52. Dye, "American Maritime Prisoners," 297–98; John Mitchell to James Prince, n.d. but c. Jan. 1, 1813 ("Here"), JMP, 1:153, LC; Mitchell to James Monroe, Sept. 11, 1813 ("of all men"), RG 94, ser. 127, box 3, folder 4, USNA.

53. Thomas Barclay and John Mason, prisoner cartel, May 12, 1813 ("sound and wholesome"), in *SBD*, 3, part 2:799; Reuben G. Beasley to Mason, Oct. 28, 1813, RG 94, ser. 127, box 7, folder 2, USNA; Robert Gardner to Francis Kempt, Oct. 12, 1813, RG 94, ser. 127, box 9, folder 5, USNA; Kempt to Gardner, Oct. 12, 1813, RG 94, ser. 127, box 19, folder 6, USNA; Mason to Barclay, Dec. 27, 1813, RG 8, 692:6, reel C-3233, LAC; Dietz, "Prisoner of War," 150–51. The British prisoner-of-war ration provided about 2,400 calories per day, a little short of the 2,800 needed by a male of average height. See Dye, "American Maritime Prisoners of War," 312.

54. Thomas Barclay to James Dick, Aug. 6, 1814 ("British and French"), RG 94, ser. 127, box 10, folder 2, USNA; Reuben G. Beasley to John Mason, Mar. 22, 1814, RG 94, ser. 127, box 9, folder 3, USNA; Waterhouse, ed., *Journal*, 21 ("American eats") and 204 ("a third more"). For the taller average height and better diet of American men, compared to Britons, see Galenson, "Settlement and Growth," 192–93.

55. Waterhouse, ed., *Journal*, 39 ("mess"), 43 and 163 ("To young men"); Hawthorne, ed., *Yarn*, 203–4; A. Walker, *Journal*, 78; Cooper, ed., *Ned Myers*, 81–84.

56. John Mitchell to John Borlase Warren, Oct. 12, 1814 ("Spirit"), RG 94, ser. 127, box 13, folder 4, USNA; Warren to Mitchell, Oct. 14, 1812, JMP, 1:97, LC; Waterhouse, ed., *Journal*, 11 and 24 ("formerly intemperate"); S. White, *History of the American Troops*, 55.

57. William D. Clark, report, Mar. 5, 1815, RG 94, ser. 127, box 21, folder 3, USNA; Daniel James Woodruff to William H. Robinson, June 14, 1813, RG 8, 689:101, reel C-3232, LAC. From July 25, 1813, to Nov. 16, 1813, forty-nine American prisoners died at Quebec. See Robert Gardner to John Mason, Jan. 16, 1814, RG 94, ser. 127, box 19, folder 3, USNA. Despite holding larger numbers of prisoners for longer stretches, Halifax lost only eighty-six dead from Aug. 10, 1812, to Jan. 31, 1814, and nine of those deaths came from wounds initially suffered in combat. See William Miller, register, Jan. 31, 1814, RG 94, ser. 127, box 21, folder 3, USNA. For American praise for the British medical care, see Gardner to Mason, Oct. 10, 1813, RG 94, ser. 127, box 19, folder 6, USNA; James Winchester to Major Aspenwall, July 17, 1813, RG 8, 689:197, reel C-3232, LAC; John Mitchell to Mason, Aug. 2, 1814, RG 94, ser. 127, box 3, folder 1, USNA.

58. William Miller to John Mitchell, Nov. 29, 1813, JMP, 3:458, LC; Miller to Mitchell, Jan. 30, 1814, RG 94, box 3, folder 5, USNA; Mitchell to John Cochet, Nov. 16, 1814 ("necessarys"), RG 94, box 3, folder 1, USNA; Dietz, "Prisoner of War," 151–52.

59. Robert Gardner to John Mason, Apr. 24, 1814, RG 94, M 2019, one reel, USNA; John Mitchell to Mason, Jan. 30, 1814 ("truly surprising"), and May 30, 1814, RG 94, ser. 127, box 3, folder 1, USNA; Waterhouse, ed., *Journal*, 154 ("never saw" and "passion"); Andrews, *Prisoners' Memoirs*, 52.

60. A. Walker, *Journal*, 73; Atherton, *Narrative*, 124; Andrews, *Prisoners' Memoirs*, 11; Dye, "American Maritime Prisoners," 295; Reuben G. Beasley to James Monroe, Oct. 28, 1812, RG 94, ser. 127, box 2, folder 2, USNA; Robert Gardner to John Mason, Mar. 25, 1814, RG 94, ser. 127, box 9, folder 2, USNA; Gardner to Mason, Jan. 31, 1815, RG 94, ser. 127, box 11, folder 1, USNA; Mitchell to Mason, Sept. 2, 1813, and July 11, 1814, RG 94, ser. 127, box 3, folder 1, USNA; William Miller to Mitchell, Sept. 7, 1813 ("true born Citizen"), JMP, 3:382, LC; Gardner to Mason, Apr. 24, 1814 ("We have lost"), RG 94, M 2019, one reel, USNA.

61. James Winchester to John Mason, Aug. 23, 1814 ("recruit"), RG 45, ser. RE 1812–15, box 592, folder 3, USNA; Reuben G. Beasley to Mason, Jan. 22, 1813 ("only way"), RG 94, ser. 127, box 2, folder 1, USNA; Beasley to Mason, Oct. 28, 1813, RG 94, ser. 127, box 7, folder 2, USNA; John Mitchell to Mason, May 4, 1814, RG 94, ser. 127, box 3, folder 1, USNA; Thomas Swaine et al., petition, n.d. but c. May 14, 1814, RG 45, ser. 464, box 567, folder 9, USNA.

62. Reuben G. Beasley to John Mason, Mar. 24, 1813 ("from the prison"), RG 94, ser. 127, box 9, folder 4, USNA; Beasley, "List of American Prisoners, who have entered into the British Service," July 4, 1813–Mar. 24, 1814, RG 94, ser. 127, box 21, folder 3, USNA; Dye, "American Maritime Prisoners," 306; Andrews, *Prisoners' Memoirs*, 69; John Mitchell to William Miller, Sept. 8, 1813, and Mitchell to Mason, July 20, 1814, RG 94, ser. 127, box 3, folder 1, USNA.

63. Waterhouse, ed., *Journal*, 126 ("Tenders"); Atherton, *Narrative*, 120; Andrews, *Prisoners' Memoirs*, 78 ("shortly reduce" and "their subjects").

64. Atherton, *Narrative*, 110; Andrews, *Prisoners' Memoirs*, 126 ("the keepers"); Waterhouse, ed., *Journal*, 144 ("Sometimes"), 169: Benjamin F. Palmer, "Prisoner's Journal," Feb. 2 and 13, 1814, NYPL; Archer, ed., "Journal of Major Roach," 309; Benjamin Hodge, Jr., "An Account," July 15, 17, and 25, 1814, HP, box 6, folder 72A, HL.

65. Waterhouse, ed., *Journal*, 76–77, 134–35 ("Captivity"), 142 ("Bloody villains!"), and 217; Benjamin Hodge, Jr., "An Account," July 4, 1814, HP, box 6, folder 72A, HL; Hawthorne, ed., *Yarn*, 245; Andrews, *Prisoners' Memoirs*, 96–99; Bolster, *Black Jacks*, 115–16.

66. Charles Calvert Egerton to John Mason, Aug. 2, 1813, and D. Chalmers to John Mason, Oct. 16, 1813, RG 45, ser. RE 1812–15, box 590, USNA; Waterhouse, ed., *Journal*, 53, 81 ("God of nature"), 166–67 ("hard-hearted"), and 207–8.

67. Fabel, "Self-Help in Dartmoor," 165 and 170–71.

68. Waterhouse, ed., *Journal*, 193 ("the largest"); Bolster, *Black Jacks*, 102–3, 105–6; Horsman, "Paradox of Dartmoor," 12–17. When captured, King Dick was Richard Crafus, but after the war he preferred the name Richard Seaver.

69. Hawthorne, ed., *Yarn*, 181–87 and 193–94; Waterhouse, ed, *Journal*, 194–97; Fabel, "Self-Help in Dartmoor," 181–82.

70. Waterhouse, ed., *Journal*, 193–97; Hawthorne, ed., *Yarn*, 181–83; Bolster, *Black Jacks*, 108–12.

71. Thomas Barclay to Transport Board, June 5, 1813 ("British Prisoners"), in Rives, ed., *Correspondence of Barclay*, 334–35; Benjamin Hodge, Jr., "An Account," June 18, 1814 ("finds friends" and "fares better"), HP, box 6, folder 72A, HL; Waterhouse, ed., *Journal*, 60 ("An American"); Atherton, *Narrative*, 143; Dietz, "Prisoner of War," 134–35.

72. John Mason to George Cockburn, June 7, 1813, and Mason to Benjamin Henry Latrobe, Apr. 19, 1814, RG 45, ser. RE 1812–15, boxes 589 and 597, folder 2, USNA; Thomas Steel to John Mason, Jan. 22, 1814 ("Farmers"), and John Martin to

Mason, May 20, 1814, RG 94, ser. 127, box 12, folder 1, USNA; Mason to John Armstrong, July 28, 1814 ("constant habit"), RG 107, M 221, reel 64, USNA.

73. Thomas Barclay to Commissioners of Transport, Apr. 15, 1813, in Rives, ed., *Correspondence of Barclay*, 326; John Mason to Barclay, June 7, 1813, RG 94, box 17, folder 4, USNA; William Jones to Mason, June 8, 1813, RG 45, ser. 464, box 607, folder 2, USNA; Alexander Macomb to John Armstrong, June 10, 1813, RG 107, M 221, reel 55, USNA; Graves, ed., *Merry Hearts*, 220.

74. Reuben G. Beasley to James Monroe, Nov. 9, 1812, RG 59, T168, reel 10, USNA; John Borlase Warren to James Monroe, Mar. 8, 1813 ("seduced from"), RG 59, M 179, reel 27, USNA; Thomas Barclay to George Prevost, May 20, 1813, RG 8, 689:61, reel C-3232, LAC; Barclay to Transport Board, June 24, 1813, in MPHS, *MHC*, 25:482; William Winkley et al. to William Jones, Dec. 12, 1813, RG 45, ser. 464, RV 1812–15, box 567, folder 10, USNA; John Mason to Benjamin Henry Latrobe, Apr. 19, 1814, RG 45, ser. RK 1812–15, box 597, folder 2, USNA; John Mitchell to James Prince, n.d., but c. Jan. 1, 1813, JMP, 1:153, LC; Mason to Thomas Barclay, June 7, 1813 ("every British Prisoner" and "that sort"), RG 94, ser. 127, box 17, folder 4, USNA.

75. William Winkley et al. to William Jones, Dec. 12, 1813, RG 45 ("birth right" and "British Subjects"), ser. 464, RV 1812–15, box 567, folder 10, USNA.

76. James Prince to John Mason, Nov. 27 and 29, 1813, RG 94, ser. 127, box 1, folder 4, USNA; Waterhouse, ed., *Journal*, 60.

77. Arthur Sinclair to John Hartwell Cocke, Oct. 10, 1813 ("to enlist"), in Malcomson, ed., *Sailors of 1812*, 57; Richard Dennis to John Armstrong, Dec. 6, 1813, RG 107, M 221, reel 52, USNA.

78. Tobias Lear to John Mason, July 21, 1814 ("amiable" and "industry"), RG 45, ser. RE 1812–15, box 592, folder 2, USNA; J. E. A. Smith, *History of Pittsfield*, 192–96, 206–7, and 398–99.

79. Thomas Melville to Elisha Jenkins, July 13, 1813, RG 94, ser. 127, box 4, folder 2, USNA; Jenkins to John Armstrong, July 13, 1813, RG 94, ser. 127, box 4, folder 1, USNA; and Melville to John Mason, July 22, 1814, RG 94, ser. 127, box 20, folder 5, USNA; J. E. A. Smith, *History of Pittsfield*, 192–99.

80. Thomas Melville, Jr., to Elisha Jenkins, July 13, 1813, RG 94, ser. 127, box 4, folder 2, USNA; James Prince to John Mason, Aug. 18, 1813, RG 94, ser. 127, box 11a, folder 1, USNA; Melville to John Mason, Aug. 19, 1813, RG 94, ser. 127, box 9, folder 2, USNA; Jonathan Allen, Solomon Clark, and Hosea Merrill to Melville, Oct. 19, 1815, RG 94, ser. 127, box 20, folder 4, USNA; Walter Kerr, parole, Aug. 20, 1813, RG 8, 695:128, reel C-3234, LAC; J. E. A. Smith, *History of Pittsfield*, 212; Dietz, "Prisoner of War," 160–70.

81. Thomas Melville, Jr., to James Prince, Apr. 29, 1815 ("By the system"), RG 94, ser. 127, box 20, folder 4, USNA; Melville to John Mason, Nov. 9, 1813, and Oct. 19, 1814, RG 94, ser. 127, box 9, folder 1, USNA; Melville to Mason, Mar. 22, 1814, RG 94, ser. 127, box 2, folder 3, USNA; Thomas W. Moore to Melville, Dec. 12, 1813, J. S. Tyeth et al. to Moore, Dec. 12, 1813 ("a Gentleman"), and Melville to Mason, Apr. 30, 1815, RG 94, ser. 127, box 20, folder 4, USNA; P. R. Wybault to Melville, Dec. 27, 1814, RG 94, ser. 127, box 9, folder 1, USNA; Robert R. Loring, memorandum, Jan. 23, 1815, RG 8, 694:25, reel C-3233, LAC.

82. William H. Merritt, "Journal of Events," in *SBD*, 3, part 2:626–36 ("real democrat" and "old routine" on 631, "carousing" on 632, and "unwell" on 633); Merritt to Catherine Prendergast, Oct. 1, 1814 ("allowed" and "Gout").

83. Robert R. Loring, memorandum, Jan. 23, 1815 ("ruinous" and "general liberty"), RG 8, 694:25, reel C-3233, LAC.

84. Thomas Melville, Jr., to John Mason, Jan. 9, 1814 ("relations"), and Melville, printed handbill, Jan. 9, 1814, RG 94, ser. 127, box 20, folder 5, USNA; Melville, printed handbill, Jan. 19, 1814, and Melville to Mason, Jan. 20, 1814, RG 94, ser. 127, box 20, folder 4, USNA; Thomas G. Walker to Melville, Feb. 16, 1814, RG 94, ser. 127, box 2, folder 3, USNA.

85. Robert Gardner to John Mason, Oct. 11, 1813, RG 94, ser. 127, box 19, folder 6, USNA; James Winchester to David Winchester, Dec. 2, 1813, Gratz Coll., box 35, HSP; George Prevost to Thomas Barclay, Nov. 13, 1813 ("retaliating system"), in MPHS, *MHC*, 25:546; William Winder to James Monroe, Nov. 5, 1813 ("interest"), RG 45, ser. 464, box 606, folder 2, USNA; Winder to Prevost, Dec. 17, 1813 ("the horrible"), RG 8, 691:147, reel C-3233, LAC.

86. James Monroe to William Winder, Mar. 19, 1814, and Mar. 22, 1814 ("not to relinquish"), and Winder to Monroe, Apr. 30, 1814, RG 45, ser. RE 1812–15, box 591, USNA; Winder to Monroe, Mar. 28, 1814, RG 45, ser. 464, box 606, folder 3A, USNA; Brant, *James Madison: Commander in Chief*, 243.

87. Edward Baynes to William Winder, Apr. 10, 1814 ("inadmissible"), and Apr. 12, 1814, in Richardson, *Richardson's War*, 276–77 and 281–82; Winder to Baynes, Apr. 10, 1814 ("linger out"), and Apr. 11, 1814, Baynes to Winder, Apr. 12, 1814, and Winder to Baynes, included in George Prevost, general order, July 2, 1814, RG 8, 693:66, reel C-3233, LAC; Baynes to Winder, Apr. 11, 1814, RG 45, ser. 464, box 606, folder 3A, USNA; Dietz, "Prisoner of War," 292–93.

88. William Winder and Edward Baynes, prisoner convention, Apr. 15, 1814, RG 45, ser. RE 1812–15, box 591, USNA. See also *ASP-FR*, 1st ser., 1:728.

89. George Prevost, general order, Apr. 16, 1814, in Richardson, *Richardson's War*, 272; William Winder to James Monroe, May 20, and 22, 1814, RG 45, ser. RE 1812–15, box 591, USNA; Brant, *James Madison: Commander in Chief*, 255; Dietz, "Prisoner of War," 294–96; Reuben G. Beasley to John Mason, Mar. 18, 1814, RG 94, ser. 127, box 9, folder 4, USNA; Thomas Melville, Jr., to George Prevost, June 9, 1814, RG 94, ser. 127, box 20, folder 4, USNA; James Monroe to Tobias Lear, June 27, 1814, in *ASP-FR*, 1st ser., 1:727–28. In November 1814 Beasley reported that one of the twenty-three had died and another had "entered into the British service," but one of the men stated that three of the twenty-three had died. See Henry Kelly to unknown, July 2, 1813, RG 94, M 2019, one reel, USNA; Beasley to John Mason, Nov. 15, 1814, RG 45, ser. RL 1812–15, box 597, folder 3, USNA.

90. Earl Bathurst to George Prevost, May 13, 1813 ("take on the Spot"), and Prevost to Bathurst, Oct. 30, 1813, in MPHS, *MHC*, 15:288 and 25:540–41; Bathurst to Prevost, Mar. 5, 1814 ("after Conviction"), in *SBD*, 3, part 2: 840; Prevost to Gordon Drummond, July 5, 1814, RG 5, 16:6929, reel C-4508, LAC.

91. Thomas Melville, Jr., to John Mason, July 6, and 17, 1814, RG 94, ser., 127, box 20, folder 5, USNA; George Prevost to Edward Baynes and E. B. Brenton, July 14, 1814, RG 8, 693: 57, reel C-3233, LAC; Lear and Baynes, prisoner convention, July 16, 1814, in *SBD*, 3, part 2:844; Mason to John Armstrong, July 28, 1814, RG 107, M 221, reel 64, USNA; Melville to Alexander Macomb, Sept. 29, 1814, RG 94, ser. 127, box 14, folder 3, USNA.

92. John Mason to marshal of Kentucky, June 16, 1814, RG 45, ser. RE 1812–15, box 592, folder 1, USNA; Richardson, *Richardson's War*, 285–92; John Martin to John Mason, Sept. 7, 1814, and John Hamm to Mason, Oct. 8, 1814, and Oct. 26, 1814, RG

94, ser. 127, box 12, folder 1, USNA; John Erly to John Harvey, Nov. 9, 1814, RG 8, 693:150, reel C-3233, LAC. For Brown's responsibility, see Edmund P. Kennedy to William Jones, July 22, 1814, in Dudley, ed., *Naval War,* 3:546; Jacob Brown to Monroe, Nov. 15, 1814, RG 107, M 221, reel 59, USNA.

93. J. L. Hill to Gordon Drummond, Sept. 22, 1814, and Adam Muir to William Evans, n.d., but c. Oct. 25, 1814 ("some dead"), in *DHCNF-1814,* 2:454 and 455; Richardson, *Richardson's War,* 289–92; John Erly to John Harvey, Nov. 9, 1814 ("more generous"), RG 8, 693:150, reel C-3233, LAC; Gordon Drummond to George Prevost, Nov. 5, 1814, MG 11, 355:175, reel B-295, LAC; C. Van de Venter to William Winder, Nov. 18, 1814, Van de Venter to Edward Baynes, Nov. 24, 1814, Baynes to Van de Venter, Dec. 2, 1814, and Van de Venter to John Mason, Dec. 11, 1814, RG 45, ser. RE 1812–15, box 593, folder 1, USNA.

94. Graves, *Right and Glory,* 205 ("The lot"). Dietz, "Prisoner of War," is a useful but unpublished dissertation that covers American prisoner policy.

Chapter Fourteen: Honor

1. John Armstrong to Jacob Brown, Aug. 7, 1814, in Edmund Kirby, orderly book, GP, box 2, BECHS.

2. Morris, *Sword of the Border,* 3–13; Graves, *Field of Glory,* 45; William B. Skelton, "Jacob Jennings Brown," *ANB,* 3:682–83.

3. Morris, *Sword of the Border,* 13–17; Graves, *Field of Glory,* 45.

4. Jacob Brown to Nathan Williams, Nov. 20, 1812, and Brown to Williams, Dec. 11, 1813, JBP, 1:118 and 126, OCHS; Morris, *Sword of the Border,* 17–18 and 33–36; Graves, *Field of Glory,* 45 and 320; Hickey, *War of 1812,* 183; Skelton, "High Army Leadership," 270.

5. Jacob Brown, general order, Feb. 21, 1814 ("gain a name"), RG 98, ser. 52, vol. 439, USNA; Brown to Nathan Williams, May 10, 1814 ("Let us meet"), JBP, 1:138, OCHS.

6. Earl Bathurst to George Prevost, Apr. 24, 1814, in *DHCNF,* 9:307; Hickey, *War of 1812,* 159–60, 166, and 183; John Armstrong to Jacob Brown, June 10, 1814, in Dudley, ed., *Naval War,* 3:500–501; Brown to Armstrong, June 17, 1814, RG 107, M 221, reel 59, USNA; Stagg, *Madison's War,* 386–90; Graves, *Right and Glory,* 17 and 20–22.

7. Horton, ed., "Original Narrative," 4 ("a wide"); Jonas Harrison to Joseph Ellicott, June 25, 1814, HLCP, reel 9, BECHS; Ketchum, *History of Buffalo,* 2:414 and 419; Charles K. Gardner to Daniel Parker, July 17, 1814 ("I would rather"), DPP, box 3, HSP.

8. Rufus McIntire to John Holmes, Aug. 1, 1814 ("General Brown"), War of 1812 Coll., box 1, folder 2, AAS; Scott, *Memoirs,* 18–52 and 116–18; Morgan Lewis to John Armstrong, July 5, 1813, RG 107, M 222, reel 8, USNA; Benjamin F. Perry quoted in Graves, *Right and Glory,* 24–26 ("God"); T. D. Johnson, *Winfield Scott,* 9–18; Stagg, *Madison's War,* 370.

9. Winfield Scott to John Armstrong, May 17, 1814 ("broken"), RG 107, M 221, reel 57, USNA; John B. Murdock to Charles K. Gardner, May 26, 1814 ("General Scott"), CKGP, box 2, NYSL; Alexander McMullen, narrative, and Erastus Granger to Peter B. Porter, May 28, 1814, in *DHCNF,* 9:368–72 and 400; Scott, *Memoirs,* 1:119–21; Left Division, Order Book, May 31, 1814, and June 3, 1814, NYSL; Graves, *Right and Glory,* 28.

10. Winfield Scott to John Armstrong, May 17, 1814, RG 107, M 221, reel 57, USNA; Left Division, Order Book, Apr. 28, 1814 ("scrupulous"), June 2, 13, and 23, 1814, NYSL; Graves, *Right and Glory*, 27 and 45–46; Rufus MacIntire to John Holmes, Apr. 15, 1814 in Fredriksen, ed., "War of 1812 in Northern New York," 311; John B. Murdock to Charles K. Gardiner, May 26, 1814, CKGP, box 2, NYSL.

11. Alexander McMullen, narrative, in *DHCNF*, 9:372 ("constant exercise"); Fredriksen, ed., "Pennsylvania Volunteers," 149–50 ("regular troops"); Ketchum, *History of Buffalo*, 2:418.

12. Winfield Scott to John Armstrong, May 17, 1814, RG 107, M 221, reel 57, USNA; Peter B. Porter to Armstrong, Feb. 11, 1814, RG 107, M 221, reel 65, USNA; Porter to Daniel D. Tompkins, July 3, 1814, Porter to Jacob Brown, July 13, 1814, and July 29, 1814 ("assert its equal rights"), in *DHCNF-1814*, 2:26, 27, and 101; Porter and John Swift, "To the Inhabitants of the Western District," Mar. 25, 1814, manuscript #11202, NYSL; William B. Rochester to Porter, Apr. 22, 1814 ("Appeals"), PBPP, reel 2, BECHS; Porter to Nathan Williams, May 6, 1814, NWP, box 2, folder 91, OCHS.

13. Peter B. Porter to Jacob Brown, June 23, 1814, and Porter to Daniel D. Tompkins, July 3, 1814, in *DHCNF-1814*, 1:392, and 1:406, and 2:26; Fredriksen, ed., "Pennsylvania Volunteers," 126; Joseph Willcocks, morning report, July 14, 1814, PBPP, reel 3, BECHS.

14. Jacob Brown to John Armstrong, June 17, 1814 ("All private property"), RG 107, M 221, reel 59, USNA; Brown, general order, July 2, 1814 ("Profligate men"), in *DHCNF-1814*, 2:37; Graves, *Right and Glory*, 46–50.

15. John B. Campbell to John Armstrong, May 18, 1814, in Dudley, ed., *Naval War*, 3:486; Amelia Ryerse Harris, "Historical Memoranda," in Talman, ed., *Loyalist Narratives*, 147 (all quotations); Alexander McMullen, narrative, and Mathias Steele, deposition, May 31, 1814, in *DHCNF-1814*, 1:370–71 and 2:16–17; Thomas Talbot to Phineas Riall, May 16, 1814, in *SBD*, 3, part 1:88–90.

16. John B. Campbell to John Armstrong, May 18, 1814 ("I determined" and "we must"), and Arthur Sinclair to William Jones, May 19, 1814 ("old revolutionary Tories"), in Dudley, ed., *Naval War*, 3:486–87 and 488; S. White, *History of the American Troops*, 6–7; Robert R. Loring to E. B. Brenton, June 18, 1814, RG 5, 16:6840, reel C-4508, LAC; Cruikshank, "Study of Disaffection," 49.

17. Gordon Drummond to George Prevost, June 28, 1814, in *SBD*, 3, part 1:109; Campbell Court of Enquiry, June 20, 1814 ("admiration"), in *DHCNF-1814*, 2:18; Cruikshank, "The County of Norfolk," 33; Graves, *Right and Glory*, 41.

18. Thomas Sidney Jesup, "Memoir of the Campaign," TSJP, 1:183 ("If we could," "Every one," and "point"), LC; Hector Shields to David L. Shields, July 7, 1814 ("if I continue"), War of 1812 Coll., box 1, folder 1, AAS.

19. Thomas Sidney Jesup, "Memoir of the Campaign," TSJP, 1:185, LC; Scott, *Memoirs*, 1:123 ("had to swim"); Hector Shields to David L. Shields, July 7, 1814, War of 1812 Coll., box 1, folder 1, AAS; Peter B. Porter to William L. Stone, May 25, 1840, PBPP, reel 4, BECHS; Graves, *Right and Glory*, 75–77.

20. Phineas Riall to Gordon Drummond, July 6, 1814, and July 11, 1814, in *SBD*, 3, part 1:115–17 and 123–24; Horton, ed., "Original Narrative," 9.

21. Peter B. Porter to William Leete Stone, May 25, 1840 ("scenes"), PBPP, reel 4, BECHS; Graves, *Right and Glory*, 81–82; Benn, *Iroquois*, 160–62.

22. Peter B. Porter to Jacob Brown, c. July 10, 1814, in *DHCNF-1814*, 1:410–11; Gordon Drummond to George Prevost, July 10, 1814, and James Maclachlan to

Phineas Riall, July 12, 1814 ("their Troops"), in *SBD*, 3, part 1:121 and 136; Horton, ed., "Original Narrative," 9; Graves, *Right and Glory*, 82–89.

23. Phineas Riall to Gordon Drummond, July 6, 1814, and July 11, 1814, in *SBD*, 3, part 1:115–17 and 123–24; Cate, ed., "Benjamin Ropes' Autobiography," 119 ("the groans"); Graves, *Right and Glory*, 90 (includes Merritt quotation: "very unpleasant").

24. Peter B. Porter to William Leete Stone, May 25, 1840 ("the first decisive"), PBPP, reel 4, BECHS; Jacob Brown, general order, July 6, 1814, in *DHCNF-1814*, 1:412; Brown to Nathan Williams, July 10, 1814 ("fancy nothing"), JBP, 1:148, OCHS; Charles K. Gardner to Daniel Parker, July 17, 1814 ("most important" and "an assurance"), DPP, box 3, HSP; Scott, *Memoirs*, 1:133.

25. Jacob Brown to John Armstrong, July 7, 1814 ("every officer"), in *DHCNF-1814*, 2:40; Henry Leavenworth to Winfield Scott, July 24, 1814 ("My feelings"), TSJP, 1:202, LC; Brown to Armstrong, July 10, 1814, RG 107, M 221, reel 59, USNA; Graves, *Right and Glory*, 96–97.

26. Hector Shields to David L. Shields, July 7, 1814, War of 1812 Coll., box 1, folder 1, AAS; Horton, ed., "Original Narrative," 10 ("the beginning").

27. Indian interpreter Henry Johnson quoted in Peter B. Porter to William Leete Stone, May 25, 1840 ("that we ought"), PBPP, reel 4, BECHS; S. White, *History of the American Troops*, 18–21; Henry Bull to Charles K. Gardner, Oct. 24, 1814, CKGP, box 2, NYSL.

28. Jacob Brown, narrative, in *DHCNF-1814*, 2:464–65; Phineas Riall to Gordon Drummond, July 9, 1814, in *SBD*, 3, part 1:126; Benn, *Iroquois*, 165; Graves, *Right and Glory*, 93–95.

29. Left Division, Order Book, July 7, 12, and 14, 1814, NYSL; Phineas Riall to Gordon Drummond, July 17, 1814, Daniel McFarland to wife, undated, and Riall to Drummond, July 20, 1814, in *DHCNF-1814*, 2:70–71, 73, and 76; William H. Merritt, "Journal of Events," in *SBD*, 3, part 2: 617 ("daily skirmishing"); Scott, *Memoirs*, 1:138; Graves, *Right and Glory*, 97 and 99–100.

30. Phineas Riall to Gordon Drummond, July 15, 1814, and John G. P. Tucker to Riall, July 15, 1814 ("Canadian Militia"), in *DHCNF-1814*, 2:65 and 66; Gordon Drummond to George Prevost, July 10, 1814, and Riall to Drummond, July 19, 1814 ("almost the whole"), in *SBD*, 3, part 1:114 and 138.

31. Peter B. Porter, brigade orders, July 13, 1814 ("through the breast"), and Porter to Jacob Brown, July 16, 1814 ("the victims" and "were advised"), in *DHCNF-1814*, 2:63 and 68; Left Division, Order Book, July 13, 1814, NYSL.

32. David Secord, memorial, n.d., Daniel McFarland to wife, c. July 20, 1814, and Loyal and Patriotic Society, Report, 1816, in *DHCNF-1814*, 2:72, 73, and 324–27; *Buffalo Gazette*, July 26, 1814; "The Army," [Canandaigua, N.Y.] *Ontario Messenger*, July 26, 1814; Graves, *Right and Glory*, 100–101. For Stone, see O. Turner, *History of the Pioneer*, 585.

33. Left Division, Order Book, July 19, 1814, NYSL; Isaac W. Stone to David D. Tompkins, July 25, 1814, in *DHCNF-1814*, 2:74; Claudius V. Boughton to Peter B. Porter, n.d. but c. July 25, 1814 ("is tumbled"), PBPP, reel 3, BECHS.

34. Peter B. Porter, "Description of the Battle of Chippawa," in Hastings, ed., *Papers of Tompkins*, 1:91; Porter to William L. Stone, May 25, 1840, PBP, reel 4, BECHS; Jacob Brown, "Narrative," in *DHCNF-1814*, 2:465; Benn, *Iroquois*, 168.

35. Jacob Brown to John Armstrong, July 6, 1814, in *SBD*, 3, part 1:110–11; Brown to Isaac Chauncey, July 13, 1814, in *DHCNF-1814*, 2:64; Graves, *Right and Glory*, 97–98.

36. Isaac Chauncey to William Jones, Dec. 17, 1813, in *DHCNF-1814*, 2:5; Chauncey to Jones, Mar. 15, 1814 ("expected Contest"), and Mar. 30, 1814, in Dudley, ed., *Naval War*, 3:406 and 412; Malcomson, *Lords*, 288.

37. Isaac Chauncey to William Jones, Apr. 11, 1814, in *DHCNF-1814*, 1:287–88; Jones to James Madison, May 25, 1814 ("one fourth"), and Chauncey to Jones, June 15, 1814, in Dudley, ed., *Naval War*, 3:496 and 522–23; Malcomson, *Lords*, 250–54.

38. Isaac Chauncey to Jacob Brown, June 25, 1814, in Dudley, ed., *Naval War* 3: 527; Chauncey to Brown, Aug. 10, 1814 ("higher destiny" and "a convenience"), in *DHCNF-1814*, 2:130.

39. Anonymous to John Armstrong, July 20, 1814 ("a fine opportunity"), and Jacob Brown to Armstrong, July 25, 1814, in *DHCNF-1814*, 2:77 and 87; E. P. Gaines to Armstrong, July 23, 1814, RG 107, M221, reel 61, USNA; William Jones to Isaac Chauncey, Aug. 3, 1814, in Dudley, ed., *Naval War*, 3:556–57; Malcomson, *Lords*, 290.

40. Gordon Drummond to George Prevost, July 16, 1814 ("the decided" and "extraordinary"), Phineas Riall to Drummond, July 12, 16, and 21, 1814, Drummond to Prevost, July 24, 1814, and Jacob Brown to John Armstrong, c. July 27, 1814, in *SBD*, 3, part 1:132–33, 133–34, 137, 140–41, 144, and 157–58.

41. Graves, *Right and Glory*, 107–41; Quimby, *U.S. Army*, 2:532–38 and 544.

42. Jacob Brown to John Armstrong, July 27, 1814, in *SBD*, 3, part 1:159–60; Graves, ed., *Merry Hearts*, 178 ("from going"); Graves, *Right and Glory*, 142–81; Quimby, *U.S. Army*, 2:538–40.

43. Jacob Brown to John Armstrong, July 27, 1814, in *SBD*, 3, part 1:159–60; Thomas Sidney Jesup, "Memoir of the Campaign," TSJP, 1:194, LC; Graves, *Right and Glory*, 182–88; Quimby, *U.S. Army*, 2:541–42.

44. Graves, ed., *Merry Hearts*, 179 (all quotations); Graves, *Right and Glory*, 186–88.

45. Gordon Drummond to George Prevost, July 27, 1814, MG 11, 355:136, reel B-295, LAC; Jacob Brown to John Armstrong, c. July 27, 1814, in *SBD*, 3, part 1:161; Brown, "Narrative," in *DHCNF-1814*, 2:472–73; Graves, *Right and Glory*, 190–92; Quimby, *U.S. Army*, 2:541–43.

46. Alexander McMullen, "Narrative," in *DHCNF-1814*, 2:377 ("slow," "shattered," "lay down," and "of all nights"); Graves, *Right and Glory*, 190–92; Quimby, *U.S. Army*, 2:541–43.

47. Jacob Brown to John Armstrong, c. July 27, 1814, in *SBD*, 3, part 1:164; Graves, *Right and Glory*, 195–99; Quimby, *U.S. Army*, 2:544.

48. E. W. Bull to unknown, July 31, 1814 ("scene of carnage"), in *DHCNF-1814*, 2:104; Lord, ed., "War of 1812," 209; Graves, *Right and Glory*, 188–89.

49. Dunlop, "Recollections," 34–35 ("an Army Surgeon" and "The weather"); Graves, *Right and Glory*, 197–204; Douglas, *Medical Topography*, 31–32.

50. Richard Goodsell, Jr., to Richard Goodsell, Aug. 3, 1814, Misc. Mss., Goodsell Folder, NYHS; Eleazar W. Ripley, brigade order, July 28, 1814 ("died on the field"), in *DHCNF-1814*, 2:420; Charles K. Gardner to Daniel Parker, July 29, 1814 ("Our victory" and "the slaughter"), DPP, box 3, HSP.

51. Thomas Sidney Jesup, "Memoir of the Campaign," TSJP, 1:196, LC; Peter B. Porter to Daniel D. Tompkins, July 29, 1814, and Jacob Brown, "Narrative," in *DHCNF-1814*, 2:101 and 472–73; Brown to John Armstrong, Aug. 7, 1814, in Dudley, ed., *Naval War*, 3:577–79; Eleazar W. Ripley to James Monroe, Sept. 4, 1814; RG 107, M 221, reel 65, USNA; Quimby, *U.S. Army*, 2:544–45.

52. Peter B. Porter to Daniel D. Tompkins, Aug. 9, 1814 ("Our position"), in *DHCNF-1814*, 2:431; Graves, *Right and Glory*, 211–16.

53. Gordon Drummond to George Prevost, Aug. 4, 1814, and John G. P. Tucker to General Conran, Aug. 4, 1814, in *SBD*, 3, part 1:167–68 and 177–78; Drummond, general order, Aug. 5, 1814 ("Crouching" and "the duty"), in *DHCNF-1814*, 2:427; Fredriksen, *Green Coats*, 56–58; Graves, *Right and Glory*, 214–15.

54. Dunlop, "Recollections," 40–41; Gordon Drummond to George Prevost, Aug. 15, 1814, in *SBD*, 3, part 1:178; Edmund P. Gaines to John Armstrong, Aug. 23, 1814, in *DHCNF-1814*, 2:152–53; Quimby, *U.S. Army*, 2:550–51; Graves, *Right and Glory*, 216–18.

55. Gordon Drummond to George Prevost, Aug. 15, 1814, and Drummond to Victor Fischer, Aug. 14, 1814 ("valuable weapon"), in *SBD*, 2, part 1:178–79, and 185–87; Dunlop, "Recollections," 51; Quimby, *U.S. Army*, 2:551.

56. Victor Fischer to John Harvey, Aug. 15, 1814, in *SBD*, 3, part 1:188–89; Graves, ed., *Merry Hearts*, 189; Quimby, *U.S. Army*, 2:551–53.

57. Hanks, "Memoir," in Graves, ed., *Soldiers of 1814*, 39; Edmund P. Gaines to John Armstrong, Aug. 23, 1814, in *DHCNF-1814*, 2:54–56; Graves, *Right and Glory*, 220.

58. Horton, ed., "Original Narrative," 29 ("every sound" and "the centre"); unnamed American quoted in Graves, *Right and Glory*, 220 ("cartridge boxes"); Hanks, "Memoir," in Graves, ed., *Soldiers of 1814*, 39; Quimby, *U.S. Army*, 2:554.

59. Graves, ed., *Merry Hearts*, 189–91 ("roasted" and "I found"); Dunlop, "Recollections," 53 ("along the road"); Graves, *Right and Glory*, 220.

60. Hanks, "Memoir," in Graves, ed., *Soldiers of 1814*, 39–40 ("legs"); Joseph B. Varnum to A. Bradley, Aug. 15, 1814 ("I never"), RG 107, M 222, reel 11, USNA; Gordon Drummond to George Prevost, Aug. 16, 1814, in *SBD*, 3, part 1:192–93; Graves, *Right and Glory*, 220–21; Quimby, *U.S. Army*, 2:554–55.

61. Gordon Drummond to George Prevost, Aug. 15, 1814, and Aug. 16, 1814 ("agony "), in *SBD*, 3, part 1:178–80 and 189–91; Edmund P. Gaines to John Armstrong, Aug. 23, 1814, in *DHCNF-1814*, 2:151–52; Dunlop, "Recollections," 39; John Harvey, "Journal of a Staff Officer," 114, AO; Graves, *Right and Glory*, 220–21.

62. For British explanations, see Edward McMahon to William Jarvis, Aug. 22, 1814, in *DHCNF-1814*, 2:167; R. E. Armstrong to Hugh Swayne, Sept. 1, 1814, in Stacey, ed., "Upper Canada at War," 41–42. For American explanations, see O'Reilly, "One of Philadelphia's Soldiers," 303; Hanks, "Memoir," in Graves, ed., *Soldiers of 1814*, 39.

63. Peter B. Porter to Jacob Brown, July 28, 1814, and A. Matteson to Eleazar W. Ripley, Sept. 5, 1814 ("Of Col. Willcocks"), and Ripley, General Order, Sept. 6, 1814, in *DHCNF-1814*, 2:194, 418, and 445–46; Ripley to John Armstrong, Aug. 25, 1814, RG 107, M 221, reel 65, USNA; "The Late Colonel Wilcocks," [New York] *Shamrock*, Nov. 19, 1814 ("ardent friend" and "member of"); Dunlop, "Recollections," 48; Quimby, *U.S. Army*, 2:548–50 and 557–58; Fredriksen, *Green Coats*, 58–59.

64. John Harvey, "Journal of a Staff Officer," 115, AO; Harvey to John Strachan, Sept. 8, 1814 ("Arch Rebel"), Strachan Papers, reel MS-35, AO; Barrett, *Journal*, 105; Cruikshank, "Study of Disaffection," 51.

65. Gordon Drummond to George Prevost, Aug. 12, 1814 ("prompt acquiescence"), in *DHCNF-1814*, 1:134; Samuel D. Harris to brother, Aug. 31, 1814 ("enveloping" and "Miserably bruised"), Harris folder, BECHS; Eleazar W. Ripley to

James Monroe, Sept. 4, 1814 ("Nothing saves"), RG 107, M 221, reel 65, USNA; Graves, *Right and Glory*, 221–22; Quimby, *U.S. Army*, 2:557–58.

66. Jacob Brown to Daniel D. Tompkins, Aug. 1, 1814, in *DHCNF-1814*, 1:103–4; Eleazar W. Ripley to James Monroe, Sept. 4, 1814 ("No Military man"), RG 107, M 221, reel 65, USNA; Quimby, *U.S. Army*, 2:557–58.

67. Jacob Brown to Daniel D. Tompkins, Aug. 1, 1814, in *DHCNF-1814*, 1:103; Peter B. Porter to Tompkins, Aug. 9, 1814, Edmund P. Gaines to Porter, Aug. 16, 1814, and Porter to the militia of the western counties, Aug. 21, 1814 ("the moment" and "That army"), in *DHCNF-1814*, 2:431, 433, and 436–37.

68. Peter B. Porter, general order, Sept. 4, 1814, *Buffalo Gazette*, Sept. 20, 1814, Jacob Brown to George Izard, Sept. 10, 1814, George Fleming to Porter, Sept. 4, 1814 ("The Militia"), and Porter, general order, Sept. 8, Brown to Porter, Sept. 8, 1814, and Porter, general order, Sept. 11, 1814, in *DHCNF-1814*, 1:197, 2:444, 2:448–49, 2:450, and 2:451.

69. Harvey, "Journal of a Staff Officer," 111, AO; James Commins to Mr. Davidson, Aug. 28, 1815 ("obliged"), in Lord, ed., "War of 1812," 211; Gordon Drummond to George Prevost, Aug. 21, 1814, Aug. 24, 1814, Sept. 11, 1814, and Sept. 14, 1814, in *DHCNF-1814*, 1:185, 186, 198–99, and 200; Drummond to Prevost, Sept. 21, 1814 ("Camp"), MG 11, 355:158, reel B-295, LAC; Dunlop, "Recollections," 37–39; Douglas, *Medical Topography*, 26.

70. Jacob Brown, "Memoranda of Occurrences" ("would prefer" and "to make"), GP, box 1, BECHS; Graves, *Right and Glory*, 225–26; Quimby, *U.S. Army*, 2: 559–61.

71. Louis de Watteville to Gordon Drummond, Sept. 19, 1814, in *SBD*, 3, part 1:196–98; Drummond to George Prevost, Sept. 19, 1814, MG 11, 355:152, reel B-295, LAC; Jacob Brown to John Armstrong, Sept. 18, 1814, Brown to Daniel D. Tompkins, Sept. 20, 1814, and Peter B. Porter to Brown, Sept. 23, 1814, in *DHCNF-1814*, 1:206, 207, and 208–9; Graves, *Right and Glory*, 226–27; Quimby, *U.S. Army*, 2:564–66.

72. Jacob Brown to Daniel D. Tompkins, Sept. 20, 1814 ("The militia" and "good conduct"), in *DHCNF-1814*, 1:207; Brown to Nathan Williams, Nov. 27, 1814, JBP, 1:158, OCHS; Brown to Ambrose Spencer, Nov. 27, 1814 ("He *drinks*"), Gratz Coll., box 32, HSP; Hitsman, *Incredible War*, 240–45.

73. Fredriksen, "George Izard," *ANB*, 11:728–30; Fredriksen, ed., "Georgia Officer," 687–89; George Izard to James Monroe, Sept. 28 and Oct. 7, 1814, in *DHCNF-1814*, 2:233–34 and 241; Jonas Harrison to Joseph Ellicott, Oct. 30, 1814 ("meandering"), HLCP, reel 9, BECHS; Graves, *Right and Glory*, 227–28; Quimby, *U.S. Army*, 2:566–569.

74. George Izard to John Armstrong, Aug. 11, 1813, RG 107, M 221, reel 62, USNA; Alexander Macomb to James Monroe, Sept. 15, 1814, in *SBD*, 3, part 1:358–60; Hickey, *Don't Give Up the Ship!* 75–76; Quimby, *U.S. Army*, 2:598–600 and 604–33.

75. Alicia Cockburn to Charles Sandys, Oct. 20, 1814, and "A Free Speaker," and "Englishman," *Halifax Gazette*, Oct. 1, 1814 ("true republicans"), in *SBD*, 3, part 1:387–90 and 391; "The Old Soldier, *Canadian Courant*, Dec. 3, 1814; Malcolmson, *Lords*, 316–17; Latimer, *War of 1812*, 354 and 359–60; Quimby, *U.S. Army*, 2:629–33.

76. George Izard to James Monroe, Oct. 16, 1814, and Oct. 23, 1814, in *DHCNF-1814*, 2:254–56 and 275; Daniel Bissel to Izard, Oct. 22, 1814, and Izard to James Monroe, Dec. 16, 1814 ("so distant" and "thinly settled"), RG 107, M 221, reel 62, USNA; Graves, *Right and Glory*, 228–29; Quimby, *U.S. Army*, 2:570–73.

77. Peter B. Porter, general order, Nov. 2, 1814, in *DHCNF,* 2:283–84; Jacob Brown to Nathan Williams, Nov. 2, 1814 ("Chauncey will"), JBP, 1:156, OCHS; Brown to Ambrose Spencer, Nov. 27, 1814 ("We of course"), Gratz Coll., box 32, HSP; Malcomson, *Lords,* 293.

78. John McMillan court-martial, Oct. 25–27, 1814, RG 9, I-B-1, box 3, Lincoln County folder, LAC; Gordon Drummond, militia general order, Oct. 28, 1814, in *DHCNF-1814,* 2:279; Couture, *Study,* 111; Graves, "Canadian Volunteers," 116.

79. George Izard to James Monroe, Nov. 2, 1814, and Nov. 8, 1814, and S. Romilly to Drummond, Nov. 10, 1814 ("Snake Hill"), in *DHCNF-1814,* 2:284–86, 298, and 299; Jacob P. Norton to his father, Nov. 12, 1814 ("The explosion"), in D. Porter, ed., "Jacob Porter Norton," 54; Quimby, *U.S. Army,* 2:573.

80. William H. Merritt, "Journal of Events," in *SBD,* 3, part 2:645 ("The campaign"); Gordon Drummond to Lord Bathurst, Nov. 20, 1814, MG 11, 355:124, reel B-295, LAC; Graves, *Right and Glory,* 231–33.

81. John Walworth to Jonas Simonds, Sept. 6, 1814, MG 24, F 16 (Simonds fonds), one folder, LAC; James Curry to Duncan McArthur, Sept. 25, 1814 ("The business"), DMP, 16:3087, LC; "An American Soldier," *Buffalo Gazette,* Oct. 4, 1814; John C. Calhoun, speech, Oct. 25, 1814, in Meriwether et al., eds., *Papers of Calhoun,* 1:257–58.

82. John Armstrong to Jacob Brown, Aug. 7, 1814 ("You have"), in Edmund Kirby, orderly book, GP, box 2, BECHS; Thomas S. Jesup to unknown, Sept. 8, 1814, TSJP, 1:220, LC.

83. James Miller to wife, Sept. 19, 1814 ("every major"), in *DHCNF-1814,* 2:223.

84. Dunlop, "Recollections," 35 (all quotations).

85. Gordon Drummond to George Prevost, Nov. 5, 1814, MG 11, 355:179, reel B-295, LAC.

86. George Izard to James Monroe, Oct. 16, 1814, in *DHCNF-1814,* 2:254; Izard, general orders, Oct. 16 and Nov. 2, 1814, in James Preston/James Paxton Order Book, PFP, 8D:141, LC. For the absence of other punishments for crimes against Canadians, see Orderly Book of a Rifle Detachment, 1813–15, RG 98, vol. 439, USNA. Covering October–December 1814, this orderly book records many prosecutions and punishments of common soldiers for stealing from civilians in Buffalo but none for stealing when in Canada.

87. A. S. Langhan to William Bradford, Dec. 11, 1814 ("we have nothing" and "our late movements"), DMP, 20:3896, LC; George Izard to James Monroe, Nov. 26 and Dec. 16, 1814, RG 107, M 221, reel 62, USNA.

88. Jacob Brown to John Armstrong, Nov. 2, 1814 ("a few brave men"), quoted in Barbuto, *Niagara,* 318; Brown to Nathan Williams, Sept. 13, 1814 ("We have been"), Nov. 27 and Dec. 14, 1814, JBP, 1:154 and 160, OCHS; Brown to Moss Kent, Sept. 24, 1814, and Brown to Ambrose Spencer, Nov. 27, 1814, Gratz Coll., box 32, HSP.

89. For the backbiting, see Eleazar W. Ripley to James Monroe, Sept. 15, 1814, and Daniel Parker, general order, Mar. 4, 1815, RG 107, M 221, reel 65, USNA; Jacob Brown to Nathan Williams, Sept. 23, 1815, JBP, 1:166, OCHS; [Charles K. Gardner], "An Officer," *Buffalo Gazette,* July 29, 1815; Graves, *Right and Glory,* 239–40 and 242–43. For celebration of the Niagara campaign for developing better military leadership, see Quimby, *U.S. Army,* 2:578–79; Barbuto, *Niagara,* xii–xiii, 314–15, and 318–19.

90. Gordon Drummond to George Prevost, July 27, 1814, MG 11, 355:136, reel B-295, LAC; Hickey, *War of 1812,* 309.

Chapter Fifteen: Peace

1. Robert McDouall to Frederick P. Robinson, Oct. 4, 1815, in MPHS, *MHC*, 16:310.

2. J. J. Talman, "William Hamilton Merritt," *DCB*, 9:544; William H. Merritt to Catherine Prendergast, Feb. 9, 1814 ("this unnatural" and "I am grieved"), WHMP, reel MS-74 (5), AO.

3. William H. Merritt to Catherine Prendergast, Feb. 9, 1814, Merritt to Prendergast, Aug. 6, 1814, Prendergast to Merritt, Aug. 13, 1814 ("*despotic* governments"), and Merritt to Prendergast, Oct. 29, 1814 ("You accuse" and "magnanimous"), WHMP, reel MS-74 (5), AO.

4. William H. Merritt to Catherine Prendergast, July 27, 1814, Aug. 9, 1814, Dec. 11, 1814, and Dec. 23, 1814 ("desert"), WHMP, reel MS-74 (5), AO; J. J. Talman, "William Hamilton Merritt," *DCB*, 9:544.

5. Catherine Prendergast to William H. Merritt, Jan. 12, 1815 ("Situated"), Merritt to Prendergast, Feb. 10, 1815, WHMP, reel MS-74 (5), AO.

6. J. Gordon to Catherine Prendergast Merritt, Apr. 8, 1815, and Penelope Prendergast to C. P. Merritt, May 30, 1815, WHMP, reel MS-74 (5), AO; Tallman, "William Hamilton Merritt," *DCB*, 9:544; Graves, *Midst of Alarms*, 80–81.

7. Harrison, ed., *Philadelphia Merchant*, 290 ("principal subject"); James Madison to Congress, Nov. 4, 1812, in *PJM-PS*, 5:430; James Monroe to Thomas Jefferson, Nov. 11, 1812, in S. M. Hamilton, ed., *Writings of Monroe*, 5: 226–27; Viscount Castlereagh quoted in Reuben G. Beasley to Monroe, Nov. 19, 1812 ("as England"), RG 59, T 168, reel 10, USNA; Perkins, *Castlereagh and Adams*, 3–4, and 10–16; Hickey, *War of 1812*, 282–83; Stagg, *Madison's War*, 508.

8. James Monroe to John Borlase Warren, Oct. 27, 1812, in [Philadelphia] *Aurora*, Nov. 7, 1812; Felix Grundy, speech, Jan. 15, 1814, *AC*, 13th Congress, 2d session, 991; Monroe to Albert Gallatin, May 6, 1813, in S. M. Hamilton, ed., *Writings of Monroe*, 5:256–58; Stagg, *Madison's War*, 295–97; Perkins, *Castlereagh and Adams*, 14–16 and 51–52.

9. Hickey, *War of 1812*, 283–85; Jenkins, *Henry Goulburn*, 82; Latimer, *1812*, 222–23; Perkins, *Castlereagh and Adams*, 20–22 and 39–42.

10. Henry Goulburn, "Memoirs," in W. D. Jones, ed., "British View," 486 ("unprovoked aggression"); Jenkins, *Henry Goulburn*, 77–81 and 84–85; Latimer, *1812*, 361; Perkins, *Castlereagh and Adams*, 59–61.

11. James Monroe to Albert Gallatin, May 5, 1813, and Monroe to James A. Bayard, May 6, 1813, in S. M. Hamilton, ed., *Writings of Monroe*, 5:252–53 and 254; Monroe, instructions, Jan. 28, 1814 ("degrading practice"), in Hopkins et al., eds., *Papers of Clay*, 1:857; Monroe to Gallatin and Bayard, June 23, 1813, in Donnan, ed., "Papers of Bayard," 2:227–28.

12. James A. Bayard to Henry Clay, Apr. 22, 1814, and Albert Gallatin to Clay, Apr. 22, 1814, in Hopkins et al., eds., *Papers of Clay*, 1:882 and 884; Jenkins, *Henry Goulburn*, 82–83; Perkins, *Castlereagh and Adams*, 25, 44, 56–57, and 62–63; Stagg, *Madison's War*, 392–93.

13. Perkins, *Castlereagh and Adams*, 53; Stagg, *Madison's War*, 394–95.

14. Henry Clay, Journal, Aug. 7–8, 1814, in Hopkins et al., eds., *Papers of Clay*, 1:953; Burt, *United States*, 351; Jenkins, *Henry Goulburn*, 83; Latimer, *1812*, 362–63; Perkins, *Castlereagh and Adams*, 63–69; Stagg, *Madison's War*, 395.

15. Isaac Brock to George Prevost, Sept. 28, 1812, and Prevost to Lord Bathurst,

Oct. 5, 1812, in *DHCNF,* 3:299 and 4:36–38; Prevost to Bathurst, July 10, 1814, MPHS, *MHC,* 25:584–85; Prevost to Robert Dickson, Jan. 14, 1813, and Robert McDouall, speech, June 5, 1814, in Esarey, ed., *Messages and Letters,* 2:618–19 and 653–55; "Peace with America," *Quebec Gazette,* June 8, 1814.

16. Henry Clay, Journal, Aug. 7–8 and 19, 1814, British commissioners to American commissioners, Sept. 19, 1814, and American commissioners to British commissioners, Sept. 26, 1814, in Hopkins et al., eds., *Papers of Clay,* 1:953, 969–70, 978, and 980; John Quincy Adams to James Monroe, Sept. 5, 1814, American commissioners to British commissioners, Sept. 25, 1814, and reply, Oct. 8, 1814, in Manning, ed., *Diplomatic Correspondence,* 1:647–48, 665, and 672; Nevins, ed., *Diary of John Quincy Adams,* 126–27, 131 ("American Government"), 134, and 138–39; Perkins, *Castlereagh and Adams,* 74–77 and 103–4.

17. Henry Clay to James Monroe, Aug. 18, 1814 ("savage tribes"), and British commissioners to American commissioners, Sept. 4, 1814, in Hopkins et al., eds., *Papers of Clay,* 1:963–65 and 973; American commissioners to British commissioners, Sept. 25, 1814, in Manning, ed., *Diplomatic Correspondence,* 1:665–66; Nevins, ed., *Diary of John Quincy Adams,* 124–25, 131–32 ("To condemn" and "a feather"), and 136–37; Henry Goulburn quoted in Jenkins, *Henry Goulburn,* 86 ("till I came"); Perkins, *Castlereagh and Adams,* 88.

18. James Monroe to William B. Giles, Oct. 17, 1814 ("the object" and "relinquish no right"), in *ASP-MA,* 1:514–17; John C. Calhoun, speech, Oct. 25, 1814, in Meriwether et al., eds., *Papers of Calhoun,* 1:258–59; Hickey, *War of 1812,* 237–38 and 291; Perkins, *Castlereagh and Adams,* 79, 100, and 112.

19. Nathan Ford to David Ford, Sept. 3, 1814, FFP, reel MS-7695, AO; Horsman, "Nantucket's Peace Treaty," 180–98; Andrews, *Prisoners' Memoirs,* 144–45; Hickey, *War of 1812,* 215–16.

20. Buel, *America on the Brink,* 219–22; Hickey, *War of 1812,* 269–74.

21. James Monroe to Daniel D. Tompkins, Nov. 26, 1814, and Monroe to Thomas S. Jesup, Nov. 26, 1814, RG 107, M 7, reel 1, USNA; Jesup to Monroe, Dec. 31, 1814, and Jan. 2, 1815 ("We should"), RG 107, M 221, reel 63, USNA.

22. Buel, *America on the Brink,* 226–29; Hickey, *War of 1812,* 275–78; Latimer, *1812,* 367.

23. Hickey, *War of 1812,* 233 and 235; Skeen, *John Armstrong,* 198–204; Stagg, *Madison's War,* 428–32.

24. Hickey, *War of 1812,* 222–25, 231, and 247–51; Stagg, *Madison's War,* 426–27.

25. Duncan McArthur to James Monroe, Jan. 14, 1815, Monroe to McArthur, Jan. 17, 1815, and Benjamin F. Stickney to McArthur, Jan. 17, 1815, DMP, 22:4177, 4193, and 4196, LC; Anthony Butler to McArthur, Feb. 12, 1815 ("wretched situation"), DMP, 23:4451, LC; Thomas Melville, Jr., to John Mason, Oct. 19, 1814, RG 94, ser. 127, box 9, folder 1, USNA; Melville to Mason, Jan. 13, 1815, RG 94, ser. 127, box 20, folder 5, USNA.

26. Morris S. Miller to Jacobus S. Bruyn, Nov. 30, 1814, M.S. Miller file, NYHS; Hickey, *War of 1812,* 221–22 and 241–44.

27. Anonymous to John E. Wool, July 4, 1814 ("Men's Souls"), JEWP, box 7, NYSL; William North to William Eustis, Aug. 28, 1814, ms #14492, NYSL; Lewis Cass to Duncan McArthur, Jan. 13, 1815, and McArthur to Cass, Jan. 22, 1815, DMP, 21:4163 and 4248, LC; Stagg, *Madison's War,* 503.

28. Henry Goulburn to Henry Clay, Oct. 3, 1814 ("Brussels"), and Clay to William H. Crawford, Oct. 17, 1814 ("I tremble"), in Hopkins et al., eds., *Papers of*

Clay, 1:982 and 989; Nevins, ed., *Diary of John Quincy Adams,* 139; Perkins, *Castlereagh and Adams,* 95–98.

29. Henry Goulburn, "Memoirs," in Jones, ed., "British View," 486; Lord Liverpool quoted in Hickey, *War of 1812,* 292 ("inconvenience"); Jenkins, *Henry Goulburn,* 86–87; Perkins, *Castlereagh and Adams,* 99–109; Hitsman, *Safeguarding Canada,* 109.

30. American commissioners to British commissioners, Nov. 10, 1814, and Albert Gallatin to James Monroe, Dec. 25, 1814 ("I really think"), in Manning, ed., *Diplomatic Correspondence,* 1:687–96 and 709; Jenkins, *Henry Goulburn,* 86–87; Perkins, *Castlereagh and Adams,* 85–90 and 128 (Edward Cooke quoted: "to return").

31. James Monroe, instructions, Apr. 15, 1813, in Donnan, ed., "Papers of Bayard," 2:204–5; American commissioners to British commissioners, Nov. 10, 1814, in Manning, ed., *Diplomatic Correspondence,* 1:687–96; Perkins, *Castlereagh and Adams,* 120–21.

32. Nevins, ed., *Diary of John Quincy Adams,* 144; Hickey, *War of 1812,* 294–96; Jenkins, *Henry Goulburn,* 87–88; Perkins, *Castlereagh and Adams,* 103–6 and 117–21.

33. Carroll, *Good and Wise Measure,* 29; Perkins, *Castlereagh and Adams,* 126–28; Hickey, *War of 1812,* 295–96.

34. Henry Clay to James Monroe, Dec. 25, 1814 ("undoubtedly"), in Hopkins et al., eds., *Papers of Clay,* 1:1007.

35. Hickey, *War of 1812,* 295–97 (296 includes Viscount Castlereagh quotation: "released"); Jenkins, *Henry Goulburn,* 88–89; Perkins, *Castlereagh and Adams,* 128 and 132–36.

36. Hickey, *War of 1812,* 297–98; Perkins, *Castlereagh and Adams,* 138–42.

37. Fredriksen, ed., " 'Poor but Honest Sodger,' " 152; Rufus McIntire to John Holmes, Mar. 4, 1815, War of 1812 Coll., box 1, folder 2, AAS; Graves, ed., *Merry Hearts,* 222 ("Several American officers") and 223–24 ("a hot"); Butler Cocke to Alexander J. Dallas, June 20, 1815, RG 107, M 221, reel 60, USNA.

38. Thomas P. Cope, diary, Feb. 12, 1815 ("cheering" and "continuation"), Feb. 16, 1815, and Feb. 17,1815 ("public manifestations"), in Harrison, ed., *Philadelphia Merchant,* 303–4; Leverett Saltonstall to Nathaniel Saltonstall, Feb. 18, 1815 ("Our Town"), in Moody, ed., *Saltonstall Papers,* 2:569; Hickey, *War of 1812,* 297–98; Perkins, *Castlereagh and Adams,* 138–42.

39. Hickey, *War of 1812,* 298–99 (includes quotations from James Robertson to Timothy Pickering, Feb. 14, 1815—"a war"—and from James Madison to Congress, Feb. 18, 1815—"an event") and 308 (Federalist quoted: "attempted"); Perkins, *Castlereagh and Adams,* 145–47.

40. Daniel D. Tompkins to the New York State Legislature, Feb. 21, 1815, in Hastings, ed., *Papers of Tompkins,* 3:638; James Monroe to Winfield Scott, Feb. 21, 1815, RG 107, M 7, reel 1, USNA; Monroe to the United States Senate, Feb. 22, 1815 ("our Union" and "By the war"), in S. M. Hamilton, ed., *Writings of Monroe,* 5:321–22.

41. Hickey, *War of 1812,* 211–13; Latimer, *1812,* 381–88; Quimby, *U.S. Army,* 2:897–919.

42. Bellesiles, "Experiencing the War," 227–28; Hickey, *War of 1812,* 211–12; Hickey, *Don't Give Up the Ship!* 284–85; Quimby, *U.S. Army,* 2:916–17.

43. For the persistent myth that the battle was fought after the peace, see Latimer, *1812,* 388. For the reality, see Hickey, *Don't Give Up the Ship!* 278 and 295–96; Quimby, *U.S. Army,* 2:937–38.

44. Waterhouse, ed., *Journal,* 216 ("Nothing now").

45. Buel, *America on the Brink*, 229–34; Hickey, *War of 1812*, 279–80 and 308–9; Latimer, *1812*, 399–400; Quimby, *U.S. Army*, 2:938.

46. Perkins, *Castlereagh and Adams*, 175–76; Hickey, *War of 1812*, 307–8 (includes Joseph Story quotation: "Never").

47. Fredriksen, ed., " 'Poor But Honest Sodger,' " 152 and 161; Porter, ed., "Jacob Porter Norton," 56; Jacobs, *Tarnished Warrior*, 314–16; Skelton, *American Profession of Arms*, 62–63; Skelton, "High Army Leadership," 271–73.

48. Abraham Markle to James Monroe, Feb. 24, 1815, and Peter B. Porter to Monroe, Feb. 27, 1815, RG 107, M 221, reel 65, USNA; Markle to Porter, Feb. 24, 1816, PBPP, reel 3, BECHS; D. R. Beasley, "Andrew Westbrook," *DCB*, 6:809; Robert Lochiel Fraser, "Abraham Markle," *DCB*, 6:490–91; Fraser, "Benajah Mallory," *DCB*, 8:609.

49. John Mason to marshal of Virginia, Feb. 22, 1815, and Mason to marshal of North Carolina, Mar. 14, 1815 ("From the disposition"), RG 45, ser. RE 1812–15, box 593, folder 3, USNA; Thomas Melville, Jr., to George Prevost, Mar. 5, 1815, and Melville to John Mason, Mar. 13, 1815, RG 94, ser. 127, box 20, folder 3, USNA. For the escape from the Baltimore jail, see John S. Skinner to Mason, Mar. 7, 1815, and Apr. 20, 1815, RG 45, ser. RE 1812–15, box 593, folders 4 and 5.

50. Waterhouse, ed., *Journal*, 186 ("momentary stupor") and 217–19; Hawthorne, ed., *Yarn*, 261–62; Reuben G. Beasley to John Mason, Feb. 10, 1815, and Beasley to Thomas G. Shortland, Mar. 31, 1815, RG 94, ser. 127, box 9, folder 4, USNA; Perkins, *Castlereagh and Adams*, 165; Dye, "American Maritime Prisoners," 306–8.

51. Hawthorne, ed., *Yarn*, 273–79; Waterhouse, ed., *Journal*, 239–47; Perkins, *Castlereagh and Adams*, 165.

52. Reuben G. Beasley to John Mason, Apr. 19, 1815, RG 94, ser. 127, box 9, folder 4, USNA; Hawthorne, ed., *Yarn*, 283–87; Waterhouse, ed., *Journal*, 222–23, 235–36, and 239–56; Perkins, *Castlereagh and Adams*, 165–66; Hickey, *War of 1812*, 306.

53. Reuben G. Beasley to John Mason, Apr. 30, 1815, and Beasley, undated table of released prisoners, RG 94, ser. 127, box 9, folder 4, USNA; Beasley to Mason, June 10, 1815, RG 94, ser. 127, box 7, folder 2, USNA; John Odiorne to Mason, June 10, 1815, and Beasley to Mason, Apr. 15, 1815, RG 94, ser. 127, box 3, folders 2 and 5, USNA; Andrews, *Prisoners' Memoirs*, 220; Hawthorne, ed., *Yarn*, 288–89, 292–94, and 300–305; Dye, "American Maritime Prisoners," 308.

54. W. Scott, *Memoirs*, 81; "Shipping News," *New-York Evening Post*, Aug. 12, 1815; G. W. Gardner, certificate, Aug. 10, 1815, RG 45, ser. 464-RV, box 566, folder 5, USNA. Scott's version has misled subsequent scholars, including Robinson, "Retaliation," 70.

55. Jacob Brown to Nathan Williams, Mar. 30, 1815, JJBP, 1:4, OCHS; Einstein, ed., "Recollections," 75–77 ("came on deck"); Isaac Chauncey to James L. Yeo, Mar. 3, 1815, in Dudley, ed., *Naval War*, 3:698; Malcomson, *Lords*, 320–21.

56. Lord Bathurst to Gordon Drummond, Jan. 10, 1815, and Robert McDouall to Colley Foster, May 15, 1815, in *SBD*, 3, part 1:507–8 and 534–35; William McGillivray to John Harvey, Apr. 19, 1815, and Black Hawk, speech, Aug. 3, 1815, in MPHS, *MHC*, 16:76 and 196; R. Allen, *His Majesty's Indian Allies*, 168 and 175–76 (Little Crow quoted: "After we"); Calloway, "End of an Era," 1–4 and 11–18.

57. William McGillivray and John Richardson to Gordon Drummond, Apr. 20, 1815, John Harvey to McGillivray and Richardson, Apr. 24, 1815, and Robert McDouall to Frederick P. Robinson, Oct. 4, 1815 ("Enigma"), in MPHS, *MHC*,

16:77–80, 80–81, and 310; McDouall to Colley Foster, May 15, 1815, in *SBD*, 3, part 1: 535; James Monroe to John Quincy Adams, July 21, 1815, in Manning, ed., *Diplomatic Correspondence*, 1:231–32.

58. Gordon Drummond to Lord Bathurst, May 20 and Aug. 15, 1815, in MPHS, *MHC*, 25:628 and 630; James Monroe to Anthony St. John Baker, June 3, 1815, in Manning, ed., *Diplomatic Correspondence*, 1:226–27; Anthony Butler to Duncan McArthur, July 3, 1815, DMP, 26:5210, LC; Butler to Alexander J. Dallas, Aug. 6, 1815, RG 107, M 221, reel 59, USNA; Gough, *Fighting Sail*, 128–30.

59. John McDonnell to Quetton St. George, Jan. 15, 1808, BFP, reel MS-88 (1), AO; Duncan McArthur to John Armstrong, July 16, 1814, RG 107, M 221, reel 64, USNA; John McDonnell to Lewis Cass, Dec. 4, 1822, in MPHS, *MHC*, 36:458–61; Beal, "John McDonnell," 332–35 and 341–47; Clarke, *Land, Power, and Economics*, 107–14.

60. John McDonnell, deposition, June 13, 1815, and McDonnell to Lewis Cass, Dec. 4, 1822, in MPHS, *MHC*, 36:379–82 and 458–61; McDonnell to Quetton St. George, Jan. 30, 1815, J. Raye to St. George, Apr. 23, 1815 ("To assist"), and George H. Detler to St. George, July 11, 1815, BFP, reel MS-88 (1), AO.

61. William Henry Puthuff to Lewis Cass, May 14, 1816, RG 107, M 221, reel 68, USNA; Puthuff, public notice, Sept. 9, 1815, Puthuff to Elizabeth Mitchell, Oct. 5, 1815, Robert McDouall to Frederick P. Robinson, Sept. 24, 1815, McDouall to Talbot Chambers, Oct. 2, 1815, Chambers to McDouall, Oct. 5, 1815, Puthuff to McDouall, Oct. 5, 1815, McDouall to Colley Foster, Oct. 10, 1815, and Oct. 26, 1815, and McDouall to Robinson, Dec. 2, 1815, in MPHS, *MHC*, 16:252, 254, 289–90, 307, 315, 316–18, 327, 369, 399–401, and 731n253; D. Mitchell to McDouall, Dec. 29, 1815, RG 5, A 1, 25:11159, reel C-4545, LAC.

62. Hickey, *War of 1812*, 146–51; Latimer, *1812*, 219–21 and 402–3; Prucha, *Sword of the Republic*, 118, 120.

63. Anthony Butler to Duncan McArthur, Mar. 1, 1815, DMP, 23:4573, LC; John Johnston to Alexander J. Dallas, July 5, 1815, RG 107, M 221, reel 63, USNA; Lewis Cass to Dallas, July 7, 1815, RG 107, M 221, reel 60, USNA; Jacob J. Brown to Nathan Williams, Aug. 13, 1815, JBP, 1:164, OCHS; Allen, *His Majesty's Indian Allies*, 169; Calloway, "End of an Era," 5; Prucha, *Sword of the Republic*, 120–23.

64. Lewis Cass, "On the Black Swamp Road," in MPHS, *MHC*, 36: 369–78; William Woodbridge to Edward Tiffin, Mar. 24, 1815, and Woodbridge to Alexander J. Dallas, May 10, 1815, and Woodridge to Josiah Meigs, May 1815, in Carter, ed., *Territorial Papers*, 10:523, 536–37, and 545; William H. Crawford to Daniel D. Tompkins, Jan. 22, 1816 ("an object"), RG 75, M 15, reel 3, USNA; Gilpin, *Territory of Michigan*, 117–18; Klunder, *Lewis Cass*, 25–26.

65. Reginald James to Frederick P. Robinson, Sept. 6, 1815, James, speech, Sept. 14, 1815, and Robert McDouall to Robinson, Sept. 22, 1815 ("Merciless Jackson"), and Sept. 24, 1815, in MPHS, *MHC*, 16:244, 270–71, 284, and 289.

66. Reginald James, speech, Sept. 14, 1815, and Robert McDouall, speech, Sept. 17, 1815 ("to frighten you"), in MPHS, *MHC*, 16:270–71 and 273–74.

67. C. Jouett to Alexander J. Dallas, July 23, 1815 ("This is the time"), RG 107, M 221, reel 63, USNA; Prucha, *Sword of the Republic*, 123–25.

68. Robert McDouall to Colley Foster, June 17, 1816, and McDouall to John C. Sherbrooke, Aug. 7, 1816, in MPHS, *MHC*, 16:465 and 510–11; John Quincy Adams and Lewis Cass quoted in Calloway, "End of an Era," 8 ("bitter experience") and 9–10

("iron frontier"); Allen, *His Majesty's Indian Allies,* 169–70; Prucha, *Sword of the Republic,* 126–28 and 136–37.

69. William McGillivray to John Harvey, Apr. 19, 1815, Robert McDouall to Andrew Bulger, May 5, 1815, McDouall to George Murray, June 24, 1815 ("the whole"), and June 25, 1815, McDouall to Frederick P. Robinson, Aug. 21, 1815 ("the hordes"), and McDouall to Colley Foster, Oct. 10, 1815, and Oct. 26, 1815, in MPHS, *MHC,* 16:76, 90, 137, 139, and 325; Drummond to Lord Bathurst, Aug. 27, 1815 ("faithful allies"), in MPHS, *MHC,* 25: 632–33; William McKay quoted in Calloway, "End of an Era," 17 ("Great Father's orders").

70. Edward Owen to Gordon Drummond, Jan. 17, 1816 ("aggravating"), RG 8, 674:11, reel C-3171, LAC.

71. Augustus B. Woodward to James Monroe, Mar. 5, 1815, in Carter, ed., *Territorial Papers,* 10:513; Reginald James to George Murray, July 4, 1815, in MPHS, *MHC,* 16:150; Lewis Cass to Alexander J. Dallas, July 20, 1815, RG 107, M 221, reel 60, USNA; James to Indian chiefs, Sept. 14, 1815 ("pillow"), and J. Maule to Lt. Col. Addison, Aug. 10, 1816, in MPHS, *MHC,* 16:270–72 and 515.

72. Anthony St. John Baker to James Monroe, June 15, 1815, and Reginald James, "Proceedings of a Court of Inquiry held at Malden," Aug. 12, 1815, in Manning, ed., *Diplomatic Correspondence,* 1:716–18 and 757–60; Baker to Monroe, July 12, 1815, and Lewis Cass to Edward Barwick, July 28, 1815, in MPHS, *MHC,* 16:163 and 186–87; Cass to Alexander J. Dallas, July 20, 1815 ("prevent"), RG 107, M 221, reel 60, USNA; James to Frederick P. Robinson, Oct. 25, 1815, RG 5, A 1, 25:11060, reel C-4545, LAC; Allen, *His Majesty's Indian Allies,* 170–71.

73. Robert Richardson to William Caldwell, Oct. 5, 1815, in MPHS, *MHC,* 16:319; William Smith, coroner's inquest, Oct. 6, 1815, and Richardson, inquest, Oct. 9, 1815, RG 5, A 1, 25:11072 and 11078, reel C-4545, LAC.

74. Reginald James to Lewis Cass, Oct. 6, 1815, Cass to James, Oct. 8, 1815, James, memorandum, Oct. 12, 1815, James to Frederick P. Robinson, Nov. 2, 1815 ("to cut off"), and James to Cass, Nov. 1, 1815 ("fulfillment"), RG 5, A 1, 25:10888, 10895, 11065, 11067, and 11068, reel C-4545, LAC.

75. Lewis Cass to Reginald James, Oct. 7, 1815 ("a British officer"), in MPHS, *MHC,* 16:314; Cass to James, Oct. 8, 1815, James, memorandum, Oct. 12, 1815, William Caldwell to James, Oct. 21, 1815, James to Cass, Oct. 22, 1815, and Cass to James, Oct. 26, 1815 ("The Jurisdiction"), RG 5, A 1, 25:11067, 11068, 10890, 10891, and 10892, reel C-4545, LAC.

76. Lewis Cass to Edward Owen, Sept. 5, 1815, in MPHS, *MHC,* 36:334; Cass to Reginald James, Sept. 6, 1815, in MPHS, *MHC,* 16:242–43.

77. Lewis Grant to Frederick P. Robinson, May 16, 1815, William Granger and John McGee, deposition, June 7, 1815, and Robinson to Gordon Drummond, Aug. 16, 1815, RG 8, 167:55, 72, and 118, reel C-2774, LAC; Anthony St. John Baker to James Monroe, July 7, 1815 ("several Sergeants"), in Manning, ed., *Diplomatic Correspondence,* 1:719–20; Robinson to Francis Gore, Sept. 26, 1815 ("Neither the Army"), in MPHS, *MHC,* 16:304; Whitfield, *Tommy Atkins,* 62; Burroughs, "Tackling Army Desertion," 30.

Burroughs calculates 1,061 deserters during 1815, but the original monthly returns of rank-and-file strength report 1,163 deserters. In addition, in October 1815 at Amherstburg, Lieutenant Colonel Reginald James reported 111 "casualties during preceding Months not accounted for." Given the lack of any fighting on that front, those "casualties" must have been deserters, which James was too ashamed to report by that name. So I calculate the number of deserters in 1815 as 1,163 + 111 = 1,274. The decline in desertions in June reflected the reduced British troop strength in Canada, which fell from 24,201 rank and file in May to just 9,197 by the end of June. See Monthly Returns of Rank and File, Jan. 25, 1815, to Dec. 25, 1815, MG 13, War Office 17, 1519:6-219, reel B-1571, LAC.

78. Reginald James to George Murray, May 29, 1815, James to Lewis Cass, Sept. 3, 1815, James to Frederick P. Robinson, Sept. 4, 1815, Cass to James, Sept. 6, 1815, and James to Robinson, Sept. 6, 1815 ("punctilio"), and Sept. 7, 1815 ("System of desertion"), in MPHS, *MHC*, 16:118, 235, 236, 242, 243, and 251.

79. Edward Owen to unknown, Sept. 5, 1815, and Owen to Anthony St. John Baker, Sept. 10, 1815, in MPHS, *MHC*, 16:238-39 and 258-59; Owen to Lewis Cass, Sept. 6, 1815 ("irritable feelings"), John Miller, deposition, Sept. 8, 1815, John Meldrum, deposition, Sept. 8, 1815, and Owen to Baker, Sept. 9, 1815, MPHS, *MHC*, 36:321-22, 326-27, 330, and 332-33.

80. Lewis Cass to Edward Owen, Sept. 7, 1815, Owen to Cass, Sept. 7, 1815, and Owen to Anthony St. John Baker, Sept. 9, 1815, in MPHS, *MHC*, 36:323-24, 325, and 332-33; Owen to Baker, Sept. 10, 1815 ("extraordinary"), and Alexander Vidal to Owen, Nov. 8, 1815, in MPHS, *MHC*, 16:258-59 and 387.

81. Alexander Vidal to Edward Owen, Oct. 16, 1815, and Nov. 8, 1815, James Monroe to Charles Bagot, June 12, 1816, Alexander Macomb to William H. Crawford, June 20, 1816, and Monroe to Bagot, July 20, 1816, in MPHS, *MHC*, 16:350-51, 387, 460, 474, and 490; Monroe to Anthony St. John Baker, Dec. 6, 1815, and Reginald James to John Harvey, Mar. 2, 1816, in Manning, ed., *Diplomatic Correspondence*, 1:236 and 797.

82. James Monroe to John Quincy Adams, Nov. 16, 1815, and July 8, 1816, and Monroe to Charles Bagot, Aug. 14, 1816, in Manning, ed., *Diplomatic Correspondence*, 1:235, 246, and 251; John R. Williams to Lewis Cass, July 24, 1816, and Alexander Macomb to William H. Crawford, July 25, 1816, and Cass to Monroe, July 26, 1816 ("From the tone"), in MPHS, *MHC*, 16:496, 500-501 and 502; Gough, *Fighting Sail*, 131-33.

83. John Quincy Adams to James Monroe, Feb. 8, 1816, Lord Bathurst to Gordon Drummond, Mar. 13, 1816, and Lord Castlereagh to Adams, Sept. 12, 1816, in Manning, ed., *Diplomatic Correspondence*, 1:783-84, 793-94, and 808; Drummond to Bathurst, May 20, 1816, in MPHS, *MHC*, 25:648-49; Monroe to Charles Bagot, Aug. 14, 1816, Lord Bathurst to John C. Sherbrooke, Sept. 9, 1816 ("strictly Conformable"), and Bagot to Monroe, Nov. 18, 1816, in MPHS, *MHC*, 16:520-21, 529, and 546-47; Perkins, *Castlereagh and Adams*, 196-201.

84. Charles Bagot to John C. Sherbrooke, Aug. 14, 1816, in MPHS, *MHC*, 16:517-19; Bagot to James Monroe, Nov. 18, 1816, and Bagot to Sherbrooke, Dec. 5, 1816, RG 8, 674:134 and 141, reel C-3171, LAC; Perkins, *Castlereagh and Adams*, 240-44.

85. Calloway, "End of an Era," 9-10; Perkins, *Castlereagh and Adams*, 272-75.

86. Gordon Drummond to George Prevost, Feb. 8, 1814, and Prevost to Drummond, Feb. 17, 1814, in *DHCNF*, 9:169-70 and 188; Drummond to Prevost, July 10, 1814, and July 13, 1814, in *SBD*, 3, part 1:121 and 128; Graves, ed., *Merry Hearts*, 146 ("Mohawks"); Stacey, ed., "Upper Canada at War," 42; Lord, ed., "War of 1812," 200 and 209.

87. Gordon Drummond to George Prevost, Feb. 8, 1814, in *DHCNF*, 9:169-70;

Samuel, Levi, and John Green to Gordon Drummond, June 17, 1815 ("Dispoiled"), RG 5, A 1, 23:10086, reel C-4545, LAC; Klinck and Talman, eds., *Journal of Norton*, 367–69; Benn, *Iroquois*, 135 and 235n50.

88. William Claus to Frederick P. Robinson, Sept. 10, 1815, Claus to Colley Foster, Sept. 10, 1815, and Red Jacket speech, Sept. 1, 1815, in MPHS, *MHC*, 16:260, 261, and 265; Benn, *Iroquois*, 178 and 181.

89. Daniel D. Tompkins to James Monroe, May 7, 1814, in Hastings, ed., *Papers of Tompkins*, 3:470–71; Tompkins to Alexander J. Dallas, June 28, 1815, RG 107, M 221, reel 66, USNA; Benn, *Iroquois*, 183; Hauptman, *Conspiracy of Interests*, 8–9 and 136–43.

90. Allen, *His Majesty's Indian Allies*, 177; Surtees, "Land Cessions," 112–19.

91. Jedediah Morse to John C. Calhoun, Aug. 5, 1821, in Morse, *Report to the Secretary of War*, 19; Allen, *His Majesty's Indian Allies*, 178–84.

92. Furstenberg, "Significance of the Trans-Appalachian Frontier," 674–75.

93. Lewis Cass to Alexander J. Dallas, July 20, 1815, RG 107, M 221, reel 60, USNA: Gordon Drummond to Lord Bathurst, Aug. 27, 1815, in MPHS, *MHC*, 25:632–33; Robert McDouall to John C. Sherbrooke, Aug. 7, 1816 ("total extinction" and "anxiety"), in MPHS, *MHC*, 16:509–10; Perkins, *Castlereagh and Adams*, 2.

94. Daniel D. Tompkins to the New York State Legislature, Feb. 2, 1816, in Hastings, ed., *Papers of Tompkins*, 3:646–47; Albert Gallatin to Matthew Lyon, May 7, 1816 ("The people"), in Adams, ed., *Writings of Gallatin*, 1:700; Perkins, *Castlereagh and Adams*, 150.

95. John Quincy Adams to John Adams, May 29, 1816 ("my country men" and "rather more proud"), quoted in Perkins, *Castlereagh and Adams*, 147 and 155.

Chapter Sixteen: Aliens

1. William Lyon Mackenzie, in the [Toronto] *Constitution*, July 5, 1837, quoted in Craig, *Upper Canada*, 244.

2. J. E. Rea, "Alexander McDonell," *DCB*, 7:544; Rea, *Bishop Alexander Macdonell*, 1–9 and 14; W. Johnston, *Glengarry Light Infantry*, 300; McLean, *People of Glengarry*, 131–33.

3. Alexander Macdonell to Lord Bathurst, Dec. 20, 1814, RG 5, A 1, 21:9049, reel C-4544, LAC; Rea, "McDonell," *DCB*, 7:544–45; McLean, *People of Glengarry*, 78–97, 133–36, and 144–48; Rea, *Bishop Alexander Macdonell*, 19–21 (includes, on 21, Macdonell quotation: "strong barrier") and 33; Graves, *Field of Glory*, 118–19.

4. Alexander Macdonell to Lord Bathurst, Dec. 20, 1814 ("Contagion," "the place," "under an irritation"), RG 5, A 1, 21:9049, reel C-4544, LAC.

5. Alexander Macdonell to Lord Bathurst, Dec. 20, 1814 ("strong population"), RG 5, A 1, 21:9049, reel C-4544, LAC.

6. Edward Baynes to George Prevost, June 15, 1814 ("American Interloper"), RG 5, A 1, 20:8495, reel C-4544, LAC; John Strachan, "Remarks . . . to be sent to Sir George Murray," in Spragge, ed., *John Strachan Letterbook*, 91; John Strachan to unknown, June 22, 1818, JSP, reel MS-35 (10), AO; James Strachan, *Visit*, v–vi, 62 ("to lose"), and 63–66; Errington, *Lion*, 166; Wilton, *Popular Politics*, 34. A visitor from Scotland, James Strachan was John's brother; John served as the *Visit*'s primary source.

7. William Dummer Powell, "First Days in Upper Canada," 1044 ("His Head"), MG 23 H-I-4 (Powell Papers), LAC.

8. Romney, "Reinventing Upper Canada," 78–79.

9. Mrs. John Heard, diary, Aug. 3–4, 1815 ("not a house"), MHS; Barlow and

Powell, eds., "Physician's Journey," 90; Buttrick, *Voyages*, 53 ("struck with"); Goldie, *Diary*, 33 ("the Americans").

10. Barrett, *Journal*, 39, 42–43 ("complained" and "thorough detestation"), and 51; Mrs. John Heard, Diary, Aug. 5, 1815, MHS; Goldie, *Diary*, 33 ("hate the Yankies"); Gourlay, ed., *Statistical Account*, 1:249n; F. Hall, *Travels*, 154; Howison, *Sketches*, 275–76; Young, ed., "Bishop Peters," 621; McOuat, ed., "Diary of William Graves," 23 ("A stranger").

11. F. Hall, *Travels*, 128 ("obstreperously loyal"); John Beverley Robinson quoted in Brode, *Robinson*, 26 ("for the purpose").

12. Akenson, *Irish in Ontario*, 138; Errington, *Lion*, 89–92; Mills, *Idea of Loyalty*, 27–28 and 31; Burt, *United States*, 184; Howison, *Sketches*, 77 ("last American war"); *Kingston Chronicle*, Sept. 20, 1815 ("line of separation"), quoted in Craig, *Upper Canada*, 85.

13. Isaac Brock to Lord Liverpool, Dec. 3, 1811, MG 11, 351:146, reel B-295, LAC; French, *Parsons & Politics*, 70; Gordon Drummond to Lord Bathurst, Apr. 30, 1814 ("Previous to the war"), MG 11, 355:52, reel B-295, LAC; French, *Parsons & Politics*, 67–76; Ivison and Rosser, *Baptists*, 56–62 and 138–40; Adamson, "God's Continent Divided," 435–36; Moir, "American Influences," 447–51 (448 includes quotation from A. K. Buell to A. Peters, Apr. 11, 1821: "We must be"); Gregg, *History of the Presbyterian Church*, 191–206; Playter, *History of Methodism*, 143–44; Moir, "Early Methodism," 58.

14. French, *Parsons & Politics*, 72; Adamson, "God's Continent Divided," 437–43 (442: Strachan quoted: "to separate").

15. Gourlay, ed., *Statistical Account*, 1:14n; Johnson, *Becoming Prominent*, 76–77 and 129–31; Talman, *Loyalist Narratives*, lx–lxi.

16. Strachan, *Sermon Preached at York*, 16–17, 34, and 36 ("friends from our foes"); Reuben Sherwood to Johnstown District magistrates, Nov. 14, 1815 ("the most dangerous"), Ira Schofield to William Halton, Dec. 24, 1815, and D'Arcy Boulton to Halton, Oct. 28, 1815, RG 5, A 1, 25:10985, 11296, and 11334, LAC; Joel Stone to Giles Stone, Oct. 29, 1815, JSP, box 1, folder 3, QUA; Errington, *Lion*, 166; Craig, *Upper Canada*, 89.

17. John Strachan to John Harvey, July 27, 1818, Strachan Papers, reel MS-35 (10), AO; Strachan, *Sermon Preached at York*, 16–17, 34, 36, and 37; Mills, *Idea of Loyalty*, 25–26; Gourlay, ed., *Statistical Account*, 1:567 ("Magistrates"); Strachan quoted in Johnson, *Becoming Prominent*, 116 ("The power"); Dunham, *Political Unrest*, 41–45; Errington, *Lion*, 92–93 and 107–8; B. Wright, "Sedition in Upper Canada," 10–13.

18. Brode, *Robinson*, 3–8 and 10 (John Beverley Robinson quote: "Democratic"); Robert E. Saunders, "John Beverley Robinson," *DCB*, 9:668.

19. Brode, *Robinson*, 8–60; Saunders, "Robinson," *DCB*, 9:668–79.

20. Craig, *Upper Canada*, 108–10 and 111 (*Upper Canada Gazette*, July 7, 1825 quoted: "universal order"); Mills, *Idea of Loyalty*, 27–28 and 31; Romney, "From the Types Riot to Rebellion," 134 and 137; B. Wright, "Sedition in Upper Canada," 10–12.

21. McNairn, *Capacity to Judge*, 29–32 and 40; Mills, *Idea of Loyalty*, 40–42 (42 includes the John Matthews quotation: "Loyalty") and 51.

22. Howison, *Sketches*, 79–81 and 115 ("bustle, improvement"); Craig, "American Impact," 333–34; "A Briton," from the *Kingston Chronicle*, quoted in Errington, *Lion*, 127 ("I dislike"); Gourlay, ed., *Statistical Account*, 1:251; Mills, *Idea of Loyalty*, 48.

23. George Murray to Lord Melville, Mar. 27, 1815, in Graham, ed., "Views of General Murray," 162–63; Craig, *Upper Canada*, 85 (includes Strachan quote: "power-

ful"); Spragge, ed., *John Strachan Letterbook*, 93–94; Brode, *Robinson*, 33; Romney, "From the Types Riot to Rebellion," 137.

24. Gordon Drummond to Earl Bathurst, July 12, 1814, and Drummond to George Prevost, Feb. 19, 1814, MG 11, 355:118 and 120, reel B-295, LAC; Bathurst to Drummond, Jan. 10, 1815, RG 5, A 1, 23:9956, reel C-4545, LAC; Epp, *Mennonites in Canada*, 71; J. K. Johnson, *Becoming Prominent*, 113; Wood, *Making Ontario*, 26 and 40.

25. Thomas Whitehead to Joel Stone, July 31, 1816, JSP, box 1, folder 4, QUA; Howison, *Sketches*, 79–81; McOuat, ed., "Diary of William Graves," 12–14 and 21–22; Cruikshank, "Post-War Discontent," 15 and 23–24; Dunham, *Political Unrest*, 47–48; Sheppard, *Plunder*, 175–86.

26. Mills, *Idea of Loyalty*, 34–35 and 51; reformer quoted in Errington, *Lion*, 172 ("Americans"); John Matthews quoted in Romney, "John Matthews," *DCB*, 6:498 ("the King").

27. Craig, *Upper Canada*, 90–91; Cruikshank, "Post-War Discontent," 14–19; Errington, *Lion*, 95 and 120–28; Bruce G. Wilson, "William Dickson," *DCB*, 7:250–51; Dunham, *Political Unrest*, 49; Sheppard, *Plunder*, 186–87 and 189–92.

28. Gourlay quoted in S. F. Wise, "Robert Fleming Gourlay," *DCB*, 9:331–32 ("peculiar" and "quite a radical"); Cruikshank, "Post-War Discontent," 19–21; Dunham, *Political Unrest*, 51–52; Wilton, *Popular Politics*, 27–29.

29. Gourlay, ed., *Statistical Account*, 1:275, 305, 313, 317, 319, 321, 346, 348, 379, 425, 467, and 480 ("Such lands"); Cruikshank, "Post-War Discontent," 20–21; Dunham, *Political Unrest*, 53; Wood, *Making Ontario*, 52.

30. Gourlay, ed., *Statistical Account*, 1:614; Sheppard, *Plunder*, 197; Wise, "Gourlay," *DCB*, 9:332–33 (includes Gourlay quotations: "system," "the vile," and "monstrous"); Cruikshank, "Post-War Discontent," 25–26; Wilton, *Popular Politics*, 29–30.

31. John Strachan to John Macaulay, Dec. 8, 1818, MFP, reel MS-78, AO; Wise, "Gourlay," *DCB*, 9:332–35 (includes Gourlay quotation:"a radical change"); Dunham, *Political Unrest*, 54–59; Errington, *Lion*, 109–10; Wilton, *Popular Politics*, 32.

32. Boyd, "Barnabas Bidwell," 51–68; G. H. Patterson, "Barnabas Bidwell," *DCB*, 6:54–55.

33. Boyd, "Barnabas Bidwell," 71–74; Patterson, "Bidwell," *DCB*, 6:55; Bidwell, *Address to the People*, 23–24 ("between," "taxes," and "shall acquire"); Bidwell, *Summary*, 7–21.

34. Samuel Taggart to John Taylor, Dec. 24, 1805 ("Mr. Bidwell"), Jan. 12, 1806 ("talents"), and Feb. 2, 1806 ("right hand man"), in Hayes, ed., "Letters of Samuel Taggart," 167, 173, and 174; Boyd, "Barnabas Bidwell," 76–83; Patterson, "Bidwell," *DCB*, 6:55.

35. Barnabas Bidwell to trustees of the Kingston Presbyterian Church, Aug. 14, 1817, Bidwell file, LC; Patterson, "Bidwell," *DCB*, 6:55.

36. John Bethune, Jr., to John Macaulay, Nov. 16, 1810, MFP, reel MS-78, AO; Patterson, "Bidwell," *DCB*, 6:55–56; John B. Robinson to John Macaulay, Feb. 15, 1811, MFP, reel MS-78, AO; "The Wars of the Gulls," 1812, in *SBD*, 1:564.

37. John Strachan to John Macaulay, June 13, 1820, June 26, 1820, and Nov. 18, 1821, and John B. Robinson to Macaulay, Nov. 18, 1821 ("old vagabond" and "made me sick"), and Dec. 13, 1821, MFP, reel MS-78, AO; Patterson, "Bidwell," *DCB*, 6:56–57; Riddell, "Bidwell Elections," 237; Brode, *Robinson*, 67–68 and 70; Romney, "Reinventing Upper Canada," 80–81.

38. Jonas Jones and Mahlon Burwell, quoted in Patterson, "Bidwell," *DCB*, 6:578 ("incapable"); William Macaulay to John Macaulay, Dec. 31, 1821 ("more than half"), MFP, reel MS-78, AO.

39. William Macaulay to John Macaulay, Dec. 31, 1821 ("was born" and "do not think"), MFP, reel MS-78, AO; Romney, "Reinventing Upper Canada," 84–87.

40. John B. Robinson to John Macaulay, Dec. 13, 1821 ("dispose of"), MFP, reel MS-78, AO; Brode, *Robinson*, 70–72; Errington, *Lion*, 169–70; Romney, "Reinventing Upper Canada," 81–82.

41. Patterson, "Bidwell," *DCB*, 6:57; Brode, *Robinson*, 96; Dunham, *Political Unrest*, 75–76; Romney, "Reinventing Upper Canada," 82.

42. Brode, *Robinson*, 96–97 and 122; Errington, *Lion*, 173.

43. Mills, *Idea of Loyalty*, 37; Romney, "Reinventing Upper Canada," 91–93.

44. Brode, *Robinson*, 97–98, 122, and 126–28; Dunham, *Political Unrest*, 77.

45. Mills, *Idea of Loyalty*, 39, 43 (John Matthews quoted: "divide and govern"), 45 (John Beverley Robinson quoted: "would suffer death"), and 49; Brode, *Robinson*, 128–30; Craig, *Upper Canada*, 119; Dunham, *Political Unrest*, 77–78; Errington, *Lion*, 178–79.

46. Brode, *Robinson*, 135–38; Craig, *Upper Canada*, 120–21; Dunham, *Political Unrest*, 79–80; Romney, "Robert Randal," *DCB*, 6:632; Wilton, *Popular Politics*, 42.

47. Brode, *Robinson*, 138–39; Dunham, *Political Unrest*, 80–81; Errington, *Lion*, 181; Bowsfield, "Sir Peregrine Maitland," *DCB*, 8:600–603; Wilton, *Popular Politics*, 43.

48. McNairn, *Capacity to Judge*, 66–69, 119–20, and 174; the reformer John Willson quoted in Bowsfield, "Sir Peregrine Maitland," *DCB*, 8:600 ("difficult"); Mills, *Idea of Loyalty*, 46–47.

49. Lord Bathurst to Gordon Drummond, Jan. 10, 1815, in *SBD*, 3, part 1:507; to George Prevost, Sept. 8, 1814, and to Drummond, Mar. 20, 1815 ("to the British Colonies"), in *SBD*, 3, part 2:786–87 and 788–89; Graham, ed., "Views of General Murray," 162; Craig, *Upper Canada*, 88; McLean, *People of Glengarry*, 151–56; Klinck and Ross, eds., *Tiger Dunlop's Upper Canada*, 105–6 ("grateful"); Gourlay, ed., *Statistical Account*, 1:617.

50. Gourlay, ed., *Statistical Account*, 1:549; Howison, *Sketches*, 61–64; Martin, "Regiment de Watteville," 27–29; Craig, *Upper Canada*, 125–30; J. K. Johnson, *Becoming Prominent*, 113; Wood, *Making Ontario*, 26 and 40; Higgins, *Life of Gould*, 41.

51. John Strachan to John Macauley, Nov. 18, 1821, MFP, reel MS-78, AO; Frederick H. Armstrong and Ronald J. Stagg, "William Lyon Mackenzie," *DCB*, 9:496–501; Craig, *Upper Canada*, 228–32; Romney, "From the Types Riot to Rebellion," 139–40.

52. Brode, *Robinson*, 188–93; Craig, *Upper Canada*, 232–39 (236 includes Sir Francis Bond Head quote: "to contend"); Read and Stagg, eds., *Rebellion of 1837*, xxv–xxviii; Mills, *Idea of Loyalty*, 106–7; J. E. Rea, "Alexander McDonell," *DCB*, 7:550; Wilton, *Popular Politics*, 179 (Sir Francis Bond Head quoted: "moral war") and 180–87.

53. Craig, *Upper Canada*, 241–44; John Beverley Robinson quoted in Brode, *Robinson*, 188 ("a strange person").

54. Brode, *Robinson*, 194–200; Mills, *Idea of Loyalty*, 104–8; Craig, *Upper Canada*, 245–49 and 255; Armstrong and Stagg, "William Lyon Mackenzie," *DCB*, 9:502–3; Ruth McKenzie, "James FitzGibbon," *DCB*, 9:265–66; Read and Stagg, eds., *Rebellion of 1837*, xi–lvii and xc; Wilton, *Popular Politics*, 189–90.

55. William Lyon Mackenzie quoted in Craig, *Upper Canada*, 250; Armstrong and Stagg, "William Lyon Mackenzie," *DCB*, 9:503.

56. Craig, *Upper Canada*, 249–51, 256, and 258–59; Armstrong and Stagg, "William Lyon Mackenzie," *DCB*, 9:503–4; George Rude, "Elijah Crocker Woodman," *DCB*, 7:923–24; Read and Stagg, eds., *Rebellion of 1837*, lxxviii and lxxxiii–xcii; R. C. Stuart, *United States Expansionism*, 130–31 and 135–38; Wilton, *Popular Politics*, 190.

57. R. C. Stuart, *United States Expansionism*, 126–37.

58. Bothwell, *Penguin History of Canada*, 182–83; Mills, *Idea of Loyalty*, 108–10; R. C. Stuart, *United States Expansionism*, 131.

59. R. C. Stuart, *United States Expansionism*, 128–34 and 259–61; J. H. Thompson and Randall, *Canada and the United States*, 24–30.

60. Sir Francis Bond Head quoted in Mills, *Idea of Loyalty*, 108 ("The struggle"); Bothwell, *Penguin History of Canada*, 183–86; Craig, *Upper Canada*, 252–276; Wilton, *Popular Politics*, 194–220.

Bibliography

Adams, Henry. *History of the United States of America During the Administrations of James Madison*. New York: Library of America, 1986.

———. *History of the United States of America During the Administrations of Thomas Jefferson*. New York: Library of America, 1986.

———, ed. *The Writings of Albert Gallatin*. 3 vols. Philadelphia: J. B. Lippincott, 1879.

Adamson, Christopher. "God's Continent Divided: Politics and Religion in Upper Canada and the Northern and Western United States, 1775 to 1814." *Comparative Studies in Society and History* 36 (July 1994): 417–46.

Akenson, Donald Harman. *The Irish in Ontario: A Study in Rural History*. Montreal: McGill-Queen's University Press, 1999.

Allen, Robert S. *His Majesty's Indian Allies: British Indian Policy in the Defence of Canada, 1774–1815*. Toronto: Dundurn Press, 1992.

———. "His Majesty's Indian Allies: Native Peoples, the British Crown, and the War of 1812." *Michigan Historical Review* 14 (fall 1988): 2–24.

Anderson, Fred W. *A People's Army: Massachusetts Soldiers and Society in the Seven Years War*. Chapel Hill: University of North Carolina Press, 1979.

Andrews, Charles. *The Prisoners' Memoirs, or Dartmoor Prison . . .* New York: Charles Andrews, 1815.

[Anonymous]. *An Account of the Beginning, Transactions and Discovery of Ransford Rogers, Who Seduced Many By Pretended Hobgoblins and Apparitions, And Thereby Extorted Money from their Pockets*. Newark, N.J.: unknown pub., 1792.

———."Canadian Letters: Description of a Tour thro' the Provinces of Lower and Upper Canada in the Course of the Years 1792 and '93." *Canadian Antiquarian and Numismatic Journal*, 3d ser., 9 (1912):85–168.

———.*The Capitulation, or, A History of the Expedition Conducted by William Hull, Brigadier-General of the Northwestern Army by an Ohio Volunteer*. Chilicothe, Ohio: James Barnes, 1812.

———. "The First Campaign of an A.D.C." *Military and Naval Magazine of the United States* 1 (1833): 153–62 and 257–67; 2(1833–34):10–20, 73–82, 200–210, and 278–88; 3 (1834): 437–46; 4 (1834–35): 26–34 and 85–93; and 5 (1835): 253–61.

———. "The Last War in Canada." *Colburn's United Service Magazine and Naval and Military Journal*, part 2, 271–83. London: H. Hurst, 1848.

———, ed. *A Sketch of the Life of Lieut. Mathew Hughes, Late of the United States Army, Serving on the Niagara Frontier During the Late War*. Alexandria, Va.: Corse and Rounsanvell, 1815.

Antal, Sandy, *A Wampum Denied: Procter's War of 1812*. Ottawa: Carleton University Press, 1997.

Appleby, Joyce. *Capitalism and a New Social Order: The Republican Vision of the 1790s.* New York: New York University Press, 1984.

Archer, Mary R., ed. "Journal of Major Isaac Roach, 1812–1824." *Pennsylvania Magazine of History and Biography* 17 (1893): 129–58 and 281–315.

Armitage, David. "Greater Britain: A Useful Category of Historical Analysis?" *American Historical Review* 15 (Apr. 1999): 427–45.

Armstrong, Frederick H. *Handbook of Upper Canadian Chronology.* Toronto: Dundurn Press, 1985.

Atherton, William. *Narrative of the Suffering & Defeat of the North-Western Army, Under General Winchester.* Frankfort, Ky.: A. G. Hodges, 1842.

Barbuto, Richard V. *Niagara 1814: America Invades Canada.* Lawrence: University Press of Kansas, 2000.

Barlow, William, and David O. Powell, eds. "A Physician's Journey through Western New York and Upper Canada in 1815." *Niagara Frontier* 25 (1978): 85–95.

Barrett, Richard. *Richard Barrett's Journal: New York and Canada, 1816.* Winfield, Kans.: Wedgeston Press, 1983.

Bartlett, C. J., and Gene A. Smith. " 'A Species of Milito-Nautico-Guerilla Warfare': Admiral Alexander Cochrane's Naval Campaign against the United States, 1814–1815." In Julie Flavell and Stephen Conway, eds., *Britain and America Go to War: The Impact of War and Warfare in Anglo-America, 1754–1815*, 173–204. Gainesville: University Press of Florida, 2004.

Bartlett, Thomas. "Clemency and Compensation: The Treatment of Defeated Rebels and Suffering Loyalists after the 1798 Rebellion." In Jim Smyth, ed., *Revolution, Counter-Revolution, and Union: Ireland in the 1790s*, 99–127. New York: Cambridge University Press, 2000.

Baseler, Marilyn C. *"Asylum for Mankind": America, 1607–1800.* Ithaca, N.Y.: Cornell University Press, 1998.

Bayly, C. A. *Imperial Meridian: The British Empire and the World, 1780–1830.* London: Addison, Wesley, Longman, 1989.

Beal, Vernon L. "John McDonnell and the Ransoming of American Captives after the River Raisin Massacre." *Michigan History* 35 (Sep. 1951): 331–51.

Beall, William K. "Journal of William K. Beall." *American Historical Review* 17 (July 1912): 783–808.

Bell, Charles H. *The Bench and Bar of New Hampshire.* Boston: Houghton Mifflin, 1894.

Bellesiles, Michael A. "Experiencing the War of 1812." In Julie Flavell and Stephen Conway, eds., *Britain and America Go to War: The Impact of War and Warfare in Anglo-America, 1754–1815*, 205–40. Gainesville: University Press of Florida, 2004.

Ben-Atar, Doron, and Barbara B. Oberg. "Introduction: The Paradoxical Legacy of the Federalists." In Ben-Atar and Oberg, eds., *Federalists Reconsidered*, 1–16. Charlottesville: University of Virginia Press, 1998.

Benn, Carl. *The Battle of York.* Belleville, Ont.: Mika, 1984.

———. *The Iroquois in the War of 1812.* Toronto: University of Toronto Press, 1998.

Berlin, Ira. *Many Thousands Gone: The First Two Centuries of Slavery in North America.* Cambridge, Mass.: Harvard University Press, 1998.

Bidwell, Barnabas. *An Address to the People of Massachusetts.* Boston: no pub., 1805.

———. *A Summary, Historical, and Political Review of the Revolution, the Constitution, and Government of the United States.* Pittsfield, Mass.: Phinehas Allen, 1805.

[Bidwell, Barnabas]. "Sketches of Upper Canada Written by an Inhabitant." In Robert Gourlay, ed., *Statistical Account of Upper Canada, Compiled with a View to a Grand System of Emigration,* vol. 1. London, 1822.

Bigelow, Timothy. *Journal of a Tour to Niagara Falls in the Year 1805.* Boston: John Wilson, 1876.

Bingham, Robert W., ed. *Reports of Joseph Ellicott.* 2 vols. Buffalo: Buffalo Historical Society, 1937, 1941.

Binns, John. *Recollections of the Life of John Binns.* Philadelphia: Parry & McMillan, 1854.

Boerstler, Charles G. *Battle of the Beaver Dams.* Baltimore: no pub., 1816.

Bolster, W. Jeffrey. *Black Jacks: African American Seamen in the Age of Sail.* Cambridge, Mass.: Harvard University Press, 1997.

Bond, Phineas. "Letters of Phineas Bond." *American Historical Association, Annual Report* 1(1896): 568–86.

Bonney, Catharina Van Rensselaer, ed. *A Legacy of Historical Gleanings.* 2 vols. Albany: J. Munsell, 1875.

Bothwell, Robert. *The Penguin History of Canada.* Toronto: Penguin Canada, 2006.

Boulton, D'Arcy. *Sketch of His Majesty's Province of Upper Canada.* London, 1805. Reprint, Toronto: Baxter, 1961.

Boyd, Julian P. "Barnabas Bidwell, 1768–1833." *Wyoming Historical and Geological Society, Proceedings and Collections* 20(1929): 51–102.

———. *Number 7: Alexander Hamilton's Secret Attempts to Control American Foreign Policy, with Supporting Documents.* Princeton: Princeton University Press, 1964.

Boyd, Julian P., et al., eds. *The Papers of Thomas Jefferson.* 28 vols. to date. Princeton: Princeton University Press, 1950–.

Bradburn, Douglas. *The Citizenship Revolution: Politics and the Creation of the American Union, 1774–1804.* Charlottesville: University of Virginia Press, 2009.

Brant, Irving. *James Madison: Commander in Chief, 1812–1836.* New York: Bobbs-Merrill, 1961.

———. *James Madison: The President, 1809–1812.* New York: Bobbs-Merrill, 1956.

Brayman, Daniel, ed. "A Pioneer Patriot." In Buffalo Historical Society, *Publications* 9 (1906):364.

Bric, Maurice J. "The Irish and the Evolution of the 'New Politics' in America." In P. J. Drudy, ed., *The Irish in America: Emigration, Assimilation, and Impact,* 143–67. New York: Cambridge University Press, 1985.

———. "The Irish Immigrant and the Broadening of the Polity in Philadelphia, 1790–1800." In Eliga H. Gould and Peter S. Onuf, eds., *Empire and Nation: The American Revolution in the Atlantic World,* 159–77. Baltimore: Johns Hopkins University Press, 2005.

Brigham, Clarence, ed. "Letters of Abijah Bigelow, Member of Congress, to his Wife, 1810–1815." *American Antiquarian Society, Proceedings* 40 (Oct. 1930): 305–406.

Brode, Patrick. *Sir John Beverly Robinson: Bone and Sinew of the Compact.* Toronto: University of Toronto Press, 1984.

Brooke, John L. "Consent, Civil Society, and the Public Sphere in the Age of Revolution and the Early American Republic." In Jeffrey L. Pasley, Andrew W. Robertson, and David Waldstreicher, eds., *Beyond the Founders: New Approaches to the Political History of the Early American Republic,* 207–38. Chapel Hill: University of North Carolina Press, 2004.

Brown, Richard D. "The Disenchantment of a Radical Whig: John Adams Reckons with Free Speech." In Richard Alan Ryerson, ed., *John Adams and the Founding of the Republic*, 171–85. Boston: Massachusetts Historical Society, 2001.

Brown, Richard D., " 'No Harm to Kill Indians': Equal Rights in a Time of War." *New England Quarterly* 81 (Mar. 2008): 34–62.

———, ed. *Major Problems in the Era of the American Revolution, 1760–1791*. Lexington, Mass.: D.C. Heath, 1992.

Brown, Richard Maxwell. "Back Country Rebellions and the Homestead Ethic." In Brown and Don E. Fehrenbacher, eds., *Tradition, Conflict, and Modernization: Perspectives on the American Revolution*, 73–98. New York, 1977.

Brown, Roger H. *Redeeming the Republic: Federalists, Taxation, and the Origins of the Constitution*. Baltimore: Johns Hopkins University Press, 1993.

———. *The Republic in Peril: 1812*. New York: Norton, 1971.

Brown, Wallace. "Loyalists and Non-Participants." In John Parker and Carol Urness, eds., *The American Revolution: A Heritage of Change*, 120–34. Minneapolis: Associates of the James Ford Bell Library, 1975.

Brown, Wallace, and Hereward Senior. *Victorious in Defeat: The Loyalists of the American Revolution in Exile*. New York: Facts on File, 1984.

Brunson, Alfred. *A Western Pioneer: or, Incidents of the Life and Times of Rev. Alfred Brunson, A.M., D.D.* 2 vols. Cincinnati: Hitchcock and Walden, 1872, 1879.

Brymner, Douglas, ed., "Note B: Anticipation of the War of 1812." In Brymner, ed., *Report on Canadian Archives, 1896*, 24–75. Ottawa: S. E. Dawson, 1897.

———. "Note D: French Republican Designs on Canada." In Brymner, ed., *Report on Canadian Archives, 1891*. Ottawa: S. E. Dawson, 1892.

———. "Political State of Upper Canada in 1806–7." In Brymner, ed., *Report on Canadian Archives, 1892*, 32–135. Ottawa: S. E. Dawson, 1893.

Budka, Metchie J. E., ed. "Journey to Niagara, 1805: From the Diary of Julian Ursyn Niemcewicz." *New-York Historical Society, Quarterly* 44 (Jan. 1960): 72–113.

Buel, Richard, Jr., *America on the Brink: How the Political Struggle over the War of 1812 Almost Destroyed the Young Republic*. New York: Palgrave MacMillan, 2005.

———. *Securing the Revolution: Ideology in American Politics, 1789–1815*. Ithaca, N.Y.: Cornell University Press, 1972.

Bunn, Matthew. "Narrative of Matthew Bunn." *Buffalo Historical Society, Publications* 7 (1904): 379–434.

Burkholder, Lewis J. *A Brief History of the Mennonites in Ontario*. N.p.: Livingstone Press, 1935.

Burroughs, Peter. "Tackling Army Desertion in British North America." *Canadian Historical Review* 61 (Mar. 1980): 28–68.

Burt, Alfred Leroy. *The Old Province of Quebec*. 2 vols. Toronto: McClelland and Stewart, 1968.

———. *The United States, Great Britain, and British North America from the Revolution to the Establishment of Peace after the War of 1812*. New Haven: Yale University Press, 1940.

Bushman, Richard L. *King and People in Provincial Massachusetts*. Chapel Hill: University of North Carolina Press, 1985.

Buttrick, Tilly, Jr. *Voyages, Travels, and Discoveries of Tilly Buttrick, Jr.* Boston: John Putnam, 1831.

Byfield, Shadrach. "A Common Soldier's Account." In John Gellner, ed., *Recollections of the War of 1812: Three Eyewitness Accounts*, 1–45. Toronto: Baxter, 1964.

Calloway, Colin G. *Crown and Calumet: British-Indian Relations, 1783–1815*. Norman: University of Oklahoma Press, 1987.
———. "The End of an Era: British–Indian Relations in the Great Lakes Region after the War of 1812." *Michigan Historical Review* 12 (fall 1986): 1–20.
Cameron, Kenneth Walter, ed. *The Papers of Loyalist Samuel Peters*. Hartford, Conn.: Transcendental Books, 1978.
Campbell, Maria [Hull]. *Revolutionary Services and Civil Life of General William Hull; Prepared from his Manuscripts*. New York: D. Appleton, 1848.
Campbell, Patrick. *Travels in the Interior Inhabited Parts of North America in the Years 1791 and 1792*. Edited by H. H. Langton. Toronto: Champlain Society, 1937.
Campbell, William W., ed. *The Life and Writings of De Witt Clinton*. New York: Baker and Scribner, 1849.
Carroll, Francis M. *A Good and Wise Measure: The Search for the Canadian–American Boundary, 1783–1842*. Toronto: University of Toronto Press, 2001.
Carter, Clarence Edwin, ed. *The Territorial Papers of the United States*. 28 vols. Washington, D.C.: Government Printing Office, 1934–75.
Carter, Edward C., Jr. "A 'Wild Irishman' Under Every Federalist's Bed: Naturalization in Philadelphia, 1789–1806." *Pennsylvania Magazine of History and Biography* 94 (July 1970): 331–46.
Cartwright, C. E., ed. *Life and Letters of the Late Hon. Richard Cartwright*. Toronto: Belford Brothers, 1876.
[Cartwright, Richard]. *Letters From an American Loyalist in Upper Canada to His Friend in England*. Kingston, Upper Canada: no pub., 1810.
Cate, Mary R., ed. "Benjamin Ropes' Autobiography." *Essex Institute, Collections* 91 (Apr. 1955): 105–27.
Christie, Nancy. " 'In These Times of Democratic Rage and Delusion': Popular Religion and the Challenge to the Established Order, 1760–1815." In George A. Rawlyk, ed., *The Canadian Protestant Experience, 1760 to 1990*, 9–47. Burlington, Ont.: Welch, 1990.
Clarke, John. *Land, Power, and Economics on the Frontier of Upper Canada*. Montreal: McGill-Queen's University Press, 2001.
Cogswell, Nathaniel. *An Oration Delivered Before the Republican Citizens of Newburyport in the Rev. John Giles's Meeting House on the Fourth of July*. Newburyport, Mass.: W. & J. Gilman, 1808.
Coles, Isaac A. *To the Public*. Washington, D.C.: n.p., 1814.
Colgate, William, ed. "Letters from the Honourable Chief Justice William Osgoode." *Ontario History* 46 (1954): 77–96 and 149–68.
Colley, Linda. *Britons: Forging the Nation, 1707–1837*. New Haven: Yale University Press, 1992.
———. *Captives*. New York: Pantheon Books, 2002.
Cometti, Elizabeth, ed. *The American Journals of Lt. John Enys*. Syracuse, N.Y.: Syracuse University Press, 1976.
Conway, Stephen. *War, State, and Society in Mid-Eighteenth-Century Britain and Ireland*. New York: Oxford University Press, 2006.
Cookson, J. E. *The British Armed Nation, 1793–1815*. Oxford: Clarendon Press, 1997.
Cooper, James Fenimore, ed. *Ned Myers; Or a Life Before the Mast*. New York: Putnam, 1912.
Copeland, Pamela C., and Richard K. MacMaster. *The Five George Masons: Patriots and Planters of Virginia and Maryland*. Charlottesville: University of Virginia Press, 1975.

Countryman, Edward. "Indians, the Colonial Order, and the Social Significance of the American Revolution." *William and Mary Quarterly*, 3d ser., 53 (April, 1996): 342–62.

———. *A People in Revolution: The American Revolution and Political Society in New York, 1760–1790*. Baltimore: Johns Hopkins University Press, 1981.

Couture, Paul Morgan. *A Study of the Non-Regular Military Forces on the Niagara Frontier: 1812–1814*. Ottawa: National Historic Parks and Sites Branch, Microfiche Report Series #193, 1985.

———. *War and Society on the Detroit Frontier, 1791 to 1815*. Ottawa: National Historic Parks and Sites Branch, Microfiche Report Series, #289, 1986.

Coventry, Alexander. *Memoirs of an Emigrant: The Journal of Alexander Coventry, M.D.* 2 vols. Albany: Albany Institute, 1978.

Coyne, James H., ed. *The Talbot Papers*. Ottawa: Royal Society of Canada, 1909.

Crackel, Theodore J. *Mr. Jefferson's Army: Political and Social Reform of the Military Establishment, 1801–1809*. New York: New York University Press, 1987.

Craig, Gerald M. "The American Impact on the Upper Canadian Reform Movement Before 1837." *Canadian Historical Review* 29 (1948):333–52.

———. *Upper Canada: The Formative Years, 1784–1841*. Toronto: McClelland and Stewart, 1963.

Crawford, Mary M., ed. "Mrs. Lydia B. Bacon's Journal, 1811–1812." *Indiana Magazine of History* 40 (Dec. 1944):367–86 and 41 (Mar. 1945): 59–79.

Cray, Robert E., Jr. "Remembering the U.S.S. *Chesapeake*: The Politics of Maritime Death and Impressment." *Journal of the Early Republic* 25 (fall 2005): 445–74.

Creighton, Donald G. *The Empire of the St. Lawrence, 1760–1850*. Toronto: Ryerson Press, 1956.

Crocker, J. D., ed. *Letters and Journals of Samuel and Laura Sherwood, 1813–1823*. Delhi, N.Y.: no pub., 1967.

Crombie, John N. "The Papers of Major Daniel McFarland: A Hawk of 1812." *Western Pennsylvania Historical Magazine* 51 (Apr. 1968):101–25.

Cruikshank, E. A. "Blockade of Fort George, 1813." *Niagara Historical Society, Publications* 3 (1898): 21–76.

———. "The Chesapeake Crisis as It Affected Upper Canada." *Ontario Historical Society, Papers and Records* 24 (1927): 281–322.

———. *The Fight in the Beechwoods: A Study in Canadian History*. Welland, Ont.: Lundy's Lane Historical Society, 1895.

———. "General Hull's Invasion of Canada in 1812." *Royal Society of Canada, Transactions*, 3d ser., 1 (1907), part 2: 211–90.

———. "John Beverley Robinson and the Trials for Treason in 1814." *Ontario History* 25 (1929): 191–219.

———. "The King's Royal Regiment of New York." *Ontario Historical Society, Papers and Records* 27 (1931): 193–323.

———. "A Memoir of Lieutenant-General Peter Hunter." *Ontario Historical Society, Papers and Records* 30 (1934): 5–32.

———. "Notes on the Early Settlement of Burford." *Ontario Historical Society, Papers and Records* 26 (1930): 380–89.

———. *The Political Adventures of John Henry: The Record of an International Imbroglio*. Toronto: Macmillan, 1936.

———. "Post-War Discontent at Niagara in 1818." *Ontario Historical Society, Papers and Records* 29 (1933): 14–46.

————. *The Settlement of the United Empire Loyalists on the Upper St. Lawrence and Bay of Quinte in 1784, A Documentary Record.* Toronto: Ontario Historical Society, 1934.

————. "A Sketch of the Public Life and Services of Robert Nichol." *Ontario Historical Society, Papers and Records* 19 (1922): 6–81.

————. "A Study of Disaffection in Upper Canada in 1812–15." *Royal Society of Canada, Transactions,* 3d ser., 6 (1912), section 2:11–65.

Cruikshank, E. A., ed., "An Account of the Operations of the Indian Contingent with our Forces on the Niagara Frontier in 1812–13." *Niagara Historical Society, Publications* 9 (1934): 23–46.

————, ed. *The Correspondence of the Honourable Peter Russell.* 3 vols. Toronto: Ontario Historical Society, 1932–36.

————, ed. *The Correspondence of Lieut. Governor John Graves Simcoe, with Allied Documents Relating to His Administration of the Government of Upper Canada.* 5 vols. Toronto: Ontario Historical Society, 1923–31.

————, ed. "The County of Norfolk in the War of 1812." *Ontario Historical Society, Papers and Records* 20 (1923): 9–40.

————, ed. *Documentary History of the Campaigns upon the Niagara Frontier in 1812–1814.* 9 vols. Welland, Ont.: Tribune Press, 1896–1908.

————. *Documents Relating to the Invasion of Canada and the Surrender of Detroit, 1812.* Ottawa: Government Printing Bureau, 1912.

————, ed. "The Early History of the London District." *Ontario Historical Society, Papers and Records* 24 (1927): 145–280.

————, ed. "Petitions for Grants of Land, 1792–6." *Ontario Historical Society, Papers and Records* 24 (1927): 17–144.

————. "Petitions for Grants of Land in Upper Canada, Second Series, 1796–99." *Ontario Historical Society, Papers and Records* 26 (1930): 97–379.

————, ed. "Records of Niagara, 1784–7." *Niagara Historical Society, Publications* 39 (1928): 3–134.

————. "Records of Niagara, 1784–9." *Niagara Historical Society, Publications* 40 (1929): 3–100.

————. "Records of Niagara, 1805–1811." *Niagara Historical Society, Publications* 42 (1931): 3–132.

————. "Records of Niagara: A Collection of Contemporary Letters and Documents, 1812." *Niagara Historical Society, Publications* 43 (1934): 9–77.

————. "Records of Niagara: A Collection of Contemporary Letters and Documents, January to July 1813." *Niagara Historical Society, Publications* 44 (1939): 9–87.

Curry, Frederick C., ed. "A Letter from Ogdensburg in 1814." *Ontario History* 41 (1949): 207–12.

Curtin, Nancy J. *The United Irishmen: Popular Politics in Ulster and Dublin, 1791–1798.* Oxford: Clarendon Press, 1994.

Dallas, Alexander J. *Report of the Secretary of the Treasury . . . in Relation to Expenses in the Prosecution of Offenses Against the United States . . . 1808 to the Year 1815.* Washington, D.C.: William A. Davis, 1818.

Darnell, Elias. *A Journal Containing an Accurate and Interesting Account of the Hardships, Sufferings, Battles, Defeat, and Captivity of those Heroic Kentucky Volunteers and Regulars Commanded by General Winchester in the Years 1812–13.* Philadelphia: Lippincott, Grambo, 1854.

Davis, Richard Beale, ed. *Jeffersonian America: Notes on the United States of America Col-

lected in the Years 1805–6–7 and 11–12 by Sir Augustus John Foster, Bart. San Marino, Calif.: Huntington Library, 1954.

Dawe, Brian. *"Old Oxford is Wide Awake!": Pioneer Settlers and Politicians in Oxford County, 1793–1853.* N.p., 1980.

DeConde, Alexander. *The Quasi-War: The Politics and Diplomacy of the Undeclared War with France, 1797–1801.* New York: Scribner, 1966.

Densmore, Christopher. *Red Jacket: Iroquois Diplomat and Orator.* Syracuse, N.Y.: Syracuse University Press, 1999.

Dickson, William, "Correspondence Between Hon. William Dickson, Prisoner of War and Gen. Dearborn, 1813." *Niagara Historical Society, Publications* 28 (1915–16): 1–5.

Dietz, Anthony George. "The Prisoner of War in the United States During the War of 1812." Ph.D. diss., American University, 1964.

Donnan, Elizabeth, ed. "Papers of James A. Bayard, 1796–1815." In American Historical Association, *Annual Report for the Year 1913.* 2 vols. Washington, D.C.: American Historical Association, 1915.

Dorland, Arthur. *A History of the Society of Friends (Quakers) in Canada.* Toronto: Macmillan, 1927.

Douglas, John. *Medical Topography of Upper Canada.* London, 1819. Reprint, Boston: Science Publications, 1985.

Duane, William. "Selections from the Duane Papers." *Historical Magazine* 4 (Aug. 1868): 60–75.

Dudley, William S., ed. *The Naval War of 1812: A Documentary History.* 3 vols. Washington, D.C.: Department of the Navy, 1992.

Duffy, John J., ed. *Ethan Allen and His Kin: Correspondence, 1772–1819.* 2 vols. Hanover, N.H.: University Press of New England, 1998.

Dunham, Aileen. *Political Unrest in Upper Canada, 1815–1836.* Toronto: McClelland and Stewart, 1963.

Dunnigan, Brian Leigh. "Fortress Detroit, 1701–1826." In David Curtis Skaggs and Larry L. Nelson, eds., *The Sixty Years' War for the Great Lakes, 1754–1814,* 167–86. East Lansing: Michigan State University Press, 2001.

———. "The Michigan Fencibles." *Michigan History* 57 (winter 1973): 277–95.

———. "Military Life at Niagara, 1792–1796." In Richard Merritt, Nancy Butler, and Michael Power, eds., *The Capital Years: Niagara-on-the-Lake, 1792–1796,* 67–102. Toronto: Dundurn Press, 1991.

Durey, Michael. "Marquess Cornwallis and the Fate of Irish Rebel Prisoners in the Aftermath of the 1798 Rebellion." In Jim Smyth, ed., *Revolution, Counter-Revolution, and Union: Ireland in the 1790s,* 128–45. New York: Cambridge University Press, 2000.

———. *Transatlantic Radicals and the Early American Republic.* Lawrence: University Press of Kansas, 1997.

———. "The United Irishmen and the Politics of Banishment, 1798–1807." In Michael T. Davis, ed., *Radicalism and Revolution in Britain, 1775–1848,* 96–109. New York: St. Martin's Press, 2000.

Dye, Ira. "American Maritime Prisoners of War, 1812–1815." In Timothy J. Runyan, ed., *Ships, Seafaring, and Society: Essays in Maritime History,* 298–320. Detroit: Wayne State University Press, 1987.

———. "Early American Merchant Seafarers." *American Philosophical Society, Proceedings* 120 (Oct. 1976): 331–60.

———. *The Fatal Cruise of the Argus: Two Captains in the War of 1812.* Annapolis: Naval Institute Press, 1994.

———. "Physical and Social Profiles of Early American Seafarers, 1812–1815." In Colin Howell and Richard J. Twomey, eds., *Jack Tar in History: Essays in the History of Maritime Life and Labour,* 220–35. Fredericton, N.B.: Acadiensis Press, 1991.

Edgar, Matilda, ed. *Ten Years of Upper Canada in Peace and War, 1805–1815.* Toronto: William Briggs, 1890.

Edmunds, R. David. "Forgotten Allies: The Loyal Shawnees and the War of 1812." In David Curtis Skaggs and Larry L. Nelson, eds., *The Sixty Years' War for the Great Lakes, 1754–1814,* 337–51. East Lansing: Michigan State University Press, 2001.

Egan, Clifford L., ed. "The Path to War in 1812 through the Eyes of a New Hampshire 'War Hawk.'" *Historical New Hampshire* 30 (fall 1975): 147–77.

Egerton, Douglas R. "The Empire of Liberty Reconsidered." In James Horn, Jan Ellen Lewis, and Peter S. Onuf, eds., *The Revolution of 1800: Democracy, Race, and the New Republic,* 309–30. Charlottesville: University of Virginia Press, 2002.

Einstein, Lewis, ed. "Recollections of the War of 1812 by George Hay, Eighth Marquis of Tweeddale." *American Historical Review* 32 (Oct. 1926): 69–78.

Elkins, Stanley, and Eric McKitrick. *The Age of Federalism.* New York: Oxford University Press, 1993.

Ellery, Harrison, ed. *The Memoirs of Gen. Joseph Gardner Swift, LL.D., U.S.A.* Worcester, Mass.: privately printed, 1890.

Ellis, David Maldwyn. *Landlords and Farmers in the Hudson-Mohawk Region, 1790–1850.* Ithaca, N.Y.: Cornell University Press, 1946.

———. "The Rise of the Empire State, 1790–1820." *New York History* 56 (Jan. 1975): 5–27.

Emsley, Clive. "An Aspect of Pitt's 'Terror': Prosecutions for Sedition during the 1790s." *Social History* 6 (May 1981): 155–84.

Epp, Frank H. *The Mennonites in Canada, 1786–1920: The History of a Separate People.* Toronto: Macmillan of Canada, 1974.

Erney, Richard Alton. *The Public Life of Henry Dearborn.* New York: Arno Press, 1979.

Ernst, Robert. *Rufus King: American Federalist.* Chapel Hill: University of North Carolina Press, 1968.

Errington, Jane. *The Lion, the Eagle, and Upper Canada: A Developing Colonial Ideology.* Montreal: McGill-Queen's University Press, 1987.

Esarey, Logan, ed. *Messages and Letters of William Henry Harrison.* 2 vols. Indianapolis: Indiana Historical Commission, 1922.

Evans, Paul D. *The Holland Land Company.* Buffalo: Buffalo Historical Society, 1924.

Everest, Allan S. *The War of 1812 in the Champlain Valley.* Syracuse, N.Y.: Syracuse University Press, 1981.

Fabel, Robin F. A. "Self-Help in Dartmoor: Black and White Prisoners in the War of 1812." *Journal of the Early Republic* 9 (summer 1989): 165–90.

Fahey, Curtis. *In His Name: The Anglican Experience in Upper Canada, 1791–1854.* Ottawa: Carleton University Press, 1991.

Fairchild, George M., Jr., ed. *Journal of an American Prisoner at Fort Malden and Quebec in the War of 1812.* Quebec: Frank Carrell, 1909.

Farmer, Silas. *The History of Detroit and Wayne County and Early Michigan.* Detroit: Silas Farmer, 1890.

Fecteau, Jean-Marie, F. Murray Greenwood, and Jean Pierre Wallot. "Sir James Craig's 'Reign of Terror' and Its Impact on Emergency Powers in Lower Canada,

1810–13." In F. Murray Greenwood and Barry Wright, eds., *Canadian State Trials*, 2 vols., 1:323–78. Toronto: Osgoode Society and University of Toronto Press, 1996.

Fiege, Mark. "Gettysburg and the Organic Nature of the American Civil War." In Richard P. Tucker and Edmund Russell, eds., *Natural Enemy, Natural Ally: Toward an Environmental History of Warfare*, 93–109. Corvallis: Oregon State University Press, 2004.

Finan, P. "An Onlooker's View." In John Gellner, ed., *Recollections of the War of 1812: Three Eyewitness Accounts*, 46–107. Toronto: Baxter, 1964.

Firth, Edith G., ed. *The Town of York, 1793–1815: A Collection of Documents of Early Toronto*. Toronto: Champlain Society, 1962.

Fischer, David Hackett. *The Revolution of American Conservatism: The Federalist Party in the Era of Jeffersonian Democracy*. New York: Harper & Row, 1965.

Foner, Jack D. *Blacks and the Military in American History: A New Perspective*. New York: Praeger, 1974.

Ford, Worthington C., ed. "Letters of William Duane." *Massachusetts Historical Society, Proceedings* 20 (May 1906): 257–394.

Fraser, Alexander, ed. *Fourth Report of the Bureau of Archives for the Province of Ontario, 1906*. Toronto: L. K. Cameron, 1907.

Fraser, Robert Lochiel. "Politics at the Head of the Lake in the Era of the War of 1812: The Case of Abraham Markle." *Hamilton Heritage/Wentworth Bygones* 14 (1984): 18–27.

Fredriksen, John C. *Green Coats and Glory: The United States Regiment of Riflemen, 1808–1821*. Youngstown, N.Y.: Old Fort Niagara Association, 2000.

Fredriksen, John C., ed. "Chronicle of Valor: The Journal of a Pennsylvania Officer in the War of 1812." *Western Pennsylvania Historical Magazine* 67 (July 1984): 243–84.

Fredriksen, John C. "Colonel James Burn and the War of 1812: The Letters of a South Carolina Officer." *South Carolina Historical Magazine* 90 (Oct. 1989): 299–312.

———. "A Georgia Officer in the War of 1812: The Letters of William Clay Cumming." *Georgia Historical Quarterly* 71 (winter 1987): 668–92.

———. "Lawyer, Soldier, Judge: Incidents in the Life of Joseph Lee Smith of New Britain, Connecticut." *Connecticut Historical Society, Bulletin* 51 (spring 1986): 103–21.

———. "The Letters of Captain John Scott, 15th U.S. Infantry: A New Jersey Officer in the War of 1812." *New Jersey History* 107 (fall/winter 1989): 61–82.

———. "Memoirs of Ephraim Shaler: A Connecticut Yankee in the War of 1812." *New England Quarterly* 57 (Sep. 1984): 411–20.

———. "A New Hampshire Volunteer in the War of 1812: The Experiences of Charles Fairbanks." *Historical New Hampshire* 40 (fall/winter 1985): 156–78.

———. "The Pennsylvania Volunteers in the War of 1812: An Anonymous Journal of Service for the Year 1814." *Western Pennsylvania Historical Magazine* 70 (April 1987): 123–57.

———. " 'A Poor But Honest Sodger': Colonel Cromwell Pearce, the 16th U.S. Infantry, and the War of 1812." *Pennsylvania History* 52 (July 1985): 131–61.

———. *Surgeon of the Lakes: The Diary of Usher Parsons, 1812–1814*. Erie, Pa.: Erie County Historical Society, 2000.

———. "The War of 1812 in Northern New York: General George Izard's Journal of the Chateauguay Campaign." *New York History* 76 (Apr. 1995): 173–200.

———. "The War of 1812 in Northern New York: The Observations of Captain Rufus McIntire." *New York History* 68 (July 1987): 297–324.

Freeman, Joanne B. "Corruption and Compromise in the Election of 1800: The Process of Politics on the National Stage." In James Horn, Jan Ellen Lewis, and Peter S. Onuf, eds., *The Revolution of 1800: Democracy, Race, and the New Republic,* 87–120. Charlottesville: University of Virginia Press, 2002.

French, Goldwin S. *Parsons & Politics: The Role of the Wesleyan Methodists in Upper Canada and the Maritimes from 1780 to 1855.* Toronto: Ryerson Press, 1962.

Fryer, Mary Beacock, and Christopher Dracott. *John Graves Simcoe, 1752–1806: A Biography.* Toronto: Dundurn Press, 1998.

Furstenberg, François. "The Significance of the Trans-Appalachian Frontier in Atlantic History." *American Historical Review* 113 (June 2008): 647–77.

Galenson, David W. "The Settlement and Growth of the Colonies: Population, Labor, and Economic Development." In Stanley L. Engerman and Robert E. Gallman, eds., *The Cambridge Economic History of the United States,* 135–207. New York: Cambridge University Press, 1996.

Garner, John. *The Franchise and Politics in British North America.* Toronto: University of Toronto Press, 1969.

Gates, Lillian F. *Land Policies of Upper Canada.* Toronto: University of Toronto Press, 1968.

———. "Roads, Rivals, and Rebellion: The Unknown Story of Asa Danforth, Jr." *Ontario History* 76 (Sep. 1984): 233–54.

Gentilcore, R. Louis, and John David Wood. "A Military Colony in a Wilderness: The Upper Canada Frontier." In Wood, ed., *Perspectives on Landscape and Settlement in Nineteenth-Century Ontario,* 32–50. Toronto: McClelland and Stewart, 1975.

Geoghegan, Patrick. *Robert Emmet, a Life.* Dublin: Gill & Macmillan, 2002.

Gilje, Paul A. *Liberty on the Waterfront: American Maritime Culture in the Age of Revolution.* Philadelphia: University of Pennsylvania Press, 2004.

———. *Rioting in America.* Bloomington: Indiana University Press, 1996.

Gilpin, Alec R. *The Territory of Michigan, 1805–1837.* East Lansing: Michigan State University Press, 1970.

Giunta, Mary A., ed. *The Emerging Nation: A Documentary History of the Foreign Relations of the United States under the Articles of Confederation, 1780–1789.* 3 vols. Washington, D.C.: NHPRC, 1996.

Goldie, John. *Diary of a Journey through Upper Canada and Some of the New England States, 1819.* Toronto: privately published, 1967.

Golovin, Anne Castrodale, ed. "William Wood Thackara, Volunteer in the War of 1812." *Pennsylvania Magazine of History and Biography* 91 (July 1967): 299–325.

Gough, Barry. *Fighting Sail on Lake Huron and Georgian Bay: The War of 1812 and Its Aftermath.* St. Catharines, Ont.: Vanwell, 2002.

Gould, Eliga H. "American Independence and Britain's Counter-Revolution." *Past and Present,* no. 154 (Feb. 1997): 107–41.

———. "The Making of an Atlantic State System: Britain and the United States, 1795–1825." In Julie Flavell and Stephen Conway, eds., *Britain and America Go to War: The Impact of War and Warfare in Anglo-America, 1754–1815,* 241–65. Gainesville: University Press of Florida, 2004.

———. *The Persistence of Empire: British Political Culture in the Age of the American Revolution.* Chapel Hill: University of North Carolina Press, 2000.

Gourlay, Robert, ed. *Statistical Account of Upper Canada, Compiled with a View to a Grand System of Emigration.* 2 vols. London, 1822.

Grabbe, Hans-Jurgen. "European Immigration to the United States in the Early National Period, 1783–1820." *American Philosophical Society, Proceedings* 133 (June 1989): 190–214.

Graffagnino, J. Kevin. " 'Twenty Thousand Muskets!!!': Ira Allen and the Olive Branch Affair, 1796–1800." *William and Mary Quarterly* 48 (July 1991): 409–31.

Graham, Gerald S. *British Policy and Canada, 1774–1791: A Study in Eighteenth-Century Trade Policy.* London, 1930. Reprint, Westport, Conn.: Greenwood Press, 1974.

———, ed. "Views of General [Sir George] Murray on the Defense of Upper Canada, 1815." *Canadian Historical Review* 34 (June 1953): 158–65.

Graham, John Andrew. *A Descriptive Sketch of the Present State of Vermont.* London, 1797. Reprint, Bennington: Vermont Heritage Press, 1987.

Grant, John Webster. *A Profusion of Spires: Religion in Nineteenth-Century Ontario.* Toronto: University of Toronto Press, 1988.

Graves, Diana. *In the Midst of Alarms: The Untold Story of Women and the War of 1812.* Cap-Saint-Ignace, Quebec: Robin Brass Studio, 2007.

Graves, Donald E. "The Canadian Volunteers, 1813–1815." *Military Collector & Historian* 31 (fall 1979): 113–17.

———. *Field of Glory: The Battle of Crysler's Farm, 1813.* Toronto: Robin Brass Studio, 1999.

———. *Where Right and Glory Lead!: The Battle of Lundy's Lane, 1814.* Toronto: Robin Brass Studio, 2000.

Graves, Donald E. ed. *Merry Hearts Make Light Days: The War of 1812 Journal of Lieutenant John Le Couteur, 104th Foot.* Ottawa: Carleton University Press, 1993.

Graves, Donald E. *Soldiers of 1814: American Enlisted Men's Memoirs of the Niagara Campaign.* Youngstown, N.Y.: Old Fort Niagara Association, 1995.

Gray, Leslie R., ed. "From Bethlehem to Fairfield—1798." *Ontario History* 46 (winter and spring 1954): 37–61 and 107–30.

———. "From Fairfield to Schonbrun–1798." *Ontario History* 49 (winter 1957): 63–96.

Graymont, Barbara. *The Iroquois in the American Revolution.* Syracuse, N.Y.: Syracuse University Press, 1972.

Green, Ernest. "John De Cou, Pioneer." *Ontario Historical Society, Papers and Records* 22 (1925): 92–116.

Greenwood, F. Murray. *Legacies of Fear: Law and Politics in Quebec in the Era of the French Revolution.* Toronto: University of Toronto Press, 1993.

Greenwood, F. Murray, and Barry Wright. "Parliamentary Privilege and the Repression of Dissent in the Canadas." In Greenwood and Wright, eds., *Canadian State Trials,* 2 vols., 409–49. Toronto: University of Toronto Press, 1996.

Gregg, William. *History of the Presbyterian Church in the Dominion of Canada from the Earliest Times to 1834.* Toronto: Presbyterian Printing, 1885.

Grew, John. *Journal of a Tour from Boston to Niagara Falls and Quebec, 1803.* N.p., n.d.

Griffin, Patrick *American Leviathan: Empire, Nation, and Revolutionary Frontier.* New York: Hill & Wang, 2007.

Guest, Harry H. "Upper Canada's First Political Party." *Ontario History* 54 (Dec. 1962): 275–96.

Guillet, Edwin C. *Early Life in Upper Canada.* Toronto: Ontario Publishing Co., 1933.

Hacker, Louis M. "Western Land Hunger and the War of 1812." *Mississippi Valley Historical Review* 10 (1923–24): 365–95.

Hadfield, Joseph. *An Englishman in America, 1785, Being the Diary of Joseph Hadfield.* Edited by Douglas S. Robertson. Toronto: Hunter-Rose, 1933.

Hall, Amos. "Militia Service of 1812–1814, as Shown by the Correspondence of Major General Amos Hall." *Buffalo Historical Society, Publications* 5 (1902): 26–62.

Hall, Francis. *Travels in Canada and the United States in 1816 and 1817.* Boston: Wells & Lilly, 1818.

Hamil, Fred Coyne. *Lake Erie Baron: The Story of Colonel Thomas Talbot.* Toronto: Macmillan of Canada, 1955.

Hamilton, Milton W., ed. "Guy Johnson's Opinions on the American Indian." *Pennsylvania Magazine of History and Biography* 77 (July 1953): 311–27.

Hamilton, Stanislaus Murray, ed. *The Writings of James Monroe: Including a Collection of his Public and Private Papers and Correspondence.* 7 vols. New York: Putnam, 1901.

Hanks, Jarvis Frary. "The Memoir of Drummer Jarvis Frary Hanks, 11th Infantry." In Donald Graves, ed., *Soldiers of 1814: American Enlisted Men's Memoirs of the Niagara Campaign,* 19–49. Youngstown, N.Y.: Old Fort Niagara Association, 1995.

Hansen, Marcus Lee, and John Bartlett Brebner. *The Mingling of the Canadian and American Peoples.* New Haven: Yale University Press, 1940.

Hare, John S. "Military Punishments in the War of 1812." *Journal of the American Military Institute* 4 (winter 1940): 225–39.

Harlow, Vincent T. *The Founding of the Second British Empire, 1763–1793.* 2 vols. London: Longmans, Green, 1964.

Harrison, Eliza Cope, ed. *Philadelphia Merchant: The Diary of Thomas P. Cope, 1800–1851.* South Bend, Ind.: Gateway Editions, 1978.

Hastings, Hugh, ed. *Public Papers of Daniel D. Tompkins, Governor of New York: 1807–1817.* 3 vols. Albany: Wynkoop, Hallenbeck, & Crawford, 1898.

Hauptman, Laurence M. *Conspiracy of Interests: Iroquois Dispossession and the Rise of New York State.* Syracuse, N.Y.: Syracuse University Press, 1999.

Hawthorne, Nathaniel, ed. *The Yarn of a Yankee Privateer.* New York: Funk and Wagnalls, 1926.

Hayes, George H., ed. "Letters of Samuel Taggart, Representative in Congress, 1803–1814." *American Antiquarian Society, Proceedings* 33 (Apr. 1923): 113–226.

Healey, Robynne Rogers. *From Quaker to Upper Canadian: Faith and Community among Yonge Street Friends, 1801–1850.* Montreal: McGill-Queen's University Press, 2006.

Heitman, Francis B., ed. *Historical Register and Dictionary of the United States Army, 1789–1903.* Washington, D.C.: Government Printing Office, 1903.

Henderson, Dwight F., *Congress, Courts, and Criminals: The Development of Federal Criminal Law, 1801–1829.* Westport, Conn.: Greenwood Press, 1985.

Henderson, J. L. H., ed. *John Strachan: Documents and Opinions, a Selection.* Toronto: McClelland and Stewart, 1969.

Hendrickson, David C., *Peace Pact: The Lost World of the American Founding.* Lawrence: University Press of Kansas, 2003.

Heriot, George. *Travels Through the Canadas, Containing a Description of the Picturesque Scenery on some of the Rivers and Lakes.* Philadelphia, 1813. Reprint, Toronto: Coles, 1971.

Hickey, Donald R. *Don't Give Up the Ship!: Myths of the War of 1812.* Urbana: University of Illinois Press, 2006.

———. *The War of 1812: A Forgotten Conflict.* Urbana: University of Illinois Press, 1989.

Higgins, W. H. *The Life and Times of Joseph Gould, Ex-Member of the Canadian Parliament.* Toronto: C. Blackett Robinson, 1887.

Hinde, Wendy. *Castlereagh.* London: William Collins, 1981.

Hinderaker, Eric. *Elusive Empires: Constructing Colonialism in the Ohio Valley, 1673–1800.* New York: Cambridge University Press, 1997.

Hitsman, J. Mackay. "David Parish and the War of 1812." *Military Affairs* 26 (winter 1962–63): 171–77.

———. *The Incredible War of 1812: A Military History.* Toronto: Robin Brass Studio, 1999.

———. *Safeguarding Canada, 1763–1871.* Toronto: University of Toronto Press, 1968.

———. "Spying at Sacker's Harbor," *Inland Seas* 15 (summer 1959): 120–22.

Hodge, William. "The William Hodge Papers." *Buffalo Historical Society, Publications* 26 (1922): 169–314.

Holmden, H. R., ed. "Baron de Gaugreben's Memoir on the Defence of Upper Canada." *Canadian Historical Review* 2 (Mar. 1921): 58–68.

Holton, Woody. " 'From the Labour of Others': The War Bonds Controversy and the Origins of the Constitution in New England." *William and Mary Quarterly* 61 (Apr. 2004): 271–316.

Hopkins, James F., et al., eds. *The Papers of Henry Clay.* 11 vols. Lexington: University of Kentucky Press, 1959–1992.

Horsman, Reginald. "British Indian Policy in the Northwest, 1807–1812," *Mississippi Valley Historical Review* 45 (June 1958): 51–66.

———. *The Causes of the War of 1812.* Philadelphia: University of Pennsylvania Press, 1962.

———. *Expansion and American Indian Policy, 1783–1812.* East Lansing: Michigan State University Press, 1967.

———. "Nantucket's Peace Treaty with England in 1814." *New England Quarterly* 54 (1981):180–98.

———. "On to Canada: Manifest Destiny and United States Strategy in the War of 1812." *Michigan Historical Review* 13 (fall 1987): 1–24.

———. "The Paradox of Dartmoor Prison." *American Heritage Magazine* 26 (Feb. 1975): 12–17.

Horton, John T., ed. "An Original Narrative of the Niagara Campaign of 1814," *Niagara Frontier* 46 (Spring 1964): 1–36.

Hough, Franklin B. *A History of Jefferson County in the State of New York from the Earliest Period to the Present Time.* Albany: Joel Munsell, 1854.

———. *A History of St. Lawrence and Franklin Counties New York from the Earliest Period to the Present Time.* Albany: Little & Co., 1853.

Howe, Ebenezer D. "Recollections of a Pioneer Printer." *Buffalo Historical Society, Publications* 9 (1906): 377–406.

Howe, John R., Jr. "Republican Thought and the Political Violence of the 1790s." *American Quarterly* 19 (1967): 147–65.

Howison, John. *Sketches of Upper Canada: Domestic, Local, and Characteristic.* Edinburgh: Oliver & Boyd, 1821.

Hughes, Thomas. *A Journal by Thos. Hughes, for his Amusement.* Edited by E. A. Benians. Cambridge, U.K.: University of Cambridge Press, 1947.

Humphries, Charles W. "The Capture of York." *Ontario History* 51 (winter 1959): 1–24.

Hunter, Robert, Jr. *Quebec to Carolina in 1785–1786, Being the Travel Diary and Obser-*

vations of Robert Hunter, Jr., a Young Merchant of London. Edited by Louis B. Wright and Marion Tinling. San Marino, Calif.: Huntington Library, 1943.

Hutchinson, William T., et al., eds. *The Papers of James Madison: Congressional Series.* 17 vols. Charlottesville: University of Virginia Press, 1959–91.

Ignatiev, Noel. *How the Irish Became White.* New York: Routledge, 1995.

Innis, Mary Quale, ed. *Mrs. Simcoe's Diary.* Toronto: Macmillan, 1965.

Irwin, Ray W. *Daniel D. Tompkins: Governor of New York and Vice-President of the United States.* New York: New-York Historical Society, 1968.

Isenberg, Nancy. *Fallen Founder: The Life of Aaron Burr.* New York: Viking, 2007.

Ivison, Stuart, and Fred Rosser. *The Baptists in Upper and Lower Canada before 1820.* Toronto: University of Toronto Press, 1956.

Jackman, Sidney W., ed. "Two Simcoe Letters." *Ontario History* 49 (1957): 42–45.

Jacobs, James Ripley. *Tarnished Warrior: Major-General James Wilkinson.* New York: Macmillan, 1938.

Jacobsen, Edna L. "Aaron Hamton's Diary." *New York History* 21 (July 1940): 324–34 and (Oct. 1940): 431–42.

James, C. C. "The First Legislators of Upper Canada." *Royal Society of Canada, Transactions,* 2d ser., 8, sec. 2 (1902): 93–119.

Jasanoff, Maya. "The Other Side of Revolution: Loyalists in the British Empire." *William and Mary Quarterly,* 3d ser., 65 (Apr. 2008): 205–32.

Jenkins, Brian, *Henry Goulburn, 1784–1856: A Political Biography.* Montreal: McGill-Queen's University Press, 1996.

Johnson, J. K. *Becoming Prominent: Regional Leadership in Upper Canada, 1791–1841.* Montreal, 1989.

Johnson, J. K., and Bruce G. Wilson, eds. *Historical Essays on Upper Canada: New Perspectives.* Ottawa: Carleton University Press, 1989.

Johnson, Timothy D. *Winfield Scott: The Quest for Military Glory.* Lawrence: University of Kentucky Press, 1998.

Johnston, Charles M. "An Outline of Early Settlement in the Grand River Valley." *Ontario History* 54 (Mar. 1962):43–67.

———, ed. *The Valley of the Six Nations: A Collection of Documents on the Indian Lands of the Grand River.* Toronto: Champlain Society and University of Toronto Press, 1964.

Johnston, Henry P., ed. *The Correspondence and Public Papers of John Jay.* New York: Putnam, 1891.

Johnston, Winston. *The Glengarry Light Infantry, 1812–1816: Who Were They and What Did They Do in the War?* Charlottetown, P.E.I.: Benson, 1998.

Jones, Wilbur Devereux, ed. "A British View of the War of 1812 and the Peace Negotiations." *Mississippi Valley Historical Review* 45 (Dec. 1958):481–87.

Judd, Peter. *The Hatch and Brood of Time.* Boston: Newbury Street Press, 1999.

Kaplan, Roger. "The Hidden War: British Intelligence Operations during the American Revolution." *William and Mary Quarterly,* 3d ser., 47 (Jan. 1990):115–38.

Keegan, John. *The Face of Battle: A Study of Agincourt, Waterloo, and the Somme.* New York: Random House, 1976.

Ketchum, William. *An Authentic and Comprehensive History of Buffalo.* 2 vols. Buffalo: Rockwell, Baker, and Hill, 1864–65.

Kettner, James H. *The Development of American Citizenship, 1608–1870.* Chapel Hill: University of North Carolina Press, 1978.

Klinck, Carl F., and Malcolm Ross, eds. *Tiger Dunlop's Upper Canada*. Toronto: McClelland and Stewart, 1967.

Klinck, Carl F., and J. J. Talman, eds. *Journal of Major John Norton, 1816*. Toronto: Champlain Society, 1970.

Kline, Mary-Jo, ed. *Political Correspondence and Public Papers of Aaron Burr*. 2 vols. Princeton: Princeton University Press, 1983.

Klunder, Willard Carl. *Lewis Cass and the Politics of Moderation*. Kent, Ohio: Kent State University Press, 1996.

Koenigsberger, H. G. "Composite States, Representative Institutions, and the American Revolution." *Historical Research* 63 (1989):135–53.

Kutolowski, John F., and Kathleen Smith Kutolowski, "Commissions and Canvasses: The Militia and Politics in Western New York, 1800–1845." *New York History* 63 (Jan. 1982):5–38.

Lanctot, Gustave. *Canada and the American Revolution, 1774–1783*. Cambridge, Mass.: Harvard University Press, 1967.

Landon, Fred. *Western Ontario and the American Frontier*. Toronto: Ryerson Press, 1941.

Landon, Harry F. "British Sympathizers in St. Lawrence County During the War of 1812." *New York History* 35 (April 1954): 131–38.

Lathem, Edward Connery. *Chronological Tables of American Newspapers, 1690–1820*. Barre, Mass., 1972.

Latimer, Jon. *1812: War with America*. Cambridge, Mass.: Harvard University Press, 2007).

Lavery, Brian. *Nelson's Navy: The Ships, Men, and Organisation, 1793–1815*. London: Conway Maritime Press, 1989.

Lawson, Philip. *Imperial Challenge: Quebec and Britain in the Age of the American Revolution*. Montreal: McGill-Queen's University Press, 1989.

Lemmon, Sarah McCulloh. *Frustrated Patriots: North Carolina and the War of 1812*. Chapel Hill: University of North Carolina Press, 1973.

Lender, Mark E., and James Kirby Martin, eds. *Citizen-Soldier: The Revolutionary War Journal of Joseph Bloomfield*. Newark: New Jersey Historical Society, 1982.

Lewis, James E., Jr. " 'What Is to Become of Our Government': The Revolutionary Potential of the Election of 1800." In James Horn, Jan Ellen Lewis, and Peter S. Onuf, eds., *The Revolution of 1800: Democracy, Race, and the New Republic*, 3–29. Charlottesville: University of Virginia Press, 2002.

Lewis, Michael. *A Social History of the Navy, 1793–1815*. London: George Allen & Unwin, 1960.

Lincoln, Benjamin. "Journal of a Treaty Held in 1793 with the Indian Tribes North West of the Ohio by Commissioners of the United States." *Massachusetts Historical Society, Collections*, 3d ser., 5 (1836): 109–76.

Lindley, Jacob. "Account of a Journey to Attend the Indian Treaty Proposed to Be Held at Sandusky in the Year 1793." *Michigan Pioneer and Historical Society, Historical Collections* 18 (1890): 565–632.

Lipscomb, Andrew A., and Albert Ellery Bergh, eds. *The Writings of Thomas Jefferson*. 20 vols. Washington, D.C.: Thomas Jefferson Memorial Association, 1903–4.

Lord, Norman C., ed. "The War of 1812 on the Canadian Frontier, 1812–1814: Letters Written by Sergeant James Commins, 8th Foot." *Journal of the Society for Army Historical Research* 18 (winter 1939): 199–211.

Macauley, James. *The Natural, Statistical and Civil History of the State of New-York* . . . 3 vols. New York, 1829.

MacLeod, Malcolm. "Fortress Ontario or Forlorn Hope?: Simcoe and the Defence of Upper Canada." *Canadian Historical Review* 53 (1972): 149–78.

Malcomson, Robert. *Capital in Flames: The American Attack on York, 1813.* Annapolis: Naval Institute Press, 2008.

———. *Lords of the Lake: The Naval War on Lake Ontario, 1812–1814.* Annapolis: Naval Institute Press, 1998.

———. *A Very Brilliant Affair: The Battle of Queenston Heights, 1812.* Annapolis: Naval Institute Press, 2003.

———, ed. *Sailors of 1812: Memoirs and Letters of Naval Officers on Lake Ontario.* Youngstown, N.Y.: Old Fort Niagara Association, 1997.

Malone, Dumas. *Jefferson, the President: Second Term, 1805–1809.* Boston: Little, Brown, 1974.

Mancke, Elizabeth. "Another British America: A Canadian Model for the Early Modern British Empire." *Journal of Imperial and Commonwealth History* 25 (Jan. 1997): 1–36.

———. "Early Modern Imperial Governance and the Origins of Canadian Political Culture." *Canadian Journal of Political Science* 32 (Mar. 1999): 3–20.

Mann, James. *Medical Sketches of the Campaigns of 1812, 13, 14.* Dedham, Mass.: H. Mann, & Co., 1816.

Manning, William R., ed. *Diplomatic Correspondence of the United States: Canadian Relations, 1784–1860.* 3 vols. Washington, D.C.: Carnegie Endowment for International Peace, 1940.

Martin, James Kirby, and Mark Edward Lender. *A Respectable Army: The Military Origins of the Republic, 1763–1789.* Arlington Heights, Ill.: Harlan Davidson, 1982.

Martin, John D. P. "The Regiment de Watteville: Its Settlement and Service in Upper Canada." *Ontario History* 52 (Mar. 1960): 17–30.

Mason, Keith. "The American Loyalist Diaspora and the Reconfiguration of the British Atlantic World." In Eliga H. Gould and Peter S. Onuf, eds., *Empire and Nation: The American Revolution in the Atlantic World*, 239–59. Baltimore: Johns Hopkins University Press, 2005.

Maude, John. *Visit to the Falls of Niagara in 1800.* London: Longman, Rees, 1826.

McCalla, Douglas. *Planting the Province: The Economic History of Upper Canada, 1784–1870.* Toronto: University of Toronto Press, 1992.

McCartney, James R. "Sectarian Strife in Dundas County: A Lutheran-Episcopalian Land Endowment Controversy." *Ontario History* 54 (June 1962): 69–86.

McClure, George. *Causes of the Destruction of the American Towns on the Niagara Frontier.* Bath, N.Y.: Benjamin Smead, 1817.

McConville, Brendan. *The King's Three Faces: The Rise & Fall of Royal America, 1688–1776.* Chapel Hill: University of North Carolina Press, 2006.

McCusker, John J. "British Mercantilist Policies and the American Colonies." In Stanley L. Engerman and Robert E. Gallman, eds., *The Cambridge Economic History of the United States*, vol. 1, *The Colonial Era*, 337–62. New York: Cambridge University Press, 1996.

McDowell, R. B. "The Age of the United Irishmen: Revolution and the Union, 1794–1800." In T. W. Moody and W. E. Vaughan, eds., *A New History of Ireland*, vol. 4, *Eighteenth-Century Ireland, 1691–1800*, 339–73. Oxford: Clarendon Press, 1986.

———. "Ireland in 1800." In T. W. Moody and W. E. Vaughan, eds., *A New History of Ireland*, vol. 4, *Eighteenth-Century Ireland, 1691–1800*, 657–712. Oxford: Clarendon Press, 1986.

———. *Ireland in the Age of Imperialism and Revolution, 1760–1801*. Oxford: Clarendon Press, 1979.

McFarland, Elaine. "Scotland and the 1798 Rebellion: The Limits of 'Common Cause.' " In Thomas Bartlett et al., eds., *1798: A Bicentenary Perspective*, 565–76. Dublin: Four Courts Press, 2003.

McKee, Christopher. "Foreign Seamen in the United States Navy: A Census of 1808." *William and Mary Quarterly*, 3d ser., 42 (July 1985): 383–93.

McKenna, Katherine M. J. *A Life of Propriety: Anne Murray Powell and Her Family, 1755–1849*. Montreal: McGill-Queens University Press, 1994.

McKenzie, Ruth. *James FitzGibbon: Defender of Upper Canada*. Toronto: Dundurn Press, 1983.

McLean, Marianne. *The People of Glengarry: Highlanders in Transition, 1745–1820*. Montreal: McGill-Queen's University Press, 1991.

———. "Peopling Glengarry County: The Scottish Origins of a Canadian Community." In J. K. Johnson and Bruce G. Wilson, eds., *Historical Essays on Upper Canada: New Perspectives*, 151–73. Ottawa: Carleton University Press, 1989.

McLellan, Hugh, and Charles Woodberry McLellan, eds. "Garrison Orders: Burlington, Vermont, July 13–August 4, 1813." *Moorsfield Antiquarian* 1 (August 1937): 79–103.

McMaster, Guy Humphrey. *History of the Settlement of Steuben County, N.Y. including Notices of the Old Pioneer Settlers and their Adventures*. Bath, N.Y.: R. S. Underhill, 1853.

McNairn, Jeffrey L. *The Capacity to Judge: Public Opinion and Deliberative Democracy in Upper Canada, 1791–1854*. Toronto: University of Toronto Press, 2000.

McOuat, Donald F., ed. "The Diary of William Graves." *Ontario Historical Society, Papers and Records* 43 (1951): 1–26.

Melish, John. *Travels Through the United States of America, in the Years 1806 & 1807 and 1809, 1810, & 1811*. 2 vols. Philadelphia: T. & G. Palmer, 1812.

Meriwether, Robert C., et al., eds. *The Papers of John C. Calhoun*. 28 vols. Columbia: University of South Carolina Press, 1959–2003.

Middleton, Jesse Edgar, and Fred Landon, eds. *The Province of Ontario: A History, 1615–1927*. Toronto: Dominion, 1928.

Miller, Genevieve, ed. *William Beaumont's Formative Years: Two Early Notebooks, 1811–1821*. New York: Henry Schulman, 1946.

Miller, John C. *Crisis in Freedom: The Alien and Sedition Acts*. Boston: Little, Brown, 1951.

Miller, Kerby A., and Arnold Schrier, Bruce D. Boling, and David N. Doyle, eds. *Irish Immigrants in the Land of Canaan: Letters and Memoirs from Colonial and Revolutionary America, 1675–1815*. New York: Oxford University Press, 2003.

Mills, David. *The Idea of Loyalty in Upper Canada, 1784–1850*. Kingston, Ont.: McGill-Queens University Press, 1988.

Milobar, David. "Conservative Ideology, Metropolitan Government, and the Reform of Quebec, 1782–1791." *International History Review* 12 (Feb. 1990): 45–64.

Moir, John S. "American Influences on Canadian Protestant Churches Before Confederation." *Church History* 26 (Dec. 1967): 440–55.

———. "Early Methodism in the Niagara Peninsula." *Ontario Historical Society, Papers and Records* 43 (Apr. 1951): 51–58.

———. "An Early Record of Laura Secord's Walk." In Morris Zaslow, ed., *The Defended Border: Upper Canada and the War of 1812*, 312–14. Toronto: Macmillan, 1964.

Moody, Robert E., ed. *The Saltonstall Papers, 1607–1815.* 2 vols. Boston: Massachusetts Historical Society, 1972–74.

Moore, Christopher. "The Disposition to Settle: The Royal Highland Emigrants and Loyalist Settlement in Upper Canada, 1784." In J. K. Johnson and Bruce G. Wilson, eds., *Historical Essays on Upper Canada: New Perspectives*, 53–79. Ottawa: Carleton University Press, 1989.

———. *The Loyalists: Revolution, Exile, Settlement.* Toronto: Macmillan of Canada, 1984.

Moore, Joseph. "Journal of a Tour to Detroit . . ." In MPHS, *MHC* 17: 623–68. Lansing: Wynkoop, Hallenbeck, Crawford, 1910.

Morgan, Edmund S. *Inventing the People: The Rise of Popular Sovereignty in England and America.* New York: Norton, 1988.

Morley, Vincent. *Irish Opinion and the American Revolution, 1760–1783.* New York: Cambridge University Press, 2002.

Morris, John D. *Sword of the Border: Major General Jacob Jennings Brown, 1775–1828.* Kent, Ohio: Kent State University Press, 2000.

Morris, Richard B. *The Peacemakers: The Great Powers and American Independence.* New York: Harper & Row, 1965.

Morris, Roger. *Cockburn and the British Navy in Transition: Admiral Sir George Cockburn, 1772–1853.* Columbia: University of South Carolina Press, 1997.

Morse, Jedediah. *A Report to the Secretary of War of the United States on Indian Affairs, Comprising a Narrative of a Tour Performed in the Summer of 1820.* New Haven: S. Converse, 1822.

Mortimer, Benjamin. "The Ohio Frontier in 1812: Diary of the Indian Congregation at Goshen on the River Muskingum for the Year 1812." *Ohio Archaeological and Historical Quarterly* 22 (Apr. 1913): 205–58.

Moser, Harold D. et al., eds. *The Papers of Andrew Jackson.* 5 vols. to date. Knoxville: University of Tennessee Press, 1980–.

Muir, R. C. "Burford's First Settler, Politician, and Military Man—Benajah Mallory." *Ontario Historical Society, Papers and Records* 26 (1930): 492–97.

Murray, J. M., ed. "A Recovered Letter: W. W. Baldwin to C. B. Wyatt." *Ontario Historical Society, Papers and Records* 35 (1943): 49–55.

Murrin, John M. "The Jeffersonian Triumph and American Exceptionalism." *Journal of the Early Republic* 20 (spring 2000): 1–25.

Nash, Gary B., and Jean R. Soderlund. *Freedom by Degrees: Emancipation in Pennsylvania and Its Aftermath.* New York: Oxford University Press, 1991.

Neatby, Hilda. *Quebec: The Revolutionary Age, 1760–1791.* Toronto: McClelland and Stewart, 1966.

Neel, Joanne Loewe. *Phineas Bond: A Study in Anglo-American Relations, 1786–1812.* Philadelphia: University of Pennsylvania Press, 1968.

Nelson, William H. *The American Tory.* Boston: Northeastern University Press, 1964.

Newman, Richard S. *Freedom's Prophet: Bishop Richard Allen, the AME Church, and the Black Founding Fathers.* New York: New York University Press, 2008.

Newman, Simon. "Reading the Bodies of Early American Seafarers." *William and Mary Quarterly*, 3d ser., 55 (Jan. 1998): 59–82.

O'Brien, Brendan. *Speedy Justice: The Tragic Last Voyage of His Majesty's Vessel Speedy.* Toronto: University of Toronto Press, 1992.

O'Connell, Maurice R. *Irish Politics and Social Conflict in the Age of the American Revolution.* Philadelphia: University of Pennsylvania Press, 1965.

O'Donnell, Ruan. *Robert Emmet and the Rising of 1803.* Dublin: Irish Academic Press, 2003.

Ogden, John Cosens. *A Tour Through Upper and Lower Canada by a Citizen of the United States.* Litchfield, Conn.: 1799.

Onuf, Peter S. "The Expanding Union." In David Thomas Konig, ed., *Devising Liberty: Preserving and Creating Freedom in the New American Republic*, 50–80. Stanford, Calif.: Stanford University Press, 1995.

———. *Jefferson's Empire: The Language of American Nationhood.* Charlottesville: University of Virginia Press, 2000.

O'Reilly, Isabel M. "One of Philadelphia's Soldiers in the War of 1812," American Catholic Historical Society of Philadelphia, *Records* 12 (1901): 294–321, and 419–51.

———, ed. "A Hero of Fort Erie." *Buffalo Historical Society, Publications* 5 (1902): 63–93.

Palmer, R. R. *The Age of Democratic Revolution: A Political History of Europe and America, 1760–1800.* 2 vols. Princeton: Princeton University Press, 1959.

Parish, John C., ed. *The Robert Lucas Journal of the War of 1812 during the Campaign under General William Hull.* Iowa City: Iowa State Historical Society, 1906.

Parker, D. W., ed. "Secret Reports of John Howe, 1808." *American Historical Review* 17 (Oct. 1911): 70–102 and 17 (Jan. 1912): 332–54.

Parmet, Herbert S., and Marie B. Hecht, *Aaron Burr: Portrait of an Ambitious Man.* New York: Macmillan, 1967.

Pasley, Jeffrey L. "1800 as a Revolution in Political Culture: Newspapers, Celebrations, Voting, and Democratization in the Early Republic." In James Horn, Jan Ellen Lewis, and Peter S. Onuf, eds., *The Revolution of 1800: Democracy, Race, and the New Republic*, 121–52. Charlottesville: University of Virginia Press, 2002.

———. *"The Tyranny of Printers": Newspaper Politics in the Early American Republic.* Charlottesville: University of Virginia Press, 2001.

Patterson, Graeme H. "Whiggery, Nationality, and the Upper Canadian Reform Tradition." *Canadian Historical Review* 56 (March 1975): 25–44.

Pauley, Philip J. "Fighting the Hessian Fly: American and British Responses to Insect Invasion, 1776–1789." *Environmental History* 7 (2002): 377–400.

Perkins, Bradford. *Castlereagh and Adams: England and the United States, 1812–1823.* Berkeley: University of California Press, 1964.

———. *The First Rapprochement: England and the United States, 1795–1805.* Philadelphia: University of Pennsylvania Press, 1955.

———. *Prologue to War: England and the United States, 1805–1812.* Berkeley: University of California Press, 1963.

Perrin, Noel. " 'So Good Bye, You Jackall': An Annotated Copy of John Andrew Graham's *Descriptive Sketch of the Present State of Vermont.* 1797)." *Vermont History* 43 (spring 1975): 95–102.

Phillips, Kim Tousley. *William Duane, Radical Journalist in the Age of Jefferson.* New York: Garland Publishing, 1989.

Playter, George. *The History of Methodism in Canada.* Toronto: Anson Green, 1862.

Porter, Daniel R., ed. "Jacob Porter Norton: A Yankee on the Niagara Frontier in 1814." *Niagara Frontier* 12 (summer 1965): 51–57.

Porter, Kenneth Wiggins. *John Jacob Astor: Business Man.* 2 vols. Cambridge, Mass.: Harvard University Press, 1931.

Potter, Janice. *The Liberty We Seek: Loyalist Ideology in Colonial New York and Massachusetts.* Cambridge, Mass.: Harvard University Press, 1983.

Pratt, Julius W. *Expansionists of 1812.* New York: Peter Smith, 1949.

Preston, Richard A., ed. "The Journals of General Sir F. P. Robinson, G.C.B." *Canadian Historical Review* 37 (Dec. 1956): 352–55.

———. *Kingston Before the War of 1812: A Collection of Documents.* Toronto: Champlain Society, 1959.

Prucha, Francis Paul. *The Sword of the Republic: The United States Army on the Frontier, 1783–1846.* Toronto: Macmillan, 1969.

Purvis, Thomas L. "Patterns of Ethnic Settlement in Late Eighteenth-Century Pennsylvania." *Western Pennsylvania Historical Magazine* 70 (April 1987): 107–22.

Quaife, Milo M. *The Yankees Capture York.* Detroit: Wayne State University Press, 1955.

———, ed. "The Chronicles of Thomas Vercheres de Boucherville." In Quaife, ed., *War on the Detroit,* 3–178. Chicago: Lakeside Press, 1940.

———. "From Marietta to Detroit in 1815." *Historical Society of Northwestern Ohio, Quarterly Bulletin* 4 (1942): 134–55.

———. *The John Askin Papers.* 2 vols. Detroit: Library Commission, 1928–31.

Quimby, Robert S. *The U.S. Army in the War of 1812: An Operational and Command Study.* 2 vols. East Lansing: Michigan State University Press, 1997.

Quinn, Dermot. *The Irish in New Jersey: Four Centuries of American Life.* New Brunswick, N.J.: Rutgers University Press, 2004.

Rakove, Jack N. *Original Meanings: Politics and Ideas in the Making of the Constitution.* New York: Knopf, 1996.

Rawlyk, George. *The Canada Fire: Radical Evangelicalism in British North America, 1775–1812.* Montreal: McGill-Queen's University Press, 1994.

Rea, James E. *Bishop Alexander Macdonell and the Politics of Upper Canada.* Toronto: Ontario Historical Society, 1974.

Read, Colin, and Ronald J. Stagg, eds. *The Rebellion of 1837 in Upper Canada: A Collection of Documents.* Toronto: Champlain Society, 1985.

Reaman, G. Elmore. *The Trail of the Black Walnut.* Toronto: McClelland & Stewart, 1957.

Reed, T. A., ed. "John Strachan's Journey from Montreal to Kingston in December 1799." *Ontario Historical Society, Papers and Records* 42 (1950): 213–17.

Reuter, Frank T. " 'Petty Spy' or Effective Diplomat: The Role of George Beckwith." *Journal of the Early Republic* 10 (1990): 471–92.

Richards, Eric. "Scotland and the Uses of the Atlantic Empire." In Bernard Bailyn and Philip D. Morgan, eds., *Strangers Within the Realm: Cultural Margins of the First British Empire,* 67–114. Chapel Hill: University of North Carolina Press, 1991.

Richardson, John. *Richardson's War of 1812 with Notes and a Life of the Author.* Toronto: Historical Publishing, 1902.

Riddell, William Renwick. "The Ancaster 'Bloody Assize' of 1814." *Ontario Historical Society, Papers and Records* 20 (1923): 107–25.

———. "Benajah Mallory, Traitor." *Ontario Historical Society, Papers and Records* 26 (1930): 573–78.

———. "The Bidwell Elections: A Political Episode in Upper Canada a Century Ago." *Ontario Historical Society, Papers and Records* 21 (1924): 236–44.

———. "Joseph Willcocks: Sheriff, Member of Parliament and Traitor." *Ontario History* 24 (1927): 475–99.

———. *The Life of John Graves Simcoe, First Lieutenant Governor of the Province of Upper Canada, 1792–96.* Toronto: McClelland & Stewart, 1926.

———. *The Life of William Dummer Powell, First Judge at Detroit and Fifth Chief Justice of Upper Canada.* Lansing: Michigan Historical Commission, 1924.

———, ed. *La Rochefoucault-Liancourt's Travels in Canada, 1795.* Toronto: Ontario Bureau of Archives, 1917.

Riordan, Liam. *Many Identities, One Nation: The Revolution and Its Legacy in the Mid-Atlantic.* Philadelphia: University of Pennsylvania Press, 2007.

Ritcheson, Charles R. *Aftermath of Revolution: British Policy Toward the United States, 1783–1795.* Dallas: Southern Methodist University Press, 1969.

Rives, George Lockhart, ed. *Selections from the Correspondence of Thomas Barclay, Formerly British Consul-General at New York.* New York: Harper & Brothers, 1894.

Robinson, Ralph. "Retaliation for the Treatment of Prisoners in the War of 1812." *American Historical Review* 49 (Oct. 1943): 65–70.

Rodger, N. A. M. "Mutiny or Subversion?: Spithead and the Nore." In Thomas Bartlett et al., eds., *1798: A Bicentenary Perspective,* 549–64. Dublin: Four Courts Press, 2003.

———. "Sea-Power and Empire, 1688–1793." In P. J. Marshall, ed., *The Oxford History of the British Empire, vol. 2, The Eighteenth Century,* 169–83. New York: Oxford University Press, 1998.

Rogers, Henry C. *History of the Town of Paris and the Valley of the Sauquoit.* Utica, N.Y.: Utica Printing, 1881.

Rohrbough, Malcolm J. *The Land Office Business: The Settlement and Administration of American Public Lands, 1789–1837.* New York: Oxford University Press, 1968.

Roland, Charles G. "Health, Disease, and Treatment in Early Upper Canada." In Richard Merritt, Nancy Butler, and Michael Power, eds., *The Capital Years: Niagara-on-the-Lake, 1792–1796,* 223–50. Toronto: Dundurn Press, 1991.

Romney, Paul. "From the Types Riot to Rebellion: Elite Ideology, Anti-Legal Sentiment, Political Violence, and the Rule of Law in Upper Canada." *Ontario History* 79 (June 1987): 113–44.

———. *Mr. Attorney: The Attorney General for Ontario in Court, Cabinet, and Legislature, 1791–1899.* Toronto: Osgoode Society, 1986.

———. "Reinventing Upper Canada: American Immigrants, Upper Canadian History, English Law, and the Alien Question." In Roger Hall et al., eds., *Patterns of the Past: Interpreting Ontario History,* 78–107. Toronto: Dundurn Press, 1988.

Romney, Paul, and Barry Wright. "State Trials and Security Proceedings in Upper Canada During the War of 1812." In F. Murray Greenwood and Barry Wright, eds., *Canadian State Trials,* 2 vols., 379–405. Toronto: Osgoode Society and University of Toronto Press, 1996.

Rorabaugh, W. J. *The Alcoholic Republic: An American Tradition.* New York: Oxford University Press, 1979.

Sabathy-Judd, Linda, ed. *Moravians in Upper Canada: The Diary of the Indian Mission of Fairfield on the Thames, 1792–1813.* Toronto: Champlain Society, 1999.

Schrauwers, Albert. "The Politics of Schism: The Separation of the Children of Peace, 1812." *Ontario History* 80 (Mar. 1988): 31–52.

Schultz, Christian. *Travels on an Inland Voyage.* New York: Isaac Riley, 1810.

Scott, Winfield. *Memoirs of Lieut.-General Scott, L.L.D., Written by Himself.* New York: Sheldon, 1864.

Scotti, N. David, ed. "Additions to the Letters of Abijah Bigelow." *American Antiquarian Society, Proceedings* 79 (Oct. 1970): 245–52.

Senter, Nathaniel G. M. *A Vindication of the Character of Nathaniel G. M. Senter Against the Charge of Being a Spy and a Traitor.* Hallowell, Me.: Ezekiel Goodale, 1815.

Severance, Frank H., ed. "The Case of Alexander Smyth." *Buffalo Historical Society, Publications* 18 (1914): 215–55.

———, ed. "Extracts from Joseph Ellicott's Letterbooks and Early Correspondence." *Buffalo Historical Society, Publications* 26 (1922): 49–166.

Shalhope, Robert E. *A Tale of New England: The Diaries of Hiram Harwood, Vermont Farmer, 1810–1837.* Baltimore: Johns Hopkins University Press, 2003.

Sharp, James Roger. *American Politics in the Early Republic: The New Nation in Crisis.* New Haven, 1993.

Sheaffe, Roger Hale. "Documents Relating to the War of 1812: The Letter-Book of Gen. Sir Roger Hale Sheaffe." *Buffalo Historical Society, Publications* 17 (1913): 271–382.

Shepard, Elihu H. *The Autobiography of Elihu H. Shepard, Formerly Professor of Languages in St. Louis College.* St. Louis: George Knapp, 1869.

Sheppard, George. *Plunder, Profit, and Paroles: A Social History of the War of 1812 in Upper Canada.* Montreal: McGill-Queen's University Press, 1994.

Sherk, A. B. "The Pennsylvania Germans in Waterloo County." *Ontario Historical Society, Papers and Records* 6 (1906): 98–109.

Shortt, Adam, and Arthur G. Doughty, eds. *Documents Relating to the Constitutional History of Canada, 1759–1791: Part Two, 1774–1791.* Ottawa: J. de L. Tache, 1918.

Shy, John. "Ian Steele as Military Historian." In Nancy L. Rhoden, ed., *English Atlantics Revisited: Essays Honouring Professor Ian K. Steele,* 18–29. Montreal: McGill-Queen's University Press, 2007.

———. *A People Numerous and Armed.* New York: Oxford University Press, 1976.

Sider, E. Morris. "The Early Years of the Tunkers in Upper Canada." *Ontario History* 51 (spring 1959): 121–29.

Siebert, W. H. "The Loyalists and the Six Nation Indians in the Niagara Peninsula." *Royal Society of Canada, Transactions,* 3d ser., 9 (1915–16), section 2: 79–128.

Silver, Peter. *Our Savage Neighbors: How Indian War Transformed Early America.* New York: W. W. Norton, 2008.

Simcoe, John Graves. "Remarks on the Travels of the Marquis de Chastellux (1787)." *Magazine of History* 43, extra no. 172 (1931): 8–49.

———. *Simcoe's Military Journal.* London, 1787. Reprint, Toronto: Baxter, 1962.

Sissons, C. B. "The Martyrdom of McCarty: Fact or Myth?" *Canadian Journal of Religious Thought* 4 (1927): 12–18.

Skeen, C. Edward. *Citizen Soldiers in the War of 1812.* Lexington: University of Kentucky Press, 1999.

———. *John Armstrong, Jr., 1758–1843: A Biography.* New York: Syracuse University Press, 1981.

Skelton, William B. *An American Profession of Arms: The Army Officer Corps, 1784–1861.* Lawrence: University Press of Kansas, 1992.

———. "High Army Leadership in the Era of the War of 1812: The Making and Remaking of the Officer Corps." *William and Mary Quarterly,* 3d ser., 51 (April 1994):253–74.

Smith, Alison. "John Strachan and Early Upper Canada, 1799–1814." *Ontario History* 52 (Sep. 1960): 159–73.

Smith, David W. *A Short Topographical Description of His Majesty's Province of Upper Canada, in North America.* London: W. Paden, 1799.

Smith, J. E. A. *The History of Pittsfield (Berkshire County), Massachusetts, From the Year 1800 to the Year 1876.* Springfield, Mass.: C.W. Bryan, 1876.

Smith, James Morton. *Freedom's Fetters: The Alien and Sedition Laws and American Civil Liberties.* Ithaca, N.Y.: Cornell University Press, 1966.

Smith, Michael. *A Geographical View of the Province of Upper Canada; and Promiscuous Remarks on the Government.* Philadelphia: Thomas and Robert Desilver, 1813.

———. *Human Sorrow and Divine Comfort; or a Short Narrative of the Suffering, Travel, and Present Feelings and Situation of M. Smith, Preacher of the Gospel.* Richmond, Va.: Samuel Pleasants, 1814.

Smith, Paul H. *Loyalists and Redcoats: A Study in British Revolutionary Policy.* Chapel Hill: University of North Carolina Press, 1964.

———, ed. *Letters of Delegates to Congress, 1774–1789.* 25 vols. Washington, D.C.: Library of Congress, 1976–.

Smith, Peter J. "Civic Humanism Versus Liberalism: Fitting the Loyalists In." In Janet Abzenstat and Peter J. Smith, eds., *Canada Origins: Liberal, Tory, or Republican,* 109–35. Ottawa: Carleton University Press, 1995.

Snyder, Charles M., ed. *Red and White on the New York Frontier, a Struggle for Survival: Insights from the Papers of Erastus Granger, Indian Agent, 1807–1819.* Harrison, N.Y.: Harbor Hill Books, 1978.

Spafford, Horatio Gates. *A Gazetteer of the State of New York.* Albany: H. C. Southwick, 1813.

Spalding, Lyman A. *Recollections of the War of 1812 and Early Life in Western New York.* Lockport, N.Y.: Niagara County Historical Society, 1949.

Spragge, George W., ed. *The John Strachan Letterbook: 1812–1834.* Toronto: Ontario Historical Society, 1946.

Stacey, Charles P. "An American Plan for a Canadian Campaign: Secretary James Monroe to Major General Jacob Brown, February 1815." *American Historical Review* 46 (Jan. 1941): 348–58.

———, ed. "Upper Canada at War, 1814: Captain Armstrong Reports." *Ontario History* 48 (winter 1956): 37–42.

Stagg, J. C. A. "Between Black Rock and a Hard Place: Peter B. Porter's Plan for an American Invasion of Canada in 1812." *Journal of the Early Republic* 19 (fall 1999): 383–422.

———. "Enlisted Men in the United States Army, 1812–1815: A Preliminary Survey." *William and Mary Quarterly,* 3d ser., 43 (1986): 615–45.

——— *Mr. Madison's War: Politics, Diplomacy, and Warfare in the Early American Republic, 1783–1830.* Princeton: Princeton University Press, 1983.

Stagg, J. C. A., et al., eds., *The Papers of James Madison: Presidential Series.* 6 vols. to date. Charlottesville: University of Virginia Press, 1984–.

Stanley, George F. G. *The War of 1812: Land Operations*. Toronto: Macmillan of Canada, 1983.

Strachan, James. *A Visit to the Province of Upper Canada in 1819*. 1820. Reprint, New York: Johnson Reprint Corp., 1968.

Strachan, John. *A Discourse on the Character of King George the Third, Addressed to the Inhabitants of British America*. Montreal: Nahum Mower, 1810.

————. *A Sermon Preached at York before the Legislative Council and House of Assembly, August 2nd 1812*. York, Upper Canada: John Cameron, 1812.

Stray, Albert. "Canadian Volunteers Burn Old Niagara." *Canadian Genealogist* 6 (Dec. 1984): 220–42.

Strum, Harvey. " 'A Most Cruel Murder': The Isaac Underhill Affair, 1809." *Ontario History* 80 (Dec. 1988): 293–310.

Stuart, Charles. "Lord Shelburne." In Hugh Lloyd-Jones, Valerie Pearl, and Blair Worden, eds., *History and Imagination: Essays in Honour of H. R. Trevor-Roper*, 243–53. London: Gerald Duckworth, 1981.

Stuart, Reginald C. *United States Expansionism and British North America, 1775–1871*. Chapel Hill: University of North Carolina Press, 1988.

Surtees, Robert J. "Land Cessions, 1763–1830." In Edward S. Rogers and Donald B. Smith, eds., *Aboriginal Ontario: Historical Perspectives on the First Nations*, 92–121. Toronto: Dundurn Press, 1994.

Syndergaard, Rex. "Wild Irishmen and the Alien and Sedition Acts," *Eire-Ireland* 9 (spring 1971): 14–24.

Syrett, Harold C. et al., eds. *The Papers of Alexander Hamilton*. 27 vols. (New York: Columbia University Press, 1961–87.

Szatmary, David P. *Shays' Rebellion: The Making of an Agrarian Insurrection*. Amherst: University of Massachusetts Press, 1980.

Talman, James J., ed. *Loyalist Narratives from Upper Canada*. Toronto: Champlain Society, 1946.

Taylor, Alan. *The Divided Ground: Indians, Settlers, and the Northern Borderland of the American Revolution*. New York: Knopf, 2006.

————. "The Early Republic's Supernatural Economy: Treasure Seeking in the American Northeast, 1780–1830." *American Quarterly* 38 (spring 1986): 6–34.

————. " 'The Hungry Year': 1789 on the Northern Border of Revolutionary America." In Alessa Johns, ed., *Dreadful Visitations: Confronting Natural Catastrophe in the Age of Enlightenment*. New York: Routledge, 1999.

————. "Land and Liberty on the Post-Revolutionary Frontier." In David T. Konig, ed., *Devising Liberty: Preserving and Creating Freedom in the New American Republic*, 81–108. Stanford, Calif.: Stanford University Press, 1995.

————. "A Northern Revolution of 1800?: Upper Canada and Thomas Jefferson." In James Horn, Jan Ellen Lewis, and Peter S. Onuf, eds., *The Revolution of 1800: Democracy, Race, and the New Republic*, 383–409. Charlottesville: University of Virginia Press, 2002.

————. " 'To Man Their Rights': The Frontier Revolution." In Ronald Hoffman, ed., *The Transforming Hand of Revolution: Reconsidering the American Revolution as a Social Movement*, 231–57. Charlottesville: University of Virginia Press, 1995.

————. *William Cooper's Town: Power and Persuasion on the Frontier of the Early American Republic*. New York: Knopf, 1995.

Taylor, Robert J. et al., eds. *The Adams Papers: Papers of John Adams.* 14 vols. Boston: Massachusetts Historical Society, 1977–.

Thompson, E. P. *The Making of the English Working Class.* New York: Vintage Books, 1966.

Thompson, John Herd, and Stephen J. Randall. *Canada and the United States: Ambivalent Allies.* Athens: University of Georgia Press, 1997.

Thompson, Mabel W., ed. "Billy Green, 'the Scout.' " *Ontario History* 44 (Oct. 1952): 173–82.

Tillyard, Stella. *Citizen Lord: Edward Fitzgerald, 1763–1798.* London: Chatto & Windus, 1997.

Tucker, Robert W., and David C. Hendrickson. *Empire of Liberty: The Statecraft of Thomas Jefferson.* New York: Oxford University Press.

Tucker, Spencer C., and Frank T. Reuter. *Injured Honor: The Chesapeake-Leopard Affair, June 22, 1807.* Annapolis: Naval Institute Press, 1996.

Turner, Orsamus. *History of the Pioneer Settlement of Phelps and Gorham's Purchase and Morris' Reserve.* Rochester, N.Y.: William Alling, 1851.

Turner, Wesley B. *British Generals in the War of 1812: High Command in the Canadas.* Montreal: McGill-Queen's University Press, 1999.

United States. *American State Papers, Class I: Foreign Relations,* 6 vols. Washington, D.C.: Gales and Seaton, 1832–1861.

United States. *American State Papers, Class V: Military Affairs.* Washington, D.C.: Gales and Seaton, 1832–1861.

United States Congress. *Biographical Directory of the American Congress, 1774–1961.* Washington, D.C.: Government Printing Office, 1961.

———. *Debates and Proceedings in the Congress of the United States, 1789–1825.* 42 vols. Washington, D.C., 1834–56. Scholarly convention abbreviates this compilation as the *Annals of Congress (AC).*

———. *The Public Statutes at Large of the United States of America. Vol 2.* Boston: Charles C. Little and James Brown, 1845.

Upton, Leslie F. S. *The Loyal Whig: William Smith of New York & Quebec.* Toronto: University of Toronto Press, 1969.

———, ed. *The Diary and Selected Papers of Chief Justice William Smith, 1784–1793.* 2 vols. Toronto: Champlain Society, 1963.

Valenti, Nicholas C. "Cyrenius Chapin: Doctor and Pioneer." Master's thesis, Niagara University, 1972.

Van Doren, Carl. *Secret History of the American Revolution.* New York: Viking Press, 1941.

Varga, Nicholas. "Election Procedures and Practices in Colonial New York." *New York History* 41 (1960): 249–77.

Walker, Adam. *A Journal of Two Campaigns of the Fourth Regiment of U.S. Infantry in the Michigan and Indian Territories.* Keene, N.H.: Sentinel Press, 1816.

Wallace, W. Stewart. "The First Journalists in Upper Canada." *Canadian Historical Review* 26 (Dec. 1945): 372–81.

———, ed. "Captain Miles Macdonell's Journal of a Jaunt to Amherstburg in 1801." *Canadian Historical Review* 25 (June 1944): 166–76.

Walters, Philip G., and Raymond Walters, Jr. "The American Career of David Parish." *Journal of Economic History* 4 (Nov. 1944): 149–66.

———. "David Parish: York State Land Promoter." *New York History* 26 (April 1945): 146–61.

Warner, R. I., ed. "The Bold Canadian: A Ballad of the War of 1812." In Morris Zaslow, ed., *The Defended Border: Upper Canada and the War of 1812*, 303–5. Toronto: Macmillan, 1964.

Waterhouse, Benjamin, ed. *A Journal of a Young Man of Massachusetts, Late a Surgeon on Board an American Privateer* New York: William Abbott, 1911.

Waters, Thomas P. "An Episode of the War of 1812." *Massachusetts Historical Society, Proceedings*, 3d ser., 48 (June 1915): 496–504.

Watson, J. Steven. *The Reign of George III, 1760–1815*. Oxford: Clarendon Press, 1960.

Watts, Steven. *The Republic Reborn: War and the Making of Liberal America, 1790–1820*. Baltimore: Johns Hopkins University Press, 1987.

Webster, Noah. *An American Selection of Lessons, in Reading and Speaking, Calculated to Improve the Minds and Refine the Taste of Youth and also Instruct them in the Geography, History and Politics of the United States*. Albany: Charles R. and George Webster, 1800.

Weld, Isaac. *Travels Through the States of North America and the Provinces of Upper and Lower Canada during the Years 1795, 1796, and 1797*. 2 vols. London, 1807. Reprint, New York: Johnson Reprint Co., 1968.

Wells, Roger. *Insurrection: The British Experience, 1795–1803*. Gloucester, Mass.: Allan Sutton, 1983.

Werner, Raymond C. "War Scare and Politics in 1794." *New York State Historical Association, Quarterly Journal* 11 (Oct. 1930): 324–34.

Whelan, Kevin "The Green Atlantic: Radical Reciprocities between Ireland and America in the Long Eighteenth Century." In Kathleen Wilson, ed., *A New Imperial History: Culture, Identity, and Modernity in Britain and the Empire, 1660–1840*, 216–38. New York: Cambridge University Press, 2004.

White, Patrick C. T., ed. *Lord Selkirk's Diary, 1803–1804: A Journal of His Travels in British North America and the Northeastern United States*. Toronto: Champlain Society, 1958.

White, Richard. *The Middle Ground: Indians, Empires, and Republics in the Great Lakes Region, 1650–1815*. New York: Cambridge University Press, 1991.

White, Samuel. *History of the American Troops during the Late War Under the Command of Colonels Fenton and Campbell*. 1830. Reprint, Rochester, N.Y.: George P. Humphrey, 1896.

Whitfield, Carol M. *Tommy Atkins: The British Soldier in Canada, 1759–1870*. Ottawa: Parks Canada, 1981.

Wickwire, Franklin, and Mary Wickwire. *Cornwallis: The Imperial Years*. Chapel Hill: University of North Carolina Press, 1980.

Wilbur, J. B. *Ira Allen, Founder of Vermont*. 2 vols. Boston: Houghton Mifflin, 1928.

Wilkinson, James. *Memoirs of My Own Times*. 3 vols. Philadelphia: Abraham Small, 1816.

Willcox, William B. *Portrait of a General: Sir Henry Clinton in the War of Independence*. New York: Knopf, 1964.

———, ed. *The American Rebellion: Sir Henry Clinton's Narrative of His Campaigns, 1775–1782, with an Appendix of Original Documents*. New Haven: Yale University Press, 1954.

Wilson, Bruce G. *The Enterprises of Robert Hamilton: A Study of Wealth and Influence in Early Upper Canada, 1776–1812*. Ottawa: Carleton University Press, 1983.

———. "Patronage and Power: The Early Political Culture of the Niagara Peninsula." In Richard Merritt, Nancy Butler, and Michael Power, eds., *The Capital Years: Niagara-on-the-Lake, 1792–1796*. Toronto: Dundurn Press, 1991.

Wilson, David A. *United Irishmen, United States: Immigrant Radicals in the Early Republic.* Ithaca, N.Y.: Cornell University Press, 1998.

Wilton, Carol. *Popular Politics and Political Culture in Upper Canada, 1800–1850.* Kingston, Ont.: McGill-Queen's University Press, 2000.

Winks, Robin W. *The Blacks in Canada: A History.* New Haven: Yale University Press, 1971.

Wise, S. F. *God's Peculiar Peoples: Essays on Political Culture in Nineteenth-Century Canada.* Ottawa: Carleton University Press, 1993.

Wood, Gordon S., *The Creation of the American Republic, 1776–1787.* Chapel Hill: University of North Carolina Press, 1969.

———. "Interests and Disinterestedness in the Making of the Constitution." In Richard Beeman, Stephen Botein, and Edward C. Carter, Jr., eds., *Beyond Confederation: Origins of the Constitution and American National Identity,* 69–109. Chapel Hill: University of North Carolina Press, 1987.

———. *The Radicalism of the American Revolution.* New York: Knopf, 1992.

Wood, J. David. *Making Ontario: Agricultural Colonization and Landscape Re-Creation before the Railway.* Montreal, 2000.

Wood, William, ed. *Select British Documents of the Canadian War of 1812.* 3 vols. Toronto: Champlain Society, 1920–28.

Woodford, Frank B. *Mr. Jefferson's Disciple: A Life of Justice Woodward.* East Lansing: Michigan State University Press, 1953.

Wright, Barry. "Sedition in Upper Canada: Contested Legality." *Labour/Le Travail* 29 (spring 1992): 7–57.

Wright, Henry Clarke. *Human Life, Illustrated in my Individual Experience as a Child, a Youth, and a Man.* Boston: B. Marsh, 1849.

Wright, J. Leitch, Jr. *Britain and the American Frontier, 1783–1815.* Athens: University of Georgia Press, 1975.

Wylie, William N. T. "Instruments of Commerce and Authority: The Civil Courts in Upper Canada, 1789–1812." In David H. Flaherty, ed., *Essays in the History of Canadian Law,* 3–28. Toronto: University of Toronto Press, 1983.

Young, A. H., ed. "Bishop Peters." *Ontario History* 27 (1931): 583–623.

———. "Letters from the Secretary of Upper Canada and Mrs. Jarvis, to her father, the Rev. Samuel Peters." In *Women's Canadian Historical Society of Toronto, Transactions* 23 (1922–23): 11–63.

———. "More Langhorn Letters." *Ontario Historical Society, Papers and Records* 29 (1933): 47–71.

———. "Revd. John Langhorn." *Ontario Historical Society, Papers and Records* 23 (1926): 534–60.

Young, Alfred F. *The Democratic Republicans of New York: The Origins, 1763–1797.* Chapel Hill: University of North Carolina Press, 1967.

Zagarri, Rosemarie. "Gender and the First Party System." In Doron Ben-Atar and Barbara B. Oberg, eds., *Federalists Reconsidered,* 118–34. Charlottesville: University of Virginia Press, 1998.

Zahediah, Nuala. "Overseas Expansion and Trade in the Seventeenth Century." In Nicholas Canny and Alaine Low, eds., *The Origins of Empire: British Overseas Enterprise to the Close of the Seventeenth Century,* 398–422. New York: Oxford University Press, 1998.

Zeichner, Oscar. "The Loyalist Problem in New York After the Revolution." *New York History* 19 (July 1940): 289–95.

Zeisberger, David. *Diary of David Zeisberger: A Moravian Missionary among the Indians of Ohio*. Edited by Eugene F. Bliss. 2 vols. Cincinnati: Historical and Philosophical Society of Ohio, 1885.

Zimmerman, James Fulton. *Impressment of American Seamen*. Port Washington, N.Y.: Kennikat Press, 1966.

Acknowledgments

Historians depend on the insightful assistance of librarians and archivists, and I have been especially fortunate to work with the staff at the Library and Archives of Canada, the Provincial Archives of Ontario, the Toronto Reference Library, and the New York State Archives and State Library. At the Library and Archives of Canada, I benefited from the generous insights provided by Patricia Kennedy. I had a very productive visit to the Buffalo and Erie County Historical Society because of the generous help of Patricia Virgil. My visits to Buffalo also benefited from the hospitality of Tamara Plakins Thornton, Donald McGuire, and Martha Malamud. At the St. Lawrence University Archives, Mark McMurray and Darlene Leonard proved especially helpful. As my scholarly home away from home, the American Antiquarian Society has been indispensable to this project. I am especially grateful for the deft guidance offered by Gigi Barnhill, Joanne Chasen, Philip Lampi, and Marie Lamoureux. Two of my graduate students, Elizabeth Covart and Marcus Gallo, also offered valuable research leads, as did Tiffany Edwards and Beth Lew.

The University of California's Washington Center provided me with a residency which became an invaluable base for my research at the U.S. National Archives. As the administrator for the U.C. Davis program, Sara Lombardo was a paragon of help and guidance. And Larry Berman provided exemplary leadership. At the U.S. National Archives, I benefited from the lively help of Lucy Barber, who has a special talent for accessorizing historic figures and tableaux. For my presentation at the Society of the Cincinnati, Preston Russell and Jack D. Warren, Jr., proved extraordinarily generous.

The Society for Historians of the Early American Republic (SHEAR) has provided a great scholarly network of kindred spirits. For helping me through my year as that society's president, I thank Amy Baxter-Bellamy, Daniel Richter, Richard Dunn, James Green, and Peter Agree. The annual SHEAR conference also enables me to renew a special bond with my *amigos*: Paul Gilje, Annette Gordon-Reed, Jan Lewis, Peter Onuf, and El Jefe (David Konig). Their insights and good company have enriched my life as a historian. As editor of SHEAR's journal, Roderick McDonald shepherded to publication an essay that helped me to develop this book. I am also grateful to the good spirits, in all senses of that word, provided by Roderick and Michelle McDonald during my visits to Philadelphia.

I also benefited from the opportunity to present draft work to scholarly audiences at several universities. Tom Chambers and Douglas Kohler hosted my visit to Niagara University. I especially enjoyed a dinner with them and Ann Chambers at the Lewiston landing, where we could look across the Niagara River at the battlefield of Queenston Heights. I thank Marc Egnal for hosting my visit to York University and H. V. Nelles and John Weaver for giving so generously of their time and insights during my visit to McMaster University. I am also grateful to Allan Greer and Heidi Bohaker for hosting my visit to the Munk Center of the University of Toronto, where I also benefited from the gracious assistance of Robert Bothwell, Elspeth Brown, and Louis Pauley. At Duke University, Elizabeth Fenn, Peter Wood, Jane and Pete Moss, and John H. Thompson were gracious hosts, as were my old friends Kathleen Duval and Marty Smith—and new friend Quinton Duval-Smith, who beat me like a drum at Chutes-and-Ladders. I'm grateful to Gaines Foster, Nancy Isenberg, Alecia Long, and Suzanne Marchand for welcoming me to Louisiana State University, where I also saw a tiger and an animatronic Huey Long. At Yale University my generous hosts included John Demos, Laura Engelstein, Joanne Freeman, and Kariann Yokota. That visit was also enriched by my dear and generous sister, Carole Goldberg, and her husband Marty, a paragon in all things save his devotion to the Steinbrenner dynasty. Richard Dunn, Daniel Richter, and Michael Zuckerman hosted my visit to the University of Pennsylvania, where the feedback proved invaluable at an early stage in this project. Elizabeth Leonard, Hank and Pam Gemery, and Jason Opal were similarly helpful to me during my return to speak at Colby College. At the University of Cincinnati I benefited from the hospitality of Daniel Glenn, Wendy Kline, Geoffrey Plank, and Karim Tiro.

Several leading scholars generously gave of their time and expertise to review draft chapters despite the pressing demands of their own work. For this, I thank Carl Benn, Paul Gilje, Allan Greer, Elizabeth Mancke, H. V. Nelles, Peter Onuf, Jared Orsi, Louis Pauley, Gene Smith, and Samuel Watson. My friend and colleague Ari Kelman proved an especially insightful, witty, and tenacious reader.

For assistance with arranging illustrations, I thank Paul Banfield (Queens University Archives), Gigi Barnhill and Jackie Penny (American Antiquarian Society), Fred Bassett and H. E. Weltin (New York State Library), Steven Brisson and Brian Jaeschke (Mackinac Island State Park Commission), Brian Dunnigan and Clayton Lewis (William L. Clements Library), Deborah Emmons-Andarawis (Historic Cherry Hill), Ila Furman (Corcoran Gallery of Art), Robert Hanshew (Naval Heritage Center), Tania Henley and Alan Walker (Toronto Reference Library), Sylvia Lassam (University of Trinity College, Toronto), Walter Mayer (Buffalo and Erie County Historical Society), Marsha Mullin (The Hermitage), Kathleen Mylen-Coulombe (Yale University Art Gallery), Stéphanie Poisson (McCord Museum), Lizanne Garrett Reger (National Portrait Gallery, Smithsonian Institution), Amy Rupert (Rensselaer Polytechnic Institute Archives and Special Collections), Laura Shafer (Arkansas Arts Center), Jill Slaight (New-York Historical Society), Richard Trask (Danvers Archival Center), Courtney A. Troeger (Albany Institute of History and Art), and Nicola Woods (Royal Ontario Museum). I am also indebted to Jeffrey L. Ward for his usual excellent work in preparing two maps for this work.

For literary representation, I thank Andrew Wylie, Rebecca Nagel, and Scott Moyers of the Wylie Agency. For the editing and production of the book, I was again fortunate to work with Jane Garrett, who has so expertly shepherded two previous books of mine to publication. I also thank her very able and patient assistant, Leslie Levine.

Several friends sustained morale and listened patiently to more than they had bargained for on the War of 1812. They include Wendy and Bruce Hazard, Cynthia Robinson, Warren Leon, Jim and Sandy McCann, Bill Ainsworth, Lesley Kelman, Jack Crowley, Chris Clark, and Margaret Lamb, Nina Dayton, David Jaffee, Barbara Brooks, Chris Reynolds, Alessa Johns, Pablo Ortiz, Ana Peluffo, Bob Powell, Cecelia

Colombi, Rosamaria and Emil Tanghetti, Ruma and Rahul Chopra. For sharing his expertise on piracy, the Boston Celtics, the newspaper business, fine food, and Celtic music, I again thank Kevin R. Convey. For their insights on borders and borderlands in the Americas, I am grateful to Ari Kelman, Lorena Oropeza, Andres Resendez, Chuck Walker, and Louis Warren (aka Theory Man). For regal generosity, none can match Clarence Walker. And Spring Warren was an inspiration for her artistic, literary, and gardening talents, as well as for her tales of hard-drinking adventure in the pool halls of the Australian Outback.

I've dedicated the book to Sheila McIntyre, Michael Von Herff, and their children William, Silas, and Lucy (and dog Maggie), for taking me in to share in their lives and laughter during my many visits to the world's greatest basement and for helping me to decipher the past and present of Canada. I even grew to like (sort of) my sustained exposure to "Wonder Pets," including the turtle talking on the telephone. They have all been the best of friends. And they never made me go to the Experimental Farm.

Through the entire journey, Emily Albu remained an inspiration and (in Maine parlance) "wicked sweet."

Index

A Note About the Author

Alan Taylor is a professor of history at the University of California at Davis and a contributing editor at *The New Republic*. He is the author of *Liberty Men and Great Proprietors*, *American Colonies*, *The Divided Ground*, and *William Cooper's Town*, which won the Bancroft and Pulitzer prizes for American History.

A Note on the Type

This book was set in Janson, a typeface long thought to have been made by the Dutchman Anton Janson, who was a practicing type-founder in Leipzig during the years 1668–1687. However, it has been conclusively demonstrated that these types are actually the work of Nicholas Kis (1650–1702), a Hungarian, who most probably learned his trade from the master Dutch typefounder Dirk Voskens. The type is an excellent example of the influential and sturdy Dutch types that prevailed in England up to the time William Caslon (1692–1766) developed his own incomparable designs from them.

Composed by North Market Street Graphics, Lancaster, Pennsylvania

Printed and bound by Berryville Graphics, Berryville, Virginia

Book design by Robert C. Olsson

Maps by Jeffrey L. Ward